SLAVERY

IN THE

UNITED STATES

SLAVERY

IN THE

UNITED STATES

A SOCIAL, POLITICAL,
AND HISTORICAL ENCYCLOPEDIA

VOLUME TWO

Junius P. Rodriguez, Editor

A B C ⬤ C L I O

Santa Barbara, California   Denver, Colorado   Oxford, England

Library of Congress Cataloging-in-Publication Data
Slavery in the United States : a social, political, and historical
   encyclopedia / Junius P. Rodriguez, editor.
      p. cm.
   Includes bibliographical references and index.
   ISBN-13: 978-1-85109-544-5 (hardcover : alk. paper)
   ISBN-13: 978-1-85109-549-0 (e-book)
   ISBN-10: 1-85109-544-6 (hardcover : alk. paper)
   ISBN-10: 1-85109-549-7 (e-book)
   1. Slavery—United States—History—Encyclopedias. 2.
Slavery—Political aspects—United States—History—Encyclopedias. 3.
Slavery—Social aspect—United States—History—Encyclopedias. 4.
United States—Biography—Encyclopedias. I. Rodriguez, Junius P.

E441.S635 2007
306.3'6209703—dc22

                                            2006101351
11   10   09   08   /   2   3   4   5   6   7   8   9   10

Production Editor: Anna A. Moore
Editorial Assistant: Sara Springer
Production Manager: Don Schmidt
Media Editor: Jason Kniser
Media Resources Coordinator: Ellen Brenna Dougherty
Media Resources Manager: Caroline Price
File Manager: Paula Gerard

ABC-CLIO, Inc.
130 Cremona Drive, P.O. Box 1911
Santa Barbara, California 93116-1911

This book is also available on the World Wide Web as an ebook.
Visit http://www.abc-clio.com for details.

This book is printed on acid-free paper. ∞
Manufactured in the United States of America

Contents

—ɱ—

Volume One

Contextual Essays

Entries

A

B

E

F

G

H

I

J

K

L

M

Volume Two

N

O

P

Q

R

S

T

U

V

W

Y

Primary Source Documents

Contributors

Valerie Abrahamsen
Tunde Adeleke
Thanet Aphornsuvan
Andrea M. Atkin
Jim Baugess
Jackie R. Booker
Stefan Brink
Christopher L. Brown
Ron D. Bryant
Beverly Bunch-Lyons
Keith Byerman
Sydney J. Caddel-Liles
Charles W. Carey
Mark Cave
Constance J. S. Chen
William L. Chew III
Boyd Childress
David M. Cobin
Philip R.P. Coelho
Dallas Cothrum
Charles D'Aniello
Enrico Dal Lago
Brian Dirck
Elizabeth Dubrulle
Jonathan Earle
Raingard Eßer
Patience Essah
Peter S. Field
Roy E. Finkenbine
James C. Foley
Daniel L. Fountain
Dan R. Frost
DoVeanna S. Fulton
Gwilym Games
Larry Gara
Henry H. Goldman
Marquetta L. Goodwine

John Grenier
Sally E. Hadden
Judith E. Harper
Sharon A. Roger Hepburn
Timothy S. Huebner
Anthony A. Iaccarino
Eric R. Jackson
Claude F. Jacobs
Mark L. Kamrath
Frances Richardson Keller
Stephen C. Kenny
Yitzchak Kerem
Jeffrey R. Kerr-Ritchie
Hyong-In Kim
Stewart King
Sharon Landers
Tom Lansford
Lori Lee
Kurt E. Leichtle
David J. Libby
Richard D. Loosbrock
David B. Malone
Chandra M. Manning
Jennifer Margulis
Charles H. McArver, Jr.
Dwight A. McBride
Robert A. McGuire
Scott A. Merriman
Debra Meyers
Mary Jo Miles
Dennis J. Mitchell
Andrew P. Morriss
Bruce L. Mouser
Caryn E. Neumann
Elsa A. Nystrom
Onaiwu W. Ogbomo
Craig S. Pascoe

Julieanne Phillips
Michael Phillips
Jan Pilditch
Michael Polley
James M. Prichard
John W. Pulis
Maria Elena Raymond
Douglas S. Reed
Richard A. Reiman
Junius P. Rodriguez
Barbara Ryan
Arnold Schmidt
Jason H. Silverman
Malik Simba
Frederick J. Simonelli
Manisha Sinha
James L. Sledge, III

Dale Edwyna Smith
Gene A. Smith
John David Smith
Richard D. Starnes
John Stauffer
Torrance T. Stephens
Harold D. Tallant
Anthony Todman
Eric Tscheschlok
Peter Wallenstein
Nagueyalti Warren
Michael Washington
Mary Ellen Wilson
Yolandea Wood
John J. Zaborney
Robert J. Zalimas, Jr.

Maps

—∿—

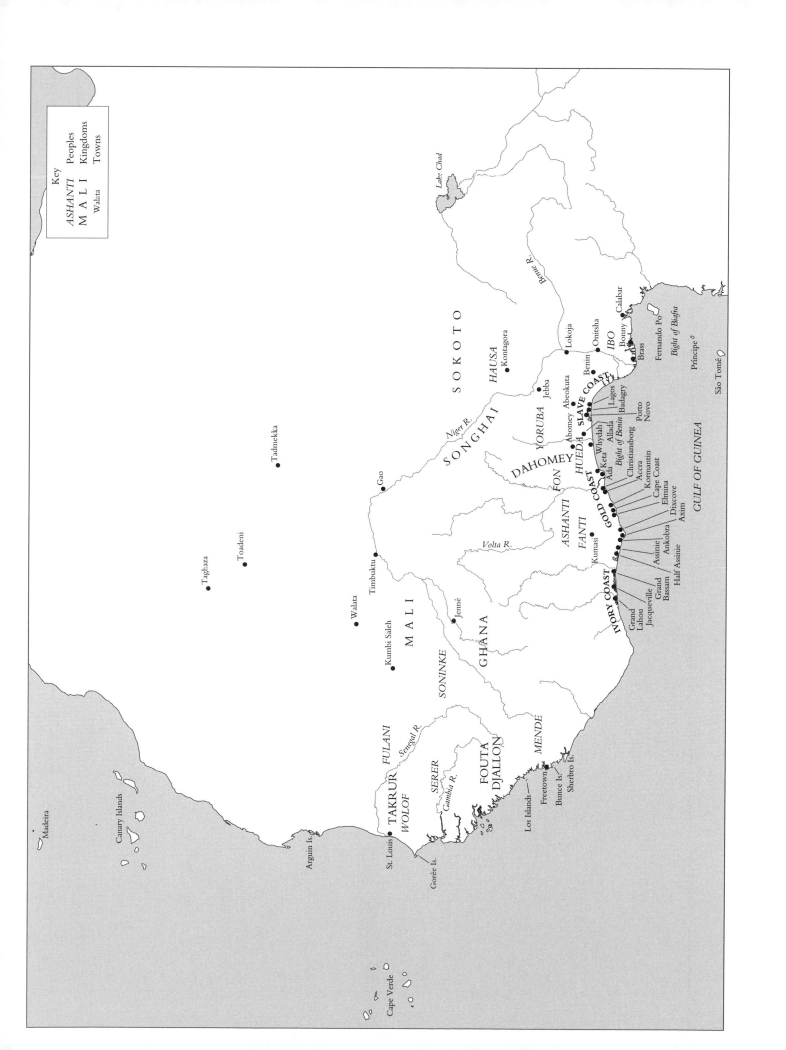

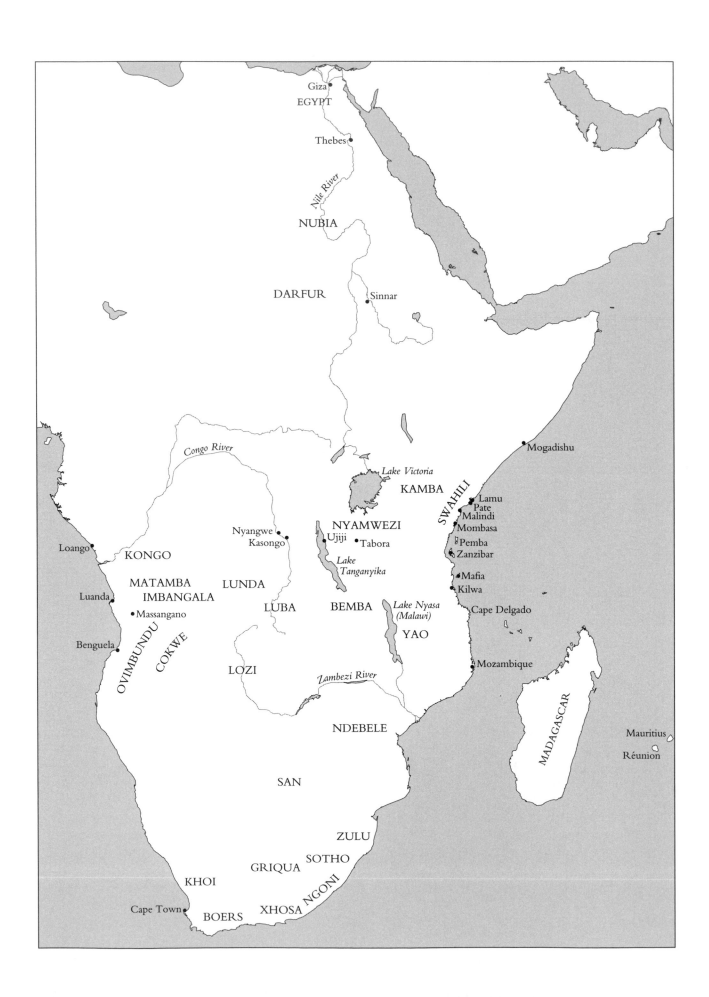

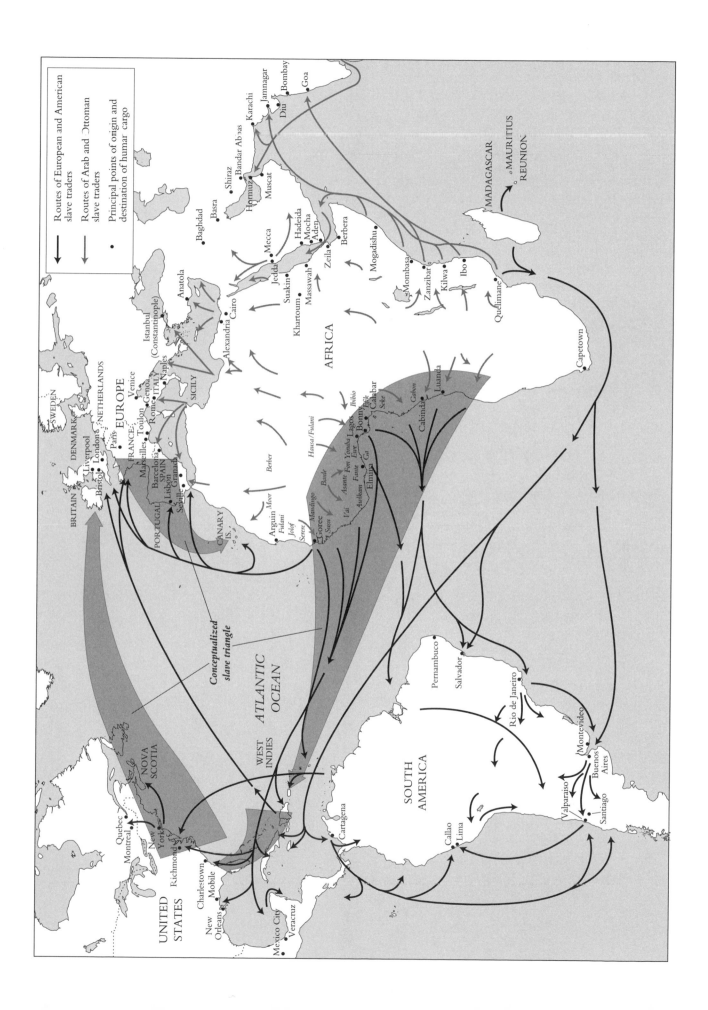

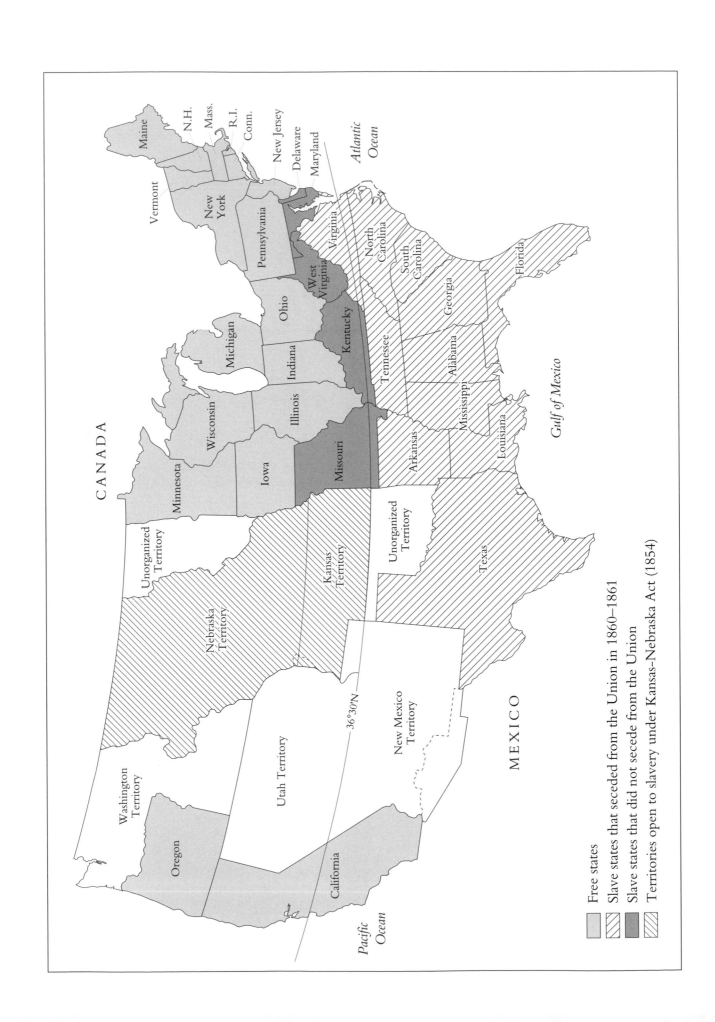

Free states

Slave states that seceded from the Union in 1860–1861

Slave states that did not secede from the Union

Territories open to slavery under Kansas–Nebraska Act (1854)

CANADA

MEXICO

Pacific
Ocean

Atlantic
Ocean

Gulf of Mexico

Maine

N.H.

Mass.

R.I.

Conn.

New Jersey

Delaware

Maryland

Vermont

New
York

Pennsylvania

Virginia

West
Virginia

Ohio

Michigan

Indiana

Kentucky

North
Carolina

South
Carolina

Georgia

Tennessee

Alabama

Wisconsin

Illinois

Mississippi

Florida

Minnesota

Iowa

Missouri

Arkansas

Louisiana

Unorganized
Territory

Kansas
Territory

Unorganized
Territory

Texas

Nebraska
Territory

36°30′N

Washington
Territory

Utah Territory

New Mexico
Territory

Oregon

California

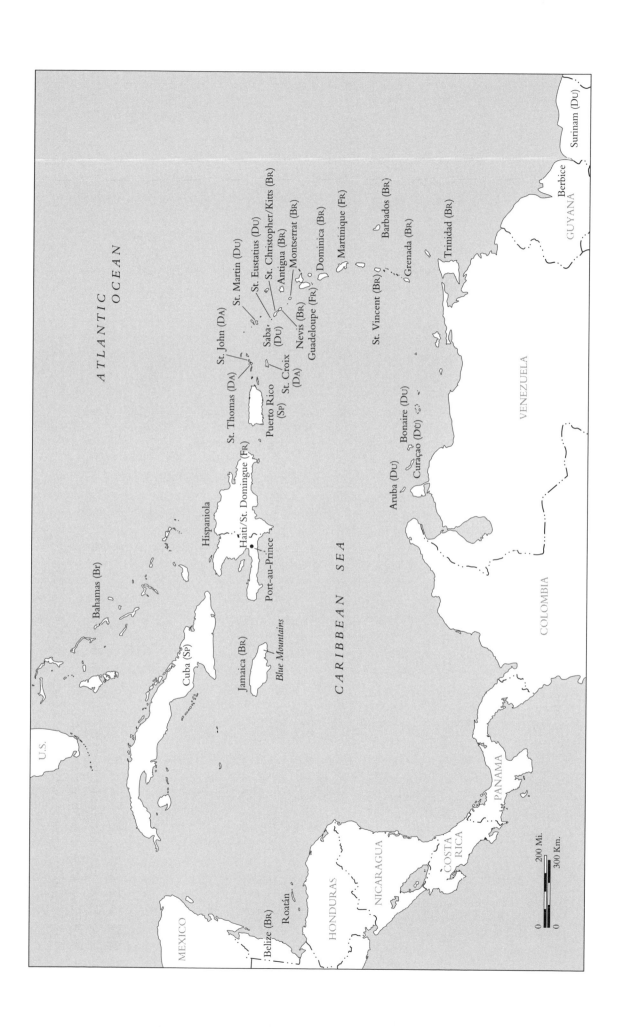

SLAVERY
IN THE
UNITED STATES

Entries

~ N ~

NAMES AND NAMING

The idea that all human beings must have a unique social identification is found in all cultures and all strata in a society. Besides being an identifying tool, names may also have a classifying role. The question here is how slaves, the human category on the lowest level in society, have been named and socially identified. For proprietal identification, a normal custom was to mark a slave by piercing the ears, branding with a hot iron, cutting of the ears or the nose, scoring the nostrils, or tattooing the name of the slaveowner on the skin. Another way to "mark" the slave was to give the individual a special kind of slave name—a type of name used only for slaves.

In nearly all cultures, a name is more or less intimately tied to an individual, the persona, but it has been stated that this tendency was not the case for slaves, for the slave had no "personality" and owned neither his body nor his name. The name was bestowed upon him by the salesman or a master, and hence, it was "owned" by the master. It may be correct that the slave did not own his official name, but when discussing the name of slaves, it is important to make clear that there are at least two vital aspects regarding naming and the use of proper names. A name is a kind of social identification label, and a name may be part of one's self-identifica-

tion, tied to one's persona. These two linguistic labels may not be the same, and it is obvious that slaves often had names of both these two categories: one name or "social identification label" given by the owner and another (or several) name(s) used by the slave and by friends and relatives in a close social context.

In Ancient Greece and Rome, slaves could be given a name indicating their place of origin (*Lydos, Syros, Asia*). Some were given eponyms (*Hermes, Eros, Cleopatra*). A special case for Rome was the slave names with the master's *praenomen* (the first of the usual three names) in the genitive with the suffix *-por* (*-puer,* that is, 'boy'), for example, *Marcipor, Publipor, Quintipor.*

The West Africans who were deported to the United States during the eighteenth and nineteenth centuries were normally given a new single, simple name. The most common of these slave names were *John, Henry, George, Sam, Jim, Jack, Tom, Charles, Peter,* and *Joe* for males; *Mary, Maria, Nancy, Lucy, Sarah, Harriett, Hannah, Eliza, Martha,* and *Jane* for females. Of course, this practice led to a frequent duplication of names, and to avoid confusion, there was often a descriptive addition—*Old, Big, Fat, Little,* and so on. Another naming practice used was to name the slave after the birthplace or the place where the slave was bought: *Richmond, Williamsburg, Albemarle.* A third naming principle used by the slaveowner was to bestow upon him or her a name from the classical world, such as *Cato, Caesar, Hector, Pompey, Jupiter, Titus, Virgil, Cupid, Primus, Cato, Scipio, Venus, Diana, Juno, Flora, Agamemnon.* For Jamaica records show that classical names, such as *Venus, Bacchus,* and *Chloe,* were popular. A fourth case was to give the slave a biblical name: *Abraham, Moses, Solomon, Isaac, Noah, Cain, Abel, Esther, Rachel, Leah, Delilah, Rhoda, Sarah.*

There are some interesting records from the year 1741 from Barbados, where we get an insight into the different naming and addressing practices among the slaves. These records give us both the Christian name (probably given by the slaveowner) on the slave as well as the plantation name (probably used by the slave and friends and relatives). Among the men, the Christian name *Joseph* had a plantation equivalent (*Cuffey*); *Samuel* was *Etto* or *Sambo*; *Davis* was *Quashey*; and *Thomas* was *Quoffey*. Similarly, females given the Christian name *Philis* were known as *Occo*; *Jane* was *Adjubah* or *Jiba*; and *Diana* was *Dada*. For boys, *Thomas* was *Tuma*; *Anthony* was *Tong*; *Danie* was *Quaccoe*; and *Edward* was *Cuffey*. For girls, *Mercy* was *Gong*; *Penelope* was *Jobbah*; *Pheoby* was *Affiba*; and *Orrinda* was *Obah*.

Many of the slaves of West African origin already had a Christian personal name, but whether that Christian saint's name was kept is uncertain. It has been assumed that a Konglolese name such as *João* can lurk behind many *Johns* and *Johnnies*. A few anglicized Fanti and Ibo names are also recorded—for example, *Duke* (*Orek*), *Cobham* (*Akabom*), and *Becky* (*Beke*).

Early slave lists from the two Carolinas show that about 15 to 20 percent of the slaves had kept their African names, such as *Quamino, Musso, Cush, Footbea, Teebee, Banabar, Gimba, Ankque, Juba, Mingo, Simba*. Hence few slaves in the North America and the British Caribbean were known by their original name, but there is at least one kind of name that is found in the early records of sales and shipments all over the area that saw an import of African slaves, namely, the so-called West African day names, such as *Cuffee, Cudjo, Quashee* for males and *Phibba, Cubba, Quasheba* for females. In the Fanti language, a male born on a Sunday could be named *Quisi*, a female *Akosua*, on Monday *Kujot : Ajua*, Tuesday *Quabina : Abmaba*, Wednesday *Quaku : Ekua*, Thursday *Quahu : Aba*, Friday *Kufi : Efua* and Saturday *Quamina : Ama*. On Jamaica the same set of names has been recorded as for Sunday *Quashie* (male): *Quasheba* (female), *Cudjoe : Juba*, *Cubena : Beneba*, *Quaco : Cubba*, *Quao : Abba*, *Cuffie : Phibba*, and for Saturday *Quamin : Mimba*. Of these, the most common in the United States was *Cuffee* ("male born on Friday").

A name such as *Sambo* bears witness to another naming principle that West African slaves took with them to North America, namely, the principle of naming the child according to the order of its birth in relation to its brothers and sisters. *Sambo* means "the second son."

— *Stefan Brink*

For Further Reading:

DeCamp, David. 1967. "African Day-Names in Jamaica." *Language* 43: 139–149.

Ebeogu, Afam. 1993. "Onomastics and the Igbo Tradition of Politics." *African Languages and Cultures* 6: 133–146.

Handler, Jerome S., & Jacoby, JoAnn. 1996. "Slave Names and Naming in Barbados 1650–1830." *The William and Mary Quarterly,* 3rd Series 53: 685–728.

Inscoe, John C. 1983. "Carolina Slave Names: An Index to Acculturation." *The Journal of Southern History* 49: 527–554.

Jeffreys, M. D. W. 1948. "Names of American Negro Slaves." *American Anthropologist* 50: 571–573.

Thornton, John. 1993. "Central African Names and African-American Naming-Patterns." *The William and Mary Quarterly,* 3d Series 50: 727–742.

NARRATIVES

Critics define slave narratives as first-person autobiographies written by slaves and ex-slaves that describe their lives in servitude and their efforts to become free. In the process, the narratives create for the speakers both individual identities and a collective history. Many slave narratives consist of written versions of speeches given at abolition meetings by escaped or free slaves, and they often retain an oral flavor.

More than six thousand slave narratives exist, ranging in length from hundreds of pages like those of Olaudah Equiano and Frederick Douglass to one-page interviews conducted with slaves and ex-slaves by abolitionist periodicals, historians, and the Federal Writers Project of the 1930s. During the struggle for abolition, more than one hundred book-length slave narratives appeared in America, Brazil, Great Britain, Cuba, France, and Germany, which often proved commercially successful for their publishers. For example, the *Narrative of the Life of Frederick Douglass* sold 11,000 copies in the United States between 1845 and 1847, and 30,000 copies in Britain by 1860.

Slave narratives served as powerful weapons in the abolition struggle. Plantocrats justified slavery because they saw Africans as subhuman. Slaves wrote their narratives to refute those who believed Africans incapable of reason, socialization, and moral improvement. In that sense, writes Henry Louis Gates, Jr., the "slave narrative represents the attempts of blacks to *write*

Title page from the narrative of Olaudah Equiano. More than six thousand slave narratives exist; they range in length from several-hundred-page recountings to one-page interviews conducted with slaves and ex-slaves. (Library of Congress)

themselves into being" (Davis and Gates, 1985, p. xxiii). Because of this, most slave narratives contain a central scene in which the slave first encounters a "talking book" and ultimately becomes literate.

Writers like David Hume, Georg Wilhelm Hegel, and Immanuel Kant viewed Africans as inferior because their nations lacked written histories; slave narratives respond to this challenge, according to Gates (1988). "Accused of lacking a formal and collective history, blacks published individual histories that, taken together, were intended to narrate, in segments, the larger yet fragmented history of blacks in Africa, then dispersed throughout a cold New World" (Davis and Gates, 1985, p. xxvi). Fragmentation thus becomes part of the narrative structure because the speakers often interrupt their autobiographies proper to relate the experiences of other slaves. Consequently, most slave narratives share common scenes and an organization that is more anecdotal than chronological. This structure allows slave narrators to present themselves as both unique individuals and representatives of slaves generally.

Rhetorically, slave narratives advance two lines of argument. The first appeals for freedom based on the "natural rights" discourse of John Locke and Jean-Jacques Rousseau. The second appeal relies on eighteenth-century sentimentalism, decrying such practices as the public flogging of women, the separation of families, and sexual violence, at the same time raising religious concerns about the Africans' potential Christian salvation.

Frances Smith Foster groups slave narratives into two categories: according to their characterizations of slavery and their presentations of the narrators. Those published between 1760 and 1807, when both Great Britain and America outlawed the slave trade (though not slavery itself), often recount tales of adventure told by African narrators of noble birth, who condemn slavery for its brutality and curtailment of physical freedom, rather than for its dehumanization. One example is *The Interesting Narrative of the Life of Olaudah Equiano, or Gustavus Vassa, The African (Written by Himself)*, published in 1789. Both honest and evil masters owned Equiano, a child of Igbo nobility. During the Seven Years' War, he served in Canada with General James Wolfe and sailed the Mediterranean with Admiral Boscawen, accompanied the Phipps expedition to the Arctic, and lived in Central America with the Miskito Indians. Pre–1807 narratives describe Edenic moments in Africa where family and traditional life are being enjoyed and then come the kidnapping, the Middle Passage, the slave auction, and finally, after portraying the daily evils of slave life, freedom.

The emphasis of slave narratives changed between 1831 and 1868, a period corresponding with the rise of antebellum interest in African American issues after the Missouri Compromise and the *Dred Scott* decision. These later texts, which feature American-born slave narrators of common ancestry, indict slavery as an institution. Both categories of slave narratives share common features, such as biblical imagery, in particular references to Moses leading the Israelites out of slavery. Both use Christianity as a basis for abolition, arguing that blacks have souls and therefore must be saved. Post–1831 narratives begin with the innocence of childhood, contrasted with the moment when the child first comprehends the meaning of slavery. Next follows a desire to be free, escape or manumission, and freedom, though in the end, racism often confronts the disillusioned ex-slave on arrival in "free" states or Canada.

The published narrative customarily included material by white abolitionist intermediaries attesting to the voracity of the narrative and the (usually Christian) character of the narrator. For example, the second edition of *The History of Mary Prince,* which appeared in London and Scotland in 1831, opens with a "Supplement" by her abolitionist sponsor and editor Thomas Pringle, and closes with letters of character reference, one from her former master. The third edition even includes testimony by Pringle's wife Margaret, verifying that she had inspected Prince's body and seen the scars received from her whippings. Consequently, it resembles legal evidence as much as autobiography, for while Prince does speak for herself, the text also includes material that uses her own body as evidence.

Prince's *History,* then, makes a sentimental appeal as it describes her beatings, ill treatment, excessive amounts of work, and emotional trauma, while the supplemental material adds an empirical defense of Prince's claims. For critics and historians, the editorial apparatus that accompanied the slaves' narratives illuminates the power inequities between abolitionist publishers and slave narrators, particularly in the roles that religion, violence, and sexuality played in constructing the slave narrators' personae. The former slave felt and responded to pressure to conform to an "improved" image of the black person in order to "deserve" freedom. At the same time, many slave narratives appear "double voiced" and, by sophisticated rhetorical strategies, resist this pressure.

The slave narrative profoundly influenced the stylistic and thematic development of the African American novel, as seen in such works as Ralph Ellison's *Invisible Man,* Zora Neale Hurston's *Their Eyes Were Watching God,* Richard Wright's *Black Boy,* and the works of Toni Morrison and Alice Walker.

— *Arnold Schmidt*

See also: Autobiographies; Proslavery Argument; Works Progress Administration Interviews.

For Further Reading
Carretta, Vincent, and Phillip Gould, eds. 2001. *Genius in Bondage: Literature of the Black Atlantic.* Lexington: University Press of Kentucky.

Davis, Charles T., and Henry Louis Gates, Jr., eds. 1985. *The Slave's Narrative.* Oxford: Oxford University Press.

Gates, Henry Louis, Jr., ed. 1988. *Six Women's Slave Narratives.* New York: Oxford University Press.

Rawick, George P. 1979. *The American Slave: A Composite Autobiography.* Westport, CT: Greenwood.

Smith Foster, Frances. 1979. *Witnessing Slavery: The Development of Ante-bellum Slave Narratives.* Madison: University of Wisconsin Press.

Taylor, Yuval, ed. 1999. *I Was Born a Slave: An Anthology of Classic Slave Narratives.* Chicago: Lawrence Hill Books.

NATIONALISM. *See* Black Nationalism.

NUMBERS. *See* Volume of the Slave Trade.

NASHOBA PLANTATION

One of the grandest experiments ever conceived, Tennessee's Nashoba plantation promised to end slavery. Based on cooperative labor and established by the first American woman to act publicly against slavery, this colony hoped to emancipate slaves gradually by demonstrating how they might be responsibly educated and then freed.

Nashoba plantation began in response to the common belief that slavery had left African Americans morally and intellectually unfit for freedom. Rather than argue for the immediate freedom of African Americans, Scottish-born Frances Wright proposed a plan to wean slaves from the confines of bondage and convince slaveholders of the merits of another system. As a foreigner, she may not have realized just how deep the roots of slavery were in the South or that it constituted much more than an economic structure.

Located on 1,940 acres one and one-third miles from Memphis along both sides of the Wolf River (Nashoba is the Chickasaw word for "wolf"), the project may have been doomed from the start by its poor location. Although cheerfully described by its seller as pleasant woodland, the plantation's virgin land was later described as containing second-rate soil. The property may have been cheap because it was malarial, as nearby swamps were filled with mosquitoes that rose in huge clouds at dusk.

Blissfully unaware of the inherent barriers to prosperity, Nashoba's founders moved boldly ahead in late 1825. Influenced by the French Marquis de Lafayette's attempt to emancipate bond servants gradually on his New Guinea plantation, his protégé Wright decided to make her own attempt at destroying slavery. Considering both the masters' and the slaves' positions, Wright hoped to make emancipation financially appealing to slaveholders while simultaneously demonstrating the ability of African Americans to prosper.

At Nashoba, slaves earned freedom through the requirement that they perform enough labor to reimburse the plantation for their purchase price plus 6 percent interest as well as food and clothing costs. As they worked, adult slaves would learn a trade and how to read, to figure, and to write, while slave children received a full education. The slaves, understanding the noble purpose of the experiment, would theoretically work much harder than slaves normally worked. The plantation's profits would be used to buy additional slaves and continue the expanding enterprise. Slaveholders, seeing that this sort of enterprise was more profitable than slavery itself, would copy it, which before very long would lead to the end of slavery in America.

Wright opposed colonization, but she bowed to political realities and made colonization a basic part of the Nashoba plan. She expected the freed slaves to leave the United States, perhaps emigrating to Haiti or move into the Mexican territory. No recorded African American reaction to the plan appears in any black-published books or newspapers, but the Nashoba plan may have been regarded as just another colonization scheme. The Nashoba slaves did not have a vote. Most whites also lacked enthusiasm for the project.

A wealthy woman, Wright bought Nashoba's land with her own money and ultimately lost half her wealth in the venture. She spent most of the funds buying tools, building cabins, and purchasing slaves. In 1826 newly bought slaves Willis, Jacob, Grandison, Redick, Henry, Nelly, Peggy, and Kitty arrived at Nashoba. The cheapest slave cost $500 and the most expensive $1,500. A pregnant woman with five small children later joined the group. Wright and her sister Camilla, along with an ever-changing number of whites, completed Nashoba's population.

Despite the project's ambitious goals, Nashoba's slaves remained subordinate to the whites. Although no corporal punishment occurred while Wright remained on the premises, this experimental plantation probably did not appear too different from any other to the blacks, particularly since they still were expected to complete the heaviest tasks. Once Wright left the area in 1827 because of ill health, Nashoba's managers abandoned her goal of slowly trying to build a sense of importance and self-respect in people who had earlier been denied the right to develop those traits. The whites now demanded unconditional obedience and used beating as a punishment.

Wright planned that Nashoba would be much more than an emancipation experiment. She saw it as a prototype of advanced living, with women having equal status with men and free education provided to all children regardless of color. But, worried by her illness, Wright decided to change Nashoba's legal structure, for she feared that the blacks might be returned to slavery if she were to die. In Nashoba's revised deed, Wright shared property ownership with ten other trustees: Lafayette, Camilla Wright, famed utopian socialist Robert Owen and his son Robert Dale Owen, Owenite socialist and merchant William Maclure, socialist James Richardson, Robert Jennings, Illinois pioneer George Flower, former Shaker Richesson Whitby, and prominent New York lawyer Cadwallader Colden.

While Wright was away, Richardson, the plantation overseer, created a huge scandal by advocating and practicing free love with one of the African Americans under his charge. Sexual relations between white masters and black slaves were certainly not uncommon in the South, but open advocacy of miscegenation was taboo. The colony, beset by bad publicity, sickness, and business setbacks, failed in 1830.

Wright kept her promise to free the remaining colonists by escorting them to Haiti, paying the expenses out of her own pocket. Although the plantation failed, Nashoba remains an innovative attempt at abolition, the remarkable dream of a most remarkable woman.

— *Caryn E. Neumann*

See also: Gradualism; Wright, Frances.

For Further Reading
Eckhardt, Celia Morris. 1984. *Fanny Wright: Rebel in America.* Cambridge, MA: Harvard University Press.
Lane, Margaret. 1972. *Frances Wright and the "Great Experiment."* Manchester, England: Manchester University Press.
Stiller, Richard. 1972. *Commune on the Frontier: The Story of Frances Wright.* New York: Thomas Y. Crowell.

NASHVILLE CONVENTION (1850)

The mid-nineteenth century sectional debate in the United States about slavery threatened to drive a permanent wedge between North and South. Although the Missouri Compromise (1820) maintained a shaky balance between free and slave states, new territorial acquisition led to heated arguments about slavery's expansion into the new areas.

The debate continued throughout the Mexican War (1846–1848), as people wondered about slavery's status in territories that might be gained from Mexico. Pennsylvania representative David Wilmot introduced a proviso prohibiting slavery in any territory ceded from Mexico, which outraged southerners. The northern-dominated House of Representatives passed the Wilmot Proviso, but southerners blocked its passage in the Senate. Angered by attempts to block slavery's expansion, South Carolina statesman John C. Calhoun called for action. In 1849 he called on the slave states to hold a convention in Nashville, Tennessee, the following year to discuss plans to protect slaveholders' rights.

Meanwhile, Kentucky senator Henry Clay proposed a congressional compromise that seemingly offered a solution to the conflict. Clay's plan divided the land ceded from Mexico by admitting California as a free state and allowing residents of the New Mexico and Utah territories to choose their status. Two elements of the plan favored antislavery supporters, as Clay's bill would end both the Washington, D.C., slave trade and Texan claims for a wider western border. In addition, Clay's compromise benefited slaveholders by creating the tough Fugitive Slave Law, which would promise federal support in returning runaway slaves.

By June 1850 enthusiasm for the Nashville Convention had dwindled considerably in light of Clay's proposal. The convention's 175 delegates represented only nine of fifteen slave states, with 102 of the delegates representing Tennessee. As the convention opened, radicals led by the South Carolina delegation called for immediate secession. They were overruled by more moderate colleagues, who hoped to find a solution while remaining loyal to the Union.

Delegates proposed twenty-eight resolutions stressing their convictions that as U.S. citizens, slaveholders had the constitutional right to take property (slaves) into the territories. Furthermore, delegates believed that the Constitution gave slaveholders the privilege of federal protection of their property. They stressed that any violation of these rights was unconstitutional. As evidence of goodwill, the convention reluctantly agreed to accept the dividing line established by the Missouri Compromise and urged Congress to settle the matter, either by recognizing slaveholders' rights or fairly dividing the territories.

After offering these resolutions, the convention adjourned to await the outcome of Clay's proposal. After much debate, Congress passed Clay's bill, which became known as the Compromise of 1850. Although fifty-nine delegates reconvened the Nashville Convention to protest the Compromise of 1850, most southerners accepted the Compromise and remained loyal to the Union, hoping for a permanent solution to the slavery expansion debate.

Ultimately, the Nashville Convention accomplished little, but it gave Americans a preview of the debates that would arise during the following decade. Not only did the Nashville Convention give secessionists a chance to express their ideas, but it also indicated the measures that some southerners were prepared to take to protect their way of life and the institution of slavery.

— *Jason H. Silverman*

See also: Calhoun, John C.; Compromise of 1850; Fire-Eaters; Wilmot Proviso.

For Further Reading
Hamilton, Holman. 1964. *Prologue to Conflict: The Crisis and Compromise of 1850.* Lexington: University of Kentucky Press.
Jennings, Thelma. 1980. *The Nashville Convention: Southern Movement for Unity, 1848–1851.* Memphis, TN: Memphis State University Press.

NATIONAL ANTI-SLAVERY STANDARD

The *National Anti-Slavery Standard* was the official journal of the American Anti-Slavery Society from June 1840 to April 1870. The society then published from May to July 1870, the *Standard: A Journal of Reform and Literature;* from July 30, 1870 to December 23, 1871, the *National Standard: An Independent Reform and Literary Journal;* and from January to December 1872, the *National Standard: A Temperance and Literary Journal.* The *National Anti-Slavery Standard* was published weekly, and except between July 1854 and November 1865, when it was published in Philadelphia, it was published in New York City. The *Standard* was well served by a distinguished succession of editors, among them, most notably, Lydia Maria Child, who was technically coeditor with husband, David L. Child, from May 1841 to May 1843.

Immediate emancipation was the goal of the American Anti-Slavery Society, and the *Standard* made a strong religious appeal for abolition. Chastising the American church and calling God abolition's "most efficient ally," it also initially recognized the value of political action. The year of its founding saw the American Anti-Slavery Society torn apart over tactics (specifically William Lloyd Garrison's nonresistant contention that governments are by nature immoral, which offended the politically minded abolitionists) and over the rights of women. Some dissenters founded the American and Foreign Anti-Slavery Society, and others founded the Liberty Party. Consequently, the language of that party's prospectus was inclusive and appropriate for an umbrella organization, in regard to both gender and tactics. But in 1844, David Lee Child, now serving as editor after charges of meek editorial style had prompted his wife to resign, resigned himself after disunionism and nonresistance (a form of Christian anarchism) became the official creed of the society. Modes of action were no longer to be left up to individual members. Later, the American Civil War brought the society firmly behind the president and the Republican Party.

Founded by William Lloyd Garrison in 1832, the New England Anti-Slavery Society distinguished itself from other antislavery societies by resisting colonization and openly promoting "immediatism," the belief that immediate, determined measures must be adopted for the emancipation of every slave. (Corbis)

Recruited in 1840 by William Lloyd Garrison, who supported women's rights, Lydia Maria Child (1802–1880), appointed with her husband, first served alone because of his poor health. She gave the *Standard* a literary flavor that made it appealing to educated readers. The *Standard,* in fact, was the first American journal to publish William Blake's poetry ("The Little Black Boy" on March 10, 1842), which appealed to the Unitarian circle that contributed to the society. Child's "Letters from New York," describing life in the city and commenting on current events and reforms such as nonresistance and the woman question, were published in the *Standard* and then published in two volumes in 1843 and 1844. However, they were refused by the publisher because of the letters' abolitionist assertions, which had already been muted by the author in an act of self-censorship.

The *Standard* published material from the American Anti-Slavery Society and from other abolitionist groups in America and abroad; letters from frequent correspondents such as Charles K. Whipple, "D.Y.," Samuel J. May, Jr., Henry C. Wright, Harriet Beecher Stowe, and Wendell Phillips; extracts from a wide range of newspapers; and material from various religious denominations. A miscellany of news, not always focused on reform, was regular, along with excerpts or works by prominent authors. Reform causes other than slavery were discussed, and after the onset of the Civil War, the focus of coverage changed from abolition to prospects and potentialities for the life of the slaves as freemen and freewomen.

— *Charles D'Aniello*

See also: American Anti-Slavery Society; Child, Lydia M.; Garrison, William Lloyd.

For Further Reading

Blassingame, John W., Mae G. Henderson, and Jessica M. Dunn, eds. 1980–1984. *Antislavery Newspapers and Periodicals, Volume IV (1840–1860) and Volume V*

(1861–1871) Annotated Index of Letters in the National Anti-Slavery Standard. Boston: G.K. Hall.

Mills, Bruce. 1994. *Cultural Reformations: Lydia Maria Child and the Literature of Reform.* Athens: University of Georgia Press.

Karcher, Carolyn L. 1994. *The First Woman in the Republic: A Cultural Biography of Lydia Maria Child.* Durham, NC: Duke University Press.

NEGRO CONVENTION MOVEMENT (1830–1854)

In August 1830, reacting to the Cincinnati antiblack riots of the previous year, prominent blacks officially convened in Philadelphia, Pennsylvania, to launch the Negro convention movement. This annual tradition involved black delegates from different parts of the country, coming together to deliberate and exchange ideas about their problems and determine appropriate solutions. The movement, which also signaled the beginning of organized black abolitionism, was equally a response to the larger challenges of slavery, discrimination, and the denial to blacks of citizenship rights and privileges. The Cincinnati riots, therefore, were just the precipitating force. In the aftermath of the riots, Hezekiah Grice, a free black from Baltimore, corresponded with leading blacks across the nation on the imperative of organizing to more effectively deal with the challenges of slavery and discrimination. The convention movement brought together blacks of diverse social backgrounds. The first national convention officially opened in August 1831 in Philadelphia. Delegates at this convention affirmed their strong antislavery commitments and embraced moral suasion, believing that improvement in the material and moral condition of blacks would influence public sentiment in favor of abolishing slavery and discrimination. Moral suasion also nurtured a universalist ethos, inducing blacks to embrace the doctrine of one humanity and to welcome white participants. Blacks held five national conventions from 1831 to 1835, all but one of them in Philadelphia. Convinced of the potency of moral suasion, blacks deemphasized political strategies and demands, while emphasizing self-effort and moral and material elevation instead.

By the late 1830s, however, the confidence blacks reposed in moral suasion had evaporated. The moral and material elevation of blacks had not made any significant dent in slavery and racism. Instead of acceptance and commendation for their efforts, successful blacks became the targets of angry antiabolitionist mobs. The conventions of the 1840s, both state and national, therefore, assumed a racially exclusive and political character. Delegates condemned slavery and demanded full citizenship rights. Although a few delegates seriously considered violence, the convention never officially adopted the policy. Despite increasing radicalization of the convention movement, moral suasion was not totally jettisoned as a reform strategy. Blacks continued to believe in and to propagate the doctrine of moral reform.

The passage of the Fugitive Slave Act in 1850 launched the movement's next phase. The federal government's pledge to assist in apprehending fugitives threatened free blacks with reenslavement. Though threatened, free blacks concentrated on cultivating group unity and institutional development, and the national and state conventions of the 1850s evinced a strong resolve to intensify the struggle against slavery and discrimination.

A few of the 1850s conventions, however, favored more radical emigrationist and separatist solutions. This reflected a growing ideological cleavage among black leaders. Two of the three national conventions of the decade illustrate this phenomenon. On the one hand, the convention of 1853 in Rochester, New York, unequivocally declared the commitment of blacks to the pursuit and acquisition of social and political equality within the United States. The emigrationist convention of 1854 in Cleveland, Ohio, on the other hand, perceived racism as invincible and opted for establishing an independent black nationality abroad. Though inspired by separatist consciousness, the Cleveland convention failed to activate any serious emigration momentum.

The state conventions of the 1850s overwhelmingly espoused integrationist aspirations. Black Americans committed themselves to resisting slavery and degradation, and they petitioned state legislatures and published addresses and appeals asserting their claims to meaningful freedom and equality within the United States.

The coming of the Civil War and the abolition of slavery by the Thirteenth Amendment did not terminate the convention movement. Freedom did not obliterate discrimination and degradation. The convention movement continued, and it instilled in blacks a sense of responsibility, while nurturing group consciousness and identity. It also provided forums in which black values and aspirations were articulated and their material and intellectual resources harnessed.

— *Tunde Adeleke*

See also: Antiabolition Riots; Fugitive Slave Act (1850).

For Further Reading

Bell, Howard H. 1969. *A Survey of the Negro Convention Movement, 1830–1861.* New York: Arno Press.

Pease, William H., and Jane H. Pease. 1971. "The Negro Convention Movement." In *Key Issues in the Afro-American Experience.* Ed. Nathan I. Higgins, et al. New York: Harcourt Brace Jovanovich.

Reed, Harry. 1994. *Platform for Change: The Foundation of the Northern Free Black Community, 1775–1865.* East Lansing: Michigan State University Press.

NEW ENGLAND
ANTI-SLAVERY SOCIETY

Founded by William Lloyd Garrison in 1832, the New England Anti-Slavery Society distinguished itself from other antislavery societies by resisting colonization and openly promoting "immediatism," the belief that immediate, determined measures must be adopted for the emancipation of every slave. Although it was short-lived and its role and impact were limited in a national sense, the society played a pivotal role in advancing later, more broadly effective antislavery activity.

After initially meeting in Samuel Sewall's law office on November 13, 1831, to hear Garrison's proposal, about one dozen Bostonian men assembled again on December 16, 1831, and then in January 6, 1832, in the basement schoolroom of a Boston African Baptist church to discuss formation of the abolitionist society. Seeing that the British societies succeeded only after they adopted the principle of immediate emancipation, the group accepted "immediatism" as the new organization's guiding principle. It appointed Arnold Buffum as its first president and Garrison as its corresponding secretary.

In drafting their constitution, which was published in Garrison's *Liberator* on February 18, 1832, Sewall, Garrison, and others made the society's objectives clear. As stated in its second article, the purpose of the New England Anti-Slavery Society was to "endeavor, by all means sanctioned by law, humanity and religion, to effect the Abolition of Slavery in the United States, to improve the character and condition of the free people of color, to inform and correct public opinion in relation to their situation and rights, and obtain for them equal civil and political rights and privileges with the whites" (NEAS, 1832). In its *Address to the Public,* which the society sent to editors of newspapers in New England, the group affirmed that the object of their society was "neither war nor sedition" and that the "fundamental principle" of their constitution was

"OUR SAVIOR'S GOLDEN RULE," that is, the idea that "*All things whatsoever ye would that men should do to you, do ye even so unto them*" (NEAS, 1832). Unlike its constitution, the *Address* outlined what was meant by "immediate abolition" and critiqued the objectives of the American Colonization Society, a society Garrison would criticize more heavily in his pamphlet *Thoughts of African Colonization* (1832). Although blacks were not involved in the initial founding of the society, they later had substantial numbers in its ranks. When the society's constitution was approved, for instance, about one-fourth of the seventy-two signers were of African descent.

Membership increased slowly, but after three years the name was changed to the Massachusetts Anti-Slavery Society. As indicated in its annual report for 1835, the formation and designs of the larger, recently organized American Anti-Slavery Society were making an impact. Also, the fact that state societies had already been established in Maine, New Hampshire, and Vermont caused the New England Anti-Slavery Society, which already was confining its activities to Massachusetts, to be a state-only society. By 1837 Massachusetts had 145 societies, and the American Anti-Slavery Society had taken the lead nationally in promoting immediate emancipation. Despite these later developments, the New England Anti-Slavery Society played a vital role in encouraging debate and discussion concerning the antislavery movement and in persuading people to take up the cause.

— *Mark L. Kamrath*

See also: American Anti-Slavery Society; American Colonization Society; Garrison, William Lloyd; Immediatism.

For Further Reading

Barnes, Gilbert Hobbs. 1933. *The Anti-Slavery Impulse 1830–1844.* New York: Harcourt Brace.

Cain, William E. 1995. *William Lloyd Garrison and the Fight against Slavery: Selections from the* Liberator. Boston: Bedford.

Dumond, Dwight Lowell. 1961. *Antislavery: The Crusade for Freedom in America.* Ann Arbor: University of Michigan Press.

Myers, John L. 1983. "Antislavery Agents in Connecticut, 1833–1838." *Connecticut History* 24: 1–28.

New England Anti-Slavery Society. 1832. *Constitution of the New England Anti-Slavery Society: With an Address to the Public* [by Rev. Moses Thacher]. Boston: Garrison and Knapp.

Zorn, Roman J. 1957. "The New England Anti-Slavery Society: Pioneer Abolition Organization." *Journal of Negro History* 42: 157–176.

NORTH STAR

The *North Star* (1847–1851), later called *Frederick Douglass' Paper* (1851–1860), was a weekly abolitionist newspaper owned and edited by Frederick Douglass, the American abolitionist. This newspaper records Douglass's changing views on slavery's constitutionality, legislation regarding African Americans, the antislavery movement and its leaders, and American and international politics. It also describes Douglass's activities and includes many of his orations.

A large donation from British abolitionists enabled Douglass to start the *North Star* in Rochester, New York, in 1847. Douglass argued that his paper would demonstrate African Americans' abilities and present their point of view. This point of view was apparently lacking in other antislavery newspapers, which had few black employees and rarely addressed the interests of northern blacks. Only four other black newspapers operated at that time.

Several white leaders, most prominently William Lloyd Garrison and Maria Weston Chapman, tried to dissuade Douglass from starting this paper. They were ostensibly worried about competition among antislavery papers, but actually their arguments revealed the racism that tainted the antislavery movement. Chapman thought Douglass was not intellectually capable of producing a newspaper. After he proceeded anyway, against their advice, she and Garrison thought that his action was a betrayal and a sign of impertinence. This conflict, and Douglass's very public movement away from Garrisonian antislavery, precipitated an acrimonious split between Douglass and Garrison, his former mentor and friend.

Like other antislavery newspapers, the *North Star* constantly faced financial crises. The subscription list was never large, and subscribers did not always pay. Although Douglass refused Gerrit Smith's proposal to merge the *North Star* with the *Syracuse Standard,* the Liberty Party organ, Smith assisted Douglass financially for many years. Douglass supported Smith's foray into congressional politics but did not follow any party line; he took his own positions in the paper and offered its columns to other abolitionists, even those who disagreed with him. The paper operated more efficiently when Julia Griffiths, a British abolitionist with good business sense, took over its finances in the 1850s. Still, Douglass found it necessary to conduct lecture tours to raise money to keep his newspaper going. From 1859 to 1863 he also published a magazine, *Douglass' Monthly.*

Douglass believed his newspaper would reach a wide audience, but more people knew of his views through his public speaking. As editor and owner of a newspaper, he held an authoritative position, one that loudly proclaimed his equality with other abolitionist leaders, particularly Garrison, and his leadership among black Americans. The paper allowed Douglass to express himself through the written word, which had been his central desire from his days as a slave. In many ways, the newspaper represented his freedom and independence.

— *Andrea M. Atkin*

See also: Douglass, Frederick; Garrison, William Lloyd.

For Further Reading
    Fishkin, Shelly Fisher, and Carla L. Peterson. 1990. "'We Hold These Truths to Be Self-Evident': The Rhetoric of Frederick Douglass' Journalism." In *Frederick Douglass: New Literary and Historical Essays.* Ed. Eric J. Sundquist. Cambridge: Cambridge University Press.
    Foner, Philip S. 1950. *Life and Writings of Frederick Douglass.* 5 vols. New York: International Publishers.
    McFeely, William S. 1991. *Frederick Douglass.* New York: Norton.

NORTH STAR. *See* United States–Canadian Relations on Fugitives.

NORTHWEST ORDINANCE (1787)

The Northwest Ordinance was enacted on July 13, 1787, by the United States Congress under the Articles of Confederation as "An Ordinance for the Government of the Territory of the United States, Northwest of the River Ohio." Building on Thomas Jefferson's idea of a territorial system in the Land Ordinance (1785), a committee headed by James Monroe organized a governmental structure for the western lands. This Northwest Ordinance addressed the challenges of westward movement, representative government, federal-state relations, individual rights, and sectionalism and slavery in the Northwest Territory. The preamble and first article established republican principles that foreshadowed the Bill of Rights: trial by jury, proportionate representation, common law courts, prohibition of primogeniture and entail, and guarantees of writ of habeas corpus.

The ordinance also provided a means by which a territory could become a state on the basis of equality with the existing states, laid the foundation for a national system of free public education, and outlawed slavery and involuntary servitude north and west of the Ohio River. The ordinance supplied the governmental structure for the Northwest Territory and the process by which the territories would become states.

A governor, secretary, and three judges made up the governmental structure of the territory. When the territory consisted of 5,000 free male inhabitants, they could elect representatives to a general assembly. After the territory claimed 60,000 free inhabitants, it could be admitted to the Union as a state on equal footing with the original states. The ordinance created the states of Ohio (1803), Indiana (1816), Illinois (1818), Michigan (1837) and Wisconsin (1848). The Northwest Ordinance set the basic pattern of settlement and statehood throughout the United States.

The ordinance also maintained that "Religion, Morality and knowledge being necessary to good government and the happiness of mankind, Schools and the means of education shall forever be encouraged." This article of the Northwest Ordinance reinforced the Land Ordinance (1785), which had set aside funds in each township for the establishment of schools. The Ohio General Assembly established Ohio University (1804) and Miami University (1809) as land-grant colleges, which became the cornerstones for higher education across the nation. These provisions laid the foundation for the nationwide system of public education.

Nathan Dane and Rufus King from Massachusetts proposed Article Six of the ordinance, which excluded slavery and involuntary servitude in the territories. It also stated that fugitive slaves "may be lawfully reclaimed and conveyed to the person claiming" them. The common interpretation by territorial governors and judges was that the article prohibited the introduction of new slaves but did not affect the status of slaves and their descendants already in the territory. These slaves and their children continued to live in servitude and were sold and bequeathed in wills.

An extended controversy over the meaning of Article Six developed between anti- and proslavery factions. Questions of states' rights, popular sovereignty, and appropriateness of agricultural regions and their labor systems developed. Northwesterners also argued over the original intent of Article Six's authors and its constitutional authority. In 1806 the Ohio legislature stated that it would "never permit the foul form of slavery to tread on their sacred soil," while in 1823, Illinois's slavery proponents claimed that the economy matured and the population grew most rapidly where slavery was legal.

Indiana proslavery settlers circumvented the Article Six controversy by passing a system of slavery thinly disguised as indentured servitude. "An Act concerning the Introduction of Negroes and Mulattoes into This Territory," passed in 1805, permitted any person owning or purchasing slaves outside the territory to bring them into Indiana and bind them to service. Records show that slaves were frequently made to sign contracts for periods of service that extended beyond their lifetime—sometimes for ninety years. Many wealthy men in the territory, including Governor William Henry Harrison, held blacks under the indenture law.

In practice, there was little difference in the status and treatment of slaves who had been in the territory prior to 1787 and those serving under indentures after 1787. Territorial laws borrowed from the southern slave codes regulated their conduct and provided punishments for offenses different from those accorded free persons. Eventually, antislavery delegates dominated at constitutional conventions, and all states formed from the Northwest Territory excluded slavery in their state constitutions.

The dilemma over slavery that surfaced in the Northwest Territory reappeared in the establishment of Oregon and California in 1848 and throughout the country in the 1850s before the Civil War. Men like Senator Thomas Corwin from Ohio and President Abraham Lincoln from Illinois took their "stand upon the Ordinance of 1787" to eventually abolish slavery in the United States.

— *Julieanne Phillips*

See also: Coles, Edward; *Strader v. Graham.*

For Further Reading

Festa, Matthew J. 2002. "Property Rights and the Northwest Ordinance." M.A. thesis, Department of History, Vanderbilt University, Nashville, Tennessee.

Hammond, John Craig. 2004. "Slavery and Freedom in the Early American West: from the Northwest Ordinance to the Missouri Controversy, 1787–1821." Ph.D. dissertation, Department of History, University of Kentucky, Lexington, Kentucky.

Onuf, Peter. 1987. *Statehood and Union: A History of the Northwest Ordinance.* Bloomington: Indiana University Press.

Taylor, Robert M., Jr., ed. 1987. *The Northwest Ordinance 1787: A Bicentennial Handbook.* Indianapolis: Indiana Historical Society.

NOTES ON VIRGINIA (JEFFERSON)

Notes on Virginia (1785) was Thomas Jefferson's only published book. He wrote it in 1780–1781 to answer a French official's queries concerning aspects of society in the United States and the country's natural history. In the *Notes,* Jefferson discussed slavery in two chapters, "Laws" and "Manners."

In "Laws," he described a gradual emancipation plan calling for education of blacks "at the public expense, to tillage, arts or sciences, according to their geniuses." Once freed, blacks would be supplied with arms, tools, seeds, and domestic animals; declared a "free and independent people"; and colonized abroad, under U.S. protection. Jefferson discussed black "physical distinctions" like dark skin color, lack of facial expression, less facial and body hair, greater heat tolerance, lower sleep requirements, and greater "adventuresome[ness]."

In "Faculties," he said blacks were equal to whites in memory, and inferior in both reason and imagination. He stated that "to justify a general conclusion" about blacks would require more scientific study and observation, and such a conclusion "would degrade a whole race of men from the rank in the scale of beings which their Creator may perhaps have given them." Without justification, he offered, "as a suspicion only" the "opinion" that blacks were inferior to whites "in the endowments both of body and mind."

In "Manners," Jefferson wrote that slavery had "an unhappy influence," for it prompted "unremitting despotism" in whites and "degrading submissions" in blacks. Whites became immoral tyrants, while blacks were forced to "lock up the faculties" and "live and labour for another." Pointing to slavery's injustice, Jefferson hoped that "a total emancipation" would be achieved "with the consent of the masters, rather than by their extirpation."

Jefferson's comments were both praised and denounced by antislavery and proslavery forces, respectively. Jefferson knew his comments were controversial, and so he delayed publishing them for fear they would polarize and "indispose the people toward . . . the emancipation of slaves."

Opponents of slavery praised Jefferson's condemnation of the institution and his call for emancipation. In 1785 John Adams wrote that the passages about slavery would have more effect than volumes written by philosophers. Following Nat Turner's Rebellion, Virginia legislators in 1832 debated a plan of gradual emancipation based on that in the *Notes*. In Charles Sumner's "Landmark of Freedom" speech (1854), the abolitionist senator used Jefferson's own words from the *Notes* to depict slavery as a corrupting influence. In David Walker's *Appeal* (1829), that black writer declared Jefferson's *Notes* to be "as great a barrier to our emancipation, as any thing."

Proponents of slavery embraced Jefferson's comments on black inferiority while rejecting both his call for emancipation and his assertion that slavery harmed white morals. By the middle of the nineteenth century, advocates of scientific racism, like Dr. Josiah C. Nott, continued where Jefferson left off by describing black inferiority in terms of quasiscientific methods.

Thomas R. Dew, in the first southern proslavery book, *Review* (1832), argued that emancipation was economic suicide, and he refuted Jefferson's comments that slavery had harmful effects on the morals of southern whites. Jefferson's comments also initiated a colonization movement that culminated in the founding of the American Colonization Society in 1816.

— *Mary Jo Miles*

See also: American Colonization Society; Jefferson, Thomas; Nott, Josiah Clark; Turner, Nat; Virginia's Slavery Debate; Walker, David.

For Further Reading
Jefferson, Thomas. 1955. *Notes on Virginia*. Ed. William Peden. Chapel Hill: University of North Carolina Press.
    Jordan, Winthrop D. 1968. *White over Black: American Attitudes toward the Negro, 1550–1812*. Baltimore, MD: Penguin Books.
    Peterson, Merrill D. 1962. *The Jefferson Image in the American Mind*. New York: Oxford University Press.
    Randell, Willard Sterne. 1993. *Thomas Jefferson: A Life*. New York: Henry Holt.

JOSIAH CLARK NOTT (1804–1873)

Josiah Clark Nott was a physician, ethnologist, educator, and influential nineteenth-century racist whose writings provided much of the scientific justification for the establishment of strict racial segregation in the United States. Nott was born in Columbia, South Carolina, on March 31, 1804, to Abraham and Angelica Mitchell Nott. His well-to-do family was socially prominent in the antebellum South.

After graduating from South Carolina College in 1824, Nott continued his medical education at Columbia University and the College of Physicians and Surgeons in New York City and at the University of Pennsylvania in Philadelphia, where he received his medical degree in 1827. After several years of teaching at the University of Pennsylvania and studying in Europe, Nott established a private practice in Mobile, Alabama, where he became one of the South's most prominent surgeons. While in private practice, Nott continued teaching medicine, holding various posts at the University of Louisiana and the Medical College of Alabama.

In 1832 Nott married Sarah Deas of Columbia, South Carolina, and they had eight children; in 1853 a yellow fever epidemic in Mobile, Alabama, claimed the lives of four of them. At the outbreak of the Civil War, Nott joined the Confederate army and served as a

Josiah Clark Nott was a physician, ethnologist, educator, and influential nineteenth-century racist whose writings provided much of the scientific justification for the establishment of strict racial segregation in the United States. (Library of Congress)

field surgeon throughout the conflict. Two of Nott's sons died in the service of the Confederacy, one at the battle of Shiloh, the other at the battle of Chickamauga. After the Civil War, Nott lived and practiced medicine in Baltimore and New York City for five years before returning to Mobile where he spent the remainder of his life.

Although Nott was a productive and well-respected contributor to the medical literature of his day, including innovative work on yellow fever and surgical techniques, his most lasting impact on society in the United States was through his published works on ethnology, which helped lay the foundation for nineteenth-century American racism. Nott believed that humankind was divided, ever since the Creation, into several "fixed types," that these fixed types corresponded to what he identified as the five "races" of humankind, and that these five races could be distinguished by a clear and immutable hierarchy of

physical, mental, and moral characteristics. In Nott's hierarchy, Caucasians occupied the highest position and Ethiopians the lowest. Nott concluded that Ethiopians, meaning Africans and African Americans, had little potential for roles in modern society beyond that of slaves or menial laborers.

Nott introduced his theories on immutable racial characteristics in a widely read book, *Connection Between the Biblical and Physical History of Man* (1849), and his theories became fixed in popular consciousness with the publication of *Types of Mankind* (1854), which he wrote with George R. Gliddon. Editions of *Types of Mankind* were eventually published and became a standard textbook in biology and medicine during the late nineteenth century. Nott wrote *Indigenous Races of the Earth* (1857), also with Gliddon, which expanded upon and reinforced his racial theories.

Nott died in Mobile, probably of throat cancer, on his sixty-ninth birthday, March 31, 1873.

— *Frederick J. Simonelli*

For Further Reading

Nott, Josiah Clark. 1849. *Connection Between the Biblical and Physical History of Man.* New York: Bartlett and Welford.

Nott, Josiah Clark, and George R. Gliddon. 1854. *Types of Mankind.* Philadelphia: Lippincott, Grambo, and Company.

Nott, Josiah Clark, and George R. Gliddon. 1857. *Indigenous Races of the Earth.* Philadelphia: Lippincott.

NULLIFICATION DOCTRINE

As a constitutional argument to protect southern social and economic interests, the doctrine of nullification played a significant role in the debate over slavery in the United States. Nullification was founded on the premise that sovereignty resided with the people but was exercised by the states with the people's consent. Believing that the Tenth Amendment granted such powers, advocates of nullification believed that the states could declare null and void any federal law they deemed unconstitutional.

Nullification had its roots in protests arising in 1798 in response to the Alien and Sedition Acts and previously proposed Hamiltonian banking measures. Fearing such federal laws could stifle free speech and hamper southern state economies, James Madison and Thomas Jefferson articulated their beliefs concerning the right of states to limit the power of the federal government. In the Virginia Resolution of 1798, Madison argued that the federal government possessed only those powers specifically granted to it by the U.S.

Constitution. Therefore, Madison believed that individual states could interpose their authority between the federal government and the citizenry to prevent the enforcement of oppressive or inequitable legislation. In the Kentucky Resolution of the same year, Jefferson took Madison's idea of interposition one step further and argued that states could nullify federal laws that were deemed by the state legislature to be unconstitutional. In Jefferson's argument, states became the final arbiters of the Constitution. These important documents firmly asserted the supremacy of state sovereignty and served as important precedents in a debate that grew more heated during the nineteenth century.

This strict construction of the Constitution with regard to states' rights became one of the fundamental principles of the Democratic-Republican Party in 1792, and the doctrine of nullification resurfaced in a firestorm of debate surrounding the tariff of 1828. In an effort to decrease public debt and protect American manufacturers, Congress passed the highest protective tariff to date in 1827, and southern politicians, most notably from Virginia and South Carolina, vehemently opposed it. Labeling it "the tariff of abominations," they protested the increase in the cost of manufactured goods in the South. When Andrew Jackson was elected in 1828, southerners were confident the new chief executive would identify with their cause. Their confidence was misplaced, however, as Jackson had never made his position on the tariff clear. In fact, he saw the protective tariff as a way to garner support for the Democratic Party in the North.

However, southern antitariff leaders did have a vocal, articulate champion in the administration. Vice President John C. Calhoun considered the tariff to be an unconstitutional act that favored one section of the country over another, and in 1828 the South Carolina legislature published anonymously Calhoun's *South Carolina Exposition and Protest,* in which he resurrected a remedy for such blatantly oppressive legislation: nullification. Drawing on the ideas of Madison and Jefferson, Calhoun argued that the Union was a compact of individually sovereign states and that these states had the authority to nullify federal laws they deemed oppressive. This action could not be taken arbitrarily. In order to nullify a law, a special state convention had to be elected to consider the question, thereby following the same procedures as the ratification of the Constitution. If this body determined a law to be unconstitutional, the state could prevent its enforcement within state boundaries. The federal government would then be forced to repeal the law or to seek a constitutional amendment to guarantee its va-

lidity. In October 1832, the South Carolina legislature endorsed Calhoun's doctrine and called for a convention to consider nullifying the tariff of 1828. Meeting the following month, the convention adopted an ordinance that nullified both the 1828 and the 1832 tariffs, reasoning that these duties placed an unfair economic hardship on the citizens of South Carolina.

Jackson reacted swiftly. In December, he declared his intention to continue collecting the tariff in South Carolina, as well as his belief that nullification was both unconstitutional and detrimental to the Union. To demonstrate federal resolve, Jackson dispatched troops and naval vessels to Charleston; in response, the South Carolina legislature mobilized the state militia. In January, Jackson asked Congress to formalize his authority to use troops to enforce federal law in South Carolina. While this bill, called the Force Act, was being debated, moderates in Congress, led by Henry Clay of Kentucky, were formulating a compromise that lowered tariff rates gradually until 1842. This solution allowed both Jackson and the nullifiers to claim victory—and it was hoped it would avoid an armed confrontation. Jackson signed both the Force Act and the new tariff into law on March 2, 1833. In response, the South Carolina convention rescinded the ordinance of nullification, and, in an effort to assert the supremacy of states' rights, nullified the Force bill. Thus ended the nullification crisis, but nullification, and the corollary doctrine of states' rights, remained important themes in antebellum politics.

As historian Richard Ellis has argued, though not directly involved in the nullification crisis itself, slavery was directly linked to this important doctrine in the minds of northerners and southerners alike. Many northerners, and even Jackson himself, believed that the nullification crisis had raised divisive sectional issues that the Missouri Compromise had merely masked. Southerners, in many ways for the first time, began to view themselves as a minority within the nation whose interests were considered secondary to those of the majority. Nullification, while unsuccessful in 1833, offered an important new course of action for the South. Faced with abolitionist attacks on the slave system and fearing federal intervention, nullification was a doctrine that offered white southerners a measure of protection of the two things they cherished most, state sovereignty and slave property.

After 1833, a vocal, influential minority of southern politicians, the fire-eaters, embraced the idea of nullification to the ultimate extreme. They reasoned that states could do more than nullify oppressive federal legislation; when faced with a national government that was detrimental to their interests and the interest of their citizens, states could also dissolve the bonds that held them in the Union. Secession, therefore, can be seen as the most extreme example of nullification in practice.

— *Richard D. Starnes*

See also: Calhoun, John C.; Hayne–Webster Debate; United States Constitution.

For Further Reading

Ellis, Richard. 1987. *The Union at Risk: Jacksonian, States' Rights and the Nullification Crisis.* New York: Oxford University Press.

Freehling, William. 1966. *Prelude to Civil War: The Nullification Controversy in South Carolina, 1818–1836.* New York: Harper and Row.

Potter, David. 1976. *The Impending Crisis, 1848–1861.* New York: Harper and Row.

OCTOROONS

Octoroons were mixed-race individuals who were recognized as having one-eighth African American ancestry. Still recognized as being black by the law and custom of the antebellum South, octoroons were rarely slaves and most were recognized as free persons of color.

In the race-conscious antebellum South, and in the generations that followed Civil War and Reconstruction, the extent of one's blackness was perceived as a statistic that was worthy of note. Until the civil rights era of the 1960s, many southern states continued to carry laws that defined a person as black if one-sixty-fourth or greater of their ancestry was black. Not surprisingly, there were no comparable statutes to define what was meant by whiteness. Under such a system, a black ancestor seven generations removed could still transmit the "stain" of blackness upon a descendant.

It had been possible in Spanish colonial America to purchase a legal document, the *Cédula de Gracias al Sacar*—a "certificate of whiteness"—that allowed an individual to pass from one race to another. Though such legal tools did not exist in the United States, there was a de facto system of passing that occurred on a regular basis when one's skin color became light enough that they could identify themselves as being white. Many African Americans of mixed-ancestry, notably author Jean Toomer, have struggled with the moral dilemma of whether or not to pass themselves as white or to affirm the African heritage they carry within themselves.

New Orleans, Louisiana, and Charleston, South Carolina, were two urban centers of the antebellum era that contained large mixed-race populations. The unique cultural population often provided ready fodder for authors who sought to pique the moral sensibilities of the antebellum South. Such was the case in Dion Boucicault's play *The Octoroon, or Life in Louisiana,* which first opened in New York just four days after abolitionist John Brown was hanged in 1859.

Despite their nebulous place within southern society, octoroons did make efforts to advance the cause of civil rights for all persons of color. Homer Plessy, the person who initiated the lawsuit in the infamous *Plessy v. Ferguson* (1896) case that legalized Jim Crow era "separate but equal" facilities, was a New Orleans octoroon. Plessy had been denied permission to ride in a railcar that was designated as white only.

Like mulattoes, quadroons, and other mixed-race individuals, octoroons fashioned a strong cultural bond in their sense of otherness because they never felt themselves totally welcomed either within white or black society. Much of this sense of racial exclusivity persisted many generations beyond the days of antebellum slavery.

— *Junius P. Rodriguez*

See also: Black Slaveowners; Mulattoes; Passing; Quadroons.

For Further Reading

Ball, Edward. 1998. *Slaves in the Family.* New York: Farrar, Straus and Giroux.

Degler, Carl N. 1971. *Neither Black Nor White: Slavery and Race Relations in Brazil and the United States.* New York: Macmillan.

Johnston, James Hugo. 1972 [1939]. *Miscegenation in the Ante-Bellum South.* New York: AMS Press.

O'Toole, James. M. 2002. *Passing for White: Race, Religion, and the Healy Family, 1820–1920.* Amherst: University of Massachusetts Press.

❧ P ❧

PASSING

The *Oxford English Dictionary* offers more than sixty usages for the word "pass." One of these meanings suggests the sense in which the word relates to slavery, although it scarcely encompasses the ramifications we have come to associate with this concept: "To be accepted," the fifteenth meaning says, to be "received or held in repute, often with the implication of being something else" *(OED)*.

Yet many of the examples provided in the other usages verge, if sometimes remotely, on conditions relevant to consequences of slavery. In 1662 an English character cried "God made him and therefore let him passe for a man." Another writer early mused, "Had Lucretia been only a poet, this might have passed for a handsomely described fable." Martin Gil spoke to a stranger: "You pass," he said, "for a kind-hearted gentleman." Another Englishman, a political commentator, remarked "Something happened which at least passed for a regular election," while still another and later speaker said "Most of those who now pass as Liberals are Tories of a new type."

In the modern American sense, however, "passing" carries the dimension of color. It usually refers to persons of at least partial African American descent whose skin color is light and who therefore could seem to be white persons. It also carries an implication that the person who passes wishes to hide his or her true origins.

Beyond doubt there are many shades of meaning associated with this term in literature and in law. This situation was conspicuous in the period from the close of the Civil War well into the late nineteenth century. As the American South rushed toward laws ensuring white supremacy, it became legally possible to declare persons known to have some African American heritage to be white persons, that is, legally to be permitted to pass. Thus the Mississippi Code of 1885 drew the line at one-fourth Negro blood, and by 1890 in Mississippi all persons of one-eighth Negro blood were legally white. In Louisiana a descendant of a white person and a quadroon was a white person. Before the war, in Ohio a person was legally white if he or she was more than half white. South Carolina concluded that "where color or feature is doubtful" a jury must decide by reputation, by reception into society, and by the exercise of the privileges of a white man, as well as by admixture of blood. But in Georgia, the term *person of color* meant "all such as have an admixture of Negro blood." Interracial marriage was forbidden in all eleven of the former Confederate states. Clearly, these varying distinctions and prohibitions reflected the desire of white politicians to maintain control in areas where black populations outnumbered whites.

This problem, however, is not an exclusively American problem. Never within memory have two races existed side by side in whatever circumstances without intermingling. In some instances, in ancient Egypt and in some other societies, accommodation has progressed at a less harrowing, even beneficial pace. In the United States, however, the coexistence of two races has proved divisive, with the consequences recurrent. The effects of "passing" have given rise not only to legal complexities but to a poignant literature.

We can discern several patterns of "passing" in American literature since the twentieth century. In his novel *The House Behind the Cedars*, Charles W. Chesnutt, a writer of partial African American descent, told the story of Rena. Beautiful, complex, sensitive, of a deep emotional nature, Rena lived the tragedy of the outcast struggling to discover an acceptable style of life. The daughter of a white father and a light-skinned Negro mother of pre–Civil War days, Rena grew up at the edge of town. Because Rena's mother could never hope for marriage, she and her children lived as lonely exiles in a house provided by her white paramour. But Rena watched her older brother John learn the law while working as an office boy for a well-meaning white man. Then John left to go to South Carolina to pass as a white person. Despite his success, John felt some discomfiture. He returned to offer Rena a home. Moved by Rena's beauty and her natural dignity, George Toyon, one of John's clients, soon finds himself in love and proposes marriage. But because Rena cannot forget her mother, Toyon learns of her Negro blood and rejects her. Still he desires her, but only for what he knows to be the supreme insult, a liaison without a marriage. Sick from this vindication of her worst fears, Rena returns to her childhood home. Driven into the dangerous cypress swamps of the North Carolina lands abetting the Cape Fear River, Rena meets her death.

This story touches several situations that frequently arose in the pre–Civil War South. In other instances, white families lived close to second black families. They shared the same father. Inevitably, sisters and brothers who might resemble one another came into contact. Or those who successfully "passed" suffered mental distress from the loss of family connections, or they felt the embarrassment of daily denials on one level or another. Many variations of these situations have provided literary themes.

In another facet of the situation, some made conscious choices and lived with them. Charles Chesnutt was a light-skinned Negro child born to free Negro parents. Although some of his relatives left the circumstances in which they were born and effectively severed themselves from their past, and although he could himself have "passed," Chesnutt conceived a life project to champion black people. He always insisted on his own racial connections. In stark contrast is the twentieth-century writer Anatole Broyard, who was for many years an editor and book reviewer for *The New York Times;* he "passed" and went to great lengths to conceal his heritage. Broyard, a gifted intellectual, resolved in the words of Henry Louis Gates, Jr., "to pass so that he could be a writer, rather than a Negro writer" (*New Yorker,* June 17, 1996). Whatever the individual means of dealing with the situation of being born into one race in America and yet looking more like the other race, built-in cruelties of mental and social dimensions seemed to provide a sure accompaniment.

— *Frances Richardson Keller*

See also: Mulattoes; Octoroons; Quadroons.

For Further Reading

Chesnutt, Charles W. 1988. *The House Behind the Cedars.* Athens: University of Georgia Press.

Gates, Henry Louis, Jr. 1996. "White Like Me." *New Yorker.* June 17: 66–81.

Keller, Frances Richardson. 1978. An *American Crusade: The Life of Charles Waddell Chesnutt.* Provo, UT: Brigham Young University Press.

Monfredo, Miriam Grace. 1993. *North Star Conspiracy.* New York: Berkley Publishing Group.

O'Toole, James M. 2002. *Passing for White: Race, Religion, and the Healy Family, 1820–1920.* Amherst: University of Massachusetts Press.

PATERNALISM

Developed during the colonial period and later modified in response to northern abolitionist rhetoric critical of southern slavery in the antebellum period, paternalism in the United States was the result of the quandary produced by the ownership of human property. The image of the Old South popularized by historian Ulrich Bonnell Phillips was based on the English model of a hierarchical social order derived from extended family units. Ulrich, using the journals and plantation records of antebellum slaveowners, conveyed the gentility and family sympathy, pastoral beauty, elegance, and ease of the Old South, all of which belied the reality of southern slavery.

In the American colonial period, the extended family exemplified stability. The wife was subservient to the husband, as were the children and servants; the husband did not take advantage of his power but generously provided for his household. This model stressed the complementary nature of the relationships. Men assumed higher political office as an extension of this role, expanding their duty to the care of the larger community. The result was almost perfect order, and it was believed that assumptions of equal status in society were invitations to disorder, even chaos. Since the people on the very bottom were cared for, there was a benefit for all involved.

The racist assumption inherent in the rationale of the time was that their presumption of superiority allowed whites to approach their black slaves with benevolent "affection." This attitude was enhanced by Enlightenment ideals concerning both "natural rights" and a morality dictating protection of society's weak and disadvantaged. Thus, slaveholders practiced what they considered to be "a good and wise despotism." An alternative view suggests that the lives of the slaves were circumscribed by constant white interference. Whites arbitrarily inflicted many detailed rules for slave behavior, not only in the areas of work and religious belief, but also in a slave's choice of mate, child rearing, and use of time when not working. Such rules were enforced by various punishments ranging from subtle threats to whipping or sale.

During the antebellum period, paternalism increasingly came to be seen as a form of benign interference. One form this interference took was a heightened interest in the slaves' spiritual lives, or perhaps, in what slaves believed and how those beliefs might affect their attitudes and behavior. Thus white ministers wrote and sermonized on the Christian responsibility of slaveowners to their slaves. Absentee slaveowners frequently included specific instructions to overseers concerning their slaves' religious activities. The Second Great Awakening, a series of fundamentalist revivals in the antebellum period, resulted in an internal missionary movement to increase slave converts to Protestant Christianity. Yet literacy continued to be prohibited to slaves, and the Christian message to slaves was carefully monitored and emphasized biblical injunctions to work hard and obey the master.

Paternalism was also seen as a justification for increasing restrictions on slaves and even for physical punishments. Respect, if not veneration, of slaveowners by slaves was desired and slaves would not "respect" an overly lenient master, so punishment was expected and required. Thus, to be more truly "benevolent," some slaveowners might limit the practice of allowing slaves private garden patches (which they worked on during "off" hours after a full day's work for the owner), visitor's passes, or approval for marriages off the "home" place. In South Carolina and Georgia, the task system was seen as a paternalistic innovation because it allowed slaves to budget their own time once a particular task was completed.

The emphasis on family stability was quite ironic in lieu of the great disruption of slave families; indeed, the slaveowners depended on the threat of that disruption to instill "order." The picture of "our family black and white" that is so often described in plantation journals and correspondence was depicted fictionally in Harriet Beecher Stowe's *Uncle Tom's Cabin, or Life Among the Lowly* (1852), which was credited with widely disseminating antislavery views. The novel was groundbreaking in being the first widely read publication to treat seriously the idea of a black family, albeit one broken by sale.

The folklore tales of plantation slaves, particularly the "trickster" tales, which highlighted the triumph of an underdog character by wiles and subtlety, are evidence of the slaves' recognition of their unequal status rather than reliance on territorial control, as some historians have suggested. The former slaves' report of both cruelty and affection from the slaveowners also suggests the complexity of paternalism as a slaveholding strategy.

Paternalist slaveowners consistently recorded their confusion as to the motives of rebellious slaves—slaves who refused to work, feigned sickness, or ran away; they saw such behavior as being, at the very least, ungrateful. This purported puzzlement was always based on the firm conviction of black inferiority, so that slaveowners generally were serious when they attributed a slave insurrection or any other organized activity as showing the influence of outside agitators, most often from the North; they truly believed that their slaves had neither the intelligence nor the skill to plan such actions.

The laws passed by southern slaveholders indicate how they themselves defined paternalism. Slave mobility was severely restricted and tied to the prohibition on slave literacy since slaves required written permission to be away from their own home place. Such restrictions increased after the Nat Turner Rebellion in 1831, as did the ability of slaves to congregate in groups, especially for the purpose of religious worship. Laws also made it increasingly difficult to manumit slaves or for freed slaves to remain in the state where they were freed.

Laws that made it a criminal act for a white person to kill a slave most often reflected the slave's monetary rather than human value, and laws defining the criminal culpability of slave acts against whites were sometimes moot since, in the heat of the moment, slaves were sometimes summarily executed. Historians interpret the existence of such laws as an attempt to live up to a paternalistic ideal—and to occasional instances when slaves received trial at law for offenses against the slave regime.

In the wake of the Civil War and the sweeping climax to the era of American race slavery, paternalism took on a new face, one in which race or gender was eclipsed by the emergence of modern notions of social class. Free northern blacks (such as Philadelphia activist Charlotte Forten) and former southern planters alike now took charge of the lives of freed southern slaves in what they considered a benign and generous spirit. Most often, however, such guidance assumed that freed slaves were incapable of taking charge of their own destinies.

In more recent times, paternalism has been reborn as an attitude of condescension on the part of men in their dealings with women, especially but not limited to interactions in professional settings. Clearly, a strategy based in power relations between individuals or groups, the legacy of U.S. slavery and paternalism is replicated today in a variety of forms.

— *Dale Edwyna Smith*

See also: Forten, Charlotte; Phillips, Ulrich Bonnell; Turner, Nat.

For Further Reading
Kolchin, Peter. 1993. *American Slavery, 1619–1877.* New York: Hill and Wang.
Oakes, James. 1982. *The Ruling Race.* New York: Alfred A. Knopf.
Parish, Peter J. 1989. *Slavery: History and Historians.* New York: Harper and Row.

SLAVE PATROLS

The existence of runaway slaves in every slave system of the world led directly to the creation of formal slave patrols after 1500. Both professional and amateur slave catchers flourished in other slave-based societies, and in the New World, regardless of whether settlements were French, Spanish, Portuguese or English, men found employment as slave catchers. The earliest New World antecedents of patrols were slave-hunting groups of owners in the 1530s, the volunteer militia *hermandad,* who looked for fugitives in Cuba. Gradually, the *hermandad* was displaced by professional slave hunters, *ranchadores,* who were paid for each individual capture.

Free blacks and slaves in Caribbean and South American colonies also chased fugitive slaves, and in Peru, these hunters were called *cuadrilleros.* In Barbados, by the mid-seventeenth century, the English militia operated like the *hermandad* in many ways, designating a portion of its men to serve as slave patrollers. As English planters migrated to the North American mainland in the seventeenth century, particularly to South Carolina, they carried well-established views on the proper steps to take in recapturing fugitive slaves.

On the mainland, colonial legislatures enacted laws creating formal slave patrols after enough slaves had been imported to warrant the effort. The earliest patrol laws in South Carolina (1704), Virginia (1727), and North Carolina (1753) were responses to rising slave populations, threatened slave revolts, and white insecurities about personal safety. In South Carolina, the existence of a black majority early in the eighteenth century convinced white lawmakers that some form of community-based slave control was necessary to supplement individual slaveowners' efforts.

The South Carolina laws soon found emulation in colonial Georgia, and as settlers migrated into the Deep South, copies of South Carolina's or Virginia's slave laws, and slave patrols, migrated with them. Patrols existed in all slave states prior to the Civil War, created by law and sanctioned by state authority. Only the Civil War formally ended the legal use of slave patrols in the United States. After the Civil War, the Ku Klux Klan copied the patroller methods of violence and intimidation formerly directed at slaves and used them against freedmen.

In most colonies, and later states, patrollers were drawn from the local militia, often chosen directly from membership rolls by captains of militia districts. This created problems in the nineteenth century, as militia groups fell into general decline. In North Carolina, county courts had authority over the patrols from the beginning, and patrollers, or "searchers" as they were first called, were exempt from militia duty for their term of service as patrollers. In Virginia and North Carolina, patrollers eventually received exemptions from jury service, militia duty, and road work duty during their term of service.

North Carolina usually paid patrollers for their work on a per-night or per-hour basis. Some cities (e.g., Wilmington, Raleigh, Charleston, and Columbia) adopted a form of payment for urban patrollers instead of relying solely on exemptions. Paid urban patrollers occasionally substituted for official police forces in southern cities, whose residents viewed slaves as more troublesome than mere criminals. After the Civil War, police forces displaced urban patrollers in southern cities.

Patrollers had three main tasks, First, they were to contain slaves' activities once they left the plantation or residence of their owner. Patrollers did most of their work at night on roads, in fields, and between the farms of their neighbors, making sure that slaves went where their masters intended them to go. Their duty required them to chase and interrogate slaves, and they frequently used violence in these nocturnal encounters. Traveling slaves were supposed to carry passes, stating their owners' name, their destination, and when they were to return home. Many planters resisted giving their slaves passes of any kind, while others gave them freely. In towns, passes complicated everyday life, since no owner wanted to have to write a new pass for every errand. Many towns resorted to having slaves wear metal badges, purchased once a year, which clearly indicated their status.

The second job of patrollers was to disperse illegal slave gatherings wherever they might occur. Such assemblies could be used to plot insurrections, which southern whites dreaded. In breaking up meetings, patrols routinely disrupted religious gatherings that slaves organized on their own.

Their third main task was to enter slave quarters and search for runaway slaves or any items (e.g., guns, papers, or books) forbidden to slaves. Some white slavemasters, however, forbade patrollers to encroach on their property, even though the law gave them legal rights to enter and search slave quarters.

Unlike slave catchers, patrollers were sanctioned by law, appointed by their neighbors, (sometimes) paid for their work, and did more than just hunt fugitives. Their work was local, whereas the slave catcher might range widely, hunting only runaways. Patrols always worked in groups, led by a "captain," the leader appointed to supervise the patrol group's activities.

Many historians claim that patrollers were from the lowest classes, that they were the "poor whites" or "white trash" of a community, chosen by their social superiors to perform an unsavory social duty. They have typically been cast as poor nonslaveowners who were being used by the richer slaveowning class. These assertions are often supported with statements drawn from the WPA interviews conducted with ex-slaves, who routinely stated that patrollers were poor whites.

Studies by Sally Hadden and Charles Bolton, however, indicate that patrollers were chosen from the middle strata of southern society, not exclusively from the poor, and that patrol groups usually in-

Men pointing guns at Fort Scott Peace Convention. Hoping to prevent the destruction of the Union during the 1860–1861 secession crisis, 133 delegates met in Washington, D.C. to discuss a compromise that would keep the Union together and avert possible civil war. However, the political motives of both sides were questioned. (Bettmann/Corbis)

cluded at least one affluent slaveowner. This makes sense, when we consider that slaves as property were too valuable to allow propertyless poor whites to injure and perhaps kill them. Some sort of supervision by the landed gentry was required to keep the slave patrols from brutalizing slaves too much. The presence of slaveowners on patrols provided just such a restraint.

— *Sally E. Hadden*

See also: Slave Catchers; Narratives; Passing; Punishment.

For Further Reading

Bolton, Charles C. 1994. *Poor Whites of the Antebellum South: Tenants and Laborers in Central North Carolina and Northeast Mississippi.* Durham, NC: Duke University Press.

Fry, Gladys-Marie. 1991. *Night Riders in Black Folk History.* Athens: University of Georgia Press.

Hadden, Sally E. 2001. *Slave Patrols: Law and Violence in Virginia and the Carolinas.* Cambridge, MA: Harvard University Press.

Henry, H. M. 1914. "The Police Control of the Slave in South Carolina." Emory: n.p.

Russ, Williams, E., ed. 1972. "Slave Patrol Ordinances of St. Tammany Parish, Louisiana, 1835–1838." *Louisiana History* 13 (1972): 399–412.

PEACE CONVENTION (1860–1861)

Hoping to prevent the destruction of the Union during the 1860–1861 secession crisis, 133 delegates met in Washington, D.C., to discuss a compromise that would keep the Union together and avert possible civil war. Representatives from Connecticut, Delaware, Indiana, Illinois, Iowa, Kansas, Kentucky, Maine, Maryland, Massachusetts, Missouri, New Hampshire, New York, North Carolina, Ohio, Pennsylvania, Rhode Island, Virginia and Wisconsin faced the formidable task of creating a compromise to keep the North and South together. Former president John Tyler of Virginia chaired the proceedings.

Members of the convention stressed the theme of a

conciliation between North and South. The Democratic and Republican parties were urged to lay aside their political differences for the good of the nation. However, the political motives of both sides were questioned. By the time the convention began debating the issues dividing the country, some of its members had resorted to insulting remarks toward fellow delegates and their states. Disagreements on how to proceed with the convention led to bitter arguments that threatened to end the peace conference before any concrete proposals could be made. Further difficulties in the convention were caused by the exclusion of the press. These closed-door sessions created tension and suspicion, not only with the press, but also within the political community.

Some of the key points for peace between the North and South were included in the compromise proposed by Kentucky Senator John J. Crittenden. His proposal stated that the Missouri Compromise line of 36°30' would be maintained and be extended to the Pacific and slavery would be permitted south of the line, although new states would have the option to remain free. Slavery on public lands could not be prohibited, and slavery in the District of Columbia could not be abolished as long as slavery existed in Virginia and Maryland, or until a majority of the citizens in those states voted for emancipation. Congress could not interfere with the interstate transportation of slaves, and compensation would be given to slaveowners who could not retrieve their runaway slaves due to the activities of abolitionists. Also, Crittenden's proposals could not be nullified by future legislation.

The Peace Convention formally presented its proposals, a modified version of the Crittenden Compromise, to both houses of Congress on February 27, 1861. The subjects of slave territory and the rights of slaveowners constantly came up for debate, and the convention finally did propose protection for the slaveowner's rights to hold slave property. At the same time, it also stated its desire to see the slave trade suppressed by all means necessary. Congress took the convention's report under advisement, but after a brief review of its report, the House and Senate failed to act on any of the proposals. The rejection of the Peace Convention's proposals by Congress was evidence of the severe divisions in the nation. Congress's lack of interest in the work of the convention, disagreements within the convention itself, and Virginia's rejection of its proposals doomed the work of the convention to failure. Within a matter of months, the United States was plunged into civil war.

— *Ron D. Bryant*

See also: Civil War; Compensated Emancipation; Crittenden Compromise.

For Further Reading
Keene, Jesse Lynn. 1961. *The Peace Convention of 1861.* Tuscaloosa, AL: Confederate Publishing.
Kirwan, Albert D. 1962. *John J. Crittenden: The Struggle for the Union.* Lexington: University Press of Kentucky.

JAMES W. PENNINGTON (1809–1870)

A committed minister, teacher, writer, and dedicated abolitionist, James W. Pennington, was a former slave whose writings and activities helped generate a worldwide revulsion against slavery. Like other blacks of his generation, Pennington grew up shadowed by the brutalities and inhumanities that slavery and racial discrimination entailed.

Born a slave on Maryland's Eastern Shore, Pennington was moved at the age of four to Washington County, Maryland, where he began active plantation labor. A brilliant and versatile man, Pennington learned and became expert in stone masonry and black-smithing. Having never reconciled himself to slavery, he frequently contemplated escape and finally succeeded when he fled to Pennsylvania in 1830. He began his elementary education there and later moved to Long Island, New York, where he continued his education.

In the early 1830s Pennington taught in black schools in New York and Connecticut, and after studying theology, he assumed the pastorship of churches in Long Island and Connecticut. In 1841 he was appointed president of the Union of Masonry Society, an antislavery organization whose members boycotted commodities produced by slave labor and also opposed colonization.

Pennington belongs in that category of "pioneers" of the black protest tradition who used their intellectual resources in the service of vindicating the black race. Concerned about the denial of black history, and the negative and derogatory portrayals of the black experience, Pennington published his *A Textbook of the Origin and History of the Colored People* (1841), which discussed the black's complexion and history, his intellectual capacity, and prejudice in the United States. Pennington's stated objective was to debunk false ideas, and the book remains his lasting contribution to the black's intellectual defense. Proud of his "unadulterated African blood," Pennington rejected notions of black inferiority and attributed racial characteristics to environmental factors.

In 1843 he represented Connecticut at the World Anti-Slavery Convention that convened in London.

He also represented the American Peace Convention at the World Peace Society meeting in London, where he delivered several antislavery speeches. He toured Europe, taking his antislavery crusade to Paris and Brussels. Returning to the Untied States in 1847, he lived in New York City until 1850. That same year, he attended the world peace conference in Frankfurt, Germany. His autobiography, *The Fugitive Blacksmith,* was published in London in 1849. The book is a scathing indictment of slavery. Pennington also helped organize antislavery protests in New York. He was also vehemently opposed to colonization.

With passage of the Fugitive Slave Act in 1850, Pennington felt insecure and escaped abroad, where he remained until his manumission in June 1851. He toured Europe where he delivered antislavery lectures meant to galvanize European opinion against slavery. Pennington not only condemned slavery in the United States, but also racism in Europe, particularly in England, France, and Germany. He later studied at the University of Heidelberg, where he received a doctor of divinity degree. During his time abroad, he forged links with antislavery movements and organizations in England and Scotland. The Glasgow Female Anti-Slavery Society sponsored some of his activities in Scotland.

In 1851 Pennington returned to the United States and became actively engaged in vigilante activities against the enforcement of the Fugitive Slave Act. He organized fund-raising events in defense of those arrested for obstructing the law's implementation, and in 1853 he organized the New York Legal Rights Association, which fought against discrimination on public transportation. Antislavery activities preoccupied Pennington for much of the 1850s and 1860s. He greatly admired John Brown, whose capture and execution he deplored. He moved to Jacksonville, Florida, in 1870 and founded a small black Presbyterian Church where he ministered until his death on October 20, 1870.

— *Tunde Adeleke*

See also: Fugitive Slave Act (1850).

For Further Reading

Pease, Jane H., and William H. Pease. 1990. *They Who Would Be Free: Blacks' Search for Freedom, 1830–1861.* Chicago: University of Chicago Press.

Quarles, Benjamin. 1970. *Black Abolitionists.* New York: Oxford University Press.

Thorpe, Earl. 1971. *Black Historians: A Critique.* New York: William Morrow.

White, David O. 1984. "The Fugitive Blacksmith of Hartford: James W. C. Pennington." *The Connecticut Historical Society Bulletin* 49 (Winter): 4–29.

PERSONAL LIBERTY LAWS

Fourteen northern states of the United States approved personal liberty laws before the Civil War began. The first of these were passed by many northern state legislatures between the 1780s and the 1820s in order to protect free blacks from being kidnapped by unscrupulous slave catchers and sold into bondage. Such statutes established an orderly legal process for distinguishing a free black from a fugitive slave, and the laws generally extended certain basic legal protections—the writ of habeas corpus, the right to a jury trial, and the writ of *de homine replegiando* (a process for the recovery of property)—to people who were accused of being runaway slaves. These statutes also voided the right of recaption (the right to recapture a slave without going to court) that had been claimed by slaveowners under the Fugitive Slave Act of 1793. As a result, the statutes consistently led to questions of comity (the respect of one state for the laws of another) and state sovereignty in the decades prior to the war.

The clearest rejection of southern slaveowners' claims to the right of recaption came in Pennsylvania when that state passed a new personal liberty law in 1820. This law increased the penalty for kidnapping to up to twenty-one years in prison at hard labor, and it also limited the role that state officials could play in the recovery of runaway slaves. Slaveowners and officials in Maryland, the state most affected by the act, pressed to repeal the restriction and in 1826 the Pennsylvania legislature approved a new personal liberty law. This law softened the restrictions on state officials but kept in place most of the legal protections for anyone accused of being a fugitive slave.

Proslavery interests challenged the personal liberty laws throughout the 1830s and early 1840s in the federal courts. In the case of *Prigg v. Pennsylvania* (1842), the U.S. Supreme Court acknowledged a slaveowner's right of recaption but held that state or local officials could not be required to assist in the enforcement of the Fugitive Slave Act of 1793. A second wave of personal liberty laws followed, and these ended state assistance in the recovery process and mandated the use of the writ of habeas corpus and jury trials to protect free blacks and obstruct the recovery of fugitive slaves. Between 1843 and 1847, such laws were passed in Vermont, New Hampshire, Massachusetts, Connecticut, Rhode Island, New Jersey, Pennsylvania, and Ohio.

The personal liberty laws of the 1840s were a major reason the South pushed for passage of the Fugitive Slave Act of 1850, which put the federal government in the business of capturing and returning runaway slaves. At first, northern state legislatures seemed hesitant to challenge the new act, but the notorious rendition (legal return to slavery) of Anthony Burns in 1854, and the reopening of free federal territories to slavery as a result of the Kansas–Nebraska Act in the same year, led to a third wave of personal liberty laws.

One of the strongest of the new laws was passed in 1855 in Massachusetts. It forbade any attorney in the state from acting as counsel for a slave claimant, prevented any officer of the state from issuing an arrest warrant under the Fugitive Slave Act, and appointed special commissioners to defend people who were claimed as runaway slaves. An antikidnapping section provided for a fine of up to $5,000 and imprisonment for up to five years for parties guilty of fraudulently claiming or seizing anyone as a slave. The law also guaranteed numerous protections for the accused—the writ of habeas corpus, the right to a jury trial, written evidence, witnesses—and placed the burden of proof on the claimant. Similar laws were passed in Vermont, New Hampshire, Maine, Connecticut, Rhode Island, Ohio, Michigan, and Wisconsin. These new laws successfully obstructed enforcement of the Fugitive Slave Act throughout much of the North.

In the case of *Ableman v. Booth* (1859), the U.S. Supreme Court rejected the constitutionality of the personal liberty laws. Ironically, the Wisconsin and Ohio legislatures announced their intent to practice "positive defiance" of the decision by continuing to enforce the acts as a matter of states' rights. During the secession crisis of 1860–1861, the U.S. Congress appealed to the states to repeal personal liberty laws in the spirit of sectional compromise. But they remained in force until rendered obsolete by ratification of the Thirteenth Amendment.

— *Roy E. Finkenbine*

See also: *Ableman v. Booth;* Burns, Anthony; Fugitive Slave Act (1850); *Prigg v. Pennsylvania.*

For Further Reading

Morris, Thomas. 1974. *Free Men All: The Personal Liberty Laws of the North, 1780–1861.* Baltimore, MD: Johns Hopkins University Press.

Nogee, Joseph L. 1954. "The *Prigg* Case and Fugitive Slavery 1842–1850." *Journal of Negro History* 39 (April): 185–205.

Rosenberg, Norman L. 1971. "Personal Liberty Laws and the Sectional Crisis, 1850–1861." *Civil War History* 17 (March): 25–45.

Schafer, Joseph. 1936. "Stormy Days in Court—The *Booth* Case." *Wisconsin Magazine of History* 20 (September): 89–110.

JAMES LOUIS PETIGRU (1789–1863)

Historians have traditionally portrayed prominent antebellum white southerners as monolithic in their support of slavery and states' rights. Such a view minimizes the role of an important minority who criticized slavery, supported the Union, and attacked the social and economic foundations of southern life. No southern dissenter was more important than James Louis Petigru.

Petigru was born near Abbeville, South Carolina, on May 10, 1789, the first of eight children. His father, William Petigrew, soon lost his land to gambling and drinking and came to rely on his wife's brother to support his family. James grew up doing farm chores much as did any youth of the period. However, his mother imbued him with a deep intellectual curiosity and schooled him at home until he was fifteen, when he entered a local academy. Two years later, he began his studies at South Carolina College in Columbia. Graduating in 1809, James read law with Beaufort attorney William Robertson and was admitted to the bar in 1812. During this time, he also changed the spelling of his name to "Petigru," a reflection of his poor relationship with his father. Then he embarked on one of the most brilliant and controversial legal careers in the history of southern jurisprudence.

Petigru's legal practice was initially lackluster, but he found success after David Hugen, a prominent South Carolina lawyer and politician, took an interest in his career. In rapid succession, Petigru became a state solicitor, a partner in a powerful Charleston firm, and state attorney general. In court, he often made arguments that were unpopular with other white southerner elites, and on several occasions, he took cases brought by slaves against their masters, arguing for the extension of basic human rights for slaves. As attorney general, he argued that South Carolina's Negro Seaman Law, which prohibited black sailors from coming ashore in the state, was unconstitutional. These actions do not mean that Petigru was a racial egalitarian. Rather, he believed that slavery was an impediment to the South, one that prevented social reform and economic development. To end the institution, he favored manumission, a controversial practice that involved owners freeing their slaves by bequest.

Petigru's opposition to slavery was not the only view that placed him in conflict with prominent leaders in his state and region. He also opposed nullification, a stand that placed him at odds with powerful politicians such as John C. Calhoun. Petigru considered nullification an unconstitutional act. In Petigru's view, federal law superseded state laws, and if a state took issue with a federal act, it should seek relief through the judicial and legislative channels established by the U.S. Constitution. Armed confrontation, according to Petigru, was not a viable solution. For many of the same reasons, he later opposed secession, becoming a vocal unionist until his death in 1863. His views on slavery, nullification, and secession set James Louis Petigru at odds with the prevailing opinions of the day and made him one of the great southern dissenters of the antebellum period.

— *Richard D. Starnes*

See also: Nullification Doctrine; Proslavery Argument; Seamen's Acts.

For Further Reading

Degler, Carl. 1974. *The Other South: Southern Dissenters in the Nineteenth Century.* New York: Harper and Row.

Eaton, Clement. 1964. *The Freedom of Thought Struggle in the Old South.* New York: Harper and Row.

Pease, William, and Jane Pease. 1995. *James Louis Petigru: Southern Conservative, Southern Dissenter.* Athens: University of Georgia Press.

PHILADELPHIA FEMALE ANTI-SLAVERY SOCIETY (1833–1870)

The Philadelphia Female Anti-Slavery Society was the longest-lived of all female antislavery societies in the United States. It was also the first biracial antislavery organization in Pennsylvania. The society consciously tried to recruit women of diverse backgrounds and welcomed blacks as members and officers throughout its nearly forty-year existence. Although the society was open to all women, most of its membership consisted of Hicksite Quakers—those who followed the tenets of the antislavery Quaker preacher Elias Hicks.

The American Anti-Slavery Society held its founding convention in Philadelphia on December 4–6, 1833, and invited several women to witness the event silently. Although it was intended that women would be present but nonparticipatory, several of them, especially Lucretia Mott, entered the debate and contributed suggestions for the national society's constitution and its declaration of sentiments. Three days later, Mott and the other women present at the convention invited women interested in the abolitionist cause to a meeting where they founded the Philadelphia Female Anti-Slavery Society. These women pioneered female participation in state and national antislavery societies in addition to founding autonomous female antislavery societies.

The Philadelphia Female Anti-Slavery Society boasted many members besides Lucretia Mott, though she is probably the best-known member. Sarah Pugh was the society's president for most of the 1838–1866 era, and Mary Grew was the society's corresponding secretary from 1834 to 1870. Lydia White, Sydney Ann Lewis, and Alba Alcott (wife of Bronson Alcott and mother of Louisa May Alcott) were all active members. There were also active members from several prominent Philadelphia families, including the Fortens—Charlotte, Marguerite, Sarah, and Harriet Forten Purvis (wife of Robert Purvis); the Douglasses—Grace and Sarah; and the Grimké sisters—Sarah and Angelina.

Initially, the society's activities included circulating petitions, recruiting new members, and sponsoring public lectures by black and white abolitionists. Its mission was to end slavery and racial discrimination. Besides its history of racial cooperation, the society hosted the second annual Convention of American Anti-Slavery Women in 1838, during which the antiabolitionist mobs burned the newly built Pennsylvania Hall.

As conditions changed within the antislavery movement, owing to dissension over whether women should be allowed to take an active role in the movement and the use of political means to end slavery, the Philadelphia Female Anti-Slavery Society became more focused on both its membership and its activities. Emphasis shifted from various public works to concentrating on the organization of and producing items for the annual fair. Although this change appears to have reduced the society's effectiveness, the women continued to raise substantial funds for the antislavery movement. They saw their years of work bear fruit toward the end of the society's long life when the state legislature passed laws prohibiting discrimination against blacks on public transportation.

— *Sydney J. Caddel-Liles*

See also: Forten, Charlotte; Grimké, Angelina; Grimké, Sarah Moore; Mott, Lucretia Coffin; Quakers; Women and the Antislavery Movement.

For Further Reading

Bacon, Margaret Hope. 1986. *Mother of Feminism: The Story of Quaker Women in America.* San Francisco: Harper and Row.

Brown, Ira V. 1978. "Cradle of Feminism: The Female Anti-Slavery Society, 1833–1840." *Pennsylvania Magazine of History and Biography* 102: 143–166.

Soderland, Jean R. 1994. "Priorities and Power: The Philadelphia Female Anti-Slavery Society." In *The Abolitionist Sisterhood: Women's Political Culture in Antebellum America.* Ed. Jean Fagan Yellin and John C. Van Horne. Ithaca, NY: Cornell University Press.

Williams, Carolyn. 1994. "The Female Antislavery Movement: Fighting against Racial Prejudice and Promoting Women's Rights in Antebellum America." In *The Abolitionist Sisterhood: Women's Political Culture in Antebellum America.* Ed. Jean Fagan Yellin and John C. Van Horne. Ithaca, NY: Cornell University Press.

Williams, Carolyn. 1991. "Religion, Race, and Gender in Antebellum American Radicalism: The Philadelphia Female Anti-Slavery Society 1833–1870." Ph.D. dissertation, Department of History, University of California at Los Angeles.

ULRICH BONNELL PHILLIPS (1877–1934)

Born in LaGrange, Georgia, in 1877, Ulrich Bonnell Phillips studied history with William A. Dunning at Columbia University (receiving his Ph.D. in 1902) and became the most prolific and influential historian of slavery of the first half of the twentieth century. Phillips's writings combined postbellum proslavery attitudes, conservative racial views, and Progressive Era "scientific" historical methodology. He published nine books and almost sixty articles, most of them dealing with slavery. Phillips's major works were his in-depth economic and institutional history, *American Negro Slavery* (1918), and his broadly conceived social history, *Life and Labor in the Old South* (1929).

In *American Negro Slavery,* Phillips defined slavery and the plantation regime as part of an organic whole, one that rendered the Old South unique. Drawing heavily on plantation sources (diaries, manuscripts, account books, and letters) and on newspapers, Phillips argued that slavery was a patriarchal system that was beneficial to slaves, whom he considered "inert." He pronounced the plantation "a school constantly training and controlling pupils who were in a backward state of civilization." Paternalistic planters, Phillips contended, fed, clothed, and "civilized" their slaves, often sacrificing economic profits in order to keep their slave families together and to maintain social and racial order.

After carefully studying slavery's costs and the slaves' productivity, he pronounced the institution an economic burden for white southerners. To Phillips's mind, slavery "was less a business than a life; it made fewer fortunes than it made men." By this statement, Phillips meant that slavery succeeded less as an economic system than as a social system. It bound master and slave together in a relationship characterized by "propriety, proportion and cooperation." Under slavery, Phillips insisted, the races were interdependent—the blacks "always within the social mind and conscience of the whites, as the whites in turn were within the mind and conscience of the blacks."

In *Life and Labor in the Old South,* Phillips broadened his net to include the Old South's hitherto neglected people—Indians, Latins, yeomen, and mountain folk. Even though Phillips had discovered new plantation sources in the decade since he published *American Negro Slavery,* his interpretation of slavery in *Life and Labor* remained virtually unchanged. He continued to hammer home his earlier themes—the duality of slavery as unprofitable but its necessity as a vehicle of racial control, slavery's benign and paternalistic qualities, and his belief in the slaves' inherent inferiority. Fewer racial slurs appeared in 1929 than in 1918, but Phillips's racism remained unchanged.

Although contemporary black critics, most notably Carter G. Woodson and W. E. B. DuBois, attacked Phillips's racial bias and criticized his one-dimensional view of slavery, most scholars and laypersons greeted *American Negro Slavery* and *Life and Labor* enthusiastically. Writing in 1929, Henry Steele Commager praised *Life and Labor* as "perhaps the most significant contribution to the history of the Old South in this generation" (review in *New York Herald Tribune,* May 19, 1929). Not surprisingly, white historians from the 1920s until the 1950s applied Phillips's essential method and biases to their research and amassed what scholars term "the Phillips School" of studies on slavery. Phillips reigned as the master of slave historiography until he was ousted by Kenneth M. Stampp and his revisionist book, *The Peculiar Institution* (1956).

On balance, Phillips's works exhibited all the strengths and weaknesses of first-rate white scholars during the age of legally sanctioned social discrimination against blacks. Deeply researched in primary sources, carefully focused on the social and economic aspects of slavery, and gracefully written, his many books and articles set a high scholarly standard for his contemporaries. Phillips also played a major role in locating plantation-generated archival sources, in editing texts, and in delineating the themes and topics that later generations of historians of slavery would study.

Today, Phillips is best remembered for his overt sympathy with the master class and his condescending treatment of blacks as intellectually, culturally, and morally inferior to whites. Phillips's romanticized interpretation of the Old South, where gracious masters succored their grateful slaves, has been thoroughly repudiated by almost a half century of scholarship.

— *John David Smith*

See also: DuBois, W. E. B.; Stampp, Kenneth M.

For Further Reading
Dillon, Merton L. 1985. *Ulrich Bonnell Phillips:*

Historian of the Old South. Baton Rouge: Louisiana State University Press.

Roper, John Herbert. 1984. *U.B. Phillips: A Southern Mind.* Macon, GA: Mercer University Press.

Smith, John David. 1991. *An Old Creed for the New South: Proslavery Ideology and Historiography, 1865–1918.* Athens: University of Georgia Press.

Smith, John David, and John C. Inscoe, eds. 1993. *Ulrich Bonnell Phillips: A Southern Historian and His Critics.* Athens: University of Georgia Press.

POINTE COUPÉE CONSPIRACY (1795)

The Pointe Coupée conspiracy, an abortive slave revolt, created such a legacy of paranoia that it was sometimes called an uprising in early histories of Louisiana. In spring 1795, when Louisiana was under Spanish colonial control, the remote Pointe Coupée district located on the Mississippi River about 150 miles upriver from New Orleans was not an unlikely place for slave revolt. In 1783 Spanish colonial governor Esteban Rodriguez Miró sent an expedition to Pointe Coupée to help deal with a problem with large numbers of runaway slaves. The reason for the runaway problem was probably harsh treatment, and by the 1790s economic troubles in the colony had caused reductions in already meager rations. Another problem that made Pointe Coupée a likely place for slave revolt was that masters, isolated from each other on plantations stretched along the river, were significantly outnumbered by their slaves. In fact, the district's population included approximately two thousand whites and seven thousand slaves, a differential that would certainly have given rebelling slaves reason to be optimistic about their chances for success.

The night of April 12–13 was set for the revolt, which was to be initiated on the estate of Julien Poydras, a bachelor who lived alone except for his slaves. Poydras, a prominent Louisiana literary figure, was considered one of the most humane planters in his treatment of slaves. He had planned to visit the United States in April, which may have been a factor in timing the rebellion. The slaves planned to steal guns and ammunition from Poydras's store and then set fire to a building on the estate. It was hoped that masters from neighboring estates would come to help extinguish the blaze, and when they arrived, they would be killed. Slaves would then march on other estates, killing both the masters and those slaves who refused to participate in the rebellion.

On April 10, two Tunica Indian women betrayed the rebellion when they informed Spanish authorities of a conversation they had overheard. Upon learning that the slaves intended to kill all the whites except for the young women, the Indian women apparently feared for their own safety if the revolt were successful. Patrols were immediately dispatched with orders to arrest all blacks assembling at plantations other than their own and any strangers found in the slave quarters. Authorities found several witnesses who confirmed the story told by the Tunica women. Governor Hector de Carondelet was informed of the plot, and he ordered all commandants of Louisiana to make a simultaneous raid on slave quarters, to confiscate all firearms, and to arrest any strangers found there.

A total of sixty-three people were implicated in the conspiracy—mostly black slaves, but three free men of color and four white men were also convicted. Trials began on May 8, 1795, and continued through May 19. More than twenty slaves were sentenced to be hanged while the remainder of the conspirators were sentenced to military duty or simply banished from the colony. During the trial, residents discovered that the conspiracy had not been isolated to Pointe Coupée but that the slaves in other parts of the region had known of the conspiracy and had intended to revolt simultaneously. In response to this threat and as a grisly deterrent to rebellion, Spanish authorities placed the severed heads of those who had been executed on posts throughout the region.

The slaves at Pointe Coupée and elsewhere in Louisiana conspired to revolt for many reasons, but perhaps the most fundamental was a realistic hope for freedom. Political chaos caused by war between France and Spain and an anticipated French invasion of the colony made the timing ideal, and the French National Convention's abolition of slavery in all its colonies in 1794 made freedom a real possibility. The trial summary also indicated the slaves' awareness of the success of the St. Domingue revolt in 1791, which certainly provided inspiration.

In response to the conspiracy, Louisiana prohibited all slave imports even though there was an increasing dependency on slave labor in the colony as a result of expanding sugar and cotton production. The slave trade later reopened in November 1800 to satisfy the merchants' interests. Colonial officials attempted to assert greater control over slaves by restricting their movement between plantations and giving whites the authority to arrest slaves without a pass "or for any other reason." Perhaps the conspiracy's most significant effect was that it created a legacy of paranoia that plagued Louisiana's plantation economy throughout the antebellum period.

— *Mark Cave*

See also: Louisiana; Resistance.

For Further Reading

Din, Gilbert C. 1980. "Cimarrones and the San Malo Band in Spanish Louisiana." *Louisiana History* 21: 237–262.

Hall, Gwendolyn Midlo. 1992. *Africans in Colonial Louisiana: The Development of Afro-Creole Culture in the Eighteenth Century.* Baton Rouge: Louisiana State University Press.

Holmes, Jack D. L. 1970. "The Abortive Slave Revolt at Pointe Coupée, Louisiana, 1795." *Louisiana History* 11: 341–362.

POPULAR SOVEREIGNTY

A controversial approach to the problem of slavery in the territories, popular sovereignty was envisioned as a democratic solution to this divisive issue. Popular sovereignty did not solve the problem of slavery expansion. However, in many ways, it heightened sectional tensions and brought the nation closer to civil war.

By the 1840s the issue of slavery in the territories was as old as the Union itself. Congress first attempted to regulate slavery in newly acquired lands through the Northwest Ordinance of 1787. Prohibiting the extension of slavery north of the Ohio River, this legislation set an important precedent. Congress assumed the role of regulating slavery in the territories, and this role became important in 1820 when a conflict over the admission of Missouri to the Union brought the issue to the forefront. A compromise brokered by the Speaker of the House Henry Clay provided for the admission of Missouri and Maine, thereby preserving the numerical balance between slave and free states in Congress. More importantly, the Missouri Compromise established that slavery would be prohibited in the Louisiana Purchase north of 36°30' minutes north latitude. This agreement defused the immediate conflict over the admission of Missouri, but it was merely a temporary solution to the question of slavery in the territories.

Slavery in the territories was the most divisive issue in American politics by the 1840s, and this single issue split both political parties and threatened to dissolve the Union itself. Several important factors contributed to this tension. During the previous decade, northern abolitionists such as Theodore Dwight Weld, William Lloyd Garrison, and Lyman Beecher had been increasingly vocal and politically influential. Moreover, they had begun to attack the morality of southern slaveowners, not simply the institution itself. As a result of these attacks, a high protective tariff, and other factors, southerners came to believe that the federal govern-

Illinois Senator Stephen A. Douglas as a gladiator. He ran against Lincoln in 1860 and supported the doctrine of popular sovereignty, framed the Kansas–Nebraska bill, and advocated strict economy and prompt payment of government salaries. (Bettmann/ Corbis)

ment was not serving their social and economic interests. Southerners became vocal proponents of states' rights in an effort to protect these interests, which in reality was a thinly veiled euphemism for slavery.

This sectional debate over the future of the institution became more pronounced after the Mexican War (1846–1848) when Congress debated the future of slavery expansion. Abolitionists, some northern Democrats, and antislavery Whigs demanded that slavery be excluded from the lands acquired from Mexico because that nation had previously abolished the institution. The most famous articulation of this position was the 1846 Wilmot Proviso. Southern slaveowners and proslavery Whigs argued that any attempt to regulate slavery in the territories, even the Missouri Compromise line, was unconstitutional, as territories were a collective possession of the states and the federal government was obliged by the Constitution to protect the property of any citizen taken there.

These extreme positions threatened to dissolve the Union, but Michigan senator Lewis Cass offered a solution to the problem. Cass, who had previously served as territorial governor of Michigan, secretary of war, and minister to France, was a moderate who believed that the extreme positions of David Wilmot and John C. Calhoun would never satisfactorily settle the question of slavery expansion. Therefore in 1848, Cass offered a proposal that would transfer the political burden of deciding the issue from Congress to the territorial legislatures. Cass argued that the federal government should not decide such internal matters, as such action was both corrosive to the bonds of Union and fundamentally undemocratic. Therefore, he proposed that the territorial legislatures, as the elected representatives of the people, decide the slave question in each individual territory. According to Cass, Congress had no constitutional authority to regulate slavery in the territories, and popular sovereignty, or squatter sovereignty as it was sometimes known, offered the best solution to the problem of slavery expansion.

Popular sovereignty had many political benefits. It was a democratic solution to a pressing national issue; it also, at least on the surface, had something to offer both southern slaveowners and northern abolitionists. Southerners and their property would be protected if they chose to migrate to a territory, where they would have an equal voice in the final determination of slavery through the electoral process. Northern free soil advocates understood that much of the land in the territories was unsuitable for slave-based agriculture. Moreover, it was assumed that the new territories would be quickly populated by midwestern farmers, who would dominate the legislature and ban slavery in the territories. Despite these theoretical appeals to both sides, the ambiguity of popular sovereignty undermined its popularity. Cass was never clear on the precise point at which a territory could act on slavery, nor on the proper method for taking this action. Southerners realized their property would never be truly protected in the territories, and free soil activists would not entertain a proposal that might protect the institution of slavery.

Despite this initially lackluster appeal, popular sovereignty was destined to have far-reaching political implications. Cass won the 1848 Democratic presidential nomination, but the debate over popular sovereignty deepened the gap between the northern and southern wings of the party. Though Cass lost the election to Zachary Taylor, popular sovereignty continued to have political resonance. The Compromise of 1850 allowed territorial legislatures broad legislative powers, which some people interpreted as an unstated endorsement of popular sovereignty. However, the most important manifestation of the concept arose in 1854 during debates over the Kansas and Nebraska Territories.

Stephen A. Douglas, a U.S. senator from Illinois, was one of the most influential converts to popular sovereignty. He used this approach to appeal to southern Democrats whose support Douglas needed to establish a transcontinental railroad with an eastern terminus in his native state. In 1854 he sponsored a bill that created two new territories, Kansas and Nebraska, both of which were north of 36°30' minutes north latitude, the old Missouri Compromise line. According to the bill, the territorial legislatures would have full authority to determine the future of slavery within their respective borders. More importantly, Douglas agreed to an amendment that repealed the Missouri Compromise altogether, arguing that popular sovereignty was the best method for deciding the future of slavery in the territories.

The Kansas–Nebraska Act had far-reaching implications. The Whig Party ceased to exist as a cohesive political entity, as its members split into proslavery and free soil factions over this issue. The Republican Party, which embraced free soil ideology, united its members by its stand on the Kansas–Nebraska Act, and Douglas's own presidential hopes were dashed by this sponsorship of his controversial bill. More immediately, and more importantly, violence erupted in Kansas, as proslavery and free soil interests literally fought for the power to determine the future of slavery in the territory. This division and violence were important steps toward, and in many ways a rehearsal for, the American Civil War.

— *Richard D. Starnes*

See also: Border War (1854–1859); Compromise of 1850; Democratic Party; Douglas, Stephen A.; Kansas–Nebraska Act; Whig Party; Wilmot Proviso.

For Further Reading

Freehling, William. 1990. *The Road to Disunion.* New York: Harper and Row.

Potter, David. 1976. *The Impending Crisis, 1848–1861.* New York: Harper and Row.

Rawley, James. 1969. *Race and Politics: "Bleeding Kansas" and the Coming of the Civil War.* Philadelphia: Lippincott.

PORT ROYAL EXPERIMENT

Called the "Rehearsal for Reconstruction," the Port Royal Experiment was an effort by federal officials, military officers, abolitionists, teachers, and missionar-

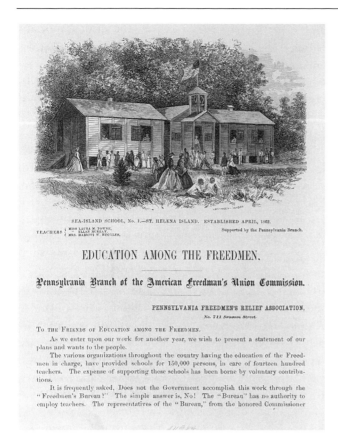

SEA-ISLAND SCHOOL, No. 1.—ST. HELENA ISLAND. ESTABLISHED APRIL, 1862.

TEACHERS { MISS LAURA M. TOWNE, / ELLEN MURRAY, / MRS. HARRIOT W. RUGGLES.   Supported by the Pennsylvania Branch.

EDUCATION AMONG THE FREEDMEN.

Pennsylvania Branch of the American Freedman's Union Commission.

PENNSYLVANIA FREEDMEN'S RELIEF ASSOCIATION,
No. 711 Sansom Street.

TO THE FRIENDS OF EDUCATION AMONG THE FREEDMEN.

As we enter upon our work for another year, we wish to present a statement of our plans and wants to the people.

The various organizations throughout the country having the education of the Freedmen in charge, have provided schools for 150,000 persons, in care of fourteen hundred teachers. The expense of supporting these schools has been borne by voluntary contributions.

It is frequently asked, Does not the Government accomplish this work through the "Freedmen's Bureau?" The simple answer is, No! The "Bureau" has no authority to employ teachers. The representatives of the "Bureau," from the honored Commissioner

The Port Royal Experiment was an effort to demonstrate that freedmen could be converted from slave labor to free labor. It was also a way to prepare for the upcoming emancipation of the slaves and to deal with the numerous slaves who had attached themselves to advancing Union forces. (Library of Congress)

ies to demonstrate that freedmen could be converted from slave labor to free labor. The Port Royal Experiment also was a way to prepare for the upcoming emancipation of the slaves and to deal with the numerous slaves who had attached themselves to advancing Union forces.

On November 7, 1861, the U.S. Navy bombarded the town of Beaufort, South Carolina, located on the island of Port Royal a few miles north of Savannah, Georgia. Most of the island's whites had already fled, leaving behind ten thousand slaves, referred to as contraband. The "contrabands," who were technically still slaves, showed a strong reluctance to working the slave crop of cotton. Instead, they concentrated on growing subsistence crops and hunting and fishing in order to live. Both contrabands and freedmen preferred to distance themselves from any contact with whites, northern or southern.

Northern entrepreneurs and U.S. Treasury officials responsible for administering confiscated property, which included slaves, considered the acquisition of Port Royal an economic opportunity for the federal treasury. But federal officers and the Treasury Department, under the direction of Secretary Salmon P. Chase, faced the problem of how to manage the thousands of slaves who remained on the plantations. Chase appointed Edward L. Pierce to establish a new labor system on the island. Pierce implemented a system that resembled the former antebellum plantation, complete with plantation supervisors, the gang system of labor, and restricted movement of laborers. Instead of providing cash wages for work performed on the plantation, workers received basic necessities and free education.

Northern missionaries like the Gideonites and the American Missionary Association believed that with guidance and education, freedmen could be transformed into an obedient and effective workforce. Missionaries and teachers also advocated giving land to freedmen, but their impact on the direction of the experiment was minimal. Entrepreneurs like Edward S. Philbrick wanted to convert the former slaves into a large "free labor" workforce that was also tied to a market economy (i.e., to make them both laborers and consumers). Unlike Pierce, Philbrick implemented a wage labor system on his plantation based on the example of northern labor. Philbrick replaced the gang system with a labor program based on incentives, giving families their own garden plots and paying cash wages to field laborers. Federally supervised plantations soon converted to Philbrick's model.

In 1863 and 1864 Treasury officials auctioned Port Royal Island plantations for nonpayment of taxes. Northern speculators purchased most of the 60,000 acres of confiscated land. Officials had reserved over 16,000 acres for purchase by freedmen at $1.25 per acre, but only a few freedmen who pooled their meager resources were able to purchase land. The island's military governor, General Rufus Saxton, tried to help freedmen by allowing them to acquire land through preemption. President Abraham Lincoln overturned Saxton's policy in 1864.

By 1865 Philbrick realized that his experiment to prove that African Americans working as wage laborers could be more profitable than slave labor had failed. Throughout the experiment to establish a new economic system based on wage labor, freedmen resisted working in the cotton fields, and cotton production never reached pre–Civil War rates. Philbrick divided his plantation into small lots and sold them to former workers and returned North. On other plantations, military authorities required freedmen to sign labor contracts or leave.

On January 12, 1865, General Tecumseh Sherman issued Special Field Order No. 15, which entitled freedmen to 40-acre plots of land in an area along the coast from Charleston, South Carolina, to Jacksonville, Florida. Later that year, President Andrew Johnson commanded that all confiscated lands be returned to their owners. Many of the Port Royal freedmen who had acquired land during the experiment lost their claims to those plots, and the Port Royal Experiment came to a close.

— *Craig S. Pascoe*

See also: Civil War; Contrabands; Emancipation Proclamation; Gullah; Sea Islands; South Carolina.

For Further Reading

Foner, Eric. 1988. *Reconstruction: America's Unfinished Revolution*. New York: Harper & Row.

Gerteis, Louis S. 1973. *From Contraband to Freedmen: Federal Policy Toward Southern Blacks, 1861–1865*. Westport, CT: Greenwood.

Jacoway, Elizabeth. 1980. *Yankee Missionaries in the South: The Penn School Experiment*. Baton Rouge: Louisiana State University Press.

Ochiai, Akiko. 2001. "The Port Royal Experiment Revisited: Northern Visions of Reconstruction and the Land Question." *New England Quarterly* 74 (1): 94–117.

Rose, Willie Lee Nichols. 1976. *Rehearsal for Reconstruction: The Port Royal Experiment*. New York: Oxford University Press.

POTTAWATOMIE MASSACRE

The Pottawatomie massacre occurred on May 24, 1856, at Pottawatomie Creek, Kansas Territory, and initiated John Brown's rise to national prominence. Brown and seven followers executed five proslavery settlers in retaliation for a proslavery raid on Lawrence, an antislavery center in the territory. The massacre highlighted the controversy over popular sovereignty and revealed the volatile consequences of the Kansas–Nebraska Act (1854).

Brown arrived in Kansas Territory on October 7, 1855, to help several of his sons establish claims under the terms of popular sovereignty. Owing to a prolonged drought, which destroyed their crops, Brown's sons had left Ohio in spring 1855 to start anew in the unorganized territory. Besides their financial motivation, the younger Browns were also eager to rush to Kansas and reinforce antislavery settlers there.

Throughout the first year of settlement, tensions mounted between proslavery and antislavery pioneers, and many prepared for war. Prior to his move west, Brown solicited funds from sympathetic abolitionists and purchased a shipment of arms in preparation for what he thought would be imminent bloodshed. The crate included a cache of broadswords, medieval weapons symbolic of Brown's self-imposed image as an antislavery crusader ordained by Christ.

During his adult life, Brown called for guerrilla warfare against southern plantations and the execution of slave catchers. In Kansas, he put his words into action. Shortly after he arrived at Brown's Station near Pottawatomie Creek, Kansas turned bloody. In late November 1855, proslavery and antislavery forces mobilized at Lawrence in a prelude to the impending confrontation. Although a treaty averted bloodshed, tensions smoldered during the winter months as both sides issued calls for arms and men. In April 1856 Brown gained regional attention by publicly announcing that he would kill any peace officer who attempted to enforce territorial laws banning abolitionist activity. A month later, after years of agitating for a violent end to slavery, Brown moved toward fulfillment of his destiny.

On May 21, 1856, a proslavery militia force raided Lawrence with impunity. The following morning, Brown and his sons marched with a company known as the Pottawatomie Rifles to help repel the attack. A messenger stopped them and ordered Brown to turn back since the proslavery men had retreated following the arrival of federal troops. After the Pottawatomie company refused to press forward, an exasperated Brown called for volunteers for a secret mission. Further electrified by the news of Preston Brooks's assault upon Charles Sumner on the floor of the U.S. Senate on May 22, Brown led a small squad, including four of his sons, back to Pottawatomie Creek. There, on May 24, 1856, Brown and his men wielded sharpened broadswords and hacked to death five proslavery residents. The slaughter sent proslavery settlers into a frenzy and sparked unbridled guerrilla warfare throughout southeastern Kansas.

Coupled with the raid on Lawrence, the Pottawatomie massacre brought both sides to local civil war. In this unruly environment, known as Bleeding Kansas, Brown and his men avoided prosecution for their night of carnage and fought in several small skirmishes. Brown left Kansas in October 1856 and gained national attention as an antislavery guerrilla fighter and speaker. This recognition helped him recruit men and garner financial support for another secret mission waged at Harpers Ferry, Virginia, in October 1859, a mission that ultimately played a major role in plunging the whole nation into civil war.

— *Robert J. Zalimas, Jr.*

See also: Border War (1854–1859); Brown, John; Harpers Ferry Raid.

For Further Reading

Malin, James C. 1942. *John Brown and the Legend of Fifty-six.* Philadelphia: American Philosophical Society.

Oates, Stephen B. 1984. *To Purge This Land with Blood: A Biography of John Brown.* Amherst: University of Massachusetts Press.

Potter, David M. 1976. *The Impending Crisis, 1848–1861.* New York: Harper and Row.

Yang, Liwen. 1992. "John Brown's Role in the History of the Emancipation Movement of Black Americans." *Southern Studies* 3: 135–142.

SLAVE PREACHERS

African American slave preachers often occupied an uncomfortable middle position between white and black worlds in the antebellum South. Targets of distrust by white slaveholding society, which suspected them of being fomenters of slave rebellion, slave preachers had to rely on their master's protection to maintain their positions. They, in return, were expected to indoctrinate their black flock to the idea that heaven awaited slaves who faithfully served white rulers. Within the slave community, slave clergy preserved African cultural practices while disseminating the Christian gospel. Revered as bold leaders and reviled as craven sellouts in slave folklore, black preachers constructed a worldview that largely preserved black cultural autonomy while accommodating the reality of antebellum power relations.

The slave preacher filled a spiritual vacuum left by white masters who often feared that Christianity, with its message that slaves possessed souls worth saving and were as human as whites, undermined the slave economy's racist tenets. Slaveowners long resisted attempts to Christianize their chattel. When white preachers were sent to evangelize slaves, their obvious political mission to encourage black acceptance of servitude undermined their credibility with black congregations. In this atmosphere, slaves often learned an Africanized version of Christianity from other slaves— slave preachers, both licensed and unlicensed; exhorters, individuals who spontaneously "got the spirit" and began preaching with or without training; and conjurers, who often maintained traditional African magic practices and beliefs in earthly ghosts and divinations.

Many slave preachers faced ridicule by white elites for illiteracy and the lack of formal theological training. Historians Eugene Genovese and Albert J. Raboteau both argue that slave preachers were no more likely to be illiterate than southern poor white preachers. Bible tales, in any case, had become part of the slave oral tradition. Certain slave preachers gained fame for their command of scripture, fiery eloquence, and multilingual fluency.

Some preachers often enjoyed a freedom of movement unknown by other slaves, being exempted from manual labor by approving masters and invited to lead white congregations and preside over white funerals. Before white or racially mixed audiences, slave preachers at times bowed to reality and ignored slavery or delivered accommodationist sermons. Such preachers suffered harsh lampooning in slave folklore, but others delivered subtle, highly symbolic antislavery messages.

Historian Sterling Stuckey believes that an essential element of slave preacher oratory incorporated an ostensibly Christian message with an African performance style with "the rhythms of [the slave preacher] stirring some to jump and clap their hands and others to shriek" (Stuckey, 1987). Such sermonizing followed West African norms of the ring shout, a style of religious celebration incorporating a call-and-response interplay between an exhorter and the gathered faithful, clapping of hands, and African dances. The ring shout was performed in a circle during weddings, funerals, and other religious rituals throughout West and Central Africa, Stuckey reveals, and served as a method of achieving union with God. Slave preachers incorporated the ring shout into black Protestant practices as well.

Black worship styles heavily influenced southern white Christianity, even when critics condemned slave religious practices as barely disguised heathenism. Slave preachers differed from white counterparts not only in style, but also in substance. Although white preachers emphasized the slave's duty to obey masters, slave preachers frequently noted that all men were descended from Adam and Eve, in subtle rebuke of white supremacist thinking. Others used tales of Moses and the Israelites as metaphor for the eventual deliverance of black slaves from white domination.

Southern slaveholders were fully aware of the black church's insurrectionary potential, and, while blacks were given relative freedom to preach in the eighteenth century, nineteenth-century southern state and local governments sought to limit slave preaching. Black preachers were implicated in several actual or threatened slave revolts, such as those led by Gabriel Prosser (1800), Denmark Vesey (1822), and Nat Turner (1831). Each abortive insurrection led to a suppression of slave preaching.

Laws were passed throughout the South that prohibited free blacks from preaching to slaves, required slave preachers to register with local authorities, and/or mandated that whites be present when any black preacher presided over a meeting. Some independent black churches that had developed in the 1700s were required to merge with white churches. Yet, the black church had become too entrenched in the slave community to be repressed legally, and slave preaching thrived until the Civil War.

Regardless of some slaveowners' fears, slave preachers have often been painted by many leftist critics as collaborators. As Genovese argues, traditional African religions had a distinctly nonmessianic, nonmillenarian cast emphasizing community and fidelity to tradition as a means of fulfillment and promoted a long view on immediate issues of social justice. Time is cyclical in the African view, Genovese states, which encouraged slave clergy to preach an eventual reversal of fortune, to carry a gospel that, with time, the last shall be first and the first shall be last. Imbued with African sensibility, these preachers constructed a universe that was morally self-correcting, one in which justice would be restored and imbalances of power reversed over time's vast stretches.

Rather than being accommodationists, in Genovese's view slave preachers were hard realists, recognizing the vastly unequal power relations between the African American and white communities. They responded accordingly, providing the slave community with psychological defenses against slavery's assault while bearing in mind the African long view that justice awaits the virtuous and that time, inevitably, is on the African American community's side. What has been typically interpreted by leftists as accommodation has not been a lapse into passivity but a strategy for survival.

— *Michael Phillips*

See also: Chavis, John; Prosser, Gabriel; Turner, Nat; Vesey, Denmark.

For Further Reading

Blassingame, John W. 1979. *The Slave Community: Plantation Life in the Antebellum South.* New York: Oxford University Press.

Genovese, Eugene D. 1976. *Roll, Jordan, Roll: The World the Slaves Made.* New York: Vintage Books.

Raboteau, Albert J. 1978. *Slave Religion: The "Invisible Institution" in the Antebellum South.* New York: Oxford University Press.

Stuckey, Sterling. 1987. *Slave Culture: Nationalist Theory and the Foundations of Black America.* New York: Oxford University Press.

Wimbush, Vincent L. 1997. *Rhetorics of Resistance: a Colloquy on Early Christianity as Rhetorical Formation.* Atlanta, GA: Scholars Press.

PRIGG V. PENNSYLVANIA (1842)

Perhaps the most famous fugitive slave case decided by the U.S. Supreme Court before the Civil War, *Prigg v. Pennsylvania* [41 U.S. 539 (1842)] concluded that the Fugitive Slave Act of 1793 was constitutional and that states could not tack on additional requirements to hinder people who captured runaway slaves. An 1826 Pennsylvania statute (one of many such state laws, usually called personal liberty laws) required that slave catchers obtain a "certificate of removal" before they could take fugitives back to the South and a life of slavery.

One slave catcher, Edward Prigg, requested a certificate of removal from a Pennsylvania official for a fugitive slave, Margaret Morgan, and several of her children, one of whom was born in Pennsylvania and thus considered free by state law. After his request was refused, Prigg took Morgan and her children from Pennsylvania back to slavery in Maryland. Prigg was indicted in Pennsylvania for kidnapping and was convicted; he appealed his conviction to the U.S. Supreme Court.

At issue was whether states had the ability to pass laws that might interfere or burden the performance of existing federal laws. Justice Joseph Story, in the majority opinion, wrote that any state law that impeded the Fugitive Slave Act was unconstitutional, and thus Pennsylvania's personal liberty law was null and void. He added that the federal Fugitive Slave Act of 1793 was thoroughly constitutional and that any slaveowner or slave catcher could enforce it privately, if recapturing the fugitive could be accomplished without breaking the law. If they complied with the federal Fugitive Slave Act, professional slave catchers could operate freely in the North, without having to notify state or local officials about their actions.

In the opinion's stunning conclusion, Story wrote that state judges and all state officials should enforce the federal Fugitive Slave Act, but that the national government could not require them to do so. Many southerners objected to this caveat to *Prigg*'s opinion, since virtually no northern officials would willingly volunteer to help slave catchers in their work, and without their assistance, it might be extremely difficult to recapture runaway slaves.

Chief Justice Roger B. Taney wrote a concurring opinion in *Prigg*, in which he took issue with Story's conclusion. Taney believed that, with this exception in place, slave recapture would become a dead letter, since only federal officials would enforce the Fugitive Slave Act and assist slave catchers in returning runaways to the South. Taney was correct, as many northern state judges began to refuse hearing fugitive slave cases, and state assemblies passed laws barring the use of state facilities (like jails) in the process of slave recapture.

Prigg v. Pennsylvania and *Jones v. Van Zandt* (1847), another fugitive slave case, set the stage for rewriting the 1793 Fugitive Slave Act as part of the Compromise of 1850, which included a much harsher series of penalties for harboring or assisting runaway slaves. These cases, and related slavery cases like *Dred Scott v. Sandford* (1857), significantly heightened sectional tensions in the decades preceding the Civil War.

— *Sally E. Hadden*

See also: *Ableman v. Booth;* Abolitionism in the United States; *Dred Scott v. Sandford; Jones v. Van Zandt;* Taney, Roger B.; United States Constitution.

For Further Reading

Cover, Robert. 1975. *Justice Accused: Antislavery and the Judicial Process.* New Haven, CT: Yale University Press.

Finkelman, Paul. 1979. "Prigg v. Pennsylvania and Northern State Courts: Anti-Slavery Use of a Pro-Slavery Decision." *Civil War History* 25: 5–35.

Finkelman, Paul. 1981. *An Imperfect Union: Slavery, Federalism, and Comity.* Chapel Hill: University of North Carolina Press.

Morris, Thomas. 1974. *Free Men All: The Personal Liberty Laws of the North, 1780–1861.* Baltimore, MD: Johns Hopkins University Press.

Wiecek, William E. 1978. "Slavery and Abolition before the United States Supreme Court, 1820–1860." *Journal of American History* 65 (1978): 34–59.

PROSLAVERY ARGUMENT

The proslavery argument in the United States was a philosophical rationale for slavery as the core component of the antebellum southern culture and worldview. Defense of slavery began in the colonial period, when it became a wholly southern ideology espoused by the best theological, political, and scientific thinkers of the time.

Religion led the way, and one historian believes that the Bible was an indispensable tool of the "proslavery mainstream" since, like manifest destiny, proslavery theory was based in Scripture. Slaveholders noted that Jesus had not specifically prohibited slaveholding and that, in the Old Testament, Noah's descendants through Canaan had been "cursed" to labor as slaves. When all else failed, Christianity was presented as a "civilizing" influence for Africans.

Slavery was also seen as a practical method of controlling the population and maintaining social order. Blacks were viewed as inherently disruptive, imposing pagan ways and sexual license upon an otherwise orderly society. Although slaves consistently resisted their enslavement, this resistance occasionally took the form of violent insurrection against the slave regime. The three most well-known such insurrections were the 1739 Stono Rebellion in South Carolina, the 1822 Denmark Vesey revolt in South Carolina, and the 1831 insurrection led by Nat Turner in Virginia. In the wake of these revolts, laws were implemented requiring even more stringent restrictions on the activities of black slaves, as well as free blacks and mulattoes. These laws, generally known as black codes, included limitations on or outright prohibition of black slave preachers, restrictions on gatherings of blacks, prohibition of black slave literacy, and surveillance or prohibition of slaves engaging in activities with free blacks.

After the 1831 Nat Turner insurrection, white attitudes toward blacks, free and slave, hardened. Thomas Roderick Dew published the *Review of the Debate in the Virginia Legislature of 1831 and 1832* (1832), a debate over whether to abolish slavery because of the Turner rebellion, which had served to reinforce proslavery sentiment. Dew concluded that large-scale emancipation was impractical, echoing the Founding Fathers' doubts that blacks could fit into society in the United States.

The most forceful argument in the southern defense of slavery was based on the assumption of white superiority. Medical arguments by Dr. Samuel Cartwright, who worked in the field of ethnology, were presented as proof of black inferiority. Similarly, the physician Josiah Nott contributed comparisons of cranial capacity to buttress physiological arguments supporting the theory of the superior intelligence of whites. However, suggestions that blacks actually represented a separate species from whites were generally viewed with skepticism because they clashed with the Christian doctrine of the creation.

Finally, retaining slavery was portrayed as an economically sound policy, an argument that was tied to the individual's right to private property. Accordingly, southern slavery was declared to be both more efficient and more humane than free labor in the industrial North. Apologist George Fitzhugh echoed those sentiments, arguing that expanding slavery to include white slaves was a logical extension of the patriarchal family model wherein white children and wives were subservient to the husband and father.

One of the critical elements of southern politics was the position of race-based slavery in their society, especially of the right to establish and maintain internal systems without outside interference. Political arguments favoring slavery also had a racial component, attempting to convince slaveless whites that the presence of black slaves ensured white equality. Indeed, rather than thinking that white liberty founded on black slavery was a "paradox," white southern politicians pointed to black slavery as indispensable to white liberty.

Occasional opposition to slavery from within the South, such as Hinton Rowan Helper's pamphlet *The Impending Crisis of the South* (1857), recognized that slavery was a drain on the southern economy rather than a boost to it. However, slaveholders insisted that because their slaves freed them from being encumbered by the mundane details of daily life, they were able to elevate their community.

And indeed, southern politics was dominated by slaveholders until the Civil War. James Henry Hammond, for example, ardently defended the necessity of a "mudsill" class of black slaves for the achievement of political and cultural greatness. In 1857, as a freshman congressman from South Carolina, Hammond defended slavery as a "positive good" requiring defense to the point of civil war. Such politicians and writers eventually defended slavery in secession conventions, as not merely a component part of southern culture, but rather, as the vice president of the Confederate States of America, Alexander Stephens, described it, "the cornerstone of the Confederacy" (Oakes, 1982).

For some historians, the development of the proslavery ideology was perhaps evidence of antebellum guilt over slavery, although it is more likely that these writings were meant for southerners' own edification, not to persuade northern abolitionists of the rightness of their views. Feminist analyses have variously speculated on an identity or sympathy of attitude between white slaveholding women and black slave women, although recent scholarship shows that white slaveholding women, by their attitudes and actions, contributed to the hegemony of the slave regime. Scholars of American literature perceive the energy exerted by antebellum southern writers and intellectuals as leading to the paucity of important literary contributions by southerners during a period of marked literary production in New England.

— *Dale Edwyna Smith*

See also: Dew, Thomas R.; Fitzhugh, George; Hammond, James H.; Helper, Hinton Rowan; Nott, Josiah Clark.

For Further Reading

Bleser, Carol, ed. 1988. *Secret and Sacred: The Diaries of James Henry Hammond, a Southern Slaveholder.* New York: Oxford University Press.

Faust, Drew Gilpin. 1981. *The Ideology of Slavery: Proslavery Thought in the Antebellum South, 1830–1860.* Baton Rouge: Louisiana State University Press.

Fox-Genovese, Elizabeth. 1988. *Within the Plantation Household: Black and White Women of the Old South.* Chapel Hill: University of North Carolina Press.

Morrow, Ralph E. 1961. "The Proslavery Argument Revisited." *Mississippi Valley Historical Review* 47 (June): 79–93.

Oakes, James. 1982. *The Ruling Race.* New York: Alfred A. Knopf.

Tise, Edward. 1979. "The Interregional Appeal of Proslavery Thought: An Ideological Profile of the Antebellum American Clergy." *Plantation Society in the Americas* 1 (February): 63–72.

GABRIEL PROSSER (1776–1800)

Gabriel Prosser (also referred to as Prosser's Gabriel), a slave, a highly skilled blacksmith, and a literate black, was born in 1776 when the United States was fighting to rid itself of British hegemony. The historical event that historians refer to as Gabriel's plot or rebellion was an abortive slave revolt in half a dozen counties of Virginia, and it was organized against the backdrop of the changing circumstances in the Revolutionary era in America. The rhetoric that all men were created equal and have certain natural and inalienable rights, including "life, liberty, and the pursuit of happiness," unfortunately did not apply to slaves. Although the American War of Independence did not lead to freedom for blacks, it gave the slaves a lasting impression of the importance of liberty and freedom. Some slaves used the war to escape as runaways, and all slaves took to heart the lesson that the possibility of freedom existed. One of the regions in which this hope was played out was postwar Virginia.

In 1800 Richmond, Virginia, was inhabited by about fifty-seven hundred people, and about half were slaves and free blacks. As a growing port city, Richmond had a thriving merchant class that benefited from the new wealth, of which slave labor contributed a substantial amount. One condition that prepared a fertile ground for the slaves to revolt was the collapse of control over slaves in Virginia, and more importantly, in the city of Richmond. Economic and social changes occurring in the post–Revolutionary War era were also significant.

The major economic development of the period was the production of such crops as wheat, hemp, flax, and cotton and the introduction of small-scale local manufacturing industries. These industries relied on skilled slave labor to effect the changes and chart new directions for the economy. In addition to economic changes, a new evangelical movement (the First Great

Awakening, 1720–1770) challenged both the religious and the social order in Virginia—the Baptists and the Methodists were especially motivated by this new evangelism. This new wave of Christianity emphasized an unusual fellowship between the preachers, the congregation, and the slaves. The humanity of the slaves was recognized, and they were accepted as equals in the sight of God. Emancipation and freedom became the slaves' creed.

It was in this climate that Gabriel and his co-conspirators planned the destruction of Richmond in 1800. Gabriel belonged to the Prosser plantation of Brookfield, which was about 6 miles north of Richmond. The plantation was owned by Thomas Prosser, who owned fifty-three slaves, including Gabriel, his parents, and two of his brothers, Martin and Solomon. Prosser and his wife, Ann, had two children, Elizabeth and Thomas Henry, the latter born on November 5, 1776. Since Thomas Henry and Gabriel were born the same year; and because they grew in the same plantation, they were said to have been playmates in their childhood. In spite of the close companionship, their fortunes were quite different because of the accident of their birth—one a slave and the other a freeborn. It has also been speculated that Gabriel in his early years might have been taught to read either by Thomas Henry or by Ann Prosser. Whoever did so gave Gabriel a head start over most slaves of his time and age. As Gabriel grew older, the class differences between him and Thomas Henry became more apparent, and while Thomas Henry was being trained by his father to take over as the master of the plantation, Gabriel and his brother were learning a trade, blacksmithing.

Owing to his size, courage, and intellect, Gabriel was respected by both whites and blacks. He was never afraid to fight back if he felt he was wronged—for example, in 1799 it was reported that he bit off the left ear of one Absalom Johnson in an argument over a stolen hog. For this action, Gabriel spent a month in jail. In order to avoid any possible confrontation with Gabriel, his master, Thomas Prosser, was said to have granted him considerable freedom and autonomy. For instance, Prosser never subjected Gabriel's wife, Nanny, to abuse as he might have done. Following the death of Thomas Prosser on October 7, 1798, the leadership of Prosser's plantation passed to Thomas Henry who was then twenty-two. Having inherited the plantation, Thomas Henry was determined not only to keep it solvent but also to increase its profit margins.

In order to secure productivity from his slaves, it is said that the young Prosser was harsh to them. More importantly, he adopted the strategy of hiring out surplus slaves to people who needed their services. The slaves worked either in farms or as house help or craftsmen in urban centers. This highly profitable practice of hiring out slaves without doubt freed the bondsmen from the control of their masters. Consequently, Gabriel and such other insurrectionists as Martin, Solomon, Jack Ditcher (also called Jack Bowler), Sam Byrd, Jr., and George Smith, took advantage of the relaxed control to plot their insurrection. Douglas Egerton argues that in addition to the practice of hiring out slaves, the cash they earned "conferred a degree of psychological and social independence on the wage-earning bondsman" (Egerton, 1993). In the process of being hired, slaves like Gabriel were either underpaid or cheated by wicked employers. This injustice violated Gabriel's and others' sense of justice and fair play, and they felt the unscrupulous employers had to be taught a lesson. Also subjected to harsh economic and social discrimination were free blacks and poor unskilled whites, and in time, slaves formed an alliance with them to challenge the status quo.

Gabriel and his fellow accomplices chose 1800 to strike back. The year was unique in many ways—it was the year Nat Turner and John Brown were born and the year Denmark Vesey bought his freedom. The plot began early in the spring of 1800. Initially, the leadership of the plot was uncertain. A number of sources have pointed out that in spite of Gabriel's early involvement with the conspiracy, it was not his brainchild and he first heard of the scheme from fellow conspirator Jack Ditcher. The twenty-four-year-old Gabriel, however, emerged as the leader of the group, and Gerald Mullin contends that "more than any other organizer he sensed the narcotic and self-justifying effects of revolutionary rhetoric and organization. Because he was able to make decisions, delegate responsibilities, and pursue routine tasks to their completion in order to avert the strong possibility of disaster, the rebellion came to be his. And it bore his own quietly methodical, businesslike character" (Mullin, 1972). Although Gabriel may have been a methodical, businesslike, and skillful leader, it is debatable if he really averted "the strong possibility of disaster" as Mullin claims. From what we know, the plot was nipped in the bud.

The level of success the conspiracy achieved depended on the recruitment strategy and effort. The main recruiters were Gabriel, Jack Ditcher, George Smith, Sam Byrd, Jr., and Ben Woolfolk, and they employed various strategies and locations to recruit potential participants. The enlistment of a slave was for the most part based on the litmus test, "Was he willing to fight the white people for his freedom?" More often than not, the leaders of the plot found slaves who in addition to hating whites were willing to kill to secure their freedom. The goal of the plot was a coup that would result in an insurrection. The number of insurrectionists was estimated at about one thousand, and this was the core of the group that was expected to launch the attack on Richmond and subsequently count on the support of slaves, free blacks, and lower-class whites in the region. The conspirators believed that the capture of Richmond would result in the end of slavery in Virginia and "subdue the whole country where slavery was permitted" (Dillon, 1990). In carrying out their plan, Gabriel cautioned his co-conspirators not to hurt the Quakers, Methodists, and French people. Nonetheless, they planned to enter Richmond carrying a flag with the inscription "Death or liberty."

The insurrectionists had planned to strike at midnight on August 30, 1800, but a violent storm at about noon that day led them to postpone the rebellion until the following night. Meanwhile, two slaves had broken their oath of secrecy, and Virginia state authorities, led by Governor James Monroe, acted swiftly by calling out about six hundred troops. The slaves were subsequently arrested, tried, and executed. Gabriel was arrested in late September 1800 while trying to escape in the schooner *Mary*. Governor Monroe tried to interview Gabriel as to his motives but to no avail. Gabriel along with others was executed on October 7, 1800. Although Gabriel and his co-conspirators failed to achieve their ultimate goal of ending slavery, they undoubtedly drew attention to the plight of the slaves. More important, they made it clear that slaves were anything but docile.

— *Onaiwu W. Ogbomo*

See also: Turner, Nat; Vesey, Denmark.

For Further Reading

Dillon, Merton L. 1990. *Slavery Attacked: Southern Slaves and Their Allies, 1619–1865.* Baton Rouge: Louisiana State University Press.

Egerton, Douglas R. 1993. *Gabriel's Rebellion: The Virginia Slave Conspiracies of 1800 and 1802.* Chapel Hill: University of North Carolina Press.

Mullin, Gerald W. 1972. *Flight and Rebellion: Slave Resistance in Eighteenth-Century Virginia.* New York: Oxford University Press.

Mullin, Michael. 1992. *Africa in America: Slave Acculturation and Resistance in the American South and the Caribbean, 1736–1831.* Chicago: University of Chicago Press.

PROVISION GROUNDS

Beyond the initial expenditure associated with the purchase of a slave, the only other financial burdens that slaveowners experienced during the slave's lifetime were maintenance costs—provision of food, shelter, and clothing sufficient to keep the laborer alive and productive. In an agricultural economy in which profitability varied owing to fluctuating commodity prices and the fickle nature of weather patterns, slaveowners always tried to keep their overhead costs of maintaining their plantations and farms at the lowest possible level in order to maximize profits. The costs of slave maintenance were thus marginalized to the point where the slaves themselves were expected to grow a significant portion of their own food. Slave gardens—or provision grounds—became an integral part of the plantation system that helped to sustain the lives of slaves, and on occasion, provide a limited source of revenue that might be used for purchasing one's own freedom.

It was common on many plantations to have small plots of land set aside for the specific use of slaves as their own personal provision grounds. Sometimes these garden plots might be located near the slave quarters, but more often they were located on some of the less productive low-lying marginal lands that were not deemed suitable for the particular monoculture staple that was cultivated on the estate. Other plots were provided in wooded or hilly areas of the estate that were unsuited for large-scale agricultural activity. Slaves were permitted to farm their own provision grounds only during their spare time, so the slaves often worked these gardens on Sundays and holidays or in scarce moments near dawn or at dusk. The former slave Charles Ball acknowledged that "there were about thirty of these patches, cleared in the woods, and fenced—some with rails, and others with brush—the property of the various families" on a Georgia plantation where he had labored (Ball, 1836).

The primary function of the provision ground was to grow enough produce to supplement the slave's diet or provide a sustainable alternative to standard plantation fare. The slave gardens usually included corn, okra, beans, squash, sweet potatoes, onions, and various types of "greens" (mustard, collards, and turnip). Aside from the beans that were grown, there was very little to add protein to the slave's diet, and the foodstuffs grown in the provision grounds were heavy in carbohydrates and limited in dietary fiber. It was the rare slave who regularly attained the 2,000 calorie per day minimum regimen deemed necessary to prevent malnourishment and sustain one's health. The limited diet of the slave and the absence of medicine and healthcare made slavery even more brutal.

One of the most unique aspects of the provision ground was the understanding that a slave owned the produce that was grown in the garden—it became the property of the slave. The slaveowner determined what the slave might do with the excess produce. In some circumstances, such excess produce could be sold in the local community or at Sunday "market days," and the slave who grew the produce could reap all or part of the revenues earned from such sales. As a result, on some plantations and farms there were industrious slaves who were able to accumulate some wealth that was often used to purchase their own freedom and effect self emancipation.

One additional benefit provided by the provision grounds was the sense of autonomy they gave the slave. As they tended to their garden plots in wooded areas or hilly ground, the slaves could evade the watchful eyes of owners and overseers and gain some very welcome solitude. This sense of limited independence, coupled with the understanding that their labors were serving their own and their kin's well-being, made their time in the garden especially meaningful.

The slave gardens and the supplemental foodstuffs they produced figure prominently in many of the slave narratives collected during the 1930s. Katie Brown, who grew up as a slave on Georgia's Sapelo Island, recalled the central place that provision grounds played in the life of the slave. "Oh yes, de slaves had dey own garden dat de work at night en especially moonlight nights coarse de had to work in de fields all day till sundown. Mamma had a big garden en plant collards en everything like dat you want to eat" (Georgia, 1940). In a world of slavery where practically all aspects of one's life was proscribed, the provision grounds of the slaves nourished both body and soul.

— Junius P. Rodriguez

For Further Reading

Ball, Charles. 1836. *Slavery in the United States: The Life and Adventures of Charles Ball, a Black Man.* Lewistown, PA: Fisher.

Crader, Diana C. 1990. "Slave Diet at Monticello." *American Antiquity* 55 (4): 690–717.

Georgia Writer's Project, Works Progress Administration. 1940. *Drums and Shadows: Survival Studies among the Georgia coastal Negroes.* Athens: University of Georgia Press.

Hilliard, Sam B. 1972. *Hog Meat and Hoecake: Food Supply in the Old South, 1840–1860* Carbondale: Southern Illinois University Press.

Westmacott, Richard. 1992. *African American Gardens and Yards in the Rural South.* Knoxville: University of Tennessee Press.

PUNISHMENT

The study of slavery is incomplete unless one considers the consequences slaves suffered while yearning to be free. The European form of slavery differed from other world slavery systems in that the master had absolute property rights and the slaves had little protection by law. In addition, slaves' marriages were not recognized as legally binding, and slaves were typically viewed as tools. In contrast, slaves in Africa were considered to be members of their master's family and were workers with rights. Slavery under Islam was also quite different from European slavery: Muslims were bound by a religious code of treatment for slaves as ordered by the Qur'an.

Since the role of slaves in the Western world was clearly demarcated by the master's successful ability to strip them of their active, collective, and individual personalities by treating and thinking of them as less than human, the punishment of slaves evolved into a significant part of the institution. The psychological benefits to the master class included the maintenance of the system as well as lucrative profits generated by free labor. However, such psychological and physical oppression could neither be implemented nor maintained without the use of brute force, mob violence, and punishment. The basic historical picture of the punishment of slaves has focused on the lash. The practice of punishing slaves seemed to have little relationship to the crime; rather, it had more to do with the master's desire to maintain control and instill fear.

Extending the boundaries of the European worldview to the colonies through the transatlantic slave trade led to the conception of Africans as distinctly inferior creatures, and because of this belief, Africans and other indigenous populations were treated like chattel in the New World. Workhouse irons and brands were commonly applied, as were laws that reinforced the inferiority of slaves and justified cruel and unusual punishment for minor offenses. For example, slaves were not allowed to leave their master's property without passes and could not meet in large groups, carry weapons, or strike a white person. At the same time, however, masters were free to impart punishment whenever and however it was deemed necessary without legal prosecution. In areas where large numbers of slaves were concentrated, white men were required to form patrols. Slaves were also punished for playing with white children, running away, being disobedient, and committing crimes against the Sabbath, such as selling liquor on Sunday. A common punishment for slaves who had attained reading or writing skills was amputation—slave narratives indicate that the removal

THE LASH.

Public floggings were used to degrade, discipline, and deter slaves from engaging in activities that masters perceived as disruptive to the public good. (Library of Congress)

of a finger from the joint was considered a warning for stealing a book and that beheading was punishment for a repeat offense. Slaves could also be punished by death if they attempted to harm others. However, the basic punishment for most offenses was based on Hebraic law and required a whipping of approximately thirty-nine lashes.

In one case that occurred in 1640 in Virginia, three slaves (one white) were punished for running away. The white man had the terms of his labor extended for four years, but one of the Africans, one John Punch, was sentenced to work for his master for the remainder of his life. In Richmond, Virginia, a slave could receive nearly forty lashes for stealing a pair of boots, and there are countless accounts of burning

slaves on selected parts of the anatomy as well. After the New York rebellions in 1741, slaves were denied legal counsel, and the authorities expressed regret that nothing more extreme was available than hanging or burning Africans at the stake: eighteen were hanged and thirteen burned alive at the stake. After the 1800 Virginia slave conspiracy, said to have been organized by one Gabriel Prosser, at least twenty-five slaves were ordered to death by the courts of Virginia. Outside of particular punishment of slaves, history is ripe with accounts of random murder. The twentieth-century historian Gilberto de Mello Freyre often reported rampant murders of African slaves by colonialists in Brazil.

The historical records are also replete with evidence regarding the psychological aspect of the punishment of slaves. As mentioned, whites recognized neither fatherhood nor marriage among the slaves because such recognition would impinge on the concept of property rights. Slave narratives are replete with descriptive punishments for slaves. One woman recalled a slave boy who killed his master was given a swift trial by six white men who, upon his confession, took an ax and cut off his head. Another tells of whites taking slaves to a bridge in South Carolina, lining the slaves up, and shooting them off of the bridge. Still another makes reference to her mother being punished by fifty lashes when she refused to obey her white master.

Punishment of slaves in the New World by their masters was generally brutal and inhumane and served primarily to help uphold the institution of slavery and all the economic benefits it entailed to the planter class. Punishment was implemented for a range of so-called crimes to facilitate the slaveowners' ability to hold other men and women in perpetual bondage.

— *Torrance T. Stephens*

See also: Mutilation; Narratives; Slave Patrols.

For Further Reading
Bancroft, Frederick. 1931. *Slave Trading in the Old South.* Baltimore, MD: J.H. Furct.
Cornelius, Janet. 1983. "We Slipped and Learned to Read: Slave Accounts of the Literacy Process, 1830–1865." *Phylon* 44 (3): 171–86.
Freyre, Gilberto. 1966. *The Masters and the Slaves: A Study in the Development of Brazilian Civilization.* 2nd English language edition. New York: Alfred A. Knopf.
Hurmence, Belinda. 1989. *Before Freedom: When I Just Can Remember.* Winston-Salem, NC: John Blair.
Pinn, Anthony B. 2002. *Moral Evil and Redemptive Suffering: a History of Theodicy in African-American Religious Thought.* Gainesville: University Press of Florida.

Viar, Kristin D. 1997. "'Don't Let de Paddle Rollers Catch You': Punishment, Control, and Resistance in the Slave South." M.A. thesis, Department of History, Virginia Polytechnic Institute and State University, Blacksburg, Virginia.

NUTRITION. *See* Diet.

QUADROONS

Quadroons were mixed-race individuals who were recognized as having one-fourth African American ancestry. Still recognized as being black by the law and custom of the antebellum South, some quadroons were slaves, but many were manumitted and became recognized as free persons of color. There were some quadroons who either inherited slaves or purchased them outright, thus creating the paradox of the black slaveowner.

Perhaps one of the most horrid aspects of slavery in the United States was the sexual exploitation of slave women, which occurred all too frequently. There was a certain hypocrisy to southern moralists who preached about the dangers of racial "amalgamation" but cast a blind eye to interracial dalliances, self-defined as the crime of miscegenation, which transpired in communities throughout the slaveholding South. The mixed-race offspring that resulted from these encounters often found their situations circumscribed by white society's fear of otherness, but some of these individuals did manage to achieve a level of social prominence and economic affluence within a world that deemed one's skin color as a sign of merit and worth.

The vast majority of interracial births involved children who were born to slave mothers. The paternity in such cases often involved a white person who was in a position of power—often an owner, an owner's son or relative, or an overseer. Slave codes throughout the antebellum South always deemed that the status of the child followed that of the mother, so unless special provisions were made to emancipate the child through manumission, such children were relegated to begin their lives as slaves. The birth of mixed-race children to white women was rare in the slaveholding South as law

codes defined such an encounter as the rape of a white woman and the slave or free black male guilty of the offence would be punished with death.

Slave women found no sympathy from white women—be they plantation mistresses or their daughters—who usually remained silent, though obviously aware, as the exploitation of black women persisted. White women often felt powerless and marginalized in a patriarchal society, and they often took out their frustrations on the slave women who were themselves victimized by the patriarchal tyranny of the plantation South. As a result of this deflected angst, black women were perceived as being lustful and lascivious, therefore inviting their own exploitation. In a slaveholding society where everything seemed to be turned around, lust was viewed with greater horror than the crime of rape. In some slave codes, black women were required to wear kerchiefs or turbans on their head to make them less attractive.

In the race-conscious antebellum South, and in the generations that followed the Civil War and Reconstruction, the extent of one's blackness was perceived as a statistic that was worthy of note. Until the civil rights era of the 1960s, many southern states continued to carry laws that defined a person as black if one-sixty-fourth or greater of their ancestry was black. Not surprisingly, there were no comparable statutes to define what was meant by whiteness. Under such a system, a black ancestor seven generations removed could still transmit the "stain" of blackness upon a descendant.

The quadroon was often the subject of literary interest in the nineteenth century. Henry Wadsworth Longfellow reflected the moral double standard that existed in the South when he wrote the poem "The Quadroon Girl":

His heart within him was at strife
With such accursed gains:
For he knew whose passions gave her life,
Whose blood ran in her veins.

A rudimentary typography developed in society—something akin to a caste system—to identify individuals of mixed-race parentage based on the relative percentage of blackness they carried. According to this system, a mulatto was a child born to a black and a white parent who thus carried 50 percent black (or African) ancestry. A quadroon was a child who had one black grandparent and was thus 25 percent black. Similarly, an octoroon was a child who had one black great-grandparent and was thus 12.5 percent black. These individuals, along with countless other permutations of ancestry, formed a mixed-race population whose membership represented a vast range of skin color.

During the Reconstruction era, many African Americans of mixed-ancestry rose to positions of prominence in social and political circles. Booker T. Washington, a mulatto, became the preeminent spokesperson for African Americans in the late nineteenth century. Many of the black men who were elected to the U.S. Senate and House of Representatives, along with many other statewide offices, were persons of mixed-race origin. Not surprisingly, in D.W. Griffith's stereotypical-racist film *Birth of a Nation"* (1915), a light-skinned mulatto named Silas Lynch is portrayed as a power-hungry villain who seeks political power in South Carolina.

In Spanish colonial America, an individual could purchase a legal document, the *Cédula de Gracias al Sacar*—a "certificate of whiteness"—that allowed one to pass from one race to another. Although such legal tools did not exist in the United States, there was a de facto system of passing that occurred on a regular basis when one's skin color became light enough that they could identify themselves as being white. Many African Americans of mixed-ancestry, notably author Jean Toomer, have struggled with the moral dilemma of whether to pass themselves as white or to affirm their African heritage.

New Orleans, Louisiana, and Charleston, South Carolina, were two urban centers of the antebellum era that contained large mixed-race populations. Among some members of these communities, the status of mixed-ancestry was viewed as one of racial uniqueness, and certain social and fraternal organizations developed exclusively for those whose skin color was light enough to qualify for admission. In the late nineteenth and early twentieth centuries, some social organizations for mixed-race persons limited their membership to those whose skin color was lighter than the color of a standard paper grocery sack. In New Orleans the quadroon balls that were held regularly became important and fashionable events in the social and cultural scene where white men gathered to meet the acquaintance of light-skinned quadroon women.

Like mulattoes, octoroons, and other mixed-race individuals, quadroons fashioned a strong cultural bond in their sense of otherness because they never felt themselves totally welcomed within either white or black society. Much of this sense of racial exclusivity persisted many generations beyond the days of antebellum slavery.

— *Junius P. Rodriguez*

See also: Black Slaveowners; Mulattoes; Octoroons; Passing.

For Further Reading

Ball, Edward. 1998. *Slaves in the Family.* New York: Farrar, Straus and Giroux.

Degler, Carl N. 1971. *Neither Black Nor White: Slavery and Race Relations in Brazil and the United States.* New York: Macmillan.

Johnston, James Hugo. 1972 [1939]. *Miscegenation in the Ante-Bellum South.* New York: AMS Press.

O'Toole, James. M. 2002. *Passing for White: Race, Religion, and the Healy Family, 1820–1920.* Amherst: University of Massachusetts Press.

QUAKERS

The Society of Friends (Quakers) has played a fundamental role in the history of American slavery and its abolition. From the society's founding in Great Britain in the 1650s, Friends promoted a spiritualistic and rigorous Christianity. Quakers faced persecution for rejecting both the established church and contemporary class and sexual distinctions. This radicalism led to a questioning attitude toward slavery, as is seen as early as 1657 when their earliest leader, George Fox, advised Friends with slaves to convert them and treat them as brothers. On a visit to Barbados in 1671 Fox controversially preached to slaves, and later he suggested that Quakers should limit the service of slaves to thirty years and give them compensation. Fox's companion, William Edmondson, went further in a 1676 tract stating that Christian freedom could not coexist alongside physical slavery and justified slave rebellion. However, as Quakers sought religious and political freedom by creating settlements in Rhode Island and Pennsylvania, they also discovered that their work ethic and links with trustworthy West Indian and English brethren gave them economic advantages in the transatlantic trade. American Quaker merchants found that the West Indies was a natural market for their products, and this led on to transshipment of sugar and direct participation in the slave trade. Eventually Newport, Rhode Island, would become America's largest slave-trading port. By the eighteenth century, these wealthy Quaker merchants, who were by nature proslavery, formed part of an increasingly secularized elite, while ordinary Quakers tended to become more quietistic and conservative.

Nevertheless, the Germantown Protest in Philadelphia in 1688 is one example of how slavery remained problematic for some Quakers. From 1711 onward, the

Philadelphia Yearly Meeting faced continuing controversy over slavery, mainly from Quaker farmers, but a conservative majority ensured that it went no further than advising members not to participate in the slave trade. The next two decades saw similar debates among other American Quakers and the publication of Quaker antislavery tracts, with radicals like John Farmer and Benjamin Lay being disowned for causing dissension.

Thus by the 1740s Quaker testimony against slavery was well defined, but it was only through the work of John Woolman and Anthony Benezet that it actually became widely accepted within the society. By 1755 the Philadelphia Yearly Meeting ordered that Friends who traded in slaves should be officially admonished, a step followed elsewhere. This development corresponded with a reforming drive among Friends to abandon the worldly values that their gains in political and economic power had brought. For the first time Quaker influence now made abolition a real political issue in America, leading to the first legislative attempts to outlaw the slave trade in the 1760s. By 1776 the Philadelphia Meeting ruled that Friends should free their slaves and provide them compensation, or risk dismissal; this was a groundbreaking decision, once again setting a trend to be followed even by southern Quakers. It was Quaker pressure in 1780 that led the state of Pennsylvania to declare slavery to be illegal. Furthermore, it was the prompting of American Quakers that encouraged the London Meeting to move to active abolitionism. So despite their small numbers, the Quakers provided an essential transatlantic nucleus of leadership and financial backing for the fledgling abolitionists. The long tradition of Quaker female activism and separate women's meetings also meant that it was among Quakers that female abolition found its beginnings and many of its greatest figures.

After the slave trade was banned in 1808 American Quakers became ever more withdrawn and sectarian in feeling; they disliked public controversy and, in addition, were distracted by the Hicksite theological schism in the 1820s. Thus abolitionist Friends generally followed a gradualist position advocating peaceful lobbying, publishing campaigns, boycotts of slave produce, plans for educating freed slaves, and colonizing them in Africa; or more radically being prominent in the sanctuary offered by the Underground Railroad. The Quakers' commitment to gradualism meant that the society in the North and South remained united and it seemed to help their lobbying against the Fugitive Slave Law, but it meant that they forfeited the leadership role they had before 1808. In Britain after 1807 where abolition was less contentious, Quakerism

was more radical; abolition was vital to the triumph of British abolition in 1833. The British Quakers example and influence inspired some American Friends like Arnold Buffum and John Greenleaf Whitter to support the immediatist American Anti-Slavery Society. To most American Quakers, immediatism seemed divisive and un-Christian. Some local meetings prohibited Friends from joining the society. As a result of the disputes aroused by immediatism, Friends like the Grimké sisters left or were expelled; the culmination of this internal unrest came in 1842 in a local schism, with Charles Osborn forming the Indiana Anti-Slavery Friends. With the approach of the Civil War most Friends, no matter how committed they were to abolition, remained true to their pacifist principles and refused to support it. Involvement in Reconstruction after the war was more suited to Quaker ideals, and so they were conspicuous in philanthropic attempts to help and educate ex-slaves and to transform the South. Friends have continued to be leaders in campaigns against slavery and forced labor throughout the world right up to the present day.

— *Gwilym Games*

See also: Abolitionism in the United States; Coffin, Levi; Grimké, Angelina; Grimké, Sarah Moore; Mott, Lucretia Coffin; Woolman, John.

For Further Reading

Aptheker, Herbert. 1940. "The Quakers and Negro Slavery." *Journal of Negro History* 25 (July): 331–362.

Barbour, Hugh, and J. William Frost. 1988. *The Quakers.* Westport, CT: Greenwood.

Braithwaite, William. 1961. *The Second Period of Quakerism.* Cambridge: Cambridge University Press.

Drake, Thomas. 1954. *Quakers and Slavery in America.* New Haven, CT: Yale University Press.

Frost, J. William. 1978. "The Origins of the Quaker Crusade against Slavery: A Review of Recent Literature." *Quaker History* 67: 42–58.

Hewitt, Nancy A. 1986. "Feminist Friends: Agrarian Quakers and the Emergence of Women's Rights in America." *Feminist Studies* 12 (Spring): 27–49.

Knee, Stuart E. 1985. "The Quaker Petition of 1791: A Challenge to Democracy in Early America." *Slavery & Abolition* 6 (September): 151–159.

Soderlund, Jean R. 1985. *Quakers and Slavery: A Divided Spirit.* Princeton, NJ: Princeton University Press.

JOHN A. QUITMAN (1798–1858)

A staunch defender of slavery and states' rights, Mississippian John A. Quitman was a southern nationalist in the pivotal secession era. Quitman was born near Kingston in Rhinebeck, New York, to a Lutheran minister; he was one of eight children. He graduated from Harwick Seminary in 1816, studied law, and in 1821 was admitted to the Ohio bar. He taught briefly in Pennsylvania but began a legal practice in Natchez, Mississippi, in 1821.

Quitman was a large landowner with several plantations and hundreds of slaves. Although it is difficult to determine just how many slaves he held at any one time, records indicate that his largest plantation at Palmyra included 311 slaves (1848). At Monmouth, his base of operations, he had primarily house servants, but on smaller holdings, Quitman's slaves numbered thirty-nine, forty-five, and eighty-five at various times.

From 1821 to 1858 Quitman was a significant figure in Mississippi politics as a representative, senator, governor, and, from 1855 to 1858, as a U.S. congressman. During his years of leadership in state politics, he became associated with the nullification movement, was a protégé of John C. Calhoun, and became the most recognized figure in antebellum Mississippi.

When Calhoun and South Carolina advocated nullification of the 1828 and 1832 tariffs, Henry Clay pushed a compromise through Congress to lower tariff rates over a ten-year period. South Carolina reacted by repealing its tariff nullification. In Mississippi, Quitman nevertheless encouraged support for the principle of nullification and formation of a states' rights party, which culminated in a May 1834 nullification convention in Jackson, Mississippi.

Quitman envisioned himself as a military man. He led an expedition in 1836 to support Texas independence and, although the unit saw no combat, the effort enabled Quitman to pursue his military interests. During the Mexican War (1846–1848), Quitman was commissioned a brigadier-general under General Zachary Taylor. Active at Monterey, Mexico (September 1846), Quitman's troops were the first to enter Mexico City after its surrender (November 1846). Commanding General Winfield Scott appointed the Mississippian military governor of the city, and Quitman became a major-general in April 1847.

Quitman was considered for the presidential nomination at the Democratic Convention in 1848 in Baltimore but was elected governor of Mississippi in 1849 instead. Inaugurated in January 1850, Quitman had a brief and, at best, a stormy term in office. The governor opposed the Compromise of 1850 and called a state legislative session to protest Henry Clay's latest compromise measures, thus reaffirming his role as leader of Mississippi's proslavery forces.

After becoming a co-conspirator with Cuban fili-bustering leader Narciso Lopez, Quitman was indicted by a New Orleans grand jury for violating neutrality laws. He resigned the governor's office in February 1851, but was later acquitted. Quitman served in Congress from 1855 until he died in office on July 17, 1858.

The question remains: Was Quitman a secessionist? Evidently he did support secession (as governor in 1850) when he responded to what he deemed an attack on states' rights, but he never became an extreme southern nationalist.

— Boyd Childress

See also: Lopez, Narciso.

For Further Reading

Claiborne, J. F. H. 1860. *Life and Correspondence of John A. Quitman, Major-General, U.S.A., and Governor of the State of Mississippi.* New York: Harper.

May, Robert E. 1985. *John A. Quitman: Old South Crusader.* Baton Rouge: Louisiana State University Press.

∾ R ∾

JAMES THOMAS RAPIER (1837–1883)

James Thomas Rapier was a teacher, newspaperman, planter, and congressman from Alabama and one of the most prominent African American politicians in the United States during the Reconstruction era. He was born in Florence, Alabama, in 1837 to John H. and Sally Rapier, both free blacks. His father was a barber, one of the few occupations legally open to free blacks in antebellum Alabama, and a very successful businessman. He accumulated substantial property, and most of his children received an education—out of the state, for it was illegal for free blacks to be educated in Alabama. At the age of seven, James Rapier was sent to live with his slave grandmother and uncle in Nashville, Tennessee, in order to attend school there. After receiving a basic education in Nashville, Rapier spent a year working on steamboats on the Cumberland, Mississippi, and Tennessee rivers. At the age of nineteen, Rapier left the South and moved to Canada to continue his education at the Buxton School.

The Buxton School was located in Buxton, Ontario,

a prosperous black utopian community of over two thousand founded by ex-slaves in the late 1840s and home to Rapier's aunt and uncle with whom he lived. At first Rapier seemed preoccupied with acquiring material wealth through various business schemes, but following a religious conversion during a Methodist revival, he applied himself to his studies and determined to return to the South to aid enslaved blacks. Rapier left Buxton in 1860 and enrolled in a normal college in Toronto where he received a teaching certificate in 1863. After a year of teaching school in Buxton, Rapier returned to Nashville in 1864 to begin working among the newly freed blacks.

Rapier leased land for cotton planting and served as a correspondent for a northern newspaper. With the end of the Civil War, he became active in the fight for civil rights for the former slaves. The Tennessee state government's failure to enact legislation guaranteeing black equality disgusted Rapier, and in 1866 he returned to Florence, Alabama. Renting several hundred acres of rich land, Rapier quickly became one of the most prosperous cotton planters in northern Alabama, and after passage of the Congressional Reconstruction Act (1867), he actively recruited and organized black political activists in Alabama.

Rapier attended the first Republican state convention in Alabama and quickly became one of the party's most prominent leaders. In 1870 he was the first black to run for statewide office (secretary of state) in Alabama, and although he was defeated in this first bid for political office, two years later he was elected as one of Alabama's representatives to the Forty-third Congress. During his time in the U.S. House of Representatives, Rapier became known for his fights for civil rights and educational opportunities for blacks and for his efforts to improve transportation and commerce in Alabama. Rapier was defeated in his bid for reelection in 1874 and ran for Congress for the last time, unsuccessfully, in 1876.

Rapier devoted the remainder of his life to black labor organizations, encouraging blacks to migrate west; Republican Party politics; and raising cotton. In 1878 Rutherford B. Hayes appointed him as collector of internal revenue for the Second District of Alabama, a position he held for the next four years. In 1883 James Rapier died in Montgomery, Alabama, of tuberculosis. Although he was only forty-five years old at the time of his death, Rapier had lived a remarkably full life, not only as one of the South's most prominent Republican politicians, but also as a prominent symbol of African Americans' accomplishments in the mid-nineteenth century.

— *James L. Sledge, III*

For Further Reading

Schweninger, Loren. 1979. *James T. Rapier and Reconstruction.* Chicago: University of Chicago Press.

RICHARD REALF (1834–1878)

A poet and radical abolitionist, Richard Realf became a member of John Brown's band of insurgents that hoped to liberate slaves in the United States by invading the mountainous regions of Virginia and inciting a slave insurrection. He abandoned the mission prior to Brown's attack on the federal arsenal at Harpers Ferry in 1859, and after the Civil War, he became a well-known poet who often described in verse the efforts to abolish slavery in the United States.

Realf was born in Sussex County, England, into a poor peasant family. He left home at age seventeen to pursue a literary career and became a protégé of Lady Noel Byron, widow of the famous poet, George Gordon (Lord) Byron. Realf arranged through Lady Byron to settle on one of her estates in Leicestershire in order to learn estate management and cultivate his literary ambition.

But shortly after beginning his new career, he became the center of a scandalous event that underscored a central tension throughout his adult life: the romantic struggle between the "real" and the "ideal," between the worldly passions of the flesh and those of the mind and spirit. He fell in love with the eldest daughter of the estate, despite what he realized were "great [social] gulfs between us that could never be bridged." She became pregnant, and he, "desirous of finding some other place in which to dwell" and having "instincts" that "were democratic and republican," fled to the United States (Johnson, 1879).

Realf settled in New York City, worked briefly for the evangelical reformer Louis Pease at the House of Industry, and soon became a self-described "radical abolitionist"—meaning that he sought the immediate abolition of slavery and was willing to go to great lengths to effect it. He went to Kansas in 1856 to help defend the territory against slavery, and in the following year he joined John Brown's company of revolutionaries. In 1858 the group met with some expatriate African Americans in Chatham, Canada, to recruit new members and to establish a "provisional constitution" to govern areas in the southern part of the United States that Brown hoped to liberate from slavery. Realf was appointed secretary of state of Brown's provisional government.

Shortly after the Chatham meeting, however, Realf read Francis Wayland's *Limitations of Human*

Responsibility, and that work caused him to abandon his radical abolitionism. The "book taught me," he said (Johnson, 1879), that certain ideals should never be acted upon. Instead of working to abolish the sins of the world, he now decided to escape them. In 1859, therefore, he began training to become a Jesuit priest at the Jesuit College at Spring Hill, Alabama, and the following year he joined a utopian Shaker community at Union Village, Ohio, a perfectionist and millennialist sect that required from its members, among other things, absolute celibacy and restraint from all carnal pleasures.

In 1862 Realf renewed his fight against slavery by joining the Eighty-eighth Illinois Volunteer Infantry. He continued to write highly romantic verse, fashioned after that of Byron and Percy Bysshe Shelley, and some of his poems were published in *Atlantic* and *Harper's* monthlies. His efforts to abolish slavery—whether while serving with John Brown or during his service with the Union army—represented the only sustained periods in which he was able to act on his spiritual and reform ideals and reconcile the struggle between the passions of the flesh and those of the mind and spirit.

In 1865, after his discharge from the Union army, Realf married Sophia Emery Graves. But he abandoned her within months and began making plans to join John Humphrey Noyes's Oneida, New York, utopian community, a community that practiced group marriage and a sacred form of free love. "I wanted always to live in accord with the Invisible Truth," Realf told Noyes, "and very many times it seems to me that the struggle in my nature between the beast and the seraph, the flesh and the spirit, was greater than I could bear." He wanted to escape the "howl of the beast" in a world "so very atheistic," and to "become alive to all righteousness" at Noyes's sacred community in Oneida (Johnson, 1879).

But Realf never made it to Oneida. He got as far as Rochester, New York, before succumbing to what he described as a "prolonged debauch" that included a bigamist marriage to a prostitute named Catherine Cassidy. He tried to abandon her as well, but she followed him wherever he went. After she caught up with him in San Francisco in 1878, Realf took a fatal dose of morphine, "as the only final relief" from her "incessant persecutions" (Johnson, 1879).

— *John Stauffer*

See also: Border War (1854–1859); Brown, John; Harpers Ferry Raid; Romanticism and Abolitionism.

For Further Reading
Hinton, Richard J., ed. 1898. *Poems by Richard Realf: Poet, Soldier, Workman.* New York: Funk & Wagnalls Company.

Johnson, Rossiter. 1879. "Richard Realf." *Lippincott's Magazine* (March): 293–300.

Realf, Richard. Testimony in "Mason Report" 1860. *U.S. Senate Committee Reports, 1859–60, II,* 21 January, 91–113.

Stimson, John Ward. 1903. "An Overlooked American Shelley." *The Arena* (July): 15–26.

RECONSTRUCTION. *See* Frederick Douglass; Fifteenth Amendment; Fourteenth Amendment; George Washington Julian; Freedmen's Bureau; James Thomas Rapier.

CHARLES LENOX REMOND (1810–1873)

Charles Lenox Remond was born in Salem, Massachusetts, to John and Nancy Remond, both noted black abolitionists. His mother played a significant part in establishing the Salem Antislavery Society in the early 1830s, and in 1835 his father became a lifetime member of the Massachusetts Anti-Slavery Society. John and Nancy Remond's involvement in antislavery activities greatly influenced the future direction of their son's life.

Charles began participating in the American Antislavery Society at an early age and became a staunch supporter of white abolitionist William Lloyd Garrison. In his early years, Remond found Garrison's philosophy of nonresistance appealing, but his own abolitionist philosophy would eventually become much more radical as he came to the conclusion that white abolitionists did not fully understand the problems facing African Americans.

In 1838 Remond was hired by the Massachusetts Anti-slavery Society to lecture—the first black to hold the position. For the next two years he traveled throughout New England delivering antislavery speeches and organizing new antislavery societies. In summer 1838, two new antislavery societies were established in Maine shortly after a visit from Remond.

Remond also spoke out in favor of women's involvement in antislavery activities. In most cities, women were encouraged to create their own auxiliary societies rather than just work alongside men. When women delegates were refused seating at the World's Anti-Slavery Convention in London in 1840, where Remond was serving as one of four representatives of the American Anti-Slavery Society, he voiced his disapproval and proceeded to remove himself from the assembly. Remond's trip to London had been financed by several female antislavery societies.

Remond continued on the lecture circuit for the

next year, returning to the United States in 1841. His speeches were well received, especially in London and Ireland, but this was frequently not the case in the United States. Remond became increasingly disillusioned with Garrison's belief that voting constituted tacit support of a proslavery government operating in compliance with a proslavery constitution. In 1848 Remond cast his ballot for Free Soil candidate Stephen C. Phillips, who, if elected governor, pledged greater appropriations for the support of black schools.

By 1850 Remond was supporting a more radical approach to abolition. At a convention held in New Bedford, Massachusetts, to discuss the *Dred Scott* decision, Remond stated that he was prepared to write an address encouraging slaves to revolt. He also suggested that change in the South would likely be the result of violence. He believed that the efforts of abolitionists had been a failure because conditions for most blacks remained dismal.

During the Civil War, Remond recruited soldiers for the Union army; this was further evidence of his growing discontent and radicalism. He eventually became less involved in public life, owing to failing health that was exacerbated by the death of his second wife. Remond died in Boston in 1873.

— *Beverly Bunch-Lyons*

See also: Women and the Antislavery Movement.

For Further Reading
Quarles, Benjamin. 1969. *Black Abolitionists.* New York: Oxford University Press.
Ripley, C. Peter, ed. 1992. *The Black Abolitionist Papers: Volume V, The United States, 1859–1865.* Chapel Hill: University of North Carolina Press.
Salzman, Jack, David Lionel Smith, and Cornel West, eds. 1996. *Encyclopedia of African-American Culture and History.* New York: Simon & Schuster, Macmillan.
Usrey, Mirian L. 1970. "Charles Lenox Remond: Garrison's Ebony Echo at the World's Anti-Slavery Convention 1840." *Essex Institute Historical Collections* 106 (April): 112–125.

REPUBLICAN PARTY. *See* Emancipation Proclamation; Free Soil Party; Abraham Lincoln; Whig Party.

RICE CULTIVATION AND TRADE

The English established colonial outposts along the eastern seaboard of North America in the seventeenth century, seeking to accumulate great profits. Hoping to capitalize on great wealth in gold or silver as the Spanish had done in the previous century in the Americas, many in England believed that the acquisition of the New World's fortune would be an easy task. Only after realizing that Virginia and surrounding regions were not replete with precious metals did the English settlers understand that the task of planting colonies, and of making them economically viable was a long and arduous process.

The North American colonists turned to agriculture in the hope that a "cash crop" might emerge that would make the colonial ventures profitable. Tobacco, a plant previously cultivated by the Native American inhabitants of the region, emerged as the staple crop of Virginia and the Carolinas. Farther to the south, in coastal areas of South Carolina and Georgia, planters began to cultivate indigo and rice. Of these crops, rice would emerge as the most successful and most profitable for the low country regions.

Rice cultivation was not an indigenous form of agriculture in South Carolina and Georgia, but rather, it was introduced by outsiders. Rice was not cultivated in Europe in the seventeenth century—it was a cereal grain whose cultivation was limited at the time to vast portions of southeastern Asia and two geographical regions of Africa. Rice cultivation was prevalent among the Malagasy, the indigenous people who inhabited the island of Madagascar. African peoples of the Upper Guinea coast, a region corresponding to modern-day Senegal, Gambia, Guinea-Bissau, Guinea, Sierra Leone, and Liberia, were also familiar with rice culture.

The cultivation of rice is a true Africanism, an African cultural survival that endured the harshness of the Middle Passage and managed to take root, literally, in the soil of the Americas. Africans brought rice cultivation to Brazil, to parts of the Caribbean basin, and eventually to the North American colonies of Georgia and South Carolina. The introduction of the grain was successful, bringing tremendous profits to the planter class of the low country region. Interestingly, the planters' profits were due to both the labor and the intellect of the enslaved Africans who worked the coastal plantations and farms.

It was common knowledge among coastal South Carolina and Georgia planters that the higher prices traders demanded for African slaves drawn from the Senegambia region was because these slaves possessed skills and experience in the cultivation of rice. The expertise of the Senegambian slaves was so valued that these slaves may have had some bargaining rights with their owners with respect to how their labor would be employed in the rice fields. Some historians have suggested that the "task system" may have originated in the coastal rice plantations as slaves sought to mitigate against the more brutal labor regime associated with the "gang system" that was commonly used. The planters' awareness of the true value of their slave property was evident as Georgia and South Carolina planters became more discriminating in their purchase of new slaves, hoping to acquire only those who had previous knowledge and experience in rice cultivation.

Rice cultivation was a demanding enterprise, and anyone who did not have a respectable level of sophistication in the task was unlikely to profit from its cultivation. There is a certain time during the growing season when the rice fields must be flooded; precision in the timing of this action is critical to the quality and quantity of the harvest. In addition, the harvesting of a rice crop in a premechanical harvesting era, coupled with the perils of operating in malarial-infested regions, made cultivation especially difficult. Having a trained labor force adept at the task made the cultivation of rice more manageable in the South Carolina and Georgia coastal plantations and farms.

The use of Senegambian slaves who were experienced with rice cultivation is one expression of the "specialization of labor" that Adam Smith would later endorse in *Wealth of Nations* (1776). The successful use of trained slaves to cultivate rice also demonstrates that white planters realized that Africans came equipped with skills that could be utilized for the better management of the plantations and farms of the low country. This type of ethnic awareness, or cultural differentiation, suggests that planters were aware of the intrinsic wealth and value of African slaves as individuals.

— *Junius P. Rodriguez*

See also: Georgia; Sea Islands; South Carolina.

For Further Reading
   Carney, Judith A. 1993. "From Hands to Tutors: African Expertise in the South Carolina Rice Economy." *Agricultural History* 67: 1–30.
   Carney, Judith A. 2002. *Black Rice: The African Origins of Rice Cultivation in the Americas.* Cambridge, MA: Harvard University Press.
   Chaplin, Joyce E. 1992. "Tidal Rice Cultivation and the Problem of Slavery in South Carolina and Georgia, 1760–1815." *William and Mary Quarterly* 49: 29–61.
   Dusinberre, William. 1996. *Them Dark Days: Slavery in the American Rice Swamps.* New York: Oxford University Press.
   Littlefield, Daniel C. 1981. *Rice and Slaves: Ethnicity and the Slave Trade in Colonial South Carolina.* Baton Rouge: Louisiana State University Press.
   Smith, Julia Floyd. 1985. *Slavery and Rice Culture in Low Country Georgia, 1750–1860.* Knoxville: University of Tennessee Press.

NORBERT RILLIEUX (1806–1894)

By making what many people consider to be the most significant technological advancement in the history of sugar refining, Norbert Rillieux, a free octoroon (a person who is one-eighth black), dramatically changed the nature of labor on nineteenth-century sugar plantations. Having been born the son of a Louisiana sugar planter, Rillieux was familiar with the refining process. Later as a student at L'Ecole Centrale in Paris, he devoted himself to the study of engineering and developed expertise in the emerging steam technology. Returning to Louisiana in 1840, he applied his knowledge of steam technology to sugar refining—gaining patents in 1843 and 1846 for variations of his multiple-effect vacuum pan evaporator.

Before Rillieux's technological breakthrough, plantations employed a wasteful and dangerous sugar-refining system known as "the Jamaica train." In this process, a series of large, open kettles were heated, and a line of slaves stood beside the hot steaming kettles pouring boiling sugarcane juice from one kettle to another. As the juice was passed along, it gradually became thicker and eventually crystallized. It was extremely uncomfortable work, and many slaves received disfiguring scars from the boiling juice. The process was slow, labor intensive, wasteful of fuel, and produced a poor-quality sugar.

Rillieux's adaptation of the vacuum pan distillation process applied the latent heat in the steam to economize on fuel. Using a partial vacuum, he was able to heat a number of kettles with the steam produced by the first. In addition to the obvious fuel savings, the system produced higher-quality sugar. Initially, there was some resistance in implementing the new system. There was a significant start-up cost, and many plantation owners were concerned that their uneducated slave labor force would be unable to run the equipment. Although, in the end, most plantations had to hire a skilled laborer to maintain and oversee the operation of the machinery, the new technology was compatible with the slave system, and the enormous savings the process brought, made sugar production very profitable. Producers were able to lower prices and thus make fine-quality sugar affordable to a much larger market, which in turn drastically increased demand.

In order to feed this growing market, sugar plantations expanded, and thus the demand for slaves to grow and harvest the sugarcane increased. Although Rillieux's technological advancement ended the unpleasant and wasteful system of the Jamaica train, it caused the sugar industry to expand and resulted in greater economic incentives to defend the plantation economy. It serves as an interesting contradiction to the prevailing notion that technological evolution minimized the economic attractiveness of the slave economy.

As the slave system became progressively more difficult to maintain, greater restrictions were placed on all people of color, which made life in Louisiana increasingly difficult for Rillieux. Having profited significantly from his patents in the United States, Rillieux returned to France in 1854 and developed an interest in Egyptology. His interests in evaporation and sugar machinery were rekindled later in life however, and in 1881 he patented a system for heating juice with vapors in multiple effect, a system that is still used in sugar refineries today.

— *Mark Cave*

See also: Louisiana; Octoroons; Sugar Cultivation and Trade.

For Further Reading

Aufhauser, R. Keith. 1974. "Slavery and Technological Change." *The Journal of Economic History* 34: 36–50.

Heitmann, John Alfred. 1987 *The Modernization of the Louisiana Sugar Industry 1830–1910*. Baton Rouge: Louisiana State University Press.

Klein, Aaron E. 1971. *The Hidden Contributors: Black Scientists and Inventors in America*. New York: Doubleday and Company.

Meade, George P. 1946. "A Negro Scientist of Slavery Days." *Scientific Monthly* 62: 317–326.

ROMANTICISM AND ABOLITIONISM

More than mere coincidence accounted for the concomitant rise of romanticism and abolitionism in the United States and Europe. Romanticism placed its emphasis on the natural world and the natural rights of man, and made it possible, for the first time, to write about and dramatize the life and plight of the common man and to elevate such to the level of art.

This was an important development at a time when there was much civil unrest among the growing underclass in Europe, and it predated the Reform Act of 1832 in England as well as the enfranchisement of the propertyless in other European nations and the United States. In many ways, romantic philosophy gave rise to the democratization of Europe and of the United States, and it provided much of the foundation for huge social and political eruptions like the French and American revolutions. It is not surprising, then, that abolitionism as an organized movement got under way

at about the same time as romantic thought was sweeping Europe and the United States. In fact, the language of "natural rights" and the "rights of man"— which romanticism borrowed in part from the Enlightenment and extended—was fused with the moral rhetoric of the Bible to provide the substance of the philosophical, moral, and political positions of early abolitionist rhetoric.

Although much historical attention has been devoted to abolitionism and much literary attention has been given to British and U.S. romanticism, little has been written on the relationships between romanticism and the rise of racial politics in the nineteenth century. Such a discussion should not be limited to considerations of the appearance of traditional romantic themes and tropes in texts by black authors—for example, the "innocence" of childhood versus the "experience" of slave identity consciousness, the use of sentimentalism, the emphasis on "self-reliance," the valorizing of the meek and lowly or the "natural man." But it should also include some speculation about the rise of romanticism in light of the political upheavals surrounding the issue of slavery and the rise of a natural rights philosophy.

In other words, literary romanticism (here the rise of Nature in opposition to ordered civilization associated with the Enlightenment) is less about escaping the political realities and anxieties of civilization than it is about choosing in Nature a more uncertain, or less determined, terrain on which to work out those political anxieties. Thinkers and writers found that contemporary issues associated with civilization—most notably the French Revolution and its aftermath, rampant poverty among a growing underclass, and abolitionism—which so plagued the creative imagination were more easily worked out in the coded poetic language of Nature than in the highly charged and volatile political terms of the public debates of the day. Such cross-cultural readings offer new ways of understanding and reading romanticism as well as the romantics.

In *Romanticism and Gender* (1993), Anne Mellor poses a monumental question to romanticists and, more broadly, to students of literature. She asks her readers to reconfigure what they have traditionally known as romanticism by centering women's writings in that period instead of on works by men. We are instructed that by doing so, new dominant themes emerge and new aesthetic principles become normative. Such an inquiry, then, gets to the heart of the ways in which dominant representations of literary romanticism get established and maintained through an emphasis on male-authored texts and the suppression of female-authored texts.

Similarly, any serious consideration of romanticism's relationship to abolitionism must focus on the literary production and the concerns of blacks during the romantic period, which would inevitably include a number of slave narrative texts as they were the most common literary form among blacks. Even a cursory perusal of these texts demonstrates the extent to which romantic thought so thoroughly permeated the discourse of the abolitionists. An equally cursory glance at the canonical romantic writers demonstrates the opposite directional flow of such influences.

— Dwight A. McBride

For Further Reading

Davis, David Brion. 1966. *The Problem of Slavery in Western Culture.* Oxford: Oxford University Press.

Gaull, Marilyn. 1988. *English Romanticism: The Human Context.* New York: Norton.

Gossett, Thomas. 1965. *Race: The History of an Idea in America.* New York.

Mellor, Anne K. 1993. *Romanticism and Gender.* New York and London: Routledge.

Raimond, Jean, and J. R. Watson, eds. 1992. *A Handbook to English Romanticism.* New York: St. Martin's.

Edmund Ruffin, one of the most vocal "fire-eaters" of the proslavery South, was said to have fired the first shot against Fort Sumter. (Library of Congress)

EDMUND RUFFIN (1794–1865)

According to popular legend, the southern slaveholder Edmund Ruffin fired the first and last shots of the Civil War. In April 1861, at age sixty-seven, Ruffin was invited to ignite the cannon that fired on Fort Sumter in Charleston Harbor, South Carolina. On June 18, 1865, two months after the conflict had ended, Ruffin died by suicide. Ruffin's biographer enhanced his legend, describing the final moment as Ruffin wrapped himself in a Confederate flag before firing the fatal shot. This final irony lacks veracity, but Ruffin's suicide note—that he could not live in a world under Yankee rule—is accurate.

Ruffin is one of the more intriguing figures in the antebellum South. A proslavery advocate and plantation owner and ardent southern nationalist, he applied scientific farming methods at an early time. Born in Prince George County, Virginia, in 1794, Ruffin attended the College of William and Mary, served briefly in the War of 1812, and began agricultural experiments at age twenty-five on his land along the James River. His success focused on using marl, a calcium carbonate, to enrich damaged soils and greatly heighten productivity. Ruffin documented his work in *An Essay on Calcareous Manures* (1832) and in *Farmers' Register,* an agricultural journal he edited from 1833 to 1842.

In 1843 he moved to Virginia's Hanover County to a new estate named Marlbourne. Ruffin's outspoken stance on slavery significantly overshadowed his success and reputation as an agricultural reformer, but historians fully recognize his contributions to southern agriculture. He was a significant but not necessarily large slaveholder—at Marlbourne there was a total of forty-one slaves.

Politically, Ruffin had little experience at either the state or federal level, even though he served in the Virginia State Senate (1824–1828). In 1831 the moderate Ruffin skillfully defended a slave falsely accused in Nat Turner's revolt, but by 1850, he was increasingly agitated about constant attacks on slavery. His proslavery stance only solidified as the nation moved closer to war. Ruffin, fearful the South could never exist without slavery, was counted among the staunchest secessionists. Ruffin utilized his extensive network to spread proslavery views through conversation, and he used the written word to support disunion. Ruffin could be found wherever a favorable audience might be gathered across the South.

In appearance, Ruffin was an unmistakable character with long, flowing white hair in his later years. He wrote extensively for newspapers in Charleston and Richmond. One major article, "African Colonization Unveiled," was serialized in *DeBow's Review* (1859–1860) and also published as a separate pamphlet. Ruffin aired his views on secession in three other widely circulated pamphlets. A political novel, *Anticipations of the Future* (1860), pointed to the absolute necessity for secession and southern independence.

Ruffin was visible, vocal, and prolific, but his efforts probably had little impact on progress toward secession. In 1858 he and Alabamian William Lowndes Yancey formed the League of United Southerners to encourage secession, but it failed to ignite public opinion. Never one to miss an opportunity for calling attention to his cause, Ruffin joined the Virginia Military Institute Cadet Corps (December 1859) to witness John Brown's execution. He sent pikes seized from Brown's followers to southern governors for public display in order to promote secession. Finally, the excitable Ruffin joined South Carolina's Palmetto Guard to fire the first rounds aimed at Fort Sumter—the opening shots of the Civil War.

By 1861 Ruffin was not in particularly good health, and he spent the war years as a virtual exile. As his family properties were damaged and subject to raids, he finally landed at Redmoor, some 35 miles west of Richmond. As the southern cause crumbled and the inevitable became more obvious, Ruffin held steadfast to his views of southern independence. When the end came, Ruffin began preparation for suicide—a solution he had long considered.

Legend has it that just after noon on June 17, 1865, Ruffin wrapped himself in a Confederate flag and ended his own life. Although the legend is undocumented, Ruffin did pen a suicide note. Declaring his hatred for the "perfidious, malignant, and vile Yankee race," Ruffin repudiated northern rule even to the grave but chose not to attack blacks or to mention slavery. For Ruffin, though, his proslavery views survived to the end of his life.

— *Boyd Childress*

See also: Fire-Eaters.

For Further Reading
Craven, Avery O. 1932. *Edmund Ruffin, Southerner: A Study in Secession.* New York: D. Appleton.

Mathew, William M. 1988. *Edmund Ruffin and the Crisis of Slavery in the Old South: The Failure of Agricultural Reform.* Athens: University of Georgia Press.

Mitchell, Betty. 1981. *Edmund Ruffin, a Biography.* Bloomington: Indiana University Press.

Wyatt-Brown, Bertram. 2003. *Hearts of Darkness: Wellsprings of a Southern Literary Tradition.* Baton Rouge: Louisiana State University Press.

RUNAWAY SLAVES. *See* Slave Patrols; Slave Catchers; 36°30' North Latitude.

SAMBO THESIS

In *Slavery: A Problem in American Institutional and Intellectual Life* (1959), Stanley M. Elkins compared slavery in the South to Nazi concentration camps and concluded that the institution of slavery in the United States had resulted in the obliteration of the African American personality and the creation of a docile, malleable slave personality—the "Sambo." Elkins's study was motivated by what he claimed was evidence of the slaves' disinterest in resisting the slave regime, particularly the lack of consistent slave rebellions in the United States as compared to the slave regimes of Brazil and the Caribbean.

Historian Ulrich Bonnell Phillips's analysis of the Old South was based largely on the plantation records and journals of slaveowners, which had produced an enduring image of the southern plantation as a pastoral paradise where content and obsequious blacks worked under the close supervision of "paternalistic" whites. According to Phillips, slaveowners said a black "was what a white man made him." Thus black slaves were envisioned and memorialized as being highly sociable, hypersexual, musical, superstitious, subordinate, lazy, amusing, affectionate, and loyal.

Elkins's Sambo model of the slave temperament was peculiar to the United States because of the "totalitarian" nature of slavery in the antebellum South, which Elkins compared to slavery as it was institutionalized in other countries and at other times. In South America, for example, other institutions (e.g., the Catholic Church) had an almost equal impact on the lives of the slaves as did slaveowners, whereas in the United States, nothing mediated the absolute power of the slaveowner over the slave. Ultimately, Elkins found the concentration camps of twentieth-century Nazi Germany most like the closed society of the South before the Civil War, referring to the camps as a form of human slavery based on a "perverted patriarchy."

Beginning with the transportation of prisoners to the Nazi camps in closed cattle cars, which Elkins compared to the below-decks shipboard experience of Africans on the transatlantic voyage from Africa to the Americas, absolute control over the inmates of the camps was implemented. Neither camp inmate nor American slave possessed any certainty about the future. And, according to Elkins, both Nazi concentration camps and the institution of slavery in the U.S. South relied on strategies of terror: deliberate and in each case consistent punishments were intended to reduce the resistance of the prisoner/slave and to control his or her attitudes and behavior. Yet, according to Elkins, an "adjustment" to conditions was ultimately obtained, and a kind of status quo ensued.

Relying heavily on the work of the psychologist Bruno Bettelheim, Elkins proposed his own analysis of the slave personality. The experience of slavery in the United States "infantalized" the African Americans, making them "perpetual children" in need of close supervision and direction. Like the inmates of German camps, who saw their guards as father figures and assumed the demeanor of children, slaves in the U.S. South also assumed "childlike" behaviors in accepting the owner's value system, seeking to please the owner, and judging fellow slaves by the guidelines used by the owner. Because the American slave identified with her or his owner, who became, according to Elkins, the figure who was most emotionally important for slaves, resistance to slavery by the slaves in the United States was rare or nonexistent.

Other historians have pointed to the writings of French colonists in Haiti, who at least suggested that their treatment of their own slaves had produced a similar personality type or behavior, except that Haiti was the site of the hemisphere's only successful slave overthrow of a slave regime. Slaveowners in Brazil likewise memorialized their impressions of their slaves' docility. And indeed, historians have noted that slaveowners through the centuries have traditionally described their slaves as loyal but lazy, sly, and sexually promiscuous, which perhaps suggests a unified strategy of slaveholding as necessary for the close supervision or "elevation" of the enslaved group rather than the actual existence of a personality type.

Slaves had space to create full-fledged communities, which had their own value systems, and some people in those communities had a significant effect on them, so slaves were not wholly dependent on the owner or the owner's value system. One response to being a slave was the development of a theory of Afrocentrism, which placed the slave at the center of the story of slavery as subject and actor rather than as merely an object of white action. At least one historian had questioned the plausibility of reaching reasonable conclusions about an institution built around black slaves without addressing the philosophies, communities, and lives of those black slaves.

Whereas historians of slavery once relied almost exclusively on written documents as source material, documents that had often been produced by slaveowners, new attention began to focus on so-called slave sources: slave narratives written by slaves who had successfully escaped slavery, slave autobiographies and correspondence (both letters to other slaves as well as letters to owners or former owners), and especially the transcribed interviews of former slaves conducted by the Works Progress Administration in the United States in the 1930s. Also, a new look at slaveowner sources—slave bills of sale; plantation account books listing births and deaths, work assignments, and punishments; and antebellum newspapers listing runaway notices and slave auctions—provided intriguing background material for constructing the histories of the slaves themselves.

Historians have now found evidence of a community that survived despite the sale and psychological and physical coercion of its members. An extended kin network tended to include both related and "orphaned" slaves who were not necessarily related by blood. Parents and grandparents educated child slaves in the ways of both blacks (including Africans and American-born) and whites. Religious interpretations by slaves were sometimes limited by the prohibition on slave literacy, although slaves did sometimes learn to read and focused on the attainment not just of spiritual or metaphorical freedom, but also of actual physical freedom in the here and now.

Despite Elkins's support of the Sambo thesis, although spectacular resistance such as the eighteenth-century Stono Rebellion and the antebellum insurrections of Denmark Vesey and Nat Turner might have been limited, most slaves did engage in acts of daily resistance. This type of resistance included work slowdowns, feigning of illness, intentional injury to themselves, temporary escape (truancy), and successful escape beyond the reach of slavery's laws. Communities of maroons (slave runaways who set up camp along the borders of settled areas) also existed throughout the antebellum period. House slaves, especially females, were sometimes in a position to resist in more significant ways by poisoning food or water or by committing arson. Some historians have also speculated as to whether female slaves might have aborted pregnancies in order to prevent an increase of the slave population. In addition, recent discoveries in state and federal archives suggest the existence of full-fledged conspiracies of slaves to overthrow slavery in the United States; some of these conspiracies were discovered, and the slaves executed or sold. Clearly, the suggestion that U.S. slaves had been reduced to docility is soundly rebutted by a record of consistent and

Many of the marsh-strewn and palmetto-lined Sea Islands were a financial base for agricultural operations in the United States. (Library of Congress)

creative resistance to slavery from the colonial period through the Civil War.

— *Dale Edwyna Smith*

See also: Elkins, Stanley M.; Phillips, Ulrich Bonnell; Stono Rebellion; Turner, Nat; Vesey, Denmark.

For Further Reading

Blassingame, John. 1972. *The Slave Community: Plantation Life in the Antebellum South.* New York: Oxford University Press.

Jordan, Winthrop D. 1993. *Tumult and Silence at Second Creek: An Inquiry into a Civil War Slave Conspiracy.* Baton Rouge: Louisiana State University Press.

Raboteau, Albert J. 1978. *Slave Religion: The "Invisible Institution" in the Antebellum South.* New York: Oxford University Press.

Weinstein, Allen, Frank Otto Gatell, and David Sarasohn, eds. 1968. *American Negro Slavery: A Modern Reader.* New York: Oxford University Press.

White, Deborah Gray. 1985. *Ar'n't I a Woman? Female Slaves in the Plantation South.* New York: Norton.

SEA ISLANDS

The name "Sea Islands" generally identifies the Atlantic coastal islands of the South Carolina and Georgia low country and northern Florida. There have been estimates of approximately one thousand islands in the Sea Island chain. However, not all of them are inhabitable. Those that are inhabitable range from less than 15 square miles to just over 100 square miles. The inhabitable islands are the home of the Gullah and Geechee people and their associated language and culture. These islands, along with 30 miles inland onto the mainland of the states that they adjoin, form the Gullah/Geechee Nation.

The English worked to claim mainland North America before the Spanish or the French, but both of those nations had already established colonial spheres and begun settlements in the area before the English arrived. English Loyalists, called the "British Lords Proprietors," came from the sugar plantations of Barbados and began settling the region after England's

King Charles II granted a charter in 1663 that opened Carolina to colonial settlement. Those who came wanted to increase their wealth by expanding land ownership and producing crops. So, they brought with them the Africans who would one day build the base on which Gullah culture was developed and Geechee culture would grow.

During chattel slavery, many of these marsh-strewn and palmetto-lined islands served as a financial base for agricultural operations in the United States. It was in this region that long-staple Sea Island cotton was grown. This is considered to be the best cotton in the world. The islands were also the center of indigo production and shipbuilding. "Carolina Gold" rice became another major cash crop that contributed to the economic structure of the United States.

Today, many of the islands have been bought and converted into resort areas that sport huge golf courses and numerous tennis courts. This would not have been the case had the nation adhered to General William Tecumseh Sherman's Special Field Order, Number 15, issued on January 16, 1865. Within the field order, this area was specifically set aside for former enslaved Africans—"the islands from Charleston south [and] the abandoned rice fields along the rivers for thirty miles back from the sea." However, President Andrew Johnson nullified the order in September 1865, and as a result the Sea Islanders of African descent then had to purchase their property.

The descendants of these Africans still live on these islands today and continue their Gullah/Geechee culture, which first began in the plantation soil. They stood on their human right to self-determination on July 2, 2002, when they had a public ceremony declaring theirs to be the "Gullah/Geechee Nation" and enstooled their own Queen Mother as the official leader or "head on the body" of the Gullah/Geechee Nation. This leader serves as an official liaison and spokesperson who will ensure that their position is heard and that their land rights are protected for future generations.

— *Marquetta L. Goodwine*

See also: Geechee; Gullah; Rice Cultivation and Trade.

For Further Reading
Crum, Mason. 1968. *Gullah: Negro Life in the Carolina Sea Islands.* New York: Negro Universities Press.
Goodwine, Marquetta L. 1998. *The Legacy of Ibo Landing: Gullah Roots of African American Culture.* Atlanta, GA: Clarity Press.
Jones-Jackson, Patricia. 1987. *When Roots Die: Endangered Traditions in the Sea Islands.* Athens: University of Georgia Press.
Joyner, Charles W. 1989. *Remember Me: Slave Life in Coastal Georgia, 1750–1860.* Atlanta, GA: Georgia Humanities Council.
Pollitzer, William. 1999. *The Gullah People and Their African Heritage.* Athens: University of Georgia Press.
Rose, Willie Lee. 1976. *Rehearsal for Reconstruction: The Port Royal Experiment.* New York: Oxford University Press.

SEAMEN'S ACTS

In 1822, in the wake of Denmark Vesey's famous slave conspiracy in Charleston, South Carolina, that state's legislature passed an act mandating that free black sailors should be jailed while their vessels were in the state's ports. Employers were made liable for the costs of detention, and any sailor not redeemed by his employer by the time the vessel left port could be sold into slavery. Over the next four decades, this law inspired similar seamen's acts in Georgia (1829), North Carolina (1830–1831), Florida (1832), Alabama (1839, 1841), Louisiana (1842, 1859), and Texas (1859).

Southern legislators were particularly concerned about limiting contact between free black sailors and local slaves, because they were fearful that the free blacks would encourage and assist slave escapes. Although these seamen's acts were intermittently enforced, and often only as a result of public scrutiny and pressure, they raised questions of comity (the respect of one state for the laws of another) and state sovereignty and generated court challenges, protests from northern states, as well as diplomatic challenges.

The first challenge came in the federal courts, when the U.S. Supreme Court declared the South Carolina act unconstitutional in the case of *Elkison* v. *Deliesseline* (1823). But influential Charlestonians, working through a newly organized South Carolina Association, pressed for continued enforcement of the law, and state officials complied. No federal official ever saw fit to enforce the Supreme Court's decision. Long after Vesey had faded from the public mind, white southerners continued to defend these seamen's laws as a symbol of states' rights.

Northern seaboard states frequently challenged the laws. A significant number of free blacks in cities such as Boston, New York, and Philadelphia worked as sailors in the coastal trade, and the seamen's acts threatened their freedom and deprived their employers of their services while in southern ports. In 1844 Massachusetts sent attorneys Samuel Hoar and Henry Hubbard to Charleston and New Orleans, respectively, to institute suits on behalf of free black citizens of

Massachusetts who were jailed under the South Carolina and Louisiana laws. But threats of violence forced both men to return to Massachusetts before they could challenge the constitutionality of the acts. Officials in each city had informed the men that their lives were in danger and that they could not be protected from angry crowds.

Great Britain, which also used free black sailors on commercial vessels, protested enforcement of the acts to federal officials during the 1820s and 1830s. This was one of the factors behind the challenge in the *Elkison* case. In the 1850s, through a mixture of lobbying, bribery, and obsequiousness, the British consulate convinced Louisiana (1852), Georgia (1854), and South Carolina (1856) to rescind or modify their acts (such acts had already fallen into disuse in several states by this time). After the sectional controversy stirred by John Brown's 1859 raid on Harpers Ferry, Virginia, the laws were seen by many southerners as too weak and too ineffective to be revived.

— *Roy E. Finkenbine*

See also: Louisiana; South Carolina; Vesey, Denmark.

For Further Reading
Hamer, Philip M. 1935. "British Consuls and the Negro Seamen's Act, 1850–1860." *Journal of Southern History* 1 (2): 138–168.
Hamer, Philip M. 1935. "Great Britain, the United States, and the Negro Seamen's Acts, 1822–1848." *Journal of Southern History* 1 (1): 3–28.

SEMINOLE INDIANS

Slavery played an important role in both the removal and destruction of the Seminole. They are a Muskogean tribe whose original territory extended from Georgia into north Florida. As this area was first colonized by the Spanish, they were caught up in the struggle for Florida waged between British, Spanish, and American settlers. The Seminole were sympathetic to Africans, and their lenient treatment of the slaves they owned would cause them many problems after the United States gained control of Florida in 1819. Eventually, the Seminole retreated into the Everglades to escape removal to Oklahoma.

By the seventeenth century, the Seminole had learned about African culture from free blacks and slaves who had moved or been brought into Seminole land by the Spanish. Before the American Revolution, the Spanish offered freedom to slaves who escaped from the British. However some Seminoles also bought slaves during this period, paying for them with

Seminoles in Florida rose in revolt in 1835. With the help of the "black Seminoles," the Native Americans battled the United States army for nearly a decade. (Photo © Estate of Bernanda Bryson Shahn/Licensed by VAGA, New York, NY)

livestock. Most made little money from the use of slave labor, although slaveownership increased the prestige of Seminole leaders.

Seminole custom allowed slaves to live in a separate village, paying their masters a portion of the produce or livestock they grew. Because the slaves were more skilled agriculturists than the Seminole, they often prospered, eventually farming large fields and owning herds of livestock. African slaves dressed like their Seminole masters, wearing little clothing when they worked in the fields. On festive occasions, they donned turbans, shawls, beaded moccasins, leggings and the shiny metal ornaments the Seminole favored.

Slaves owned by white Americans or Creek and Cherokee Indians often fled into Spanish Florida. When their owners crossed the border to recover them, they met with resistance from both the Seminole and the Spanish. Because of their allegiance to Spain, the Seminole were considered fair game by

Americans, who killed or wounded many Seminole in several raids into Spanish territory.

Spain eventually realized it could no longer hold Florida and sold the region to the United States in 1819. The terms of the Adams-Onis Treaty (1819) guaranteed fair treatment to the Seminole, but the United States did not keep its word to the tribe. After Florida became part of the United States, slaveowners in states adjacent to Florida demanded the return of escaped slaves living in the former Spanish territory. Many escaped slaves had found refuge with the Seminole because of their lenient attitude toward slaves. As a result, white and Indian slave catchers were allowed to hunt fugitives in Seminole territory.

During the second term of James Monroe's presidency, which ended in 1825, the United States government began a policy of Indian removal. The Seminole were moved to a smaller reservation in Florida, and some of the land taken from them was given to the Creek Indians. As a result, the Seminole came into conflict with the Creek, a larger and more powerful tribe. Blacks who had been free for decades were captured and returned to slavery. There were many disputes between whites and Seminole over the return of fugitive slaves, but most were settled in favor of the white planters.

Between 1832 and 1833, the United States pressured the Seminole to leave their land in Florida and relocate to Oklahoma. The Seminole feared that if they moved to Indian Territory in Oklahoma their slaves would be taken by the Creek. However if they stayed in Florida, they would lose their slaves to the whites. Many Seminole did sign the treaties of Payne's Landing and Fort Gibson, agreeing to surrender their Florida lands and relocate within three years. Others, under the leadership of Osceola, refused to leave and started an uprising in 1835. They fled to the Everglades, where they fought the United States army for nearly a decade with the help of runaway slaves called black Seminoles who lived with them. The black Seminoles were fierce fighters and played a prominent part in the fight against removal.

The United States military captured Osceola through treachery, and he later died in prison at Fort Moultrie, South Carolina. Despite the loss of Osceola, other Seminole tribal leaders continued to fight against the American forces despite the army's attempts at systematic extermination. They had mastered the art of guerrilla warfare in the swampy Everglades and continued the struggle until 1842 when the United States abandoned the war. The Seminole War had cost the United States $20 million and the lives of fifteen hundred soldiers. Many Seminoles were also killed during the war, while some fled as far west as Texas, but the U.S. government failed in the total removal of this tribe. For this reason the Seminole are called the Unconquered People.

— *Elsa a. Nystrom*

For Further Reading
Covington, James W. 1995. *The Seminoles of Florida.* Gainesville: University Press of Florida.
McReynolds, Edwin C. 1988. *The Seminoles.* Norman: University of Oklahoma Press.
Missall, John, and Mary Missall. 2004. *The Seminole Wars: America's Longest Indian Conflict.* Gainesville: University Press of Florida.

MARY ANN SHADD (1823–1893)

As the first female editor of a North American weekly newspaper in Canada and an African American woman, Mary Ann Shadd fought for the integration of blacks into society. Fiery and immensely controversial, she promoted abolition, equal rights, and women's suffrage.

Born on October 9, 1823, in Wilmington, Delaware, as the eldest of thirteen children of wealthy shoemaker Abraham Doras Shadd and Harriet Parnell Shadd, young Mary grew up in an activist climate. Her childhood home was an Underground Railroad stop, and her father represented Delaware at national conventions for the Improvement of Free People of Color. As a youth, Shadd attended a private Quaker school for African Americans, in which several of her teachers were white abolitionists. As a young woman during the 1840s, she taught in schools for blacks in Wilmington; West Chester, Pennsylvania; New York City; and Norristown, Pennsylvania.

When the passage of the Fugitive Slave Act (1850) made life hazardous for northern blacks, Shadd joined the exodus to Canada West (present-day Ontario). As the final destination of the Underground Railroad, Canada already had a sizable black community, and after emigrating in 1851, Shadd opened a school to educate fugitive slaves and other blacks who were unable to obtain schooling. She encouraged others to emigrate and published the instruction pamphlet, *Notes of Canada West* (1852) as an aid. An immensely popular guidebook, it helped many fugitives survive the trauma of relocation.

After meeting the antislavery journalist Samuel Ringgold Ward, Shadd pressed him into helping launch one of the best fugitive slave weeklies, the staunchly integrationist *Provincial Freeman,* in 1853. Nonsectarian and apolitical, the newspaper advocated temperance, black education, and women's rights to achieve its primary goal of uplifting the black race. Although listed as editor, Ward was merely a figurehead: Shadd was the pivot on which the paper turned.

Through the *Freeman,* she continued advocating black emigration to Canada, a preference that placed her in conflict with many influential African American abolitionists. Never faint of heart, Shadd penned powerful editorials encouraging blacks in Canada West to insist on fair treatment, even if that meant being assaulted. Repelled by the begging of newly free slaves, she pushed fellow emigrants to reach for financial independence. In the *Freeman* of March 25, 1854, she asserted that the progress of the fugitives "would be a triumphant rebuke to those who once held them as chattels, and to those who hold that the slave requires to be prepared for freedom, for [former slaves] would exhibit the spectacle of a people just escaped from a galling yoke competing as free men, successfully and honorably."

Shadd's frequent attacks on black leaders for failing to adequately aid black Canadian migrants led to breaches with other African Canadian activists. Her most publicized feud was with Henry and Mary Bibb, the leaders of the black settlement at Windsor, Ontario, and the publishers of the rival newspaper, *Voice of the Fugitive.* Bibb supported an assistance program for refugees that Shadd feared would prevent blacks from becoming self-reliant.

By the late 1850s, the *Freeman* was regarded as the organ of Martin R. Delany's African Civilization Society, but it was constantly plagued by financial difficulties. The *Freeman* folded in about 1858, after the black community's sexism had forced Shadd to turn the editorship of the paper over to her brother Isaac.

Marrying Toronto barber Thomas F. Cary in 1856, Shadd bore two children before being widowed in 1860. Returning to the United States to recruit Union troops, she retired to Washington, D.C., after the U.S. Civil War to teach. A law degree earned from Howard University in 1883 went unused. She died in 1893. A legendary crusader for justice, Shadd blazed a remarkable trail.

— *Caryn E. Neumann*

See also: United States–Canadian Relations on Fugitives; Delany, Martin R.

For Further Reading

Bearden, Jim, and Linda Jean Butler. 1977. *Shadd: The Life and Times of Mary Shadd Cary.* Toronto: NC Press.

Hancock, Harold B. 1973. "Mary Ann Shadd: Negro Editor, Educator, and Lawyer." *Delaware History* 15 (3): 187–194.

Johnson, Clifton H. 1971. "Mary Shadd Cary: Crusader for the Freedom of Man." *The Crisis: A Record of the Darker Races* 78 (April/May): 89–90.

Rhodes, Jane. 1992. "Breaking the Editorial Ice: Mary Ann Shadd Cary and the *Provincial Freeman.*" Ph.D. dissertation, Department of History, University of North Carolina, Chapel Hill, North Carolina.

Silverman, Jason. 1985. *Unwelcome Guests: Canada West's Response to American Fugitive Slaves, 1800–1865.* Millwood, NY: Associated Faculty Press.

SHADRACH FUGITIVE SLAVE CASE

The first successful rescue of a runaway slave held in federal custody under the Fugitive Slave Act of 1850 occurred on February 15, 1851, when local blacks seized Shadrach Minkins from a Boston, Massachusetts, courtroom. Minkins was never recaptured, and no convictions were ever secured against the people who aided in his escape.

Prior to fleeing bondage, Minkins had been a servant in the Norfolk, Virginia, household of John Debree, a purser in the U.S. Navy. In May 1850 Minkins escaped to Boston, where he worked as a waiter in the busy commercial district near the city's wharves. To minimize the risk of capture, he often adopted the pseudonym Frederick Wilkins. On February 12, 1851, John Caphart, a Norfolk constable hired by Debree to track Minkins, arrived in Boston seeking Minkins's rendition (legal return to slavery). Caphart obtained a warrant for Minkins's arrest from George Ticknor Curtis, the federal fugitive slave commissioner in the city and, three days later, Minkins was arrested by U.S. Marshal Patrick Riley.

Minkins was immediately taken before Commissioner Curtis for a hearing on the question of his rendition. The Boston Vigilance Committee appointed six prominent local attorneys, including the black jurist Robert Morris, to serve as his counsel. After they requested and were granted a three-day delay to prepare a defense, everyone except Morris, Minkins, and several marshals left the courtroom. Suddenly, as if by a prearranged signal, several dozen local blacks pushed open the door, rushed inside, seized a surprised Minkins, and hustled him out of the building and into the street. Within minutes, they had disappeared into the African American neighborhood on Beacon Hill. Through the efforts of Morris, the black abolitionist Lewis Hayden, and their contacts on the Underground Railroad, Minkins reached the safety of Montreal within a few days.

News of the rescue reverberated throughout the nation's capital. Senator Henry Clay of Kentucky demanded a thorough investigation, and President Millard Fillmore ordered the U.S. attorney to try all persons who may have "aided, abetted, or assisted" in Minkins escape (Collison, 1997). The ensuing investigation led to the arrest of eight local abolitionists, including Morris and Hayden, for their alleged roles in the rescue. All eight were indicted by a federal grand jury and tried in U.S. district court. The initial trials in May and June 1851 showed the weakness of the government's case. Five of the accused were immediately acquitted owing to insufficient evidence; the other three were bound over for retrial on various technicalities. Although the retrials dragged on for over a year, all of the alleged rescuers were eventually acquitted and released.

The Minkins rescue, and the inability of federal authorities to convict any of his rescuers, proved a major embarrassment to the Fillmore administration and raised sectional tensions between North and South. The affair also heightened the determination of free blacks in the North, and their abolitionist colleagues, to resist enforcement of the Fugitive Slave Act of 1850.

— *Roy E. Finkenbine*

See also: Fugitive Slave Act (1850); Underground Railroad.

For Further Reading

Collison, Gary. 1997. *Shadrach Minkins: From Fugitive Slave to Citizen.* Cambridge, MA: Harvard University Press.

SHORT-STAPLE COTTON

Short-staple cotton pertains to cultivated strains of *Gossypium hirsutum* that are domesticated as a cash crop, with "short-staple" referring to the short length of the fibers of this species in comparison to other domesticated species of cotton. It is native to Central America but has been grown intensively in the southern United States since the 1790s. Like all cottons, *G. hirsutum* is a perennial in the wild, but in cultivation it is grown as an annual. As it was the chief cash crop of the South by the mid-nineteenth century, most southern slaves worked on plantations and farms that produced short-staple cotton.

Before it became a major cash crop in the 1790s, short-staple cotton was grown only for household consumption. Its fibers clung tightly to the seeds, which made seed removal a lengthy process that occupied evenings and rainy days along with spinning and weaving. Thus short-staple cotton was an integral part of the household economy in the late eighteenth cen-

tury, but it was the cotton gin, which automated the separation of the fibers from the seeds, that allowed for the cultivation of short-staple cotton as a cash crop.

Prior to the development of the cotton gin, only longer-staple cottons, with seeds that were easily separated could be grown commercially in the New World. However, these long-staple cottons (primarily *G. barbadense*) had a lengthy growing season that could only be accommodated in the Caribbean islands and the coastal islands of South Carolina and Georgia. *G. hirsutum,* however, had a shorter growing season, and grew in virtually any soil; thus it was also referred to as upland cotton.

The introduction of the cotton gin along with more productive and easily cultivated strains of *G. hirsutum* at the end of the eighteenth century spurred the reopening of the Atlantic slave trade before its final ban in the United States in 1808, and the demand for slaves suddenly grew after a period of several decades of decline. Cotton cultivation also postponed the inevitable resolution that Americans faced concerning slavery by creating a new market for the domestic slave trade. The debate over the expediency of slavery as an economic system became a moot point as cotton's economic potential became apparent. Questions concerning slavery's morality were hushed as the revitalized domestic trade increased the value of all slaveholders' property.

The cultivation of short-staple cotton also sped the migration of planters and yeomen, as well as their slaves, to the southwestern territories and states as lands there were prime for cotton production. Virginia planters, who had turned away from labor-intensive tobacco toward wheat, readily sold their excess slaves to cotton planters in the Deep South. Many of them took their entire plantation populations with them and relocated to the Southwest. Easy credit and plentiful lands made the wealth to be generated from cotton planting seem boundless, but such reckless investments in frontier lands and slaves contributed to several economic downturns throughout the first half of the nineteenth century.

Although southern planters were not often noted for widespread efforts at agricultural reform, the selective breeding of strains of short-staple cotton illustrates one exception to that generalization. As early as the first decade of the nineteenth century, southerners looked for hardier and more productive strains of *G. hirsutum.* In 1807, for instance, William Dunbar first cultivated a sample of a productive Mexican strain in Mississippi, and throughout the 1820s and 1830s, Dr. Rush Nutt crossbred that strain with several others to develop the hardy and productive Port Gibson (Mississippi) strain, which became a very popular variety throughout the South. In the 1840s and 1850s southerners developed several other new strains of *G. hirsutum,* but none were as popular as the Port Gibson strain.

For the slaves who cultivated the cotton, the specific strain mattered little as all involved the same labor patterns, although short-staple cotton cultivation was generally less labor intensive than long-staple cotton production. In almost all circumstances, the short-staple cotton routine employed the gang (rather than the task) system of labor. Cotton growing began with the clearing of the fields in late February and March; planting began after the last frost, usually on April 1; and as the young plants grew, repeated passes with the plough killed grasses and weeds that competed with the cotton plants and thinned out all but the strongest plants. By late May and early June, the slaves continually went through the fields with hoes, scraping weeds and grasses, and pushing dirt around the base of the plant. Scraping passes continued until the lay-by time, in midsummer, when the slaves tended to livestock, food crops, and plantation maintenance. The picking season began as soon as the bolls opened, usually in September, and as the bolls opened faster than they could be picked, the harvest ran into December and even January. At the height of the harvest, slaves often picked 100 or more pounds of cotton in a day, but earlier and later in the season, individual totals amounted to 15 or 20 pounds. A separate "trash gang" of children and elderly slaves followed the main gang of pickers.

Once collected, the trash gang cleaned the cotton as it dried on scaffolds while waiting to be ginned. After the gin removed the seeds, the cotton awaited baling in a separate magazine. Baling involved the use of a cotton press, and the labor of six to eight slaves as well as a horse or mule to compress as much as 500 pounds of cotton into a squared-off bale.

The production of short-staple cotton tied the southern slave economy to the Industrial Revolution and an international economy. Raw southern cotton became finished yarn and cloth in northern and European cotton mills, and some of that cloth became the clothing worn by both planters and slaves. Many plantations forsook food crops to raise cotton and thus became consumers of food grown in the northwestern states. Wealthy planters also purchased European luxury goods as displays of their wealth and elegance.

Short-staple cotton is still a major cash crop in many southern states, and its cultivation was the agricultural basis for the sharecropping economy of the "New South." The cultivation processes described here remained virtually intact until the 1950s, when planters began to invest in farm machinery to automate cotton production.

— *David J. Libby*

See also: Cotton Gin; Long-staple cotton.

For Further Reading
    Gray, Lewis C. 1933. *History of Agriculture in the Southern United States to 1860,* 2 vols. Washington, DC: Carnegie Institution.
    Moore, John Hebron. 1958. *Agriculture in Ante-Bellum Mississippi.* New York: Bookman Associates.
    Moore, John Hebron. 1988. *The Emergence of the Cotton Kingdom in the Old Southwest: Mississippi, 1770–1860.* Baton Rouge: Louisiana State University Press.

WILLIAM GILMORE SIMMS (1806–1870)

Along with Edgar Allan Poe, William Gilmore Simms was the antebellum South's leading man of letters. He was also a notable defender of slavery, and his writings helped to articulate the South's proslavery argument.

Perhaps one of the more overlooked southern antebellum literary figures, Simms stands just below Poe in reputation among the South's men of letters. Born in Charleston, South Carolina, Simms remained in the city for most of his life. His father, a failed merchant, left young Simms in his grandmother's care and traveled to Mississippi. Simms was educated in Charleston, briefly apprenticed to a druggist, married in 1826, and was admitted to the bar in 1827.

His real interest was writing, and Simms published a book of poetry by 1825. He published four more books of verse by 1830 and in 1828 began publishing the *Southern Literary Gazette,* which he edited. Although short lived, Simms's intent was to defend and promote southern literature. He published the *City Gazette* in 1829, a local newspaper that he was forced to sell in 1832. In 1830 he suffered the deaths of his father and mother, and his wife died in February 1832. To this point, his literary output was not impressive.

Simms traveled north in 1832, meeting several important writers and publishers, and produced his first important work, *Atlantis* (1832). The poem was well received in the United States and England and demonstrated his literary potential. Several works of fiction followed, including *Guy Rivers* (1834) and *The Yemassee* (1835), generally considered his best work of fiction. During this time, Simms earned up to $6,000 a year in royalties and, although this proved the high point of his literary profits, he was one of the few men in the

United States who earned a respectable living by writing. He continued with an impressive list of published works of fiction for much of the rest of his life.

The defining moment for Simms as a southerner came in 1837 when English traveler Harriet Martineau published *Society in America*, an attack on slavery. In response, Simms penned "The Morals of Slavery," which was first published in the recently begun *Southern Literary Messenger*, housed in Richmond. The essay was reprinted as a pamphlet. In 1832 Simms revised his response to Martineau for a collective volume of writings titled *The Pro-Slavery Argument, as Maintained by the Most Distinguished Writers of the Southern States*.

For Simms, defending slavery was a moral issue. He contended that God approved of the institution as a means both to rescue and preserve the savage (i.e., slave), and thus slavery represented a moral contract with God. With this direct argument, Simms became a spokesman for the South and its peculiar institution, with others like Beverley Tucker, J. B. D. DeBow, Thomas Dew, James Henry Hammond, and Edmund Ruffin.

Simms's stance on slavery also appears in his fiction, where there is natural affection between master and slave, which is generally beneficial toward the slave. He utilized his views in *The Yemassee*, where he defended the South. In another of his successful fictional works, *The Partisan* (1835), Simms uses a slave as a hero. In *Woodcraft* (1852), Simms responds to Harriet Beecher Stowe's view of slavery and southerners in *Uncle Tom's Cabin*.

During his prolific career, Simms used essays, fiction, and history to defend slavery and the southern way of life. His literary career is often overshadowed by his political views, but Simms was easily the most prolific southern novelist in the antebellum period. In 1856 a speaking tour in New York had to be abandoned when he was first abused and then ignored. Simms remained in South Carolina during the war at the "Woodlands," his Barnwell County plantation. The war interrupted and virtually ended his writing career, and he died in Charleston in 1870. His moral defense of slavery still marks him as a staunch defender of the South and clouds his successful literary achievements.

— *Boyd Childress*

See also: Literature; Proslavery Argument.

For Further Reading
Guilds, John C. 1992. *Simms: a Literary Life*. Fayetteville: University of Arkansas Press.

Singleton, Robert R. 1997. "William Gilmore Simms, Woodlands, and the Freedmen's Bureau." *Mississippi Quarterly* 50 (1): 18–36.

Waklyn, Jon L. 1973. *The Politics of a Literary Man: William Gilmore Simms*. Westport, CT: Greenwood.

Watson, Charles S. 1993. *From Nationalism to Secessionism: The Changing Fiction of William Gilmore Simms*. Westport, CT: Greenwood.

1619

The year 1619 has assumed an iconographic place in African American history and life, but its exact meaning and import are generally misunderstood. Much like other notable dates in history, 1776, for example, the proverbial certainty of popular conventional wisdom often belies the true relevance of the events that occurred. Despite the confusion, the date is one that bears historical weight.

Our knowledge of 1619 stems from a brief mention that John Rolfe included in an early history of the Virginia colony when he wrote: "About the last of August came in a dutch man of warre that sold us twenty Negars" (Rolfe, 1971). Many have made the false assumption that these Africans who were introduced at Jamestown, Virginia, represented the start of slavery in what became the United States. It is more likely that these Africans were "remaindered" captives who had not sold at auction in the Caribbean markets and were taken by the Dutch traders to Virginia where they were sold by bid as indentured servants. Slavery did not begin in 1619 at Jamestown, but it is clear that within a generation of the arrival of these African captives, Virginia law began to recognize the existence of slavery within the colony.

Some who came to America as indentured servants made prior arrangements with a master who would pay for their transoceanic journey and then contracted with the servants for a specified period of indenture during which they repaid their transportation costs. Others, who arrived unannounced, like the twenty Africans of 1619, became indentured to Virginia masters through a bidding process that was somewhat akin to later slave auctions that would become altogether too common in the slaveholding region of the United States. The laws of colonial Virginia indicate that by the early 1640s slavery had become established within the colony, and further evidence shows that many African indentured servants were variously transitioned into slavery. A black indentured servant named John Punch was made a "servant for life" in July 1640 as his punishment for running away from his master. This type of penalty was much harsher than that imposed on white indentured servants who committed the same offense in the 1640s.

It is also erroneous to claim that the twenty Africans who arrived at Jamestown in 1619 represent the first Africans to set foot on the lands that eventually became the United States. There were Africans among some of the early Spanish exploring parties that ventured along coastal and inland portions of North America. Estevanico (1503–1539) was an enslaved African who was shipwrecked in the coastal Gulf south with the Spanish explorer Álvar Núñez Cabeza de Vaca. Survivors of this misadventure (1528–1536) traveled along the Gulf Coast and into the Southwest until they made their way back to Mexico. Estevanico, also known as Esteban or Black Stephan, was likely the first person of African descent to set foot on North America—certainly the first for whom documentary evidence survives.

One would also be mistaken to claim that the presence of slavery in colonial Virginia represented the first use of that practice on soil that later formed the United States. The Spanish established the colonial outpost of St. Augustine, Florida, in 1565, and this community holds the distinction of being the oldest continuously-settled town in the United States. The founding of St. Augustine followed a failed attempt just two years prior to establish a French Huguenot refuge in the same vicinity at Fort Caroline, near modern-day Jacksonville. Slaves were used in both the Fort Caroline and St. Augustine settlements. Pedro Menédez de Avilés, the Spaniard who established the St. Augustine settlement, had permission to introduce 500 slaves within the first three years of the colony's existence, and evidence shows that slaves were used there as early as 1565.

What then is the true significance of 1619 in African American history and life? Historian Lerone Bennett captured the essence of this issue in his path-breaking work *Before the Mayflower: The History of the Negro in America 1619–1962* (1962), a study that recognizes the essential importance of the arrival of twenty involuntary African immigrants who arrived at Jamestown, Virginia, in 1619. In the common parlance of historical longevity, the place of the Pilgrim fathers and mothers who arrived aboard the *Mayflower* at Plymouth, Massachusetts, in 1620 has been elevated to a significant place in our national mythology. Bennett argues convincingly that those whose arrival antedated that of the Pilgrims should have no less import in the making of American history and national life.

The cultural significance of 1619 is also noted in the hundreds of historical monographs that include the date as a part of their title, thereby implying the larger meaning of the historical importance of the year. Few, if any, would recognize the historical significance of 1528, the arrival of Estevanico, or 1565, the founding of St. Augustine, to be as historically meaningful as 1619.

Certainly the centrality of Jamestown, Virginia, as the first permanent British settlement (1607) in North America, and the eventual understanding that the thirteen British colonies that were established on the eastern seaboard formed the nucleus of the nascent United States play a large part in embellishing the historical significance of the twenty Africans who arrived in 1619.

— *Junius P. Rodriguez*

See also: Indentured Servants; Johnson, Anthony; Virginia.

For Further Reading

Bennett, Lerone. 1962. *Before the Mayflower: The History of the Negro in America 1619–1962*. Chicago: Johnson Publishing.

Cabeza de Vaca, Álvar Núñez. [1961] 1983. *Cabeza de Vaca's Adventures in the Unknown Interior of America*. Ed. Cyclone Covey. Albuquerque: University of New Mexico Press.

Rolfe, John. 1971. *A True Relation of the State of Virginia Lefte by Sir Thomas Dale, Knight, in May Last 1616*. Charlottesville: University Press of Virginia.

SLAVE CATCHERS. *See* Catchers, Slave.

SLAVE PATROLS. *See* Patrols, Slave.

SLAVE PREACHERS. *See* Preachers, Slave.

ROBERT SMALLS (1839–1915)

Robert Smalls made a bold and heroic escape from slavery to freedom during the Civil War. In 1862 Smalls along with a slave crew of eight men commandeered the Confederate transport steamship *Planter* and navigated it out of the Port of Charleston, South Carolina, delivering it to the Union blockade fleet. His life afterwards was one of struggle, achievement, and fighting for the rights of blacks by serving in the South Carolina state legislature and the U.S. Congress.

Robert Smalls was born into slavery in Beaufort, South Carolina, on April 5, 1839. His mother Lydia was a house servant for the family of John McKee. His life was atypical of a slave, as he grew up in the household without the burden of working in the fields. After McKee's death in 1848, his son Henry owned Robert and Lydia. In 1851 he took Robert to Charleston, and hired him out for jobs such as waiter and lamplighter.

Smalls, however, was drawn to the waterfront environment, so he became a stevedore, foreman, and sailmaker. He also worked on a schooner, becoming a skilled navigator and sailor. It was at this time that he

Robert Smalls escaped from slavery to freedom during the U.S. Civil War. (Library of Congress)

engineered a financial plan to pay Henry $15 per month and keep the remainder of his wages for himself. In 1856 Smalls married a slave named Hannah Jones, and he eventually purchased freedom for her and their baby daughter Elizabeth from Hannah's master.

By July 1861 Smalls began working on the sidewheel steamer *Planter*. Once the Civil War began, the Confederate army turned *Planter* into an armed dispatch and transport vessel. Smalls never accepted his enslaved condition, teaching himself to read, write, and navigate the Charleston harbor. In his mind freedom was not impossible.

During the morning of May 13, 1862, while the captain and his crew were ashore in Charleston, Smalls, his wife, family, and a crew of twelve slaves sailed out of the harbor. They raised the South Carolina Confederate flag as they began their daring escape. Smalls, dressed as the captain, and knowledgeable of all the signals that would enable him to pass Fort Sumter, sailed *Planter* toward the Union army blockade. When out of range of the Confederate artillery, he raised a white flag and offered the ship to the Union fleet.

Smalls and his crew were welcomed as heroes. He was named captain of the *Planter* and was the only black captain in the U.S. Navy during the Civil War. His knowledge of the waterways of Charleston helped to defeat the Confederate forces through his leadership in over twelve sailing excursions. Smalls was honored by President Abraham Lincoln, and he used his influence to persuade the president to allow slaves to join the Union army.

After the war Smalls settled in Beaufort, South Carolina. He entered politics, serving in the state senate during Reconstruction from 1868–1870. In 1875 he began the first of five terms as a U.S. congressman. Smalls became an advocate of free slaves, fighting for education and equality for blacks. In 1897 he was awarded a congressional pension and in 1900 he was awarded $5,000 for his role in the capture of *Planter*.

When he left politics, Smalls served as duty and customs collector in Beaufort. He died on February 22, 1915.

— *Anthony Todman*

See also: Gullah; South Carolina.

For Further Reading
Dunkelman, Mark H. 1999. "A Bold Break for Freedom." *American History* 34 (5): 22–28.
Estell, Kenneth, ed. 1994. *The African-American Almanac*. Detroit: Gale Research.
Miller Edward A. 1995. *Gullah Statesman: Robert Smalls from Slavery to Congress 1839–1915*. Columbia: University of South Carolina Press.
Powles, James M. 2000. "South Carolina Slave Robert Smalls Put His Ship-Piloting Skills to Good Use in an Audacious Break for Freedom." *America's Civil War* 13 (4): 8, 24, 62, 64.
Salzman, Jack, David Lionel Smith, and Cornel West, eds. 1996. *Encyclopedia of African-American Culture and History*. New York: Macmillan Library Reference.
Turnage, Sheila. 2002. "Stealing a Ship to Freedom." *American Legacy: Magazine of African-American History and Culture* 8 (1): 70–73, 75–76.

GERRIT SMITH (1797–1874)

Among the most renowned American abolitionists, Gerrit Smith devoted his life and most of his great wealth to the cause of equal rights for all men and women; the immediate abolition of every sin was his most passionate desire, and he went to great lengths to effect it.

Smith was born into one of the wealthiest families in the country and grew up in the rural village of Peterboro in Madison County, which is part of the "Burned-Over District" of western New York. The young patriarch had visions of becoming a man of letters, an eminent lawyer, a respected minister, or a

Gerrit Smith worked to transform his village of Peterboro into an antebellum model of interracial harmony. In 1846 he gave roughly 50 acres of land in the Adirondacks to each of some three thousand poor blacks from New York. Smith saw this as a way for African Americans to become self-sufficient and isolated from the virulent racism in the cities. (Library of Congress)

statesman, but immediately after graduating as valedictorian from Hamilton College in 1818, a series of incidents occurred that precipitated his turn to reform work; these included the death of his mother, the death of his new bride, and the retirement of his father, who requested that Gerrit manage his vast property concerns. In little more than a year after reaching "manhood," he found himself back in the family "mansion house" overlooking the village green of Peterboro, bound to his ledger books and land office, with his dreams shattered and the two most important people in his life dead.

In 1823 he married Ann Carroll Fitzhugh Smith, a

cousin of George Fitzhugh and a fervent evangelical. She was instrumental in converting Smith to evangelicalism, fueling his religious zeal, and spawning his vision of a broad sacralization of the world. He soon became an avid temperance reformer, and in 1827 he joined the respected American Colonization Society, whose efforts to colonize blacks in Africa represented for him the most effective way to bring about gradual emancipation and an end to degradation among free blacks. In the early 1830s, when many radicals became "fanatics" by turning to immediate abolition and attacking colonization as inherently racist and unrighteous, Smith continued endorsing colonization while also flirting with immediatism. From 1834 to 1837 he was virtually unique among abolitionists in his efforts to reconcile the principles of colonization with those of the American Anti-Slavery Society; he viewed the efforts of each organization as complementary versions of the same war on slavery and racial prejudice, despite cries from immediatists that colonizationists wanted to preserve slavery and rid the country of free blacks.

Smith's final and complete repudiation of colonization occurred in 1837, two years after he formally resigned from the society; the break corresponded with an important and fundamental shift in his identity as a patriarch and a reorientation in the source of his values: he became a self-described social "outsider," turned inward, and affirmed the spiritual instincts and passions of the "heart" rather than the sin-infested conventions of social order and existing authority. His belief in the preservation of order, stability, and distinct hierarchies—values on which the principles of colonization were based—had crumbled. This was due in part to the Panic of 1837, which brought him to the brink of bankruptcy, and to the deaths of two children, one in 1835 and the other in 1836. In conjunction with his shift in values and identity, he became "born again," free from the fetters of original sin, and applied his passions to the immediate abolition of every sin.

One of the most important applications of Smith's religious vision was his reinterpretation of the Golden Rule, which he saw as a fulfillment of the ideal of empathy. He continually sought to participate in the feelings and sufferings of his black brethren and to see himself as a black man. "To recognize in every man my brother—ay, another self" was his wish, and he often described his efforts to "make myself a colored man" (Harlow, 1939). His empathic awareness had profound results: He worked to transform his own village of Peterboro into an antebellum model of interracial harmony; and in 1846 he gave to each of some three thousand poor blacks from New York roughly 50 acres of land in the Adirondacks as a way for them to attain the franchise and become self-sufficient and isolated from the virulent racism in the cities. Black leaders throughout the North hailed his efforts to effect equality: Frederick Douglass, James McCune Smith, Henry Highland Garnet, and Samuel Ringgold Ward all became respected friends and allies; the black abolitionist paper, *The Ram's Horn,* went so far as to say: "Gerrit Smith is a colored man!"

From the 1840s through the Civil War, Smith's reform work in many respects mirrored the efforts of the black abolitionist community in New York. He helped found the Liberty Party in 1840, which interpreted the Constitution as an antislavery document, and he became one of the party's staunchest supporters. He was elected to Congress in 1852, but resigned after one term, out of disgust with the culture of Washington and the existing government, which had just passed the Kansas–Nebraska Act (1854) and repealed the Missouri Compromise. Smith also abandoned nonresistance and advocated violence as a last resort for ending slavery; he became a lead underwriter in the guerrilla warfare in Kansas and one of the six lead conspirators in John Brown's raid on Harpers Ferry in 1859 in an effort to incite a massive slave insurrection. New York black leaders overwhelmingly endorsed political intervention, and by the 1850s they had little patience with the principles of nonresistance. Until his death, Smith continually championed equal rights for all and the end of exploitation, whether for blacks, women, or laborers. In 1873 Henry Highland Garnet summed up the feelings of many radicals by saying, "Among the hosts of great defenders of man's rights who in years past fought so gallantly for equal rights for all men," Smith was "the most affectionately remembered and loved" (Harlow, 1939).

— *John Stauffer*

See also: American Colonization Society; Brown, John; Harpers Ferry Raid; Immediatism; Kansas–Nebraska Act.

For Further Reading
Friedman, Lawrence J. 1982. *Gregarious Saints: Self and Community in American Abolitionism, 1830–1870.* New York: Cambridge University Press.

Frothingham, Octavius Brooks. [1878] 1969. *Gerrit Smith: A Biography.* New York: Negro Universities Press.

Harlow, Ralph Volney. 1939. *Gerrit Smith: Philanthropist and Reformer.* New York: Henry Holt and Company.

Stauffer, John. 2002. *The Black Hearts of Men: Radical Abolitionists and the Transformation of Race.* Cambridge, MA: Harvard University Press.

VENTURE SMITH (1729–1805)

Venture Smith was the author of the autobiography, *A Narrative of the Life and Adventures of Venture, A Native of Africa: But Resident Above Sixty Years in the United States of America, Related by Himself* (1798).

Venture Smith was born in Guinea in 1729. His enslavement, at age eight, occurred around 1737 when one Robert Mumford purchased him for "four gallons of rum and a piece of calico." Smith's narrative gives important details on how the transition from freedom to slavery to freedom occurred, as well as a clear picture of African village life.

Venture recollected that his father, a wealthy prince of Dukandara, Guinea, tried to appease the slave traders in his region by giving them goats and cattle, but this tactic ultimately failed and he paid for it with a tortured death at their hands, and the destruction of his village. As an adult, Venture recalled, "The shocking scene is to this day fresh in my mind, and I have often been overcome while thinking on it." He remembers his father as "a man of remarkable strength and resolution, affable, kind and gentle, ruling with equity and moderation."

Venture clearly outlined African village life as sedentary, with the production of crops and the raising of cattle, sheep, and goats. Polygamy was the norm, with wives having a veto over whether or not their husband acquired a new wife. When Venture's father attempted to take a third wife without Venture's mother's consent, she left him for a brief period for consolation. Venture remembers his mother leaving her husband's compound and not returning for some time.

Venture's narrative was published in 1798 in New London, Connecticut, and republished by his descendants in 1835. His narrative sought to "exhibit a pattern of honesty, prudence, and industry to people of his own color; and perhaps some white people would not find themselves degraded by imitating such an example." This represents the major theme in this narrative, which is not overtly antislavery, but emphasizes how frugality, hard work, and morality can uplift a man from the depths of an abyss. Antislavery is also represented in a theme that explains to whites that any black who can become a westernized version of himself is worthy of the highest rights that society can offer. In the Preface, Venture argues that slavery could inhibit the genius of George Washington or Benjamin Franklin, but his own sense of being African could not be broken and he "still exhibit[ed] striking traces of native ingenuity and good sense."

Venture's description of slave work is interesting. His obedience to his master's orders gained the master's trust. However, this trust did not alleviate the hard burden required of a slave. Venture was required, as an eight-year-old, to "pound four bushels of corn every night in a barrel for the poultry, or be rigorously punished."

A large man known for his size and strength, Venture stated that "One time my master sent me two miles after a barrel of molasses, and ordered me to carry it on my shoulders. I made out to carry it all the way to my master's house. When I lived with Captain George Mumford, only to try my strength I took upon my knees a tierce of salt containing seven bushels, and carried it two or three rods. Of this fact there are several eye witnesses now living."

Venture's loyalty was tested one day by his master's son. The son wanted Venture to quit a job that he was doing for the master so that Venture could finish a job for him. When Venture refused, a fight ensued, with neighbors called to help the son subdue Venture. Because of Venture's strength, their attempt to bind him was in vain. The son went away in tears, and nothing else came of this episode. As a proud resister to enslavement, Venture suffered a number of harrowing punishments for resisting. One was when he "was carried . . . to a gallows made for the purpose of hanging cattle on, and suspended me on it." In another episode the wife of Venture's second master attempted to beat Venture's wife, but Venture interceded and stopped his wife from being beaten. This led to a physical confrontation with his master. Eventually Venture was sold to another master and subsequently to another. The narrative demonstrates that Venture was lucky not to have been sold to the West Indies for his resistance, as one of his masters had once threatened.

Venture was wise enough to help one of his masters pay for his services because Venture saw him as benign. This master, Colonel Smith, permitted Venture to be hired out so that Venture could earn some extra money. With this money, Venture eventually paid for his freedom. Venture explained that "I hired myself at Fisher's Island, earning twenty pounds; thirteen pounds six shillings of which my master drew for the privilege, and the remainder I paid for my freedom." At Fisher's Island, Venture worked for six months in which he "cut and corded four hundred cords of wood, besides threshing out seventy-five bushels of grain, and received of my wages down only twenty pounds, which left remaining a larger sum." Following his freedom, Venture, during the next several years, purchased two of his sons, Solomon and Cuff; his wife, Meg; and eventually his daughter, Hannah.

Venture's hard work and frugality led to a degree of prosperity: he was able to purchase a 76-acre farm and

purchase several slaves himself. Venture's elevation to property holder was based on a nonmaterialistic value of thrift that prompted him to write that "All the fine clothes I despised in comparison with my interest, and never kept but just what clothes were comfortable . . . but as for superfluous finery I never thought it to be compared to . . . a good supply of money and prudence." It was this attitude and his social values that enabled Venture Smith to acquire property in estate and property in men. His effort at slaveholding was for no other reason than that the "Negro man oblige me to purchase him." This obligation and his hiring of black wage labor represent a problem area in his narrative since each worker seemed to take advantage of Venture's trusting nature. One black man, Jacklin, a comb-maker, ran off with all of Venture's investment, and another, Mingo, was taken to court when Mingo did not pay off a debt note. Black slaves and workers sought him out because of his character; and he sought them out because he needed their labor and obviously sought to lift them from the degradation he once experienced.

Venture Smith died in 1805 at the age of seventy-seven and left an inheritance of a 100-acre farm and three houses.

— *Malik Simba*

See also: Autobiographies; Narratives.

For Further Reading
Costanzo, Angelo. 1987. *Surprizing Narrative*. Westport, CT: Greenwood.
Smith, Venture. 1971. *A Narrative of the Life and Adventures of Venture Smith*. Boston: Beacon Press.
Starling, Marion Wilson. 1981. *The Slave Narrative*. Boston: G.K. Hall.

SICKNESS. *See* Diseases and African Slavery in the New World.

SOCIETY FOR THE RELIEF OF FREE NEGROES UNLAWFULLY HELD IN BONDAGE

The Society for the Relief of Free Negroes Unlawfully Held in Bondage was the first secular antislavery organization in America. Led by Philadelphia area Quakers such as Anthony Benezet, who had met yearly as early as 1758, the society organized itself in April 1775 when twenty-four men, including sixteen Quakers, met at the Sun Tavern on Second Street in Philadelphia to discuss the plight of an Indian mother who claimed that in the eyes of the law she and her four children were free. Believing that the egalitarian and humanitarian principles of the Quakers ought to be extended to others, the men attempted to remedy the situation by organizing themselves and denouncing slavery both as an injustice to the slave and a temptation to sin for the owner.

The American Revolution caused its early members to suspend meetings until 1784, when it attempted to build a broader base of support. Although the impetus for reorganizing was a situation involving two free black men accused of being runaway slaves, reluctance by many Quakers to give up their slaves and the concern that Quaker pacifism might discredit the society's antislavery testimony led to a new rationale for abolishing slavery. Relying less on moral arguments, the society used the philosophy of the Revolution, which allowed them to portray slavery as a contradiction of American political values. Slavery, they argued, not only violated the law of God, but in an age of liberation and enlightenment, it undermined the rights of man. Accordingly, during its April 23, 1787, meeting, the society revised its constitution, elected Benjamin Franklin honorary president, and renamed itself the Pennsylvania Society for Promoting the Abolition of Slavery, for the Relief of Free Negroes Unlawfully held in Bondage, and for Improving the Condition of the African Race. Strengthened, the society's membership now included non-Quakers and such well-known individuals as Thomas Paine, John Jay, Noah Webster, and Dr. Benjamin Rush.

Pursuing a more pragmatic agenda, the society became a model for similar organizations in other states, such as New York. Toward the end of the eighteenth century, the Pennsylvania Abolition Society mounted a more aggressive attack against the slave trade and slavery itself. It sought to improve the existing social order and to bring about justice by more rigorously enforcing existing laws. As part of its efforts, it promoted the development of other societies, sent petitions to Congress, publicized state laws regarding slavery, printed and distributed antislavery literature, corresponded with prominent antislavery leaders in England and France, and began a policy of assistance to free blacks and to those illegally held in bondage. In addition to forbidding members to own slaves and backing the antislavery movement, the society also sought to improve the general social and economic conditions of blacks.

Although the Society for the Relief of Free Negroes Unlawfully Held in Bondage evolved into an effective state society, its importance in the antislavery movement lies in the way early Quakers initiated antislavery thought and action and attempted to curtail the growth of slavery in colonial America. As such, its ac-

tivity contributed to the development and success of later abolitionist groups.

— *Mark L. Kamrath*

See also: Quakers.

For Further Reading
Bumbrey, Jeffrey Nordlinger. 1976. "Historical Sketch of the Pennsylvania Abolition Society." *A Guide to the Microfilm Publication of the Papers of the Pennsylvania Abolition Society at the Historical Society of Pennsylvania.* Philadelphia: The Pennsylvania Abolition Society and the Historical Society of Pennsylvania.

Dumond, Dwight Lowell. 1961. *Antislavery: The Crusade for Freedom in America.* Ann Arbor: University of Michigan Press.

Needles, Edward. 1848. *An Historical Memoir of the Pennsylvania Society, for Promoting the Abolition of Slavery, and for the Relief of Free Negroes Unlawfully Held in Bondage, and for Improving the Condition of the African Race. Compiled from the Minutes of the Society and Other Official Documents.* Philadelphia: Pennsylvania Abolition Society.

Sorin, Gerald. 1972. *Abolitionism: A New Perspective.* New York: Praeger.

Toll, John Barth, and Mildred S. Gillam. 1995. *Invisible Philadelphia: Community through Voluntary Organizations.* Philadelphia: Atwater Kent Museum.

Turner, Edward Raymond. 1912. "The First Abolition Society in the United States." *The Pennsylvania Magazine of History and Biography* 36: 92–109.

SOCIETY OF FRIENDS. *See* Quakers.

"SOLD DOWN THE RIVER"

In modern-day English slang, to have been "sold down the river" is an expression that implies that one has been duped, often through duplicitous machinations or chicanery. During the era of antebellum slavery, the peril of being "sold down the river," if spoken with a degree of certitude, was a formidable threat to the life and well-being of a slave. On many occasions this threat alone led enslaved men and women to run away in order to emancipate themselves rather than face the uncertainty of a harsher destination.

Essentially the phrase "sold down the river" became a euphemism for sending a slave down the Mississippi River to the auction block at New Orleans, Louisiana. In the conventional wisdom of the antebellum South, slavery as perceived as being more harsh in Louisiana than it was in the states of the Upper South. This reputation had as much to do with climate, heat, and humidity as it did with the type of labor regimen associated with work on the sugar and cotton plantations of south and central Louisiana, respectively. Many believed the reputed claim that slaves were worked to death on the plantations and farms near New Orleans.

In addition, the danger of being "sold down the river" made it increasingly difficult for a slave to escape. Slaves in the Upper South were often situated in locations where a few days of a stealth journey might bring them to the Ohio River—the proverbial "River Jordan" that would carry them to freedom in the North. Due to the sheer distance involved and the logistics of maintaining oneself as a fugitive for an extended period of time, slavery in Louisiana would limit the options of a slave who sought to become a fugitive.

Many slaves were actually "sold down the river," as the New Orleans auction block was one of the largest and busiest of the antebellum South. Trading slaves for sale at New Orleans was a common aspect of the domestic slave trade, which continued unabated after Congress closed the Atlantic slave trade in 1807. Slaves transported by river steamboat or coastal brigs, as well as those marched overland in long-distance coffles, regularly arrived at New Orleans where buyers gathered to acquire additional property in slaves. The flesh trade was brisk at New Orleans.

For many slaves who were threatened with being "sold down the river," their most pressing fear, beyond self-preservation, was the separation from family and friends that would ensue if they were removed from the Upper South. The bonds of kinship and family, however tenuous they might be, were one of the few elements of stability that existed within the world of the slave. Sale to the New Orleans slave market threatened to destroy these powerful bonds.

The psychological effect of being "sold down the river" had varying effects on the slaves involved. In extreme cases, it was not uncommon for a slave to commit suicide by jumping into the river and drowning rather than submitting to the untold horrors that might be waiting at New Orleans. Perhaps the most famous case of a slave being "sold down the river" appears in Harriet Beecher Stowe's novel *Uncle Tom's Cabin* (1852). In this fictional work the main character Tom is sold and becomes the victim of the contemptible overseer Simon Legree. Tom's stoic goodness and his tragic death at the hands of Legree affirmed one's worst fears about conditions on Louisiana's plantations.

Literature continued to reflect the wretchedness of plantation life in the Deep South well after the end of slavery. Mark Twain's character Roxy in the novel *The Tragedy of Pudd'nhead Wilson* (1894) expresses contempt from her experience as a slave near New Orleans when she states: "Sell a pusson down de river—*down de river!*—for de bes'! I wouldn't treat a dog so!" (Twain, 1894). Even though this fictional work was published a generation after emancipation, it still demonstrated the powerful resonance of an often-hated phrase.

— *Junius P. Rodriguez*

See also: Domestic Slave Trade; Franklin and Armfield; Louisiana; *Uncle Tom's Cabin.*

For Further Reading
   Twain, Mark. 1894. *The Tragedy of Pudd'nhead Wilson.*

SOME CONSIDERATIONS ON THE KEEPING OF NEGROES (WOOLMAN)

The Quaker abolitionist John Woolman published two antislavery tracts: *Some Considerations on the Keeping of Negroes* (Philadelphia, 1754) and *Considerations on the Keeping of Negroes, Part Second* (Philadelphia, 1762). The first presented Woolman's moral objections to slavery; the second contested rationalizations for slaveholding and implicated slaveowners in the transatlantic commerce in "fellow creatures." Both essays helped launch Quaker abolitionism and contributed to changing attitudes toward slavery that culminated in the antislavery movements of the late eighteenth and early nineteenth centuries.

Woolman first drafted *Some Considerations on the Keeping of Negroes* after witnessing plantation slavery in 1746 during visits to Quakers in Virginia and North Carolina. He withheld the manuscript until his ailing father in 1750 encouraged him to prepare it for publication. The Quaker Overseers of the Press approved and printed the essay in 1754. It was the first antislavery pamphlet endorsed and published by the Society of Friends.

Starting from a belief in human equality—"all nations are of one blood," he wrote—Woolman pleaded for charity to the oppressed and restraint in the acquisition of wealth. The Lord had provided for Quaker settlers in America. Society and family benefited more from the example of moral practice than riches. So Christians were obliged to sympathize with slaves, "make their case ours," even if at the cost of material gain. Unlike his Quaker predecessors Benjamin Lay and Ralph Sandiford, Woolman spared slaveholders from invective. Because he understood the power of habit and interest, Woolman sought merely to disquiet slaveholders by questioning custom, exposing error and inconsistency, and arousing conscience.

Woolman published the second pamphlet at his

own expense, preferring not to draw from the Quaker funds because they included contributions from Quaker slaveholders. He also believed that the book would receive more careful study if it was available only through purchase. The pamphlet exhibited the insight gleaned from several years of entreating slaveholders to free their slaves. Working from similar principles and aims but with less caution than before, Woolman confronted prevailing apologies for slavery. He spoke for the capacities of Africans and their right to equality. Drawing from travel narratives to Africa, he illustrated the "barbarous proceedings" that led to enslavement and the transportation of Africans to the Americas. It was possible in theory, said Woolman, for slaveholders to treat slaves humanely. But few, if any, acquired slaves with charitable intentions or with beneficial effects.

Both pamphlets assisted early attempts by Philadelphia Yearly Meeting to dissuade Friends from the sale, purchase, and possession of slaves. In 1754 the Overseers of the Press delivered Part One of *Considerations* to the Yearly Meetings in England and North America. Passages from the pamphlet were included in a landmark 1754 epistle to Friends from Philadelphia Yearly Meeting declaring slavery a sin.

Although the essays most influenced the Society of Friends, they circulated widely. The Quaker propagandist Anthony Benezet cited lines from the 1754 tract in the preface to his *Observations on Inslaving, Importing, and Purchasing of Negroes* (1759) and sent Parts One and Two with the antislavery pamphlets he distributed in North America and shipped to England. The essays were reprinted and bound with the first American edition of *The Journal of John Woolman* (1774) and with various editions of *The Works of John Woolman* published on both sides of the Atlantic in succeeding decades.

— *Christopher L. Brown*

See also: Quakers; Woolman, John.

For Further Reading

Cady, Edwin H. 1966. *John Woolman: The Mind of the Quaker Saint.* New York: Washington Square Press.

Drake, Thomas. 1950. *Quakers and Slavery in America.* New Haven, CT: Yale University Press.

Gummere, Amelia Mott. 1922. *The Journal and Essays of John Woolman.* New York: Macmillan.

Meranze, Michael. 2002. "Materializing Conscience." *Early American Literature* 37 (1): 71–88.

Moulton, Phillips P. "The Influence of the Writings of John Woolman." *Quaker History: The Bulletin of the Friends Historical Association* 61 (2): 3–13.

Sazama, Gerald W. 2003. "'Be Ye Therefore Perfect': Integral Christianity in *Some Considerations on the Keeping of Negroes*," in *The Tendering Presence: Essays on John Woolman: In Honor of Sterling Olmsted & Phillips P. Moulton,* Ed. Sterling Olmsted, Phillips P. Moulton, and Michael Alan Heller. Wallingford, PA: Pendle Hill Publications.

SOUTH CAROLINA

Dominated by slavery and its legacies, the history of South Carolina—as experience and example—has clearly influenced the broader historiographical twists and turns of North American slavery. There are several good reasons why this particular state figures so largely in the literature of involuntary servitude. Most obviously, there is the morbid appeal of the state's unique history of ultraconservative reactionism. Such episodes include the period of states' rights radicalism and the drafting of the ordinance of nullification in 1832, a leading role in the increasingly fanatical and racial justifications and defenses of southern slavery in the 1850s, and finally, the unilateral decision to secede in December 1860, which made the American Civil War an imminent and tragic inevitability. Together with the other great "mountain of conceit," Virginia, South Carolina has been frequently mythologized as a spiritual center of the antebellum southern aristocracy—a sentimental image still profitably employed by the region's tourist industry. Scholars of slavery on their grand tours of great southern cities, finding traces of "unofficial," neglected, and marginalized sources, have perhaps felt impelled to counter such romantic chimera by documenting some of the state's less apocryphal, but equally important, historical moments.

South Carolina was first successfully colonized by migrants from Barbados in 1670. They brought with them their well-established practice of plantation slavery and fundamental constitutions that left no doubt as to the intended status of their imported slave labor. These founding documents gave white freemen "absolute power and authority over Negro Slaves" and determined that, even allowing for a Christian conversion, Negro slaves would remain "in ye same State and Condition"—in other words, lifelong bondage (Wood, 1974). Other forms of enforced labor were tested in the early years of the colony, most notably white indentured servitude and the enslavement of Native Americans. The indentured servants proved both costly and unreliable, while the Native American option was found to be damaging to trade and seriously threatened the safety of the settlers. By contrast, African slaves allegedly posed fewer problems. Cheaply and easily secured, initially from the Caribbean, Africans were seen as an attractive source of labor because of their invaluable frontier skills. When rice cultivation began to develop in the low country, West African knowledge of the planting and processing of this profitable staple crop further stimulated slave imports and eventually led to the formation of a black majority in the colony.

Outnumbered by slaves from around 1708, the white population began to show clear signs of insecurity and enacted a series of harsh and prohibitive statutes (in particular, the acts of 1712, 1722, and 1740), allegedly "for the better ordering and governing of Negroes and Slaves" (Wood, 1974), which set the general pattern of repressive "white over black" race relations in South Carolina for the next 250 years. Despite being legally confirmed in their chattel status, subject to close social control, and exposed to the constant surveillance and arbitrary justice of white patrollers, black slaves stubbornly refused to submit to the white colonial regime. The 1739 Stono Rebellion and the mass of documentary evidence in Lathan A. Windley's third volume of *Runaway Slave Advertisements* (collected from South Carolina newspapers between the years 1730 and 1790 and published in 1983) demonstrate that point emphatically and irrefutably.

With Charleston prospering as a key area in international and interregional slave-trading systems and as a major exporter of staple crops, the low country dominated South Carolina's economy and society throughout the eighteenth century. Large-scale plantation operations and planter wealth proliferated in this area, as did slave numbers and a constant concern for their "management." Furthermore, it was this region that first gave rise to a clearly distinctive African American folk culture. From the collision of a plethora of African and European influences and in response to the demands of a new working environment, the black population creatively developed a range of composite or syncretic cultural forms. For example, a new language, Gullah, evolved, and it enabled slaves to communicate both in the language of authority and, more importantly, in code (Joyner, 1984).

From 1800 onward, as cotton began to take a firm hold in the up-country part of South Carolina, the whole state became both more economically dependent on slave labor and more marked by the rituals and tensions of the master–slave/aristocrat–yeoman social roles. Fearful of black revolt after the Denmark Vesey conspiracy of 1822 and coming under increasing attack from northern abolitionists, the South Carolina elite set about strengthening the Charleston militia and actively deploying the "positive good" proslavery defense pioneered by John C. Calhoun. However, the armor and ideology of the plantocracy failed to win the battles of the Civil War, and thereafter the state had to deal with the difficulties of Reconstruction.

A hospitable climate, a citizenry with an obvious devotion to history, and abundant archival resources detailing a rich, varied, and often tragic past ensure that armies of aspiring slavery scholars will continue to search for "the truth" about slavery in South Carolina—part of the necessary ongoing cultural analysis of "the peculiar institution."

— *Stephen C. Kenny*

See also: Gullah; Rice Cultivation and Trade; Sea Islands; Stono Rebellion; Vesey, Denmark.

For Further Reading
Dusinberre, William. 1996. *Them Dark Days: Slavery in the American Rice Swamps.* New York: Oxford University Press.

Faust, Drew Gilpin. 1982. *James Henry Hammond and the Old South: A Design for Mastery.* Baton Rouge: Louisiana State University Press.

Joyner, Charles. 1984. *Down by the Riverside: A South Carolina Slave Community.* Urbana: University of Illinois Press.

Wood, Peter H. 1974. *Black Majority: Negroes in Colonial South Carolina from 1670 through the Stono Rebellion.* New York: Norton.

SOUTH CAROLINA EXPOSITION *AND* PROTEST

The South Carolina Exposition and *Protest,* publications against federal tariff laws, were introduced in the state legislature in 1828 and mark the start of the nullification crisis. Although the *Exposition* failed to pass the legislature, its 1829 publication by the state government and John C. Calhoun's authorship of this document, even though that was initially concealed, vested it with more authority than the shorter and less confrontational *Protest.* The *Exposition* established Calhoun as a preeminent southern political theorist as it recast states' rights theory for the defense of slavery. Citing the precedent of the 1798 Virginia and Kentucky resolutions in response to the Alien and Sedition Acts, Calhoun sought to evoke state power against the actions of the federal government. But instead of an appeal to local majorities to check an undemocratic federal government, the *Exposition* devised ways and means to secure the interests of the slaveholding minority against the voice of the majority. The theory of nullification, or state veto, of federal laws outlined in the *Exposition* also violated the cardinal tenet of states' rights theory, strict construction of the constitution, as it was nowhere mentioned in the Constitution and circumvented the amendment process laid out in it.

The *Exposition* contended that the policy of protection or levying tariffs was unconstitutional and oppressive to the slave South. Calhoun made the startling and unique claim that import duties equaled export duties and thus the main burden of the tariff fell on southerners, the nation's main exporters. According to this logic, the South, rather than all consumers, paid import duties. In an interesting if implausible discovery of political economy, Calhoun claimed that producers, not consumers, paid duties levied on foreign goods—and not all producers but producers of exported crops, that is, mainly the slaveholding planter class. He claimed that this policy was the cause of the South's economic woes, and he felt that the tariff should be lowered and should mainly be a source of revenue for the government rather than protection for northern manufacturing. Calhoun concluded with the pet claim of the South Carolina nullifiers that the federal government, which now acted against the profits of the slave South, would soon attack the South's system of labor, slavery.

Calhoun's championship of slaveholders' interests informed his minority-versus-majority theory of politics. He also referred to another venerable precedent, James Madison's *Federalist* No. 10, to legitimize the grievances of southern slaveholders. For Calhoun, the minority in question was synonymous with a particular class and section, and the only solution to majority domination was state sovereignty. The state as representative of the minority would have the power to veto a federal law that it considered unconstitutional. Calhoun's notion of state sovereignty justified nullification by a single state but was contradicted by his assertion that after a state veto, the supreme power to decide the question at issue would lie with the constitution-amending authority, three-fourths of the states. Furthermore, a minority—a little more than one-fourth of the states—could make or break federal law. Calhoun's theory of nullification was not only an undemocratic prescription for minority rule but could act as an ironclad protection for southern slaveholders against any federal attempt to regulate or abolish slavery. Later Calhoun would use the term *concurrent majority* to characterize his theory and to answer accusations that he favored minority rule. He would also claim that the nullifying state had a choice either to accede to the wishes of three-fourths of the states or secede from the Union, thereby laying the foundations for the southern notion of an allegedly constitutional right to secession.

Calhoun had injected a new issue into the traditional fears of propertied minorities in majoritarian republics, and that was the specific dilemma of the southern slaveholding minority. He would have no qualms about dispensing with minority rights when it came to northern abolitionists or the unionists in his own state. A state veto or minority check that he saw epitomized in the state government of South Carolina would lead to similar undemocratic, planter-dominated politics. His concept of nullification was profoundly conservative, designed to check what South Carolinian nullifiers saw as the excesses of democracy and majoritarianism.

— *Manisha Sinha*

See also: Calhoun, John C.; Nullification Doctrine; United States Constitution.

For Further Reading
Ellis, Richard E. 1987. *The Union at Risk: Jacksonian Democracy, States' Rights and the Nullification Crisis.* New York: Oxford University Press.
Ford, Lacy, Jr. 1988. "Recovering the Republic: Calhoun, South Carolina and the Concurrent Majority." *South Carolina Historical Magazine* 89 (July): 146–159.
Freehling, William W. 1965. *Prelude to Civil War: The Nullification Controversy in South Carolina, 1816–1836.* New York: Harper.
Sinha, Manisha. 1994. "The Counter-Revolution of Slavery: Class, Politics and Ideology in Antebellum South Carolina." Ph.D. dissertation, Department of History, Columbia University, New York.

SPAIN. *See* Illegal Slave Trade; Slavery along the Spanish Borderlands.

SLAVERY ALONG THE SPANISH BORDERLANDS

The 1860 census noted that the New Mexico Territory contained eight "chattel servants" who were property of white citizens who had emigrated from Texas. Clearly, most African chattel slavery along the Spanish Borderlands was found in Texas, where it was limited by economics and geography. If we include portions of the Louisiana Purchase in an extended definition of the Spanish borderlands, we can count slaves in Missouri and Kansas in this region. Except for Texas and, to a much lower extent, in Missouri and Kansas, slavery was unprofitable in the Borderlands. The Mexican government had banned African slavery in 1829. This was one of the problems that caused the Texas Question as Americans moved into Texas, bringing their slaves with them.

This consideration does not touch on Native Americans owning African slaves. If we use a broad definition of "Spanish Borderlands," then we can consider various tribes in Florida and later in Oklahoma (Indian Territory) who brought their slaves with them during the Indian Removals of the 1830s. The question of Indian slavery was considered almost as soon as the Spanish touched the shores of the New World. Although the Spanish seemed to accept African slavery, they worked very hard to keep Indians out of slavery. Father Bartolomé de las Casas, early in his career, proposed to introduce African slaves into the Caribbean islands to spare the Indians the heavy labor, which was destroying them. Later, however, he changed his mind and opposed black slavery as well, and for similar reasons. The Spanish never fought as hard or as consistently against black slavery as they did on behalf of the Indians. Even though las Casas rejected black slavery, he owned several African slaves as late as 1544. The Spanish did not offer any concerted opposition to African slavery during the sixteenth century. The speculation is that the Iberians had become accustomed to having black Muslim slaves. There are several examples of these being a part of the Conquest (e.g., Estevanico who had been with Cabeza de Vaca and later with Coronado).

The work to emancipate African slaves in the Spanish New World was led by the Jesuits Alonso de Sandoval and Peter Claver during the seventeenth century. The Great Debate at Valladolid (1550–1551) was conducted as an inquiry into the nature of the Indian. Was he the "Natural Slave" as described in Aristotle's *Politics?* The debate concluded that Indians were not the people discussed by Aristotle.

Although slavery was expressly prohibited by law in the Spanish dominions, the Indians were subjected to the *encomienda* system and the Mission Laws of California. The *encomienda* system was devised to provide landowners with an adequate labor supply. The earliest laws on this subject went into force in 1513, under the Laws of Burgos. The laws, though humane, were unenforceable. Las Casas, in his *History of the Indies* (1520), attacked the system. He called it, "The greatest evil which has caused the total destruction of those lands and which will continue . . . is the encomienda of the Indians as it now exists. . . . also it is against God and [H]is will and [H]is Church" (Hanke, 1949). The Law of Inheritance for Two Generations (1536) permitted the *encomenderos* to pass on their *encomiendas* as inheritance (and the Indians with it) to their legitimate descendants or to their widows for one lifetime.

Another, far-reaching example of "Indian slavery" existed in the Mission System as established in California. The system, devised by the Franciscan Fathers, held the Indians in virtual slavery. The theory was that the Fathers were holding the lands in trust for the Indians until they became mature enough to handle the complexities of property and government themselves. The Indians were tied to the mission lands, they were denied free access, and the priests controlled every aspect of their lives, much as had the *encomenderos,* nearly two hundred years earlier. Even after the American conquest in 1848, California's Mission Indians tended to remain on former mission lands. Tribes even took their current names from the specific missions around which they lived.

One other aspect of slavery along the Spanish Borderlands was that of Indians who took other tribes as slaves during war and conquest. The Navajos of the American Southwest had the reputation of such a practice. Spanish chronicles of the conquest stressed the fear inspired by the Navajos' slaveholding practices.

In summary, while there was a great African slavery presence along the Spanish Borderlands, it was, in the main, limited to the American Southeast and Texas. Indian slavery was rampant in the West, with a number of tribes holding slaves during the American period and some tribes holding other Indians as slaves.

— *Henry H. Goldman*

For Further Reading

Abel, Annie Heloise. 1992. *The American Indian as Slaveholder and Secessionist.* Lincoln: University of Nebraska Press.

Bailey, L. R. 1966. *The Indian Slave Trade in the Southwest.* Los Angeles, CA: Westernlore Press.

Fuentes, Carlos. 1992. *The Buried Mirror: Reflections on Spain and the New World.* Boston: Houghton Mifflin.

Hanke, Lewis. 1949. *The Spanish Struggle for Justice in the Conquest of America.* Philadelphia: University of Pennsylvania Press.

Kessell, John L. 2002. *Spain in the Southwest: A Narrative History of Colonial New Mexico, Arizona, Texas, and California.* Norman: University of Oklahoma Press.

McNitt, Frank. 1972. *Navajo Wars: Military Campaigns, Slave Raids, and Reprisals.* Albuquerque: University of New Mexico Press.

Weber, David J. 1992. *The Spanish Frontier in North America.* New Haven, CT: Yale University Press.

KENNETH M. STAMPP (B. 1912)

Kenneth M. Stampp, a native of Milwaukee, Wisconsin, earned his Ph.D. at the University of Wisconsin in 1942 and emerged quickly as a leading historian of the Civil War era in the United States. His *Indiana Politics during the Civil War* (1949) and *And the War Came* (1950) marked him as an emerging scholar in the post–World War II years. Stampp's most influential work, however, remains his revisionist interpretation of North American slavery.

In a seminal article in the *American Historical Review* (1952) and in *The Peculiar Institution: Slavery in the Ante-Bellum South* (1956), Stampp thoroughly revised the pioneer writings of the southern historian Ulrich Bonnell Phillips. Though respectful of Phillips's earlier contributions, Stampp nonetheless attacked him for ignoring slave life on small plantations and farms, for "loose and glib generalizing" about slave life, and for failing to view slavery "through the eyes of the Negro." In describing slavery, Stampp said, Phillips overvalued the "mild and humorous side and minimized its grosser aspects." In his opinion, Phillips was incapable of taking blacks seriously.

Reflecting the anthropological findings of his day, not Phillips's, Stampp remarked that "no historian . . . can be taken seriously any longer unless he begins with the knowledge that there is no valid evidence that the Negro race is innately inferior to the white, and there is growing evidence that both races have approximately the same potentialities." Writing during the opening stages of the civil rights movement, Stampp informed readers of *The Peculiar Institution,* "I have assumed that the slaves were ordinary human beings, that innately Negroes are, after all, only white men with black skins, nothing more, nothing less."

The Peculiar Institution remained the standard work on black slavery until the 1970s. After careful research using plantation sources, Stampp described "the peculiar institution" as a dehumanizing, exploitative, but highly profitable labor system. Slaves toiled from dawn to dusk. "In terms of its broad social consequences for the South as a whole, however," he said, "slavery must be adjudged a failure." Though cognizant that not all masters overworked their bondsmen and women, Stampp nevertheless insisted that the blacks perceived slavery "as a system of labor extortion."

It was above all else a labor system, one predicated on rigid discipline. To function, slavery depended on rigid discipline and demanded unconditional submission by the black slaves to the wishes of their white masters. It also was a social system that repeatedly impressed upon the bondsmen and women their inferiority, a "closed" system determined to inculcate in them "a paralyzing fear of white men."

Whereas Phillips had defined slavery as a "school" for the allegedly heathen African Americans, Stampp interpreted it more like a prison where the slaves gained "a sense of complete dependence" and learned the whites' "code of behavior." According to Stampp, under slave law, "the slave was less a person than a thing." Whites, employing whipping as a symbol of racial control, worked hard to make the slaves "stand in fear." Challenging Phillips's notion of planter paternalism, Stampp charged that "the predominant and overpowering emotion that whites aroused in the majority of slaves was neither love nor hate but fear."

Stampp recognized that masters provided incentives to the slaves—patches of land for truck gardens, passes to visit other farms and plantations, cash payments—as ancillary modes of racial control. Unlike Phillips, Stampp argued that the slave consistently "longed for liberty and resisted bondage as much as any people could have done in their circumstances." Subjected to all manner of brutal and barbaric treatment by their captors, the slaves nevertheless remained "a troublesome property," capable of withstanding and resisting their captivity. In the end, Stampp judged that "slavery had no philosophical defense worthy of the name . . . it had nothing to commend it to posterity, except that it paid."

Stampp's view of slavery—as morally oppressive but economically profitable—generally continues to dominate theoretical approaches to the study of slavery. According to historian Peter J. Parish (1989), "Most authorities now agree that [the slaveholders] received a return on their investment which was in line with, if not superior to, that available elsewhere." But, as Stampp's critics have argued, master–slave relations were more complex, more nuanced, than the author of *The Peculiar Institution* suggested.

Stampp did not recognize change over time. He envisioned slavery, according to Carl N. Degler (1976), as "a changeless snapshot." Also, whereas Stampp, like Phillips, focused mostly on the masters and their behavior, modern scholars pay considerably more attention to the slaves' perspective of and reaction to their bondage. Few scholars today agree with Stampp's description of slaves as a "culturally rootless people."

In its day, however, *The Peculiar Institution* ranked as a major corrective to the type of writing of Phillips's era, and it thus remains one of the most influential works on the history of slavery. It influenced generations of scholars determined to understand the long history of racism in the United States.

— *John David Smith*

See also. Paternalism; Phillips, Ulrich Bonnell.

For Further Reading
Degler, Carl N. 1976. "Why Historians Change Their Minds." *Pacific Historical Review* 45: 167–184.

Degler, Carl N. 1978. "Experiencing Slavery." *Reviews in American History* 6: 277–82.

Parish, Peter J. 1989. *Slavery: History and Historians.* New York: Harper and Row.

Smith, John David. 1991. *An Old Creed for the New South: Proslavery Ideology and Historiography, 1865–1918.* Athens: University of Georgia Press.

MARIA W. STEWART (1803–1879)

Hailed as America's first black female political writer, Maria W. Stewart was an intensely active abolitionist writer and speaker. She was the first African American woman to speak before a mixed-gender audience and to leave texts of her speeches. Stewart was much more than an abolitionist, however, as she addressed varied subjects such as religion, anticolonization, political and economic exploitation, black self-determination, and women's rights.

A free black born in Hartford, Connecticut, and orphaned at an early age, Stewart lived with a clergyman's family until age fifteen when she began working as a domestic servant. Although she did not have the privilege of a formal education, her attendance at local Sunday Schools and residence in the clergyman's home offered access to books and knowledge that formed her intellectual views. Following a religious conversion, Stewart believed that born-again Christians were obligated to condemn all forms of injustice and oppression. She believed her work was part of a larger mission and declared that she possessed "that spirit of independence that were I called upon, I would willingly sacrifice my life for the cause of God and my brethren" (Richardson, 1987). She began writing antislavery tracts after the mysterious death of her friend and mentor, David Walker, whose famous *Appeal to the Colored Citizens of the World* (1829) called for black militancy to oppose slavery and racial injustice.

Stewart's first tract, *Religion and the Pure Principles of Morality, the Sure Foundation on Which We Must Build* (1831), was printed by William Lloyd Garrison and Isaac Knapp, and excerpts appeared in Garrison's abolitionist weekly, the *Liberator.* Stewart also began speaking before Boston audiences at Franklin Hall and the African-American Female Intelligence Society. Using biblical references and the values espoused in the U.S. Constitution, she denounced slavery and asserted African Americans' rights to freedom and full participation in American democracy. Stewart's lectures can be more aptly termed political sermons because they were filled with her enduring Christian beliefs even as they criticized the then current racist and sexist practices of the day.

Stewart questioned the American Colonization Society's intentions and recognized the racism of many of its members who believed blacks were inferior and unable to survive on their own in the United States. Stewart challenged colonizationists to support their claims of charity. Speaking before an audience at the African Masonic Hall in Boston, she charged, "If the colonizationists are the real friends to Africa, let them expend the money which they collect in erecting a college to educate her injured sons in this land of gospel, light, and liberty; for it would be most thankfully received on our part, and convince us of the truth of their professions, and save time, expense, and anxiety" (Richardson, 1987). Like many nineteenth-century African American abolitionists, Stewart displayed a fundamental concern with black civil rights and self-determination.

Unfortunately, Stewart's career as a public speaker was short-lived. Because social constraints impeded women's activities in the public sphere and there was insufficient responsiveness to her addresses, Stewart chose to end her speaking career in 1833 but continued working for freedom and opportunities for African Americans. Stewart published her speeches and writings in *Meditations from the Pen of Mrs. Maria W. Stewart* (1835), which was reprinted as *Productions of Mrs. Maria Stewart, Presented to the First African-Baptist Church and Society, in the City of Boston* (1879). She taught school in New York, Baltimore, and later, in Washington, D.C., during the Civil War. She was appointed matron of Washington's Freedman's Hospital in the early 1870s and supervised the hospital's service to many ill, destitute, and dispossessed former slaves until her death in 1879.

— *DoVeanna S. Fulton*

See also: American Colonization Society; Garrison, William Lloyd; Walker, David.

For Further Reading

Logan, Shirley Wilson. 1995. *With Pen and Voice: A Critical Anthology of Nineteenth-Century African-American Women.* Carbondale: Southern Illinois University Press.

Richardson, Marilyn, ed. 1987. *Maria W Stewart, America's First Black Woman Political Writer.* Bloomington: Indiana University Press.

Rycenga, Jennifer. 2001. "Maria Stewart, Black Abolitionist, and the Idea of Freedom." In *Frontline Feminisms: Women, War, and Resistance.* Ed. Marguerite R. Waller and Jennifer Rycenga. New York: Routledge.

WILLIAM STILL (1821–1902)

An abolitionist, writer, and Underground-Railroad activist, William Still was a free African American whose mother ran away from slavery and whose father purchased his own freedom. Still began working for the Pennsylvania Anti-Slavery Society in 1847. Three years later the society made him chairman of its Vigilance Committee to assist fugitives going through Philadelphia. During eight years in that job, he had contact with about eight hundred fugitive slaves, including about sixty children.

In Still's largely routine work there were some exciting moments, as evident on the day a man who purchased his own freedom contacted Still for family information. The two discovered that they were brothers, the younger having been left behind when their mother escaped from slavery. Still witnessed the arrival of such famous fugitives as Henry "Box" Brown and William and Ellen Craft. The Vigilance Committee worked closely with Thomas Garrett, Robert Purvis, and Lucretia and James Mott. Still was able to find temporary shelter for fugitives among other African Americans in Philadelphia.

One of Still's duties was to interview newly arrived slaves concerning their masters' names, their treatment, and their escape experiences. He carefully preserved these records, which years later provided source material for his book on the Underground Railroad. In 1855 Still visited former slaves in Canada and wrote a strong defense of their conduct and status, answering those who insisted that African Americans could not survive in freedom. His efforts to improve the status of African Americans continued after abolition, when, among other efforts, he led a successful eight-year struggle to desegregate Pennsylvania's streetcars.

William Still's book, *The Underground Railroad* (1872), fills an important place in the history of the Underground Railroad. One of a very few such works by African Americans, it is a significant supplement to white abolitionists' memoirs. Although he included sketches of the abolitionists, his emphasis was on the daring and ingenuity of the fugitives themselves. He did not depict them as passive passengers on an abolitionist-run railroad. Besides fugitives' accounts, his book included newspaper articles, legal documents, letters from abolitionists and former slaves, and biographical sketches. The many illustrations called attention to the role of absconding slaves in the struggle for their own freedom.

Still's book is a powerful testimony against slavery. The story of the fugitives' "heroism and desperate struggles," wrote Still, and "the terrible oppression that they were under," must be preserved for future generations. Moreover, Still argued that books by African Americans would prove their intellectual ability and demolish ideas of racial inferiority. "We very much need works on various topics from the pens of colored men to represent the race intellectually," he wrote (Still, 1883).

William Still published his book himself and sold it through his own agents. When the first edition sold out he printed another, and in 1883 a third edition. It became the most widely circulated of such accounts and is still found in many African American homes.

Yet despite its large circulation it had little influence on the way white Americans viewed the Underground Railroad, for his spotlight on the fugitives was often overshadowed by the well-publicized work of their abolitionist collaborators.

— *Larry Gara*

See also: Craft, William and Ellen; Garrett, Thomas; Underground Railroad.

For Further Reading
Blockson, Charles L. 1987. *The Underground Railroad.* New York: Prentice Hall.
Boyd, James R. "William Still: His Life and Work to This Time." In William Still. 1883. *The Underground Railroad.* Philadelphia: William Still.
Gara, Larry. 1961. "William Still and the Underground Railroad." *Pennsylvania History* (1): 33–44.

LUCY STONE (1818–1893)

Despite Lucy Stone's significant contribution to abolitionism, her involvement in the woman's rights and woman suffrage movements has overshadowed her years of labor for the antislavery movement. Born in central Massachusetts, Stone was greatly influenced by the outspoken, early feminist-abolitionists Angelina and Sarah Grimké and Abby Kelley Foster.

Stone earned her way through Oberlin College, becoming in 1847 the first Massachusetts woman to obtain a college degree. Though abolitionism was rampant at Oberlin in the mid-1840s, it shunned the radical message of the Garrisonians upon which Stone modeled her ideology and her antislavery fervor. While at Oberlin, Stone was in charge of disseminating the *Anti-Slavery Bugle,* a journal for western Garrisonians, and though women students were not permitted to speak publicly, she worked to prepare herself for a career as a women's rights and antislavery lecturer.

Shortly after Stone graduated from Oberlin, Samuel May, Jr., general agent of the American Anti-Slavery

Lucy Stone's involvement in the woman's rights and woman suffrage movements overshadowed her years of labor for the antislavery movement. (Library of Congress)

Society, hired her as an agent of the society to conduct antislavery lecture tours. When May chastised Stone for mingling women's rights issues with her antislavery message, they solved the conflict by agreeing that she would address the two concerns in separate lectures. Like her fellow Garrisonian feminist-abolitionists Lucretia Mott, Abby Kelley Foster, and Susan B. Anthony, Stone found it nearly impossible to separate the issues of political and social domination that enslaved African Americans from those that rendered women powerless.

In her first year of touring, Stone earned a solid reputation for converting people to the antislavery cause. Her success was based on a dynamic oratorical strategy—without written notes or text, she focused on relating heart-rending, true stories of families tyrannized and destroyed by slavery. Critics especially noted the persuasive power of her mellifluous voice on belligerent audiences. By the end of 1848, Stone was sharing near-equal billing with William Lloyd Garrison and Wendell Phillips. Until the late 1850s, she lectured throughout all of New England, New York, New Jersey, Ohio, Michigan, Illinois, Wisconsin, and parts of Canada.

Late in the 1850s, several years after her marriage to Cincinnati abolitionist Henry Blackwell, Stone sharply

curtailed her speaking engagements to remain home with her young daughter. In the midst of the Civil War in 1863, she joined Susan B. Anthony and Elizabeth Cady Stanton in forming the Women's National Loyal League. Stone was elected president of the league's opening convention, which determined to organize northern women to petition Congress to secure a thirteenth amendment guaranteeing the freedom of African Americans.

In 1866 Stone participated with Anthony, Stanton, and others in organizing the American Equal Rights Association and lobbied legislators to make the Fourteenth Amendment, and later the Fifteenth Amendment, ensure universal suffrage. Then, in 1869, following a major political and ideological rift with Anthony and Stanton, Stone abandoned this struggle and aligned herself with Wendell Phillips and most male abolitionists who insisted that obtaining the franchise for African American males must take precedence over all other concerns, particularly woman suffrage. Stone dedicated the remainder of her life to women's rights and woman suffrage as a major leader of the American Woman Suffrage Association and as editor of the weekly newspaper, *Woman's Journal.*

— *Judith E. Harper*

See also: American Anti-Slavery Society; Anthony, Susan B.; Foster, Abigail Kelley; Mott, Lucretia Coffin; Women and the Antislavery Movement.

For Further Reading

Blackwell, Alice Stone. 1930. *Lucy Stone: Pioneer of Women's Rights.* Boston: Little, Brown.

DuBois, Ellen Carol. 1978. *Feminism and Suffrage: The Emergence of an Independent Women's Movement in America 1848–1869.* Ithaca, NY: Cornell University Press.

Hays, Elinor Rice. 1961. *Morning Star: A Biography of Lucy Stone 1818–1893.* New York: Harcourt, Brace, World.

Kerr, Andrea Moore. 1992. *Lucy Stone: Speaking Out for Equality.* New Brunswick, NJ: Rutgers University Press.

Lepof, Amanda J. 2003. "Lucy B. Stone (1818–1893): Advocating for Abolition and Woman's Rights in Nineteenth-Century America." M.A. thesis, Department of History, Georgetown University, Washington, D.C.

Million, Joelle. 2003. *Woman's Voice, Woman's Place: Lucy Stone and the Birth of the Woman's Rights Movement.* Westport, CT: Praeger.

STONO REBELLION (1739)

A slave rebellion broke out near the Stono River in South Carolina in 1739. Known as the Stono Rebellion, it was the largest uprising of its kind to occur during the period of the American colonies. The Spanish Empire in the New World had enticed the slaves of British colonies to escape to Spanish territory, and in 1733 the Spanish monarch issued an edict to free all runaway slaves from British territory who had made their way into Spanish possessions. Five years later, the Spanish in St. Augustine, Florida, earnestly pursued the policy and publicized this news. Information about the policy reached South Carolina's slaves through the seamen who landed at Charleston, South Carolina, and throughout 1739, the colony's government had problems with an increasing number of slaves escaping to Florida. As they promised, the Spanish offered refuge to the runaways, but occasionally, they sold them to other owners.

On Sunday, September 9, 1739, about twenty slaves, most of whom were from Angola, gathered under the leadership of a slave called Jemmy near the Stono River, 20 miles away from Charleston. They massacred several white families and looted their guns and ammunition. The next day they marched south, following the Pongpong River, which ran through Georgia to St. Augustine. While they marched, the rebels cried for liberty, raised flags, and beat drums. On the road, more slaves joined the rebels, whose number reached more than sixty—some scholars estimate it was about one hundred.

In high spirits, the reinforced rebels stopped their march for a while. They began singing and dancing and tried to enlist more people by beating drums; some of them were drunk. Although they had marched more than 10 miles, the rebels had met with no obstacle and were free to burn everything they saw.

In the meantime, the militia was gathering, and when the whites pursued, the rebel ranks were soon broken, and several were killed in battle. For the following month, colonial officials arrested and executed the rebels, hanging their heads on the landmark posts along the road. In total, forty-four blacks and twenty-one whites lost their lives during the rebellion and its aftermath.

Because the leaders of the rebellion were mostly from Angola, whites later avoided purchasing Angolan slaves because they feared their rebellious nature. The Stono Rebellion shocked white South Carolinians so strongly that their assembly passed laws to place import duties on the slaves from abroad to curtail the high black population rate in the colony. Of all the British colonies in North America, South Carolina had the largest majority African population. Blacks began outnumbering white residents in 1730, and in the colony's coastal area, blacks constituted two-thirds of the population.

In 1740 the colony collected all the Negro codes that were in use in order to rearrange them into a comprehensive new law. The new legislation fortified the whites' control of blacks, both free and unfree, by strengthening patrol duties and militia training and by recommending the master's benign treatment of slaves. South Carolina's 1740 Negro Code, along with Virginia and Maryland laws, provided models for the laws governing slaves in the expanding slave territory to the west.

— *Hyong-In Kim*

See also: South Carolina.

For Further Reading
Huggins, Nathan Irvin. 1977. *Black Odyssey: The Afro-American Ordeal in Slavery.* New York: Pantheon Books.
    Thornton, John K. 1991. "African Dimensions of the Stono Rebellion." *American Historical Review* 96 (October): 1101–1113.
    Wood, Peter. 1974. *Black Majority: Negroes in Colonial South Carolina from 1670 through the Stono Rebellion.* New York: Norton.

HARRIET BEECHER STOWE (1811–1896)

Harriet Beecher Stowe, the author of *Uncle Tom's Cabin,* was born in Litchfield, Connecticut. She was the seventh of nine children born to Lyman Beecher, a leading clergyman, and his first wife, Roxana Foote. In 1816 her mother, Roxana died, but other than this early encounter with grief, Stowe's childhood seems to have been a happy one.

She first attended Dame School and later was sent to the Litchfield Academy. In 1824 she moved to Hartford where she studied and assisted her sister Catherine, a student teacher at Hartford Female Seminary. Then, in 1832, the family moved to Cincinnati, Ohio, where her father had been appointed president of Lane Theological Seminary. Harriet started to teach shortly thereafter. Although she visited a plantation in Kentucky in 1833, it was in Cincinnati that Stowe gained firsthand experience of the great moral and religious disturbances that surrounded the issue of slavery. Her father, under pressure, found himself unable to take the radical stand demanded by some of the seminary students. As a result, many of the students withdrew in 1833, under the leadership of Theodore Dwight Weld, and became the nucleus of Oberlin College in Ohio. Stowe later made use of this incident in her writing.

During her time in Cincinnati, she began writing

Harriet Beecher Stowe, U.S. author and antislavery reformer. (Library of Congress)

and published her first fiction work, *The Mayflower: Sketches and Scenes and Characters among the Descendants of the Puritans* (1843). Her life was difficult and she worked hard. Her situation did not become easier when she became the second wife of Calvin E. Stowe in 1836. He was a distinguished biblical scholar but a man hopelessly ill-equipped for married life. The family was poor, and while still in Cincinnati, Stowe lived through the births of six of her seven children, the death of one child, a cholera epidemic and race riots, before finally leaving in 1850 to move to Brunswick, Maine. Her husband had received a professorship at Bowdoin College there, and the family spent two years in Brunswick before Calvin Stowe joined the faculty of the theological seminary at Andover, Massachusetts, which remained their home until 1864 when they retired to Hartford, Connecticut. Calvin Stowe died in 1886.

For Stowe, there was no "room of one's own" in which to write, but while in Brunswick, the passage of the Fugitive Slave Act (1850) reinforced her abhorrence of slavery and led to the writing of *Uncle Tom's Cabin*

(1852). Throughout the 1840s in Cincinnati, and despite her revulsion, Stowe had never become an active member of any abolitionist organization. Eventually her work brought her into contact with Frederick Douglass and other active abolitionists, but Stowe remained on the outside of any formal abolitionist groups. Nevertheless, she had contributed articles to abolitionist papers, set up a school for the children of former slaves, and through her cook, a former slave named Eliza Buck, learned that Buck's children had been fathered by her owner. From Buck, Stowe learned that slave women were unable to help themselves. It was through its adherence to a woman's world that *Uncle Tom's Cabin* captured the emotions and imagination as no other antislavery literature had managed to do. It brought Stowe fame and, if not fortune, at least freedom from incessant money worries. The work may have sold 3 million copies in the United States alone, and in addition to being translated into many languages, it was the first American book to become a best-seller in Europe. It was admired by the Russian writers Leo Tolstoy and Feodor Dostoevski, and both Charlotte Brontë and George Eliot wrote admiringly of Stowe's courageous entry into the "political sphere" with a subject deemed unsuitable for women at that time.

Inevitably, the book was challenged, particularly in the journals and papers of the southern United States, leading Stowe to accumulate material from laws, court records, newspapers, and slave narratives that she published as *The Key to Uncle Tom's Cabin* (1853) and "Uncle Sam's Emancipation," which later appeared in a book with that title. She found the horrors of slavery more dreadful than she had imagined and continued her attack on "the peculiar institution" in *Dred: A Tale of the Great Dismal Swamp* (1856). That work developed a theme of *Uncle Tom's Cabin* to demonstrate that slaveholding demoralized the white population.

At the height of her fame, in 1853, Stowe traveled to Great Britain and was welcomed by liberals everywhere. On a second visit in 1856, she was honored by Queen Victoria, but on her third visit, in 1869, she was introduced to Lady Byron. Stowe's subsequent book, *Lady Byron Vindicated* (1870), which accused the English poet George Gordon (Lord) Byron of an incestuous relationship with his stepsister, turned many people in Britain against her. Stowe suffered personal grief, including the loss of two sons, and her talented favorite brother, Henry Ward, accused of adultery, created a scandal involving ecclesiastical and civil trials. This caused incalculable emotional upset to all concerned. Nevertheless, during the 1870s, Stowe embarked on a highly successful public speaking career, reading from *Uncle Tom's Cabin* and other works. She continued writing, contributing throughout her life to numerous magazines and journals, but her fiction after *Dred: A Tale of the Great Dismal Swamp* consisted largely of New England novels and included *The Minister's Wooing* (1859), which James Russell Lowell saw as her masterpiece. An inveterate public commentator on personal and public questions, she included in that work her attack on Calvinism, a religion she eventually deserted. In 1871 she wrote a fictional essay, "My Wife and I," in which she defended a woman's right to a career. Her own career was both long and arduous, and during the 1880s, her critical reputation, together with her health, declined. The little woman who Abraham Lincoln supposedly credited with starting the American Civil War, died on July 1, 1896, with only her nurse present.

— *Jan Pilditch*

See also: *Uncle Tom's Cabin.*

For Further Reading
Adams, John R. 1989. *Harriet Beecher Stowe.* Boston: Twayne.

Crozier, Alice C. 1969. *The Novels of Harriet Beecher Stowe.* New York: Oxford University Press.

Gerson, Noel B. 1965. *Harriet Beecher Stowe: A Biography.* New York: Praeger Publishers.

Moers, Ellen. 1996. *Literary Women.* London: Women's Press.

Wagenknecht, Edward. 1965. *Harriet Beecher Stowe: The Known and the Unknown.* New York: Oxford University Press.

STRADER V. GRAHAM (1851)

Although the question of slavery was a complex political, social, and moral issue in the generation preceding the Civil War, the topic became increasingly litigious in the decade before that conflict. Some jurists believed the courts might succeed where legislative compromise and moral suasion had failed in reckoning effectively with slavery—that judicial fiat might mandate an equitable position with respect to the South's peculiar institution and the myriad concerns it engendered. The U.S. Supreme Court's action in *Strader v. Graham* (10 How. 82 [1851]) established a short-lived precedent, a policy it later ignored when considering the infamous case of *Dred Scott v. Sandford* (1857).

Dr. Christopher Graham was a Kentucky slaveowner who regularly hired out his slaves as professional musicians for performances in Ohio and Indiana minstrel shows. Trained as performers by a freedman and recognizing their potential social and economic value in the free states, some of these bonded artisans grew disenchanted with their status as chattel property in Kentucky. In 1841 three of Graham's slaves escaped from Kentucky by crossing the Ohio River and seeking asylum as free men in Cincinnati. Since Kentucky law allowed the prosecution of anyone who aided or abetted the escape of slaves, Graham filed a lawsuit against Jacob Strader who owned the steamboat *Pike* that ferried the fugitives across the river.

The case involved several crucial legal questions that were yet unreconciled and untested in the national debate over a slaveowner's truest property rights in human capital. State law in Ohio recognized the fugitives as freedmen, and the language of the Northwest Ordinance (1787) had explicitly prohibited slavery from the region where the musicians performed and where they eventually sought their freedom. This was not merely a question of whether Ohio's laws could supersede the judicial prerogatives of Kentucky, but rather it called into question the validity of the U.S. government's assertion in the Northwest Ordinance that lands north of the Ohio River were free of slavery. Although Graham only sought compensatory damages for the value of the slaves that he had lost, the case that he filed against Strader was fraught with more potent meaning as the repercussions from legal ambiguities would have implications in the national debate on slavery.

Kentucky courts had established a precedent in *Rankin v. Lydia* (1820) that authorized emancipation for those slaves taken by their owners into free states or territories and made permanent residents there. The Kentucky Court of Appeals did not find that precedent applicable in *Strader v. Graham* because the circumstances of the case were quite different. The court held that Graham's slaves were merely sojourners who visited free states while in temporary employment and that were not taken into these regions for the purpose of establishing permanent residency outside of Kentucky. Accordingly, the Kentucky courts held Strader liable for the escape of Graham's slaves and ordered him to pay damages to Graham equivalent to the value of the three fugitives. Strader appealed the decision to the U.S. Supreme Court.

On January 6, 1851, Chief Justice Roger B. Taney announced the U.S. Supreme Court's unanimous decision to dismiss the case for lack of jurisdiction. In Taney's opinion, it was the exclusive right of each state "to determine the status, or domestic or social condition, of the persons domiciled within its territory" (Witt, 1990). In what was largely viewed as a proslavery decision, the U.S. Supreme Court had implicitly promised noninterference by federal courts with decisions that state courts had reached on slavery-related questions.

Chief Justice Taney's ruling also included other controversial statements. Taney believed that the Northwest Ordinance (1787) had been superseded by the adoption of the U.S. Constitution (1789), which provided a sense of equality (comity) to all states. Specifically, Taney held that the prohibition against slavery in the Northwest Territory ceased to exist once a territory became a state, but that states did have the right to determine the status of individuals within their respective jurisdictions. Justices John McLean and John Catron each filed separate opinions in which they challenged Taney's statements on the Northwest Ordinance and on the free navigation of rivers.

Had the U.S. Supreme Court followed its own decision in *Strader v. Graham* (1851) as a precedent, it might have similarly dismissed the case of *Dred Scott v. Sandford* (1857), but that did not happen. Apparently, the ensuing crisis fomented by the expansion of slavery into the western territories and the abject failure of popular sovereignty to remedy the situation had changed the judicial landscape by 1857.

— *Junius P. Rodriguez*

See also: *Dred Scott v. Sandford;* Northwest Ordinance (1787); United States Constitution.

For Further Reading

Finkelman, Paul. 1992. "Slavery." In *The Oxford Companion to the Supreme Court of the United States.* Ed. Kermit L. Hall. New York: Oxford University Press.

Rodriguez, Junius P. 1999. *Chronology of World Slavery.* Santa Barbara, CA: ABC-CLIO.

Siegel, Martin. 1995. *The United States Supreme Court: Volume 3, The Taney Court, 1836–1864.* Danbury, CT: Grolier Educational Corporation.

Witt, Elder, ed. 1990. *Congressional Quarterly's Guide to the U.S. Supreme Court.* Washington, DC: Congressional Quarterly.

THORNTON STRINGFELLOW
(1788–1869)

Thornton Stringfellow was perhaps the leading proslavery spokesman in the Old South to base his arguments on the Bible. Born in Fauquier County in Virginia's northern piedmont, he lived there or in neighboring Culpeper County most of his life. His part of Virginia was majority slave—Culpeper County's population in 1850 was 42 percent white, 54 percent slave, and 4 percent free black. Stringfellow himself, the son of a slaveowning family, owned about sixty slaves. He was also a Baptist minister.

In the realm of reformers in the pre–Civil War United States, Stringfellow resembled his northern counterparts in many of his ideas, but in the defense of slavery, he resembled George Fitzhugh, another eastern Virginian. Although he involved himself in temperance and in domestic and foreign missions, he also committed himself to the South's proslavery crusade. In the 1840s, when northern churches determined to exclude slaveowners from Baptist missionary activities, he convinced his fellow Baptists in the South to separate themselves and organize a Southern Baptist Convention.

As a proslavery spokesman, minister, and planter, Stringfellow contributed a scriptural variant to the proslavery writings of the South in the 1840s and 1850s. The Bible offered a sure guide to "the true principles of humanity," as he wrote in *A Brief Examination of Scripture Testimony on the Institution of Slavery* (1841). He demonstrated how God in the Old Testament ordained slavery and how Christ and the apostles in the New Testament, never challenging the institution, directed all Christians to accept their station in life, whether as servant or as master. How could it be, Stringfellow demanded of abolitionists in the North, that "God has ordained slavery, and yet slavery is the greatest of sins"? Stringfellow's writings made it easier for his fellow white southerners to view the institution of slavery as consistent with their understanding of Christianity.

Jacksonian though he was, Stringfellow contested any belief or behavior that would, in general, "level all inequalities in human condition" or, in particular, hold that "the gain of freedom to the slave, is the only proof of godliness in the master." Neither corporal punishment nor the breakup of slave families gave him pause—these, he held, were supported in Scripture. It mattered not that some translations of the Bible used the term "servants" instead of "slaves," he said, for we are talking of "not a name, but a thing." Nor did it trouble him that Abraham relied on an army of 300 of his own slaves—that so many "servants" might "bear arms"—though America's variant of slavery displayed nothing of the sort.

The "essential particulars" of slavery in the Old Testament and in the Old South, that it was "involuntary" and "hereditary," were what mattered—but then there was race. "The guardianship and control of the black race, by the white," he argued in *Scriptural and Statistical Views in Favor of Slavery* (1841), "is an indispensable Christian duty, to which we must yet look if we would secure the well-being of both races." One of Stringfellow's works, "The Bible Argument: or, Slavery in the Light of Divine Revelation," was included in an anthology of proslavery writings: E. N. Elliott, ed., *Cotton Is King, and Pro-Slavery Arguments* (1860).

See also: Fitzhugh, George.

For Further Reading

Faust, Drew Gilpin. 1977. "Evangelicalism and the Meaning of the Proslavery Argument: The Reverend Thornton Stringfellow of Virginia." *Virginia Magazine of History and Biography* 85 (January): 3–17.

Maddex, Jack P., Jr. 1979. "'The Southern Apostasy' Revisited: The Significance of Proslavery Christianity." *Marxist Perspectives* 2 (Fall): 132–141.

Snay, Mitchell. 1993. *Gospel of Disunion: Religion and Separatism in the Antebellum South.* Cambridge: Cambridge University Press.

SUGAR CULTIVATION AND TRADE

Sugar was first cultivated in Asia about two centuries before the Christian era. Sugarcane from China, Java, India, and Persia began to be cultivated in Egypt after the seventh century BCE., and was taken by Arabs through northern Africa, and from there eventually arrived in Spain, France, and Italy. Sugar was also introduced into Syria and the Byzantine Empire. Sugar was produced in small quantities and was strictly considered a luxury item, but during the fourteenth and fifteenth centuries the appreciation of its food value emerged, and sugar became a substitute for honey, the principal sweetener known in the Western world.

In both the newly discovered Atlantic islands and in the Americas, the introduction of sugar cultivation transformed this expensive luxury item into a principal food product with larger consumption in every location. In 1500 the Portuguese islands of Madeira produced about 2,000 tons of sugar each year. Sugar was the only Western product that competed profitably with Eastern spices in European markets.

Colonists in the province of Pernambuco, Brazil, experimented with sugarcane cultivation as early as 1516. In 1532 Martim Afonso de Sousa established the first *engenho* (sugar mill), and in 1549 under Tomé de Sousa, the first royal governor and captain-general, sugar growers received a ten-year tax exemption. The climate and the white, chalky, clay-like, *massapi* soil along the Brazilian coast provided excellent conditions for growing cane. Sugar quickly became the basis of Brazilian prosperity, and the colony was the world's first large-scale sugar producer. The king presented the

first governor with a difficult order: he was both to extend Portuguese authority and to make Brazil a profitable commercial venture. By 1573 Brazil shipped over 2,500 tons of sugar to Europe each year, and according to conservative estimates in 1600 Brazilian production had reached 30,000 tons. The labor requirements for the increasing sugar production promoted the development of a slave system.

Brazil's colonization really began with sugar production—when the conqueror gradually abandoned his life of trading to administer a plantation and sugar mill. Cane planting required large land tracts and an increasing supply of cheap labor. Landowners looked to Native Americans as a natural labor force, but when voluntary labor was no longer adequate, colonists began acquiring slaves. The plantations prospered, but increases in enslavement led to hostilities from Native Americans. Because they protected the Indians, the Jesuits incurred the wrath of both the *fazendeiros* and slave raiders. After 1550 there was a rapid expansion of sugar plantations, while simultaneous drought, famine, and smallpox decimated the Indian population. From that time black Africans increasingly replaced Indian slaves. They proved a more economical labor force because of their greater physical strength and their ability to survive hard work under tropical conditions. Their fear of the nearby Indian population helped deter runaways. After 1580 the number of African slaves increased rapidly, with the sugar industry providing the wealth needed for importation.

The religious orders in colonial Latin America began cultivating cane and producing sugar for profit because they did not receive the funds that they had been promised to finance their missionary efforts. In 1594 Jesuit General Aquaviva ruled that colleges could produce their own sugar without violating the Jesuits' governing rules or invalidating individual poverty vows taken by its members. Religious orders, thereafter, struggled to maintain an adequate workforce to produce sugar.

Until Brazil abolished the slave trade in 1850, Africans were the most numerous immigrants to Brazil. Many of them possessed greater skills and energies than their masters. In Brazil manumission was common, and slaves were usually allowed certain days to work for their own interests. They had legal rights—to own property, to marry without fear of being separated from their families, and to defend themselves—but actual practice at times belied the generous nature of the law.

Sugar plantations were almost self-sufficient socioeconomic units; consequently, no strong cities were established in colonial Brazil. Even after the

British and French developed sugar plantations in the Caribbean, Brazil continued to lead the American importation of African slaves. Since the working life of a sugar plantation slave was calculated at seven years, the growth and continuance of the slave trade was assured. Sugar planters made the maximum profit by working the slaves hard, feeding them meager rations, and then replacing those who died or were disabled each year. Some masters even freed nonproductive slaves so that they themselves would no longer have to provide for them.

The Dutch, when expelled from Brazil in 1656, took with them Africans familiar with all phases of sugar production. They introduced the sugar culture in the French and British islands in the Caribbean. Overproduction caused Brazil to lose its former commercial advantage. The discovery of great quantities of gold in Minas Gerais changed the economic situation and began an exodus of *fazendeiros* and slaves from the sugar-producing Northeast. The British reform movement that sought the end of slave trading provoked strong opposition in areas that depended on slave labor for sugar production. The March 1827 treaty between Great Britain and Brazil contained a clause promising the end of the slave trade by 1830, but it met with strong opposition among Brazilians.

During the eighteenth century slave labor developed an intensive sugar economy unique in history. The plantation system became all-important in the British colony of Jamaica and in French St. Domingue (present-day Haiti). Sugar became the dominant crop in Cuba, but coffee and tobacco were important as they were also on Puerto Rico. St. Domingue became the most productive of all Caribbean sugar colonies and a model for the colonial slave-holding society. By 1785 there were over five hundred thousand slaves there, a large portion of whom were African born. The mortality rate was high because of the hard labor in the tropical climate, poor sanitation, and housing, but mainly because of inhumane treatment. The supply of slaves had to be replenished continuously.

The Jesuits first introduced the cultivation of sugarcane into the French colony of Louisiana in 1751. The large-scale cultivation of sugar necessitated a more massive importation of slaves into the region, just as the sugar revolution of the previous century had caused enormous numbers of slaves to be taken to Brazil and the islands of the West Indies. Technological innovations, like the multiple-effect vacuum pan evaporator, developed by the octoroon Norbert Rillieux in the early nineteenth century served to advance the sugar-refining industry in Louisiana. In the early nineteenth century, some of the largest plantations of

the antebellum era were located in the sugar parishes of southeastern Louisiana.

— *Sharon Landers*

See also: Louisiana; Rillieux, Norbert.

For Further Reading

Azevedo, Fernando de. 1950. *Brazilian Culture: An Introduction to the Study of Culture in Brazil.* New York: Macmillan.

Follett, Richard J. 2005. *The Sugar Masters: Planters and Slaves in Louisiana's Cane World, 1820–1860.* Baton Rouge: Louisiana State University Press.

Moitt, Bernard. 2004. *Sugar, Slavery, and Society: Perspectives on the Caribbean, India, the Mascarenes, and the United States.* Gainesville: University Press of Florida.

Poppino, Rollie E. 1968. *Brazil: The Land and the People.* New York: Oxford University Press.

Rawley, James A. 1981. *The Transatlantic Slave Trade: A History.* New York: Norton.

Schwartz, Stuart. 1985. *Sugar Plantations in the Formation of Brazilian Society: Bahia, 1550–1835.* Cambridge: Cambridge University Press.

TALLMADGE AMENDMENT

The Tallmadge Amendment, an antislavery provision attached to the Missouri statehood bill of 1819, initiated the first sectional clash over slavery in the territories. In February 1819 a bill came before Congress calling for an enabling act to allow Missouri Territory to petition for statehood. As Missouri was a slaveholding territory embracing some ten thousand bondsmen, the common assumption was that Missouri would enter the Union straightaway as a slave state. Congressman James Tallmadge, Jr., of New York sought to change this scenario. He attached to the proposed enabling act an amendment closing Missouri to the further ingress of slavery and stipulating that slave children born in Missouri after its admission to the Union should be manumitted at age twenty-five. The Tallmadge Amendment proposed no regulations concerning slaves already present in the territory, but it did effectively prescribe a program of gradual emancipation that would ultimately extinguish the peculiar institution in Missouri. In short, the Tallmadge rider decreed that Missouri would, in essence, join the Union as a free state. This point held palpable political significance, for at the time the nation was composed of an equal number of free states and slave states: eleven of each. So the admission of any new state would tip the balance of power in the Union in favor of either free soil or slaveholding interests. Tallmadge's scheme gave the advantage to the free soilers.

The Tallmadge Amendment caused great alarm in the South. Some slave-state politicians, such as Nathaniel Macon of North Carolina and future president John Tyler of Virginia, denied the authority of Congress to interfere with slavery in the territories. Others predicted disunion and civil war unless northern antislavery agitation ceased. Spencer Roane, Virginia's leading state supreme court judge, suggested that the South, "if driven to it," could form with the slaveholding West a "great nation" apart from the "northern Yankies [sic]" (Roane, 1906). Georgia senator Freeman Walker went further, suggesting that Tallmadge's crusade would lead to "civil wars," to "a brother's sword crimsoned with a brother's blood" (Moore, 1953).

Congress debated the Tallmadge Amendment for a full year. Reintroduced several times, the measure repeatedly passed in the House of Representatives, where northern delegates formed a majority. The amendment continually failed in the Senate, however, where southern representation equaled that of the North owing to the exact balance between slave and free states. Illinois senator Jesse B. Thomas broke the deadlock in February 1820 when he offered an amendment to the Missouri bill that became the basis for the Missouri Compromise. The Thomas Proviso called for the admission of Missouri as a slave state without the Tallmadge restrictions and proposed the admission of Maine as a free state in order to preserve the sectional equilibrium. In addition, the Thomas Amendment excluded slavery from the remainder of the Louisiana Purchase north of 36° 30' minutes north latitude.

Henry Clay of Kentucky, who was then speaker of the House, incorporated these terms into legislation that became the Missouri Compromise. Thanks to Clay's crafty maneuvering, the act passed both chambers of Congress despite plenty of opposition. In the end, both sections grudgingly accepted the compromise. Southerners preferred an immediate short-term victory, while free-state leaders feared for the safety of the republic if they clung to the Tallmadge plan. As antislavery congressman Charles Kinsey of New Jersey explained, he opted for compromise because an antislavery victory in Missouri would be "gained at the hazard of the Union" (Fehrenbacher, 1980). Yet the Missouri Compromise solved little. It left the slavery question to a future generation of Americans, who revisited the Tallmadge controversy time and again before ultimately fulfilling Freeman Walker's prophecy of a bloody civil war between American brothers-in-arms.

— *Eric Tscheschlok*

See also: Missouri Compromise.

For Further Reading
Brown, Richard H. 1966. "The Missouri Crisis, Slavery, and the Politics of Jacksonianism." *South Atlantic Quarterly* 65 (Winter): 55–72.

Fehrenbacher, Don E. 1980. *The South and Three Sectional Crises.* Baton Rouge: Louisiana State University Press.

Moore, Glover. 1953. *The Missouri Controversy, 1819–1821.* Lexington: University of Kentucky Press.

Roane, Spencer. 1906. "Letters of Spencer Roane, 1788–1822." *New York Public Library Bulletin* 10: 167–180.

ROGER B. TANEY (1777–1864)

Roger Brooke Taney, author of the U.S. Supreme Court's opinion in the case *Dred Scott v. Sandford,* was one of the foremost judicial advocates of slavery in the nineteenth-century United States. Born on a southern Maryland tobacco plantation, Taney grew up in a wealthy planter family and never traveled far beyond Maryland's borders. After graduating from Dickinson College in Pennsylvania in 1795, he returned to his home state to study law.

As a young lawyer in Frederick County, Maryland, Taney earned somewhat of an antislavery reputation. In 1819 he defended Methodist minister Jacob Gruber, who was accused of inciting slaves to rebellion after preaching an antislavery sermon. In a passionate defense of Gruber, Taney referred to slavery as "a blot on our national character" and relied upon the Declaration of Independence to support his antislavery position. During this period, moreover, Taney freed his own slaves and joined the American Colonization Society, an organization that sought to transport American slaves to Africa. Taney's moderation on the slavery question typified southern opinion during the first two decades of the nineteenth century, particularly in a border state such as Maryland, where slaves constituted a small percentage of the total population.

Within the next decade or so, Taney adopted a more proslavery position. Appointed by President Andrew Jackson as U.S. attorney general in 1831, Taney

Chief Justice Roger B. Taney authored the U.S. Supreme Court's opinion in *Dred Scott v. Sandford* (1857). (Library of Congress)

wrote an unpublished opinion on the constitutionality of a North Carolina law regulating the immigration of free blacks that foreshadowed his ruling in the *Dred Scott* case. Taney referred to blacks as "a separate and degraded people" who "were not looked upon as citizens by the contracting parties who formed the Constitution" (Swisher, 1936). After Jackson appointed him as chief justice of the U.S. Supreme Court in 1836, Taney began a twenty-eight-year judicial career during which he consistently defended slavery and the values of the Old South.

During the 1840s, Taney began his judicial defense of slavery. In *Groves v. Slaughter* (1841), a case involving the sale of slaves in Mississippi, Taney wrote a separate, concurring opinion affirming his commitment to protecting the peculiar institution. Although the majority opinion addressed only the narrow issue of the validity of the commercial transaction in question, Taney went beyond the scope of the matter and argued that power to regulate interstate slave trading lay exclusively with the states. By doing so, Taney hoped to ensure that the national government would not interfere with slaveholders' rights.

In *Prigg v. Pennsylvania* (1842), Taney reiterated his position in another separate opinion. This case involved the constitutionality of Pennsylvania's personal liberty law of 1826, which required slave catchers to obtain a proper writ from a state judge before removing any African Americans from the state. Writing for the majority, Justice Joseph Story invalidated this state restriction on the rendition of fugitives, holding that the power to enforce the slaveholder's right of recovery lay exclusively with the U.S. Congress. Taney, who concurred in overturning the Pennsylvania law, dissented on the issue of congressional control over slavery. The U.S. Constitution, he insisted, restrained states only from interfering with slaveholders' property rights. States, in his view, possessed the power—even the obligation—to assist in protecting those rights.

As the national debate over slavery and its extension intensified during the 1850s, so too did Taney's partisan commitment to the South. In *Strader v. Graham* (1850), he dismissed a suit for damages involving several slaves who were taken briefly into Ohio and later fled from Kentucky into Canada. When the slaveowner sued several men who allegedly aided their escape, defense counsel argued that the Northwest Ordinance of 1787, which banned slavery in the Old Northwest, freed the slaves as soon as they stepped on Ohio soil. The Kentucky Court of Appeals rejected this argument, and the case went to the U.S. Supreme Court. Writing for a unanimous majority, Taney dismissed the case for lack of jurisdiction, claiming that Kentucky's laws superseded the Northwest Ordinance. Again, the chief justice hoped to preserve slaveholders' rights by upholding the states' power to protect slavery.

The pinnacle of Taney's proslavery constitutionalism came in *Dred Scott v. Sandford* (1857). Scott, a Missouri slave, accompanied his owner, an Army surgeon named John Emerson, to Illinois and later to Wisconsin Territory during the 1830s. Several years later, after Emerson's death, Scott initiated a suit against Emerson's wife claiming that by virtue of his residence in free territory, he had gained his freedom. The Missouri Supreme Court ruled against Scott, and even when he renewed his suit in federal court against his new owner, John F. A. Sanford (the name was misspelled in the official record), Scott was denied his liberty. Ultimately, he appealed to the U.S. Supreme Court.

Instead of confining himself to the specific question of Scott's status and standing to sue, Taney delivered a proslavery diatribe that revealed his deep devotion to slavery and southern values. Taney held that the lower federal court should have dismissed the case for lack of jurisdiction. Because Scott was black, according to Taney, he was not a citizen and had no right to sue. Even if he were a free black man, he was not a citizen under the U.S. Constitution. Blacks had long been considered, according to Taney, "so far inferior that they had no rights which the white man was bound to respect" (*Scott v. Sandford,* 19 Howard 393). Thus Taney not only ruled that Scott lacked standing to sue but also held, based on his interpretation of the Founders' intentions, that no African American could claim citizenship privileges under the Constitution.

The second part of Taney's opinion attacked congressional authority over slavery. Although some argued that this matter was not even before the Court, Taney attempted to steer the discussion of Scott's status to the larger question of slavery in the territories. According to Taney, Scott's sojourn in Wisconsin Territory did not make him a free man because Congress lacked the power to exclude slavery from the territories. Taney suggested that the Fifth Amendment's due process clause prohibited Congress from interfering with slavery in these areas because to do so would violate the property rights of slaveholders who settled there. In arguing that the right to hold slave property was grounded in the Constitution, Taney proved his unflagging support for slaveholders' rights. Northerners feared that Taney's proslavery rhetoric portended the nationalization of slavery—the right to take slaves anywhere in the Union—and the opinion exacerbated the sectional conflict that culminated in the Civil War.

Taney remained committed to proslavery principles for the rest of his life. Having positioned the Supreme Court squarely on the side of slaveowners in the *Dred Scott* case, he asserted the unqualified power of the national government to protect slaveholders' rights in *Ableman v. Booth* (1859). This case involved a Wisconsin abolitionist who had helped a fugitive escape, in violation of the Fugitive Slave Law of 1850. Waging a battle with the U.S. Supreme Court over jurisdiction, Wisconsin judges challenged federal authority to prosecute the alleged criminal. In response, Taney issued a sweeping statement of judicial authority, upheld the controversial law, and fanned the growing fears of those who viewed the national government as the captive of slaveholding interests.

Throughout his judicial career, Taney was a staunch advocate of slaveowners. His opinions, though occasionally flawed in their reading of history and inconsistent in their understanding of the relationship between the national government and the states, proved a powerful weapon for white southerners in their efforts to perpetuate slavery. Only a bloody civil war and the subsequent reconstruction of the nation's constitu-tional order would reverse Taney's consistently proslavery interpretation of the U.S. Constitution.

— *Timothy S. Huebner*

See also: *Ableman v. Booth; Dred Scott v. Sandford; Prigg v. Pennsylvania;* United States Constitution.

For Further Reading
Fehrenbacher, Don. 1978. *The Dred Scott Case: Its Significance in American Law and Politics.* New York: Oxford University Press.
Finkelman, Paul. 1994. "Hooted Down the Page of History": Reconsidering the Greatness of Chief Justice Taney," *Journal of Supreme Court History* : 83–102.
Huebner, Timothy S. 2003. *The Taney Court: Justices, Rulings, Legacy.* Santa Barbara, CA: ABC-CLIO.
Swisher, Carl. 1936. *Roger B. Taney.* New York: Macmillan.

TENTH AMENDMENT

The Tenth Amendment to the U.S. Constitution reads: "The powers not delegated to the United States by the Constitution, nor prohibited by it to the states, are reserved to the States respectively, or to the people." This amendment, ratified in 1791 as part of the Bill of Rights, was first used to support states' rights in the 1798 and 1799 Virginia and Kentucky Resolutions, and Thomas Jefferson had earlier cited it in his debate with Alexander Hamilton over the First Bank of the United States. Robert Hayne and John Calhoun cited the Virginia and Kentucky Resolutions during the nullification controversy of the 1830s, which concerned the right of states to declare null and void any federal law they deemed unconstitutional. The states' rights doctrine obviously related to slavery and was used as one of the main arguments for why the national government could not interfere with the issue. Even in the nullification controversy, however, states' rights took center stage and the amendment itself was relegated to secondary status, even though it was the intellectual backing for the doctrine.

Early in the history of this nation, however, the courts weakened the Tenth Amendment. In *McCulloch v. Maryland* (1819), the U.S. Supreme Court under John Marshall made several significant moves to allow the federal government to gain more power and thus reduced the importance of the Tenth Amendment. First, the Court moved to deny Maryland's right to tax the Second Bank of the United States, and generally prohibited states from taxing any "legitimate" federal function. Second, it expanded the government's powers far beyond those enumerated in the Constitution.

Third, it was in this case that Marshall crafted the term, and to some degree the idea, of the "living constitution," which means a Constitution that can grow with the times, and this Constitution is clearly one that usurps power from the states, limiting the Tenth Amendment. Marshall wrote: "We must never forget that this is a *constitution* we are expounding." By this he meant that a constitution must change with the times, as opposed to a law code, which should remain fixed.

Fourth, and most importantly for the discussion here, the Court noted that the Tenth Amendment did not have the word "expressly" in it, which meant that any power not specifically mentioned in the Constitution as being prohibited to the federal government, could be used by the federal government, as long as the power was "necessary and proper" to the carrying out of a legitimate function. This interpretation clearly limits the scope of the Tenth Amendment, even though this ruling was not noted by either Hayne or Calhoun in their speeches on nullification.

Congress, which drew up the Bill of Rights, had rejected an attempt to insert "expressly" into the Tenth Amendment (a corresponding provision in the Articles of Confederation discussed the "expressly delegated" powers of the national government), so this amendment, through Congress and the Supreme Court, was soon much more limited in scope than some had hoped it would be. Judge Spencer Roane of Virginia tried to answer *McCulloch* in a series of essays, arguing that the Supreme Court could not take away the reserved powers, but over time, obviously, *McCulloch* and Marshall carried the day.

Related to the slavery issue was also the idea that if Congress became accustomed to a wide use of a clause in the Constitution that allowed it to regulate interstate commerce, it might then try to regulate slavery as a part of commerce. Another Supreme Court case, the *Passenger Cases* (1849), removed the possibility that the transportation of persons would not be called commerce, and so the issue was fully a concern for the nation in the 1850s. Of course, as long as the balance in the Senate remained, the political guarantee of slavery was fairly certain, but the whole issue of Congress's power to regulate commerce added another part to the slavery debate. In addition, the Tenth Amendment was cited by both the majority and the dissent in *Dred Scott v. Sandford* (1857), and played a part in that ruling that further inflamed the nation.

The amendment has not been cited frequently in recent years. With regard to the power of Congress to regulate interstate commerce, the Supreme Court seemed to lay this issue to rest, for the most part, when it held for the government in *Wickard v. Filburn* in 1941. Some civil rights opponents tried to reinvigorate the whole doctrine of "states' rights" and the Tenth Amendment during the 1950s and 1960s, arguing that each state had the right to ignore the Supreme Court, nullify federal laws, and ignore civil rights reforms. It took nearly fifteen years, but civil rights reforms became the law of the land by the end of the 1960s. Finally, the Tenth Amendment was cited by both the majority and the dissent in a 1995 decision that struck down term limits for Alabama's representatives to the U.S. Congress in 1995 (*U.S. Term Limits*). Thus the issue of the bounds of federal power is still poignant, and the Tenth Amendment is not totally forgotten, even though it is not invoked that often.

— *Scott A. Merriman*

See also: *Dred Scott v. Sandford;* Hayne–Webster Debate; Nullification Doctrine; United States Constitution.

For Further Reading

Gunther, Gerald, ed. 1969. *John Marshall's Defense of McCulloch v. Maryland.* Stanford, CA: Stanford University Press.

Killenbeck, Mark R., ed. 2002. *The Tenth Amendment and State Sovereignty: Constitutional History and Contemporary Issues.* Lanham, MD: Rowman and Littlefield.

Moore, Wayne D. 1996. *Constitutional Rights and Powers of the People.* Princeton, NJ: Princeton University Press.

Shapiro, David L. 1995. *Federalism: A Dialogue.* Evanston, IL: Northwestern University Press.

36°30' NORTH LATITUDE

The boundary established at 36°30' north latitude separated Missouri (except for the so-called boot-heel region) from the Arkansas Territory and became one of the most significant borders within the United States during the antebellum era. Through the Missouri Compromise (1820), this line of demarcation limited slavery's expansion in the newly acquired Louisiana Purchase Territory to points south of the line while lands above it became free territory that prohibited slavery. Within the Louisiana Purchase Territory, the Missouri Compromise only allowed slavery to exist above the 36°30' north latitude line in Missouri, which was admitted to the Union as the twenty-second state in 1821. The decision issued by the U.S. Supreme Court in the *Dred Scott v. Sandford* (1857) case effectively nullified the portion of the Missouri Compromise that had created the line of demarcation between slave and free territory.

From the point of its inception in the Missouri Compromise, the line of 36°30' north latitude by design would have allowed slavery to expand only into the territory that eventually formed the states of Arkansas and Oklahoma. This restriction, coupled with the South's desire for additional territory where cotton and slavery might expand, encouraged southern interest in Texas and other lands of the Southwest that belonged to Mexico. When the United States and Mexico went to war in 1846, Congressman David Wilmot of Pennsylvania introduced an unsuccessful resolution (known as the Wilmot Proviso) that sought to prohibit the expansion of slavery into any territory that might be acquired from Mexico. In 1848, after the United States defeated Mexico and acquired the huge Mexican Cession territory in the Treaty of Guadalupe Hidalgo, some northern political leaders hoped that the 36°30' north latitude boundary might be extended westward to the Pacific Ocean.

By 1848 northern Democrats like Lewis Cass of Michigan and Stephen A. Douglas of Illinois believed that the answer to the slavery controversy could be settled best not by an inflexible line of demarcation, but rather by an ingenious new concept, which they termed popular sovereignty. According to this new policy, the people of a territory seeking statehood would have the opportunity to vote for or against slavery in a popular referendum. The Kansas–Nebraska Act (1854), which included a specific provision for popular sovereignty, ran counter to the decision reached in the Missouri Compromise by allowing the possibility that slavery might become established in lands north of 36°30' north latitude if such was the will expressed by territorial residents in a popular referendum. The Kansas–Nebraska Act reignited the largely sectional debate over slavery's expansion into the territories and in so doing furthered the resolve of the free soil movement in the United States, inspired the creation of the Republican Party, and led the nation, many would argue, much closer to civil war.

Protests for and against the 36°30' north latitude line became moot in 1857 when the Supreme Court ruled that slavery could effectively exist anywhere within the United States. More than an ordinary boundary between states, the line of 36°30' north latitude assumed a much larger meaning in the sectional debate over slavery's expansion into the western territories.

— *Junius P. Rodriguez*

See also: Kansas–Nebraska Act; Missouri Compromise; Popular Sovereignty.

For Further Reading

Fehrenbacher, Don E. 1980. *Sectional Crisis and Southern Constitutionalism.* Baton Rouge: Louisiana State University Press.

Ray, Perley Orman. 1909. *Repeal of the Missouri Compromise, Its Origin and Authorship.* Cleveland: A.H. Clark Company.

HENRY DAVID THOREAU (1817–1862)

Though initially a reluctant reformer, Henry David Thoreau gradually became an ardent supporter of the antislavery cause and employed his talent as a writer to persuade others of the moral imperative of abolition. Thoreau never joined an antislavery organization, primarily because he spurned organized movements in any form, but his lectures and essays helped convince thousands in the North that slavery was immoral. In the 1830s he primarily directed his energies toward his fledgling career as a writer, but he was sympathetic to the antislavery cause, and over the next thirty years, the national controversy surrounding slavery impelled him to become more active and more militant in his opposition to it.

In the early 1840s, Thoreau's essays on slavery ("Reform and the Reformers" and "Herald of Freedom") were cautious and advocated reform on an individual level. He made his own stand against slavery in 1846 by refusing to pay a poll tax. He would not support the federal government in its efforts to expand slave territory through a war with Mexico, and consequently he spent a night in the Concord, Massachusetts, jail. Thoreau saw this act of defiance as a championship of both individualism and the collective responsibility that citizens share for the actions of a representative government. After his release, he wrote the philosophical piece "Resistance to Civil Government," in which he advocated passive resistance to a government that defied the moral will of the people. His adherence to pacifism rather than violence is a central tenet of the essay. Other than his classic work *Walden* (1854), Thoreau is best remembered for his "Resistance" essay—which subsequent generations have known as "Civil Disobedience." It has been reprinted countless times and inspired Mahatma Gandhi, John F. Kennedy, and Martin Luther King, Jr.

During the 1850s events on both local and national levels caused Thoreau to revise his position that noncompliance was the only morally justifiable way to oppose slavery. He began to break the law actively by becoming part of the Underground Railroad, and he fostered friendships with abolitionists like Wendell Phillips, Horace Greeley, and Franklin Sanborn. The was appalled at how quickly New England's admiration for Brown's efforts in Kansas had turned to condemnation for his actions at Harpers Ferry. Thoreau wrote three essays in support of Brown, praising both his ideals and his willingness to act on them. All three essays—"A Plea for Captain John Brown," "Martyrdom of John Brown," and "The Last Days of John Brown"—emphasized Brown's high moral stature rather than his actions. In these works, Thoreau made it clear that he believed moral authority justified violence.

Thoreau exercised much influence in his native New England where his antislavery essays were widely read and discussed. His eloquent prose and the moral force of his arguments made him a powerful proponent of the abolitionist cause.

— Elizabeth Dubrulle

See also: Brown, John; Burns, Anthony; Fugitive Slave Act (1850); Harpers Ferry Raid; Shadrach Fugitive Slave Case; Transcendentalism; Underground Railroad.

For Further Reading

Glick, Wendell, ed. 1972. *The Writings of Henry D. Thoreau: Reform Papers.* Princeton, NJ: Princeton University Press.

Gougeon, Len. 1995. "Thoreau and Reform." In *The Cambridge Companion to Henry David Thoreau.* Ed. Joel Myerson. Cambridge: Cambridge University Press.

Harding, Walter. 1982. *The Days of Henry Thoreau: A Biography.* New York: Dover Publications.

Ostander, Gillman. 1955. "Emerson, Thoreau and John Brown." *Mississippi Valley Historical Review* 34 (March): 713–726.

Richardson, Robert D. 1986. *Henry Thoreau: A Life of the Mind.* Berkeley: University of California Press.

Taylor, Bob Pepperman. 1996. *America's Bachelor Uncle: Thoreau and the American Polity.* Lawrence: University of Kansas Press.

Worley, Sam McGuire. 2001. *Emerson, Thoreau, and the Role of the Cultural Critic.* Albany: State University of New York Press.

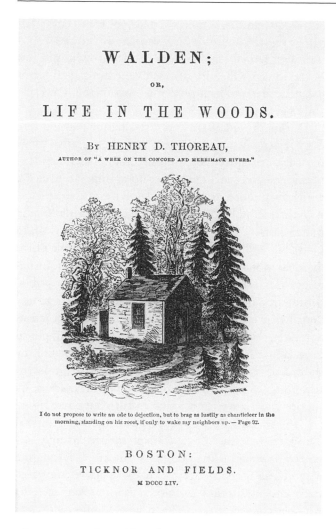

WALDEN;

OR,

LIFE IN THE WOODS.

By HENRY D. THOREAU,

AUTHOR OF "A WEEK ON THE CONCORD AND MERRIMACK RIVERS."

I do not propose to write an ode to dejection, but to brag as lustily as chanticleer in the morning, standing on his roost, if only to wake my neighbors up. — Page 92.

BOSTON:

TICKNOR AND FIELDS.

M DCCC LIV.

The cover of *Walden* depicts Thoreau's cabin at Walden Pond. (Library of Congress)

passage of the Fugitive Slave Act (1850) and the subsequent capture of Shadrach, Thomas Sims, and Anthony Burns—all in nearby Boston—ignited Thoreau's rage. In 1854 he wrote a scathing piece entitled "Slavery in Massachusetts," in which he lambasted the governor of Massachusetts for complying with the immoral Fugitive Slave Act, and he called on the state's citizens to defy it openly. Although he stopped short of advocating violence, he accepted the idea that force should be met with force when moral authority was at stake.

In 1859 John Brown's failed attempt to spark a slave insurrection at Harpers Ferry, Virginia, prompted an even stronger response from Thoreau. He had met Brown during one of Brown's fund-raising trips to New England in the mid-1850s, but although Thoreau supported Brown's cause, in a typical display of skepticism and parsimony, Thoreau refused to contribute money to the venture. After Brown's capture, however, Thoreau

TRANSCENDENTALISM

Transcendentalism was an intellectual, religious, and literary movement centered in New England in the mid-nineteenth century that helped to highlight and disseminate the moral imperative of the antislavery cause. The transcendentalist movement originated in the United States in the 1830s and 1840s as a reaction against established religion, particularly Unitarianism. Rejecting the notions that God's will could be interpreted only by ministers and that religious practice must follow guidelines specified by organized churches, transcendentalists believed that God's will was a constant, absolute truth that transcended physical phenomena and resided within everything in the universe, including man. Man could discover this higher law only by listening to his instincts and conscience rather than accepting a truth externally defined by traditional authorities like church and state. Once man discovered absolute truth, he was capable of reforming his behavior and attitudes to achieve perfection.

Reliance on instinct and conscience had two significant impacts on the movement. First, it meant that transcendentalists prized individualism and self-reliance, which produced an eclectic group whose members held varying opinions on almost every topic. The movement's spiritual center was Ralph Waldo Emerson, who relinquished his ministry in the Unitarian Church in 1836 following an intellectual crisis and shortly thereafter, in a commencement address at Harvard University, encouraged his listeners to undertake personal exploration of the soul. This spiritual call to arms, which was also articulated in his published writings, earned Emerson dozens of disciples, each of whom followed the dictates of his own conscience and many of whom followed him to Concord, Massachusetts.

Second, elevating individual conscience above society's established institutions resulted in a questioning of traditional notions concerning everything from the nature of the state to hygiene and housekeeping. This questioning coincided with and complemented the growing number of reform movements sweeping New England during the nineteenth century, and most transcendentalists sympathized with one reform cause or another. Although they desired reform, their belief in the integrity of the individual led many to spurn collective action as being too restrictive. Particularly in the movement's early years, reform on an individual basis was the only morally acceptable course of action.

From the beginning of the abolitionist movement, many transcendentalists were sympathetic to the cause, but their involvement varied. Some, like Henry David Thoreau, preferred to focus on reforming themselves before undertaking the reformation of those around them; others, like Amos Bronson Alcott, were involved in too many causes to contribute much time or energy to abolition; still others, Theodore Parker among them, threw themselves wholeheartedly into the antislavery effort. Regardless of the level of activism of individual transcendentalists, the plight of American slaves was kept at the forefront of transcendental thought by the efforts of the Concord Female Anti-Slavery Society, an extremely active and dynamic group that was organized and led by the wives, mothers, sisters, and daughters of many of transcendentalism's brightest lights. These women advocated abolition with ferocity and entertained in their homes and in the society's meetings most of the antislavery campaigners that came through the area in the late 1830s and 1840s.

During the late 1840s and 1850s, national events like the Mexican War (1846–1848) and the Fugitive Slave Act (1850) produced a unanimity among transcendentalists as such events made the moral imperative of the antislavery cause undeniable. One by one, transcendentalists concluded that slavery contaminated the moral basis of the whole country and clearly violated God's higher law. In this one issue, the principle of individual moral reform gave way to the necessity for national moral reform, leading many to seek more public forums for their advocacy. Transcendentalists maintained that the higher law that forbade such practices as slavery was not intended to work on a philosophical plane above society but through society itself, with the actions of individuals serving as the most transparent window into the true nature of that society. Thus, by supporting a government that in turn supported slavery, all Americans in effect had become slaveholders. The fact that the U.S. government increasingly appeared to sanction the peculiar institution, despite the heightened agitation against it, particularly infuriated transcendentalists and prompted them to view slavery's demise as an intensely personal responsibility.

For many transcendentalists, philosophy gave way to action when authorities decided to return the fugitive Anthony Burns to slavery. The crowd that rushed the Boston courthouse to free Burns contained many transcendentalists, including Parker and Alcott. Transcendentalists spoke out publicly against slavery, and some aided in the activities of the Underground Railroad. Several fell under John Brown's influence when he toured New England raising additional funds for his work, and the young transcendentalist Franklin Sanborn was one of "the secret six" who financially supported Brown's raid on Harpers Ferry. In commemorative addresses, Thoreau and Emerson rushed to Brown's defense after the failed insurrection, lauding Brown's high principles and idealism, although they refrained from mentioning his violent acts.

The antislavery movement gained moral strength from the transcendentalists and their increasing willingness to break man-made decrees that violated God's higher law. In this respect, the impact of transcendentalist thought was far greater than the contributions of the transcendentalists themselves. A younger generation of reformers, like Sanborn and Thomas Wentworth Higginson, believed that obedience to a higher law justified all means, including violence and coercion, that were necessary to abolish slavery. This sense of righteousness contributed to the moral backbone of the antislavery cause during the 1850s as it challenged the government on traditional notions concerning the will of the majority and the rights of the governed.

— *Elizabeth Dubrulle*

See also: Brown, John; Burns, Anthony; Fugitive Slave Act (1850); Harpers Ferry Raid; Higginson, Thomas Wentworth; Thoreau, Henry David; Underground Railroad.

For Further Reading
Boller, Paul F. 1974. *American Transcendentalism, 1830–1860: An Intellectual Inquiry.* New York: G.P. Putnam's Sons.

Brasher, Alan Dale. 1996. "Romantic Individualism, Antislavery, and Race: Transcendentalism in the Decade before the Civil War." Ph.D. dissertation. University of South Carolina, Columbia, South Carolina.

Harding, Walter. 1982. *The Days of Henry Thoreau: A Biography.* New York: Dover.

Ledbetter, Patsy S., and Billy Ledbetter. 1980. "The Agitator and the Intellectuals: William Lloyd Garrison and the New England Transcendentalists." *Mid-America* 62 (October): 173–185.

Myerson, Joel, ed. 1984. *The Transcendentalists: A Review of Research and Criticism.* New York: Modern Language Association of America.

Petrulionis, Sandra Harbert. 2001. "'Swelling That Great Tide of Humanity': The Concord, Massachusetts, Female Anti-Slavery Society." *New England Quarterly* 74 (3): 385–418.

Rose, Anne C. 1981. *Transcendentalism as a Social Movement, 1830–1850.* New Haven, CT: Yale University Press.

Worley, Sam McGuire. 2001. *Emerson, Thoreau, and the Role of Cultural Critic.* Albany: State University of New York Press.

TRANSITION FROM SLAVE LABOR TO FREE LABOR

For over two centuries, various forms of unfree labor, especially African slavery, predominated in North America. After a short civil war, free labor triumphed over slave labor. How did this come about? British settlements in the Caribbean and mainland colonies fueled the demand for agricultural labor and its social reproduction where land was plentiful, crops and markets were lucrative, and labor was scarce. The gradual decision to switch from the labor of English and Irish convicts and indentured servants to African slaves was essentially an economic one made by English merchants and planters who found a system of economic-based racial exploitation conducive to their best interests. The logical consequence of this decision to enslave was the rise of racial plantations in the British Americas worked by African slaves managed by white masters and overseers producing cash crops for consumption in European markets. Beginning in the late seventeenth century, a plantation revolution moved through the mainland Chesapeake, low country, and northern colonies as a result of the massive arrival of African slaves. This entailed the making of a regional disparity on the colonial mainland between societies with slaves in northern colonies and slave societies in the southern colonies. These regional differences were reinforced through wartime erosion, nation building, and gradual emancipation laws from the late eighteenth century onward. Many of the newly freed laborers ended up working as laborers, domestics, artisans, and sailors exchanging their labor for some form of compensation in the postrevolutionary decades.

Although this First Emancipation was significant—not least to slaves themselves—the most critical transition from slave to free labor in North America emerged as a result of a bloody civil war. During the antebellum decades, slave labor in the South and free labor in the North coexisted uneasily in the new nation. Slavery was the dominant system in the South politically and economically despite the existence of a majority of nonslaveholders. By 1860 there were 3.9 million slaves in fifteen southern states. This represented one-third of the South's population. It also represented two-thirds of all existing slaves in the New World. Meanwhile, free labor, especially wage labor, was becoming more important in the northern states, which increasingly removed independent producers from the land into the vortex of competitive market relations. These competing systems clashed over the future status of the western territories, although there seemed less dissent over the removal of Native Americans. The result was civil war.

The American Civil War began with different agendas. The North claimed it was fighting for the preservation of the Union; the South said it was fighting on behalf of states' rights. In actuality, both regions were fighting over the existence of slavery in American society. Although John Brown's raid on Harpers Ferry in 1859 provided a hint, it was the actions of the slaves themselves that revealed this social reality during the chaos of war. Drawing upon the armed struggle between the two regions for control over their own lives and labors, the slaves helped to transform the civil war into a liberation struggle. Their actions included self-emancipation toward federal lines; working as free laborers in army outposts as diggers, cooks, nurses, and servants; fighting for the Union military; work slowdowns on the plantations in the absence of white supervision; and undermining the psychological security of the slave regime. The slaves placed freedom on the Civil War agenda. As slave labor withered, free labor relations germinated according to specific regional, historical, and temporal conditions.

The military surrender at Appomattox together with passage of the Thirteenth Amendment to the U.S. Constitution in 1865 ratified an imminent social process. Slavery was legally abolished along with the material basis for the plantocracy's domination, but the central transformation occurred in master–slave relations. Former labor lords were transformed into landlords whose property and power were devastated by emancipation. Former slaves gained their personal freedom through the culmination of their successful struggle against slavery, but they were also freed from the minimum material support provided through slaveholders' economic interests. Once the former slaves were forced to work but were only minimally provided for; they were still forced to work but now free to starve.

The freed people only had their labor power to survive in a vicious marketplace of competing landlords, disgruntled former secessionists, and federal employees demanding their return to work. A myriad of labor arrangements emerged, including daily, weekly and monthly wage labor, tenancy, and crop sharing. The most popular form of free labor to emerge in the postemancipation plantation South was sharecropping as landlords sought labor and freed people sought autonomy. The crucial point about this complex postwar situation was that former slaves exchanged their labor for some form of compensation, which rendered them landless, unpropertied, and poor. The Republican Party's attempt to reshape the defeated South into a region of independent farmers existing in a free market under the rule of law essentially failed. If slave labor meant more than master–slave relations, its abolition did also. With emancipation, subsistence farmers in the South became increasingly drawn into the vortex of the cash-crop economy. The path had been cleared for northern and foreign capitalist penetration into the prostrate South on its own unimpeded terms. A similar unchecked advance of capital and social relations of free labor moved into the American West, especially after the final military subjugation of the Plains Indians during the 1870s. This free market, free labor free-for-all contributed to a prolonged economic depression from 1873 through 1896. Rural protest, the politics of Populism, and urban emigration were the consequence. This freeing of labor from the land was the ultimate rung in the emancipation ladder, and it reached across all postemancipation societies. By the 1890s the United States was poised to continue its expansion beyond its territorial borders. The recent rhetoric of making the world safe for free markets through globalization suggests that this transition remains unfinished.

— *Jeffrey R. Kerr-Ritchie*

For Further Reading
Berlin, Ira. 1998. *Many Thousands Gone: The First Two Centuries of Slavery in North America.* Cambridge, MA: Belknap Press.

Foner, Eric. 1988. *Reconstruction: America's Unfinished Revolution.* New York: Harper and Row.

Freedom Southern Society Project. 1982–. *Freedom: A Documentary History of Emancipation, 1861–1867.* Cambridge: Cambridge University Press.

Kerr-Ritchie, Jeffrey R. 1999. *Freedpeople in the Tobacco South, Virginia, 1860–1900.* Chapel Hill: University of North Carolina Press.

Reidy, Joseph P. 1992. *From Slavery to Agrarian Capitalism in the Cotton South: Central Georgia, 1800–1880.* Chapel Hill: University of North Carolina Press.

TRIANGULAR TRADE

In the triangular trade, a ship would depart from Newport, Rhode Island, for the west coast of Africa with New England rum. In Africa, most of the rum would be sold, and slaves would be purchased; a small amount of the rum would be used as currency to purchase slaves from tribal chiefs in the African interior. The slave-castle governors of the foreign powers of England, France, Holland, Portugal, and Denmark obtained the slaves from tribal chieftains and other brokers and housed the slaves in the castles until they were shipped abroad. The slaves would be chained down on small packed boats and taken to the West Indies for sale. The voyage was rough, and many slaves died en route from the terrible conditions. In the West Indies, the slaves would be sold for large sums of money, and the sugar needed for molasses and rum production would be purchased; the sugar would then be taken to New England.

In Newport there were some twenty-two stills that converted sugar into rum as early as 1730. In 1764 there were more than thirty distilling houses in Rhode Island. In the 1770s some 184 vessels in Rhode Island were involved in the slave trade—surpassed in quantity in the colonies only by South Carolina. Most owners never set foot on their ships and had no physical contact with the slaves. The owners hired slaver captains to organize the ships and conduct price negotiations with the resident governors in Africa.

For example, two New England merchants, Aaron Lopez and his father-in-law Jacob Rivera of Newport, were active in sending ships to Africa with rum and other goods in exchange for slaves. They sent their first ship, the *Grayhound,* in 1761 to Africa to buy slaves and sell them in the Caribbean. Lopez sent at least eighteen ships to Africa to purchase slaves, and after Lopez had terminated his activities in this area in about 1774 or 1775, Rivera continued to send ships to Africa. Lopez owned at least twenty-six ships and was a major, if not the foremost, merchant in Newport. The clergyman Ezra Stiles, first president of Yale University, praised Lopez by describing him as "a Merchant of the first Eminence; for Honor and Extent of Commerce probably surpassed by no Merchant in America" (Marcus, 1970). A ship of slaves could yield between £1,500 and £2,000, making the slave trade a lucrative business. The ship owners had virtually no contact with their ships or the slaves, and the slave trade was but one component of this monetary transaction connected with the triangular trade.

— *Yitzchak Kerem*

For Further Reading

Birmingham, Stephen. 1971. *The Grandees, America's Sephardic Elite.* New York: Harper and Row.

Chyet, Stanley F. 1963. "Aaron Lopez: A Study in Buenafama." *American Jewish Historical Quarterly* 52: 295–309.

Marcus, Jacob R. 1970. *The Colonial American Jew 1492–1776.* Detroit, MI: Wayne State University Press.

SOJOURNER TRUTH (C. 1797–1883)

Sojourner Truth was an emancipated slave who became a prominent independent orator for women's rights, antislavery, and freedmen's rights. In 1826 Truth left her New York owner and took refuge with a nearby white family, the Van Wagenens. When she refused to return to her owner, Isaac Van Wagenen purchased her to keep her out of jail. Freed in 1827 under New York's gradual emancipation law, Truth sued later that year to have her son freed from slavery. Most African Americans did not turn to the courts for redress, and those who did rarely succeeded, but Truth won her son's freedom. She had a religious conversion, and in 1832 she joined the Kingdom of Matthias, a religious cult that collapsed in scandal two years later. Determined to become a traveling evangelist independent of any church, she changed her name from Isabella to So-

Sojourner Truth was a former slave who became a leader in the battle against slavery. (National Archives)

journer; by some accounts, she said that God gave her the last name Truth.

Sojourner Truth did not actively work against slavery until about 1850. In the years that followed, she was an effective itinerant speaker for abolitionism and women's rights in New England, New York, Pennsylvania, and the Midwest. She spoke extemporaneously and with great power; like other ex-slave orators, she incorporated her own experiences into her speeches, and like other preachers, she drew on parables and lively images. Because Truth was illiterate, her words have come to us through accounts written by other people, accounts that are necessarily shaped by their interpretation of her.

Her best known speech, "Ar'n't I a Woman," is a case in point. Truth spoke at an 1851 women's rights meeting in Akron, Ohio; twelve years later Francis Gage, an abolitionist and women's rights leader, wrote an account of the speech, which was then included in an 1875 revision of Truth's *Narrative of the Life of Sojourner Truth.* Gage cast the speech in a caricature of slave dialect, which Truth herself did not use. Moreover, some historians argue that Truth may not have given the speech at all. Her autobiography, which she sold to help support herself, was dictated to Olive Gilbert, a white abolitionist. Truth was a shrewd woman, and she understood the value of the stories told about her effectiveness as an orator.

After the Civil War, Truth continued to work for equal rights for women and especially for African Americans. She helped resettle freedmen and campaigned for western land for them, attempted to desegregate the Washington, D.C., streetcars, and tried to vote in Michigan. "Ar'n't I a Woman" has made her important to the twentieth-century women's rights and civil rights activists, and the facts of her life justify seeing her as a strong and independent black woman fighting for justice.

— *Andrea M. Atkin*

See also: Women and the Antislavery Movement.

For Further Reading
   Mabee, Carleton. 1993. *Sojourner Truth: Slave, Prophet, Legend.* New York: New York University Press.
   Painter, Nell Irvin. 1996. *Sojourner Truth: A Life, a Symbol.* New York: Norton.
   Truth, Sojourner. 1991. *Narrative of Sojourner Truth; A Bondswoman of Olden Time.* Ed. Olive Gilbert. New York: Oxford University Press.

HARRIET TUBMAN (C.1821–1913)

Harriet Tubman was born a slave in Dorchester County, Maryland, to Harriet Greene Ross and Benjamin Ross, who had ten other children. As a child, Harriet was assigned simple domestic chores, but she was moved to the fields in her early teens, and there, despite her small stature, Tubman developed legendary physical strength and stamina. When she attempted to prevent the punishment of another slave by the overseer, Tubman was hit on the head with a two-pound weight; in later life she often wore a turban to hide the scar. Her marriage to John Tubman, a free black, did not survive her escape to freedom in Pennsylvania in 1849, for when she returned for him, he had already married another woman and refused to accompany her north. Tubman continued to use his name, however—even after she remarried.

For more than a decade, Tubman made numerous trips back into the slave South to bring slaves to freedom in the North. Her success as a "rescuer" of slaves resulted in the circulation of reward posters bearing her description throughout the South and the border states. She armed herself with a rifle, both to protect herself from slave catchers and to bolster the courage of a slave who might change his or her mind and endanger the others. Tubman's religious faith strength-

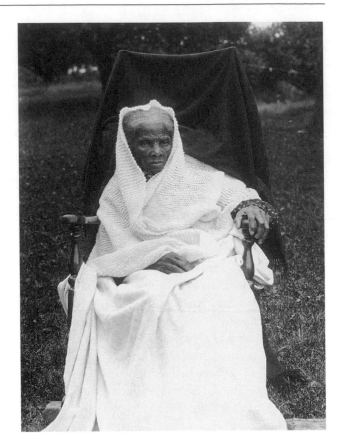

Known to many as "Moses," Harriet Tubman was the best-known leader of the Underground Railroad. (Library of Congress)

ened her in her weariness, and she often sang spirituals as she accompanied fugitives on their journey. Although she most often worked alone, Tubman was in touch with other workers along the Underground Railroad, including William Still of Pennsylvania; antislavery activists Charlotte Forten and Frederick Douglass commended her work to undermine slavery.

During the Civil War, Tubman acted as a scout for Union military operations. Because of her generosity to others, she was often penniless herself. Petitions to the War Department on Tubman's behalf for a pension for her services rendered were not successful, although in 1890 Tubman finally received a widow's pension for the service her second husband (Nelson Davis) had rendered to the Union army. Selling photographs of herself was among the methods Tubman used to support herself during tough times, a strategy she described as "selling the image to keep the substance alive" (Buhle, 2000). In this canny use of her own likeness, Tubman, like Sojourner Truth and others, demonstrated a clear awareness of her significance in the history as well as the myth of U.S. activism and social change.

After the war, Tubman focused her energies on women's rights and helping the poor, working with the National Association of Colored Women, which later granted Tubman a lifetime pension. Because of her religious convictions, Tubman also worked closely with black churches, soliciting donations of used clothing and food for the poor and elderly in New York State, where she lived.

Tubman used money from her own meager store to buy a small parcel of land adjacent to her house to erect a home for the elderly poor, which was ultimately operated by the African Methodist Episcopal Zion Church. An invalid in her old age, Tubman lived for two years at the Harriet Tubman Home for Aged and Indigent Colored People until her death in 1913. She has been honored by a U.S. postage stamp, and her home in Auburn, New York, is recognized as a national landmark.

Although she was one of a limited number of slave women who successfully escaped, because she was illiterate Tubman left no memoir. Still, historian George Rawick perhaps said it best: "Why must we always use Nat as the name for the rebellious slave? Why not Harriet?" (Sterling, 1984).

— *Dale Edwyna Smith*

See also: Forten, Charlotte; Still, William; Underground Railroad.

For Further Reading
Buhle, Paul. 2000. "The Sharecroppers' Tale." In *Civil Rights: A Reader on the Black Struggle Since 1787.* Ed. Jonathan Birnbaum and Clarence Taylor. New York: New York University Press.

Quarles, Benjamin. 1969. *Black Abolitionists.* New York: Oxford University Press.

Sterling, Dorothy, ed. 1984. *We Are Your Sisters: Black Women in the Nineteenth Century.* New York: Norton.

Thompson, Priscilla. 1986. "Harriet Tubman, Thomas Garrett, and the Underground Railroad." *Delaware History* 22 (September): 1–21.

ST. GEORGE TUCKER (1752–1827)

The author of a five-volume U.S. edition of *Blackstone's Commentaries* (1803), *Dissertation on Slavery* (1796), and noted jurist, St. George Tucker was the only prominent member of the generation who fought in the American Revolution to publish a plan for abolishing slavery in Virginia. Tucker was born in Bermuda in 1752. In 1771 he entered the North American mainland to study law under George Wythe at the College of William and Mary. Tucker became a member of the Virginia Bar in 1774, but his law practice was shortened by the Revolutionary War. He reached the rank of lieutenant colonel, and he was injured at Yorktown. After the war Tucker practiced law at the General Court, Chancery Court, and Court of Appeals. In 1786 he served as part of Virginia's delegation at the Annapolis Convention. In 1790 he was appointed professor of law and police at the College of William and Mary, replacing George Wythe.

Tucker considered the introduction of slavery as one of America's greatest misfortunes and accordingly sought advice on how it might be ended in Virginia. He initiated a correspondence with prominent figures in Massachusetts—including Jeremy Belknap, James Sullivan, and John Adams—"having observed, with much pleasure, that slavery [had] been wholly exterminated from the Massachusetts" (St. George Tucker to Jeremy Belknap, January 24, 1795). Tucker posed a series of eleven questions "respecting the Introduction, Progress, and Abolition of Slavery in Massachusetts." This correspondence continued into summer 1795, and in 1796 Tucker published *A Dissertation on Slavery: With a Proposal for the Gradual Abolition of It, in the State of Virginia.* The *Dissertation* was the only significant antislavery pamphlet to come out of Virginia in the country's early years. Tucker published his edition of *Blackstone's Commentaries* (1803), with annotations and appendices, commenting on the law of the United States and of Virginia. He included his *Dissertation on Slavery* as an appendix. Tucker clearly recognized the tragic irony of the continuance of slavery in that revolutionary age. "Whilst we were offering up vows at the shrine of liberty, and sacrificing hecatombs upon her . . . we were imposing upon our fellow men, who differ in complexion from us, *slavery,* ten thousand times more cruel than the utmost extremity of those grievances and oppressions, of which we complained" (Cullen, 1987).

Despite those impassioned sentiments, Tucker was no radical abolitionist. His plan called for a very gradual emancipation that would not eliminate all slavery in Virginia for nearly a century. Tucker himself was a substantial slaveholder, having acquired slaves upon his marriage in 1778 to Francis Bland, the widow of John Randolph of Matoax. Moreover, when given the opportunity as a jurist to rule that slavery was outlawed by the Virginia Constitution, Tucker refused.

In 1803 Tucker resigned from William and Mary and in 1804, was appointed to the Virginia Supreme Court of Appeals. *Hudgins v. Wrights* came to the Supreme

A newspaper cartoon depicts the violent slave uprising led by Nat Turner. The uprising began on August 22, 1831, when Turner killed his master and his master's family. The revolt only lasted about a week, but Turner eluded capture until October of that year. He was later tried and hanged for the crime. (Library of Congress)

Court from a ruling of Chancellor George Wythe, Tucker's teacher and predecessor at William and Mary. Wythe had ruled that the Virginia Constitution declaration that all men are free and equal abolished slavery. Judge Tucker, disagreed. He noted that this provision of the Virginia Bill of Rights was "notoriously framed with a cautious eye" and only applied to free persons [1 Hen. and M. (Va.) 134 (1806)]. Despite Tucker's limitations as an antislavery advocate, he should be remembered most as the only Virginian of the revolutionary age to make a genuine attempt to abolish slavery.

— *David M. Cobin*

See also: Compensated Emancipation; Gradualism.

For Further Reading
 Cullen, Charles T. 1987. *St. George Tucker and Law in Virginia, 1772–1804*. New York: Garland.
 Hamilton, Phillip. 1998. "Revolutionary Principles and Family Loyalties: Slavery's Transformation in the St. George Tucker Household of Early National Virginia." *William and Mary Quarterly* 55 (4): 531–556.
 Kurland, Phillip B., and Ralph Lerner. 1987. *The Founders' Constitution*. Chicago: University of Chicago Press.
 Tucker, St. George. 1996. *Blackstone's Commentaries*, 5 vols. New Jersey Law Book Exchange.

NAT TURNER (1800–1831)

Nat Turner was a black mystic who led an insurrection against white families in Southampton County, Virginia, on August 22, 1831. Turner's was the most famous of the southern slave insurrections because of its bloodiness and the fear it instilled in southern whites.

The son of slave parents, Nat was born on October 2, 1800, on Benjamin Turner's plantation near Jerusalem in Southampton County, Virginia. He attended prayer services and Sunday chapel at his Methodist master's insistence, and as a youth, he played alongside white children. He demonstrated a superior intelligence, teaching himself to read and write, and even read and studied the Bible with his master's encouragement.

Several events changed his life dramatically. Shortly after his father escaped to the North, Nat and his mother, Nancy, were loaned to master Benjamin's son, Samuel. In 1810 the elder Turner died, leaving Nat and his mother the property of Samuel Turner, a strict taskmaster who insisted that his slaves obey him. In 1812 Nat was devastated when he was put to work in the fields. No longer could he play, associate with white children, or follow intellectual pursuits.

Nat became increasingly despondent. In 1812 he escaped the plantation but returned on his own after a month of hiding, claiming that "the Spirit" had instructed him to do so. He took a wife, Cherry, shortly thereafter. In 1822 Samuel Turner died, and Nat and Cherry were sold to separate masters in Southhampton County. Although Nat was able to visit Cherry and have children by her, he was not able to have the family life he desired. His new master, Thomas Moore, demanded even more labor of him. As he grew unhappier, Nat turned to Scripture for guidance.

In his *Confessions* (1831), Nat stated that religion became the dominant motivating factor in his young adult life. He recalled that as a youth, other slaves deemed him a "prophet" because he described events that had occurred before his birth. His role as a prophet and mystic increased through early adulthood, and in 1825, he had a vision in which "white spirits and black spirits engaged in battle" appeared beneath a darkened sun as "blood flowed in streams." Shortly thereafter, he claimed to see angels in the sky, blood on the corn in the fields, and symbols on tree leaves.

Proclaiming himself a Baptist preacher, Turner described his visions to slave congregations at Sunday prayer meetings that he conducted. He emphasized the approach of Judgment Day, when God would raise the slave above the master. Preparing for his own role on Judgment Day, he gathered a small following of slaves and free blacks to assist him, telling them, "I am commissioned by Jesus Christ and act under his direction."

Turner continued laboring on weekdays and preaching on Sundays. In 1827 a white overseer asked Turner to baptize him. When local churches refused to allow Turner the use of an altar for the ceremony, he used a nearby pond. He did not forget the insult white church leaders had extended him, and his disillusionment grew. In 1828 he had another vision, which he also described in his *Confessions,* "The Spirit instantly appeared to me and said the Serpent was loosened, and Christ had laid down the yoke he had borne for the sins of men, and that I should take it on and fight against the Serpent, for the time was fast approaching when the first shall be last and the last should be first."

This vision, combined with a chain of circumstances in Turner's life, moved him toward insurrection. Upon telling his master, Thomas Moore, that slaves would be free "one day or other," he was thrashed for insubordination. When Moore died later that year, Nat became the property of the deceased's nine-year-old son until Moore's widow re-married in 1829 and Joseph Travis became Turner's new master. Turner did the work expected of him to gain Travis's "greatest confidence" and thereby be permitted to continue preaching and waiting for a sign from God. In February 1831 a solar eclipse was the first sign Turner needed to proceed with plans for insurrection. A second occurred August 13 when the sun grew dim and a black spot appeared on its surface.

In the early hours of Monday, August 22, Turner and six followers quietly entered Joseph Travis's house. Armed with axes, they killed all five whites in the home, including an infant in its cradle. From the Travis farm, Turner and his followers moved from house to house, killing whites as they went. Attracting followers and weapons on the way, they soon numbered nearly sixty men mounted on horseback and armed with axes, swords, guns, and clubs. They killed a total of fifty-five white men, women, and children.

News of the insurrection spread quickly. Confrontations with armed bands of whites resulted in the death of many of Turner's men and the dispersal of the rest. By Sunday, August 28, federal troops, militia, and armed bands of whites had killed or captured all but a handful of the insurrectionists, including Turner. He had evaded capture for nearly six weeks by hiding in a dugout under some fence rails. Finally found and captured on October 30, Turner recited his *Confessions,* an explanation of his actions, to attorney Thomas Gray on November 1. He was tried, found guilty, and sentenced to death on November 5, 1831, and hanged six days later.

Nat Turner's insurrection shocked and frightened Virginians. Because of the insurrection, Virginia's legislature held its last serious debate on ending slavery in 1832, and Virginia and most southern states eventually passed strict laws to police their slave populations and prevent insurrections. Believing that abolitionism had somehow caused the uprising, most southerners also abandoned the cause of emancipation in the aftermath of Turner's insurrection.

— *Mary Jo Miles*

See also: Virginia's Slavery Debate.

For Further Reading
Greenberg, Kenneth S. 1996. *The Confessions of Nat Turner and Related Documents.* Boston: St. Martin's Press.

Oates, Stephen B. 1990. *The Fires of Jubilee: Nat Turner's Fierce Rebellion.* New York: Harper and Row.

∿ U ∿

UNCLE TOM'S CABIN (1852)

Harriet Beecher Stowe's most famous work, *Uncle Tom's Cabin,* was intended, in common with other nineteenth-century abolitionist literature, to turn its readers against the institution of slavery. Its success was remarkable. It sold some 3 million copies in the United States alone and was translated into many languages, and it became the first U.S. book to be a European best-seller.

The Compromise of 1850, together with the Fugitive Slave Act, was the primary impetus for Stowe's novel, but letters from friends also played their part. Her sister-in-law, in particular, urged Stowe to write about the major moral issue of the day with the words: "If I could use a pen as you can, I would write something that would make this whole nation feel what accursed thing slavery is." Stowe had increasingly been driven to public and written comment on the iniquities of slavery, but on March 9, 1851, she wrote to Gamaliel Bailey, editor of the *National Era,* to tell him that the time had come when even women and children should speak out for freedom and humanity. She asked him to accept a work that painted a picture of slavery as she and her acquaintances knew it. *Uncle Tom's Cabin* began as a serial on June 5, 1851, the first installment occupying most of the front page.

Stowe's first-hand knowledge of slavery was limited, so for her facts she relied heavily on Theodore Dwight Weld's *American Slavery as It Is* (1859). Inevitably, given the large number of slave narratives being written, used and abused, in the abolitionist cause, her contemporaries searched for the "real Uncle Tom" among them. Josiah Henson, one of the best known fugitive slaves, whose autobiography, first published in 1849, told of his escape to Canada, was particularly associated with Uncle Tom. For many, Henson symbolized the successful fugitive, and versions of his autobiography that appeared after the publication of *Uncle Tom's Cabin* contained considerable alterations. As he aged, Henson, too, believed himself to be the model for Uncle Tom. His cabin and grave in rural Ontario became a tourist attraction, and the "Home of Uncle Tom" was still being advertised as such as late as the 1950s (Davis and Gates, 1990). *Uncle Tom's Cabin* was a phenomenon with far-reaching effects.

The story of *Uncle Tom's Cabin* is simple enough. Tom, a valued slave of the Shelby household, is sold to pay off debts and is thus separated from his wife,

Harriet Beecher Stowe's *Uncle Tom's Cabin* was intended to turn its readers against the institution of slavery. It sold some three million copies in the United States alone and was translated into many languages. It was the first U.S. book to become a best-seller in Europe. (Library of Congress)

Chloe, and his family. His life forms the basis of the plot. He is sold downriver, first to St. Clare whose daughter, Eva, Tom rescues from drowning, and ultimately to the evil Simon Legree, in whose ownership Tom dies. As the serial continued long past the original projection of four weeks, another story line developed. This one told of the adventures of Eliza who, having overheard Mr. Shelby agree to sell her young son flees with her son to join her runaway husband, George. Tom's story exposes the reader to the horrors of slavery as he travels deeper and deeper into the South; Eliza's story exposes the reader to the fears of the runaway as she and her family travel north to freedom.

Prior to writing *Uncle Tom's Cabin,* Stowe wrote mainly about the domestic sphere and sentimental love, subject matter that was deemed suitable for a woman. Her achievement in *Uncle Tom's Cabin* was to transfer the techniques of "the lady's novel" to a subject with which it was not associated—that of slavery. Her text insists that African American slaves should be perceived as fellow humans possessed of a moral dignity that often surpasses that of the white population. Stowe's slaves suffer when their families are disrupted and their women are exploited, and when they are lashed, they bleed.

The novel relocates the moral center of society away from those with power, that is, the white males of the text, and places it firmly in the realm of the weak and defenseless—with the women, children, and slaves. Nor are the rhetorical strategies at work in the text purely sentimental. It is made clear from the beginning of the novel that the sale of Tom is "God's curse on slavery." Mrs. Shelby's words initiate a providential plot line in which Tom is marked as God's own and all human efforts to save him are doomed to failure.

Stowe reinforces divine authority throughout the novel, emphasizing the religious view of U.S. history via a vast array of scriptural imagery, parallels, quotations, preaching, and sermons. Eliza's famous river crossing is thus both actual and symbolic, and Tom and Eva share a simplicity of faith to which all might aspire. The business of chattel slavery demanded a world without God or conscience, but the character of Tom, whose Christ-like demeanor enables his submission to the worst that slavery can offer, ensures that the first concern remains with God and salvation.

The nineteenth-century reader would have been fully aware of what was at stake: it was eternal life and the death not only of bodies, but of souls. Yet, in the twentieth century, Tom's submissiveness has created considerable debate. To many critics, his submissiveness has seemed incongruous, even objectionable, when measured against the tenets of realism, political or social, rather than in terms of a nineteenth-century Christian ideal. The most famous challenge comes from James Baldwin's "Everybody's Protest Novel" in *Notes of a Native Son* (1955), in which he argues that Eliza and George escape only because they are mulatto and can pass as white; the blacker Uncle Tom is condemned by the text to die a slave. Baldwin concludes that the text is racist.

Throughout much of the twentieth century, the designation of an "Uncle Tom" was pejorative and used to indicate an African American's unnecessarily sycophantic stance toward the white population. This usage may have come about as much through the innumerable stage and film versions of *Uncle Tom's Cabin*—none of which were authorized by Stowe and from which she received no profit—than from any reading of the texts. These stage and film versions emphasized the stereotype, brought into being the "blacked-up" character that allowed white actors to play Afro-American roles, and did much to bring into being the minstrelsy tradition. From 1853 to 1930 the play of *Uncle Tom's Cabin,* especially George L. Aiken's adaptation, was probably never off the boards, and Americans who saw no other play saw this one. There may have been as many as five hundred troupes operating in the 1890s with productions, to quote one critic, "surpassing the fantastic and bordering on the insane" (Crozier, 1969).

In 1918 Paramount produced a feature film, with Marguerite Clark playing both Eva and Topsy; Universal filmed an elaborate production in 1927; and a 1932 version by the Moscow Art Theater emphasized the miseries of the slave, had Topsy save Eva's life, and omitted all reference to religion.

It has been claimed that *Uncle Tom's Cabin* altered the course of history and that Abraham Lincoln once referred to Harriet Beecher Stowe as the woman who "started the Civil War." In its day, the work was praised by writers as diverse as George Eliot, Fyodor Dostoevski, and George Sand. More recent studies have recognized the revolutionary nature of the text in terms of women's writing. It may be that no other novel, before or since, has done so much to alter the thinking of an entire generation.

— *Jan Pilditch*

See also: Compromise of 1850; Fugitive Slave Act (1850); Stowe, Harriet Beecher; Weld, Theodore Dwight.

For Further Reading

Crozier, Alice C. 1969. *The Novels of Harriet Beecher Stowe.* New York: Oxford University Press.

Davis, Charles T., and Henry Louis Gates, Jr., eds. [1985] 1990. *The Slave's Narrative.* New York: Oxford University Press.

Foster, Charles H. 1954. *The Rungless Ladder: Harriet Beecher Stowe and New England Puritanism.* Durham, NC: Duke University Press.

Kirkham, Bruce E. 1977. *The Building of Uncle Tom's Cabin.* Knoxville: University of Tennessee Press.

Lowance, Mason I., Jr., Ellen E. Westbrook, and R. C. DeProspo, eds. 1994. *The Stowe Debate: Rhetorical Strategies in Uncle Tom's Cabin.* Amherst: University of Massachusetts Press.

UNDERGROUND RAILROAD

The Underground Railroad refers to the assistance abolitionists provided fugitive slaves going through the northern states, usually on their way to Canada.

Professional slave catchers sometimes engaged in gunfights in their efforts to capture escaped slaves and return them to the South. (Library of Congress)

Such loosely organized local activity later formed the basis for a popular legend that included stories of secret hiding places and various railroad terms as "stations" "passengers," "conductors," and even several "presidents" of the underground line. In the years after the Civil War, Underground Railroad stories frequently appeared in the northern press. Unmentioned in the legend was the role of fugitive slaves themselves, who planned and conducted their own escapes from a hostile southern environment with little available help.

Legendary accounts distorted historical reality and often exaggerated the number of slave escapes. Yet they had a basis in fact. Some abolitionists, like Levi Coffin of Cincinnati and Thomas Garrett of Wilmington, Delaware, made a personal cause of aiding fugitive slaves. Their efforts to develop efficient networks of activists gave a semblance of effective organization to their own locales. Yet most such work was on a haphazard and makeshift basis. There was no national system.

An important element in the legend was provided by memories of the vigilance committees that formed in various northern communities. Those committees assumed greater importance with passage of the Fugitive Slave Law (1850). The committees provided food, temporary housing, travel directions, and sometimes transportation to fugitive slaves passing through their communities. They also conducted some well-publicized civil disobedience, like the 1851 rescue of Jerry Henry by the Syracuse committee. Less successful was the attempt of the Boston committee to free Anthony Burns, whose return to slavery under heavy military guard sparked protest in Boston and throughout the North. Abolitionists later purchased and freed Burns.

Some rescues, like the Oberlin-Wellington Rescue of 1859, were more spontaneous. When a fugitive slave was arrested a few miles from his home in Oberlin, Ohio, an abolitionist crowd literally removed him from his place of confinement and sent him to Canada. The federal government indicted thirty-seven of the instigators of the rescue. The trials received national attention and prompted numerous demonstrations near the jail where the rescuers were held. At the same time, a county grand jury indicted the federal marshal and others for kidnapping a black. That indictment paved the way for a deal in which federal and state authorities dropped charges.

Slaves who successfully escaped their bondage were not frightened or passive, but courageous individuals who made their own daring and ingenious escape plans. Slaves who were rescued by Harriet Tubman's heroic trips into the South may have been the exception. Most escaping slaves had no such assistance. Many traveled alone by night, hiding during the day. Ellen and William Craft escaped from Georgia with Ellen disguised as an ailing master and William as his loyal servant. Frederick Douglass borrowed the free papers of a black sailor and refused to reveal his escape method in early editions of his autobiography. Henry "Box" Brown had himself literally shipped from Richmond, Virginia, to the Philadelphia antislavery office. When fugitives received help from the Underground Railroad, it was only after they had completed the most dangerous part of their journeys. Frederick Douglass, William Wells Brown, Henry Bibb, Anthony Burns, the Crafts, and thousands of others deserve recognition at least as much as white abolitionists who risked their own liberty and property to assist slave escapes.

Although secrecy was clearly essential when fugitive slaves were in danger of recapture, abolitionists were quite open at times about their fugitive slave work. In 1844 a Chicago antislavery newspaper published a cartoon captioned "The Liberty Line" that illustrated and accompanied a story describing the Underground Railroad listing the names of local "conductors." Although never arrested by authorities, Levi Coffin made no secret of his abolitionist sympathies or of his work on behalf of fugitive slaves. Each rescue had widespread notice in the press, and the violation of civil liberties of whites who helped escaping slaves served to deepen anti-southern sentiment in the North. Some fugitive slaves were featured guests at abolitionist gatherings, while others were speakers.

Abolitionists used the Underground Railroad to spread their message, and southern apologists responded by attacking the railroad as a violation of the constitutional protection of private property. Southern congressmen exaggerated both the number of escaping slaves and the monetary losses caused by those escapes. Fugitive Slave Law trials gave both sides material for their propaganda. By 1855 the law had become largely a dead letter in the North and a major cause for complaint in the South.

It was in the period after the Civil War that the idea of the Underground Railroad took hold in the American psyche. Former free soilers and abolitionist sympathizers gained inflated reputations, for hundreds of newspaper stories frequently associated all who had been antislavery with local tales of the Underground Railroad. Facts for such stories were often gleaned from interviews with family members or acquaintances of the aging activists. Several leading abolitionists wrote memoirs that later became source material for histories of the Underground Railroad. Although such memoirs contained important information, they were never supplemented by the narratives of former slaves or by information from William Still's important book on the Underground Railroad. Still, who chaired the Philadelphia Vigilance Committee, later published his own contemporary records of slave escapes and emphasized the role of the fugitives themselves. Even though the Underground Railroad clearly helped some fugitive slaves reach freedom, it was a far more complex institution than the simplest legend would suggest.

— *Larry Gara*

See also: Coffin, Levi; Fugitive Slave Act (1850); Garrett, Thomas; Still, William.

For Further Reading
Blockson, Charles L. 1987. *The Underground Railroad: First-Person Narratives of Escapes to Freedom in the North.* New York: Prentice Hall.
Gara, Larry. 1996. *The Liberty Line: The Legend of the Underground Railroad.* Lexington: University Press of Kentucky.
Siebert, Wilbur H. 1898. *The Underground Railroad from Slavery to Freedom.* New York: Macmillan.
Still, William. 1883. *The Underground Railroad.* Philadelphia: William Still.

UNION HUMANE SOCIETY

Begun by Benjamin Lundy in 1815, the Union Humane Society aimed primarily at extending humanitarian assistance to blacks in Ohio, but it also had the distinction of seeking to embrace all existing antislavery organizations. The society resembled the Quaker antislavery societies that had operated for decades in Pennsylvania to aid free blacks and fugitive slaves; its efforts to abolish slavery would eventually involve almost one thousand antislavery societies.

Lundy, a twenty-six-year-old New Jersey Quaker, organized the society in St. Clairsville, Ohio, when after much reflection over the "sad condition of the slave" he called a small number of friends to his house (Earle, 1969). Deeply affected by the frequent slave coffles he witnessed in Wheeling, Virginia, he expressed his desire to relieve those held in bondage. The society quickly grew to include nearly five hundred members, among whom were most of the influential preachers and lawyers in the state of Ohio. On January 4, 1816, Lundy (under a pseudonym) published a circular on the subject of slavery in which he appealed to the philanthropists of the whole country, urging them to organize themselves in a similar manner. He also proposed that societies should be formed wherever "a sufficient number of persons could be induced to join them," that a name common to all societies should be adopted, and that, in addition to a uniform constitution, correspondence should be kept up between all societies (Earle, 1969).

In promoting "gradual emancipation," the constitution of the society, which was drafted on April 20, 1816, relied on the Golden Rule and on statements from the Declaration of Independence asserting the inalienable rights of man. In addition, its stated goals were to remove legal restrictions, to assist blacks illegally held in bondage, and to protect the rights of free blacks entering Ohio. Beyond working for the abolition of slavery, members of the society also promised to vote only for political leaders who opposed slavery and to erase racial prejudice and various forms of discrimination. Lundy's publication of *The Genius of Universal Emancipation*, the only exclusively antislavery journal in the country at the time, aided in this cause. However, as discussion of slavery increased, Lundy discovered that any plan to abolish slavery had to deal with a range of complexities. This became evident with the founding of the American Colonization Society and Thomas Hedges Genin's attack at the semiannual meeting of the Union Humane Society at Mount Pleasant on its plan to send blacks back to Africa. Even though Lundy did not initially agree with Genin, Genin's views were part of a message delivered on behalf of the Union Humane Society at the 1819 American Convention for Promoting the Abolition of Slavery in Philadelphia.

Such internal disputes aside, the inability of the Union Humane Society to spread ideas and to limit slavery eventually led to disinterest and, ultimately, its disbanding. However, despite the society's declining effectiveness in promoting the abolition of slavery, the impact of Lundy and his organization can be seen in the effectiveness of other antislavery advocates, such as William Lloyd Garrison.

— *Mark L. Kamrath*

See also: American Colonization Society; Gradualism; Quakers.

For Further Reading

Adams, Alice. 1908. *The Neglected Period of Anti-Slavery in America*. Gloucester, MA: Peter Smith.

Dillon, Merton L. 1966. *Benjamin Lundy and the Struggle for Negro Freedom*. Urbana: University of Illinois Press.

Dumond, Dwight Lowell. 1961. *Antislavery: The Crusade for Freedom in America*. Ann Arbor: University of Michigan Press.

Earle, Thomas, ed. [1847] 1969. *The Life, Travels and Opinions of Benjamin Lundy, Including His Journeys to Texas and Mexico; with a Sketch of Contemporary Events, and a Notice of the Revolution in Hayti*. New York: Negro Universities Press.

Miller, Randall M. 1972. "The Union Human Society." *Quaker History* 61: 91–106.

UNITED STATES–CANADIAN RELATIONS ON FUGITIVES

Between the American Revolution and the Civil War, the institution of slavery influenced relations between the United States and Canada. Slavery's continued existence in the United States and its demise in Canada after 1793 strained the relationship between the two countries; the primary reason for the tensions between the two was the fact that thousands of runaway slaves from the United States sought refuge in Canadian territory. The exact number of blacks who relocated in Canada is elusive, as is the percentage of those who were fugitive slaves as opposed to free blacks. Previously estimated at thirty thousand to forty-five thousand, recent reassessments support a more modest figure of around twenty thousand blacks who relocated to Canada prior to 1860. It is probable that most blacks who left the United States and resettled in Canada were fugitive slaves, particularly after the U.S. legislature's passage of a harsh Fugitive Slave Law in 1850. Canada's rejection of U.S. appeals to extradite such fugitives led to numerous attempts to resolve the issue diplomatically. Eventually, all attempts by southern slaveholders to obtain a satisfactory solution to the fugitive slave problem—meaning, the rendition of their property—met with failure.

As Canada's reputation as a haven for runaway slaves grew in the early nineteenth century, so too did the pressure placed on the U.S. and Canadian governments by slaveowners and abolitionists alike to implement governmental policies favorable to their cause. Southern slaveholders resented the lack of assistance from the U.S. government and the lack of cooperation from the British and Canadian governments in the return of fugitive slaves. Especially aggravating to slaveowners was the Canadian courts' consistent upholding of the principle, espoused in the Upper Canadian Abolition Act (1793), that fugitive slaves who entered

Canada were thereafter free. Canadian courts rejected American appeals to extradite such refugees. Southern slaveowners were thus unable to retrieve their slaves.

The first official attempt by U.S. slaveholders to elicit aid in the recovery of fugitive slaves was made in 1819 when the owners of several slaves who had escaped from Tennessee to Canada urged the U.S. secretary of state to negotiate an arrangement whereby they could regain possession of their property. The official Canadian response was that the fugitives, by their residence in Canada, were free. This became the standard reply to such requests.

The U.S. House of Representatives resolved several times between 1821 and 1860 to engage in full-fledged diplomatic negotiations to draw up a treaty acceptable to slaveholders' interests. Successive U.S. ministers to Great Britain, including Richard Rush, Albert Gallatin, and James Barbour, were instructed to engage in negotiations for a favorable disposition of the issue. Each time, however, the British government refused to acquiesce to U.S. wishes.

Facing the continued failure of diplomacy in solving the problem of extraditing fugitive slaves, masters frequently took matters into their own hands. Some slaveowners traveled to Canada and attempted to regain their property forcibly. This type of activity violated Canadian kidnapping laws, and authorities in that country consistently protected fugitives. Slaveholders also continued to seek individual extradition orders in their quest to regain their property: most of these efforts, too, were unsuccessful.

Some slaveholders tried to extradite their runaway slaves under the pretext that the slaves faced criminal charges before southern courts. This legal stratagem was based on an 1833 Canadian statute that provided for the surrender of fugitive criminals from foreign countries. According to this law, anyone charged by a foreign country with murder, forgery, larceny, or other felonies could be extradited at the discretion of the Canadian government. This legislation seemed to threaten the freedom of all runaway slaves from the United States: first, because many slaves had committed such crimes either before or in the process of escaping; and second, because slaveowners might bring false charges in order to regain their property. Three test cases came from Kentucky, where, in the late 1830s, individual slaveowners requested the extraditions of runaways Thornton Blackburn, Solomon Mosely, and Jesse Happy.

In the first case, Blackburn's master tried to have him extradited on the basis that Blackburn had participated in the mob that had effected his rescue, but the Canadian authorities denied the extradition request. In the second case, Mosely had stolen his master's horse and had ridden it to Buffalo where he sold the animal and escaped across the Niagara River into Canada. Extradition was requested on the basis that Mosely was a horse thief. Canadian officials agreed that the crime had been proved and ordered the extradition. Mosely, however, escaped from his jailers and was never returned to his master. In the third case, Jesse Happy had also stolen his master's horse in the process of escaping, but he left the animal on the American side of the border and wrote a letter to his owner explaining where to find it. The owner later reclaimed the animal. In what is seen as the definitive ruling on extraditions arising from the 1833 Canadian statute, Canadian and British officials declared that extradition in Happy's case not be granted. The decision implied that any act a slave committed as part of his escape should be considered an act of self-defense rather than a felony.

William Parker's story further illustrates Canada's position concerning fugitives. Parker's participation in the Christiana Riot on September 11, 1851, during which one slave catcher was killed and another mortally wounded, forced him, along with several other leaders of the resistance to flee their Pennsylvania homes. Traveling to Toronto, Parker learned that Governor William Johnston of Pennsylvania had officially requested his extradition. Parker appealed in person to the governor general, Sir James Bruce, earl of Elgin and was assured that he would be considered a fugitive from slavery, not justice. Parker was not extradited.

The closest the countries came to resolving this issue came in the Webster–Ashburton Treaty (1842). Article 10 of this treaty between the United States and Great Britain provided for the mutual surrender of fugitive criminals from both countries and Canada. Yet in the end, Canadian and British officials made it clear that a liberal interpretation of Article 10 would be followed when it came to fugitive slaves and that crimes that occurred as a result of a slave's escape were not considered to be the basis for extradition. Canada remained a haven for refugee slaves until slavery was abolished in the United States.

— *Sharon A. Roger Hepburn*

See also: United States–Canadian Relations on Fugitives; Abolitionism in the United States; Webster–Ashburton Treaty.

For Further Reading

Jones, Howard. 1977. *To the Webster–Ashburton Treaty: A Study in Anglo-American Relations, 1783–1843.* Chapel Hill: University of North Carolina Press.

Lindsay, Arnett. 1920. "Diplomatic Relations between the United States and Great Britain Bearing on the Return of Negro Slaves, 1788–1828." *Journal of Negro History* 5: 261–278.

Roger Hepburn, Sharon. 1999. "Following the North Star: Canada as a Haven for Nineteenth Century American Blacks." *Michigan Historical Review* 25 (Fall): 91–126.

Silverman, Jason. 1980. "Kentucky, Canada, and Extradition: The Jesse Happy Case." *The Filson Club History* 54 (January): 50–60.

Wayne, Michael. 1995. "The Black Population of Canada West on the Eve of the Civil War." *Social History* 28: 465–85.

Winks, Robin. 1971. *The Blacks in Canada: A History.* New Haven, CT: Yale University Press.

Zorn, Roman J. 1957. "Criminal Extradition Menaces the Canadian Haven for Fugitive Slaves, 1841–1861." *Canadian Historical Review* 38: 284–294.

UNITED STATES CONSTITUTION

Despite slavery's pervasive influence on the political, economic, and social life of the United States, the country's Constitution, at ratification, did not explicitly mention the practice and institution of chattel slavery. Only with the post–Civil War amendments (the Thirteenth, Fourteenth, and Fifteenth Amendments) did the Constitution expressly acknowledge slavery's existence. The Founders spoke of slavery euphemistically, preferring ambiguous phrasing to an explicit delineation of slavery's place in the country's political order. Nonetheless, the Constitution's authors consciously designed institutions that accommodated, supported, and eventually entrenched slavery within the structures of political power. Consequently, those few euphemistic references in the original Constitution have had lasting influence on the course of political development in the United States and on constitutional interpretation.

Constitutional references to slavery fall into three classes: those that could have referred only to slavery; those that encompassed slavery and other practices or institutions; and those that did not directly touch on slavery, but had significant, indirect, and perhaps unforeseen consequences for slavery or slaveholding interests.

Five provisions fall within the first category, and they represent key compromises made at the Constitutional Convention in 1787. The first, Article I, section 2, paragraph 3 (generally called the three-fifths compromise) stipulated that both representation within the House of Representatives and any direct taxes would be apportioned to the states according to their populations, calculated "by adding to the whole Number of free Persons, including those bound to Service for a Term of Years, and excluding Indians not taxed, three fifths of all other Persons." This stipulation increased the representation of slaveholding states in Congress, but simultaneously decreased any potential direct tax liability.

Similarly, Article I, section 9, paragraph 4 ensured that all regions of the country would be equally affected by any possible "capitation" tax. This national uniformity of any possible direct taxes meant that slaveholding could not be singled out for taxation, a concern of some slaveowners who thought northerners would try to tax slavery out of existence.

Also under Article I, section 9, paragraph 1 stipulated that Congress could not ban the international slave trade until 1808. This twenty-year prohibition fostered an even greater reliance on slave labor in the South and allowed for a domestic slave market to develop. Meanwhile, the fugitive slave clause (Article IV, section 2) not only prevented free states from emancipating runaway slaves within their borders, but also required them to release any fugitive slave to his or her owner. In addition, Article 5 rendered unamendable until 1808 both the fugitive slave clause and the ban on prohibiting the international slave trade.

The second class of constitutional provisions reinforced the economic and physical domination slavery required. Article IV, section 4 required the federal government to help suppress domestic insurrections, if a state so requested, thereby putting the federal government in the position of defending slaveholders' property interests if slave rebellion occurred. Similarly, Article I, section 8, paragraph 15 allowed Congress to muster state militias to combat insurrections, including slave revolts. Article I, Sections 9 and 10 prevented the federal and state governments from taxing exports, which precluded any effort to tax the products of slave labor.

The third class of provisions generally gave political advantages to slaveholding interests that enabled them to forestall efforts to eliminate slavery. Because of the three-fifths compromise, southern states had more votes in the House of Representatives and the electoral college than if only free citizens were represented. Also the amendment process (Article 5) required the agreement of three-quarters of all states, enabling the South to veto any constitutional amendment to ban slavery. In addition, congressional powers to admit new states and adopt regulations for the territories (Article 4, section 3) created opportunities for slave states to ensure that their numbers would not diminish.

In short, the constitutional provisions that touched on slavery, either directly or indirectly, represented a significant victory for southern interests at the time of the country's founding. Why was the South able to prevail on virtually all contested issues relating to slavery at the Constitutional Convention? Mark Tushnet (1981) argues that the political concessions to slavery at the founding resulted from proslavery interests colliding with antislavery sentiment. That is, the political, economic, and social interests of slaveowning states came into conflict with the northerners' more diffuse antislavery sentiment, based on moral or religious sentiment. Consequently, the diffuse attitude could only yield in the face of such well-focused interests. Indeed, one could argue that the interests of the northern states lay primarily in promoting a political union, and slavery was the price of that union.

The question remains whether the North drove a very hard bargain in its negotiations at the Constitutional Convention. Were concessions on slavery necessary to the Union's formation? The academic debate has yet to resolve the issue, but clearly the distinctive form of the political union of the United States, its thoroughgoing federalism, emerged primarily because of the centrifugal forces of slavery. In order to form an economic and political union, the framers of the Constitution found it necessary to preserve, in large part, the existing legal arrangements that enabled slavery to flourish in the South after the American Revolution.

At the time of the country's founding, the legal framework supporting slavery lay exclusively at the state level. The then-emerging natural law position, articulated most forcefully in *Somerset v. Stewart* [98 English Reports 499 (1772)], held slavery to be contrary to natural law; therefore slavery could exist, in a legal sense, only as a creature of positive law (legislative or executive-made law). The slavery-related provisions of the U.S. Constitution recognized and validated the exclusively local law of slavery, as it then existed in the American states. Thus the constitutional priority of federalism, which allowed both legal systems to coexist under a single constitutional order, both sought to restrict federal governmental intrusion on individuals and tolerated a property right in slaves.

In doing so, the Constitution embodied a tension between the "higher law" impulses of the American Revolution and the deeply political compromises over slavery. The high-toned aspirations of "We, the people" were profoundly at odds with slavery's entrenchment, simultaneously revealing within the Constitution an idealism and a complicit pragmatism.

Through the nineteenth century, these countervailing tendencies gave rise to intense political and normative arguments over the legal meanings of the Constitution's view of slavery. Followers of William Lloyd Garrison echoed his denunciation of the Constitution

as a "covenant with hell" while other, equally ardent antislavery activists sought to confine or eliminate slavery through constitutional practices. On the other side, proslavery politicians, in both the North and the South, viewed constitutional provisions like the fugitive slave clause as the touchstone of the American union. From their perspective, defending the principle of union required a defense of slavery. Proslavery forces tried to transform the constitutional place of slavery from a necessary evil to a positive good; it was, they argued, the glue that held the American union together.

These struggles often emerged in the context of federalism because of the differing positive law of free and slave regions. Northern free states and southern slave states held fundamentally different assumptions about the legal status of blacks within their respective regions. In general, northern legal systems assumed blacks to be free citizens unless proven otherwise, while southern law viewed blacks as slaves unless proven to be free.

Conflicts over the legal status of blacks typically arose when slaves moved from a slave jurisdiction to a free one, either with or without their owners' permission. The legal status of fugitive slaves was clear within free states: the Constitution explicitly prevented northern states from emancipating them (Article 4, section 2). But some northern judges ruled that free states were not required to protect the slave property of southern masters traveling through their jurisdiction. Further legal conflicts arose over northern efforts to protect the free black population in the North from bounty hunters and from the North's refusal to cooperate with slaveowners or their agents seeking to reclaim alleged fugitive slaves.

Later, as the Civil War drew to a close, northern Republicans began laying the foundation for the constitutional abolition of slavery. Although Congress had banned slavery in the territories and the District of Columbia in 1862 and Lincoln's 1863 Emancipation Proclamation freed slaves held in the rebellious southern states, a general abolition required more than statutory or executive action. In their efforts to dismantle slavery, Republicans also aimed at the broader southern "slave power," which they believed dominated national politics before the war.

The simple language of the Thirteenth Amendment—"Neither slavery nor involuntary servitude . . . shall exist within the United States or any place subject to their jurisdiction"—not only abolished slavery but also implicitly aimed at the South's racial hierarchy. Opponents to the Thirteenth Amendment argued that it profoundly and impermissibly reconfigured the federal relationship, allowing the national polity to restructure the civil and economic life of an entire region. This opposition soon collapsed as the reelection of President Lincoln in 1864 and the installation of a large Republican majority in the House of Representatives assured passage of the Thirteenth Amendment.

The formal end of slavery in the United States came on December 6, 1865, over 240 years after a Dutch ship unloaded the first cargo of Africans in Virginia. Enormous battles lay ahead to secure basic civil and political rights for emancipated slaves, and, more broadly, to disentangle slavery from the fabric of both the Constitution and society.

— *Douglas S. Reed*

See also: Personal Liberty Laws; *Prigg v. Pennsylvania.*

For Further Reading

Cover, Robert. 1975. *Justice Accused: Antislavery and the Judicial Process.* New Haven, CT: Yale University Press.

Morris, Thomas D. 1974. *Free Men All: The Personal Liberty Laws of the North, 1780–1861.* Baltimore, MD: Johns Hopkins University Press.

Tushnet, Mark V. 1981. *The American Law of Slavery, 1810-1860.* Princeton: Princeton University Press.

Wiecek, William. 1977. *Sources of Anti-Slavery Constitutionalism.* Ithaca, NY: Cornell University Press.

DENMARK VESEY (1767–1822)

Denmark Vesey, a former slave, a skilled carpenter, a literate free black, and a man of imposing strength, was the leader of an abortive slave rebellion in Charleston, South Carolina, in 1822. He was born in 1767, and it is not clear whether his birth occurred in Africa or on the island of St. Thomas in the Caribbean. He lived as a slave boy on the island in the 1700s. In 1781 at age fourteen, Denmark and 390 other slaves were transported to St. Domingue (Haiti). The ship's master, Captain Joseph Vesey took an interest in the boy, dressed him up, and took him to his cabin. On arrival at Cape Français, St. Domingue, Denmark was sold along with other slaves.

On Captain Vesey's next trip to Cape Français, he was told that the French sugar planter who bought Denmark had rejected him, complaining that Denmark was "unsound and subject to epilepsy" (Lofton, 1948). According to the slave-trading practice at the time, Captain Vesey had to take Denmark back, and between 1781 and 1783 Denmark sailed with his master on slave-trading voyages to different ports in the Caribbean and once to Africa. As a consequence of his travels, Denmark learned to speak English, French, Danish, and Spanish.

In 1783 Captain Vesey decided to settle in Charleston, South Carolina, which, at the time, was a growing urban center and ranked as the fourth largest city after New York, Philadelphia, and Boston. One of the reasons Captain Vesey abandoned the slave trade was that in the 1780s the market for slaves in the United States began a downward slide. More importantly, in 1783 the state of South Carolina imposed heavy duties on slave imports, and beginning in 1787, it prohibited trafficking in slaves. Thus the economic climate did not favor slave trading. The suspension of the trade was only temporary, because in 1803 a boom in cotton production led to an increased trade in slaves. Captain Vesey, having given up trade in slaves, began a business in Charleston as a ship chandler, and for the next seventeen years, Denmark served his master in Charleston.

As a result of the cosmopolitan character of Charleston, external influences were bound to permeate the society. For instance, the ideological rhetoric of the French Revolution gradually crept into the city, and Denmark and others were later to borrow a leaf from the rebelling slaves of St. Domingue. As a slave in Charleston, Denmark was like most urban bondsmen who worked as domestics for the urban elites, which included shipbuilders, lawyers, doctors, engineers, merchants, and businessmen. Because of Denmark's skills as a carpenter he was hired out by his master, which provided Denmark ample opportunity not only to earn extra cash, but also to educate himself through reading about current events in Charleston and elsewhere. The freedom to move around aided Denmark in establishing a network with slaves and free blacks, and this circle of friends became the pivot around which he later organized his plot.

Another significant development in Denmark's life occurred in December 1799 when he won a lottery prize of $1,500. In January 1800 Denmark met his master, Joseph Vesey to negotiate his freedom and used $600 of the prize money to buy his freedom. As a freeman, Denmark used the $900 he had left to establish a carpenter workshop. From then on he joined the ranks of free blacks who lived in Charleston and worked as carpenters, tailors, hairdressers, barbers, cooks, seamstresses, shoemakers, blacksmiths, bricklayers, painters, contractors, merchants, coal and wood dealers, and artisans. Many of them, including Denmark, were successful in their chosen professions.

Despite the successes of free blacks, their social status in antebellum Charleston was only a level above that of slaves. Even with manumission, free blacks never achieved total freedom. For instance, despite Denmark Vesey's wealth, the law still required him to carry his manumission papers wherever he went, and until 1783, when a law was enacted against the abduction and selling of free blacks, they could be kidnapped and sold into slavery all over again. Free blacks were tried in the same manner as slaves, and they lacked legal representation. By about 1820 there were 3,165 free blacks living in Charleston whose privileges were circumscribed; it was only a matter of time before they reacted.

Based on external influences and his own conviction, Denmark became dissatisfied with the status of African Americans in the United States, and he felt the degradation of African Americans in Charleston cast an aspersion on his race. He was, therefore, impatient with blacks he considered servile and worked strenuously to galvanize those blacks who thought there was no way to change their subservient status. With time Denmark became a strong critic of the institution of slavery. His intellectual crusade was informed by reading about slavery, the American, French, and Haitian revolutions; and about abolitionists and their activities. His extensive knowledge enabled him to understand hardships inherent in the institution of slavery, and he was not afraid to express his views.

Denmark began his program for freedom by sensitizing potential participants in his plot to overthrow the slave system. He felt it was his responsibility to inform blacks in Charleston that whites were neither superior nor were they God, and he also prepared his followers psychologically to dislike whites. He used the Bible as a basis to criticize the evils of slavery—reading from the Bible how the children of Israel were delivered out of Egypt from bondage. He also made references to the success of Haitians in their bid to acquire independence from the French.

By December 1821, Denmark Vesey took a major step in achieving his objectives by picking able and trusted confidants. Among them was Peter Poyas (a slave belonging to one James Poyas), a literate ship carpenter whose job allowed him to move freely, which meant he could coordinate communication between rural and urban slaves. Others included Rolla and Ned Bennett, slaves of Governor Thomas Bennett; their closeness to the governor meant they were able to spy and inform on the white community of Charleston. Another important associate of Denmark was Jack Glenn, a literate and skilled slave whose occupation was painting. Glenn acted as the group's treasurer, collecting money from hired-out slaves who had disposable income for the purchase of weapons and horses. Monday Gell, a skilled harness maker, was also a member of Denmark's circle of confidants. Gell managed a shop on Meeting Street and was well regarded by whites, who considered him intelligent, steady, and dependable. Among Denmark Vesey's lieutenants, Jack Pritchard (Gullah Jack) was deemed to have been the most effective. He was said to possess supernatural powers and was therefore considered a conjurer. He commanded considerable respect among rural Gullah slaves who lived in the coastal Sea Islands. Denmark relied on Gullah Jack to rally the cowardly and hesitant slaves by using his assumed powers.

Once Vesey's team was in place, the business of extensive recruitment began. A number of meetings were held in Vesey's house, in Monday Gell's shop, and at Bulkley's farm on Charleston Neck, at which the leaders compared notes, exchanged information and planned strategies for the operation. The recruitment effort went beyond Charleston. Recruiters went as far as the coastal islands to the east, Georgetown to the north, the Combahee River to the south, and St. John's Parish in Berkeley County to the west. Denmark Vesey and his co-conspirators took utmost care to prevent any possible leaks, but their efforts in this regard were unsuccessful.

July 14, 1822, the second Sunday of the month, was set as the date for the rebellion. A summer month was chosen because the majority of whites would have traveled out of town, and a Sunday was picked because on that day many blacks could visit Charleston without being suspected of any sinister motive. Before the plan could be executed, a house servant who was the target of recruitment informed his master of the planned insurrection on May 30. Vesey then attempted to move the date of the uprising forward to June 16, but unfortunately, more revelations of the plot had been made by other slaves who were acting as spies. The mayor of Charleston and governor of South Carolina acted swiftly, and the insurrectionists were arrested.

Following a long trial, of the 131 African Americans who had been apprehended, 36 were hanged, 43 were banished from the state, and the charges against 51 were discharged. Peter Poyas; Ned, Rolla, and Batteau Bennett; Jessy Blackwood; and Denmark Vesey were executed on July 2, 1822.

— *Onaiwu W. Ogbomo*

See also: Gullah Jack; Sea Islands; South Carolina.

For Further Reading
Aptheker, Herbert. 1943. *American Negro Slave Revolts*. New York: Columbia University Press.

Edwards, Lillie J. 1990. *Denmark Vesey*. New York: Chelsea House Publishers.

Egerton, Douglas R. 1999. *"He Shall Go Out Free": The Lives of Denmark Vesey*. Madison, WI: Madison House.

Killens, John Oliver. 1970. *The Trial Record of Denmark Vesey*. Boston: Beacon Press.

Lofton, John M., Jr. 1948. "Denmark Vesey's Call to Arms." *Journal of Negro History* 33 (4): 395–417.

Pearson, Edward A. 1999. *Designs against Charleston: the Trial Record of the Denmark Vesey Slave Conspiracy of 1822*. Chapel Hill: University of North Carolina Press.

Robertson, David. 1999. *Denmark Vesey*. New York: Alfred A. Knopf.

VIRGINIA'S SLAVERY DEBATE

A far-reaching debate on slavery occurred in the Virginia House of Delegates in 1832. The 1831–1832 legislature convened three months after Nat Turner led a slave uprising in Southampton County on August 22–23 and only a few weeks after Turner's capture, trial, and execution. White Virginians sought security against a recurrence, and many—even some leading slaveowners in eastern Virginia—were prepared to consider an end to the institution Turner had rebelled against. Governor John Floyd hoped that a program might be launched during his administration that would bring an eventual end to slavery in Virginia and, in the meantime, greater control over all black Virginians and the expulsion of free blacks.

The legislature's lower house appointed a select committee to consider the removal of free blacks from the state and a program of graduate abolition. William O. Goode, however, introduced a resolution that it was "not expedient to legislate" on the subject of emancipation. Thomas Jefferson Randolph countered with a resolution calling for gradual emancipation. According to Randolph's measure, all children that slave mothers bore after July 4, 1840, would, if still in Virginia, become the property of the state, women when they reached age eighteen and men at age twenty-one, and would then be hired out until their labor had raised funds sufficient to pay for their transportation out of the United States. Young female slaves would begin obtaining their freedom in 1858, as would their brothers in 1861.

Half a century earlier, the state of Pennsylvania had taken the first action of any legislature in the New World to undo slavery when it passed a gradual emancipation act in 1780. By the time of Turner's uprising, every northern state had acted to end slavery, while no state south of Pennsylvania had gone any further than when Virginia, in 1782, merely eased a restriction that had previously kept slaveowners from manumitting their slaves.

Only in its broad outlines did Virginia's 1832 gradual emancipation proposal resemble Pennsylvania's. Pennsylvania's original proposal had used the same ages for freeing slaves as the Virginia proposal did, eighteen for women and twenty-one for men; it would have terminated their slavery at birth but required them to work for the mother's master until adulthood. As enacted in 1780, the Pennsylvania law postponed final freedom for slaves yet unborn to the age of twenty-eight. But that law also granted free blacks all the rights that their white neighbors enjoyed, including the right to remain in their home state and the right to vote, and it sought to protect black Pennsylvanians from being sold out of state. Virginia's proposal did nothing to expand the definition of black freedom, and its supporters anticipated that slaveowners, acting to protect their investment, would seek a market in the Deep South.

Two weeks of intense debate took place in the 1832 Virginia legislature's lower house. A western representative, William Ballard Preston, proposed an amendment to easterner Goode's resolution to declare it, instead, "expedient" that the legislature enact an emancipation measure. Proponents of abolition condemned the "evil" of slavery—sometimes because it injured slaves, always because it damaged the prospects of white Virginians. Their opponents attacked as impractical every proposed remedy for slavery, though they did agree on the expulsion of free blacks. Reformers challenged the sanctity of property as it applied to slaves; their opponents insisted on their property rights. No one advocated any proposal to end slavery anytime soon or to permit a significant continued black presence in Virginia after an end to slavery.

Virginia's legislators divided into two main groups, roughly similar in size. One group supported some immediate action toward the eventual abolition of slavery. The other stood opposed. A small but crucial swing group favored eventual emancipation but resisted any specific action at that time. Preston's amendment lost by 73 to 58. The vehemence of proslavery spokesmen had paralyzed a sufficient number of wavering delegates, so that a majority refused to take any action against slavery in 1832.

Two years earlier, in a state constitutional convention, easterners had rejected calls from western delegates for greater representation and legislative apportionment according to white population. Had the Virginia Constitution of 1830 granted westerners' wish for greater power in the legislature, the 1832 vote on slavery would have been closer, though the reformers might still have lost. The next Virginia constitution, in 1851, offered concessions to western Virginia on voting and apportionment. It also empowered the legislature to remove free blacks. But it curtailed slaveowners' right to free their slaves, and—eliminating any possible repeat of the 1832 debate—it expressly barred the legislature from acting against slavery.

The failed effort in 1832 to inaugurate gradual emancipation would have led Virginia slaves, men and women, to begin obtaining their freedom by 1861. Instead, Virginia seceded and joined the Confederacy that year. The Civil War caused Virginia to experience a transformation in the status of black residents. Slavery was ended suddenly, and without the deportation of free blacks or freed slaves. In 1866 black residents were granted citizenship; in 1867, they even received political rights.

— *Peter Wallenstein*

See also: Turner, Nat.

For Further Reading

Freehling, Alison Goodyear. 1982. *Drift toward Dissolution: The Virginia Slavery Debate of 1831–1832.* Baton Rouge: Louisiana State University Press.

Freehling, William W. 1990. *The Road to Disunion: Secessionists at Bay, 1776–1854.* New York: Oxford University Press.

Robert, Joseph Clarke. 1941. *The Road from Monticello: A Study of the Virginia Slavery Debate of 1832.* Durham, NC: Duke University Press.

Shade, William G. 1996. *Democratizing the Old Dominion: Virginia and the Second Party System, 1824–1861.* Charlottesville: University Press of Virginia.

VOLUME OF THE SLAVE TRADE

Although it is impossible to establish a precise figure, many historians have endeavored to estimate the number of Africans involved in the transatlantic slave trade. Equally important, they have sought to determine the effects of that trade on Africa.

Historians have long debated how many African slaves Europeans transported to the Americas. Edward E. Dunbar, who wrote an 1861 essay called "History of the Rise and Decline of Commercial Slavery in America," produced one of the earliest estimates. Believing that his figure was conservative, Dunbar wrote that between 1500 and 1850 almost 14 million slaves were imported into the Americas. Although Dunbar's figure was little more than a guess, historians cited it in discussions of the slave trade for over a century. More recent citations mention Robert Rene Kuczynski's work *Population Movements* (1939), which argues for a figure of 15 million. Some writers have even argued that both estimates were too low and that the figure was closer to 20 million.

Philip Curtin provided the first scholarly treatment of this question in *The Atlantic Slave Trade: A Census* (1969), which he based on an examination of various published sources. He reviewed shipping records, census data, accounts of slave merchants and ship captains, government publications, and records of slave-trading companies. From these sources, Curtin concluded that Europeans imported 274,900 slaves into the Americas prior to 1600, 1,341,100 in the seventeenth century, 6,051,700 between 1701 and 1810, and 1,898,400 between 1811 and 1870, for a total of 9,566,100. He further explained that the peak of importation occurred in the third quarter of the eighteenth century when an average of over sixty thousand Africans arrived annually. Yet Curtin emphasized that his numbers were approximations and that his total might be 20 percent too low or 20 percent too high. He intended that his study would prompt other scholars to research the substantial unpublished sources available on both sides of the Atlantic and modify his calculations.

Since Curtin's book was published, many scholars have accepted his challenge, and after examining various archival materials, several have offered revised estimates of the volume of the slave trade. Historians working on slave importations into Spanish America and North America and the Portuguese, French, Dutch, and British slave trades have argued that Curtin's estimate was too low. Joseph Inikori (1982), Curtin's most prominent critic, asserts that Dunbar and Kuczynski were closer to the truth than Curtin and that over 15 million Africans were involved.

Beyond drawing from different source materials, a major reason for the differences between Curtin and the revisionists lies in their different vantage points in observing the slave trade. Curtin largely focused on the number of slaves imported into the Americas, while scholars arguing for a higher figure have tried to determine the number of slaves exported from Africa.

The publication of a CD-ROM in 1999 offered an opportunity to resolve the controversy over the volume of the transatlantic slave trade. A team of scholars working under the auspices of the W. E. B. DuBois

Institute at Harvard University created a massive data set that includes information on over two-thirds of all transatlantic slaving voyages through 1867, a total of 27,233 voyages. Studies based on this database have provided much greater precision in analyzing the character as well as the volume of the slave trade since total numbers can be extrapolated from such a large representative sample.

Europeans shipped just over 11 million Africans across the Atlantic and, confirming Philip Curtin's estimate, 9.6 million reached the Americas. Over 60 percent came from West Central Africa and the Bight of Benin. The Portuguese carried 46 percent of the slaves, mostly to Brazil, and the English transported 28 percent mostly to the West Indies. Only about 4 percent reached North America. Less than a quarter of the slaves were children and nearly half were men. Although the proportion declined over time, 12 percent of slaves died during the passage to the Americas. Notably, shipboard mortality, contrary to the previous arguments of many historians, did not increase substantially when ship captains packed slaves more tightly into vessels. Finally, it is now evident that beyond several dozen shore-based attacks by Africans against slave ships, there was an insurrection on nearly four hundred slave voyages.

The impact of the slave trade on Africa is becoming as important to historians as the number involved in the trade. There is little evidence that profits from the slave trade contributed to economic development in Africa largely because international trade was not a significant factor in the African economy. Indeed, some scholars argue that the slave trade may have retarded economic development in Africa because it took the healthiest and strongest in the population. In some areas, the slave trade had a profound political impact. Along the Gold Coast, a combination of slave trade profits and European firearms contributed to the rise of the powerful kingdom of Dahomey. Most significant was the trade's demographic impact. Although it was not true of all areas, the slave trade contributed to a population decline in West Africa during the eighteenth century. Angola in particular suffered a significant loss of adult males, and by the 1780s, there were twice as many females as males in Angola.

Some scholars caution that, rather than the slave trade, factors like disease, drought, and famine better explain Africa's population decline. Still others contend there was no overall decline. Indeed, a few argue that because of trade with the Americas, new food crops like maize and manioc were introduced into African agriculture. Moreover, they state, the successful cultivation of those crops offset the losses to the slave trade by providing a more diverse food supply, one that was capable of sustaining larger and healthier populations.

Complicating matters in determining the impact of the large transatlantic slave trade was the substantial trans-Saharan slave trade. Largely organized by Muslims, nearly 5 million slaves were sold in North Africa and the Middle East prior to 1600, a trade that continued through the nineteenth century and may have involved over 15 million slaves.

Several questions about the volume of the slave trade remain unanswered. Notably, historians have been unable to determine the precise impact of this trade on all regions affected. One scholar, David Henige, asserts that there will never be enough data to offer an acceptable global estimate of the slave trade. Nonetheless, substantial agreement has now been reached about the volume of the transatlantic trade. Beginning with the Portuguese trade in the fifteenth century, most scholars have concluded that Europeans exported over 11 million Africans to the Americas and that about 9.6 million of them survived the trip.

— *Larry Gragg*

See also: Middle Passage.

For Further Reading
Curtin, Philip. 1969. *The Atlantic Slave Trade: A Census.* Madison: University of Wisconsin Press.
Eltis, David. 2000. *The Rise of African Slavery in the Americas.* Cambridge: Cambridge University Press.
Eltis, David, Stephen D. Behrendt, David Richardson, and Herbert S. Klein, eds. 1999. *The Trans-Atlantic Slave Trade: A Database on CD-ROM.* Cambridge: Cambridge University Press.
Ewald, Janet. 1992. "Slavery in Africa and the Slave Trades from Africa." *American Historical Review* 97 (1): 465–485.
Inikori, Joseph E., ed. 1982. *Forced Migration: the Impact of the Export Slave Trade on African Societies.* London: Hutchinson.
Klein, Herbert S. 1999. *The Atlantic Slave Trade.* Cambridge: Cambridge University Press.

WADE–DAVIS BILL

The Wade–Davis bill, passed by both houses of Congress in 1864, expressed the Radical Republicans' vision for the reconstruction of the Confederate states. Drafted by Congressman Henry Winter Davis of Maryland and Senator Benjamin F. Wade of Ohio, two Radicals who chaired the Committee on the Rebellious States in their respective chambers, the bill articulated Radical opposition to President Abraham Lincoln's own plan of restoration. In December 1863 Lincoln had issued a proclamation declaring that any seceded state could resume its normal position in the Union if one-tenth of its qualified electorate swore an oath of allegiance to the United States and formed a civil government accepting the finality of the Emancipation Proclamation. Lincoln believed that the largely Union-occupied states of Louisiana, Arkansas, and Tennessee might be reintegrated into the Union on this basis within a short time. Congressional Radicals, however, deemed the Ten Percent Plan too lenient. They wanted, not simply a restoration of the former slave states, but revolutionary measures that guaranteed civil rights for blacks and that excluded treasonous Confederates from the democratic process. Consequently, the Radical-led Congress passed the Wade–Davis bill as an alternative to Lincoln's program.

The Wade–Davis provisions were more restrictive and punitive than the president's proposals. Unlike the Ten Percent Plan, the congressional package disallowed the wartime formation of popular governments in the South and instead obliged the chief executive to appoint provisional governors to administer the states-in-revolt for the duration of the conflict. Only after hostilities ceased could the rebel states move to regain self-government, and only when a majority of a state's voters swore an "iron-clad" oath affirming their loyalty to the Union throughout the entire war. In addition, the Wade–Davis bill disfranchised former Confederates and prohibited them from holding public office. Finally, the bill required that the southern states adopt new constitutions expressly outlawing slavery.

Congress finalized the Wade–Davis bill on July 2, 1864. Two days later, just hours before the congressional session expired, Radical senators Charles Sumner of Massachusetts and Zachariah Chandler of Michigan rushed the bill to the president for a hurried signature. To their chagrin, Lincoln did not endorse the legislation. Though he agreed with several of the bill's points, he feared its harsh tone would jeopardize the erection of loyal governments in Union-held areas of the South. Moreover, Lincoln objected on constitutional grounds to the provisions mandating the abolition of slavery as a requisite for the readmission of states to the Union. When Chandler remonstrated that the bill's essential feature was "that one prohibiting slavery in the reconstructed states," Lincoln retorted, "That is the point on which I doubt the authority of Congress to act" (Oates, 1977). As the president noted, the Republican Party had always conceded the inability of the federal government to interfere with slavery in the states. Of course, Lincoln had done precisely that with the Emancipation Proclamation, but he justified the decree as a military measure within the purview of the war powers vested in the nation's commander-in-chief. Congress, however, possessed no such constitutional authority and thus could not legislate against slavery in the states. Based on this separation-of-powers argument, Lincoln did not sign the bill before Congress adjourned.

Lincoln's pocket veto of the Wade–Davis bill provoked a bitter response from the Radical wing of his party. The bill's two authors, for example, published an incendiary manifesto accusing the president of usurping legislative prerogatives and of disregarding the human rights of blacks. Such polemical saber-rattling did little to change Lincoln's views on the matter, however. Nevertheless, most of the ideas embodied in the Wade–Davis bill ultimately came to fruition during the Radical-led congressional phase of Reconstruction after 1867. The Fourteenth Amendment to the Constitution, for instance, accorded freedmen full citizenship status and guaranteed them equal protection of the laws, while it barred many ex-Confederates from holding state or national office. Likewise, the Reconstruction Acts of 1867 echoed the stern tone of the Wade–Davis bill in dividing the former Confederacy into five military districts to be occupied by Union troops and administered by provisional governors until such time as new governments, based on manhood suffrage and contingent on ratification of the Fourteenth Amendment, could be established in the southern states.

— *Eric Tscheschlok*

See also: Lincoln, Abraham.

For Further Reading

Belz, Herman. 1969. *Reconstructing the Union: Theory and Policy during the Civil War.* Ithaca, NY: Cornell University Press.

Henig, Gerald S. 1973. *Henry Winter Davis: Antebellum and Civil War Congressman from Maryland.* New York: Twayne.

Oates, Stephen B. 1977. *With Malice Toward None: The Life of Abraham Lincoln.* New York: Harper and Row.

Paludan, Philip Shaw. 1994. *The Presidency of Abraham Lincoln.* Lawrence: University Press of Kansas.

Trefousse, Hans L. 1963. *Benjamin Franklin Wade: Radical Republican from Ohio.* New York: Twayne.

WAGE SLAVERY

Antebellum northern workers critical of evolving capitalist social relations often claimed they were treated on a par with the South's slaves. This comparison of the emerging wage labor system with chattel slavery was often summarized as "wage slavery." The term originated in Great Britain in the early nineteenth century, but was refined and elevated to the status of battle cry in the North during the 1830s and 1840s. After the Civil War, the term was widely used by the Knights of Labor and Marxist writers who continued to link wage work and slavery well into the twentieth century.

The powerful image of "wage slaves," however, had special meaning in the antebellum North, where the market was rapidly transforming work and social relations in cities like New York, Philadelphia, and the new mill towns like Lowell, Massachusetts. At the same time, a vocal and highly visible group of abolitionists began to call for an immediate end to slavery, which they claimed was both a sin and the antithesis of freedom. During the 1830s, white Northern workers began (hesitantly at first) to compare themselves to enslaved African Americans.

Striking Lowell Mill workers were among the first explicitly to make this comparison. Likening their bosses and foremen to southern planters, women marched through the streets of Lowell in 1836 singing:

Oh! Isn't it a pity, such a pretty girl as I—
Should be sent to the factory to pine away and die?
Oh! I cannot be a slave,
I will not be a slave,
For I'm so fond of liberty
That I cannot be a slave (Laurie, 1989).

For male artisans, who built the nation's first labor movement, the rise of the factory system portended an ominous threat to their own independence. The same year as the Lowell strike, supporters of New York's journeymen tailors published a famous handbill emblazoned with a coffin. The coffin symbolized how the workingman's one-time liberty had been "interred by. . . . would-be masters." "Freemen of the North," the handbill warned, "are now on the level with the slaves of the South" (Commons, 1910).

Some historians of antebellum America have pointed to the use of terms like *wage slavery* (and the popular substitute *white slavery*) as evidence that labor reformers cared little about the plight of black slaves. Some have even concluded that the term embodies proslavery leanings among northern whites. But even if some northern workers viewed wage slavery as a more serious problem for the republic than chattel slavery, the very idea contained a condemnation of slavery itself. The core values of the early labor movement—which included democracy, independence, and the labor theory of value—were fundamentally at odds with the institution of slavery.

Take, for example, the labor editor and land reformer George Henry Evans, who helped make wage slavery a household term in antebellum America. As early as 1831, Evans called for an end to all forms of slavery, and wrote editorials favoring full civil rights for free African Americans. He went even further than the abolitionist William Lloyd Garrison in support of Nat Turner and his rebellion. By the 1840s Evans had hit upon a plan for universal land reform that, he thought, would end slavery, speculation in land, tenantry, and urban unemployment: free homesteads for actual settlers. For labor leaders and reformers like Evans, slavery of any type was a threat to liberty and progress.

Many of the views of labor radicals like Evans helped constitute the new, free soil ideology, which likewise opposed the expansion of southern slavery and abolitionist "fanaticism." But the concept of wage slavery was diluted in both free soil and, later, Republican politics by the more developed ideology of "free labor," which held that, with hard work and thrift, any wage earner could some day be an employer or landowner. After the Civil War, the broad-based Knights of Labor recycled the concept of wage slavery and railed against it in both print and oratory. In its combination of unionism and social reform, the Knights kept the concept before the American public even as a mature capitalist order made the abolition of work for wages an unattainable and radical dream. After the Civil War, Gilded Age labor radicals recycled the term *wage slavery* to combat the industrial system.

— *Jonathan Earle*

For Further Reading

Commons, John R., et al. 1910. *A Documentary His-*

tory of American Industrial Society. Cleveland, OH: A.H. Clark.

Cunliffe, Marcus. 1979. *Chattel Slavery and Wage Slavery: The Anglo-American Context, 1830–1860.* Athens: University of Georgia Press.

Laurie, Bruce. 1989. *Artisans into Workers: Labor in Nineteenth Century America.* New York: Noonday Press.

Roediger, David R. 1991. *Wages of Whiteness: Race and the Making of the American Working Class.* London: Verso.

DAVID WALKER (1784–1830)

A free black who left the South to settle in Boston, David Walker was an influential voice in the fight against slavery through his writing. Born the son of a slave father and a free black mother in Wilmington, North Carolina, David Walker was a free black according to North Carolina law. As a youth, he was free to travel in the antebellum South, and he observed firsthand both the harsh nature of slavery and the unfair treatment accorded his mother. From an early age, he developed an attitude of disgust toward slavery. As a result of the racial unrest and heightened restrictions placed on free blacks caused by the Denmark Vesey conspiracy in 1822, Walker left the Charleston, South Carolina, area. Exactly where he traveled is uncertain, but by 1825 he had settled in Boston.

Once in Boston, Walker learned to read and write and opened a clothing store. He was generous to a fault. He never was a business success, but he was well-respected in the black community. Tall, slender, with a dark complexion, Walker was also physically intimidating as well. It was during this period that Walker continued his self-education. He read widely on the institution of slavery, especially its history from Egypt to more contemporary slave societies. His emergence as an outspoken critic of slavery was natural considering his life experiences and his pursuit of a deeper understanding of the status of blacks in the United States.

In 1828 Walker addressed the General Colored Association of Massachusetts and made a fiery attack on slaveholders, urging blacks to oppose slavery and southern attempts to recover fugitive slaves. He urged the audience to unify in the pursuit of freedom for blacks, but within the limits of the Constitution. His address was later printed in *Freedom's Journal,* but his next published work had a far greater impact on antislavery literature.

In 1829 Walker wrote an ambitious and incendiary tract that attacked slavery and outlined a plan for organized black opposition to the institution—a plan that included violence if necessary. Only a few months before *David Walker's Appeal,* another black, Robert Alexander Young, had published *Ethiopian Manifesto,* a seven-page pamphlet stressing that God had created blacks and whites as equals, but Walker probably knew nothing of its existence.

David Walker's Appeal was published as four "articles" focusing on blacks, their degradation in slavery, and their need to revolt against their white oppressors. His writing is clear and vivid, and propounds a well-reasoned argument against slavery. Portraying whites as the enemy, Walker saw racial harmony as unlikely given white attitudes. He did lay the framework for Christian forgiveness, but only if whites admitted their crimes against blacks. Walker adopted a "kill or be killed" philosophy and saw the necessity for insurrection if blacks were to achieve eventual equality.

Walker incorporated most of the major tenets of black nationalism in the *Appeal.* He stated that blacks must have a nation of their own, they must provide for their own defense, and they must follow black leaders. He repeated the traditional messianic view for blacks. Many historians view Walker as America's earliest black nationalist. He was undoubtedly one of the more significant black ideologists and writers of the antebellum period; given his southern heritage, Walker was a remarkable figure. White southerners and slaveholders naturally held Walker in low esteem, but southern reactions to *David Walker's Appeal* were indicative of their concerns and fears if the book and its ideas were widely circulated in the South.

Walker utilized a series of unofficial agents—black sailors, newspapermen, ministers, and other free blacks—to distribute the *Appeal* in southern port cities. On December 29, 1829, only three months after initial publication, the police in Savannah, Georgia, seized sixty copies of the *Appeal* that Walker had sent to Reverend Henry Cunningham. The next month, Atlanta officials intercepted twenty copies forwarded to newspaperman Elijah Burritt, a transplanted white New Englander. After it was discovered that Burritt had requested a copy (or more) of the tract, Burritt thought it prudent to go back north. Virginia Governor William Giles alerted the state assembly that a black person had circulated copies in Richmond. Copies were discovered in Walker's birthplace of Wilmington, North Carolina, in August 1830. City officials in Charleston, South Carolina, and New Orleans were alarmed when copies of the *Appeal* reached their cities in March 1830.

Public and legislative reactions were predictable as stricter measures against slave literacy, unsupervised slave religious activity, and the freedom of slaves to interact with free blacks were enforced in some states

William Walker was the self-proclaimed president of Nicaragua from 1856 to 1857. (Library of Congress)

and passed in others. The circulation of *David Walker's Appeal* aroused the three central fears of slaveowners—that slave literacy was a dangerous skill, that black preachers posed a real threat, and that literate blacks could read to groups of illiterate slaves.

Rumors surrounding Walker's death in June 1830 were rampant. One rumor was that he had been poisoned, another was that several Georgia men had offered a reward of $1,000 for Walker dead or $10,000 for Walker alive. There is no clear evidence that Walker died from anything more than natural causes, and most likely consumption. Walker's true legacy focused on his *Appeal,* his active opposition to slavery worldwide, and his role in the evolution of black nationalism.

— *Boyd Childress*

See also: Black Nationalism; Vesey, Denmark.

For Further Reading

Aptheker, Herbert. 1965. *One Continual Cry; David Walker's Appeal to the Colored Citizens of the World, 1829–1830, Its Setting and Its Meaning, together with the Full Text of the Third, and Last, Edition of the Appeal.* New York: Humanities Press.

Burrow, Rufus. 2003. *God and Human Responsibility: David Walker and Ethical Prophecy.* Macon, GA: Mercer University Press.

Hinks, Peter P. 1997. *To Awaken My Afflicted Brethren: David Walker and the Problem of Antebellum Slave Resistance.* University Park: Pennsylvania State University Press.

WILLIAM WALKER (1824–1860)

In an era when many sought to expand slaveholding territory through the practice of "filibustering" (engaging in expansionist activities in foreign countries), the most notorious adventurer of the antebellum era in the United States, William Walker, was born on May 8, 1824, in Nashville, Tennessee. Graduating from the University of Nashville in 1838, he subsequently studied medicine at the University of Pennsylvania and received his M.D. there in 1843. He pursued medical studies in Europe but then abandoned medicine to enter the legal profession. Admitted to the bar in New Orleans, Walker then turned to journalism and by 1848 was editor and proprietor of the New Orleans *Daily Crescent.*

After emigrating to California in 1850, Walker spent three years as an editor and lawyer. However, his restless spirit led him to embrace "filibustering" as the means to fulfill his longing for fame. In 1853 he sailed from San Francisco to wrest Lower (Baja) California and Sonora from Mexico. With an "army" of only forty-five men, Walker's effort was doomed to failure from the start. By early 1854 "President Walker" of the short lived Republic of Lower California was in full retreat for the U.S. border.

Walker and his chief confederates were tried in San Francisco for violating the neutrality laws. Acquitted by a sympathetic jury, Walker then determined to make Central America his next field of operations, a region that had increasingly become the focus of attention as American and European commercial interests viewed the isthmus as a potential interocean transit route. A prolonged conflict between Nicaragua's liberal and conservative factions offered Walker a second opportunity to fulfill his destiny. Accepting an invitation to organize armed American colonists for the liberal cause, Walker landed near Realejo on June 16, 1855. With his fifty-six "immortals" he helped the liberals win several important victories, and after the death of several liberal leaders through battle and disease, Walker emerged as the faction's foremost military commander.

Walker's capture of the Nicaraguan conservative

stronghold of Granada in late 1855 effectively ended hostilities. The new government, a shaky coalition of both factions with Walker as commander-in-chief, was recognized by the United States in May 1856. The undisputed power in his adopted country, Walker became president through a controlled election in June of the same year.

However, Walker's position was far from secure. Armed and supplied by the British government, which had its own designs in the region, a coalition of Central American states launched a major invasion of Nicaragua in September 1856. Gradually losing the support of the native population, Walker filled his ranks with North Americans who poured into the country to claim land and other concessions from his administration.

Surrounded by hostile forces, Walker, in a decree dated September 22, restored African slavery in Nicaragua. Although previously regarded as a conservative on the slavery issue, Walker hoped to win support for his cause in the U.S. South. Indeed, historians contend that southern expansionists, like Pierre Soule of Louisiana, who visited Nicaragua in August, were instrumental in convincing Walker that his political survival depended on reinstituting slavery. Even though he had opposed slavery's expansion in North America earlier, Walker succeeded in convincing southerners that he was fighting for the preservation of the institution.

Despite the success of this gamble, Walker's effort was too late to prevent defeat. His rise to power had been partly owing to an alliance with the Accessory Transit Company, a U.S. corporation operating between New York and San Francisco by way of Nicaragua. However, control of the company was bitterly contested, and Walker soon found himself forced to choose between warring U.S. capitalists. When Walker withdrew his support from Cornelius Vanderbilt, one of most powerful men in the United States, his fate was sealed.

Backed by his millions, Vanderbilt obtained full legal control of the transit company and sent agents to aid the Central American alliance. Led by Vanderbilt's mercenaries, the allies seized Walker's river fleet, thus cutting him off from the coast. At the same time, the British navy began to blockade the Atlantic coast of Nicaragua. Completely surrounded and with no hope of outside aid, Walker surrendered to the U.S. Navy on May 1, 1857.

Although totally out of favor with the U.S. government, Walker returned to a hero's welcome in the United States. Undaunted, he immediately organized a second expedition to Nicaragua but was thwarted by U.S. naval forces after landing on that country's coast in November 1857. Attempting to use Honduras as a base for another invasion of Nicaragua, Walker was captured by the Royal Navy. Turned over to the Honduran authorities, the greatest of the filibusters was executed by firing squad on September 12, 1860.

One historian has written, "Walker's experience . . . offers insight into the relationship between filibustering and slavery" (Brown, 1980). Although regarded by northerners and by many future historians as an agent of proslavery interests in the United States, Walker was not a southern expansionist. Even at the height of his power he did not consider the annexation of Nicaragua by the United States, but rather dreamed of forging the republics of Central America into a "military empire" under his rule. Far from being exploited by the "slave power," Walker apparently sought to exploit the southern proslavery element in the United States in an effort to preserve his rule over Nicaragua.

— *James M. Prichard*

See also: Filibusters.

For Further Reading
Brown, Charles H. 1980. *Agents of Manifest Destiny: The Lives and Times of the Filibusters.* Chapel Hill: University of North Carolina Press.

Carr, Albert Z. 1963. *The World and William Walker.* New York: Harper and Row.

May, Robert E. 1973. *The Southern Dream of a Caribbean Empire 1854–1861.* Baton Rouge: Louisiana State University Press.

Potter, David M. 1971. *The Impending Crisis 1848–1861.* New York: Harper and Row.

THE *WANDERER*

The *Wanderer* was the most infamous slave ship of the period before the Civil War. It was built in 1857 as a sporting schooner. Southern entrepreneurs from the United States, led by Charles A. L. Lamar, commissioned the vessel in 1859 to sail to Africa to obtain a clandestine slave cargo in violation of the U.S. prohibition of the international slave trade. Purporting to sail to St. Helena in the South Atlantic, the *Wanderer*'s crew succeeded in hiding the ship's destination and their nefarious plan. Once in open water, the ship veered east for West Africa's coast and the Congo River.

Arriving at the Congo, the *Wanderer*'s officers ingratiated themselves with officers of the African Squadron patrolling the West Africa coast to enforce the abolition of the slave trade. With the British officers' tacit approval, the *Wanderer* boarded over four hundred Africans and embarked for Georgia. As the ship dashed for open seas, a U.S. vessel patrolling the coast as part of the antislavery squadron attempted to stop the *Wanderer*. Unfortunately for the slaves on board, the schooner's sleek design and top speed of nearly 20 knots was too much for the U.S. vessel.

After a six-week voyage, the *Wanderer* arrived off Jekyll Island, 60 miles south of Savannah, Georgia. Fewer than half the stolen African slaves had survived the journey. The survivors were quickly and covertly dispersed among plantations along Georgia's coast.

Federal authorities had learned of Lamar's activities, though too late to prevent the dispersion of the ship's slave cargo. However, the authorities seized the *Wanderer* and arrested three crew members for piracy. Lamar manipulated the crew members' arrests into a spectacle bemoaning abolitionist attacks on southern society. Although federal Judge James M. Wayne recommended conviction, local jurors acquitted the crew members of piracy. When Treasury Secretary Howell Cobb, also a Georgian, ordered the *Wanderer* auctioned, Lamar used intimidation, violence, and his substantial personal wealth to regain control of the ship.

Proponents for reopening the African slave trade saw the *Wanderer* case as a victory. The Civil War began before the *Wanderer* could make another slave smuggling voyage, and the U.S. Navy seized the ship and impressed it into service as a Union gunboat during the war. In 1871 the *Wanderer* was lost off Cuba.

— *John Grenier*

See also: African Squadron; Atlantic Slave Trade, Closing of; Illegal Slave Trade.

For Further Reading
Wells, Tom Henderson. 1968. *The Slave Ship Wanderer.* Athens: University of Georgia Press.

Wish, Harvey. 1941. "The Revival of the African Slave Trade in the United States, 1856–1860." *Mississippi Valley Historical Review* 27: 569–588.

WAR OF 1812

The War of 1812 was a North American conflict between the United States and Great Britain and is considered to be an outgrowth of the Napoleonic conflict in Europe. Declared by the U.S. Congress on June 18, 1812, the war concluded with the Treaty of Ghent, December 24, 1814; hostilities continued until mid-March 1815 when both sides ratified the treaty. The war's highlights included failed American invasions of Canada during the fall of 1813; American naval victories on Lakes Erie (September 1813) and Champlain (September 1814); the British conquest of Washington, D.C. (August 1814), and failed attempt to seize Baltimore (September 1814); and an American victory against Creek Indians (March 1814) at Horseshoe Bend and against British forces at New Orleans (December 1814–January 1815).

The conflict's antecedents can be traced to the French Revolution, which initiated a generation of warfare between Great Britain and France that placed all neutral nations at risk. President James Madison's June 1812 message to Congress offered four reasons why the United States should declare war:

1. British impressment of American seamen;

2. Violation of American neutral rights on the high seas and in U.S. territorial waters;

3. British blockade of U.S. ports; and

4. British refusal to revoke or modify their Orders-in-Council.

Although British maritime depredations may have prompted the war, other important causes included the British encouragement of Native American attacks in the old Northwest; manifest destiny, or the American War Hawks' desire to acquire Canadian and western Native American lands, and/or Spanish East and West Florida; an agricultural depression, which convinced some southern congressmen that war could revive the U.S. economy; and an intense American Anglophobia created by years of humiliation at the hands of Great Britain.

Estimating the number of African Americans who fought in the conflict is impossible, even though some sources suggest that more than five thousand participated. Regardless of the number, both slaves and free blacks participated with the U.S. army and navy, with the British army and navy, with the Spanish military, and alongside Native American during the conflict. While the factors that motivated these combatants to choose sides remain unclear, evidence indicates that some joined certain forces to secure their freedom, while others tried to better their material conditions, and still others fought for causes in which they believed. Black combatants provided notable U.S. service with Oliver Hazard Perry (an estimated 10 to 20 percent of his sailing force) at the battle of Lake Erie. General Samuel Smith received help from slaves and free blacks who served in the army and militia, and who dug fortifications to protect Baltimore from attack. An-

British and American forces clash at the Battle of New Orleans. A well-defended left flank anchored on the Mississippi River and a thick cypress swamp on the right forced the British assault to the center of General Andrew Jackson's defense, where Jackson had placed his thirty-five hundred men in three successive lines of defense. (National Museum of the United States Army)

drew Jackson enlisted slaves and more than two hundred "free men of color" in his defense of New Orleans.

As part of their policy of destroying the U.S. economy and breaking the American will to fight, British forces liberated and carried off slaves during their 1813 and 1814 operations in the Chesapeake Bay, along the Georgia coast, and along the Gulf of Mexico. During the Chesapeake campaign more than two hundred runaways joined British Admiral Alexander Cochrane's Colonial Marines in the late August conquest and burning of Washington, D.C., and the September attack against Baltimore. Other slaves recruited from the Gulf South served alongside black West Indian regiments during the attack on New Orleans; the West Indian forces suffered from the cold weather and ultimately contributed little to the campaign. Nonetheless, the British policy of liberating slaves combined with American fears of a British-sponsored slave insurrection prompted state and local officials to implement repressive measures to retain the *status quo*.

Not siding with British forces, many runaway slaves and free blacks instead joined renegade mulatto and Indian communities in the Gulf Spanish borderlands. The strongly armed "Negro Fort"—a former British base on the Apalachicola River occupied by runaway slaves and hostile Indians after the conflict—posed a threat to expansive-minded American frontiersmen and southern slaveholders who wanted to expand into Spanish Florida. In July 1816 an American naval force easily destroyed the bastion.

The War of 1812 ultimately strengthened slavery in the old American Southwest. After the war, the opening of farming lands in the Mississippi Territory and western Georgia, the destruction of mulatto communities along the southern frontier, and the ultimate removal of those Native Americans east of the Mississippi River provided an impetus to the growing southern plantation system and continued slavery. In the end, the conflict helped accelerate the American Civil War as it strengthened the foundations for African American slavery in an ever-expanding agricultural South.

— *Gene A. Smith*

For Further Reading

Altoff, Gerard T. 1996. *Amongst My Best Men: African-Americans and the War of 1812*. Put-in-Bay, OH: The Perry Group.

Cusick, James G. 2003. *The Other War of 1812: The Patriot War and the American Invasion of Spanish East Florida*. Gainesville: University Press of Florida.

George, Christopher T. 2000. *Terror on the Chesapeake: The War of 1812 on the Bay*. Shippensburg, PA: White Mane Books.

Hickey, Donald R. 1989. *The War of 1812: A Forgotten Conflict*. Urbana: University of Illinois Press.

Latour, Arsène Lacarrière. 1816. *Historical Memoir of the War in West Florida and Louisiana in 1814–15: With an Atlas*. Ed. Gene A. Smith. Gainesville: The Historic New Orleans Collection and the University Press of Florida, 1999.

BOOKER T. WASHINGTON (1856–1915)

Booker Taliaferro Washington was born a slave in Franklin County, Virginia, on April 5, 1856. The son of a house slave and an unknown white father, Washington grew up to become one of the most influential educators in American history. His reputation, however, extended beyond the field of education. He was a social critic and a reformer of international reputation. His educational philosophy influenced generations of black educators. He devoted his energy and resources to ameliorating the condition of blacks and healing the racial wounds inflicted by the Civil War and Radical Reconstruction. Washington spent nine years in slavery, the last four during the Civil War. Though he did not quite feel the pinch of slavery as painfully as most other blacks, Washington was nonetheless mature enough to understand the institution's destructive character.

As a young man, Washington experienced the poverty, misery and degradation, as well as the denial of education and basic necessities of life that defined the experiences of blacks in America. Despite the restrictive environment, Washington developed strong yearnings for education. After the Civil War, his mother moved him and his sister to Malden, West Virginia, to join her husband who had fled during the Civil War. Washington worked with his stepfather in the coal and salt mines. Young Washington continued to yearn for knowledge, but his early learning was largely self-taught. Fortunately, Malden's black population decided to establish a school for their children, the Kanawha Valley School, where Washington received his early formal education. He soon became a houseboy to General Lewis Rufner and his wife, Viola.

Born a slave in 1856, Booker T. Washington grew up to become one of the most influential educators in American history. (Library of Congress)

This gave him access to their rich library. He often took books home to read. At the Rufners', Washington also learned to appreciate cleanliness and industry.

Washington soon learned of the existence of the Hampton Normal Institute (an advanced school for blacks in Hampton, Virginia) founded by General Samuel Armstrong, a Civil War veteran who believed that practical education would more effectively prepare blacks for participation in the emerging New South. Washington left for Hampton in 1872; he arrived tired, penniless, and hungry but filled with an insatiable thirst for knowledge. He gained admission and performed janitorial and cleaning duties to pay for his board and tuition. Hampton also exposed him to practical education and manual labor. The curriculum emphasized agriculture, vocational skills, and self-reliance, and Washington learned to appreciate the dignity of labor. He graduated in 1875 with a strong faith in practical education as the key to black elevation.

After teaching briefly in Malden and at Wayland Baptist Seminary in Washington, D.C., Washington returned to Hampton as an instructor in 1878 and taught there until 1881 when General Armstrong recommended him to Alabama officials to help establish a similar school in that state. By 1881 Reconstruction had ended, and blacks were locked into a vicious cycle of poverty. Their rights and privileges had been sacrificed in the Compromise of 1877 (the political compromise in which Rutherford F. Hayes won the presidency and Radical Republicans agreed to pull federal troops from the South and hand complete political control back to southerners), and blacks were constantly menaced by the shadow of slavery.

With a paltry $2,000 appropriated by the state of Alabama, Washington methodically built Tuskegee Institute, patterning it after Hampton. Tuskegee emphasized practical education and the inculcation of the Christian work ethic and cleanliness. The students built their own living quarters and academic buildings; they cultivated the land and produced and cooked their own food; and they studied subjects that instructed them in practical skills. Washington warned of the dire consequences of neglecting a practical education and implored blacks to acquire vocational skills, precisely those that would enable them to function as productive members of society.

Washington organized periodic fairs to advertise the students' productive efforts, established outreach links with local farmers, and frequently toured the region garnering support for Tuskegee. The fame of the institute spread, and Washington's reputation grew. He endeared himself favorably to whites as someone with vision and prudence, and in 1895, he was invited to address the annual Atlanta Cotton Exposition. That event marked the defining moment of his career.

The speech Washington delivered catapulted him to the status of a national black leader. He addressed his observations to two key audiences—southern whites and blacks. He recommended agriculture to blacks as the key to economic elevation and meaningful freedom. Blacks needed practical skills in order to become elevated and respected members of society, he stated, and he advised them to remain in the South, where opportunities for elevation abounded. Washington deprecated and discouraged the pursuit of political rights. He even favored suffrage restrictions based on property and education if equitably applied to both races.

Washington projected progress as a gradual and cumulative process and rejected calls for social equality; he deemed social equality to be of secondary importance. The two races could remain socially separate and yet cooperate on issues pertinent to mutual progress. As he put it, "In all things that are purely social we can be as separate as the fingers, yet one as the hand in all things essential to mutual progress." This statement became the centerpiece of his entire speech, the one that most people remembered and quoted.

Washington seemingly endorsed segregation. To whites, he gave assurance that their social and political dominance would not be challenged and that blacks were interested in neither social equality nor political rights, nor were they ready for the exercise of such rights. He stressed the importance of economic cooperation between the races and appealed to the moral and economic sensibilities of whites. The speech drew deafening applause from whites who immediately catapulted Washington to the status of a national black leader.

But Washington's philosophy was much more complex. Although he publicly counseled compromise and accommodation, clandestinely he sponsored antidiscriminatory activities. He never intended second-class citizenship for blacks. His compromises were meant to heal interracial animosities and eventually facilitate full integration of blacks. His tone of compromise and reconciliation, however, was most reassuring to whites and most discomforting to blacks. His reputation among blacks suffered, even as whites elevated him to stardom. American industrialists and philanthropists responded generously and poured funds into Tuskegee. In 1901 President Theodore Roosevelt invited Washington to dine with him at the White House. He became the authority on black affairs and the person whose opinions presidents and philanthropists sought.

Washington used his position to silence blacks who disagreed with him. He envisioned a proliferation of economically self-made blacks, and toward that end, he founded the National Negro Business League in 1900. In 1905 William Monroe Trotter and William E. B. DuBois spearheaded a movement to counter "the Tuskegee machine." This was the birth of the Niagara Movement, which unequivocally rejected compromise and accommodation. In 1909 the Niagara Movement became the National Association for the Advancement of Colored People (NAACP). Neither organization succeeded in effectively undermining Washington's position and power, and he continued to control and dominate the black American struggle until his death in 1915.

— *Tunde Adeleke*

See also: DuBois, W. E. B.

For Further Reading

Harlan, Louis R. 1972. *Booker T. Washington: The Making of a Black Leader.* New York: Oxford University Press.

Harlan, Louis R. 1983. *Booker T. Washington: The Wizard of Tuskegee, 1901–1915.* New York: Oxford University Press.

Meier, August. 1963. *Negro Thought in America, 1880–1915.* Ann Arbor: University of Michigan Press.

DANIEL WEBSTER (1782–1852)

Daniel Webster was a leading orator, statesman, and lawyer in the early nineteenth century. In the area of slavery, he negotiated the Webster–Ashburton Treaty, which removed the issue of the *Creole* that had been troubling U.S.-British relations; he was the best spokesman for unity during the nullification crisis of the 1830s; and he tried unsuccessfully to serve as a voice for union during the period surrounding the Compromise of 1850.

Webster was born in Salisbury, New Hampshire, to a family that had immigrated to America in the 1630s. He was the second youngest of ten children, and he attended Dartmouth College in 1797 starting at the age of fifteen. He soon excelled in debating and was asked to deliver a Fourth of July address at age eighteen.

After graduation, he studied law and taught, moving to Boston as a clerk for Christopher Gore. He was admitted to the Boston bar in 1805. Webster returned to New Hampshire for eleven years, marrying Grace Fletcher in 1808, keeping an office in Portsmouth for most of that time and following the superior court as it traveled on its circuit. Toward the end of this period, he became more involved with politics, becoming a vocal member of the Federalist Party and opposing the War of 1812. He also made several well-received speeches across New Hampshire. He was elected to the U.S. House of Representatives in 1812 and strongly opposed the war and the embargo, but he distanced himself from talk of disunion and the Hartford Convention.

Webster was reelected in 1814. He promoted the Second Bank of the United States and opposed high tariffs on shipbuilding materials. In 1816 he moved his law office from New Hampshire to Boston and became more involved in legal work. He appeared before the U.S. Supreme Court in the case of *Dartmouth College v. Woodword* (1819) and soon became noted as one of the nation's leading lawyers. In the Dartmouth College case, Webster, a Dartmouth graduate himself, was reported to have moved John Marshall to tears by saying, "It is, sir, as I have said, a small college. And yet there are those who love it." A short time later, he reappeared in front of the court to argue successfully

Although he was an ardent opponent of slavery, Daniel Webster's reputation suffered when he voted in favor of the Fugitive Slave Act of 1850 as part of a political compromise. (Library of Congress)

for the Second Bank of the United States in *McCulloch v. Maryland* (1819). He focused on his successful law practice, which earned up to $15,000 a year, and participated in three more constitutionally significant cases: *Gibbons v. Ogden* (1824), *Osborn v. Bank of the United States* (1824), and *Ogden v. Saunders* (1827). At the height of his legal and oratorical powers, Daniel Webster was believed by some to be able to convince anyone of anything, a belief later noted in Stephen Vincent Benet's short story, "The Devil and Daniel Webster," (also later made into a movie), where Webster is retained to defend a man who has sold his soul to the devil but does not want to relinquish it.

While still involved in his law practice in 1827, Webster was elected to the U.S. Senate. Reversing his previous position, he became an active champion of tariffs because by this time, they supported the New England mills. His personal life was somewhat traumatic; both his wife Grace and his brother Ezekiel died, but he remarried Caroline Le Roy in 1829.

Webster became involved in the battle over nullification, and in 1830 he delivered his famous reply to South Carolina senator Robert Hayne, declaring that he favored "Liberty and Union, now and forever, one and inseparable" (Baxter, 1984). This battle was symptomatic of the larger early nineteenth-century conflict over America's form—whether America was going to be one country, ruled by a federal government, or a loosely disconnected union of relatively independent states (and this second form was favored by those who argued for "states' rights"). Part and parcel of this battle was the whole issue of slavery, which of course the South wanted and an increasing number (but not a majority) of northern states opposed. The South favored the states' rights theory of government when it favored slavery and its interests, as it did in the 1830s, but opposed it when it did not favor slavery, which is what occurred in the late 1850s, when the South favored a strong federal Fugitive Slave Law and the North (or at least some of it) argued for states' rights and the rights of the states to block that law.

Webster was reelected in 1833, supported the high tariffs of the period in the battle over the "compromise tariff" of 1833, and opposed President Andrew Jackson's attempts to withdraw all U.S. funds from the Bank of the United States. Throughout his career, Webster was a heavy overspender, and he was dependent on loans from friends, associates, and creditors, including the Bank of the United States, making him both a congressional and legal advocate of the Bank while also being in debt to it. Webster appeared, unsuccessfully, before the Supreme Court in 1836 in the famous *Charles River Bridge* case. He also began to overindulge increasingly in alcohol, resulting in weight gain and occasional drunkenness.

Webster was nominated by Massachusetts for president in 1836, but only received the electoral votes of that state in the contest. He was reelected to the Senate in 1839, campaigned for William Henry Harrison in the election of 1840, and was named secretary of state after Harrison's victory. Upon the accession of John Tyler, Webster remained in that office and conducted difficult negotiations regarding the Maine border and a number of other issues that were solved in the Webster–Ashburton Treaty (1842). The issues raised in the *Creole* case were addressed, as the British promised that colonial governors would avoid "officious interference" when U.S. vessels forced by violence or storm entered their ports. Webster also was successful in diplomatic ventures with China, Mexico, and Portugal.

Webster resigned in 1843 under heavy pressure from his party due to its dissatisfaction with the Tyler administration and returned to a legal career, even though he had desired a diplomatic appointment to Great Britain. He returned to the Senate in 1845, with financial assistance from his creditors, and opposed the acquisition of Texas and the later Mexican War.

Webster's second son, Edward, died in the Mexican War (1846–1848), and a daughter, Julia, died not long afterward.

After the election of 1848, a new sectional crisis loomed, and Webster tried to preserve the nation. In his famous 1850 "Seventh of March" speech, he claimed that keeping the nation together was more important than the issue of slavery. He was widely praised by the South, but condemned by his own party and northern abolitionists. Nevertheless, he became secretary of state again in 1850 and performed his duties capably. He was interested in the nomination for president in 1852 but could not carry the Whig Party. Webster began to decline physically in the summer of 1852 and died on October 24, 1852, well before the Civil War that he had tried so hard to avoid.

—Scott A. Merriman

See also: Adams, John Quincy; Calhoun, John C.; Compromise of 1850; Nullification Doctrine; Hayne–Webster Debate; Webster–Ashburton Treaty.

For Further Reading

Baxter, Maurice. 1984. *One and Inseparable: Daniel Webster and the Union.* Cambridge, MA: Belknap Press of Harvard University Press.

Peterson, Merrill. 1987. *The Great Triumvirate: Webster, Clay and Calhoun.* New York: Oxford University Press.

Remini, Robert V. 1997. *Daniel Webster: The Man and His Time.* New York: Norton.

Shewmaker, Kenneth, ed. 1990. *Daniel Webster: The 'Completest Man.'* Hanover, NH: Dartmouth College, University Press of New England.

Smith, Craig R. 1989. *Defender of the Union: The Oratory of Daniel Webster.* Westport, CT: Greenwood.

Webster, Daniel. 1969. *Speak for Yourself, Daniel: A Life of Webster in His Own Words.* Ed. Walker Lewis. Boston: Houghton Mifflin.

WEBSTER–ASHBURTON TREATY (1842)

The Webster–Ashburton Treaty (1842) settled several outstanding issues between the United States and Great Britain, including both the appropriate handling of U.S. ships carrying slaves forced into British ports and joint U.S.-British efforts to limit the African slave trade. The treaty is named for the two principal negotiators of the pact, Daniel Webster of the United States and Lord Ashburton (Alexander Baring) of Great Britain.

The main issues covered related to slavery and the

northeastern boundary of the United States, the latter having nearly brought the two nations to blows in the 1839 Aroostook War. An extradition agreement was one large part of the treaty. This grew out of the 1841 *Creole* incident, in which a slave ship of that name engaged in interstate U.S. trade and was taken over by mutinous slaves who then sailed it into Nassau in the British-controlled Bahamas, where those slaves who had not participated in the mutiny were allowed to go free. After heated debate, the British finally decided to let the mutineers go free as well. This whole incident did not please the South, and an extradition agreement covering nonpolitical crimes was inserted in the Webster–Ashburton Treaty to cover a future *Creole*-type case, as the mutinous slaves would now, at least theoretically, be returned.

In addition, there also was a provision for a joint-cruising squadron of ships off the African coast to prevent the British from having to interfere with U.S. ships, as the American squadron would do so when needed. This provision was also supposed to prevent slavers trading with Africa from illegally hiding behind the United States flag. The United States had banned the trade, but without U.S. ships patrolling off the African coast, ships flying an American flag could not be searched. The treaty was supposed to correct this problem.

The treaty also dealt with problems connected with the northeastern boundary. Although the issue may have seemed to have been solved in the Treaty of Paris (1783), which ended the American Revolution, that agreement merely established a commission, which never reached a conclusion, and later attempts to arbitrate the boundary were equally unsuccessful. Another border area that was decided by the Webster–Ashburton Treaty was the one involving the area around Lake Superior, which was settled favorably to the United States, including granting to that country the Vermilion Range in northeastern Minnesota, which—unknown then—was very rich in mineral deposits. The United States was also granted free navigation of the Saint John River in northeastern Maine and southeastern Canada.

Besides the treaty, several important notes were exchanged at the same time. One recorded the United States' disagreement with the former British practice of impressment. This practice forced British citizens into the navy, from which many deserted. The British would then stop American vessels, search them, and then "impress" all (and theoretically only) those who could not prove American citizenship into the navy. In reality, the British would often seize anyone they could lay their hands on, infuriating America. The second

note allowed for the protection of ships by the flag they flew, which theoretically covered incidents like the one in the 1830s in which the U.S. ship *Caroline* ferrying supplies to Canadian rebels was attacked and sunk by Canadians (which angered many citizens of the United States). A third note gave assurance that United States ships driven into foreign ports would be allowed to continue without interference—this note also dealt with the *Creole* incident.

— *Scott A. Merriman*

See also: Webster, Daniel.

For Further Reading

Anderson, M. S. 1993. *The Rise of Modern Diplomacy, 1450–1919.* New York: Longman.

Baxter, Maurice. 1984. *One and Inseparable: Daniel Webster and the Union.* Cambridge, MA: Belknap Press of Harvard University Press.

Jones, Howard. 1977. *To the Webster–Ashburton Treaty: A Study in Anglo-American Relations.* Chapel Hill: University of North Carolina Press.

Remini, Robert V. 1997. *Daniel Webster: The Man and His Time.* New York: Norton.

THEODORE DWIGHT WELD (1803–1895)

Theodore Dwight Weld was a social reformer and one of the most important figures in the antislavery movement. Through his work at Lane Theological Seminary and later at Oberlin College, he influenced many who became active in the national crusade against slavery. Weld was a tireless worker for the antislavery cause, but his work was virtually forgotten and unknown until the publication of Gilbert H. Barnes's *The Antislavery Impulse, 1830–1844* (1933). Barnes was the first historian to recognize Weld's huge contribution at the beginning of the antislavery movement. The *Dictionary of American Biography* says of him, "measured by his influence, Theodore Weld was not only the greatest of the abolitionists, he was also one of the greatest figures of his time."

Weld was born in Connecticut but raised in western New York in what became known as the "Burned over District." His father was a conservative, small-town pastor. Weld had little formal education, but his "learning [was] prodigious, his powers of reasoning superb." He has been described as "the nerve center of the antislavery movement until the schism of 1840" (Barnes, 1933).

Weld's early career was inextricably connected to

the work of Charles Grandison Finney. The two made antislavery a religious and moral issue, separate from politics and economics. Weld had been an early associate of Charles Stuart who interested him in the slavery question. Both Stuart and Weld fell under Finney's influence and were active members of his band of religious revivalists. Finney has long been regarded as the foremost figure of the Second Great Awakening during the second quarter of the nineteenth century. It was through Finney's teachings and Stuart's interest in reform that Finney's followers became interested and, later, heavily involved in the antislavery crusade.

Weld was interested in the slavery issue as early as 1830. He began to travel, particularly to colleges and universities in Ohio's Western Reserve, to "indoctrinate" faculties in opposition to slavery. His association with others in the movement won him respect for his leadership and his oratory. He was a close friend of James Gillespie Birney and the Grimké sisters (he later married Angelina). Birney's personal knowledge of slavery's sordid aspects developed in Weld an intense, personal patriotism that came to view the "peculiar institution" as a "cancerous growth within the body politic." Weld and Birney became active members of the American Colonization Society, and in 1832 Weld became the society's general agent for states lying southwest of the Ohio River.

Weld and his associates gradually moved away from the ideas espoused by the Colonization Society toward general emancipation. The American Anti-Slavery Society was established as the result of this change in the movement's direction. Its program was defined as, "immediate preparation for future emancipation." This group followed the lead set by Birney and others involved in, what was then, the revolutionary Kentucky Society for the Gradual Relief of the State from Slavery whose charter proclaimed, "first, that slavery shall cease to exist—absolutely, unconditionally, and irrevocably."

One of Weld's greatest contributions to the antislavery crusade came through his work at Lane Theological Seminary in Cincinnati, Ohio. That city held about twenty-five hundred African Americans, more than one-third of all blacks in Ohio. Many of these were emancipated slaves who had purchased their freedom or who were still paying for themselves or for friends and relatives still in bondage. It was here that emancipated slaves were given the opportunities to test their abilities to make economic, cultural, and social advances not otherwise available to them. They threw themselves into the task with education as their chief goal. They formed Sabbath schools, day and evening schools, a lyceum where lectures were held four

evenings a week with local and guest speakers on grammar, geography, arithmetic, philosophy, religion, and politics. In this environment Weld enjoyed his greatest successes as the leader of the theological classes.

The students shared their stories of slavery and how they managed to escape to Ohio. "They had pooled their intimate knowledge of slavery gained by long residence in the slave states, had reasoned and rationalized as became gentlemen [and ladies] trained in the school of the Great Revival, and had concluded that slavery was a sin great enough to justify their undivided attention" (Thomas, 1950). Most of the students and Weld moved to Oberlin College where their ideas about slavery were better received and where Finney had come to head the Theology Department.

It was at Oberlin, after Weld's marriage to Angelina Grimké, that he wrote and published the first widely distributed book in the United States advocating complete emancipation. *American Slavery As It Is: Testimony of a Thousand Witnesses* (1839), a devastating indictment of the institution, was his *magnum opus.* Nearly all of the episodes mentioned in the book came from the Lane-Oberlin students. It portrayed the slavery system at its worst by documenting case after case of extreme cruelty. The work was lauded by antislavery and abolitionist groups and was soundly criticized in the South. Few could read it without emotion and without hating slavery. It quickly became the abolitionists' ammunition since its impact in the North was tremendous. It was widely distributed and sold for only 37.5 cents a copy or 25 dollars per hundred. It was the preeminent book of antislavery literature until 1852 when Harriet Beecher Stowe published *Uncle Tom's Cabin* (Stowe had been one of Weld's Oberlin students, much to the chagrin of her father, Lyman Beecher). *Slavery As It Is* served as one of Charles Dickens's sources for *American Notes* (1842), though he gave Weld no credit. Weld's book became an instrument for British interest in ending slavery in their territories.

Weld also wrote a companion volume arguing that God was against slavery. *The Bible Against Slavery* (1839) dealt only with the Old Testament. That led to the publication of still another book, written together with Beriah Green and Elizur Wright, Jr., both eminent theologians; they brought the antislavery argument into the New Testament in *The Chattel Principle, The Abhorrence of Jesus Christ and the Apostles: or No Refuge for American Slavery in the New Testament* (1839).

Weld's books became instant best-sellers. A book of statistics designed to accompany *Slavery As It Is* was published in London under the title *Slavery and the Internal Slave Trade in the United States* (1841).

Weld's influence peaked in the early 1840s. The antislavery crusade continued on the roller coaster that led, inevitably, to the Civil War. Weld spent his last years in near seclusion in Massachusetts, occasionally lecturing on literature and religion. He was surrounded by the intellectuals of his day, particularly by the poet John Greenleaf Whittier, who wrote of Weld in 1884 that he had lived "a life of brave unselfishness, . . . for Freedom's need" (Thomas, 1950). Weld died on February 3, 1895, at the age of ninety-one years and two months. His life nearly spanned the entire nineteenth century, and he participated in almost every major reform movement of the age.

— *Henry H. Goldman*

See also: American Anti-Slavery Society; American Colonization Society; Garrison, William Lloyd.

For Further Reading

Barnes, Gilbert Hobbs. 1933. *The Anti-Slavery Impulse, 1830–1844.* Gloucester, MA: Peter Smith.

Dumond, Dwight Lowell. 1959. *Antislavery Origins of the Civil War in the United States.* Ann Arbor: University of Michigan Press.

Lloyd, Arthur Young. 1939. *The Slavery Controversy, 1831–1860.* Chapel Hill: University of North Carolina Press.

Thomas, Benjamin P. 1950. *Theodore Dwight Weld, Crusader for Freedom.* New Brunswick, NJ: Rutgers University Press.

PHILLIS WHEATLEY (C. 1753–1784)

As the first published black poetess in the American colonies, Phillis Wheatley, through her life and work, contributed to the eighteenth- and nineteenth-century debate about the intellectual capabilities of African Americans. Details about her early life in West Africa remain obscure. She arrived in Boston in July 1761 aboard the slaver *Phillis* and was sold to John Wheatley, a prominent local merchant.

Although the Wheatley family owned several slaves, Phillis Wheatley appears to have held a privileged position within the household. Initially, she received religious instruction and learned to speak, read, and write in English. Later, her education expanded to include literature, history, Latin, and geography. Wheatley was a bright pupil, and within four years of her arrival, she had begun to write her own poetry, an activity her owner's family encouraged. Wheatley's poems, written in the style of neoclassical verse, centered around religious themes (particularly death) and the growing tension between Great Britain and the North American colonies.

As her talent for writing matured, the Wheatley family became more involved in promoting her work to a wide audience and began a campaign to publish her poems. In December 1767, Wheatley's first poem, "On Messrs Hussey and Coffin," was published in Newport, Rhode Island. In 1770 her poem on the death of Methodist minister George Whitefield brought her considerable attention throughout New England. In 1772 the Wheatley family attempted to raise a subscription to publish a collection of Wheatley's poems but was unable to generate enough interest in the project. Instead, Wheatley and her mistress, Susanna Wheatley, traveled to London in the summer of 1773 in the hopes of finding a more enthusiastic audience for her work. Through the patronage of Selina Hastings, countess of Huntingdon, the pair engendered a great deal of interest among London society.

Subsequently, Wheatley's first and only book, *Poems on Various Subjects, Religious and Moral* (1773), was published in London. To erase doubts that a black slave, particularly a woman, could write poetry, a letter appeared in the front of the book signed by eighteen of Boston's most prestigious citizens, including Governor Thomas Hutchinson and John Hancock, testifying that a close examination of Wheatley and her work had convinced them that she had indeed written the poetry herself. The volume received good reviews and sold well in both Britain and America.

Although the success of her book boded well for Wheatley, upheaval in her personal life during and after the American Revolution put an end to her career as a poet. By 1779 most of the Wheatley family had died, and Phillis Wheatley herself had married a free black named John Peters. She bore him three children over the next five years, but all of them died young. Financial difficulties plagued the family, and Wheatley's attempts to publish additional volumes of poetry were unsuccessful. Wasted by poverty and disease, she died on December 5, 1784.

Both during her lifetime and after her death, Wheatley's work received attention primarily because she was a woman and a black slave. Serious literary evaluations of her poetry have been overshadowed by efforts to use her as an example in the debate over African American intellectual ability, or lack thereof. Thomas Jefferson, in particular, brought attention to her work when he cited her poetry in his *Notes on Virginia* (1785) as "below the dignity of criticism," a comment that vaulted her to the very center of the controversy about the capacity of African Americans to engage in intellectual pursuits and continues to influence her reputation.

In the late twentieth century, discussions concerning Wheatley have centered around her role in the demise of moral and intellectual justifications for slavery, particularly in New England. Critics condemn her for focusing her poems on the subjects of death, religion, and patriotism rather than on the plight of her fellow Africans in slavery. Supporters counter that Wheatley's concerns about slavery are implicit throughout her work and that more explicit references to slavery would not have survived the censorship of her white benefactors. This debate has led to a reevaluation of her work and additional study of her life.

— *Elizabeth Dubrulle*

See also: Whitefield, George.

For Further Reading
Mason, Julian D., Jr., ed. 1989. *The Poems of Phillis Wheatley.* Chapel Hill: University of North Carolina Press.

O'Neale, Sondra A. 1985. "Challenge to Wheatley's Critics: There Was No Other 'Game' in Town." *Journal of Negro Education* 54 (4): 500–511.

Robinson, William H. 1981. *Phillis Wheatley: A Bio-Bibliography.* Boston: G. K. Hall.

Robinson, William H. 1984. *Phillis Wheatley and Her Writings.* New York: Garland.

Wilcox, Kristin. 1999. "The Body into Print: Marketing Phillis Wheatley." *American Literature* 71 (1): 1–29.

An 1848 campaign banner for Whig Party presidential candidate Zachary Taylor (left) and his running mate Millard Fillmore (right). Taylor won the election but died after two years in office; he was succeeded by Fillmore. (Library of Congress)

WHIG PARTY

By the 1850s the issue of slavery, particularly the expansion of slavery into new territories, had come to dominate the American political scene. As the nation moved toward disunion and civil war, the dividing line was clearly drawn between those groups and people who would preserve the institution and those who would eradicate it. This division affected most institutions in American life, as political parties, religious denominations, and even families split between pro- and antislavery factions. For the Whig Party, internal divisions over slavery proved fatal.

The Whig Party originated as a political coalition against Jacksonian Democrats in 1834. Led by Henry Clay, Daniel Webster, and William Henry Harrison, the emergence of the Whigs inaugurated the second-party system in the United States. The Whigs adopted a broad construction of the U.S. Constitution, believing that the federal government should take an active role in the nation's economic life. Initially, the party was made up of a loose coalition of disaffected Democrats and others united by a hatred of Jackson and their support of a national bank, a high protective tariff, and federal aid to internal improvements. Though united on these economic issues, the Whigs divided on other policy matters, particularly slavery. This division led to the formation of two internal factions during the debates over the Wilmot Proviso in 1846.

One faction, called the Conscience Whigs, opposed the expansion of slavery into the territories. Led by Turlow Weed and William H. Seward, Conscience Whigs believed that slavery was a moral blight on the nation and should not be expanded. More radical members of this group called for immediate and uncompensated abolition. Abraham Lincoln, elected to Congress in 1846, can be described as a Conscience Whig. Although strongest in New England and in New York, this faction was present in most northern and midwestern states. In 1848 many of these Whigs left the party altogether and merged with antislavery Democrats and remnants of the Liberty Party to form the Free Soil Party. Conscience Whigs who remained in the Whig ranks continued to push for antislavery legislation and the adoption of antislavery planks in the national party platform.

Though originally used to describe proslavery Whigs in Massachusetts, the term *Cotton Whigs* can be used to describe another faction of the party. Made up of southern Whigs and northerners from states with a vested interest in the continued vitality of southern agriculture, Cotton Whigs supported the institution of slavery on social, economic, and constitutional grounds. Prominent Cotton Whigs included Alexander H. Stephens, Henry Clay, and Daniel Webster. Though labeled by Charles Sumner as a partnership between "the lords of the lash and the lords of the loom," members of the faction varied considerably in their ideology concerning slavery (Brauer, 1967). Although southerners like Stephens defended the legality of slavery under the Constitution and emphasized the racial inferiority of blacks, Webster argued that slavery should not be expanded into the territories and would die a natural death without legislative intervention. Despite these differences, Cotton Whigs agreed that the moral tone injected into the slavery debate by the 1840s heightened tension over what to them was essentially a political issue.

The internal division over slavery was the death knell of the Whig Party. By 1856 the party had imploded, with Cotton Whigs gravitating to the Democratic or American (Know-Nothing) parties, both of which refused to take a definitive stand on slavery. Many Conscience Whigs joined the Republicans, who staunchly opposed slavery. In many ways the dissolution of the Whig Party mirrored the deepening sectional tension in the nation as a whole during the 1840s and 1850s. By failing to resolve party differences over slavery, the Whigs could no longer wield meaningful political power. The split, largely along sectional lines, was an important precursor to the bloody national epoch that began in 1861.

— *Richard D. Starnes*

See also: Free Soil Party; Wilmot Proviso.

For Further Reading

Brauer, Kinley. 1967. *Cotton versus Conscience: Massachusetts Whig Party Politics and Southwestern Expansion, 1843–1848.* Lexington: University of Kentucky Press.

Freehling, William. 1990. *The Road to Disunion.* New York: Harper and Row.

Gatell, Frank Otto. 1958. "Conscience and Judgment: The Bolt of Massachusetts Conscience Whigs." *The Historian* 27 (November): 18–45.

McPherson, James M. 1963. "The Fight against the Gag Rule: Joshua Leavitt and Antislavery Insurgency in the Whig Party, 1839–1842." *Journal of Negro History* 48 (July): 177–95.

Potter, David. 1976. *The Impending Crisis, 1848–1861.* New York: Harper and Row.

GEORGE WHITEFIELD (1714–1770)

Reverend George Whitefield was a pioneering figure in Christian evangelism in the eighteenth-century Anglo-American world and so helped lay the foundations of the abolition movement, but he had mixed thoughts on the evils of slavery. Whitefield, ordained an Anglican minister in 1736, was a brilliant preacher whose innovative open-air preaching and emotional style won him an immense popular following and was part of the British revival that created Methodism. Visiting the colonial South in 1739 Whitefield observed the cruelty of plantation society, noting with displeasure the lack of religious provision for slaves, and unconventionally decided to address mixed-race meetings. In 1740 Whitefield went on his first major preaching tour in the northern colonies that helped trigger the revivals known as the Great Awakening. Following this he printed a letter entitled "To the inhabitants of Maryland, Virginia, North and South Carolina concerning their Negroes." Whitefield's letter, which exposed the harsh and un-Christian conditions slaves endured, was reprinted in newspapers across the country and aroused intense controversy that included blaming Whitefield for the Stono Uprising (1739). Whitefield's humanitarian concerns are further demonstrated by his attempts to set up a college to educate freed slaves in Delaware. All this shows why Phillis Wheatley wrote an elegy to Whitefield as a friend to those in bondage.

Despite Whitefield's concern for the physical well-being of slaves and their spiritual salvation, he never condemned the institution of slavery outright. Whitefield thought slavery was justified by scripture and that agriculture in hot climates was dependent on African labor. While he did not approve of the slave trade, he thought it could not be controlled. Slavery could also bring spiritual benefits because it exposed Africans to the Christian message. Whitefield was using exactly the type of justifications that southern evangelical churches would continue to use to defend the continuation of a properly regulated form of slavery. Whitefield's ideas were influenced by his connections with

One of colonial America's most popular preachers, George Whitefield was among the first to perform mass revivals. Sometimes preaching 40 to 50 hours a week, he was instrumental in spreading the evangelical Protestant movement known as the Great Awakening. (Library of Congress)

the struggling slave-free colony of Georgia where he had founded an orphan house. In 1747 he accepted a donation of a small slave plantation in South Carolina to support the orphanage. The profitable plantation, run on Whitefield's strict welfare guidelines, supported his long-standing belief, voiced in a letter to the Georgia trustees in 1748, that the legalization of slavery was necessary for the success of Georgia, an event that occurred two years later.

Even though Whitefield held such proslavery ideas himself, the active evangelical Christianity he promoted became a seedbed for abolitionism. This is obvious from examining the abolitionist tendencies of the movements Whitefield helped pave the way for the Methodism of his close friend John Wesley, as well as for the Anglican Evangelical movement that produced William Wilberforce and the varied fruits of the Great Awakening. One of those awakened to an intense piety by Whitefield's preaching was Quaker Anthony Benezet, who later became committed to abolition and condemned Whitefield's views on slavery. Whitefield's

emphasis on the need to convert slaves and the spiritual equality between black and white also helped encourage the formation of the Afro-American churches that had such important effects on the nature of slavery and abolition. Whitefield's unintended legacy then was the evangelical and populist ideals that were to inspire the transatlantic abolitionist crusade.

— *Gwilym Games*

See also: Abolitionism in the United States; Georgia; Stono Rebellion; Wheatley, Phillis.

For Further Reading

Dallimore, Arnold. 1970. *George Whitefield.* London: Banner of Truth Trust.

Heimert, Alan. 1966. *Religion and the American Mind: From Great Awakening to the Revolution.* Cambridge, MA: Harvard University Press.

Lambert, Frank. 1994. *Peddler in Divinity: George Whitefield and the Transatlantic Revivals.* Princeton, NJ: Princeton University Press.

Stout, Harry S. 1991. *The Divine Dramatist: George Whitefield and the Rise of Modern Evangelicalism.* Grand Rapids, MI: William B. Eerdmans.

ELI WHITNEY (1765–1825)

Eli Whitney invented the cotton gin and developed the assembly line for mass production of interchangeable parts. Whitney's cotton gin profoundly affected the American economy, revolutionized the cotton industry, and further entrenched slavery in the antebellum South. During his childhood in Westboro, Massachusetts, Whitney demonstrated an exceptional mechanical ingenuity. When he was sixteen years old, he established a successful nail-forging business to address the shortage of nails during the American Revolution. He entered Yale College in 1789 despite a friend's remark that "it was a pity that such a fine mechanical genius as his should be wasted" (Olmsted, 1846).

After graduating from Yale in 1792, Whitney went to Savannah, Georgia, to study law and tutor the children of the late General Nathanael Greene. Greene's widow and her friends continually discussed the profitability of growing cotton in the area to satisfy England's heightened demand for the fiber. The growing use of steam power to spin and weave fabric led to England's increased demand for the fiber. Georgia's inland region was favorable for growing green-seed, short-staple cotton. However, the method of separating the cotton from its seed was so tedious that it was impractical, since one worker yielded only about one pound of clean green-seed cotton per day.

Eli Whitney invented the cotton gin in 1793. (Library of Congress)

Whitney devised a machine that would address this problem. During winter 1792, he created a model cotton gin (an abbreviation for "engine") that expedited the cotton separation operation. The gin consisted of a roller with comb-like teeth that removed the seeds from the fiber and a spinning brush that removed the excess lint from the roller. After perfecting his gin by April 1793, Whitney's machine enabled one worker to process 50 pounds of cotton a day.

Soon other inventors imitated Whitney's gin, and he depleted his earnings defending his patent rights in court. Heavily in debt in 1798, he contracted with the U.S. government to make 10,000 muskets. Whitney designed a machine that produced a firearm with interchangeable parts. He created a division of labor whereby each person specialized in making one part of the musket.

The cotton gin transformed the American economy and increased the demand for slave labor. In the South, cotton became the chief crop and the basis of the region's economy. Cotton production in the South increased from about three thousand bales in 1793 to approximately one hundred seventy-eight thousand bales by 1800. Cotton was "king" and the greatest export of the country. In 1825 cotton represented $36 billion of an estimated total of $66 billion total domestic exports from the United States. By 1860 cotton production exploded to 4 million bales per year.

This profound increase in cotton production affected the northern economy as well. The bountiful cotton crop encouraged New England entrepreneurs to create a native textile industry. The manufacturing of cotton cloth enabled the North to evolve into an industrialized region.

Coupled with the increased demand for cotton was the need for more slave labor. By the late eighteenth century, slavery appeared to be in decline. The northern states took steps to abolish forced servitude, since it was never vital to their economy, and during the same period, the tobacco market collapsed in the South, and there was a decreased demand for rice and indigo, which used many slaves. By 1800 slavery appeared to be on its way to extinction in the United States.

The invention of the cotton gin revived the institution of slavery. Cotton production required an abundance of unskilled labor—plowing, planting, ditch digging, weeding, picking, ginning, baling, and shipping. Because of their role in the cotton production process, slaves became more valuable. Slave prices doubled between 1795 and 1804 in conjunction with the great demand for cotton production and expected closing of the African slave trade. Slaves who had become financial liabilities for their owners in nonproducing cotton states were sold for profit in the Deep South where cotton thrived.

Always seeking more fertile soil, cotton growers migrated west with their slaves from North Carolina and Georgia through the lower South to Alabama, Mississippi, and Louisiana, and finally to Texas by the 1840s. Between 1790 and 1860, about 1 million slaves were forced to move westward, and most found the experience extremely traumatic. This was the first large-scale dislocation of slaves since their forced immigration to colonial America. Separated from friends and families and far from their homes, slaves experienced heart-wrenching separation ordeals. By 1860 most of the 4.5 million slaves lived in the cotton-producing belt of the South.

As the North became more industrialized and the South remained agrarian, slavery became one of the dividing issues between the two regions. Whitney's invention of the cotton gin, inadvertently contributed to the coming of the Civil War and his idea of interchangeable parts for firearms ensured a Union victory. Whitney died in New Haven, Connecticut, on January 8, 1825.

— *Julieanne Phillips*

See also: Cotton Gin.

For Further Reading

Kolchin, Peter. 1993. *American Slavery: 1619–1877.* New York: Hill and Wang.

Lakwete, Angela. 2003. *Inventing the Cotton Gin: Machine and Myth in Antebellum America.* Baltimore, MD: Johns Hopkins University Press.

Olmsted, Denison. 1846. *Memoir of Eli Whitney, Esq.* New York: Arno Press.

WILMOT PROVISO

The Wilmot Proviso was perhaps the most significant piece of legislation never enacted in U.S. history. Originally proposed as an amendment to the 1846 army appropriations bill, the proviso attempted to prohibit slavery from territories acquired as a result of the Mexican War (1846–1848). A bitterly divided House of Representatives passed the measure, but it was defeated in the southern-dominated Senate. By focusing the antislavery debate on the institution's potential expansion into new western territories, the proviso set the terms of the national debate over slavery for the fifteen years preceding the Civil War.

The measure's introduction began a new era of sectional politics in the United States: nearly all northern Democrats and all northern Whigs voted in favor of the proviso, while practically every representative from districts south of the Mason–Dixon line and the Ohio River opposed it. In other words, the expansion of slavery was an issue that split both major political parties into distinct northern and southern wings. The initial vote on the Wilmot Proviso (and the dozens that followed it) were an ominous sign that the politics of the second party system (Democratic and Whig) would be unable to contain the explosive issue of slavery's expansion.

Democratic representative David Wilmot of Pennsylvania introduced the proviso on August 8, 1846, just a few months after the Mexican War began. President James K. Polk, a Democrat and a Tennessee slaveholder, had sent Congress an appropriations bill asking for $2 million to negotiate a treaty with Mexico. Wilmot, a first-term lawmaker, offered an amendment to the bill "that, as an express and fundamental condition of the acquisition of any territory from the Republic of Mexico . . . neither slavery nor involuntary servitude shall ever exist in any part of said territory."

Both the language and strategy behind the proviso were unremarkable. Its wording, for example, was lifted straight from Thomas Jefferson's Northwest Ordinance (1787), which prohibited slavery in the Old

Pennsylvania Congressman David Wilmot drafted the Wilmot Proviso in 1846; it stated that all territory gained from Mexico should be free from slavery.

Northwest, lands north and west of the Ohio River. The same legislative device had been used just two days earlier (and with little southern opposition), when the House voted to provide a territorial government for Oregon.

Several factors marked the proviso as a watershed in antebellum U.S. history. First, it was a turning point between two distinct antislavery eras. Before the measure's introduction, antislavery battles were waged over a range of issues, from the gag rule on abolitionist petitions to the U.S. Constitution's three-fifths clause, which granted southern states more representation than they would otherwise have had. Afterward, slavery's expansion into the territories absorbed every related issue. The issue of slavery's expansion initially split the major parties into sectional antagonists.

Second, the proviso represented a major shift in the antislavery movement's constituency. The group of congressmen who hatched the idea for the measure was made up of northern Democrats, most of whom represented remote, agricultural districts. Democrats like David Wilmot were not usually associated with antislavery politics, which tended to be commercially oriented, evangelical, and aristocratic. But many northern Jacksonian Democrats reached the breaking point with Polk's administration in 1846, believing it to be pro-southern and proslavery.

Some resented Polk's having received the Democratic Party's nomination for president at the expense of New Yorker Martin Van Buren in 1844. Others believed the president's acceptance of Oregon's boundary at 49° north latitude was an insult to northern sentiment and confirmed the administration's southern bias. Democrats from the Old Northwest were angered by Polk's veto of a popular rivers and harbors bill. A growing number of northerners had come to believe that a southern "conspiracy" existed to control the federal government and open the west to slavery. They believed this "Slave Power" threatened the freedom and future of white northerners because it advocated replicating the plantation system in the new territories. Taken together, these disgruntled Democrats provided the antislavery movement with the mass political appeal it needed to expand its constituency.

"The time has come," said one northern Democratic congressman in 1846, "when the Northern Democracy should make a stand. . . . We must satisfy the Northern people . . . that we are not to extend the institution of slavery as a result of this war" (Morrison, 1967). It was precisely this sentiment that turned administration loyalists like David Wilmot against Polk's administration, against southern members of their own party, and ultimately, against the expansion of slavery.

— *Jonathan Earle*

See also: Democratic Party; Free Soil Party.

For Further Reading

De Voto, Bernard A. 1989. *The Year of Decision: 1846.* Boston: Houghton Mifflin.

Foner, Eric. 1969. "The Wilmot Proviso Revisited." *Journal of American History* 61 (September): 269–79.

Going, Charles B. 1966. *David Wilmot, Free-Soiler: A Biography of the Great Advocate of the Wilmot Proviso.* Gloucester, MA: P. Smith.

Morrison, Chaplain W. 1967. *Democratic Politics and Sectionalism: The Wilmot Proviso Controversy.* Chapel Hill: University of North Carolina Press.

WOMEN AND THE ANTISLAVERY MOVEMENT (1832–1870)

Women were active in the antislavery movement, and until 1837, their contributions far outweighed their numbers. Initially in auxiliaries to men's societies and then as members of independent female antislavery societies, women circulated petitions, raised funds, distributed tracts, and organized and attended lectures on slavery and its abolition. A full appreciation of what these women did must be based on an understanding of the beliefs that influenced their actions and lives. The ideology of the "woman's sphere," the Second Great Awakening (1790s–c. 1830), various religious beliefs, and the effects of a pastoral letter are important elements in an understanding of the women's participation in and their withdrawal from the antislavery movement, as well as learning how the women's rights movement grew out of antislavery.

Women's roles centered around their homes and families as the United States moved toward having a capitalist economy. Women were not only the keepers of the home but also the guardians of religion and morality. The ideology of the "woman's sphere" gave women moral superiority over men and made them responsible for correcting any ethical wrongs they might see. Women found society corrupt and began exerting their influence in a wider circle, becoming housekeepers of social virtue.

The Second Great Awakening encouraged women to participate in the moral reform of U.S. society. Charles Grandison Finney and his troop of ministers encouraged women to participate publicly in his revivals. Finney also suggested that women might use their piety and moral superiority to reform society. The antislavery movement developed during this reforming surge, and women were drawn to the movement by both their religious beliefs and their ministers' encouragement. Slavery was perceived as a moral and domestic evil affecting women, and antislavery women were determined to end this evil through moral persuasion. Once they began, women were tireless in their efforts, collecting more petition signatures and raising more money than men. Society's housekeepers were hard at work exerting their moral influence on the people of the United States to reform the nature of slavery.

Women joined the antislavery movement with differing religious beliefs, which reflected their membership in many denominations. Initially, these divergent beliefs did not impede the women's activity, but eventually, the differing beliefs caused trouble. The religious affiliations of the women fell into two basic groups: evangelicals—those belonging to Methodist, Baptist, Presbyterian, and Congregationalist churches—and liberals—primarily Quakers and Unitarians. It is important to remember that both groups were motivated by their religious beliefs. The factions differed in that the evangelical abolitionists placed more authority in their ministers while the liberal abolitionists placed little or no authority in theirs.

On July 28, 1837, the Massachusetts General Association of Congregational Ministers issued a pastoral letter that was partly an attempt to discredit the Grimké sisters. It was also a call for men and women to limit their antislavery activity on the advice of their ministers. The conservative Congregational clergy had been under attack for several years for their weak antislavery position, and the letter was meant to reassert the clergy's authority over their congregations. The letter included a veiled threat that ministers would withdraw their guidance and support from those female parishioners who continued their antislavery activities. Evangelical women constituted most of the female antislavery group, and they responded to the pastoral letter dramatically. After 1840 the New York women discontinued their antislavery work completely, and the Boston women's society split, its effectiveness now diminished.

The women's rights movement originated in the antislavery movement. As women spoke out for the rights of slaves, they found themselves also defending their own right to speak publicly. As women's antislavery work came under attack, many antislavery women began seeing their own plight reflected in that of the slaves. Many of the most active antislavery women led the movement for women's rights, including Lucretia Mott, Angelina Grimké, Sarah Grimké, and Abby Kelley. Other leaders of the women's rights movement got their start in the antislavery movement, including Susan B. Anthony and Elizabeth Cady Stanton.

Women provided the backbone for the antislavery movement. They collected twice as many signatures as men when they circulated petitions, their fund-raising efforts kept the national organization and many of its agents functioning, and their lectures raised the conscience of northerners to the plight of slaves. Angelina and Sarah Grimké fought for the right of women to do antislavery work, Lydia Maria Child edited the *National Anti-Slavery Standard* (an abolitionist newspaper), and Abby Kelley worked tirelessly as a lecturer and fund raiser. Equally important in the antislavery movement as the individual contributions of specific women was the entire membership's continuing support and involvement.

— *Sydney J. Caddel-Liles*

See also: *An Appeal to the Christian Women of the South;* Boston Female Anti-Slavery Society; Ladies' New York City Anti-Slavery Society; Philadelphia Female Anti-Slavery Society.

For Further Reading

Hersh, Blanche Glassman. 1978. *The Slavery of Sex: Feminist Abolitionist in America.* Urbana: University of Illinois Press.

Kraditor, Aileen. 1989. *Means and Ends in American Abolitionism: Garrison and His Critics on Strategy and Tactics, 1834–1850.* Chicago: Ivan R. Dee.

Speicher, Anna M. 2001. "The Religious World of Antislavery Women: Spirituality in the Lives of Five Abolitionist Lecturers." *Journal of American History* 88 (3): 1068–1069.

Thompson, Carol. 1976. "Women and the Anti-Slavery Movement." *Current History* 70 (May): 198–201.

Van Broeckhoven, Deborah B. 1985. "A Determination to Labor . . . Female Antislavery Activity in Rhode Island." *Rhode Island History* 44 (May): 35–45.

Yellin, Jean Fagan, and John C. Van Horne, eds. 1994. *The Abolitionist Sisterhood: Women's Political Culture in Antebellum America.* Ithaca, NY: Cornell University Press.

JOHN WOOLMAN (1720–1772)

John Woolman, Quaker leader and early champion of the abolition of slavery was born on October 19, 1720, at Ancocas (later Rancocas) in New Jersey and died on October 17, 1772 of smallpox while on a visit to York, England. Woolman's integrity and purity of spirit are visible in his writing on slavery and other issues. His true piety was recognized by people of many faiths, but Woolman's beliefs were rooted in the moral and spiritual values of the Quaker religion.

Woolman was one of thirteen children born to Samuel and Elizabeth (Burr) Woolman. The family had some standing in the Northampton section of the Quaker village now called Rancocas. His grandfather had emigrated to Burlington in West Jersey from Gloucestershire, England, in 1638 and served as a proprietor of West Jersey, and Woolman's father was a candidate for the provincial assembly of that region. John received a modest formal education at the village Quaker school and continued to educate himself through extensive reading.

John Woolman later started a business as tailor and retailer in Mount Holly, New Jersey, after serving his apprenticeship, and married Sarah Ellis of Chesterfield on October 18, 1749. He was so successful in business that Woolman worried that prosperity would distract him from spiritual concerns. At one point he sent prospective customers to his competitors. These fears did not keep Woolman from working at a variety of jobs, including surveying, conveyancing, executing bills of sale, and drawing up wills. He occasionally taught school and published a primer that was reprinted several times. At his death, Woolman left an estate of several hundred acres.

John Woolman's beliefs concerning slavery and other Quaker issues, including Indian conversion and opposition to conscription and taxation for military supplies, are clearly stated in his autobiographic *Journal* and other writings. Better known in England than in the United States, he is remembered for his opposition to slavery, which was the main focus of his adult life. Woolman's *Journal* has gone through more than forty editions, prized for its content and the elegant simplicity of its writing.

Woolman's Quaker beliefs were the center of his life from early childhood. At twenty-three, he felt a calling to the Quaker ministry, and for the next thirty years he would travel as a minister from Carolina to New Hampshire and Pennsylvania and finally to Yorkshire, England. There he caught smallpox while working among the poor and died.

Woolman realized as a young man that slavery was counter to the spiritual equality of Quaker society. He was one of the first to preach against and publish tracts about the evils of slavery at a time when few thought that slavery was un-Christian even among his Quaker brethren. He witnessed the evils of slavery at first hand as many residents of New Jersey owned slaves if they could afford them, even Quakers. Slaves imported from Africa were held at Perth Amboy until they were sold. In 1734 these slaves revolted in an attempt to escape by killing their masters. Although this made Woolman's crusade against slavery unpopular, he would continue to preach against it for the rest of his life.

His opposition to slavery was triggered by an event that happened shortly after a series of spiritual "openings" had led him to the ministry. As Woolman later wrote in his *Journal,* his employer asked him as a conveyancer, to write a bill of sale for a Negro woman he had sold to another member of the Society of Friends. He wrote the bill of sale but was so troubled by the event that he told his employer he believed slavery was inconsistent with the Christian religion.

Shortly afterward, he traveled to North Carolina where he witnessed the cruelty of plantation slavery. Woolman was horrified when he realized that he himself would enjoy the benefits of a system he believed was corrupt as long as he resided in plantation country. He wrote in his *Journal,* "I saw in these Southern Provinces so many Vices and Corruptions increased by this trade and this way of life, that it appeared to me as a dark gloominess, hanging over the Land, and in the future the Consequence will be grievous to posterity."

When he returned to New Jersey after visiting the South, Woolman finished a book titled *Some Considerations of the Keeping of Negroes Recommended to the Professors of Christianity of every Description.* Seven years later in 1753, Part 1 was officially sanctioned and printed by the Philadelphia Yearly Meeting; Part 2 was printed in 1762. Woolman based his argument against slavery on his belief in the brotherhood of all men, stating also that the black people did not voluntarily come to dwell among them. Although Woolman had little success in advancing abolition during his lifetime, his writing had a great influence in England and the United States and brought many to realize that slavery was morally wrong.

— *Elsa A. Nystrom*

See also: Quakers.

For Further Reading

Brock, Peter. 1990. *The Quaker Peace Testimony, 1660–1914.* York, England: Ebor Press.

Cady, Edwin H. 1965. *John Woolman.* New York: Twayne Publishers.

Sox, David. 1999. *John Woolman, Quintessential Quaker, 1720–1772.* Richmond, IN: Friends United Press.

Trueblood, David Elton. 1966. *The People Called Quakers.* Richmond, IN: Friends United Press.

Woolman, John. 1922. *The Journal and Essays of John Woolman.* Ed. A. M. Gunmere. New York: Macmillan.

WORKS PROGRESS ADMINISTRATION INTERVIEWS

Slavery provides virtually the prototype of the historical episode involving the inarticulate. Histories of the peculiar institution must of necessity focus primarily on sources produced by white observers. Thus the Slave Narrative Collection assembled by largely white interviewers of the Works Progress Administration (WPA) long after the fact triggered a seemingly endless cycle of debate concerning its credibility and reliability even as it offered one of the rare glimpses into slavery from the viewpoint of the slaves themselves.

As a whole, the program compiled more than two thousand interviews of people, between 1937 and 1939, who were mostly children during the time of slavery. More than two-thirds were under the age of sixteen when the Civil War ended. The litany of reasons why the narratives are to be viewed skeptically as a mirror of history is a long one. The interviewers and their subjects were not chosen for their expertise but for their need (in the case of the interviewers who were on relief) or for their availability (in the case of those interviewed). The aging ex-slaves—many of whom were also facing serious privation—had good reason to tell interviewers what they imagined they wanted to hear. Ironically, the ultimate director of the project, John A. Lomax, a folklore specialist (and a southerner), was responsible for both a heightened professionalism in the subjects asked and a regrettable tendency to send more whites than blacks to interview the ex-slaves.

Historians almost universally agree that the slave narratives, despite their deficiencies, benefited from a cultural, intellectual, and professional context that prefigured a treatment of the slave of unprecedented sympathy. The American fascination with cultural pluralism in the 1920s and 1930s, the desire of black scholars to refute the racist portrait of slavery and Reconstruction in a half-century of historiography, and the humanitarianism and political calculus of the New Deal all coincided to set the stage for the narratives to be collected. A basic degree of professionalism was guaranteed by the fact that the New Deal built on earlier academic ventures. John B. Cade and Charles S. Johnson began unrelated slave narrative projects in 1929 at Southern University and at Fisk University. In 1934 the Federal Emergency Relief Administration (FERA), under the aegis of Lawrence Reddick (a protégé of Johnson's), began gathering 250 interviews in Indiana and Kentucky. Still, the FERA interviews, conducted by individuals selected unscientifically out of the relief population, were poor in quality.

The former slaves were interviewed in all southern states, the border states, New York, and Rhode Island during the two years of the program. During the first half of the program, interviewers often took notes from the interrogation and wrote accounts at a later date of what they recalled hearing, producing a chronicle of slavery twice removed by memory from the actual event. Lomax introduced greater quality control in terms of the questions asked and procedures used. Perhaps because he did not trust the memory of the interviewers, he required those in the later phase of the project to record the interviews on primitive aluminum disks. These were never intended to see the light of day but only to enhance the professionalism of the interview process; after the program was discontinued they were interred in the archives of the Library of Congress until discovered in the 1990s by a team of researchers led by historian Ira Berlin. Transcripts of these recordings have subsequently been published, and the recordings—themselves enhanced by modern restorative technology—have also been released. Therefore at the dawn of the twenty-first century, the voices of slavery could be heard again.

In 1945 B. A. Botkin wrote the first chronicle of the collection, *Lay My Burden Down: A Folk History of Slavery.* Thereafter interest waned until the 1960s spurred an interest in black history and a skepticism of the authorities that lay behind the slave interviews. Although many scholars dismissed them as unreliable curiosities, their status as a unique "Rosetta Stone" of slavery in the language of the slave himself overrode these concerns. In 1972 George P. Rawick compiled a complete published edition entitled *The American Slave: A Composite Autobiography* (1972).

The WPA Slave Narrative Program shows no sign of releasing its claim on the attention of Americans. During the 1990s continuing problems of race relations, a renewed fascination with the Civil War, and advances in technology led some scholars to set aside the credibility issue of the sources altogether in a quest to focus on the power of the recordings. A scholarly publication was released in 1998, including cassette tapes combining actual recordings with staged recreations of the interviews (with James Earl Jones, Debbie Allen, and others providing the narration). Historical verisimilitude may have suffered, but the slave narratives live on as a unique episode in the history of both slavery and the twentieth century.

— *Richard A. Reiman*

See also: Autobiographies; Literature; Narratives.

For Further Reading

Berlin, Ira, Marc Favreau, and Steven F. Miller, eds. 1998. *Remembering Slavery: Americans Talk about Their Personal Experiences of Slavery.* New York: Norton.

Botkin, B.A., ed. 1941. *Slave Narratives: A Folk History of Slavery in the United States from Interviews with Former Slaves.* Washington, DC: U.S. Government Printing Office.

Rawick, George P., ed. 1972. *The American Slave: A Composite Autobiography.* Westport, CT: Greenwood.

Yetman, Norman R. 1967. "The Background of the Slave Narrative Collection." *American Quarterly* 3: 535–553

ELIZUR WRIGHT (1804–1885)

Elizur Wright played a prominent role in establishing the American Anti-Slavery Society and promoting the abolitionist Liberty Party. Born in Connecticut, at age six he moved with his family to a farm in Ohio. His father taught Wright that slavery was evil, and he backed up his words by harboring runaway slaves in the family farmstead. Educated at Yale University, Wright returned to Ohio to teach at Western Reserve College.

Wright became a vocal advocate of immediate abolition in 1832 after reading William Lloyd Garrison's

Thoughts on African Colonization (1832), which ridiculed the efforts of the American Colonization Society to end slavery by buying slaves, freeing them, and then transporting them to Africa. The following year Wright became recording secretary of the New York Anti-Slavery Society as well as national secretary of the American Anti-Slavery Society, both of which espoused immediate abolition. For the next six years he spent most of his time supervising the American Anti-Slavery Society's field agents, keeping in touch with hundreds of state and local chapters, mailing out antislavery literature, and raising money to fund the society's many programs. From 1833 to 1837 he also edited the society's publications, which included *Anti-Slavery Reporter, Anti-Slavery Record, Human Rights,* and *Quarterly Anti-Slavery Magazine,* and wrote articles for the society's newspaper, the *Emancipator.* During his tenure as secretary, the American Anti-Slavery Society grew to become the nation's largest organization devoted to immediate abolition.

By 1839 Wright had thoroughly alienated the society's board of directors, who were much more conservative than he. Specifically, the board was put off by his blunt personality, his insistence that abolitionists should refuse to comply with the Fugitive Slave Law of 1793, and his anticlericalism. He once declared that Christian ministers presented the most formidable roadblock to abolition. Unlike Wright, the board, composed largely of Christian ministers, insisted on achieving abolition by obeying the law and working through the churches. After six years, Wright resigned as the society's national secretary and became editor of the *Massachusetts Abolitionist.* This journal supported immediate abolition but rejected the radicalism of Garrison, the editor of the rival *Liberator.* Garrison had called on abolitionists to refuse to vote in federal elections because to do so supported the very government that supported slavery.

As editor of the *Massachusetts Abolitionist,* Wright repudiated Garrison's political views and called instead for the creation of a third national political party that was committed to immediate abolition. To this end, Wright endorsed the formation of the Abolitionist Party, later known as the Liberty Party, in 1839. He attended the party's convention that same year and enthusiastically supported its candidate for president, James G. Birney, in his editorials. Many abolitionists, however, were not ready to support an abolitionist party. They preferred to work within the Whig Party, which at the time was one of the nation's two major parties, as a means of achieving their political goals. In addition, they wanted Wright to endorse William

Henry Harrison, the Whig candidate for president in the Election of 1840. As a result, about half of his subscribers canceled in protest when the *Massachusetts Abolitionist* endorsed Birney. The cancellations put the paper in a financial crisis, and shortly thereafter Wright was forced to step down as editor.

Wright concerned himself with other reforms until 1846, when he became editor of the *Chronotype* (later known as the *Commonwealth*), a Boston daily newspaper that espoused immediate abolition, among other reforms. He resigned as editor two years later but remained on the editorial staff until 1852, when he was forced to resign after being falsely accused of breaking the law by harboring a runaway slave. Shortly thereafter he faded from the abolitionist scene to concentrate on other reforms.

— *Charles W. Carey*

See also: American Anti-Slavery Society; Birney, James G.; Garrison, William Lloyd.

For Further Reading

French, David. 1976. "Elizur Wright, Jr., and the Emergence of Anti-Colonization Sentiments on the Connecticut Western Reserve." *Ohio History* 85 (Winter): 49–66.

Goodheart, Lawrence B. 1984. "Childrearing, Conscience and Conversion to Abolitionism: The Example of Elizur Wright, Jr." *Psychohistory Review* 12: 24–33.

Goodheart, Lawrence B. 1990. *Abolitionist, Actuary, Atheist: Elizur Wright and the Reform Impulse.* Kent, OH: Kent State University Press.

FRANCES WRIGHT (1795–1852)

In 1825 Frances (Fanny) Wright became the first woman in the United States to act publicly in opposition to slavery. Her plan gradually emancipated slaves by establishing Nashoba plantation to educate African Americans and to teach them a trade before releasing them and transporting them to another nation.

Born in Dundee, Scotland, to James Wright, a linen merchant, and Camilla Campbell, she was orphaned at the age of two. Sent to live with her socialite maternal grandfather in England, Wright never accepted the popular upper class belief that the many London beggars were too lazy to work. Sympathy for the poor and downtrodden would mark her for the rest of her life.

Left with a sizable inheritance by the death of an uncle, Wright traveled to the United States with her sister Camilla in 1818. Returning to Europe, she described her impressions of the visit in *Views of Society and Manners*

Frances Wright was an early nineteenth-century freethinker whose ideas were too radical for most of her contemporaries. Still, her thinking had a profound influence on later generations of American reformers. (Library of Congress)

in America (1821). Through this book, Wright developed a friendship with the marquis de Lafayette and learned of his attempt, aborted by the French Revolution, to help the less fortunate by gradually emancipating slaves on his New Guinea plantation.

Perhaps because of ties to Lafayette and her upbringing as a member of the British upper class, Wright never wholeheartedly condemned oppressors. Sympathetic to the feelings of slaveholders, she wrote in an 1826 statement to the utopian socialist *New Harmony Gazette,* "We should consider, that what we view, at first sight, as a peculiar vice and injustice, is not more so, in fact, than any other vice and injustice stamped by education on the minds and hearts of other men." Wright also decided to imitate Lafayette by supporting the gradual emancipation of slaves rather than abruptly turning African Americans loose to fend for themselves, the method that abolitionists favored.

Initially planned as a black emancipation experiment, Nashoba plantation eventually developed into an exercise in communism, racial integration, and sexual equality. It also turned into a disaster, and Wright lost half her fortune in the venture. Weakened by fever, she left for Europe in 1829, where she later began a family with William Phiquepal D'Arusmont. Except for a brief sojourn to the United States to escort Nashoba's slaves to Haiti in 1830, she remained abroad until 1836. Reports of libertine behavior on the Nashoba plantation, acts that took place while Wright was abroad, effectively destroyed her reputation on both sides of the Atlantic.

By the 1830s charges of "Fanny Wrightism" had become a popular way to discredit liberal causes. Never fazed by the scorn directed at her, Wright espoused ever more controversial issues until the end of her life. She often lectured publicly, a shocking act for an early nineteenth-century woman in the United States. Newspapers questioned her virtue and that of any woman so brazen as to attend her talks.

Wright spoke not only against slavery but also about the repressive nature of marriage and religion. Many antebellum women, particularly the Quakers, were inspired by their religious beliefs to act against slavery. Wright's theories deeply offended them and certainly did not add to her popularity in antislavery circles. Reformers distanced themselves from her in an effort to appear more respectable, but Wright's call for better working conditions for laborers made her influential among working-class women. In 1852 she died in Cincinnati, Ohio, following a fall.

An energetic and fiercely determined woman, Frances Wright was easily the most controversial woman in the United States in the antebellum period. Her willingness to experiment boldly to better the lives of downtrodden African Americans made her a household word.

— *Caryn E. Neumann*

See also: Nashoba Plantation.

For Further Reading

Bartlett, Elizabeth. 1994. *Liberty, Equality, Sorority: The Origins and Interpretations of American Feminist Thought.* Brooklyn, NY: Carlson.

Eckhardt, Celia Morris. 1984. *Fanny Wright: Rebel in America.* Cambridge, MA: Harvard University Press.

Perkins, A. J. G., and Theresa Wolfson. 1939. *Frances Wright, Free Enquirer: The Study of a Temperament.* New York: Harper.

Wright, Frances. 1972. *Life, Letters, and Lectures, 1834–1844.* New York: Arno Press.

∾ Y ∾

WILLIAM LOWNDES YANCEY
(1814–1863)

Viewed by many people as a southern rights fanatic, William Lowndes Yancey not only was an advocate for southern secession and a white supremacist, but also was known throughout the South as a fiery and brilliant orator, often called the greatest southern public speaker since Patrick Henry or John Randolph. Yancey was also noted for his virulent temper and has been compared in that regard to Adolf Hitler. In 1838 his quick temper caused him to commit manslaughter, and he was sentenced to a year in jail and fined $1,500. He served only three months, however, and $1,000 of his fine was returned.

Yancey, born August 10, 1814, in Warren County, Georgia, moved in 1821 with his mother, Caroline and stepfather, the Reverend Nathan Beman, a Presbyterian minister and abolitionist, to Troy, New York, where he attended the best New York academies and in 1830 enrolled at Williams College in Massachusetts. As a young man Yancey was of medium height, 5 feet 10 inches, and slightly built. He had fair skin, dark blue eyes, and light brown hair. In 1833 he dropped out of college without obtaining a degree and moved to South Carolina, the home of his father, to study law under the tutelage of Benjamin Perry. In 1835 Yancey married Sarah Caroline Earle, a woman with thirty-five slaves and was thus catapulted into the planter class. He then stopped his study of law and moved his wife and slaves to Dallas County, Alabama, in order to make agriculture his occupation. Yancey's uncle, his mother's brother, William E. Bird, was the county judge. They lived on his Oakland Estate, near the Alabama River. This uncle, a prominent states' rights advocate, influenced Yancey's politics. When Yancey lost his fortune in agriculture he turned to politics.

In 1840 Yancey and his brother established a weekly newspaper called *Southern Crisis* in Wetumpka, Alabama, in which Yancey tried to persuade Alabama voters to reelect Martin Van Buren president of the United States. His campaign against William Henry Harrison impressed his fellow Democrats, and he was elected to serve in the Alabama General Assembly. Following his election he passed the bar exam, sold his newspaper and became a full-time politician. In 1844

William L. Yancey of Alabama was a white supremacist and advocate for southern secession. (Library of Congress)

he moved from state to national politics when he was elected to fill a seat in the U.S. House of Representatives. Yancey's congressional experience contributed to his disenchantment with the federal government and led to his increased support for states' rights.

Yancey returned to Alabama in 1847 and settled in Montgomery where he established a law firm, Yancey and Elmore. During this time he coauthored several resolutions, known as the Alabama Platform, which forbade Congress from obstructing slavery in the territories. Although accepted by the Alabama legislature, the Alabama Platform was rejected by the 1848 Democratic Convention in Baltimore by a vote of 216 to 36. Soundly defeated and viewed by many southern Democrats as extremist, Yancey stormed out of the convention. After the Compromise of 1850, he added secession to his creed, and for the next ten years he tried to arouse white southerners to secede from the Union. Prior to the Compromise, Yancey was a strong unionist who opposed John C. Calhoun during the nullification crisis in South Carolina. In 1858 he organized southern-rights associations and helped to create the League of United Southerners. He made fiery speeches throughout the South trying to convince men of all parties to back his uncompromising proslavery states' rights position.

As a result of Yancey's unrelenting campaign, by 1860 the Alabama Platform had won support throughout the South. At the Democratic National Convention in Charleston, South Carolina, a revised version did not win an unqualified acceptance. Thus the southern delegates withdrew and nominated a rival ticket. John C. Breckinridge, a nominee of the southern wing, the Constitutional Democrats, received Yancey's support. After Lincoln became president, Yancey drafted Alabama's secession ordinance. In 1861 he spent a year in France and Great Britain where he tried to gain recognition for the Confederate government, but he was unsuccessful. He returned to Alabama in 1862 to become a member of the Confederate Senate.

Yancey claimed that "African slavery, as it exists in the Southern States of this Union, is both politically and morally right, and that the history of the world furnishes no proof that slavery is either evil or sinful" (Venable, 1945). This statement became part of a successful resolution and appeal for Alabama to secede from the Union, in which Yancey played a leading role, earning the name "The Silver-Tongued Orator of Secession" (DuBose, 1942). Yancey died on July 27, 1863, blaming Jefferson Davis for the southern military defeats at the hands of the Yankees. A great agitator for change, Yancey never was able to master the art of cooperation, and his time in the Confederate Senate led to a bitter argument with Davis, one that never was resolved.

— *Nagueyalti Warren*

See also: Alabama Platform; Compromise of 1850; Nashville Convention; Proslavery Argument.

For Further Reading

DuBose, John Witherspoon. 1942. *The Life and Times of William Lowndes Yancey.* New York: Peter Smith.

Venable, Austin L. 1942. "The Conflict between the Douglas and Yancey Forces in the Charleston Convention." *Journal of Southern History* 8 (May): 226–241.

Venable, Austin L. 1945. "The Role of William L. Yancey in the Secession Movement." M.A. thesis, Department of History, Vanderbilt University, Nashville, Tennessee.

Walther, Eric H. 1992. *The Fire Eaters.* Baton Rouge: Louisiana State University Press.

Primary Source Documents

—∿—

JOHN LOCKE PREPARES A CONSTITUTION FOR CAROLINA (1669)

The following articles pertained to the status of slave laborers in the Carolina colony:

One hundred and seven. Since charity obliges us to wish well to the souls of all men, and religion ought to alter nothing in any man's civil estate or right, it shall be lawful for slaves, as well as others, to enter themselves, and be of what church or profession any of them shall think best, and, therefore, be as fully members as any freeman. But yet no slave shall hereby be exempted from that civil dominion his master hath over him, but be in all things in the same state and condition he was in before.

One hundred and eight. Assemblies, upon what presence soever of religion, not observing and performing the above said rules, shall not be esteemed as churches, but unlawful meetings, and be punished as other riots.

One hundred and nine. No person whatsover shall disturb, molest, or persecute another for his speculative opinions in religion, or his way of worship.

One hundred and ten. Every freeman of Carolina shall have absolute power and authority over his negro slaves, of what opinion or religion soever.

THE GERMANTOWN PROTEST (1688)

This is to the monthly meeting held at Richard Worrell's:

These are the reasons why we are against the traffic of men-body, as followeth: Is there any that would be done or handled at this manner" viz., to be sold or made a slave for all the time of his life? How fearful and faint-hearted are many at sea, when they see a strange vessel, being afraid it should be a Turk, and they should be taken, and sold for slaves into Turkey. Now, what is this better done, than Turks do? Yea, rather it is worse for them, which say they are Christians; for we hear that the most part of such negers are brought hither against their will and consent, and that many of them are stolen. Now, though they are black, we cannot conceive there is more liberty to have them slaves, as it is to have other white ones. There is a saying, that we should do to all men like as we will be done ourselves; making no difference of what generation, descent, or colour they are. And those who steal or rob men, and those who buy or purchase them, are they not all alike? Here is liberty of conscience, which is right and reasonable; here ought to be likewise liberty of the body, except of evil-doers, which is another

case. But to bring men hither, or to rob and sell them against their will, we stand against. In Europe there are many oppressed for conscience-sake; and here there are those oppressed which are of a black colour. And we who know that men must not commit adultery-some do commit adultery in others, separating wives from their husbands, and giving them to others: and some sell the children of these poor creatures to other men. Ah! do consider well this thing, you who do it, if you would be done at this manner—and if it is done according to Christianity! You surpass Holland and Germany in this thing. This makes an ill report in all those countries of Europe, where they hear of [it], that the Quakers do here handel men as they handel there the cattle. And for that reason some have no mind or inclination to come hither. And who shall maintain this your cause, or plead for it? Truly, we cannot do so, except you shall inform us better hereof, viz.: that Christians have liberty to practice these things. Pray, what thing in the world can be done worse towards us, than if men should rob or steal us away, and sell us for slaves to strange countries; separating husbands from their wives and children. Being now this is not done in the manner we would be done at; therefore, we contradict, and are against this traffic of men-body. And we who profess that it is not lawful to steal, must, likewise, avoid to purchase such things as are stolen, but rather help to stop this robbing and stealing, if possible. And such men ought to be delivered out of the hands of the robbers, and set free as in Europe. Then is Pennsylvania to have a good report, instead, it hath now a bad one, for this sake, in other countries; Especially whereas the Europeans are desirous to know in what manner the Quakers do rule in their province; and most of them do look upon us with an envious eye. But if this is done well, what shall we say is done evil?

If once these slaves (which they say are so wicked and stubborn men,) should join themselves—fight for their freedom, and handel their masters and mistresses, as they did handel them before; will these masters and mistresses take the sword at hand and war against these poor slaves, like, as we are able to believe, some will not refuse to do? Or, have these poor negers not as much right to fight for their freedom, as you have to keep them slaves?

Now consider well this thing, if it is good or bad. And in case you find it to be good to handel these blacks in that manner, we desire and require you hereby lovingly, that you may inform us herein, which at this time never was done, viz., that Christians have such a liberty to do so. To the end we shall be satisfied on this point, and satisfy likewise our good friends and acquaintances in our native country, to whom it is a terror, or fearful thing, that men should be handelled so in Pennsylvania.

This is from our meeting at Germantown held ye 18th of the 2d month, 1688, to be delivered to the monthly meeting at Richard Worrell's.

Garret Henderich,

Derick op de Graeff,

Francis Daniel Pastorius,

Abram op de Graeff.

Pastorius, Daniel Franz. 1963. "The Germantown Protest, 1688." In *Documents of American History*, ed. Henry Steele Commager. New York: Appleton-Century-Crofts.

PURITANS BEGIN TO CRITICIZE SLAVERY (1700)

The Selling of Joseph

"Forasmuch as Liberty is in real value next unto Life: None ought to part with it themselves, or deprive others of it, but upon most mature Consideration". The numerousness of slaves at this day in the province, and the uneasiness of them under their slavery, hath put many upon thinking whether the foundation of it be firmly and well laid; so as to sustain the vast weight that is built upon it. It is most certain that all men, as they are the Sons of Adam, are Coheirs; and have equal right unto liberty, and all other outward comforts of life.

GOD hath given the Earth [with all its Commodities] unto the Sons of Adam, Psal 115. 16. And hath made of One Blood, all Nations of Men, for to dwell on all the face of the Earth, and hath determined the times before appointed, and the bounds of their habitation: That they should seek the Lord. Forasmuch then as we are the Offspring of GOD &c. Act 17. 26, 27, 29.

Now although the Title given by the last ADAM, doth infinitely better men's estates, respecting GOD and themselves; and grants them a most beneficial and inviolable lease under the broad seal of Heaven, who were before only tenants at will: Yet through the indulgence of GOD to our First Parents after the Fall, the outward estate of all and every of their children, remains the same, as to one another. So that originally, and naturally, there is no such thing as slavery.

Joseph was rightfully no more a slave to his brethren, than they were to him: and they had no more authority to *sell* him, than they had to *slay* him. And if *they* had nothing to do to sell him; the Ishmaelites bargaining with them, and paying down twenty pieces of sil-

ver, could not make a title. Neither could *Potiphar* have any better interest in him than the *Ishmaelites* had. Gen. 37. 20, 27, 28. For he that shall in this case plead Alteration of Property, seems to have forfeited a great part of his own claim to humanity. There is no proportion between twenty pieces of silver, and LIBERTY. The commodity it self is the claimer. If *Arabian* gold be imported in any quantities, most are afraid to meddle with it, though they might have it at easy rates; lest if it should have been wrongfully taken from the owners, it should kindle a fire to the consumption of their whole estate.

'Tis pity there should be more caution used in buying a horse, or a little lifeless dust; than there is in purchasing men and women: Whenas they are the offspring of GOD, and their Liberty is, " . . . Auro pretiosior Omni" [Isaiah 13:12]. And seeing GOD hath said, "He that stealeth a man and selleth him, or if he be found in his hand, he shall surely be put to death." Exod. 21. 16. This law being of everlasting equity, wherein man stealing is ranked amongst the most atrocious of capital crimes: What louder cry can there be made of that celebrated warning, Caveat Emptor!

And all things considered, it would conduce more to the welfare of the province, to have white servants for a term of years, than to have slaves for life. Few can endure to hear of a Negro's being made free; and indeed they can seldom use their freedom well; yet their continual aspiring after their forbidden liberty, renders them unwilling servants.

And there is such a disparity in their conditions, colour & hair, that they can never embody with us, and grow up into orderly families, to the peopling of the land: but still remain in our body politick as a kind of extravasat blood [involuntary resident].

As many Negro men as there are among us, so many empty places there are in our Train Bands, and the places taken up of men that might make husbands for our daughters. And the sons and daughters of *New England* would become more like *Jacob*, and *Rachel*, if this slavery were thrust quite out of doors.

Moreover it is too well known what temptations masters are under, to connive at the fornication of their slaves; lest they should be obliged to find them wives, or pay their fines. It seems to be practically pleaded that they might be lawless; 'tis thought much of, that the law should have satisfaction for their thefts, and other immoralities; by which means, *Holiness to the Lord*, is more rarely engraven upon this sort of servitude.

It is likewise most lamentable to think, how in taking Negros out of *Africa*, and selling of them here, That which GOD has joined together men do boldly rend asunder [Matt. 19:6]; Men from their Country, Husbands from their Wives, Parents from their Children.

How horrible is the uncleanness, mortality, if not murder, that the ships are guilty of that bring great crowds of these miserable men, and women. Methinks, when we are bemoaning the barbarous usage of our friends and kinsfolk in *Africa:* it might not be unseasonable to enquire whether we are not culpable in forcing the *Africans* to become slaves amongst our selves. And it may be a question whether all the benefit received by Negro slaves, will balance the accompt of cash laid out upon them; and for the redemption of our own enslaved friends out of *Africa.* Besides all the persons and estates that have perished there.

Obj. 1. These Blackamores are of the Posterity of Cham, and therefore are under the curse of slavery. Gen. 9. 25, 26, 27.   Answ. Of all offices, one would not beg this; *viz.* Uncalled for, to be an executioner of the vindictive wrath of God; the extent and duration of which is to us uncertain. If this ever was a commission; how do we know but that it is long since out of date? Many have found it to their cost, that a prophetical denunciation of judgment against a person or people, would not warrant them to inflict that evil. If it would, *Hazael* might justify himself in all he did against his Master, and the *Israelites,* from 2 *Kings* 8. 10, 12 [killing the king, and women].

But it is possible that by cursory reading, this text may have been mistaken. For *Canaan* is the person cursed three times over, without the mentioning of *Cham.* Good Expositors suppose the curse entailed on him, and that this prophey was accomplished in the extirpation of the *Canaanites,* and in the servitude of the *Gibeonites. Vide Pareum*

Whereas the Blackmores are not descended of *Canaan,* but of *Cush.* Psal. 68. 31. "Princes shall come out of Egypt [Mizmim] Ethiopia [Cush] shall soon stretch out her hands unto God." Under which names, all *Africa* may be comprehended; and their Promised Conversion ought to be prayed for. Jer. 13. 23. Can the Ethiopian change his skin? This shows that black men are the posterity of *Cush:* Who time out of mind have been distinguished by their colour. And for want of the true, Ovid assigns a fabulous cause of it: "Sanguine tum credunt in corpora summa vocato Æthiopum populos nigrum traxisse colorem." Metamorph. lib. 2.

Obj. 2. The Nigers are brought out of a pagan country, into places where the Gospel is preached.   *Answ.* Evil must not be done, that good may come of it. The extraordinary and comprehensive benefit accruing to the Church of God, and to Joseph personally, did not rectify his brethrens' sale of him.

Obj. 3. The Africans have Wars one with another: Our Ships bring lawful Captives taken in those Wars.

Answ. For ought is known, their wars are much such as were between *Jacob's* sons and their brother *Joseph.* If they be between town and town; provincial, or national: Every war is upon one side unjust. An unlawful war can't make lawful captives. And by receiving, we are in danger to promote, and partake in their barbarous cruelties. I am sure, if some Gentlemen should go down to the *Brewsters* to take the air, and fish: And a stronger party from *Hull* should surprise them, and sell them for slaves to a ship outward bound: they would think themselves unjustly dealt with; both by sellers and buyers.

And yet 'tis to be feared, we have no other kind of title to our Nigers. "Therefore all things whatsoever ye would that men should do to you, do ye even so to them: for this is the Law and the Prophets." Matt. 7. 12.

Obj. 4. Abraham had servants bought with his money, and born in his house.

Answ. Until the circumstances of Abraham's purchase be recorded, no argument can be drawn from it. In the mean time, Charity obliges us to conclude, that he knew it was lawful and good.

It is observable that the *Israelites* were strictly forbidden the buying, or selling one another for slaves. *Levit.* 25. 39, 46. *Jer.* 34. 8 . . . 22. And GOD gaged His Blessing in lieu of any loss they might conceipt they suffered thereby. *Deut.* 15. 18.

And since the partition wall is broken down, inordinate self love should likewise be demolished. GOD expects that Christians should be of a more ingenuous and benign frame of spirit. Christians should carry it to all the world, as the *Israelites* were to carry it one towards another. And for men obstinately to persist in holding their neighbours and brethren under the rigor of perpetual bondage, seems to be no proper way of gaining assurance that God has given them spiritual freedom. Our blessed Saviour has altered the measures of the ancient love-song, and set it to a most excellent new tune, which all ought to be ambitious of Learning. *Matt.* 5. 43, 44. *John* 13. 34. These *Ethiopians,* as black as they are; seeing they are the sons and daughters of the First *Adam,* the brethren and sisters of the Last ADAM, and the Offspring of GOD; they ought to be treated with a respect agreeable.

"Servitus perfecta voluntaria, inter Christianum & Christianum, ex parte servi patientis sæpe est licita quia est necessaria: sed ex parte domini agentis, & procurando & exercendo, vix potest esse licita: quia non convenit regulæ illi generali: Quæcunque volueritis ut faciant vobis homines, ita & vos facite eis." Matt. 7. 12.

"Perfecta servitus pænæ, non potest jure locum habere, nisi ex delicto gravi quod ultimum supplicium aliquo modo meretur: quia libertas ex naturali æstimatione proximo accedit ad vitam ipsam, & eidem a multis præferri solet."

Cap. 23. Thes. 2, 3.

Sewall, Samuel. 1700. *The Selling of Joseph: A Memorial.* Boston: Green and Allen.

COLONIAL VIRGINIA SLAVERY STATUTE (1705)

An act concerning Servants and Slaves.

I. *Be it enacted, by the governor, council, and burgesses, of this present general assembly, and it is hereby enacted, by the authority of the same,* That all servants brought into this country without indenture, if the said servants be christians, and of christian parentage, and above nineteen years of age, shall serve but five years; and if under nineteen years of age, 'till they shall become twenty-four years of age, and no longer.

II. *Provided always,* That every such servant be carried to the country court, within six months after his or her arrival into this colony, to have his or her age adjudged by the court, otherwise shall be a servant no longer than the accustomary five years, although much under the age of nineteen years; and the age of such servant being adjudged by the court, within the limitation aforesaid, shall be entered upon the records of the said court, and be accounted, deemed, and taken, for the true age of the said servant, in relation to the time of service aforesaid.

III. *And also be it enacted, by the authority aforesaid, and it is herby enacted,* That when any servant sold for the custom, shall pretend to have indentures, the master or owner of such servant, for discovery of the truth thereof, may bring the said servant before a justice of the peace; and if the said servant cannot produce the indenture then, but shall still pretend to have one, the said justice shall assign two months time for the doing thereof; in which time, if the said servant shall not produce his or her indenture, it shall be taken for granted that there never was one, and shall be a bar to his or her claim of making use of one afterwards, or taking any advantage by one.

IV. *And also be it enacted, by the authority aforesaid, and it is hereby enacted,* That all servants imported and brought into this country, by sea or land, who were not christians in their native country, (except Turks and Moors in amity with her majesty, and others that can make due proof of their being free in England, or any other christian country, before they were shipped, in order to transportation hither) shall be accounted and be slaves, and as such be here bought and sold notwithstanding a conversion to christianity afterwards.

V. *And be it enacted, by the authority aforesaid, and it is hereby enacted,* That if any person or persons shall hereafter import into this colony, and here sell as a slave, any person or persons that shall have been a freeman in any christian country, island, or plantation, such importer and seller as aforesaid, shall forfeit and pay, to the party from whom the said freeman shall recover his freedom, double the sum for which the said freeman was sold. To be recovered, in any court of record within this colony, according to the course of the common law, wherein the defendant shall not be admitted to plead in bar, any act or statute for limitation of actions.

VI. *Provided always,* That a slave's being in England, shall not be sufficient to discharge him of his slavery, without other proof of his being manumitted there.

VII. *And also be it enacted, by the authority aforesaid, and it is hereby enacted,* That all masters and owners of servants, shall find and provide for their servants, wholesome and competent diet, clothing, and lodging, by the discretion of the county court; and shall not, at any time, give immoderate correction; neither shall, at any time, whip a christian white servant naked, without an order from a justice of the peace: And if any, notwithstanding this act, shall presume to whip a christian white servant naked, without such order, the person so offending, shall forfeit and pay for the same, forty shillings sterling, to the party injured: To be recovered, with costs, upon petition, without the formal process of an action, as in and by this act is provided for servants complaints to be heard; provided complaint be made within six months after such whipping.

VIII. *And also be it enacted, by the authority aforesaid, and it is herby enacted,* That all servants, (not being slaves,) whether imported, or become servants of their own accord here, or bound by any court or church-wardens, shall have their complaints received by a justice of the peace, who, if he find cause, shall bind the master over to answer the complaint at court; and it shall be there determined: And all complaints of servants, shall and may, by virtue hereof, be received at any time, upon petition, in the court of the county wherein they reside, without the formal process of an action; and also full power and authority is hereby given to the said court, by their discretion, (having first summoned the masters or owners to justify themselves, if they think fit,) to adjudge, order, and appoint what shall be necessary, as to diet, lodging, clothing, and correction: And if any master or owner shall not thereupon comply with the said court's order, the said court is hereby authorised and impowered, upon a second just complaint, to order such servant to be immediately sold at an outcry, by the sheriff, and after charges deducted, the remainder of what the said servant shall be sold for, to be paid and satisfied to such owncr.

IX. *Provided always, and be it enacted,* That if such servant be so sick or lame, or otherwise rendered so uncapable, that he or she cannot be sold for such a value, at least, as shall satisfy the fees, and other incident charges accrued, the said court shall then order the church-wardens of the parish to take care of and provide for the said servant, until such servant's time, due by law to the said master, or owner, shall be expired, or until such servant, shall be so recovered, as to be sold for defraying the said fees and charges: And further, the said court, from time to time, shall order the charges of keeping the said servant, to be levied upon the goods and chattels of the master or owner of the said servant, by distress.

X. *And be it also enacted,* That all servants, whether, by importation, indenture, or hire here, as well some coverts, as others, shall, in like manner, as is provided, upon complaints of misusage, have their petitions received in court, for their wages and freedom, without the formal process of an action; and proceedings, and judgment, shall, in like manner, also, be had thereupon.

XI. And for a further christian care and usage of all christian servants, *Be it also enacted, by the authority aforesaid, and it is hereby enacted,* That no negros, mulattos, or Indians, although christians, or Jews, Moors, Mahometans, or other infidels, shall, at any time, purchase any christian servant, nor any other, except of their own complexion, or such as are declared slaves by this act: And if any negro, mulatto, or Indian, Jew, Moor, Mahometan, or other infidel, or such as are declared slaves by this act, shall, notwithstanding, purchase any christian white servant, the said servant shall, *ipso facto,* become free and acquit from any ser-

vice then due, and shall be so held, deemed, and taken: And if any person, having such christian servant, shall intermarry with any such negro, mulatto, or Indian, Jew, Moor, Mahometan, or other infidel, every christian white servant of every such person so intermarrying, shall, *ipso facto,* become free and acquit from any service then due to such master or mistress so intermarrying, as aforesaid.

XII. *And also be it enacted, by the authority aforesaid, and it is hereby enacted,* That no master or owner of any servant shall during the time of such servant's servitude, make any bargain with his or her said servant for further service, or other matter or thing relating to liberty, or personal profit, unless the same be made in the presence, and with the approbation, of the court of that county where the master or owner resides: And if any servants shall, at any time bring in goods or money, or during the time of their service, by gift, or any other lawful ways or means, come to have any goods or money, they shall enjoy the propriety thereof, and have the sole use and benefit thereof to themselves. And if any servant shall happen to fall sick or lame, during the time of service, so that he or she becomes of little or no use to his or her master or owner, but rather a charge, the said master or owner shall not put away the said servant, but shall maintain him or her, during the whole time he or she was before obliged to serve, by indenture, custom, or order of court: And if any master or owner, shall put away any such sick or lame servant, upon pretence of freedom, and that servant shall become chargeable to the parish, the said master or owner shall forfeit and pay ten pounds current money of Virginia, to the church-wardens of the parish where such offence shall be committed, for the use of the said parish: To be recovered by action of debt, in any court of record in this her majesty's colony and dominion, in which no essoin [a justification for an absence from court], protection, or wager of law, shall be allowed.

XIII. And whereas there has been a good and laudable custom of allowing servants corn and cloaths for their present support, upon their freedom; but nothing in that nature ever made certain, *Be it also enacted, by the authority aforesaid, and it is hereby enacted,* That there shall be paid and allowed to every imported servant, not having yearly wages, at the time of service ended, by the master or owner of such servant, viz: To every male servant, ten bushels of indian corn, thirty shillings in money, or the value thereof, in goods, and one well fixed musket or fuzee, of the value of twenty shillings, at least: and to every woman servant, fifteen bushels of indian corn, and forty shillings in money, or the value thereof, in goods: Which, upon refusal, shall be ordered, with costs, upon petition to the county court, in manner as is herein before directed, for servants complaints to be heard.

XIV. *And also be it enacted, by the authority aforesaid, and it is hereby enacted,* That all servants shall faithfully and obediently, all the whole time of their service, do all their masters or owners just and lawful commands. And if any servant shall resist the master, or mistress, or overseer, of offer violence to any of them, the said servant shall, for every such offence, be adjudged to serve his or her said master or owner, one whole year after the time, by indenture, custom, or former order of court, shall be expired.

XV. *And also be it enacted, by the authority aforesaid, and it is hereby enacted,* That no person whatsoever shall buy, sell, or receive of, to, or from, any servant, or slave, any coin or commodity whatsoever, without the leave, licence, or consent of the master or owner of the said servant, or slave: And if any person shall, contrary hereunto, without the leave or licence aforesaid, deal with any servant, or slave, he or she so offending, shall be imprisoned one calender month, without bail or main-prize; and then, also continue in prison, until he or she shall find good security, in the sum of ten pounds current money of Virginia, for the good behaviour for one year following; wherein, a second offence shall be a breach of the bond and moreover shall forfeit and pay four times the value of the things so bought, sold, or received, to the master or owner of such servant, or slave: To be recovered, with costs, by action upon the case, in any court of record in this her majesty's colony and dominion, wherein no essoin, protection, or wager of law, or other than one imparlance, shall be allowed.

XVI. *Provided always, and be it enacted,* That when any person or persons convicted for dealing with a servant, or slave, contrary to this act, shall not immediately give good and sufficient security for his or her good behaviour, as aforesaid: then, in such case, the court shall order thirty-nine lashes, well laid on, upon the bare back of such offender, at the common whipping-post of the county, and the said offender to be thence discharged of giving such bond and security.

XVII. *And also be it enacted, by the authority aforesaid, and it is hereby enacted, and declared,* That in all cases of penal laws, whereby persons free are punishable by fine, servants shall be punished by whipping, after the rate of twenty lashes for every five hundred pounds of tobacco, or fifty shillings current money, unless the servant so culpable, can and will procure some person or persons to pay the fine; in which case, the said servant shall be adjudged to serve such benefactor, after the time by indenture, custom, or order of court, to his or her then present master or owner, shall be expired, after the rate of one month and a half for every hundred pounds of tobacco; any thing in this act contained, to the contrary, in any-wise, notwithstanding.

XVIII. And if any woman servant shall be delivered of a bastard child within the time of her service aforesaid, *Be it enacted, by the authority aforesaid, and it is hereby enacted,* That in recompence of the loss and trouble occasioned her master or mistress thereby, she shall for every such offence, serve her said master or owner one whole year after her time by indenture, custom, and former order of court, shall be expired; or pay her said master or owner, one thousand pounds of tobacco; and the reputed father, if free, shall give security to the church-wardens of the parish where that child shall be, to maintain the child, and keep the parish indemnified; or be compelled thereto by order of the county court, upon the said church-wardens complaint: But if a servant, he shall make satisfaction of the parish, for keeping the said child, after his time by indenture, custom, or order of court, to his then present master or owner, shall be expired; or be compelled thereto, by order of the county court, upon complaint of the church wardens of the said parish, for the time being. And if any woman servant shall be got with child by her master, neither the said master, nor his executors administrators, nor assigns, shall have any claim of service against her, for or by reason of such child; but she shall, when her time due to her said master, by indenture, custom or order of court, shall be expired, be sold by the church-wardens, for the time being, of the parish wherein such child shall be born, for one year, or pay one thousand pounds of tobacco; and the said one thousand pounds of tobacco, or whatever she shall be sold for, shall be employed, by the vestry, to the use of the said parish. And if any woman servant shall have a bastard child by a negro, or mulatto, over and above the years service due to her master or owner, she shall immediately, upon the expiration of her time to her then present master or owner, pay down to the church-wardens of the parish wherein such child shall be born, for the use of the said parish fifteen pounds current money of Virginia, or be by them sold for five years to the use aforesaid: And if a free christian white woman shall have such bastard child, by a negro, or mulatto, for every such offence, she shall, within one month after her delivery of such bastard child, pay to the church-wardens for the time being, of the parish wherein such child shall be born, for the use of the said parish fifteen pounds current money of Virginia, or be by them sold for five years to the use aforesaid: And in both the said cases, the church-wardens shall bind the said child to be a servant, until it shall be of thirty one years of age.

XIX. And for a further prevention of that abominable mixture and spurious issue, which hereafter may increase in this her majesty's colony and dominion, as well by English, and other white men and women intermarrying with negros or mulattos, as by their unlawful coition with them, *Be it enacted, by the authority aforesaid, and it is hereby enacted,* That whatsoever English, or other white man or woman, being free, shall intermarry with a negro or mulatto man or woman, bond or free, shall, by judgment of the county court, be committed to prison, and there remain, during the space of six months, without bail or mainprize; and shall forfeit and pay ten pounds current money of Virginia, to the use of the parish, as aforesaid.

XX. *And be it further enacted,* That no minister of the church of England, or other minister, or person whatsoever, within this colony and dominion, shall hereafter wittingly presume to marry a white man with a negro or mulatto woman; or to marry a white woman with a negro or mulatto man, upon pain of forfeiting and paying, for every such marriage the sum of ten thousand pounds of tobacco; one half to our sovereign lady the Queen, her heirs and successors, for and towards the support of the government, and the contingent charges thereof; and the other half to the informer; To be recovered, with costs, by action of debt, bill, plaint, or information, in any court of record within this her majesty's colony and dominion, wherein no essoin, protection, or wager of law, shall be allowed.

XXI. And because poor people may not be destitute of employment, upon suspicion of being servants, and servants also kept from running away, *Be it enacted, by the authority aforesaid, and it is hereby enacted,* That every servant, when his or her time of service shall be expired, shall repair to the court of the county where he or she served the last of his or her time, and there, upon sufficient testimony, have his or her freedom entered; and a certificate thereof from the clerk of the said court, shall be sufficient to authorise any person to entertain or hire such servant, without any danger of this law. And if it shall at any time happen, that such certificate is won out, or lost, the said clerk shall

grant a new one, and therein also recite the accident happened to the old one. And whoever shall hire such servant, shall take his or her certificate, and keep it, 'till the contracted time shall be expired. And if any person whatsoever, shall harbour or entertain any servant by importation, or by contract, or indenture made here, not having such certificate, he or she so offending, shall pay to the master or owner of such servant, sixty pounds of tobacco for every natural day he or she shall so harbour or entertain such runaway: To be recovered, with costs, by action of debt, in any court of record within this her majesty's colony and dominion, wherein no essoin, protection, or wager of law, shall be allowed. And also, if any runaway shall make use of a forged certificate, or after the same shall be delivered to any master or mistress, upon being hired, shall steal the same away, and thereby procure entertainment, the person entertaining such servant, upon such forged or stolen certificate, shall not be culpable by this law: But the said runaway, besides making reparation for the loss of time, and charges in recovery, and other penalties by this law directed, shall, for making use of such forged or stolen certificate, or for such theft aforesaid, stand two hours in the pillory, upon a court day: And the person forging such certificate, shall forfeit and pay ten pounds current money; one half thereof to be to her majesty, her heirs and successors, for and towards the support of this government, and the contingent charges thereof; and the other half to the master or owner of such servant, if he or she will inform or sue for the same, otherwise to the informer: To be recovered, with costs, by action of debt, bill, plaint or information, in any court of record in this her majesty's colony and dominion, wherein no essoin, protection, or wager of law, shall be allowed. And if any person or persons convict of forging such certificate, shall not immediately pay the said ten pounds, and costs, or give security to do the same within six months, he or she so convict, shall receive, on his or her bare back, thirty-nine lashes, well laid on, at the common whipping post of the county; and shall be thence discharged of paying the said ten pounds, and costs, and either of them.

XXII. *Provided,* That when any master or mistress shall happen to hire a runaway, upon a forged certificate, and a servant deny that he delivered any such certificate, the *Onus Probandi* shall lie upon the person hiring, who upon failure therein, shall be liable to the fines and penalties, for entertaining runaway servants, without certificate.

XXIII. And for encouragement of all persons to take

up runaways, *Be it enacted, by the authority aforesaid, and it is hereby enacted,* That for the taking up of every servant, or slave, if ten miles, or above, from the house or quarter where such servant, or slave was kept, there shall be allowed by the public, as a reward to the taker-up, two hundred pounds of tobacco; and if above five miles, and under ten, one hundred pounds of tobacco: Which said several rewards of two hundred, and one hundred pounds of tobacco, shall also be paid in the county where such taker-up shall reside, and shall be again levied by the public upon the master or owner of such runaway, for re-imburse-ment of the same to the public. And for the greater certainty in paying the said rewards and re-imburse-ment of the public, every justice of the peace before whom such runaway shall be brought, upon the tak-ing up, shall mention the proper-name and sur-name of the taker-up, and the county of his or her resi-dence, together with the time and place of taking up the said runaway; and shall also mention the name of the said runaway, and the proper-name and sur-name of the master or owner of such runaway, and the county of his or her residence, together with the dis-tance of miles, in the said justice's judgment, from the place of taking up the said runaway, to the house or quarter where such runaway was kept.

XXIV. *Provided,* That when any negro, or other run-away, that doth not speak English, and cannot, or through obstinacy will not, declare the name of his or her masters or owner, that then it shall be sufficient for the said justice to certify the same, instead of the name of such runaway, and the proper-name and sur-name of his or her master or owner, and the county of his or her residence and distance of miles, as aforesaid; and in such case, shall, by his warrant, order the said runaway to be conveyed to the public gaol, of this country, there to be continued prisoner until the master or owner shall be known; who, upon paying the charges of the imprisonment, or give caution to the prison-keeper for the same, together with the reward of two hundred or one hundred pounds of tobacco, as the case shall be, shall have the said runaway restored.

XXV. And further, the said justice of the peace, when such runaway shall be brought before him, shall, by his warrant commit the said runaway to the next con-stable, and therein also order him to give the said run-away so many lashes as the said justice shall think fit, not exceeding the number of thirty-nine; and then to be conveyed from constable to constable, until the said runaway shall be carried home, or to the country gaol, as aforesaid, every constable through whose

hands the said runaway shall pass, giving a receipt at the delivery; and every constable failing to execute such warrant according to the tenor thereof, or refus-ing to give such receipt, shall forfeit and pay two hun-dred pounds of tobacco to the church-wardens of the parish wherein such failure shall be, for the use of the poor of the said parish: To be recovered, with costs, by action of debt, in any court of record in this her majesty's colony and dominion, wherein no essoin, protection or wager of law, shall be allowed. And such corporal punishment shall not deprive the master or owner of such runaway of the other satisfaction here in this act appointed to be made upon such servant's running away.

XXVI. *Provided always, and be it further enacted,* That when any servant or slave, in his or her running away, shall have crossed the great bay of Chesapeake, and shall be brought before a justice of the peace, the said justice shall, instead of committing such runaway to the constable, commit him or her to the sheriff, who is hereby required to receive every such runaway, accord-ing to such warrant, and to cause him, her, or them, to be transported again across the bay, and delivered to a constable there; and shall have, for all his trouble and charge herein, for every such servant or slave, five hun-dred pounds of tobacco, paid by the public; which shall be re-imbursed again by the master or owner of such runaway, as aforesaid, in manner aforesaid.

XXVII. *Provided also,* That when any runaway servant that shall have crossed the said bay, shall get up into the country, in any county distant from the bay, that then, in such case, the said runaway shall be commit-ted to a constable, to be conveyed from constable to constable, until he shall be brought to a sheriff of some county adjoining to the said bay of Chesapeake, which sheriff is also hereby required, upon such warrant, to receive such runaway, under the rules and conditions aforesaid; and cause him or her to be conveyed as aforesaid; and shall have the reward, as aforesaid.

XXVIII. And for the better preventing of delays in re-turning of such runaways, *Be it enacted,* That if any sheriff, under sheriff, or other officer of, or belonging to the sheriffs, shall cause or suffer any such runaway (so committed for passage over the bay) to work, the said sheriff, to whom such runaway shall be so com-mitted, shall forfeit and pay to the master or owner, of every such servant or slave, so put to work, one thou-sand pounds of tobacco; To be recovered, with costs, by action of debt, bill, plaint, or information, in any court of record within this her majesty's colony and dominion, wherein no essoin, protection, or wager of law, shall be allowed.

XXIX. *And be it enacted, by the authority aforesaid, and it is hereby enacted,* That if any constable, or sheriff, into whose hands a runaway servant or slave shall be committed, by virtue of this act, shall suffer such runaway to escape, the said constable or sheriff shall be liable to the action of the party grieved, for recovery of his damages, at the common law with costs.

XXX. *And also be it enacted, by the authority aforesaid, and it is hereby enacted,* That every runaway servant, upon whose account, either of the rewards aforementioned shall be paid, for taking up, shall for every hundred pounds of tobacco so paid by the master or owner, serve his or her said master or owner, after his or her time by indenture, custom, or former order of court, shall be expired, one calendar month and an half, and moreover, shall serve double the time such servant shall be absent in such running away; and shall also make reparation, by service, to the said master or owner, for all necessary disbursements and charges, in pursuit and recovery of the said runaway; to be adjudged and allowed in the county court, after the rate of one year for eight hundred pounds of tobacco, and so proportionably for a greater or lesser quantity.

XXXI. *Provided,* That the masters or owners of such runaways, shall carry them to court the next court held for the said county, after the recovery of such runaway, otherwise it shall be in the breast of the court to consider the occasion of delay, and to hear, or refuse the claim, according to their discretion, without appeal, for the refusal.

XXXII. *And also be it enacted, by the authority aforesaid, and it is hereby enacted,* That no master, mistress, or overseer of a family, shall knowingly permit any slave, not belonging to him or her, to be and remain upon his or her plantation, above four hours at any one time, without the leave of such slave's master, mistress, or overseer, on penalty of one hundred and fifty pounds of tobacco to the informer; cognizable by a justice of the peace of the county wherein such offence shall be committed.

XXXIII. *Provided also,* That if any runaway servant, adjudged to serve for the charges of his or her pursuit and recovery, shall, at the time, he or she is so adjudged, repay and satisfy, or give good security before the court, for repaiment and satisfaction of the same, to his or her master or owner, within six months after, such master or owner shall be obliged to accept thereof, in lieu of the service given and allowed for such charges and disbursements.

XXXIV. And if any slave resist his master, or owner, or other person, by his or her order, correcting such slave, and shall happen to be killed in such correction, it shall not be accounted felony; but the master, owner, and every such other person so giving correction, shall be free and acquit of all punishment and accusation for the same, as if such accident had never happened: And also, if any negro, mulatto, or Indian, bond or free, shall at any time, lift his or her hand, in opposition against any christian, not being negro, mulatto, or Indian, he or she so offending, shall, for every such offence, proved by the oath of the party, receive on his or her bare back, thirty lashes, well laid on; cognizable by a justice of the peace for that county wherein such offence shall be committed.

XXXV. *And also be it enacted, by the authority aforesaid, and it is hereby enacted,* That no slave go armed with gun, sword, club, staff, or other weapon, nor go from off the plantation and seat of land where such slave shall be appointed to live, without a certificate of leave in writing, for so doing, from his or her master, mistress, or overseer: And if any slave shall be found offending herein, it shall be lawful for any person or persons to apprehend and deliver such slave to the next constable or head-borough, who is hereby enjoined and required, without further order or warrant, to give such slave twenty lashes on his or her bare back, well laid on, and so send him or her home: And all horses, cattle, and hogs, now belonging, or that hereafter shall belong to any slave, or of any slaves mark in this her majestys colony and dominion, shall be seized and sold by the church-wardens of the parish, wherein such horses, cattle, or hogs shall be, and the profit thereof applied to the use of the poor of the said parish: And also, if any damage shall be hereafter committed by any slave living at a quarter where there is no christian overseer, the master or owner of such slave shall be liable to action for the trespass and damage, as if the same had been done by him or herself.

XXXVI. *And also it is hereby enacted and declared,* That baptism of slaves doth not exempt them from bondage; and that all children shall be bond or free, according to the condition of their mothers, and the particular directions of this act.

XXXVII. And whereas, many times, slaves run away and lie out, hid and lurking in swamps, woods, and other obscure places, killing hogs, and committing other injuries to the inhabitants of this her majesty's colony and dominion, *Be it therefore enacted, by the authority aforesaid, and it is hereby enacted,* That in all such cases, upon intelligence given of any slaves lying out, as aforesaid, any two justices (*Quorum unus*) of the peace of the county wherein such slave is supposed to lurk or do mischief, shall be and are impowered and required to issue proclamation against all such slaves, reciting their names, and owners names, if they are known, and thereby requiring them, and every of them, forthwith to surrender themselves; and also impowering the sheriff of the said county, to take such power with him, as he shall think fit and necessary, for the effectual apprehending such out-lying slave or slaves, and go in search of them: Which proclamation shall be published on a Sabbath day, at the door of every church and chapel, in the said county, by the parish clerk, or reader, of the church, immediately after divine worship: And in case any slave, against whom proclamation hath been thus issued, and once published at any church or chapel, as aforesaid, stay out, and do not immediately return home, it shall be lawful for any person or persons whatsoever, to kill and destroy such slaves by such ways and means as he, she, or they shall think fit, without accusation or impeachment of any crime for the same: And if any slave, that hath run away and lain out as aforesaid, shall be apprehended by the sheriff, or any other person, upon the application of the owner of the said slave, it shall and may be lawful for the county court, to order such punishment to the said slave, either by dismembring, or any other way, not touching his life, as they in their discretion shall think fit, for the reclaiming any such incorrigible slave, and terrifying others from the like practices.

XXXVIII. *Provided always, and it is further enacted,* That for every slave killed, in pursuance of this act, or put to death by law, the master or owner of such slave shall be paid by the public:

XXXIX. And to the end, the true value of every slave killed, or put to death, as aforesaid, may be the better known; and by that means, the assembly the better enabled to make a suitable allowance thereupon, *Be it enacted,* That upon application of the master or owner of any such slave, to the court appointed for proof of public claims, the said court shall value the slave in money, and the clerk of the court shall return a certificate thereof to the assembly, with the rest of the public claims.

Hening, William Waller. 1823. *The Statutes at Large; Be-*

ing a Collection of all the Laws of Virginia, from the First Session of the Legislature in the Year 1619. New York: R. & W. & G. Bartow.

CODE NOIR OF LOUISIANA (1724)

A Royal Edict Touching on the State and Discipline of the Black Slaves of Louisiana, Given at Versailles in the Month of March 1724

Louis, by the grace of God, King of France and Navarre, to all present and to come, Salvation. . . . We have judged that it was a matter of our authority and our justice, for the conservation of this colony, to establish there a law and certain rules to maintain there the discipline of the Roman Catholic Apostolic Church and to arrange that which concerns the state and quality of slaves in the said Isles. . . .

II. All the slaves who will be in our said province will be instructed in the Roman Catholic and Apostolic religion and baptized. . . .

III. We forbid all the exercises of a religion other than the Roman Catholic Apostolic: We wish that the offenders may be punished as rebels and disobedient persons to our commands. . . .

IV. No persons will be appointed overseers for the direction of Negroes who have not made a profession of the Roman Catholic Apostolic religion, under pain of confiscation of the said Negroes of the master who has appointed them and pain of arbitrary punishment of the overseers who have accepted the said direction.

V. We order all our subjects, of whatever condition they may be, to observe regularly Sundays and Feast days; we forbid them on the said days, from the hour of midnight all the way to the next midnight, to work or to work their slaves in the cultivation of land or in all other works on pain of fine and arbitrary punishment for the masters and of confiscation of the slaves, who will be caught at work. Yet, they [masters] will be able to send their slaves to market.

VI. We forbid our whites subjects of either sex to contract marriage with blacks under pain of punishment and arbitrary fine; [we forbid] pastors, priests, missionaries either secular or religious, and even chaplains on ships to marry them [white-black couple]. We also forbid our said white subjects, even freed blacks or those born free, to live in concubinage with slaves. We wish that those, who will have had one or several children by such a union, together with the masters who have permitted them, may be sentenced each to a fine of 300 *livres;* and if they are masters of the slave by whom they will have had the said children, they may be deprived of the slave as well as the children, who may be assigned to the workhouse of the place without the ability ever to be freed. We do not intend the present article to hold force, however, when a black man, freed or freeborn, who was not married during his concubinage with his slave woman, will espouse in the manner prescribed by the church the said slave woman, who will be freed by this means and the children rendered free and legitimate.

VII. The solemnities prescribed by the Ordinance of Blois and by the Declaration of 1639 for marriages will be observed with regard to free persons as well as slaves, yet without the consent of the mother and father of the slave being necessary, but only the consent of the master.

VIII. We very expressly forbid curates to go on with the marriage of slaves if it does not appear that they have the consent of their masters. We also forbid masters to constrain their slaves in any way to marry against their wishes.

IX. The children born of marriages between slaves will be slaves, and if the husbands and wives have different masters, the children are to belong to the masters of the female slaves and not to those of the husbands.

X. We wish, if a slave husband has married a free woman, that the children, both male and female, follow the condition of their mother and be as free as she, notwithstanding the servitude of their father; if their father is free and the mother a slave, the children are likewise slaves.

XI. Masters will be bound to bury their baptized slaves in holy ground in cemeteries set aside for this purpose; with regard to those who will die without having received baptism, they will be buried that night in some field in the neighborhood of the place where they died.

XII. We forbid slaves to bear any offensive arms or large sticks. . . .

XIII. We likewise forbid slaves belonging to different masters to gather in a crowd either day or night under the pretext of a wedding or otherwise, be it at their masters' homes or elsewhere, and still less on great thoroughfares or remote places under pain of corporal

punishment, which will not be less than the whip and [branding with] the fleur de Lis. . . .

XIV. Masters who will be convicted of having permitted or tolerated such assemblies . . . will be sentenced. . . to pay for all the damage that will have been done in their neighborhood on the occasion of such assemblies and a fine of 300 *livres* for the first offense and double that for the next.

XV. We forbid slaves to offer for sale in a market or to take to their own houses for sale any sort of provisions, even fruits, vegetables, firewood, herbs, forage for animals, any sort of grain, or any other merchandise, household things or clothing, without the express written permission of their masters. . . .

XVI. For this purpose we wish that two persons be appointed for each market. . . . to examine the produce and merchandise that will be brought by slaves together with the written notes . . . of their masters.

XVII. We permit all our subjects living in the country [Louisiana] to seize all the goods borne by slaves without tickets [written permission] from their masters to return them at once to their masters if they live in the neighborhood where the slaves will have been captured; otherwise, the good will be sent at once to the nearest company store to be warehoused until the masters have been notified.

XVIII. We wish that the officers of our Superior Council of Louisiana send their opinion on the quantity of food and the quality of clothes that would be suitable for masters to furnish their slaves; what food ought to be provided them each week and the clothing each year in order for us to make a decision about it. Meanwhile, we permit the said officers to regulate the provision of the said food and clothing. We prohibit the masters of the said slaves to give them any sort of brandy in place of the said food and clothing.

XIX. We likewise forbid them [masters] to relieve themselves of the nourishment and subsistence of their slaves by permitting them to work a certain day of the week for their own account.

XX. Slaves who are not fed, clothed, and kept up by their masters can report it to the Procurator General of the said Council or to lesser officers of justice and place their memoranda in their hands, on the basis of which . . . the masters will be pursued at the request of the said Procurator General, and without cost; this is what we wish to be observed regarding the crimes and barbarous and inhuman treatment of masters toward their slaves.

XXI. Slaves weakened by old age, illness, or otherwise, whether the illness be incurable or not, will be fed and kept up by their masters, and in case they have abandoned them, the slaves will be assigned to the nearest hospital, for which the masters will be sentenced to pay eight *sols* a day for the nourishment and maintenance of each slave ...

XXVII. The slave who will have struck his master, his mistress, the husband of his mistress, or their children, either in the face or resulting in a bruise or the outpouring of blood, will be punished by death.

XXVIII. And as to abuse and assault that will be committed by slaves against free persons, we wish that they be severely punished, even by death if it falls due. ...

XXXVIII. We also forbid all of our subjects of the said country, of whatever quality or condition they may be, to engage in, or by their private authority to have others engage in, the torture or the racking of slaves, under whatever pretext it may be; nor to do them, or to have others do them, any mutilation, under pain of confiscation of the slaves and of being proceeded against extraordinarily. We permit them [masters], when they believe their slaves will have merited it, only to bind them and to beat them with rods or cords.

XXXIX. We order the officers of justice established in the said country to proceed criminally against the masters and overseers who will have killed their slaves or will have mutilated them while under their power or under their direction and to punish the murder according to the atrocity of the circumstances. In case there is cause to discharge them, we permit the dismissal of the masters as well as the overseers without there being need to obtain from us letters of grace.

XL. We wish that the slaves be considered personal property ...

XLIII. Yet we wish that the husband, his wife, and their prepubescent children not be able to be seized or sold separately if they are all under the power of the same master: We declare null the separate seizures and sales that may be done. ...

XLIV. We also wish that slaves ages fourteen and under and up to sixty, attached to lands or to dwellings and actually working there, not to be able to be seized for debts other than one owing to the price of their purchase, unless the lands or the dwelling might actually be seized. ...

Duboys, J. 1744–1745. *Recueils de Reglemens, Edits, Declarations et Arrets, Concernant le Commerce, l'Administration de la Justice, & la Police des Colonies Francaises de l'Amerique & les Engages, avec le Code Noir et l'Addition Audit Code.* Paris: Chez les Libraires Associez.

INVESTIGATION INTO A SLAVE CONSPIRACY (1741)

At a Supreme Court of Judicature held for the province of New York, at the city-hall of the city of New York, on Tuesday, April 21, 1741–Present, Frederick Philipse, esq. Second justice; Daniel Horsmanden, esq. third justice.

The grand jury were called. The following persons appeared, and were sworn-viz.:

Mr. Robert Watts, merchant, foreman; Messrs. Jeremiah Latouche, Joseph Read, Anthony Rutgers, John M'Evers, John Cruger, jun. John Merritt, Adoniah Schuyler, Isaac De Peyster, Abraham Keteltass, David Provoost, Rene Hett, Henry Beekman, jun. David Van Horne, George Spencer, Thomas Duncan, Winant Van Zant, merchants. Mr. Justice Philipse gave the charge to the grand jury, as followeth:

Gentlemen of the grand jury,

It is not without some concern, that I am obliged at this time to be more particular in your charge, than for many preceding terms there hath been occasion. The many frights and terrors which the good people of this city have of late been put into, by repeated and unusual fires, and burning of houses, give us too much room to suspect, that some of them at least, did not proceed from mere chance, or common accidents; but on the contrary, from the premeditated malice and wicked pursuits of evil and designing persons; and therefore, it greatly behooves us to use our utmost diligence, by all lawful ways and means to discover the contrivers and perpetrators of such daring and flagitious undertakings: that, upon conviction, they may receive condign punishment; for although we have the happiness of living under a government which exceeds all others in the excellency of its constitution and laws, yet if those to whom the execution of them (which my lord Coke calls the life and soul of the law) is committed, do not exert themselves in a conscientious discharge of their respective duties, such laws which were intended for a terror to the evil-doer, and a protection to the good, will become a dead letter, and our most excellent constitution turned into anarchy and confusion; every one practising what he listeth, and doing what shall seem good in his own eyes: to prevent which, it is the duty of all grand juries to inquire into the conduct and behaviour of the people in their respective counties; and if, upon examination, they find any to have transgressed the laws of the land, to present them, that so they may by the court be put upon their trial, and then either to be discharged or punished according to their demerits.

I am told there are several prisoners now in jail, who have been committed by the city magistrates, upon suspicion of having been concerned in some of the late fires; and others, who under pretence of assisting the unhappy sufferers, by saving their goods from the flames, for stealing, or receiving them. This indeed, is adding affliction to the afflicted, and is a very great aggravation of such crime, and therefore deserves a narrow inquiry: that so the exemplary punishment of the guilty (if any such should be so found) may deter others from committing the like villainies; for this kind of stealing, I think, has not been often practised among us.

Gentlemen,

Arson, or the malicious and voluntary burning, not only a mansion house, but also any other house, and the out buildings, or barns, and stables adjoining thereto, by night or by day, is felony at common law; and if any part of the house be burned, the offender is guilty of felony, notwithstanding the fire afterwards be put out, or go out of itself.

This crime is of so shocking a nature, that if we have any in this city, who, having been guilty thereof, should escape, who can say he is safe, or tell where it will end?

Gentlemen,

Another Thing which I cannot omit recommending to your serious and diligent inquiry, is to find out and present all such persons who sell rum, and other strong liquor to negroes. It must be obvious to every one, that there are too many of them in this city; who, under pretence of selling what they call a penny dram to a negro, will sell to him as many quarts or gallons of rum, as he can steal money or goods to pay for.

How this notion of its being lawful to sell a penny dram, or a pennyworth of rum to a slave, without the consent or direction of his master, has prevailed, I know not; but this I am sure of, that there is not only no such law, but that the doing of it is directly contrary to an act of the assembly now in force, for the better regulating of slaves. The many fatal consequences flowing from this prevailing and wicked practice, are so notorious, and so nearly concern us all, that one would be almost surprised, to think there should be a necessity for a court to recommend a suppression of such pernicious houses: thus much in particular; now in general.

My charge, gentlemen, further is, to present all conspiracies, combinations, and other offences, from treasons down to trespasses; and in your inquiries, the oath you, and each of you have just now taken will, I am persuaded, be your guide, and I pray God to direct and assist you in the discharge of your duty.

Court adjourned until to-morrow morning ten o'-clock.

The grand jury having been informed, that Mary Burton could give them some account concerning the good stolen from Mr. Hogg's, sent for her this morning, and ordered she should be sworn; the constable returned and acquainted them, that she said she would not be sworn, nor give evidence; whereupon they ordered the constable to get a warrant from a magistrate, to bring her before them. The constable was some time gone, but at length returned, and brought her with him; and being asked why she would not be sworn, and give her evidence? she told the grand jury she would not be sworn; and seemed to be under some great uneasiness, or terrible apprehensions; which gave suspicion that she knew something concerning the fires that had lately happened: and being asked a question to that purpose, she gave no answer; which increased the jealousy that she was privy to them; and as it was thought a matter of the utmost concern, the grand jury was very importunate, and used many arguments with her, in public and private, to persuade her to speak the truth, and tell all she knew about it. To this end, the lieutenant governor's proclamation was read to her, promising indemnity, and the reward of one hundred pounds to any person, confederate or not, who should make discovery, etc. She seemed to despise it, nor could the grand jury by any means, either threats or promises, prevail upon her, though they assured her withal, that she should have the protection of the magistrates, and her person be safe and secure from harm; but hitherto all was in vain: therefore, the grand jury desired alderman Bancker to commit her; and the constable was charged with her accordingly; but before he had got her to jail, she considered better of it, and resolved to be sworn, and give her evidence in the afternoon.

Accordingly, she being sworn, came before the grand jury; but as they were proceeding to her examination, and before they asked her any questions, she told them she would acquaint them with what she knew relating to the goods stolen from Mr. Hogg's, but would say nothing about the fires.

This expression thus, as it were providentially, slipping from the evidence, much alarmed the grand jury; for, as they naturally concluded, it did by construction amount to an affirmative, that she could give an account of the occasion of the several fires; and therefore, as it highly became those gentlemen in the discharge of their trust, they determined to use their utmost diligence to sift out the discovery, but still she remained inflexible, till at length, having recourse to religious topics, representing to her the heinousness of the crime which she would be guilty of, if she was privy to, and could discover so wicked a design, as the firing houses about our ears; whereby not only people's estates would be destroyed, but many person might lose their lives in the flames: this she would have to answer for at the day of judgment, as much as any person immediately concerned, because she might have prevented this destruction, and would not; so that a most damnable sin would lie at her door; and what need she fear from her divulging it; she was sure of the protection of the magistrates? or the grand jury expressed themselves in words to the same purpose; which arguments at last prevailed, and she gave the following evidence, which however, notwithstanding what had been said, came from her, as if still under some terrible apprehensions or restraints.

Deposition, No. 1. -Mary Burton, being sworn, deposeth,

1. "That Prince (a) and Caesar (b) brought the things of which they had robbed Mr. Hogg, to her master, John Hughson's house, and that they were handed in through the window, Hughson, his wife, and Peggy receiving them, about two or three o'clock on a Sunday morning (c).

2. "That Caesar, prince, and Mr. Philipse's negro man (Cuffee) used to meet frequently at her master's house, and that she had heard them (the negroes) talk frequently of burning the fort; and that they would go down to the Fly (d) and burn the whole town; and that her master and mistress said, they would aid and assist them as much as they could.

3. "That in their common conversation they used to say, that when all this was done, Caesar should be governor, and Hughson, her master, should be king.

4. "That Cuffee used to say, that a great many people had too much, and others too little; that his old master had a great deal of money, but that, in a short time, he should have less, and that he (Cuffee) should have more.

5. "That at the same time when the things of which Mr. Hogg was robbed, were brought to her master's house, they brought some indigo and bees wax, which was likewise received by her master and mistress.

6. "That at the meetings of the three aforesaid negroes, Caesar, Prince and Cuffee, at her master's house, they used to say, in their conversations, that when they set fire to the town, they would do it in the night, and as the white people came to extinguish it, they would kill and destroy them.

7. "That she has known at times, seven or eight guns in her master's house, and some swords, and that she has seen twenty or thirty negroes at one time in her master's house; and that at such large meetings, the three aforesaid negroes, Cuffee, Prince and Caesar, were generally present, and most active, and that they used to say, that the other negroes durst not refuse to do what they commanded them, and they were sure that they had a number sufficient to stand by them.

8. "That Hughson (her master) and her mistress used to threaten, that if she, the deponent, ever made mention of the goods stolen from Mr. Hogg, they would poison her; and the negroes swore, if ever she published, or discovered the design of burning the town, they would burn her whenever they met her.

9. "That she never saw any white person in company when they talked of burning the town, but her master, her mistress, and Peggy."

This evidence of a conspiracy, not only to burn the city, but also destroy and murder the people, was most astonishing to the grand jury, and that any white people should become so abandoned as to confederate with slaves in such an execrable and detestable purpose, could not but be very amazing to every one that heard it; what could scarce be credited; but that the several fires had been occasioned by some combination of villains, was, at the time of them, naturally to be collected from the manner and circumstances attending them.

The grand jury therefore, as it was a matter of the utmost consequence, thought it necessary to inform the judges concerning it, in order that the most effectual measures might be concerted, for discovering the confederates; and the judges were acquainted with it accordingly.

Supreme Court, Friday, May 1.

Present, the second and third justices.

The king against Caesar and prince, negroes. On trial.

The jury called, and the prisoners making no challenge, the following persons were sworn, viz. :

Roger French, John Groesbeek, John Richard, Abraham Kipp, George Witts, John Thurman, Patrick Jackson, Benjamin Moore, William Hamersley, John Lashier, Joshua Sleydall, John Shurmur.

These two negroes were arraigned on two indictments, the twenty fourth of April last; the one for their entering the dwelling house of Robert Hogg, of this city, merchant, on the first day of March then last past, with intent then and there to commit some felony; and for feloniously stealing and carrying away then and there the goods and chattels of the said Robert Hogg, of the value of four pounds five shillings sterling, against the form of the statutes in such case made and provided, and against the peace of our sovereign lord the king, his crown and dignity.

The other for their entering the dwelling house of Abraham Meyers Cohen in this city, merchant, on the first day of March with the intent then and there to commit some felony; and for feloniously stealing and carrying away then and there the goods and chattels of the said Abraham Meyers Cohen of the value of five pounds sterling, against the form of the statutes, etc. And against the king's peace, etc.

To each of which indictments they pleaded, not guilty.

The Attorney General having opened both the indictments, he with Joseph Murray, Esq. of council for the king, proceeded to examine the witnesses, viz.,

For the king, Mrs. Hogg, Mrs. Boswell, Christopher Wilson, Rachina Guerin, Mr. Robert Hogg, Mr. Robert Watts, Margaret Sorubiero, alias Kerry, Abraham Meyers Cohen, James Mills, Thomas Wenman, John Moore, Esq. Cornelius Brower, Anthony Ham, Mary Burton.

For the prisoners, Alderman Bancker, Alderman Johnson, John Auboyneau.

The prisoners upon their defence denied the charge against them. And,

The evidence being summed up, which was very strong and full, and the jury charged, they withdrew; and being returned, found them guilty of the indictments.

Ordered, that the trials of the Hughsons and Margaret Kerry, be put off until Wednesday of the 6th inst.

Court adjourned until Monday morning, 4th May, at ten o'clock.

Supreme Court Friday, May 8

Present, the second and third justices.

The king against Caesar and Prince, negroes.

The prisoners having been capitally convicted on two several indictments for felony, and being brought to the bar the court proceeded to give sentence; which was passed by the second justice as followeth:

You, Caesar and Prince, the grand jury having found two indictments against each of you, for feloniously stealing and taking away from Mr. Hogg, and Mr. Meyers Cohen, sundry goods of considerable value. To these indictments you severally pleaded not guilty; and for your trials put yourselves upon God and the country; which country having found you guilty, it now only remains for the court to pronounce that judgment which the law requires, and the nature of your crimes deserve.

But before I proceed to sentence, I must tell you, that you have been proceeded against in the same manner as any white man, guilty of your crimes, would have been. You had not only the liberty of sending for your witnesses; asking them such questions as you thought proper; but likewise making the best defence you could; and as you have been convicted by twelve honest men upon their oaths, so the just judgement of God has at length overtaken you.

I have great reason to believe, that the crimes you now stand convicted of, are not the least of those you have been concerned in; for by your general characters you have been very wicked fellows, hardened sinners, and ripe, as well as ready, for the most enormous and daring enterprizes, especially you, Caesar: and as the time you have yet to live is to be but very short, I earnestly advise and exhort both of you to employ it in the most diligent and best manner you can, by confessing your sins, repenting sincerely of them, and praying God of his infinite goodness to have mercy on your souls: and as God knows the secrets of your hearts, and cannot be cheated or imposed upon, so you must shortly give an account to him, and answer for all your actions; and depend upon it, if you do not truly repent before you die, there is a hell to punish the wicked eternally.

And as it is not in your powers to make full restitution for the many injuries you have done the public; so I advise both of you to do all that in you is, to prevent further mischiefs, by discovering such persons as have been concerned with you, in designing or endeavouring to burn this city, and to destroy its inhabitants. This I am fully persuaded is in your power to do if you will; if so, and you do not make such discovery, be assured God almighty will punish you for it, though we do not: therefore I advise you to consider this well, and I hope both of you will tell the truth.

And now, nothing further remains for me to say, but that you Caesar, and you Prince, are to be taken hence to the place whence you came, and from thence to the place of execution, and there you, and each of you, are to be hanged by the neck until you be dead. And I pray the Lord to have mercy on your souls.

Ordered, that their execution be on Monday next, the eleventh day of this instant, between the hours of nine and one of the same day. And further ordered that after the execution of the said sentence, the body of Caesar be hung in chains.

Court adjourned till Monday morning next ten o'-clock.

Supreme Court of Judicature, New York City. n.d. "New York Conspiracy." In *Journal of the Proceedings Against the Conspirators, at New York in 1741.* New York: Author.

ARGUMENT FOR SLAVERY IN GEORGIA (1743)

" . . . But as if the difficulties arising from indifferent lands, and discouraging tenures, were not sufficient to humble and prepare them for the other severities they have met with, they were totally prohibited the importation, use, or even sight of Negroes. In spite of all endeavours to disguise this point, it is as clear as light itself, that Negroes are an essential necessary to the cultivation of Georgia, as axes, hoes, or any other utensil of agriculture. So that if a colony was designed able but to subsist itself, their prohibition was inconsistent; if a garrison only was intended, the very inhabitants were needless. But all circumstances considered, it looked as if the assistance of human creatures, who have been called slaves, as well as subject to the treatment of such, were incongruous with a system that proceeded to confer the thing, but to spare the odium of the appellation. Experience would too soon have taught them the parity of their conditions, in spite of a mere nominal difference. The only English clergymen, who were ever countenanced there, declared they never desired to see Georgia a rich, but a godly colony; and the blind subjection the poor Salzburgers are under to the Rev. Mr. Boltzius, who has furnished such extraordinary extracts in some accounts of Georgia, published here, will be too evident from some of the annexed depositions to call for any descant.

The pretended content and satisfaction of the people of Ebebezer, without Negroes, will plainly appear to be the dictates of spiritual tyranny, and only the wretched acquiescence of people, who were in truth unacquainted with the privilege of choosing for themselves.

It is acknowledged indeed that the present war, and late invasion, may furnish the enemies of the colony with the most plausible objections that could occur, against the allowance of black slaves; but these reasons have not always existed, nor have the trustees ever declared any resolution to admit them, at any other juncture. But if it plainly appears that Georgia, as a colony, cannot barely exist without them, surely an admission of them under limitations, suitable to the present situation of affairs, is absolutely necessary to its support; since want and famine must be more dreadful and insuperable invaders, than any living enemy. Besides, the honourable trustees were informed by a letter from Mr. Stirling and others, of the falsehood of the contented and comfortable situation of the people of Darien were affirmed to be in; and that they were bought with a number of cattle, and extensive promises of future rewards when they signed their petition against Negroes. "

1743. *A Brief Account of the Causes That Have Retarded the Progress of the Colony of Georgia in America.* Originally published in London. Reprinted in *Collections of the Georgia Historical Society,* II. Savannah, GA: 1842.

BENJAMIN FRANKLIN'S "OBSERVATIONS CONCERNING THE INCREASE OF MANKIND, PEOPLING OF COUNTRIES, ETC." (1751)

1. Tables of the Proportion of Marriages to Birth, of Deaths to Births, of Marriages to the Numbers of Inhabitants, &c, form'd on Observations made upon the Bills of Mortality, Christnings, &c., of populous Cities, will not suit Countries; nor will Tables form'd on Observations made on full-settled old Countries, as *Europe,* suit new Countries, as *America.*

2. For People increase in Proportion to the Number of Marriages, and that is greater in Proportion to the Ease and Convenience of supporting a Family. When families can be easily supported, more Persons marry, and earlier in Life.

3. In Cities, where all Trades, Occupations, and Offices are full, many delay marrying till they can see how to bear the Charges of a Family; which Charges are greater in Cities, as Luxury is more common: many live single during Life, and continue Servants to Families, Journeymen to Trades; &c. hence Cities do not by

natural Generation supply themselves with Inhabitants; the Deaths are more than the Births.

4. In Countries full settled, the Case must be nearly the same; all Lands being occupied and improved to the Heighth; those who cannot get land, must Labour for others that have it; when Labourers are plenty, their Wages will be low; by low Wages a family is supported with Difficulty; this Difficulty deters many from Marriage, who therefore long continue Servants and single. Only as the Cities take Supplies of People from the Country, and thereby make a little more Room in the Country; Marriage is a little more encourag'd there, and the Births exceed the Deaths.

5. *Europe* is generally full settled with Husbandmen, Manufacturers, c., and therefore cannot now much increase in People: *America* is chiefly occupied by Indians, who subsist mostly by Hunting. But as the Hunter, all of men, requires the greatest Quantity of Land from whence to draw his Subsistence, (The Husbandman subsisting on much less, the Gardner on still less, and the Manufacturer requiring least of all), the *Europeans* found *America* as fully settled as it well could be by Hunters; yet these, having large Tracks, were easily prevail'd on to part with Portions of Territory to the new Comers, who did not much interfere with the Natives in Hunting, and furnish'd them with many Things they wanted.

6. Land being thus plenty in *America,* and to cheap as that a labouring man, that understands Husbandry, can in a short Time save Money enough to purchase a Piece of new Land sufficient for a Plantation, whereon he may subsist a Family, such are not afraid to marry; for, if they even look far enough forward to consider how their Children, when grown up, are to be provided for, they see that more Land is to be had at rates equally easy, all Circumstances considered.

7. Hence Marriages in *America* are more general, and more generally early, than in *Europe.* And if it is reckoned there, that there is but one Marriage per Annum among 100 persons, perhaps we may here reckon two; and if in *Europe* they have but 4 Births to a Marriage (many of their Marriages being late), we may here reckon 8, of which if one half grow up, and our Marriages are made, reckoning one with another at 20 Years of Age, our People must at least be doubled every 20 Years.

8. But notwithstanding this Increase, so vast is the Territory of *North America,* that it will require many Ages to settle it fully; and, till it is fully settled, Labour will never by cheap here, where no Man continues long a Labourer for others, but gets a Plantation of his own, no Man continues long a Journeyman to a Trade, but goes among those new Settlers, and sets up for himself, &c. Hence Labour is no cheaper now in *Pennsylvania,* than it was 30 Years ago, tho' so many Thousand labouring People have been imported.

9. The Danger therefore of these Colonies interfering with their Mother Country in Trades that depend on Labour, Manufactures, &c., is too remote to require the attention of *Great Britain.*

10. But in Proportion to the Increase of the Colonies, a vast Demand is growing for British Manufactures, a glorious Market wholly in the Power of *Britain,* in which Foreigners cannot interfere, which will increase in a short Time even beyond here Power of supplying, tho' her whole Trade should be to her Colonies: Therefore *Britain* should not too much restrain Manufactures in her Colonies. A wise and good Mother will not do it. To distress, is to weaken, and weakening the Children weakens the whole Family.

11. Besides if the Manufactures of *Britain* (by reason of the *American* Demands) should rise too high in Price, Foreigners who can sell cheaper will drive her Merchants out of Foreign Markets; Foreign Manufactures will thereby be encouraged and increased, and consequently foreign Nations, perhaps her Rivals in Power, grow more populous and more powerful; while her own Colonies, kept too low, are unable to assist her, or add to her Strength.

12. 'Tis an ill-grounded Opinion that by the Labour of slaves, *America* may possibly vie in Cheapness of Manufactures with *Britain.* The Labour of Slaves can never be so cheap here as the Labour of working Men is in *Britain.* Any one may compute it. Interest of Money is in the Colonies from 6 to 10 per Cent. Slaves one with another cost 30 pounds Sterling per Head. Reckon then the Interest of the first Purchase of a Slave, the Insurance or Risque on his Life, his Cloathing and Diet, Expences in his Sickness and Loss of Time, Loss by his Neglect of Business (Neglect is natural to the man who is not to be benefited by his own Care or Diligence), Expence of a Driver to keep him at work, and his Pilfering from Time to Time, almost every Slave being *by Nature* a thief, and compare the whole Amount with the Wages of a Manufacturer of Iron or Wood in *England,* you will see that Labour is much cheaper there than it ever can be by Negroes here.

Why then will *Americans* purchase Slaves? Because Slaves may be kept as long as a *Man* pleases, or has Occasion for their Labour; while hired Men are continually leaving their masters (often in the midst of his Business,) and setting up for themselves.—Sec. 8.

13. As the Increase of People depends on the Encouragement of Marriages, the following Things must diminish a Nation, viz. 1. *The being conquered;* for the Conquerors will engross as many Offices, and exact as much Tribute or Profit on the Labour of the conquered, as will maintain them in their new Establishment, and this diminishing the Subsistence of the Natives, discourages their Marriages, and so gradually diminishes them, while the foreigners increase. 2. *Loss of Territory.* Thus, the *Britons* being driven into *Wales,* and crowded together in a barren Country insufficient to support such great Numbers, diminished 'till the People bore a Proportion to the Produce, while the *Saxons* increas'd on their abandoned lands; till the Island became full of *English.* And, were the *English* now driven into *Wales* by some foreign Nation, there would in a few Years, be no more Englishmen in *Britain,* than there are now people in *Wales.* 3. *Loss of Trade.* Manufactures exported, draw Subsistence from Foreign Countries for Numbers; who are thereby enabled to marry and raise Families. If the Nation be deprived of any Branch of Trade, and no new Employment is found for the People occupy'd in that Branch, it will also be soon deprived of so many People. 4. *Loss of Food.* Suppose a Nation has a Fishery, which not only employs great Numbers, but makes the Food and Subsistence of the People cheaper. If another Nation becomes Master of the Seas, and prevents the Fishery, the People will diminish in Proportion as the Loss of Employ and Dearness of Provision, makes it more difficult to subsist a Family. 5. *Bad Government and insecure Property.* People not only leave such a Country, and settling Abroad incorporate with other Nations, lose their native Language, and become Foreigners, but, the Industry of those that remain being discourag'd, the Quantity of Subsistence in the Country is lessen'd, and the Support of a Family becomes more difficult. So heavy Taxes tend to diminish a People. 6. *The Introduction of Slaves.* The Negroes brought into the *English Sugar Islands,* have greatly diminish'd the White there; the Poor are by this Means deprived of Employment, while a few Families acquire vast Estates; which they spend on Foreign Luxuries, and educating their Children in the Habit of those Luxuries; the same Income is needed for the Support of one that might have maintain'd 100. The Whites who have Slaves, not labouring, are enfeebled, and therefore not so generally prolific; the Slaves being work'd too hard, and ill fed, their Constitutions are broken, and the Deaths among them are more than the Births; so that a continual Supply is needed from *Africa.* The Northern Colonies having few Slaves, increase in Whites. Slaves also pejourate the Families that use them; the white Children become proud, disgusted with Labour, and being educated in Idleness, are rendered unfit to get a Living by Industry.

14. Hence the Prince that acquires new Territory, if he finds it vacant, or removed the Natives to give his own People Room; the Legislator that makes effectual laws for promoting of Trade, increasing Employment, improving Land by more or better Tillage, providing more Food by Fisheries; securing Property, &c. and the Man that invents new Trades, Arts, or manufactures, or new Improvements in Husbandry, may be properly called *Fathers* of their Nation, as they are the Cause of the Generation of Multitudes, by the Encouragement they afford to Marriage.

15. As to Privileges granted to the married, (such as the *Jus trium Liberorum* among the *Romans*) they may hasten the filling of a Country that has been thinned by War or Pestilence, or that has otherwise vacant Territory; but cannot increase a People beyond the Means provided for their Subsistence.

16. Foreign Luxuries and needless Manufactures, imported and used in a Nation, do, by the same Reasoning, increase the People of the Nation, that furnishes them, and diminish the People of the Nation that uses them. Laws, therefore, that prevent such Importations, and on the contrary promote the Exportation of Manufactures to be consumed in Foreign Countries, may be called (with Respect to the People that make them) *generative Laws,* as, by increasing Subsistence they encourage Marriage. Such Laws likewise strengthen a Country, doubly, by increasing its own People and diminishing its Neighbours.

17. Some *European* Nations prudently refuse to consume the Manufactures of *East-India:-* They should likewise forbid them to their Colonies; for the Gain to the Merchant is not to be compar'd with the Loss, by this Means, of People to the Nation.

18. Home Luxury in the Great increases the Nation's Manufacturers employ'd by it, who are many, and only tends to diminish the Families that indulge in it, who are few. The greater the common fashionable Expence of any Rank of People, the more cautious they are of

Marriage. Therefore Luxury should never be suffer'd to become common.

19. The great Increase of Offspring in particular Families is not always owing to greater Fecundity of Nature, but sometimes to Examples of Industry in the Heads, and industrious Education; by which the Children are enabled to provide better for themselves, and their marrying early is encouraged from the Prospect of good Subsistence.

20. If there be a Sect, therefore, in our Nation, that regard Frugality and Industry as religious Duties, and educate their Children therein, more than others commonly do; such Sect must consequently increase more by natural Generation, than any other sect in *Britain*.

21. The Importation of Foreigners into a Country, that has as many Inhabitants as the present Employments and Provisions for Subsistence will bear, will be in the End no Increase of People; unless the New Comers have more Industry and Frugality than the Natives, and then they will provide more Subsistence, and increase in the Country; but they will gradually eat the Natives out. Nor is it necessary to bring in Foreigners to fill up any occasional Vacancy in a Country; for such vacancy (if the Laws are good, sec. 14, 16) will soon be filled by natural Generation. Who can now find the Vacancy made in *Sweden, France,* or other Warlike Nations, by the Plague of Heroism, 40 years ago; in *France*, by the Expulsion of the Protestants; in *England*, by the Settlement of her Colonies; or in *Guinea*, by 100 Years Exportation of Slaves, that has flacken'd half *America?* The thinness of Inhabitants in *Spain* is owing to National Pride and Idleness, and other Causes, rather than to the Expulsion of the Moors, or to the making of new Settlements.

22. There is, in short, no Bound to the prolific Nature of Plants or Animals, but what is made by their crowding and interfering with each other's means of Subsistence. Was the Face of the Earth vacant of other Plants, it might be gradually sowed and overspread with one Kind only; as, for Instance, with Fennel; and were it empty of other Inhabitants, it might in a few Ages be replenish'd from one Nation only; as, for Instance, with *Englishmen.* Thus there are suppos'd to be now upwards of One Million *English* Souls in *North America,* (tho' 'tis thought scarce 80,000 have been brought over Sea,) and yet perhaps there is not one the fewer in *Britain,* but rather many more, on Account of the Employment the Colonies afford to Manufacturers at Home. This Million doubling, suppose but once in 25 Years, will, in another Century, be more than the People of *England,* and the greatest Number of *Englishmen* will be on this Side the Water. What an Accession of Power to the *British* Empire by Sea as well as Land! What Increase of Trade and Navigation! What Numbers of Ships and Seamen! We have been here but little more than 100 years, and yet the Force of our Privateers in the late War, united, was greater, both in Men and Guns, than that of the whole *British* navy in Queen *Elizabeth's* Time. How important an Affair then to *Britain* is the present Treaty for settling the Bounds between her Colonies and the *French,* and how careful should she be to secure Room enough, since on the Room depends so much the Increase of her People.

23. In fine, a Nation well regulated is like a Polypus; take away a Limb, its Place is soon supply'd; cut it in two, and each deficient Part shall speedily grow out of the Part remaining. Thus if you have Room and Subsistence enough, as you may be dividing, make ten Polypes out of one, you may of one make ten Nations, equally populous and powerful; or rather increase a Nation ten fold in Numbers and Strength.

And since Detachments of *English* from *Britain,* sent to *America,* will have their Places at Home so soon supply'd and increase so largely here; why should the *Palatine Boors* be suffered to swarm into our Settlements and, by herding together, establish their Language and Manners, to the Exclusion of ours? Why should *Pennsylvania,* founded by the *English,* become a Colony of *Aliens,* who will shortly be so numerous as to Germanize us instead of our Anglifying them, and will never adopt our Language or Customs any more than they can acquire our Complexion?

24. Which leads me to add one Remark, that the Number of purely white People in the World is proportionably very small. All *Africa* is black or tawny; *America* (exclusive of the new Comers) wholly so. And in *Europe,* the *Spaniards, Italians, French, Russians, and Swedes,* are generally of what we call a swarthy Complexion; as are the *Germans* also, the *Saxons* are excepted, who, with the *English,* make the principal Body of White People on the Face of the Earth. I could wish their Numbers were increased. And while we are, as I may call it, *Scouring* our Planet, by *clearing America* of Woods, and so making this Side of our Globe reflect a brighter Light to the Eyes of Inhabitants in *Mars* or *Venus,* why should we, in the Sight of Superior Beings, darken its People? Why increase the Sons of *Africa,* by planting them in *America,* where we have so fair an Opportunity, by excluding all Blacks

and Tawneys, of increasing the lovely White and Red? But perhaps I am partial to the Complexion of my Country, for such Kind of Partiality is natural to Mankind.

DEFENSE OF COLONIAL SLAVERY IN VIRGINIA (1757)

Letter excerpt from Peter Fontaine to Moses Fontaine, March 30, 1757.

. . . As to your second query, if enslaving our fellow creatures be a practice agreeable to Christianity, it is answered in a great measure in many treatises at home, to which I refer you. I shall only mention something of our present state here.

Like Adam we are all apt to shift off the blame from ourselves and lay it upon others, how justly in our case you may judge. The Negroes are enslaved by the Negroes themselves before they are purchased by the masters of the ships who bring them here. It is to be sure at our choice whether we buy them or not, so this then is our crime, folly, or whatever you will please to call it. But, our Assembly, foreseeing the ill consequences of importing such numbers amongst us, hath often attempted to lay a duty upon them which would amount to a prohibition, such as ten or twenty pounds a head, but no governor dare pass such a law, having instructions to the contrary from the Board of Trade at home. By this means they are forced upon us, whether we will or will not. This plainly shows the African Company hath the advantage of the colonies, and may do as it pleases with the ministry.

Indeed, since we have been exhausted of our little stock of cash by the war, the importation has stopped; our poverty then is our best security. There is no more picking for their ravenous jaws upon bare bones, but should we begin to thrive, they will be at the same again. All our taxes are now laid upon slaves and on shippers of tobacco, which they wink at while we are in danger of being torn from them, but we durst not do it in time of peace, it being looked upon as the highest presumption to lay any burden upon trade. This is our part of the grievance, but to live in Virginia without slaves is morally impossible. Before our troubles, you could not hire a servant or slave for love or money, so that unless robust enough to cut wood, to go to mill, to work at the hoe, etc., you must starve, or board in some family where they both fleece and half starve you. There is not set price upon corn, wheat and provisions, so they take advantage of the necessities of strangers, who are thus obliged to purchase some slaves and land. This of course draws us all into the original sin and curse of the country of purchasing slaves, and this is the reason we have no merchants, traders, or artificers of any sort but what become planters in a short time.

A common labourer, white or black, if you can be so much favoured as to hire one, is a shilling sterling or fifteen pence currency per day; a bungling carpenter two shillings or two shillings and sixpence per day; besides diet and lodging. That is, for a lazy fellow to get wood and water, £ 19. 16. 3, current per annum; add to this seven or eight pounds more and you have a slave for life.

Fontaine, James, Ann Maury, John Fontaine, James Maury, et al. 1853. *Memoirs of a Huguenot Family: Translated and Compiled from the Original Autobiography of the Rev. James Fontaine, and Other Family Manuscripts; Comprising an Original Journal of Travels in Virginia, New York, &c. in 1715 and 1716.* New York: G. P. Putnam and Sons.

JOHN WOOLMAN'S JOURNAL (1757)

"Feeling the exercise in relation to a visit to the Southern Provinces to increase upon me, I acquainted our Monthly Meeting therewith, and obtained their certificate. Expecting to go alone, one of my brothers who lived in Philadelphia, having some business in North Carolina, proposed going with me part of the way; but as he had a view of some outward affairs, to accept of him as a companion was some difficulty with me, whereupon I had conversation with him at sundry times. At length feeling easy in my mind, I had conversation with several elderly Friends of Philadelphia on the subject, and he obtaining a certificate suitable to the occasion, we set off in the Fifth Month, 1757. Coming to Nottingham week-day meeting, we lodged at John Churchman's, where I met with our friend, Benjamin Buffington, from New England, who was returning from a visit to the Southern Provinces. Thence we crossed the river Susquehanna, and lodged at William Cox's in Maryland.

Soon after I entered this province, a deep and painful exercise came upon me, which I often had some feeling of since my mind was drawn toward these parts, and with which I had acquainted my brother before we agreed to join as companions. As the people in this and the Southern Provinces live much on the labour of slaves, many of whom are used hardly, my concern was that I might attend with singleness of heart to the voice of the true Shepherd, and be so supported as to remain unmoved at the faces of men.

As it is common for Friends on such a visit to have

entertainment free of cost, a difficulty arose in my mind with respect to saving my money by kindness received from what appeared to me to be the gain of oppression. Receiving a gift, considered as a gift, brings the receiver under obligations to the benefactor, and has a natural tendency to draw the obliged into a party with the giver. To prevent difficulties of this kind, and to preserve the minds of judges from any bias, was that divine prohibition: "Thou shalt not receive any gift; for a gift blindeth the wise, and perverteth the words of the righteous" (Exod. xxiii. 8). As the disciples were sent forth without any provision for their journey, and our Lord said the workman is worthy of his meat, their labour in the gospel was considered as a reward for their entertainment, and therefore not received as a gift; yet, in regard to my present journey, I could not see my way clear in that respect. The difference appeared thus: the entertainment the disciples met with was from them whose hearts God had opened to receive them, from a love to them and the truth they published; but we, considered as members of the same religious society, look upon it as a piece of civility to receive each other in such visits; and such receptions, at times, is partly in regard to reputation, and not from an inward unity of heart and spirit. Conduct is more convincing than language, and where people, by their actions, manifest that the slave-trade is not so disagreeable to their principles but that it may be encouraged, there is not a sound uniting with some Friends who visit them.

The prospect of so weighty a work, and of being so distinguished from many whom I esteemed before myself, brought me very low, and such were the conflicts of my soul that I had a near sympathy with the prophet, in the time of his weakness, when he said: "If thou deal thus with me, kill me, I pray thee, if I have found favour in thy sight" (Num. xi. 15). But I soon saw that this proceeded from the want of a full resignation to the divine will. Many were the afflictions which attended me, and in great abasement, with many tears, my cries were to the Almighty for His gracious and Fatherly assistance, and after a time of deep trial I was favoured to understand the state mentioned by the Psalmist more clearly than ever I had done before; to wit: "My soul is even as a weaned child" (Ps. cxxxi. 2).

Being thus helped to sink down into resignation, I felt a deliverance from that tempest in which I had been sorely exercised, and in calmness of mind went forward, trusting that the Lord Jesus Christ, as I faithfully attended to Him, would be a counsellor to me in all difficulties, and that by His strength I should be enabled even to leave money with the members of society where I had entertainment, when I found that omitting it would obstruct that work to which I believed He had called me. As I copy this after my return, I may here add that oftentimes I did so under a sense of duty. The way in which I did it was thus: When I expected soon to leave a Friend's house where I had entertainment, if I believed that I should not keep clear from the gain of oppression without leaving money, I spoke to one of the heads of the family privately, and desired them to accept of those pieces of silver, and give them to such of their negroes as they believed would make the best use of them; and at other times I gave them to the negroes myself, as the way looked clearest to me. Before I came out, I had provided a large number of small pieces for this purpose, and thus offering them to some who appeared to be wealthy people was a trial both to me and them. But the fear of the Lord so covered me at times that my way was made easier than I expected; and few, if any, manifested any resentment at the offer, and most of them, after some conversation, accepted of them.

Ninth of Fifth Month.—A Friend at whose house we breakfasted setting us a little on our way, I had conversation with him, in the fear of the Lord, concerning his slaves, in which my heart was tender; I used much plainness of speech with him, and he appeared to take it kindly. We pursued our journey without appointing meetings, being pressed in my mind to be at the Yearly Meeting in Virginia. In my travelling on the road, I often felt a cry rise from the centre of my mind, thus: "O Lord, I am a stranger on the earth, hide not thy face from me. "

On the 11th, we crossed the rivers Patowmack and Rapahannock, and lodged at Port Royal. On the way we had the company of a colonel of the militia, who appeared to be a thoughtful man. I took occasion to remark on the difference in general betwixt a people used to labour moderately for their living, training up their children in frugality and business, and those who live on the labour of slaves; the former, in my view, being the most happy life. He concurred in the remark, and mentioned the trouble arising from the untoward, slothful disposition of the negroes, adding that one of our labourers would do as much in a day as two of their slaves. I replied that free men, whose minds were properly on their business, found a satisfaction in improving, cultivating, and providing for their families; but negroes, labouring to support others who claim them as their property, and expecting nothing but slavery during life, had not the like inducement to be industrious.

After some further conversation I said, that men having power too often misapplied it; that though we made slaves of the negroes, and the Turks made slaves of the Christians, I believed that liberty was the natural right of all men equally. This he did not deny, but said the lives of the negroes were so wretched in their own country that many of them lived better here than there. I replied, "There is great odds in regard to us on what principle we act"; and so the conversation on that subject ended. I may here add that another person, some time afterwards, mentioned the wretchedness of the negroes, occasioned by their intestine wars, as an argument in favour of our fetching them away for slaves. To which I replied, if compassion for the Africans, on account of their domestic troubles, was the real motive of our purchasing them, that spirit of tenderness being attended to, would incite us to use them kindly, that, as strangers brought out of affliction, their lives might be happy among us. And as they are human creatures, whose souls are as precious as ours, and who may receive the same help and comfort from the Holy Scriptures as we do, we could not omit suitable endeavours to instruct them therein; but that while we manifest by our conduct that our views in purchasing them are to advance ourselves, and while our buying captives taken in war animates those parties to push on the war and increase desolation amongst them, to say they live unhappily in Africa is far from being an argument in our favour.

I further said, the present circumstances of these provinces to me appear difficult; the slaves look like a burdensome stone to such as burden themselves with them; and that, if the white people retain a resolution to prefer their outward prospects of gain to all other considerations, and do not act conscientiously toward them as fellow-creatures, I believe that burden will grow heavier and heavier, until times change in a way disagreeable to us. The person appeared very serious, and owned that in considering their condition and the manner of their treatment in these provinces he had sometimes thought it might be just in the Almighty so to order it.

Having travelled through Maryland, we came amongst Friends at Cedar Creek in Virginia, on the 12th; and the next day rode, in company with several of them, a day's journey to Camp Creek. As I was riding along in the morning, my mind was deeply affected in a sense I had of the need of divine aid to support me in the various difficulties which attended me, and in uncommon distress of mind I cried in secret to the Most High, "O Lord, be merciful, I beseech Thee, to Thy poor afflicted creature!" After some time I felt inward relief, and soon after a Friend in company began to talk in support of the slave-trade, and said the negroes were understood to be the offspring of Cain,

their blackness being the mark which God set upon him after he murdered Abel, his brother; that it was the design of Providence they should be slaves, as a condition proper to the race of so wicked a man as Cain was. Then another spake in support of what had been said.

To all which I replied in substance as follows: that Noah and his family were all who survived the flood, according to Scripture; and as Noah was of Seth's race, the family of Cain was wholly destroyed. One of them said that after the flood Ham went to the land of Nod and took a wife; that Nod was a land far distant, inhabited by Cain's race, and that the flood did not reach it; and as Ham was sentenced to be a servant of servants to his brethren, these two families, being thus joined, were undoubtedly fit only for slaves. I replied, the flood was a judgment upon the world for their abominations, and it was granted that Cain's stock was the most wicked, and therefore unreasonable to suppose that they were spared. As to Ham's going to the land of Nod for a wife, no time being fixed, Nod might be inhabited by some of Noah's family before Ham married a second time; moreover the text saith "That all flesh died that moved upon the earth" (Gen. vii. 21). I further reminded them how the prophets repeatedly declare "that the son shall not suffer for the iniquity of the father, but every one be answerable for his own sins."

I was troubled to perceive the darkness of their imaginations, and in some pressure of spirit said, "The love of ease and gain are the motives in general of keeping slaves, and men are wont to take hold of weak arguments to support a cause which is unreasonable. I have no interest on either side, save only the interest which I desire to have in the truth. I believe liberty is their right, and as I see they are not only deprived of it, but treated in other respects with inhumanity in many places, I believe He who is a refuge for the oppressed will, in His own time, plead their cause, and happy will it be for such as walk in uprightness before Him." And thus our conversation ended."

Woolman, John. 1910. *The Journal and Other Writings of John Woolman.* London: J. M. Dent and Sons.

SLAVES PETITION FOR FREEDOM DURING THE REVOLUTION (1773)

Province of the Massachusetts Bay To His Excellency Thomas Hutchinson, Esq; Governor; To The Honorable His Majesty's Council, and To the Honorable House of Representatives in General Court assembled at Boston, the 6th Day of January, 1773.

The humble PETITION of many Slaves, living in the Town of Boston, and other Towns in the Province is this, namely

That your Excellency and Honors, and the Honorable Representatives would be pleased to take their unhappy State and Condition under your wise and just Consideration.

We desire to bless God, who loves Mankind, who sent his Son to die for their Salvation, and who is no respecter of Persons; that he hath lately put it into the Hearts of Multitudes on both Sides of the Water, to bear our Burthens, some of whom are Men of great Note and Influence; who have pleaded our Cause with Arguments which we hope will have their weight with this Honorable Court.

We presume not to dictate to your Excellency and Honors, being willing to rest our Cause on your Humanity and justice; yet would beg Leave to say a Word or two on the Subject.

Although some of the Negroes are vicious, (who doubtless may be punished and restrained by the same Laws which are in Force against other of the King's Subjects) there are many others of a quite different Character, and who, if made free, would soon be able as well as willing to bear a Part in the Public Charges; many of them of good natural Parts, are discreet, sober, honest, and industrious; and may it not be said of many, that they are virtuous and religious, although their Condition is in itself so unfriendly to Religion, and every moral Virtue except Patience. How many of that Number have there been, and now are in this Province, who have had every Day of their Lives embittered with this most intollerable Reflection, That, let their Behaviour be what it will, neither they, nor their Children to all Generations, shall ever be able to do, or to possess and enjoy any Thing, no, not even Life itself, but in a Manner as the Beasts that perish.

We have no Property! We have no Wives! No Children! We have no City! No Country! But we have a Father in Heaven, and we are determined, as far as his Grace shall enable us, and as far as our degraded contemptuous Life will admit, to keep all his Commandments: Especially will we be obedient to our Masters, so long as God in his sovereign Providence shall suffer us to be holden in Bondage.

It would be impudent, if not presumptuous in us, to suggest to your Excellency and Honors any Law or Laws proper to be made, in relation to our unhappy State, which, although our greatest Unhappiness, is not our Fault; and this gives us great Encouragement to pray and hope for such Relief as is consistent with your Wisdom, justice, and Goodness.

We think Ourselves very happy, that we may thus address the Great and General Court of this Province, which great and good Court is to us, the best judge, under God, of what is wise, just-and good.

We humbly beg Leave to add but this one Thing more: We pray for such Relief only, which by no Possibility can ever be productive of the least Wrong or Injury to our Masters; but to us will be as Life from the dead.

Signed,
FELIX

"A Petition for Freedom in Massachusetts." In *Sources of the African American Past: Primary Sources in American History,* ed. Roy E. Finkenbine. New York: Longman, 1997.

LORD DUNMORE'S PROCLAMATION (1775)

By His Excellency the Right Honorable JOHN Earl of DUNMORE, His MAJESTY'S Lieutenant and Governor General of the Colony and Dominion of VIRGINIA, and Vice Admiral of the Same.

A PROCLAMATION. As I have ever entertained Hopes that an Accommodation might have taken Place between GREAT-BRITAIN and this colony, without being compelled by my Duty to this most disagreeable but now absolutely necessary Step, rendered of by a Body of armed Men unlawfully assembled, bring on His MAJESTY'S [Tenders], and the formation of an Army, and that Army now on their March to attack His MAJESTY'S troops and destroy the well disposed Subjects of this Colony. To defeat such unreasonable Purposes, and that all such Traitors, and their Abetters, may be brought to Justice, and that the Peace, and good Order of this Colony may be again restored, which the ordinary Course of the Civil Law is unable to effect; I have thought fit to issue this my Proclamation, hereby declaring, that until the aforesaid good Purposes can be obtained, I do in Virtue of the Power and Authority to ME given, by His MAJESTY, determine to execute Martial Law, and cause the same to be executed throughout this Colony: and to the end that Peace and good Order may the sooner be [effected], I do require every Person capable of bearing Arms, to [resort] to His MAJESTY'S STANDARD, or be looked upon as Traitors to His MAJESTY'S Crown and Government, and thereby become liable to the Penalty the Law inflicts upon such Offences; such as forfeiture of

Life, confiscation of Lands, &c. &c. And I do hereby further declare all indentured Servants, Negroes, or others, (appertaining to Rebels,) free that are able and willing to bear Arms, they joining His MAJESTY'S Troops as soon as may be, for the more speedily reducing this Colony to a proper Sense of their Duty, to His MAJESTY'S Leige Subjects, to retain their [Quitrents], or any other Taxes due or that may become due, in their own Custody, till such Time as Peace may be again restored to this at present most unhappy Country, or demanded of them for their former salutary Purposes, by Officers properly authorized to receive the same.

GIVEN under my Hand on board the ship WILLIAM, off NORPOLE, the 7th Day of NOVEMBER, in the SIXTEENTH Year of His MAJESTY'S Reign.

DUNMORE.

(GOD save the KING.)

By his Excellency the Right Honourable John Earl of Dunmore, His Majesty's Lieutenant and Governor-General of the Colony and Dominion of Virginia, and Vice-Admiral of the Same: A Proclamation [Declaring Martial Law, and to Cause the Same to be Executed Throughout This Colony], broadside. 1775. Williamsburg, Virginia.

VERMONT ABOLISHES SLAVERY (1777)

Constitution of the State of Vermont

A Declaration of the Rights of the Inhabitants of the State of Vermont.   Chapter I, Article 1st—That all men are born equally free and independent, and have certain natural, inherent, and unalienable rights, amongst which are the enjoying and defending life and liberty, acquiring, possessing and protecting property, and pursuing and obtaining happiness and safety; therefore no person born in this country, or brought from over sea, ought to be holden by law, to serve any person as a servant, slave or apprentice, after he arrives to the age of twenty-one years, unless he is bound by his own consent, after he arrives to such age, or bound by law for the payment of debts, damages, fines, costs, or the like.

United States Congress. 1909. *The Federal and State Constitutions Colonial Charters, and Other Organic Laws of the States, Territories, and Colonies Now or Heretofore Forming the United States of America Compiled and Edited Under the Act of Congress of June 30, 1906 by Francis Newton Thorpe.* Washington, DC: Government Printing Office.

PENNSYLVANIA ABOLISHES SLAVERY (1780)

An Act for the Gradual Abolition of Slavery

I. When we contemplate our abhorrence of that condition to which the arms and tyranny of Great Britain were exerted to reduce us, when we look back on the variety of dangers to which we have been exposed, and how miraculously our wants in many instances have been supplied, and our deliverances wrought, when even hope and human fortitude have become unequal to the conflict, we are unavoidably led to a serious and grateful sense of the manifold blessings, which we have undeservedly received from the hand of that Being from whom every good and perfect gift cometh. Impressed with these ideas, we conceive that it is our duty, and we rejoice that it is in our power to extend a portion of that freedom to others which hath been extended to us, and release from that state of thraldom to which we ourselves were tyrannically doomed, and from which we now have every prospect of being delivered. It is not for us to inquire why in the creation of mankind the inhabitants of several parts of the earth were distinguished by a difference in feature or complexion. It is sufficient to know that all are the work of an Almighty Hand. We find in the distribution of the human species that the most fertile as well as the most barren parts of the earth are inhabited by Men of complexions different from ours and from each other; from whence we may reasonably as well as religiously infer that He who placed them in their various situations, hath extended equally His care and protection to all, and that it becometh not us to counteract His mercies.

We esteem it a peculiar blessing granted to us, that we are enabled this day to add one more step to universal civilization, by removing as much as possible the sorrows of those who have lived in undeserved bondage, and from which by the assumed authority of the Kings of Great Britain no effectual legal relief could be obtained. Weaned, by a long course of experience, from those narrow prejudices and partialities we have imbibed, we find our hearts enlarged with kindness and benevolence toward men of all conditions and nations, and we perceive ourselves at this particular period extraordinarily called upon by the blessings which we have received, to manifest the sincerity of our profession to give substantial proof of our gratitude.

II. And, whereas, the condition of those persons who have heretofore been denominated Negro and Mulatto slaves, has been attended with circumstances which not only deprived them of the common blessings that they were by nature entitled to, but has cast them into the deepest afflictions by an unnatural separation and sale of husband and wife from each other and from their children, an injury the greatness of which can only be conceived by supposing that we were in the same unhappy case. In justice, therefore, to persons so unhappily circumstanced, and who, having no prospect before them whereon they may rest their sorrows and hopes, have no reasonable inducement to render their services to society, which they otherwise might, and also in grateful commemoration of our own happy deliverance from that state of unconditional submission to which we were doomed by the tyranny of Britain.

III. *Be it enacted, and it is hereby enacted,* That all persons as well Negroes and Mulattoes, as others, who shall be born within this State from and after the passing of this Act shall not be deemed and considered as servants for life, or slaves; and that all servitude for life, or slavery of children in consequence of the slavery of their mothers, in the case of all children born within this State from and after the passing of this Act, as aforesaid, shall be, and hereby is, utterly taken away, extinguished, and forever abolished.

IV. *Provided always, and be it further enacted,* That every Negro and Mulatto child, born within this State after the passing of this act as aforesaid (who would, in case this act had not been made, have been born a servant for years, or life, or a slave) shall be deemed to be, and shall be, by virtue of this act, the servant of such person, or his or her assigns, who would in such case have been entitled to the service of such child, until such child shall attain the age of twenty-eight years, in the manner, and on the conditions, whereon servants bound, by indenture for four years are or may be retained and holden; and shall be liable to like corrections and punishment, and entitled to like relief, in case he or she be evilly treated by his or her master or mistress, and to like freedom dues and other privileges, as servants bound by indenture for four years are or may be entitled, unless the person, to whom the service of any such child shall belong, shall abandon his or her claim to the same; in which case the Overseers of the Poor of the city, township, or district, respectively, where such child shall be abandoned, shall, by indenture, bind out every child so abandoned, as an apprentice, for a time not exceeding the age herein before limited for the service of such children.

V. *And be it further enacted,* That every person, who is or shall be the owner of any Negro or Mulatto slave or servant for life, or till the age of thirty-one years, now within this State, or his lawful attorney, shall, on or before the said first day of November next, deliver, or cause to be delivered, in writing, to the Clerk of the peace of the county, or to Clerk of the court of record of the city of Philadelphia, in which he or she shall respectively inhabit, the name and surname, and occupation or profession of such owner, and the name of the county and township, district or ward, wherein he or she resideth; and also the name and names of such slave and slaves, and servant and servants for life, or till the age of thirty-one years, together with their ages and sexes, severally and respectively set forth and annexed, by such persons owned or statedly employed, and then being within this State, in order to ascertain and distinguish the slaves and servants for life, and till the age of thirty-one years, within this State, who shall be such on the said first day of November next, from all other persons; which particulars shall, by said Clerk of the sessions and Clerk of the said city court, be entered in books to be provided for that purpose by the said Clerks; and that no Negro or Mulatto, now within this State, shall, from and after the said first day of November, be deemed a slave or servant for life, or till the age of thirty-one years, unless his or her name shall be entered as aforesaid on such record, except such Negro and Mulatto slaves and servants as herein excepted; the said Clerk to be entitled to a fee of two dollars for each slave or servant so entered as aforesaid, from the Treasurer of the county to be allowed to him in his accounts.

VI. *Provided always,* That any person, in whom the ownership or right to the service of any Negro or Mulatto shall be vested at the passing of this act, other than such as are hereinbefore accepted, his or her heirs, executors, administrators, and assigns, and all and every of them, severally, shall be liable to the Overseers of the city, township, or district, to which any such Negro or Mulatto shall become chargeable, for such necessary expense, with costs of suit thereon, as such Overseers may be put to through the neglect of the owner, master, or mistress of such Negro or Mulatto, notwithstanding the name and other descriptions of such Negro or Mulatto shall not be entered as aforesaid, unless his or her master or owner shall, before such slave or servant attain his or her twenty-eighth year, execute and record in the proper county, a deed or instrument, securing to such slave or servant his or her freedom.

VII. *And be it further enacted,* That the offences and crimes of Negroes and Mulattoes, as well slaves and servants as freemen, shall be enquired of, adjudged, corrected, and punished, in like manner as the offences and crimes of the other inhabitants of this State are, and shall be enquired of, adjudged, corrected, and punished, and not otherwise, except that a slave shall not be admitted to bear witness against a freeman.

VIII. *And be it further enacted,* That in all cases wherein sentence of death shall be pronounced against a slave, the jury before whom he or she shall be tried shall appraise and declare the value of such slave; and in such case sentence be executed, the court shall make an order on the State Treasurer, payable to the owner for the same, and for the costs of prosecution, but in case of remission or mitigation, for costs only.

IX. *And be it further enacted,* That the reward for taking up runaway and absconding Negro and Mulatto slaves and servants, and the penalties for enticing away, dealing with or harboring, concealing or employing Negro and Mulatto slaves and servants, shall be the same, and shall be recovered in like manner, as in case of servants bound for four years.

X. *And be it further enacted,* That no man or woman of any nation, or color, except the Negroes or Mulattoes who shall be registered as aforesaid, shall, at any time, be deemed, adjudged, and holden within the territories of this commonwealth as slaves and servants for life, but as free men and free women; except the domestic slaves attending upon Delegates in Congress from other American States, foreign Ministers and Consuls, and persons passing through or sojourning in this State, and not becoming resident therein, and seamen employed in ships not belonging to any inhabitant of this State, nor employed in any ship owned by such inhabitants; provided such domestic slaves be not aliened or sold to any inhabitant, nor (except in the case of Members of Congress, foreign Ministers and Consuls) retained in this State longer than six months.

XI. *Provided always, and be it further enacted,* That this act, or anything in it contained, shall not give any relief or shelter to any absconding or runaway Negro or Mulatto slave or servant, who has absented himself or shall absent himself, from his or her owner, master or mistress, residing in any other State or country, but such owner, master or mistress, shall have like right and aid to demand, claim, and take away his slave or servant, as he might have had in case this act had not been made; and that all Negro and Mulatto slaves now owned and heretofore resident in this State, who have absented themselves, or been clandestinely carried away, or who may be employed abroad as seamen, and have not returned or been brought back to their owner, masters or mistresses, before the passing of this act, may, within five years, be registered, as effectually as is ordered by this act concerning those who are now within the State, on producing such slave before any two Justices of the Peace, and satisfying the said Justices, by due proof, of the former residence, absconding, taking away, or absence of such slaves as aforesaid, who thereupon shall direct and order the said slave to be entered on the record as aforesaid.

XII. And whereas attempts may be made to evade this act, by introducing into this State Negroes and Mulattoes bound by covenant to serve for long and unreasonable terms of years, if the same be not prevented.

XIII. *Be it therefore enacted,* That no covenant of personal servitude or apprenticeship whatsoever shall be valid or binding on a Negro or Mulatto for a longer time than seven years, unless such servant or apprentice were, at the commencement of such servitude or apprenticeship, under the age of twenty-one years, in which case such Negro or Mulatto may be holden as a servant or apprentice, respectively, according to the covenant, as the case shall be, until he or she shall attain the age of twenty-eight years, but no longer.

XIV. *And be it further enacted,* That an act of Assembly of the Province of Pennsylvania, passed in the year one thousand seven hundred and five, entitled *An Act for the trial of Negroes;* and another act of Assembly of the said Province, passed in the year one thousand seven hundred and twenty-five, entitled *An Act for the better regulating of Negroes in this Province;* and another act of Assembly of the said Province, passed in the year one thousand seven hundred and sixty-one, entitled *An Act for laying a duty on Negro and Mulatto slaves imported into this Province;* and also another act of Assembly of the said Province, passed in the year one thousand seven hundred and seventy-three, entitled *An Act for making perpetual an act for laying a duty on Negro and Mulatto slaves imported into this Province, and for laying an additional duty on said slaves,* shall be, and are hereby, repealed, annulled, and made void.

Pennsylvania Law Book, Vol. I: 339

COMMONWEALTH V. JENNISON (1783)

Charge of Chief Justice Cushing.

As to the doctrine of slavery and the right of Christians to hold Africans in perpetual servitude, and sell and treat them as we do our horses and cattle, that (it is true) has been heretofore countenanced by the Province Laws formerly, but nowhere is it expressly enacted or established. It has been a usage—a usage which took its origin from the practice of some of the European nations, and the regulations of British government respecting the then Colonies, for the benefit of trade and wealth. But whatever sentiments have formerly prevailed in this particular or slid in upon us by the example of others, a different idea has taken place with the people of America, more favorable to the natural rights of mankind, and to that natural, innate desire of Liberty, with which Heaven (without regard to color, complexion, or shape of noses—features) has inspired all the human race. And upon this ground our Constitution of Government, by which the people of this Commonwealth have solemnly bound themselves, sets out with declaring that all men are born free and equal—and that every subject is entitled to liberty, and to have it guarded by the laws, as well as life and property—and in short is totally repugnant to the idea of being born slaves. This being the case, I think the idea of slavery is inconsistent with our own conduct and Constitution; and there can be no such thing as perpetual servitude of a rational creature, unless his liberty is forfeited by some criminal conduct or given up by personal consent or contract . . .

Blaustein, Albert P. and Robert L. Zangrando, eds. 1968. *Civil Rights and the Black American: A Documentary History.* New York: Simon & Schuster.

QUAKER ANTI-SLAVERY SENTIMENTS (1785)

When the General Congress first assembled, they prefaced the reason of their separation from Great Britain, with the following sentence, 'We hold these truths to be self-evident, That all men are created equal, that they are endowed by their Creator, with certain unalienable rights; that among these are life, liberty and the pursuit of happiness.' And in the declaration on the 6th of July 1775, Congress have in very forcible language declared their opinion 'that it was contrary to the intent of the Divine Author of our existence, that a part of the human kind should hold an absolute property over others, marked out by infinite goodness and wisdom, as objects of a Legal Domination.—That reverence for our great Creator, principles of humanity, and the dictates of common sense, must convince all those who reflect upon the subject, that Government was instituted to promote the welfare of mankind, and ought to be administered for the attainment of that end. 'As these reflections apply however diversified by colour and other distinctions, how far the situation of the Negroes still kept in slavery, on this continent is consonant thereto, is a matter which calls for the most serious attention of all those who, indeed believe, in a general Providence, and that the good Author of our being multiplies his blessings in proportion as we render ourselves worthy by the practice of Justice and Love. Hence it becomes a matter of the utmost weight to Americans, in a peculiar manner, duly to consider how they can justify a conduct so abhorrent from these sacred truths as that of dragging these oppressed Strangers from their native land and all those tender connections which we hold so dear.' . . .

How inconsistent is this abhorrent practice, with every idea of Liberty, every principle of humanity. Nay is it not of public notoriety that those masters or overseers who by ill usage or by an unrelenting scourge, have brought their Slaves to an untimely end, have scarce been called to any account, by those who ought not to bear the sword in vain: Scarce an instance can be mentioned even of any man's being capitally arraigned for the willful murder of a slave. Nay, dreadful to mention, do not the laws in some of the islands, and frequent advertisements in the Southern States, in effect encourage the murder of a Negroe who has absented himself for a certain time from his master's service, by giving a reward greater for the poor fugitive's head than for bringing him home alive.

When this unjust and cruel treatment of the Negroes is considered, and brought to the test of the above declarations, will it not appear wonderfully inconsistent and a matter of astonishment, to the whole world, that an alteration of conduct towards them, has not yet taken place, preparatory to a general abolition of Slavery on the continent; a step which every principle of honour, reason and humanity call for, and which may well be effected in such a manner as will conduce to the happiness of the master as well as the slave. . . .

To assist in eradicating the deep rooted prejudice which an education amongst Slaves has planted in many minds, let us attend to what the Abbe Raynal, that celebrated philosopher and friend to Mankind, has said on the subject of Slavery.

"I will not," says he, "disgrace myself by adding one to the list of venal writers who have prostituted their pens in defense of a trade so abhorrent from the laws of universal justice. No principles of policy can justify the breach of her Sacred Laws. In so enlightened as age, an age where so many errors are boldly laid open, it would be shameful to conceal any truth that is interesting to humanity. We will first prove that no reason of state can authorize Slavery. In doing this we shall not hesitate to arraign, before the Tribunal of Eternal Light and Justice, all those governments who tolerate the cruel practice, or are not ashamed to make it the basis of the basis of their power. The great Montesquieu could not prevail upon himself to treat the question concerning slavery, in a furious light. In reality it is degrading to reason to employ it. I will not say in defending, but even in refuting an abuse so repugnant to it; whoever justifies so odious a system deserves the utmost contempt. . . . "

The writer of the foregoing introductory observations, i.e., A. Benezet, teacher of a school established by private subscription, in Philadelphia, for the instruction of the Black Children and others of that people, has, for many years, had opportunity of knowing the temper and genius of the Africans; particularly of those under his tuition, who have been many, of different ages; and he can with Truth and Sincerity declare, that he has found amongst them as great variety of Talents, equally capable of improvements, as amongst a like number of Whites; and he is bold to assert, that the notion entertained by some, that the Blacks are inferior to the Whites in their capacities, is a vulgar prejudice, founded on the Pride or Ignorance of their lordly Masters, who have kept their Slaves at such a distance, as to be unable to form a right judgement of them.

Benezet, Anthony. 1785. *Short Observations on Slavery.* Philadelphia: Enoch Story.

PREAMBLE OF THE FREE AFRICAN SOCIETY (1787)

Philadelphia

[12th, 4th mo., 1787]—Whereas, Absalom Jones and Richard Allen, two men of the African race, who, for their religious life and conversation have obtained a good report among men, these persons, from a love to the people of their complexion whom they beheld with sorrow, because of their irreligious and uncivilized state, often communed together upon this painful and important subject in order to form some kind of religious society, but there being too few to be found under the like concern, and those who were, differed in their religious sentiments; with these circumstances they labored for some time, till it was proposed, after a serious communication of sentiments, that a society should be formed, without regard to religious tenets, provided, the persons lived an orderly and sober life, in order to support one another in sickness, and for the benefit of their widows and fatherless children.

Articles

[17th, 5th mo., 1787]—We, the free Africans and their descendants, of the City of Philadelphia, in the State of Pennsylvania, or elsewhere, do unanimously agree, for the benefit of each other, to advance one shilling in silver Pennsylvania currency a month; and after one year's subscription from the date hereof, then to hand forth to the needy of this Society, if any should require, the sum of three shillings and nine pence per week of the said money: provided, this necessity is not brought on them by their own imprudence.

And it is further agreed, that no drunkard nor disorderly person be admitted as a member, and if any should prove disorderly after having been received, the said disorderly person shall be disjointed from us if there is not nit amendment, by being informed by two of the members, without having any of his subscription money returned.

And if any should neglect paying his monthly subscription for three months, and after having been informed of the same by two of the members, and no sufficient reason appearing for such neglect, if he do not pay the whole the next ensuing meeting, he shall be disjointed from us, by being informed by two of the members its an offender, without having any of his subscription money returned.

Also, if any person neglect meeting every month, for every omission he shall pay three pence, except in case of sickness or any other complaint that should require the assistance of the Society, then, and in such a case, he shall be exempt from the fines and subscription during the said sickness.

Also, we apprehend it to be just and reasonable, that the surviving widow of a deceased member should enjoy the benefit of this Society so long as she remains his widow, complying with the rules thereof, excepting the subscriptions.

And we apprehend it to be necessary, that the children of our deceased members be under the care of the Society, so far as to pay for the education of their children, if they cannot attend the free school; also to put them out apprentices to suitable trades or places, if required.

Also, that no member shall convene the Society together; but, it shall be the sole business of the committee, and that only on special occasions, and to dispose of the money in hand to the best advantage, for the use of the Society, after they are granted the liberty at a monthly meeting, and to transact all other business whatsoever, except that of Clerk and Treasurer.

And we unanimously agree to choose Joseph Clarke to be our Clerk and Treasurer; and whenever another should succeed him, it is always understood, that one of the people called Quakers, belonging to one of the three monthly meetings in Philadelphia, is to be chosen to act as Clerk and Treasurer of this useful Institution.

The following persons met, viz., Absalom Jones, Richard Allen, Samuel Baston, Joseph Johnson, Cato Freeman, Caesar Cranchell, and James Potter, also William White, whose early assistance and useful remarks we found truly profitable. This evening the articles were read, and after some beneficial remarks were made, they were agreed unto.

Douglass, William. 1862. *Annals of the First African Church in the United States of America Now Styled the African Episcopal Church of St. Thomas, Philadelphia.* Philadelphia: King & Baird Printers.

THE FUGITIVE SLAVE ACT (1793)

Chap. VII.—An Act respecting fugitives from justice, and persons escaping from the service of their masters.

Section 1. *Be it enacted by the Senate and House of Representatives of the United States of America in Congress assembled,* That whenever the executive authority of any state in the Union, or of either of the territories northwest or south of the river Ohio, shall demand any person as a fugitive from justice, of the executive authority of any such state or territory to which such person shall have fled, and shall moreover produce the copy of an indictment found, or an affidavit made before a magistrate of any state or territory as aforesaid, charging the person so demanded, with having committed treason, felony or other crime, certified as authentic by the governor or chief magistrate of the state or territory from whence the person so charged fled, it shall be the duty of the executive authority of the state or territory to which such person shall have fled, to cause him or her to be arrested and secured, and notice of the arrest to be given to the executive authority making such demand, or to the agent of such authority appointed to receive the fugitive, and to cause the fugitive to be delivered to

such agent when he shall appear: But if no such agent shall appear within six months from the time of the arrest, the prisoner may be discharged. And all costs or expenses incurred in the apprehending, securing, and transmitting such a fugitive to the state or territory making such demand, shall be paid by such state or territory.

Section 2. *And be it further enacted,* That any agent, appointed as aforesaid, who shall receive the fugitive into his custody, shall be empowered to transport him or her to the state or territory from which he or she shall have fled. And if any person or persons shall by force set at liberty, or rescue the fugitive from such agent while transporting, as aforesaid, the person or persons so offending shall, on conviction, be fined not exceeding five hundred dollars, and be imprisoned not exceeding one year.

Section 3. *And be it also enacted,* That when a person held to labour in any of the United States, or in either of the territories on the northwest or south of the river Ohio, under the laws thereof, shall escape into any other of the said states or territory, the person to whom such labour or service may be due, his agent or attorney, is hereby empowered to seize or arrest such fugitive from labour, and to take him or her before any judge of the circuit or district courts of the United States, residing or being within the state, or before any magistrate of a county, city or town corporate, wherein such seizure or arrest shall be made, and upon proof to the satisfaction of such judge or magistrate, either by oral testimony or affidavit taken before and certified by a magistrate of any such state or territory, that the person so seized or arrested, doth, under the laws of the state or territory from which he or she fled, owe service or labour to the person claiming him or her, it shall be the duty of such judge or magistrate to give a certificate thereof to such claimant, his agent or attorney, which shall be sufficient warrant for removing the said fugitive from labour, to the state or territory from which he or she fled.

Section 4. *And be it further enacted,* That any person who shall knowingly and willingly obstruct or hinder such claimant, his agent or attorney in so seizing or arresting such fugitive from labour, or shall rescue such fugitive from such claimant, his agent or attorney when so arrested pursuant to the authority herein given or declared; or shall harbor or conceal such person after notice that he or she was a fugitive from labour, as aforesaid, shall, for either of the said offences, forfeit and pay the sum of five hundred dollars. Which penalty may be recovered by and for the benefit of such claimant, by action of debt, in any court proper to try the same; saving moreover to the person claiming such labour or service, his right of action for or on account of the said injuries or either of them.

Approved, February 12, 1793.

U.S. Congress. 1793. *United States Statutes at Large.* 2nd Cong., 2nd sess., ch. 7.

THE FORMATION OF A BLACK CONGREGATION IN PHILADELPHIA (1794)

Whereas, a few of our race did in the NAME and FEAR Of GOD, Associate for the purpose Of advancing our friends in a true knowledge of God, of true religion, and of the ways and means to restore our long lost race, to the dignity of men and of christians;—and Whereas, God in mercy and wisdom, has exceeded Our most sanguine wishes, in blessing our undertakings, for the above purposes, and has opened the hearts of our white brethren, to assist in our undertakings therein;—and

Whereas the light of the glorious gospel of God, our Saviour, has begun to shine into our hearts, who were strangers to the true and living God, and aliens to the commonwealth of this spiritual Israel; and having seen the dawn of the gospel day, we are zealously concerned for the gathering together our race into the sheep-fold of the great Shepherd and Bishop of our souls; and as we would earnestly desire to proceed in all our ways therein consistent with the word of God or the scripture of the revelation of God's will, concerning us and our salvation;—and

Whereas, through the various attempts we have made to promote our design, God has marked out [and] made our ways with blessings. And we are now encouraged through the grace and divine assistance of the friends and God opening the hearts of our white friends and brethren, to encourage us to arise out of the dust and shake ourselves, and throw off that servile fear, that the habit of oppression and bondage trained us up in. And in meekness and fear we would desire to walk in the liberty wherewith Christ has made us free. That following peace with all men, we may have our fruit unto holiness, and in the end, everlasting life.

And in order the more fully to accomplish the good purposes of God's will, and organize ourselves for the purpose of promoting the health [of] the people all, but more particularly our relatives, of color. We, after many consultations, and some years deliberation thereon, have gone forward to erect a house for the glory of God, and our mutual advantage to meet in for clarification and social religious worship. And more particularly to keep an open door for those of our race, who may be into assemble with us, but would not attend divine worship in Other places; and

Whereas, faith comes by hearing, and hearing by the word of God, we are the more encourage thereto, believing God will bless our works and labors of love;—and

Whereas, for all the above purposes, it is needful that we enter into, and forthwith establish some orderly, Christian-like government and order of former usage in the Church of Christ; and, being a way to avoid all appearance of evil, by self-conceitedness, or an intent to promote or establish any new human device among us.

Now be it known to all the world and in all eyes thereof, that we the founders and trustees of said house did on Tuesday the twelfth day of August, in the year of our Lord, one thousand seven hundred and ninety four.

RESOLVE AND DECREE, To resign and conform ourselves to the Protestant Episcopal Church of North America.—And we dedicate ourselves to God, imploring his holy protection; and our house to the memory of St. Thomas, the Apostle, to be henceforward known and called by the name and title of St. Thomas's African Episcopal Church of Philadelphia; to be governed by us and our successors for ever as follows.

Given under our hands, this Twelfth day of August, 1794.

Founders and Trustees.

William Gray, Absalom Jones, William White, William Gardner, Henry Stewart, William Gray, for William Wiltshire.

Douglass, William. 1862. *Annals of the First African Church in the United States of America now Styled the African Episcopal Church of St. Thomas, Philadelphia.* Philadelphia: King & Baird Printers.

GEORGE WASHINGTON FREES HIS SLAVES (1799)

The Last Will and Testament of George Washington [Excerpt]

July 9, 1799

In the name of God, amen!

I, George Washington of Mount Vernon, a citizen of the United States and lately President of the same, do make, ordain and declare this instrument, which is written with my own hand and every page thereof subscribed with my name, to be my last Will and Testament, revoking all others.

Imprimus. All my debts, of which there are but few, and none of magnitude, are to be punctually and speedily paid, and the legacies hereinafter bequeathed are to be discharged as soon as circumstances will permit, and in the manner directed.

Item. To my dearly beloved wife, Martha Washington, I give and bequeath the use, profit and benefit of my whole estate, real and personal, for the term of her natural life, except such parts thereof as are specially disposed of hereafter—my improved lot in the town of Alexandria, situated on Pitt and Cameron Streets, I give to her and her heirs forever, as I also do my household and kitchen furniture of every sort and kind with the liquors and groceries which may be on hand at the time of my decease, to be used and disposed of as she may think proper.

Item. Upon the decease of my wife, it is my will and desire, that all the slaves which I hold in my own right shall receive their freedom. To emancipate them during her life, would tho earnestly wished by me, be attended with such insuperable difficulties, on account of their intermixture by marriages with the dower negroes as to excite the most painful sensations—if not disagreeable consequences from the latter while both descriptions are in the occupancy of the same proprietor, it not being in my power under the tenure by which the dower Negroes are held to manumit them. And whereas among those who will receive freedom according to this devise there may be some who from old age, or bodily infirmities and others who on account of their infancy, that will be unable to support themselves, it is my will and desire that all who come under the first and second description shall be comfortably clothed and fed by my heirs while they live and that such of the latter description as have no parents living, or if living are unable, or unwilling to provide for them, shall be bound by the Court until they shall arrive at the age of twenty-five years, and in cases where no record can be produced whereby their ages can be ascertained, the judgment of the Court upon its own view of the subject shall be adequate and final. The negroes thus bound are (by their masters and mistresses) to be taught to read and write and to be brought up to some useful occupation, agreeably to the laws of the Commonwealth of Virginia, providing for the support of orphans and other poor children—and I do hereby expressly forbid the sale or transportation out of the said Commonwealth of any slave I may die possessed of, under any pretense, whatsoever—and I do moreover most positively, and most solemnly enjoin it upon my executors hereafter named, or the survivors of them to see that this clause respecting slaves and every part thereof be religiously fulfilled at the epoch at which it is directed to take place without evasion, neglect or delay after the crops which may then be on the ground are harvested, particularly as it respects the aged and infirm, seeing that a regular and permanent fund be established for their support so long as there are subjects requiring it, not trusting to the uncertain provisions to be made by individuals. And to my mulatto man, William (calling himself William Lee) I give immediate freedom or if he should prefer it (on account of the accidents which have befallen him and which have rendered him incapable of walking or of any active employment) to remain in the situation he now is, it shall be optional in him to do so. In either case, however, I allow him an annuity of thirty dollars during his natural life which shall be independent of the victuals and clothes he has been accustomed to receive; if he chooses the last alternative, but in full with his freedom, if he prefers the first, and this I give him as a testimony of my sense of his attachment to me and for his faithful services during the Revolutionary War.

Abbot, W. W., ed. 1999. *The Papers of George Washington, Retirement Series, vol. 4, April–December 1799.* Charlottesville: University Press of Virginia.

THOMAS JEFFERSON ON RACE AND SLAVERY (1801)

It will probably be asked, Why not retain and incorporate the blacks into the state, and thus save the expense of supplying, by importation of white settlers, the vacancies they will leave? Deep rooted prejudices entertained by the whites; ten thousand recollections, by the blacks, of the injuries they have sustained; new provocations; the real distinctions which nature has made; and many other circumstances, will divide us into parties, and produce convulsions, which will probably never end but in the extermination of the one or the other race.—To these objections, which are political, may be added others, which are physical and moral. The first difference which strikes us is that of colour.—Whether the black of the negro resides in the reticular membrane between the skin and scarf-skin, or in the scarf-skin itself; whether it proceeds from the colour of the blood, the colour of the bile, or from that of some other secretion, the difference is fixed in nature, and is as real as if its seat and cause were better known to us. And is this difference of no importance? Is it not the foundation of a greater or less share of beauty in the two races? Are not the fine mixtures of red and white, the expressions of every passion by greater or less suffusions of colour in the one, preferable to that eternal monotony, which reigns in the countenances, that immovable veil of black which covers all the emotions of the other race? Add to these, flowing hair, a more elegant symmetry of form, their own judgment in favour of the whites, declared by their preference of them, as uniformly as is the preference of the Oranootan for the black women over those of his own species. The circumstance of Superior beauty, is thought worthy attention in the propagation of our horses, dogs, and other domestic animals; why not in that of man? Besides those of colour, figure, and hair, there are other physical distinctions proving a difference of race. They have less hair on the face and body. They secrete less by the kidneys, and more by the glands of the skin, which gives them a very strong and disagreeable odour. This greater degree of transpiration renders them more tolerant of heat, and less so of cold than the whites. Perhaps too a difference of structure in the pulmonary apparatus, which a late ingenious experimentalist has discovered to be the principal regulator of animal heat, may have disabled them from extricating, in the act of inspiration, so much of that fluid from the outer air, or obliged them in expiration, to part with more of it. They seem to require less sleep. A black after hard labour through the day, will be induced by the slightest amusements to sit up till midnight, or later, though knowing he must be out with the first dawn of the morning. They are at least as brave, and more adventuresome. But this may perhaps proceed from a want of forethought, which prevents their seeing a danger till it be present.—When present, they do not go through it with more coolness or steadiness than the whites. They are more ardent after their female: but love seems with them to be more an eager desire, than a tender delicate mixture of sentiment and sensation. Their griefs are transient. Those numberless afflictions, which render it doubtful whether heaven has given life to us in mercy or in wrath, are less felt, and sooner forgotten with them. In general, their existence appears to participate more of sensation than reflection. To this must be ascribed their disposition to sleep when abstracted from their diversions, and unemployed in labour. An animal whose body is at rest, and who does not reflect, must be disposed to sleep of course. Comparing them by their faculties of memory, reason, and imagination, it appears to me that in memory they are equal to the whites; in reason much inferior, as I think one could scarcely be found capable of tracing and comprehending the investigations of Euclid; and that in imagination they are dull, tasteless, and anomalous. It would

be unfair to follow them to Africa for this investigation.

We will consider them here, on the same stage with the whites, and where the facts are not apocryphal on which a judgment is to be formed. It will be right to make great allowances for the difference of condition, of education, of conversation, of the sphere in which they move. Many millions of them have been brought to, and born in America. Most of them indeed have been confined to tillage, to their own homes, and their own society: yet many have been so situated, that they might have availed themselves of the conversation of their masters; many have been brought up to the handicraft arts, and from that circumstance have always been associated with the whites. Some have been liberally educated, and all have lived in countries where the arts and sciences are cultivated to a considerable degree, and have had before their eyes samples of the best works from abroad.

The Indians, with no advantages of this kind, will often carve figures on their pipes not destitute of design and merit. They will crayon out an animal, a plant, or a country, so as to prove the existence of a germ in their minds which only wants cultivation. They astonish you with strokes of the most sublime oratory; such as prove their reason and sentiment strong, their imagination glowing and elevated. But never yet could I find that a black had uttered a thought above the level of plain narration; never saw even an elementary trait of painting or sculpture. In music they are more generally gifted than the whites with accurate ears for tune and time, and they have been found capable of imagining a small catch. Whether they will be equal to the composition of a more extensive run of melody, or of complicated harmony, is yet to be proved. Misery is often the parent of the most affecting touches in poetry. Among the blacks is misery enough, God knows, but no poetry. Love is the peculiar oestrum of the poet. Their love is ardent, but it kindles the senses only, not the imagination. Religion indeed has produced a Phillis Wheatley but it could not produce a poet. The compositions published under her name are below the dignity of criticism. The heroes of the Dunciad are to her, as Hercules to the author of that poem. Ignatius Sancho has approached nearer to merit in composition; yet his letters do more honour to the heart than the head. They breathe the purest effusions of friendship and general philanthropy, and show how great a degree of the latter may be compounded with strong religious zeal. He is often happy in the turn of his compliments, and his style is easy and familiar, except when he affects a Shandean fabrication of words. But his imagination is wild and extravagant, escapes incessantly from every restraint of reason and taste, and, in the course of its vagaries, leaves a tract of thought as incoherent and eccentric, as is the course of a meteor through the sky. His subjects should often have led him to a process of sober reasoning: yet we find him always substituting sentiment for demonstration. Upon the whole, though we admit him to the first place among those of his own colour who have presented themselves to the public judgment, yet when we compare him with the writers of the race among whom he lived and particularly with the epistolary class, in which he has taken his own stand, we are compelled to enrol him at the bottom of the column. This criticism supposes the letters published under his name to be genuine, and to have received amendment from no other hand; points which would not be of easy investigation. The improvement of the blacks in body and mind, in the first instance of their mixture with the whites, has been observed by every one, and proves that their inferiority is not the effect merely of their condition of life. We know that among the Romans, about the Augustan age especially, the condition of their slaves was much more deplorable than that of the blacks on the continent of America. The two sexes were confined in separate apartments, because to raise a child cost the master more than to buy one. Cato, for a very restricted indulgence to his slaves in this particular, took from them a certain price. But in this country the slaves multiply as fast as the free inhabitants. Their situation and manners place the commerce between the two sexes almost without restraint. The same Cato, on a principle of economy, always sold his sick and superannuated slaves. He gives it as a standing precept to a master visiting his farm, to sell his old oxen, old wagons, old tools, old and diseased servants, and every thing else become useless. . . . The American slaves cannot enumerate this among the injuries and insults they receive. It was the common practice to expose in the island Esculapius, in the Tyber, diseased slaves, whose cure was like to become tedious. The emperor Claudius, by an edict, gave freedom to such of them as should recover, and first declared that if any person chose to kill rather than expose them, it should be deemed homicide. The exposing them is a crime of which no instance has existed with us; and were it to be followed by death, it would be punished capitally. We are told of a certain Vedius Pollio, who, in the presence of Augustus, would have given a slave as food to his fish, for having broken a glass. With the Romans, the regular method of taking the evidence of their slaves was under torture. Here it has been thought better never to resort to their evidence. When a master was murdered, all his slaves, in the same house, or within hearing, were condemned to death. Here punishment falls on the guilty only, and as precise proof is required against him as against a freeman. Yet notwithstanding these and other discouraging circumstances among the Romans, their slaves were often their rarest artists. They excelled too in science, insomuch as to be usually employed as tutors to their masters' children. Epictetus, Terence, and Phaedrus, were slaves. But they were of the race of whites. It is not their condition then, but nature, which has produced the distinction. Whether further observation will or will not verify the conjecture, that nature has been less bountiful to them in the endowments of the head, I believe that in those of the heart she will be found to have done them justice. That disposition to theft with which they have been branded, must be ascribed to their situation, and not to any depravity of the moral sense. The man, in whose favour no laws of property exist, probably feels himself less bound to respect those made in favour of others. When arguing for ourselves, we lay it down as a fundamental, that laws, to be just, must give a reciprocation of right; that, without this, they are mere arbitrary rules of conduct, founded in force, and not in conscience: and it is a problem which I give to the master to solve, whether the religious precepts against the violation of property were not framed for him as well as his slave? And whether the slave may not as justifiably take a little from one, who has taken all from him, as he may slay one who would slay him? That a change in the relations in which a man is placed should change his ideas of moral right or wrong, is neither new, nor peculiar to the colour of the blacks. Homer tells us it was so 2600 years ago.

Jove fix'd it certain, that whatever day
Makes man a slave, takes half his worth away.

But the slaves of which Homer speaks were whites. Notwithstanding these considerations which must weaken their respect for the laws of property, we find among them numerous instances of the most rigid integrity, and as many as among their better instructed masters, of benevolence, gratitude and unshaken fidelity. The opinion, that they are inferior in the faculties of reason and imagination, must be hazarded with great diffidence. To justify a general conclusion, requires many observations, even where the subject may be submitted to the anatomical knife, to optical classes, to analysis by fire, or by solvents. How much more then where it is a faculty, not a substance, we are examining; where it eludes the research of all the

Senses; where the conditions of its existence are various and variously combined; where the effects of those which are present or absent bid defiance to calculation; let me add too, as a circumstance of great tenderness, where our conclusion would degrade a whole race of men from the rank in the scale of beings which their Creator may perhaps have given them. To our reproach it must be said, that though for a century and a half we have had under our eyes the races of black and of red men, they have never yet been viewed by us as subjects of natural history. I advance it therefore as a suspicion only, that the blacks, whether originally a distinct race, or made distinct by time and circumstances, are inferior to the whites in the endowments both of body and mind. It is not against experience to suppose, that different Species of the same genus, or varieties of the same species, may possess different qualifications. Will not a lover of natural history then, one who views the gradations in all the races of animals with the eye of philosophy, excuse an effort to keep those in the department of man as distinct as nature has formed them?

This unfortunate difference of colour, and perhaps of faculty, is a powerful obstacle to the emancipation of these people. Many of their advocates, while they wish to vindicate the liberty of human nature are anxious also to preserve its dignity and beauty. Some of these, embarrassed by the question *'What further is to be done with them?'* join themselves in opposition with those who are actuated by sordid avarice only. Among the Romans emancipation required but one effort. The slave, when made free, might mix with, without staining the blood of his master. But with us a second is necessary, unknown to history. When freed, he is to be removed beyond the reach of mixture.

The particular customs and manners that may happen to be received in that state? It is difficult to determine on the standard by which the manners of a nation may be tried, whether catholic, or particular. It is more difficult for a native to bring to that standard the manners of his own nation, familiarized to him by habit. There must doubtless be an unhappy influence on the manners of our people produced by the existence of slavery among us. The whole commerce between master and slave is a perpetual exercise of the most boisterous passions, the most unremitting despotism on the one part, and degrading submissions on the other. Our children see this, and learn to imitate it; for man is an imitative animal. This quality is the germ of all education in him. From his cradle to his grave he is learning to do what he sees others do. If a parent could find no motive either in his philanthropy or his self love, for restraining the intemperance of passion towards his slave, it should always be a sufficient one that his child is present. But generally it is not sufficient. The parent storms, the child looks on, catches the lineaments of wrath, puts on the same airs in the circle of smaller slaves, gives a loose to the worst of passions, and thus nursed, educated, and daily exercised in tyranny, cannot but be stamped by it with odious peculiarities. The man must be a prodigy who can retain his manners and morals undepraved by such circumstances. And with what execration should the statesman be loaded, who, permitting one half the citizens thus to trample on the rights of the other, transforms those into despots, and these into enemies, destroys the morals of the one part, and the amor patriae of the other. For if a slave can have a country in this world, it must be any other in preference to that in which he is born to live and labour for another; in which he must lock up the faculties of his nature, contribute as far as depends on his individual endeavours to the evanishment of the human race, or entail his own miserable condition on the endless generations proceeding from him. With the morals of the people, their industry also is destroyed. For in a warm climate, no man will labour for himself who can make another labour for him. This is so true, that of the proprietors of slaves a very small proportion indeed are ever seen to labour. And can the liberties of a nation be thought secure when we have removed their only firm basis, a conviction in the minds of the people that these liberties are of the gift of God? That they are not to be violated but with his wrath? Indeed I tremble for my country when I reflect that God is just: that his justice cannot sleep for ever: that considering numbers, nature and natural means only, a revolution of the wheel of fortune, an exchange of situation is among possible events: that it may become probable by supernatural interference! The almighty has no attribute which can take side with us in such a contest.—But it is impossible to be temperate and to pursue this subject through the various considerations of policy, of morals, of history natural and civil. We must be contented to hope they will force their way into every one's mind. I think a change already perceptible, since the origin of the present revolution. The spirit of the master is abating, that of the slave rising from the dust, his condition mollifying, the way I hope preparing, under the auspices of heaven, for a total emancipation, and that this is disposed, in the order of events, to be with the consent of the masters, rather than by their extirpation.

Thomas Jefferson. 1801. *Notes on the State of Virginia.* Philadelphia: R. T. Rawle.

FEAR THAT ST. DOMINGO MIGHT INFLUENCE AMERICAN SLAVES (1804)

Petition by the Citizens of Pointe Coupée
Post of Pointe Coupée, November 9th, 1804.

His Excellency Wm. C. C. Claibourn, Governor of The Territory of Orleans, etc. We, the inhabitants of Pointe Coupée, have deputed Dr. E. Cooley, Planter of this Place, to lay before your Excellency the precarious Situation of the lives and property of the Inhabitants of this Post. The news of The revolution of St. Domingo and other Places has become common amongst our Blacks—and some here who relate the tragical history of the Revolution of that Island with the General Disposition of the most of our Slaves has become very serious—a Spirit of Révolt and mutyny has crept in amongst them. A few Days since we happyly Discovered a Plan for our Distruction.

Our Nombre [*sic*] and fource [*sic*] being so extrêaly [*sic;* i. e., "extremely"] in favour of the Blacks and almost destitute of any kind of Arms for our defence, we must humbly beg your Excellency Goodness to assist us in this Cloud of Danger—in Sending immediately for our temporary Relief, a Detachment of a Company of Military force and the loan of a hundred Stand of Arms to defend the lives and Property of your new friends and fellows Citizens we subscribe with the higheste Esteem for your Excellency and a sympathetic Regret, for your irretrievable Domestic Calamity. Your most Obt Fellow-citizens and very Huble Servants—

This is followed by one hundred and seven signatures—probably all the landholders in Pointe Coupée.

James Alexander Robertson. 1911. *Louisiana under the Rule of Spain, France, and the United States, 1785–1807.* Vol. 2. Cleveland, OH: Arthur H. Clark Company.

PUNISHMENT OF SLAVES (C. 1810)

About a week afterwards, I was sent by my master to a place a few miles distant, on horseback, with some letters. I took a short cut through a lane, separated by gates from the high road, and bounded by a fence on each side. This lane passed through a part of the farm owned by my master's brother, and his overseer was in the adjoining field, with three negroes, when I went by. On my return, half an hour afterwards, the overseer was sitting on the fence, but I could see nothing of the black fellows. I rode on, utterly unsuspicious of any trouble; but as I approached, he jumped off the fence, and at the same moment two of the negroes sprang up from under the bushes where they had been concealed, and stood with him immediately in front of me, while the third sprang over the fence just behind me. I was thus enclosed between what I could no longer doubt were hostile forces. The overseer seized my horse's bridle and ordered me to alight, in the usual elegant phraseology addressed by such men to slaves. I asked what I was to alight for. "To take the worst flogging you ever had in your life, you black scoundrel. " He added many oaths that I will not repeat. "But what am I to be flogged for, Mr. L.?" I asked. "Not a word," said he, "but 'light at once, and take off your jacket. " I saw there was nothing else to be done, and slipped off the horse on the opposite side from him. "Now take off your shirt," cried he; and as I demurred at this he lifted a stick he had in his hand to strike me, but so suddenly and violently that he frightened the horse, which broke away from him and ran home. I was thus left without means of escape to sustain the attacks of four men as well as I might. In avoiding Mr. L.'s blow, I had accidentally got into a corner of the fence where I could not be approached except in front. The overseer called upon the negroes to seize me; but they, knowing something of my physical power, were slow to obey. At length they did their best, and as they brought themselves within my reach I knocked them down successively; and I gave one of them, who tried to trip up my feet, when he was down, a kick with my heavy shoe, which knocked out several teeth, and sent him howling away.

Meanwhile Bryce Litton beat my head with a stick, not heavy enough to knock me down, but it drew blood freely. He shouted all the while, "Won't you give up! Won't you give up!" adding oath after oath. Exasperated at my defence, he suddenly seized a heavy fence-rail and rushed at me with rage. The ponderous blow fell; I lifted my arm to ward it off, the bone cracked like a pipe-stem, and I fell headlong to the ground. Repeated blows then rained on my back till both shoulder-blades were broken, and the blood gushed copiously from my mouth. In vain the negroes interposed. "Didn't you see the nigger strike me?" Of course they must say "Yes," although the lying coward had avoided close quarters, and fought with his stick alone. At length, his vengeance satisfied, he desisted, telling me "to remember what it was to strike a white man."

Meanwhile an alarm had been raised at the house by the return of the horse without his rider, and my master started off with a small party to learn what the trouble was. When he first saw me he swore with rage. "You've been fighting, you mean nigger!" I told him Bryce Litton had been beating me, because he said I shoved him the other night at the tavern, when they had a fuss. Seeing how much I was injured, he became still more fearfully mad; and after having me carried home, mounted his horse and rode over to Montgomery Court House to enter a complaint. Little good came of it. Litton swore that when he spoke to me in the lane I "sassed" him, jumped off my horse, attacked him, and would have killed him but for the help of his negroes. Of course no negro's testimony was admitted against a white man, and he was acquitted. My master was obliged to pay all the costs of court; and although he had the satisfaction of calling Litton a liar and scoundrel, and giving him a tremendous bruising, still even this partial compensation was rendered less gratifying by what followed, which was a suit for damages and a heavy fine.

My sufferings after this cruel treatment were intense. Besides my broken arm and the wounds on my head, I could feel and hear the pieces of my shoulder-blades grate against each other with every breath. No physician or surgeon was called to dress my wounds, and I never knew one to be called on Riley's estate on any occasion whatever. "A nigger will get well anyway," was a fixed principle of faith, and facts seemed to justify it. The robust, physical health produced by a life of outdoor labour, made our wounds heal with as little inflammation as they do in the case of cattle. I was attended by my master's sister, Miss Patty, as we called her, the Esculapius of the plantation. She was a powerful, big-boned woman, who flinched at no responsibility, from wrenching out teeth to setting bones. I have seen her go into the house and get a rifle to shoot a furious ox that the negroes were in vain trying to butcher. She splintered my arm and bound up my back as well as she knew how. Alas! it was but cobbler's work. From that day to this I have been unable to raise my hands as high as my head. It was five months before I could work at all, and the first time I tried to plough, a hard knock of the coulter against a stone shattered my shoulder-blades again, and gave me even greater agony than at first. And so I have gone through life maimed and mutilated. Practice in time enabled me to perform many of the farm labours with considerable efficiency; but the free, vigorous play of the muscles of my arm was gone for ever.

Josiah Henson. 1876. *"Uncle Tom's Story of His Life" An Autobiography of the Rev. Josiah Henson (Mrs. Harriet Beecher Stowe's "Uncle Tom"), from 1789 to 1876.* John Lobb, ed. London: Christian Age Office.

A KENTUCKY SLAVE CODE (1811)

An act for the more effectual prevention of crimes, conspiracies and insurrections of slaves, free negroes and mulattoes, and for their better government.

Section 1. *Be it enacted by the general assembly of the commonwealth of Kentucky,* That if any negroes or other slaves, shall, at any time hereafter conspire to rebel or make insurrection, every such conspiring shall be adjudged and deemed felony, and the slave or slaves, duly convicted thereof, shall suffer death.

Section 2. *Be it further enacted,* That where any slave or slaves shall hereafter be convicted of administering to any person or persons, any poison or medicine with the evil intent, that death may thereupon ensue, such slave or slaves shall suffer death.

Section 3. *Be it further enacted,* That any slave or slaves, free negro or mulatto, hereafter duly convicted of voluntary manslaughter, shall suffer death.

Section 4. *Be it further enacted,* That any slaver or slaves hereafter duly convicted of an attempt to commit a rape on the body of any white woman, such slave, or slaves, so convicted, shall suffer death.

Section 5. *Be it further enacted,* That it shall be lawful for any trustee of a town to issue his warrant, to cause any slave, free negro, or mulatto, misbehaving within the limits of the town, to be apprehended and brought before him, or some other trustee of said town, who shall have power to punish such slave or slaves, free negro or mulatto, as is now vested by law in a justice of the peace.

Section 6. *Be it further enacted,* That if any negro or other slave, shall, at any time hereafter, consult or advise the murder of any person or persons whatever, every such consulting or advising, shall be punished by any number of stripes, not exceeding one hundred, in the discretion of a jury, to be empanelled by order of any justice or justices of the peace, before whom such slave or slaves may be brought for trial.

Section 7. All laws, sections or parts of laws, coming within the provisions or purview of this act, are hereby repealed; *Provided however,* that nothing in this section contained shall be construed to prevent any justice of the peace from exercising the powers given to trustee.

Kentucky Reporter, February 11, 1811.

PAUL CUFFEE VISITS SIERRA LEONE (1811)

"On the first of the present month of August, 1811, a vessel arrived at Liverpool, with a cargo from Sierra Leone, the owner, master, mate, and whole crew of which are free Negroes. The master, who is also owner, is the son of an American Slave, and is said to be very well skilled both in trade and navigation, as well as to be of a very pious and moral character. It must have been a strange and animating spectacle to see this free and enlightened African entering, as an independent trader, with his black crew, into that port which was so lately the nidus of the Slave Trade."—*Edinb. Review,* August, 1811.

We are happy in having an opportunity of confirming the above account, and at the same time of laying before our readers an authentic memoir of Capt. Paul Cuffee, the master and owner of the vessel above referred to, who sailed from this port on the 20th ult. with a licence from the British Government, to prosecute his intended voyage to Sierra Leone.

The father of Paul Cuffee, was a native of Africa, whence he was brought as a Slave into Massachusetts.—He was there purchased by a person named Slocum, and remained in slavery a considerable portion of his life.—He was named Cuffee, but as it is usual in those parts took the name of Slocum, as expressing to whom he belonged. Like many of his countrymen he possessed a mind superior to his condition, and although he was diligent in the business of his Master and faithful to his interest, yet by great industry and economy he was enabled to purchase his personal liberty.

At this time the remains of several Indian tribes, who originally possessed the right of soil, resided in Massachusetts; Cuffee became acquainted with a woman descended from one of those tribes, named Ruth Moses, and married her.—He continued in habits of industry and frugality, and soon afterwards purchased a farm of 100 acres in Westport in Massachusetts.

Cuffee and Ruth has a family of ten children.—The three eldest sons, David, Jonathan, and John are farmers in the neighborhood of Westport, filling respectable situations in society, and endowed with good intellectual capacities.—They are all married, and have families to whom they are giving good educations. Of six daughters four are respectably married, while two remain single.

Paul was born on the Island of Cutterhunkker, one of the Elizabeth Islands near New Bedford, in the year 1759; when he was about 14 years of age his father died leaving a considerable property in land, but which being at that time unproductive afforded but little provision for his numerous family, and thus the care of supporting his mother and sisters devolved upon his brothers and himself.

At this time Paul conceived that commerce furnished to industry more ample rewards than agriculture, and he was conscious that he possessed qualities which under proper culture would enable him to pursue commercial employments with prospects of success; he therefore entered at the age of 16 as a common hand on board of a vessel destined to the bay of Mexico, on a Whaling voyage. His second voyage was to the West Indies; but on his third he was captured by a British ship during the American war about the year 1776: after three months detention as a prisoner at New York, he was permitted to return home to Westport, where owing to the unfortunate continuance of hostilities he spent about 2 years in his agricultural pursuits. During this interval Paul and his brother John Cuffee were called on by the Collector of the district, in which they resided, for the payment of a personal tax. It appeared to them, that, by the laws of the constitution of Massachusetts, taxation and the whole rights of citizenship were untied.—If the laws demanded of them the payment of personal taxes, the same laws must necessarily and constitutionally invest them with the rights of representing, and being represented, in the state Legislature. But they had never been considered as entitled to the privilege of voting at Elections, nor of being elected to places of trust and honor.—Under these circumstances, they refused payment of the demands.—The Collector resorted to the force of the laws, and after many delays and vexations, Paul and his brother deemed it most prudent to silence the suit by payment of the demands. But they resolved, if it were possible, to obtain the rights which they believed to be connected with taxation.

Liverpool *Mercury*

EFFORTS TO STOP SLAVE SMUGGLING (1817)

Extract of a letter from Captain Charles Morris to the Secretary of the Navy.
U.S. Frigate Congress,
Off the Balize, 10th June, 1817.

"Most of the goods carried to Galveston are introduced into the United States; the more bulky and least valuable, regularly through the custom house; the more valuable, and the slaves, are smuggled in through the numerous inlets to the Westward, where the people are but too much disposed to render them every possible assistance. Several hundred slaves are now at Galveston, and persons have gone from New Orleans to purchase them. Every exertion will be made to intercept them, but I have little hopes of success."

United States' brig Boxer, off the Balize,
June 28th, 1817.

"From cape Catouche to La Vera Cruz, the piratical boats are very numerous, and commit their depredations without respect to flag or nation. Should it meet your approbation, sir, it would afford me infinite pleasure to protect our commerce on that coast.

I shall leave this on Monday, to cruise off the Sabine river: it is reported that attempts will be made to smuggle slaves into Louisiana from Galveston, and the natural presumption is, they will attempt the Sabine or Atchafalya rivers; the depth of the water off those rivers are very inaccurately represented on the charts, and it will not be in my power to approach nearer the shore than within ten miles off the Sabine, and not nearer than thirty off the Atchafalya. Whatever can be done to prevent their being brought clandestinely into the country, will have to be performed by the boats, which, sir, shall be actively employed the moment we arrive on the ground."

Extract of a letter from the Secretary of the Navy, to captain John H. Elton, commanding the U.S. brig Saranac, New York
Navy Department, July 16th 1817.

"The recent occupation of Amelia Island by an officer in the service of the Spanish revolutionists, occasions just apprehensions that from the vicinity to the coast of Georgia, attempts will be made to introduce slaves into the United States, contrary to the existing laws, and further attempts at illicit trade in smuggling goods in violation of our revenue laws, you are hereby directed to detain and search every vessel under whatever flag, which may enter the river St. Mary's, or be found hovering upon the coast under suspicious circumstances, and seize every vessel freighted with slaves, or whose doubtful character and situation shall indicate an intention of smuggling. In the execution of these orders, you will take special care not to interrupt or detain any vessels sailing with regular papers and of a national character, upon lawful voyages to or from a port or ports of the United States. The traffic in slaves is intended to be restrained, and in the performance of this duty, you will exercise your sound judgment in regard to all vessels you may visit."

Bauer, K. Jack, ed. *The New American State Papers—Naval Affairs.* 1981. Vol. 2, *Diplomatic Activities.* Wilmington, DE: Scholarly Resources.

MEMORIAL TO THE CONGRESS FROM THE AMERICAN COLONIZATION SOCIETY (1820)

To the Senate and House of Representatives of the United States:

The President and Board of Managers of the American Colonization Society respectfully represent that, being about to commence the execution of the object to which their views have been long directed, they deem it proper and necessary to address themselves to the legislative council of their country. They trust that this object will be considered, in itself, of great national importance, will be found inseparably connected with another, vitally affecting the honor and interest of this nation, and leading, in its consequences, to the most desirable results.

Believing that examination and reflection will show that such are its connexions and tendency, they are, encouraged to present themselves, and their cause, where they know that a public measure, having these advantages, cannot fail to receive all the countenance and aid it may require.

The last census shows the number of free people of color of the United States, and their rapid increase. Supposing them to increase in the same ratio, it will appear how large a proportion of our population will, in the course of even a few years, consist of persons of that description.

No argument is necessary to show that this is very far indeed from constituting an increase of our physical strength; nor can there be a population, in any country, neutral as to its effects upon society. The least observation shows that this description of persons are not, and cannot be, either useful or happy among us; and many considerations, which need not be mentioned, prove, beyond dispute, that it is best, for all the parties interested, that there should be a separation; that those who are now free may become so those who hereafter, should be provided with the means of attaining to a state of respectability and happiness, which, it is certain, they have never yet reached, and, therefore, can never be likely to reach, in this country.

The two last reports of the Society, to which your memorialists beg leave to refer, show the success of their mission to Africa, and the result of their inquiries upon that continent. From those it is manifest that a situation can be readily obtained, favorable to commerce and agriculture, in a healthy and fertile country, and that the natives are well disposed to give every encouragement to the establishment of such a settlement among them. Thus, it appears, that an object of great national concern, already expressly desired by some of the States, and truly desirable to all, receiving, also, the approbation of those upon whom it is more immediately to operate, is brought within our reach.

But this subject derives, perhaps, its chief interest from its connexion with a measure which has, already, to the honor of our country, occupied the deliberations of the Congress of the United States.

Your memorialists refer, with pleasure, to the act, passed at the last session of Congress, supplementary to the act formerly passed for the suppression of the slave trade. The means afforded, by the provisions of that act, for the accomplishment of its object are certainly great; but the total extirpation of this disgraceful trade cannot, perhaps, be expected from any measures which rely alone upon the employment of a maritime force, however considerable.

The profits attending it are so extraordinary, that the cupidity of the unprincipled will still be tempted to continue it, as long as there is any chance of escaping the vigilance of the cruisers engaged against them. From the best information your memorialists have been able to obtain, of the nature, causes, and course of this trade, and of the present situation of the coast of Africa, and the habits and dispositions of the natives, they are well assured that the suppression of the African slave trade, and the civilization of the natives, are measures of indispensable connexion. . . .

Since the establishment of the English settlement at Sierra Leone, the slave trade has been rapidly ceasing upon that part of the coast.

Not only the kingdoms in its immediate neighborhood, but those upon the Sherbro and Bagroo rivers, and others with whom the people of that settlement have opened a communication, have been prevailed upon to abandon it, and are turning their attention to the ordinary and innocent pursuits of civilized nations.

That the same consequences will result from similar settlements cannot be doubted. When the natives there see that the European commodities, for which they have been accustomed to exchange their fellow-beings, until vast and fertile regions have become almost depopulated, can be more easily and safely obtained by other pursuits, can it be believed that they will hesitate to profit by the experience? Nor will the advantages of civilization be alone exhibited. That religion, whose mandate is "peace on earth and good will

towards men," will "do its errand"; will deliver them from the bondage of their miserable superstitions, and display the same triumphs which it is achieving in every land.

No nation has it so much in its power to furnish proper settlers for such establishments as this; no nation has so deep an interest in thus disposing of them. By the law passed at the last session, and before referred to, the captives who may be taken by our cruisers, from the slave ships are to be taken to Africa, and delivered to the custody of agents appointed by the President. There will then be a settlement of captured negroes upon the coast, in consequence of the measures already adopted. And it is evidently most important, if not necessary, to such a settlement, that the Civilized people of color of this country, whose industry, enterprise, and knowledge of agriculture and the arts, would render them most useful assistants, should be connected with such an establishment.

When, therefore, the object of the Colonization Society is viewed in connection with that entire suppression of the slave trade which your memorialists trust it is resolved shall be effected, its importance becomes obvious in the extreme.

The beneficial consequences resulting from success in such a measure, it is impossible to calculate. To the general cause of humanity it will afford the most rich and noble contribution, and for the nation that regards that cause, that employs its power in its behalf, it cannot fail to procure a proportionate reward. It is by such a course that a nation insures to itself the protection and favor of the Governor of the World. Nor are there wanting views and considerations, arising from our peculiar political institutions, which would justify the sure expectation of the most signal blessings to ourselves from the accomplishment of such an object. If one of these consequences shall be the gradual and almost imperceptible removal of a national evil, which all unite in lamenting, and for which, with the most intense, but, hitherto, hopeless anxiety, the patriots and statesmen of our country have labored to discover a remedy, who can doubt, that, of all the blessings we may be permitted to bequeath to our descendants, this will receive the richest tribute of their thanks and veneration?

Your memorialists cannot believe that such an evil, universally acknowledged and deprecated, has been irremovably fixed upon us. Some way will always be opened by Providence by which a people desirous of acting justly and benevolently may be led to the attainment of a meritorious object. And they believe that, of all the plans that the most sagacious and discerning of our patriots have suggested, for effecting what they have so greatly desired the colonization of Africa, in the manner proposed, present the fairest prospects of success. But if it be admitted to be ever so doubtful, whether this happy result shall be the reward of our exertions, yet, if: great and certain benefits immediately attend them, why may not others, still greater, follow them?

In a work evidently progressive, who shall assign limits to the good that zeal and perseverance shall be permitted to accomplish? Your memorialists beg leave to state that, having expended considerable funds in prosecuting their inquiries and making preparations, they are now about to send out a colony, and complete the purchase, already stipulated for with the native kings and chiefs of Sherbro, of a suitable territory for their establishment. The number they are now enabled to transport and provide for, is but a small proportion of the people of color who have expressed their desire to go; and without a larger and more sudden increase of their funds than can be expected from the voluntary contributions of individuals, their progress must be slow and uncertain. They have always flattered themselves with the hope that when it was seen they had surmounted the difficulties of preparation, and shown that means applied to the execution of their design would lead directly and evidently to its accomplishment, they would be able to obtain for it the national countenance and assistance. To this point they have arrived; and they, therefore, respectfully request that this interesting subject may receive the consideration of your honorable body, and that the Executive Department may be authorized, in such way as may meet your approbation, to extend to this object such pecuniary and other aid as it may be thought to require and deserve.

Your memorialists further request, that the subscribers to the American Colonization Society may be incorporated, by act of Congress, to enable them to act with more efficiency in carrying on the great and important objects of the Society, and to enable them, with more economy, to manage the benevolent contributions intrusted to their care.

Signed by John Mason, W. Jones, E. B. Caldwell, and F. S. Key, committee.

Washington

February, 1, 1820

Blaustein, Albert P. and Robert L. Zangrando. 1968. *Civil Rights and the Black American: A Documentary History.* New York: Simon & Schuster.

PROSPECTUS OF *THE EMANCIPATOR* (1820)

Address of the Editor.

The EMANCIPATOR will be published monthly in *Jonesborough,* Ten. By *ELIHU EMBREE,* on a fine superroyal sheet of paper, in octava form, at *One Dollar* per annum, payable on receipt of the first number.

This paper is especially designed by the editor to advocate the abolition of slavery, and to be a repository of tracts on that interesting and important subject. It will contain all the necessary information that the editor can obtain of the progress of the abolition of slavery of the descendants of Africa, together with a concise history of their introduction into slavery, collected from the best authorities.

The constitutions and proceedings of the several benevolent societies in the United States and elsewhere who have had this grand object in view will be carefully selected and published in the *Emancipator.*

A correspondence between those societies, and between individuals in different parts of the nation on the subject, of emancipation, will be kept up through the medium of this paper by inserting in its pages all interesting communications, letters &c. that may come to the knowledge of the editor.

The speeches of those who have been and are eminently advocating this glorious cause, either in the Congress of the United States, the state legislatures, or in the parliaments and courts of the nations, will be strictly attended to.

Biographical sketches of the lives of those who have been eminent in this cause will also occasionally find a place in this work.

A portion of this paper is intended to be devoted to a history of the abolition of the African Slave Trade, in every part of the world, from its first dawn, down to the present times.

In the prosecution of this work the editor professes that he expects (like other periodical editors) to live much upon the borrow; and to make use of such materials as he may find in his way, suited to his object, without being very particular to take up much time or room in acknowledging a loan, unless he may think it necessary, willing that others should use the same freedom with him, & hoping that by offering such a fair exchange, such borrowing will be thought no robbery.

Communications on the subject, and materials for the work are solicited and will be thankfully received both from societies and individuals friendly to the abolition of slavery. Such communications, if approved of by the editor, will find a harty welcome in the *Emancipator.*

The Manumission Society of Tennessee in particular, it is expected, will afford many tracts on the subject of slavery, which the editor assures them he will feel inclined to respect; and where his judgment should not otherwise dictate, will give them an early and gratuitous insertion. They will find the *Emancipator* a true chronicle of the proceedings of that benevolent society, as far as the editor is enabled–And for this purpose the clerks of the conventions, and of each branch of the society are requested to forward from time to time true copies of all their minutes, which may not be really improper to publish (and it is hoped there will be none such) together with the names of their members, their places of residence, &c. All which particulars we are of opinion will not be unprofitable to the cause of abolition to be published.

Letters from one individual to another, with the names of both, we think will be often beneficial to be published. If they do nothing more they will shew that all are not asleep nor dumb to the cries of suffering humanity.

Those who have had, or may have law suits on hand for the freedom of such as are unlawfully held in bondage, are desired to forward the true history of the facts, their progress, final decision, &c. with the places of residence and the names of plaintiffs and defendants, with every interesting particular, and they shall find in the *Emancipator* a true repository.

Although the editor is as far from being a man of leisure as any in his acquaintance, and not the owner of the office where the paper will be printed, and therefore shall have to hire the printing of it; and although he has spent several thousand dollars already in some small degree abolishing and in endeavoring to facilitate the general abolition of slavery, yet he feels not satisfied without continuing to throw in his mite, hoping that if the weight of it should not at present be felt that when the scale comes nearly to a preponderancy, it will be more sensibly perceived and in some small degree hasten an even balance of equal rights to the now neglected sons of Africa.

And as it will be at considerable trouble and expense that the work will be published, agreeably to the editor's intention, it is hoped that none who have any love for African liberty will think hard of paying $1 annually to the support of the only paper of this kind in the United States. And as the sum is too small and the income by no means expected to be sufficient to warrant the editor in travailing over the country to procure subscribers he takes the liberty of sending the *Emancipator* to a good many whose names and places of residence he has become acquainted with, without their having subscribed. And he requests, and from the nature of the work, he will expect that those to whom they are sent, will, on receiving the first number, and having time to peruse it, remit to the editor, by mail or otherwise, *One Dollar* in some good current bank paper; or if they do not wish it continued, will carefully wrap it in a separate paper to preserve it from being injured, and direct it to the editor at Embree's Ironworks.

All communications by mail to the editor must be directed as follows—*Elihu Embree, post-master, Embree's Ironworks, Sullivan County, Tennessee*—By this mean the postage will be free, both to and from the editor; the government bearing the expense, as it righteously ought, of distributing these communications through the country, for the purpose of preparing the public mind for a practical reform from imposing unconditional slavery on a portion of its subjects.—

It is intended that each number bear date the last day of each month.

Those who procure 12 subscribers and pay for them shall be entitled to one gratis.

The Emancipator, April 30, 1820: 1.

FUGITIVES FOLLOW THE NORTH STAR TO ESCAPE (C. 1820)

At sixteen she went to live with her young mistress, who was married to a planter in that fertile country known as the "Eastern Shore." At eighteen Margaret was a large woman, tall and well formed, her complexion black as jet, her countenance always pleasant, though she seldom laughed. She talked but little, even to those of her own race. At twenty years of age she became the wife of a worthy young man to whom she had given her best affections. Not long after, her young master became very angry with her for what he called stubbornness and resistance to his will, and threatened to chastise her by whipping—a degradation that she had always felt that she could not submit to, and yet to obey her master in the thing he demanded would be still worse. She therefore told him that she would not be whipped, she would rather die, and gave him warning that any attempt to execute his threat would surely result in the death of one of them. He knew her too well to risk the experiment, and decided to punish her in another way. He sold her husband, and she saw him bound in chains and driven off with a large drove of men and women for the New Orleans market. He then put her in the hands of a brutal overseer, with directions to work her to the extent of her ability on a tobacco plantation, which command was enforced up to the day of the birth of her child. At the end of one week she was driven again to the field and compelled to perform a full task, having at no time any abatement of her work on account of her situation, with exception of one week. It was the custom on the plantation to establish nurseries, presided over by old, broken down slaves, where mothers might leave their infants, but this privilege was denied to Margaret. She was obliged to leave her child under the shade of a bush in the field, returning to it but twice during the long day. On returning to the child one evening she found it apparently senseless, exhausted with crying, and a large serpent lying across it. Although she felt that it would be better for both herself and child if it were dead, yet a mother's heart impelled her to make an effort to save it, and by caressing him and careful handling she resuscitated it.

As soon as she heard its feeble, wailing cry, she made a vow to deliver her boy from the cruel power of slavery or die in the attempt, and falling prostrate, she prayed for strength to perform her vow, and for grace and patience to sustain her in her suffering, toil, and hunger; then pressing her child to her bosom, she fled with all the speed of which she was capable toward the North Star. Having gone a mile or two, she heard something pursuing her; on looking round she saw Watch, the old house dog. Watch was a large mastiff, somewhat old, and with him Margaret had ever been a favorite, and since she had been driven to the field, Watch often visited her at her cabin in the evening. She feared it would not be safe to allow Watch to go with her, but she could not induce him to go back, so she resumed her flight, accompanied by her faithful escort. At break of day she hid herself on the border of a plantation and soon fell asleep.

Toward evening she was aroused by the noise made by the slaves returning to their quarters, and seeing an old woman lingering behind all the others, she called her, told her troubles, and asked for food. The old woman returned about midnight with a pretty good supply of food, which Margaret divided with Watch, and then started on, taking the north star for her guide. The second day after she left, the Overseer employed a hunter with his dogs to find her. He started with an old slut and three whelps, thinking, no doubt, that as the game was only a woman and her infant child, it would be a good time to train his pups.

Margaret had been missed at roll call the morning after her flight, but the Overseer supposed she was hiding near the place for a day or two, and that hunger would soon drive her up; therefore, when the hunter started, he led the old dog, expecting to find her in an

hour or two, but not overtaking her the first day, on the next morning, he let his hounds loose, intending to follow on horseback, guided by their voices. About noon, the old dog struck the track at the place where Margaret had made her little camp the day before, and she bounded off with fresh vigor, leaving the man and the younger dogs beyond sight and hearing. The young dogs soon lost the track where Margaret forded the streams, and the old dog was miles away, leaving the hunter without a guide to direct him.

Margaret had been lying in the woods on the bank of a river, intending to start again as soon as it was dark, when she was startled by the whining and nervous motions of old Watch, and listening, she heard the hoarse ringing bay of a blood-hound. Although she had expected that she would be hunted with dogs, and recalled over and over again the shocking accounts related by Overseers to the slaves, of fugitives overtaken and torn in pieces by the Spanish blood-hounds, she had not, until now, realized the horrors of her situation. She expected to have to witness the destruction of her child by the savage brute, and then be torn in pieces herself. Meanwhile, old Watch lay with his nose between his feet, facing the coming foe. The hound, rendered more fierce by the freshness of the track, came rushing headlong with nose to the ground, scenting her prey, and seemed not to see old Watch, until, leaping to pass over him, she found her windpipe suddenly collapsed in the massive jaws of the old mastiff. The struggle was not very noisy, for Watch would not even growl, and the hound could not, for it was terribly energetic. The hound made rapid and persuasive gestures with her paws and tail, but it was of no use, the jaws of old Watch relaxed not until all signs of life in his enemy had ceased. Margaret came back from the river, and would have embraced her faithful friend, but fearing that a stronger pack was following, she hastily threw the dead hound into the river and pursued her journey.

Within a few hours after her providential escape by the aid of her faithful friend, old Watch, from the fangs of the slave hunter's hound, she fell into the hands of friends, who kept her secreted until she could be sent into a free State; while there, she learned about the pursuit by the hunter, and that he never knew what became of his best hound. After the chase was abandoned, she, through a regular line, similar to our Underground Railroad, was sent to Philadelphia and then to New York, where she became a celebrated nurse, and always befriended the poor of all colors and all nationalities.

Pettit, Eber M. 1879. *Sketches in the History of the Underground Railroad, Comprising Many Thrilling Incidents of the Escape of Fugitives from Slavery, and the Perils of Those Who Aided Them.* Fredonia, NY: W. McKinstry & Son.

CHARLES BALL DESCRIBES THE PROVISIONS GRANTED SLAVES (C. 1820)

At the time of which I now speak, the rice was ripe, and ready to be gathered. On Monday morning, after our feast, the overseer took the whole of us to the rice field, to enter upon the harvest of this crop. The field lay in a piece of low ground, near the river, and in such a position that it could be flooded by the water of the stream, in wet seasons. The rice is planted in drills, or rows, and grows more like oats than any of the other grain, known in the north.

The water is sometimes let in to the rice fields, and drawn off again, several times, according to the state of the weather. Watering and weeding the rice is considered one of the most unhealthy occupations on a southern plantation, as the people are obliged to live for several weeks in the mud and water, subject to all the unwholesome vapours that arise from stagnant pools, under the rays of a summer sun, as well as the chilly autumnal dews of night. At the time we came to cut this rice, the field was quite dry; and after we had reaped and bound it, we hauled it upon wagons, to a piece of hard ground where we made a threshing floor, and threshed it. In some places, they tread out the rice, with mules or horses, as they tread wheat in Maryland; but this renders the grain dusty, and is injurious to its sale.

After getting in the rice, we were occupied for some time in clearing and ditching swampy land, preparatory to a more extended culture of rice, the next year; and about the first of August, twenty or thirty of the people, principally women and children, were employed for two weeks in making cider, of apples which grew in an orchard of nearly two hundred trees, that stood on a part of the estate. After the cider was made, a barrel of it was one day brought to the field, and distributed amongst us; but this gratuity was not repeated. The cider that was made by the people, was converted into brandy, at a still in the corner of the orchard.

I often obtained cider to drink, at the still, which was sheltered from the weather by a shed, of boards and slabs. We were not permitted to go into the orchard at pleasure; but as long as the apples continued, we were allowed the privilege of sending five or six persons every evening, for the purpose of bringing apples to the quarter, for our common use; and by taking large baskets, and filling them well, we generally contrived to get as many as we could consume.

When the peaches ripened, they were guarded with more rigour—peach brandy being an article which is nowhere more highly prized than in South Carolina. There were on the plantation, more than a thousand peach trees, growing on poor sandy fields which were no longer worth the expense of cultivation. The best peaches grow upon the poorest sandhills.

We were allowed to take three bushels of peaches every day, for the use of the quarter; but we could, and did eat, at least three times that quantity, for we stole at night that which was not given us by day. I confess, that I took part in these thefts, and I do not feel that I committed any wrong, against either God or man, by my participation in the common danger that we ran, for we well knew the consequences that would have followed detection.

After the feast at laying by the corn and cotton, we had no meat for several weeks; and it is my opinion that our master lost money, by the economy he practised at this season of the year.

In the month of August, we had to save the fodder. This fodder-saving is the most toilsome, and next to working in the rice swamps, the most unhealthy job, that has to be performed on a cotton plantation, in the whole year. The manner of doing it is to cut the tops from the corn, as is done in Pennsylvania; but in addition to this, the blades below the ear, are always pulled off by the hand. Great pains is taken with these corn-blades. They constitute the chosen food of race, and all other horses, that are intended to be kept with extraordinary care, and in superior condition. For the purpose of procuring the best blades, they are frequently stripped from the stock, sometimes before the corn is ripe enough in the ear, to permit the top of the stalk to be cut off, without prejudice to the grain. After the blades are stripped from the stem, they are stuck between the hills of corn until they are cured, ready for the stack. They are then cut, and bound in sheaves, with small bands of the blades themselves. This binding, and the subsequent hauling from the field, must be done either early in the morning, before the dew is dried up, or in the night, whilst the dew is falling.

This work exposes the people who do it, to the fogs and damps of the climate, at the most unhealthy season of the year. Agues, fevers, and all the diseases which follow in their train, have their dates at the time of fodder-saving. It is the only work, appertaining to a cotton estate, which must of necessity be done in the night, or in the fogs of the morning; and the people at this season of the year, and whilst engaged in this very fatiguing work, would certainly be better able to go through with it, if they were regularly supplied, with proper portions of sound and wholesome salted provisions.

If every master would, through the months of August and September, supply his people with only a quarter of a pound of good bacon flitch to each person, daily, I have no doubt but that he would save money by it; to say nothing of the great comfort it would yield to the slaves, at this period, when the human frame is so subject to debility and feebleness.

Early in August, disease made its appearance amongst us. Several were attacked by the ague, with its accompanying fever; but in South Carolina the "ague," as it is called, is scarcely regarded as a disease, and if a slave, has no ailment that is deemed more dangerous, he is never withdrawn from the roll of the field hands. I have seen many of our poor people compelled to pick cotton, when their frames were shaken so violently, by the ague, that they were unable to get hold of the cotton in the burs, without difficulty. In this, masters commit a great error. Many fine slaves are lost, by this disease, which superinduces the dropsy, and sometimes the, consumption, which could have been prevented by arresting the ague at its onset. When any of our people were taken so ill that they were not able to go to the field, they were removed to the great house, and placed in the "sick room," as it was termed. This sick room was a large, airy apartment, in the second story of a building, which stood in the garden.

The lower part of this building was divided into two apartments, in one of which was kept the milk, butter, and other things connected with the dairy. In the other, the salt provisions of the family, including fish, bacon, and other articles, were secured. This apartment also constituted the smoke house; but as the ceiling was lathed, and plastered with a thick coat of lime and sand, no smoke could penetrate the "sick room," which was at all seasons of the year, a very comfortable place to sleep in. Though I was never sick myself, whilst on this plantation, I was several times in this "sick room," and always observed, when there, that the sick slaves were well attended to. There a hanging partition, which could be let down at pleasure, and which was let down when it was necessary, to divide the rooms into two apartments, which always happened when there were several slaves of different sexes, sick at the same time. The beds, upon which the sick lay, were of straw, but clean and wholesome, and the patients when once in this room, were provided with every thing necessary for persons in their situation. A physician attended them daily, and proper food, and even wines, were not wanting.

The contrast between the cotton and rice fields, and

this little hospital, was very great; and it appeared to me at the time, that if a part of the tenderness and benevolence, displayed here, had been bestowed upon the people whilst in good health, very many of the inmates of this infirmary, would never have been here.

Ball, Charles. 1836. *Slavery in the United States. A Narrative of the Life and Adventures of Charles Ball, a Black Man, Who Lived Forty Years in Maryland, South Carolina and Georgia, as a Slave Under Various Masters, and Was One Year in the Navy with Commodore Barney, During the Late War.* Lewistown, PA: J. W. Shugert.

DESCRIPTION OF DENMARK VESEY (1822)

As Denmark Vesey has occupied so large a place in the conspiracy, a brief notice of him will, perhaps, be not devoid of interest. The following anecdote will show how near he was to the chance of being distinguished in the bloody events of San Domingo. During the revolutionary war, Captain Vesey, now an old resident of this city, commanded a ship that traded between St. Thomas and Cape Francais (San Domingo). He was engaged in supplying the French of that Island with Slaves. In the year 1781, he took on board at St. Thomas 390 slaves and sailed for the Cape; on the passage, he and his officers were struck with the beauty, alertness and intelligence of a boy about 14 years of age, whom they made a pet of, by taking him into the cabin, changing his apparel, and calling him by way of distinction Telemaque, (which appellation has since, by gradual corruption, among the negroes, been changed to Denmark, or sometimes Tebaak.) On the arrival, however, of the ship at the Cape, Captain Vesey, having no use for the boy, sold him among his other slaves, and returned to St. Thomas. On his next voyage to the Cape, he was surprised to learn from his consignee that Telemaque would be returned on his hands, as the planter, who had purchased him, represented him unsound, and subject to epileptic fits. According to the custom of trade in that place, the boy was placed in the hands of the king's physician, who decided that he was unsound, and Captain Vesey was compelled to take him back, of which he had no occasion to repent, as Denmark proved, for 20 years, a most faithful slave. In 1800, Denmark drew a prize of $1500 in the East-Bay-Street Lottery, with which he purchased his freedom from his master, at six hundred dollars, much less than his real value. From that period to day of his apprehension he has been working as a carpenter in this city, distinguished for great strength and activity. Among his colour he was always looked up to with awe and respect. His temper was impetuous and domineering in the extreme, qualifying him for the despotic rule, of which he was ambitious. All his passions were ungovernable and, savage; and to his numerous wives and children, he displayed the haughty and capricious cruelty of Eastern Bashaw. He had nearly effected his escape, after information had been lodged against him. For three days the town was searched for him without success. As early as Monday, the 17th, he had concealed himself. It was not until the night of the 22d of June, during a perfect tempest, that he was found secreted in the house of one of his wives. It is to the uncommon efforts and vigilance of Mr. Wesner, and Capt. Dove, of the City Guard, (the latter of whom seized him) that public justice received its necessary tribute, in the execution of this man. If the party had been one moment later, he would, in all probability, have effected his escape the next day in some outward bound vessel.

Coffin, Joshua. 1860. *An Account of Some of the Principal Slave Insurrections, and Others, Which Have Occurred, or Been Attempted, in the United States and Elsewhere, During the Last Two Centuries, with Various Remarks.* New York: American Anti-Slavery Society.

CONSTITUTION OF THE MANUMISSION SOCIETY OF NORTH CAROLINA (1824)

The delegates appointed to revise and amend the constitution of the society of North Carolina for the gradual abolition of slavery are of opinion, that at this eventful era, when the attention of Europe and America is excited by the suffering of the African race, it is incumbent on us to consider whether we are acting up to the principles we profess. We take the liberty briefly to observe, that we adhere to the declaration of 1776, viz. "that all men are endowed by the great Creator with certain unalienable rights; that among these are life, liberty, and the pursuit of happiness." We think that declaration holds good, without respect to color, and that it is the duty of nations and states, as well as individuals, and more especially those who profess to be actuated by the republican principle, to suppress involuntary slavery among them, and endeavor to remove this dishonor of the christian character from a free people. In accordance with these principles, we have adopted the following articles as a constitution.

Article 1. This society shall be known by the title of "The Manumission Society of North Carolina," for promoting the gradual abolition of slavery, and for meliorating the condition of the African race among us.

Article 2. This society shall convene once in each year, or oftener if necessary, which meeting shall be denominated the "General Association."

Article 3. This society shall consist of such branch meetings as shall adopt this constitution, and be represented in the general association.

Article 4. The general association shall elect a president, secretary and treasurer, by ballot, for the term of two years. Twelve members shall constitute a quorum; but a smaller number may adjourn from time to time, until a quorum shall be formed.

Article 5. It shall be the duty of the association when met, to transact the business of the society, and endeavour to promote the objects of this institution. The money for the use of the society is to be raised by free donation of the branches, and by voluntary contribution of individuals who may wish to promote the views of this society.

Article 6. Each branch meeting who may adopt this constitution, shall be entitled to two representatives in the general association, but may send one delegate for every ten members. Each branch may choose their own officers, and make their own by-laws, consistent with the stipulations of this constitution. Each branch meeting shall convene once in six months, or oftener if they think proper.

Article 7. The reception of members shall take place at the respective branch meetings; each branch shall keep a record of their members, and report the number annually to the association.

Article 8. The general association may choose a board of managers, if they think proper, to transact the business of the society in the recess of its sittings. With regard to the emigration of free colored persons who may be disposed to remove, the society reserve to themselves the privilege to act as circumstances may justify, to promote emigration to any place which in their judgement may be most likely to produce the desired effect.

Article 9. It shall be the duty of the president to preside at each meeting of the association, keep order and decorum, and give such information to the meeting as he may be in possession of, relative to the affairs of the society, and recommend such measures as in his opinion may have a tendency to promote the views of this institution; shall have power to adjourn as occasion may require, and may call a special meeting of the association at the request of two, or more, of the branches. In case of absence of the president, the meeting shall appoint one pro tempore.

Article 10. It shall be the duty of the secretary to keep fair records of the proceeding of each association, so as to form a regular journal of the transactions of the society. In case of absence of the secretary, the meeting shall appoint a secretary pro tempore.

Article 11. It shall be the duty of the treasurer to receive the money collected for the use of the society; he shall make regular entries of all money received or paid out, but shall not pay out any money without an order from the president, or the chairman of the board of managers; he shall exhibit a true statement of the funds at each annual meeting.

Article 12. In case any member shall violate the principles of this institution, he may be disowned by the branch meeting unto which he belongs, subject to an appeal to the general association.

Article 13. The general association shall have power to alter or amend this constitution whenever two thirds of the branches concur therein.

> Ratified in general association,
> held at Deep river meeting-house,
> in Guilford county, the 19th of
> October, 1824.
>
> RICHARD MENDENHALL, *Pres't.*
> AARON COFFIN, *Sec,ry.*

Genius of Universal Emancipation and Baltimore Courier, October 8, 1825.

QUAKER ATTITUDES TOWARD SLAVERY (1824)

Observations and Remarks on Slavery, 1824.

I had at Fredericksburg a very large meeting in the Presbyterian meeting house. The prospect of having a meeting at that place, where I have repeatedly seen the poor slaves treated with great cruelty, felt awful to me. But the dear Master helped his poor servant to do the work required. I was enlarged in setting forth the love of Him who has loved us whilst sinners, and has commanded us to love one another as he has loved us. His love is to all men, he has died for all, and we must love all, and do to others as we would they should do to us. Were this the case, could men oppress one another?

could they wage war against one another? could they hold their fellow men, of any colour or nation, in a state of bondage? The Lord's power came over the meeting in such a manner as to bring conviction to the minds of the people, and seriousness prevailed over all. But, alas! it may prove to many on only the passing of the morning cloud.

On the way to Richmond, stopping on the road to feed our horses, we saw a large concourse of slaves in an orchard. They were holding a meeting, previous to the burial of an aged fellow negro. Such a meeting was allowed them on the occasion, and a magistrate was with them to see that order was maintained. There was no need however of his interference, for they were very quiet and serious. One of the number was preaching to them. He was earnest and fluent in his communication, and the matter was good and appropriate. It was pleasant to me to stand a while among them, listening to what was said. I doubt not that many of them were offering unto the Lord acceptable worship.

I had two meetings at Richmond; one was largely attended by the inhabitants. I had several times, before now, apprehended that there are in this place, among much of what is evil, some well-disposed, pious persons; to these the Lord gave me to minister, for their encouragement in the ways of righteousness and holiness.

The Quarterly Meeting at Wain Oak was a time of suffering to me; things are very low among them, and there is a great departure, among the young people, from the purity and Christian simplicity of our religious profession. Many of these have been sorely wounded by associations with slaveholders . . .

I had meeting throughout that part of Virginia, as far as Suffolk. These meetings were numerously attend[ed] by slave-holders. I cannot describe the weight of distress brought on my mind on these occasions; for the yoke of slavery has become heavy here; their treatment, and the oppressive laws against the free people of colour, are not less so. It is very evident that their Colonizaiton Society, under fair, specious appearances, has for its object to drive the free negroes away from the country, so that slaves, by not seeing any of their colour in the enjoyment of liberty, may the better submit to their state of bondage. They have so increased the penalties on the free blacks, that if any one of these is charged with having stolen to the value of *one dollar and fifty cents,* he is to be sold as a slave, and transported out of the country. Those that have been set free of late, must leave the state within one year, or else they are liable to be sold again as slaves. Free people of colour are liable to be taken up as suspected slaves, and confined in prison till they can give proof that they are free; but, being shut up, they have not an opportunity to obtain this proof; or, should they obtain it, if they cannot pay the expenses incurred by their imprisonment, they are also sold as slaves. Will not the Lord plead with his people for these things? Will He not arise for the cry of the poor and oppressed descendants of Africa? I feel deeply for them, and not less awfully for their oppressors. . . .

I passed thence into the lower parts of North Carolina, attended their Quarterly Meeting for those counties, held this time as Sutton's Creek, which was very satisfactory. The public meetings were baptizing seasons. Great crowds attend them, and the Lord was pleased to extend his gracious invitation to return to him with full purpose of heart. Through those counties I had several large meetings. Some entirely among the slave-holders. Others, chiefly among the slaves; for, although it was given me to proclaim the Truth, without disguise, to the masters, their hearts appeared to be open towards me, and they made way very readily for the meetings I appointed for their slaves. Some of the masters attended, but generally they said, that they were persuaded that I would not say anything in their absence, that I would not say in their presence. The Lord was very preciously near in several of these religious opportunities. . . .

25th [7th month, 1824]. I had two meetings; one in the forenoon with Friends, the other in the Methodists large house at Lynchburg, attended by the people of the various religious denominations in the place. The Lord was near and good; he strengthened me to proclaim his Gospel, which is designed to be glad tidings of great joy to all people; a joy that all may become partakers of, if, by their own fault, they do not frustrate the purpose of the Redeemer's love towards them. In his love and free mercy he has come to deliver us from the bondage of sin, and has commanded us to love one another as he has loved us. Can we say that we love him if we observe not his commandments? Can we say that we love our fellow men, if we act toward them contrary to what we would they should do towards us? Should we think, that those who are now held under the galling yoke of bondage, acted justly towards us, were they to rivet the same heavy chains upon us that they are now laden with? It will not avail us to say that slaves are of another colour than ourselves; they, equally with us, are the children of the same Almighty Father. He has made all the nations of the earth one blood; Christ Jesus has died for all men, and he commands us to love all men. I entreated with them, to live in the Divine fear, to do justly, to love mercy, and to walk humbly with God. Much serious-

ness was over the assembly, and none made any opposition, though I fully set before them the unrighteousness of slavery, and the guilt of slave-holders.

Grellet, Stephen. 1877. *Memoirs of the Life and Gospel Labors of Stephen Grellet.* Benjamin Seebohm, ed. Philadelphia: H. Longstreth.

FEARS ABOUT PENDING EMANCIPATION OF SLAVES IN TEXAS (1826)

Emancipation of Slaves in Texas.

We learn by a gentleman of this place, who arrived a few days since from Miller County that a citizen of that county had returned before he started from the province of Texas, bringing information that great excitement prevailed throughout the several colonies in that country, when he left there, in consequence of the recent passage of a law by the *Mexican Government,* for the *Emancipation of all the Slaves in the* Province of Texas, and that orders had been received for carrying it into immediate effect. As may be well supposed, this information produced the greatest consternation among the slave holders, all of whom had emigrated to that country under an assurance, as we are informed, from the local authorities of Texas, that they could hold their slaves, though we are under the impression that slavery is prohibited throughout the Republic, by the Constitution of Mexico.

The large slave holders were hurrying off their slaves in great numbers, into Louisiana and Arkansas, and we have heard of several persons who emigrated from this Territory, who have recently crossed the line into Louisiana, with their slaves. Those persons, who have but few slaves have held meetings, at which it was resolved, that they would stand by each other in resisting the execution of the law until they can gather this year's crop, after which they have determined to leave the country.

We also learn, that the Indians have been very troublesome for some time past, to the colonists, and that in many settlements they were under the necessity of erecting forts for their protection, and retreating into them for security. Several persons had been killed by the Indians within a few months, but at the latest advices, the alarm was subsiding. The crops are said to be short this season, and the country very sickly.

Arkansas Gazette, November 11, 1826.

FREEDOM'S JOURNAL EDITORIAL (1827)

To Our Patrons

In presenting our first number to our Patrons, we feel all the diffidence of persons entering upon a new and untried line of business. But a moment's reflection upon the noble objects, which we have in view by the publication of this journal; the expediency of its appearance at this time, when so many schemes are in action concerning our people encourage us to come boldly before an enlightened publick. For we believe, that a paper devoted to the dissimination of useful knowledge among our brethren, and to their moral and religious improvement, must meet with the cordial approbation of every friend to humanity.

The peculiarities of this Journal, renders it important that we should advertise to the world our motives by which we are actuated, and the objects which we contemplate.

We wish to plead our own cause. Too long have others spoken for us. Too long has the publick been deceived by misrepresentations, in things which concern us dearly, though in the estimation of some mere trifles; for though there are many in society who exercise towards us benevolent feelings; still (with sorrow we confess it) there are others who make it their business to enlarge upon the least trifle, which tends to the discredit of any person of colour; and pronounce anathemas and denounce our whole body for the misconduct of this guilty one. We are aware that there are many instances of vice among us, but we avow that it is because no one has taught its subjects to be virtuous; many instances of poverty, because no sufficient efforts accommodated to minds contracted by slavery, and deprived of early education have been made, to teach them how to husband their hard earnings, and to secure to themselves comfort.

Education being an object of the highest importance to the welfare of society, we shall endeavour to present just and adequate views of it, and to urge upon our brethren the necessity and expediency of training their children, while young, to habits of industry, and thus forming them for becoming useful members of society. It is surely time that we should awake from this lethargy of years, and make a concentrated effort for the education of our youth. We form a spoke in the human wheel, and it is necessary that we should understand our pendence on the different parts, and theirs on us, in order to perform our part with propriety.

Though not desiring of dictating, we shall feel it our incumbent duty to dwell occasionally upon the general principles and rules of economy. The world has grown too enlightened, to estimate any man's character by his personal appearance. Though all men acknowledge the excellency of Franklin's maxims, yet comparatively few practise upon them. We may deplore when it is too late, the neglect of these self-evident truths, but it avails little to mourn. Ours will be the task of admonishing our brethren on these points.

The civil rights of a people being of the greatest value, it shall ever be our duty to vindicate our brethren, when oppressed; and to lay the case before the publick. We shall also urge upon our brethren, (who are qualified by the laws of the different states) the expediency of using their elective franchise; and of making an independent use of the same. We wish them not to become the tools of party.

And as much time is frequently lost, and wrong principles instilled, by the perusal of works of trivial importance, we shall consider it a part of our duty to recommend to our young readers, such authors as will not only enlarge their stock of useful knowledge, but such as will also serve to stimulate them to higher attainments in science.

We trust also, that through the columns of the FREEDOM'S JOURNAL, many practical pieces, having for their bases, the improvement of our brethren, will be presented to them, from the pens of many of our respected friends, who have kindly promised their assistance.

It is our earnest wish to make our journal a medium of intercourse between our brethren in the different states of this great confederacy: that through its columns an expression of our sentiments, on many interesting subjects which concern us, may be offered to the publick: that plans which apparently are beneficial may be candidly discussed and properly weighed; if worth, receive our cordial approbation; if not, our marked disapprobation.

Useful knowledge of every kind, and everything that relates to Africa, shall find a ready admission into our columns; and as that vast continent becomes daily more known, we trust that many things will come to light, proving that the natives of it are neither so ignorant nor stupid as they have generally been supposed to be.

And while these important subjects shall occupy the columns of the FREEDOM'S JOURNAL, we would not be unmindful of our brethren who are still in the iron fetters of bondage. They are our kindred by all the ties of nature; and though but little can be effected by us, still let our sympathies be poured forth, and our prayers in their behalf, ascend to Him who is able to succour them.

From the press and the pulpit we have suffered much by being incorrectly represented. Men whom we equally love and admire have not hesitated to represent us disadvantageously, without becoming personally acquainted with the true state of things, nor discerning between virtue and vice among us. The virtuous part of our people feel themselves sorely aggrieved under the existing state of things—they are not appreciated.

Our vices and our degradation are ever arrayed against us, but our virtues are passed by unnoticed. And what is still more lamentable, our friends, to whom we concede all the principles of humanity and religion, from these very causes seem to have fallen into the current of popular feeling and are imperceptibly floating on the stream   actually living in the practice of prejudice, while they abjure it in theory, and feel it not in their hearts. Is it not very desirable that such should know more of our actual condition; and of our efforts and feelings, that in forming or advocating plans for our amelioration, they may do it more understandingly? In the spirit of candor and humility we intend by a simple representation of facts to lay our case before the public, with a view to arrest the progress of prejudice, and to shield ourselves against the consequent evils. We wish to conciliate all and to irritate none, yet we must be firm and unwavering in our principles, and persevering in our efforts.

If ignorance, poverty and degradation have hitherto been our unhappy lot; has the Eternal decree gone forth, that our race alone are to remain in this state, while knowledge and civilization are shedding their enlivening rays over the rest of the human family? The recent travels of Denham and Clapperton in the interior of Africa, and the interesting narrative which they have published; the establishment of the republic of Hayti after years of sanguinary warfare; its subsequent progress in all the arts of civilization; and the advancement of liberal ideas in South America, where despotism has given place to free governments, and where many of our brethren now fill important civil and military stations, prove the contrary.

The interesting fact that there are FIVE HUNDRED THOUSAND free persons of colour, one half of whom might peruse, and the whole be benefitted by the publication of the journal; that no publication, as yet, has been devoted exclusively to their improvement—that many selections from approved standard authors, which are within the reach of few, may occasionally be made—and more important still, that this large body of our citizens have no public channel—all serve to prove the real necessity, at present, for the appearance of the FREEDOM'S JOURNAL.

It shall ever be our desire so to conduct the editorial department of our paper as to give offence to none of our patrons; as nothing is farther from us than to make it the advocate of any partial views, either in politics or religion. What few days we can number, have been devoted to the improvement of our brethren; and it is our earnest wish that the remainder may be spent in the same delightful service.

In conclusion, whatever concerns us as a people, will ever find a ready admission into the FREEDOM'S JOURNAL, interwoven with all the principal news of the day.

And while every thing in our power shall be performed to support the character of our journal, we would respectfully invite our numerous friends to assist by their communications, and our coloured brethren to strengthen our hands by their subscriptions, as our labour is one of common cause, and worthy of their consideration and support. And we most earnestly solicit the latter, that if at any time we should seem to be zealous, or too pointed in the inculcation of any important lesson, they will remember, that they are equally interested in the cause in which we are engaged, and attribute our zeal to the peculiarities of our situation; and our earnest engagedness in their well-being.

Freedom's Journal, March 16, 1827.

FREEDOM FOR AN AFRICAN PRINCE (1828)

The Captive African Restored to Liberty

Letter from a gentleman of Natchez to a Lady of Cincinnati.   Natchez, April 7, 1828.

This letter will be handed to you by a very extraordinary personage—no less than your old acquaintance Prince (or Ibrahim) who is now FREE, and on his way to his own country; where he was captured in battle nearly forty years ago, and has been in slavery nearly the whole of that long period upon the plantation of Mr. Thomas Foster of this county. I am much gratified to have been the instrument of his emancipation—although from his advanced age (sixty-six years), he can but possess merely a glimpse of the blessings to which he was entitled from his birth.

As I happen to have a leisure half hour, I will give you a sketch of the manner in which his liberation has been brought about; you may recollect that I frequently suggested to him that if he would write a letter to his country, I would have it conveyed for him to his own country. I think it was early in the spring of 1826, that he wrote the letter in my office, which I directed to the care of our Consul General (Captain John Mulloway). Thomas B. Reed, Esq., one of our Senators, took charge of the letter to Washington, from whence it was sent by the Department of State to its destination. During last summer, I received a letter from the Department of State, informing me that the letter had been forwarded, and a translation of it returned, and I was requested to inquire on what terms Mr. Foster would liberate Prince, to the intent that he might be returned to his own country. On applying to Mr. F. he agreed to give him up without any compensation, conditioned, that he should not enjoy his liberty in this country. I informed the President of the result of my inquiry, and a few weeks ago, received a letter from Mr. Clay, asking of me to complete the agency and to send Prince on to Washington City, for which purpose I was authorized to draw for a sum of money necessary to defray the expenses of his journey and to clothe him if necessary.

But the poor old man, when the news was communicated to him that he was to be free and return to his country, where he is, we have no doubt a lawful king, [of a country called Timboo,] he looked at the old companion of his slavery—the mother of his nine children—he could not agree to part with her—she too—how could she part with him!—She wished to follow him to the end of the world. What was to be done? I had no authority to interfere as to her, and I felt almost grieved that I had taken a solitary step in the business believing that the separation of the old couple would no doubt accelerate the death of both. However, it rejoices me to tell you Isabella is with Prince—they will both call and see "Miss Jane"—as the old man, you recollect always called you. I applied again to Mr. Foster, who is a truly amiable and worthy man; he could not find in his heart to separate his old and faithful servants, and for a very small sum (compared to the value of Isabella as a servant), he agreed to give her up. So soon as his intentions were known, I requested a young gentleman of the bar to head a subscription paper for Prince, asking of his friends to assist him to purchase his wife. Two hundred dollars was the sum required. In a very few days he had a surplus of $33. Several gentlemen gave him 10 dolls. One gave him 15, many gave 5 and very few less than 1 dollar.

Prince has also several certificates voluntarily given to him, of his uncommon good conduct for twenty four years. N. A. Ware, Esq. has kindly undertaken to see him to Washington City. I expect he will remain three or four days in Cincinnati, and as he will call on you in all his finery, (I have had an elegant Moorish dress made for him), and perhaps attract some attention. I write you this long history, that you may be enabled to give some account of your distinguished visitor.

Prince is really a most extraordinary man—born to a kingdom—well educated, for he now writes Arabic in a most elegant style—brought a slave in a foreign country, he has sustained a character for honesty and integrity which is almost beyond parallel; he has been faithful, honest, humble, and industrious, and although he adheres strictly to the religion of his country (Mahometism) he expresses the greatest respect for the Christian religion and is very anxious to obtain a testament in his own language, that he may read the history of Jesus Christ. I wrote to the President to request one for him, but that part of my letter was not answered. I am however in hopes, if one is to be had at Washington City, he will be gratified on his own application for it.

Prince called to see us yesterday, with his wife and sons, who are really the finest looking young men I have seen. They were all genteelly dressed; and although they expressed themselves pleased with the freedom of their parents, there was a look of *silent agony* in their eyes I could not bear to witness. I hope the old man will be able to realize his prospects and regain his property; which if he does, he says he can buy them free at TEN PRICES.

Freedom's Journal, 2:8 (May 16, 1828).

DAVID WALKER ADDRESSES FREE PERSONS OF COLOR (1828)

Address, Delivered before the General Colored Association at Boston, by David Walker

Mr. President,—I cannot but congratulate you, together with my brethren on this highly interesting occasion, the first semi-annual meeting of this Society. When I reflect upon the many impediments through which we have had to conduct its affairs, and see, with emotions of delight, the present degree of eminency to which it has arisen, I cannot, sir, but be of the opinion, that an invisible arm must have been stretched out on our behalf. From the very second conference, which was by us convened, to agitate the proposition respecting this society, to its final consolidation, we were by some, opposed, with an avidity and zeal, which, had it been on the opposite side, would have done great honor to themselves. And, sir, but for the undeviating, and truly patriotic exertions of those who were favorable to the formation of this institution, it might have been this day, in a yet unorganized condition. Did I say in an unorganized condition? Yea, had our opponents their way, the very notion of such an institution might have been obliterated from our minds. How strange it is, to see men of sound sense, and of tolerably good judgment, act so diametrically in opposition to their interest; but I forbear making any further comments on this subject, and return to that for which we are convened.

First, then, Mr. President, it is necessary to remark here, at once, that the primary object of this institution, is, to unite the colored population, so far, through the United States of America, as may be practicable and expedient; forming societies, opening, extending, and keeping up correspondences, and not withholding any thing which may have the least tendency to meliorate *our* miserable condition—with the restrictions, however, of not infringing on the articles of its constitution, or that of the United States of America. Now, that we are disunited, is a fact, that no one of common sense will deny; and, that the cause of which, is a powerful auxiliary in keeping us from rising to the scale of reasonable and thinking beings, none but those who delight in our degradation will attempt to contradict. Did I say those who delight in our degradation? Yea, sir, glory in keeping us ignorant and miserable, that we might be the better and the longer slaves. I was credibly informed by a gentleman of unquestionable veracity, that a slaveholder upon finding one of his young slaves with a small spelling book in his hand (not opened) fell upon and beat him almost to death, exclaiming, at the same time, to the child, you will acquire better learning than I or any of my family.

I appeal to every candid and unprejudiced mind, do not all such men glory in our miseries and degradations; and are there not millions whose chief glory centers in this horrid wickedness? Now, Mr. President, those are the very humane, philanthropic, and charitable men who proclaim to the world, that the blacks are such a poor, ignorant and degraded species of beings, that, were they set at liberty, they would die for the want of something to subsist upon, and in consequence of which, they are compelled to keep them in bondage, to do them good.

O Heaven! what will not avarice and the love of despotic sway cause men to do with their fellow creatures, when actually in their power? But, to return whence digressed; it has been asked, in what way will the *General Colored Association* (or the Institution) unite the colored population, so far, in the United States as may be practicable and expedient? To which

enquiry I answer, by asking the following: Do not two hundred and eighty years [of] very intolerable sufferings teach us the actual necessity of a general among us? do we not know indeed, the horrid dilemma into which we are, and from which, we must exert ourselves, to be extricated? Shall we keep slumbering on, with our arms completely folded up, exclaiming every now and then, against our miseries, yet never do the least thing to ameliorate our condition, or that of posterity? Shall we not, by such inactivity, leave, or [farther] entail a hereditary degradation on our children, but a little, if at all, inferior to that which our fathers, under all their comparative disadvantages and privations, left on us? In fine, shall we, while almost every other people under Heaven, are making such mighty efforts to better their condition, go around from house to house, enquiring what good associations and societies are going to do for us? Ought we not to form ourselves into a general body, to protect, aid, and assist each other to the utmost of our power, with the beforementioned restrictions?

Yes, Mr. President, it is indispensably our duty to try every scheme that we think will have a tendency to facilitate our salvation, and leave the final result to that God, who holds the destinies of people in the hollow of his hand, and who ever has, and will, repay every nation according to its works.

Will any be so hardy as to say, or even to imagine, that we are incapable of effecting any object which may have a tendency to hasten our emancipation, in consequence of the prevalence of ignorance and poverty among us? That the major part of us are ignorant and poor, I am at this time unprepared to deny. —But shall this deter us from all lawful attempts to bring about the desired object? Nay, sir, it should rouse us to greater exertions; there ought to be a spirit of emulation and inquiry among us, a hungering and thirsting after religion; these are requisitions, which, if we ever be so happy as acquire, will fit us, for all the departments of life; and, in my humble opinion, ultimately result in rescuing us from an oppression, unparalleled, I had almost said, in the annals of the world.

But some may even think that our white breathren and friends are making such mighty efforts, for the amelioration of our condition, that we may stand as neutral spectators of the work. That we have very good friends yea, very good, among that body, perhaps none but a few of those who have, ever read at all will deny; and that many of them have gone, and will go, all lengths for our good, is evident, from the very works of the great, the good, and the godlike Granville Sharpe [sic], Wilberforce, Lundy, and the truly patriotic and lamented Mr. Ashmun, late Colonial Agent of Liberia, who, with a zeal which was only equaled by the goodness of his heart has lost his life in our cause, and a host of others too numerous to mention: a number of private gentlemen too, who, though they say but little, are nevertheless engaged for good. Now, all of those great, and indeed, good friends whom God has given us I do humbly, and very gratefully acknowledge. But, that we should co-operate with them, as far as we are able by uniting and cultivating a spirit of friendship and of love among us, is obvious, from the very exhibition of our miseries, under which we groan.

Two millions and a half of colored people in these United States, more than five hundred thousand of whom are about two thirds of the way free. Now, I ask, if no more than these last were united (which they must be, or always live as enemies) and resolved to aid and assist each other to the utmost of their power, what mighty deeds could be done by them for the good of our cause?

But, Mr. President, instead of a general compliance with these requisitions, which have a natural tendency to raise us in the estimation of the world, we see, to our sorrow, in the very midst of us, a gang of villains, who, for the paltry sum of fifty or a hundred dollars, will kidnap and sell into perpetual slavery their fellow creatures! and, too, of one of their fellow sufferers, whose miseries are a little more enhanced by the scourges of a tyrant, would abscond from his pretended owner, to take a little recreation, and unfortunately fall in their way, he is gone! Brethren and fellow sufferers, I ask you, in the name of God, and of Jesus Christ, shall we suffer such notorious villains to rest peaceably among us? will they not take our wives and little ones, more particularly our *little ones,* when a convenient opportunity will admit and sell them for money to slave holders, who will doom them to *chains, handcuffs,* and even unto death? May God open our eyes on these children of the devil and enemies of all good!

But, sir, this wickedness is scarcely more infernal than that which was attempted a few months since, against the government of our brethren, the Haytians, by a consummate rogue, who ought to have, long since, been *haltered,* but who, I was recently informed, is nevertheless, received into company among some of our most respectable men, with a kind of brotherly affection which ought to be shown only to a gentleman of honor.

Now, Mr. President, all such mean, and more than disgraceful actions as these, are powerful auxiliaries, which work for our destruction, and which are abhorred in the sight of God and of good men.

But, sir, I cannot but bless God for the glorious anticipation of a not very distant period, when these things which now help to degrade us still no more be practiced among the sons of Africa—for, though this, and perhaps another, generation may not experience the promised blessings of Heaven, yet, the dejected, degraded, and now enslaved children of Africa will have, in spite of all their enemies, to take their stand among the nations of the earth. And, sir, I verily believe that God has something in reserve for us, which, when he shall have poured it out upon us, will repay us for all our suffering and miseries.

Freedom's Journal, December 19, 1828.

KEY ARGUMENTS FROM DAVID WALKER'S *APPEAL* (1829)

My dearly beloved Brethren and Fellow Citizens.

Having travelled over a considerable portion of these United States, and having, in the course of my travels, taken the most accurate observations of things as they exist—the result of my observations has warranted the full and unshaken conviction, that we, (coloured people of these United States,) are the most degraded, wretched, and abject set of beings that ever lived since the world began; and I pray God that none like us ever may live again until time shall be no more. They tell us of the Israelites in Egypt, the Helots in Sparta, and of the Roman Slaves, which last were made up from almost every nation under heaven, whose sufferings under those ancient and heathen nations, were, in comparison with ours, under this enlightened and Christian nation, no more than a cypher—or, in other words, those heathen nations of antiquity, had but little more among them than the name and form of slavery; while wretchedness and endless miseries were reserved, apparently in a phial, to be poured out upon, our fathers, ourselves and our children, by *Christian Americans!*

. . . I call upon the professing Christians, I call upon the philanthropist, I call upon the very tyrant himself, to show me a page of history, either sacred or profane, on which a verse can be found, which maintains, that the Egyptians heaped the *insupportable insult* upon the children of Israel, by telling them that they were not of the *human family.* Can the whites deny this charge? Have they not, after having reduced us to the deplorable condition of slaves under their feet, held us up as descending originally from the tribes of *Monkeys* or *Orang-Outangs?* O! my God!

I appeal to every man of feeling—is not this insupportable? Is it not heaping the most gross insult upon our miseries, because they have got us under their feet and we cannot help ourselves? Oh! pity us we pray thee, Lord Jesus, Master.—Has Mr. Jefferson declared to the world, that we are inferior to the whites, both in the endowments of our bodies and our minds? It is indeed surprising, that a man of such great learning, combined with such excellent natural parts, should speak so of a set of men in chains. I do not know what to compare it to, unless, like putting one wild deer in an iron cage, where it will be secured, and hold another by the side of the same, then let it go, and expect the one in the cage to run as fast as the one at liberty. So far, my brethren, were the Egyptians from heaping these insults upon their slaves, that Pharaoh's daughter took Moses, a son of Israel for her own, as will appear by the following.

The world knows, that slavery as it existed was, man's, (which was the primary cause of their destruction) was, comparatively speaking, no more than a *cypher,* when compared with ours under the Americans. Indeed I should not have noticed the Roman slaves, had not the very learned and penetrating Mr. Jefferson said, "when a master was murdered, all his slaves in the same house, or within hearing, were condemned to death."—Here let me ask Mr. Jefferson, (but he is gone to answer at the bar of God, for the deeds done in his body while living,) I therefore ask the whole American people, had I not rather die, or be put to death, than to be a slave to any tyrant, who takes not only my own, but my wife and children's lives by the inches? Yea, would I meet death with avidity far! far!! in preference to such *servile submission* to the murderous hands of tyrants. Mr. Jefferson's very severe remarks on us have been so extensively argued upon by men whose attainments in literature, I shall never be able to reach, that I would not have meddled with it, were it not to solicit each of my brethren, who has the spirit of a man, to buy a copy of Mr. Jefferson's "Notes on Virginia," and put it in the hand of his son.

But let us review Mr. Jefferson's remarks respecting us some further. Comparing our miserable fathers, with the learned philosophers of Greece, he says: "Yet notwithstanding these and other discouraging circumstances among the Romans, their slaves were often their rarest artists. They excelled too, in science, insomuch as to be usually employed as tutors to their master's children; Epictetus, Terence and Phaedrus, were slaves,—but they were of the race of whites. It is not their *condition* then, but *nature,* which has produced the distinction. "See this, my brethren! ! Do you believe that this assertion is swallowed by millions of the whites? Do you know that Mr. Jefferson was one of as great characters as ever lived among the whites? See his writings for the world, and public labours for the United States of America. Do you believe that the assertions of such a man, will pass away into oblivion unobserved by this people and the world? If you do you are much mistaken—See how the American people treat us—have we souls in our bodies? Are we men who have any spirits at all? I know that there are many *swell-bellied* fellows among us, whose greatest object is to fill their stomachs. Such I do not mean—I am after those who know and feel, that we are MEN, as well as other people; to them, I say, that unless we try to refute Mr. Jefferson's arguments respecting us, we will only establish them.

. . . I must observe to my brethren that at the close of the first Revolution in this country, with Great Britain, there were but thirteen States in the Union, now there are twenty-four, most of which are slave-holding States, and the whites are dragging us around in chains and in handcuffs, to their new States and Territories to work their mines and farms, to enrich them and their children—and millions of them believing firmly that we being a little darker than they, were made by our Creator to be an inheritance to them and their children for ever—the same as a parcel of *brutes.*

Are we MEN!!—I ask you, O my brethren, are we MEN? Did our Creator make us to be slaves to dust and ashes like ourselves? Are they not dying worms as well as we? Have they not to make their appearance before the tribunal of Heaven, to answer for the deeds done in the body, as well as we? Have we any other Master but Jesus Christ alone? Is he not their Master as well as ours?—What right then, have we to obey and call any other Master, but Himself? How we could be so *submissive* to a gang of men, whom we cannot tell whether they are as good as ourselves or not, I never could conceive. However, this is shut up with the Lord, and we cannot precisely tell—but I declare, we judge men by their works.

The whites have always been an unjust, jealous, unmerciful, avaricious and blood-thirsty set of beings, always seeking after power and authority.

. . . to my no ordinary astonishment, [a] Reverend gentleman got up and told us (coloured people) that slaves must be obedient to their masters—must do their duty to their masters or be whipped—the whip was made for the backs of fools, &c. Here I pause for a moment, to give the world time to consider what was my surprise, to hear such preaching from a minister of my Master, whose very gospel is that of peace and not of blood and whips, as this pretended preacher tried to make us believe. What the American preachers can think of us, I aver this day before my God, I have never been able to define. They have newspapers and monthly periodicals, which they receive in continual succession, but on the pages of which, you will scarcely ever find a paragraph respecting slavery, which is ten thousand times more injurious to this country than all the other evils put together; and which will be the final overthrow of its government, unless something is very speedily done; for their cup is nearly full. —Perhaps they will laugh at or make light of this; but I tell you Americans! that unless you speedily alter your course, *you* and your *Country are gone!!!!!*

If any of us see fit to go away, go to those who have been for many years, and are now our greatest earthly friends and benefactors—the English. If not so, go to our brethren, the Haytians, who, according to their word, are bound to protect and comfort us. The Americans say, that we are ungrateful—but I ask them for heaven's sake, what should we be grateful to them for—for murdering our fathers and mothers ?—Or do they wish us to return thanks to them for chaining and handcuffing us, branding us, cramming fire down our throats, or for keeping us in slavery, and beating us nearly or quite to death to make us work in ignorance and miseries, to support them and their families. They certainly think that we are a gang of fools. Those among them, who have volunteered their services for our redemption, though we are unable to compensate them for their labours, we nevertheless thank them from the bottom of our hearts, and have our eyes steadfastly fixed upon them, and their labours of love for God and man.—But do slave-holders think that we thank them for keeping us in miseries, and taking our lives by the inches?

Let no man of us budge one step, and let slave-holders come to beat us from our country. America is more our country, than it is the whites—we have enriched it with our *blood and tears.* The greatest riches in all America have arisen from our blood and tears:—and will they drive us from our property and homes, which we have earned with our *blood?* They must look sharp or this very thing will bring swift destruction upon them. The Americans have got so fat on our blood and groans, that they have almost forgotten the God of armies. But let them go on.

Do the colonizationists think to send us off without first being reconciled to us? Do they think to bundle us up like brutes and send us off, as they did our brethren of the State of Ohio? Have they not to be reconciled to us, or reconcile us to them, for the cruelties with which they have afflicted our fathers and us? Methinks colonizationists think they have a set of brutes to deal with, sure enough. Do they think to drive us from our country and homes, after having enriched it with our blood and tears, and keep back millions of our dear brethren, sunk in the most barbarous wretchedness, to dig up gold and silver for them and their children? Surely, the Americans must think that we are brutes, as some of them have represented us to be. They think that we do not feel for our brethren, whom they are murdering by the inches, but they are dreadfully deceived.

What nation under heaven, will be able to do any thing with us, unless God gives us up into its hand? But Americans. I declare to you, while you keep us and our children in bondage, and treat us like brutes, to make us support you and your families, we cannot be your friends. You do not look for it, do you? Treat us then like men, and we will be your friends. And there is not a doubt in my mind, but that the whole of the past will be sunk into oblivion, and we yet, under God, will become a united and happy people. The whites may say it is impossible, but remember that nothing is impossible with God.

I count my life not dear unto me, but I am ready to be offered at any moment. For what is the use of living, when in fact I am dead. But remember, Americans, that as miserable, wretched, degraded and abject as you have made us in preceding, and in this generation, to support you and your families, that some of you, (whites) on the continent of America, will yet curse the day that you ever were born. You want slaves, and want us for your slaves!!! My colour will yet, root some of you out of the very face of the earth!!!!!! You may doubt it if you please. I know that thousands will doubt—they think they have us so well secured in wretchedness, to them and their children, that it is impossible for such things to occur.

See your Declaration Americans!!! Do you understand your own language? Hear your languages, proclaimed to the world, July 4th, 1776—"We hold these truths to be self evident—that ALL MEN ARE CREATED EQUAL!! that they *are endowed by their Creator with certain unalienable rights; that among these are life, liberty, and the pursuit of happiness! !"* Compare your own language above, extracted from your Declaration of Independence, with your cruelties and murders inflicted by your cruel and unmerciful fathers and yourselves on our fathers and on us—men who have never given your fathers or you the least provocation!!!!!!

Walker, David. 1830. *David Walker's Appeal, In Four Articles: Together with a Preamble to the Coloured Citizens of the World, but in Particular, and Very Expressly, to those of the United States of America.* Boston: D. Walker.

ADDRESS TO THE FREE PEOPLE OF COLOUR OF THESE UNITED STATES (1830)

Brethren,

Impressed with a firm and settled conviction, and more especially being thought by that inestimable and invaluable instrument, namely, the Declaration of Independence, that all men are born free and equal, and consequently are endowed with unalienable rights, among which are the enjoyments of life, liberty, and the pursuits of happiness.

Viewing these as incontrovertible facts, we have been led to the following conclusions; that our forlorn and deplorable situation earnestly and loudly demand of us to devise and pursue all legal means for the speedy elevation of ourselves and brethren to the scale and standing of men.

And in pursuit of this great object, various ways and means have been resorted to; among others, the African Colonization Society is the most prominent. Not doubting the sincerity of many friends who are engaged in that cause; yet we beg leave to say, that it does not meet with our approbation. However great the debt which these United States may owe to injured Africa, and however unjustly her sons have been made to bleed, and her daughters to drink of the cup of affliction, still we who have been born and nurtured on this soil, we, whose habits, manners, and customs are the same in common with other Americans, can never consent to take our lives in our hands, and be the bearers of the redress offered by that Society to that much afflicted country.

Tell it not to barbarians, lest they refuse to be civilised, and eject our christian missionaries from among them, that in the nineteenth century of the christian era, laws have been enacted in some of the states of this great republic, to compel an unprotected and harmless portion of our brethren to leave their homes and seek an asylum in foreign climes: and in taking a view of the unhappy situation of many of these, whom the oppressive laws alluded to, continually crowd into the Atlantic cities, dependent of their support upon their daily labour, and who often suffer for want of employment, we have had to lament that no means have yet been devised for their relief.

These considerations have led us to the conclusion, that the formation of a settlement in the British province of Upper Canada, would be a great advantage of the people of colour. In accordance with these views, we pledge ourselves to aid each other by all honourable means, to plant and support one in that country, and therefore we earnestly and most feelingly appeal to our coloured brethren, and to all philanthropists here and elsewhere, to assist in this benevolent and important work.

To encourage our brethren earnestly to co-operate with us, we offer the follwing, viz.

1st. Under that government no inviduous distinction of colour is recognised, but there we shall be entitled to all the rights, privileges, and immunities of other citizens.

2nd. That the language, climate, soil, and productions are similar to those in this country.

3rd. That land of the best quality can be purchased at the moderate price of one dollar and fifty cents per acre, by the one hundred acres. 4th. The market for different kinds of produce raised in that colony, is such as to render a suitable reward to the industrious farmer, equal in our opinion to that of the United States. And lastly, as the erection of buildings must necessarily claim the attention of the emigrants, we would invite the mechanics from our large cities to embark in the enterprise; the advancement of architecture depending much on their exertions, as they must consequently take with them the arts and improvements of our well regulated communities.

It will be much to the advantage of those who have large families, and desire to see them happy and respected, to locate themselves in a land where the laws and prejudices of society will have no effect in retarding their advancement to the summit of civil and religious improvement. There the diligent student will have ample opportunity to reap the reward due to industry and perseverence; whilst those of moderate attainments, if properly nurtured, may be enabled to take their stand as men in the several offices and situations necessary to promote union, peace, order and tranquility. It is to these we must look for the strength and spirit of our future prosperity.

Before we close, we would just remark, that it has been a subject of deep regret to this convention, that we as a people, have not availingly appreciated every opportunity placed within our power by the benevolent efforts of the friends of humanity, in elevating our condition to the rank of freemen. That our mental and physical qualities have not been more actively engaged in pursuits more lasting, is attributable in a great measure to a want of unity among ourselves; whilst our only stimulus to action has been to become domestics, which at best is but a precarious and degraded situation.

It is to obviate these evils, that we have recommended our views to our fellow-citizens in the foregoing instrument, with a desire of raising the moral and political standing of ourselves; and we cannot devise any plan more likely to accomplish this end, than by encouraging agriculture and mechanical arts: for by the first, we shall be enabled to act with a degree of independence, which as yet has fallen to the lot of but few among us; and the faithful pursuit of the latter, in connection with the sciences, which expand and ennoble the mind, will eventually give us the standing and condition we desire.

To effect these great objects, we would earnestly request our brethren throughout the United States, to co-operate with us, by forming societies *auxiliary* to the Parent Institution, about being established in the city of Philadelphia, under the patronage of the GENERAL CONVENTION. And we further recommend to our friends and brethren, who reside in places where, *at present,* this may be impracticable, so far to aid us, by contributing to the funds of the Parent Institution; and, if disposed, to appoint one delegate to represent them in the next Convention, to be held in Philadelphia the first Monday of June next, it being fully understood, that organized societies be at liberty to send any number of delegates not exceeding *five.*

Signed by order of the Convention,

Rev. Richard Allen, *President,*

Senior Bishop of the African
Methodist Episcopal Churches.

Junius C. Morel, *Secretary.*

Constitution of the American Society of Free Persons of Colour, for Improving Their Condition in the United States; for Purchasing Lands; and for the Establishment of a Settlement in Upper Canada, also the Proceedings of the Convention, with Their Address to the Free Persons of Colour in the United States. 1831. Philadelphia: J. W. Allen.

THE LIBERATOR (1831)

To the Public:

In the month of August, I issued proposals for publishing "*The Liberator*" in Washington city; but the enterprise, though hailed in different sections of the country, was palsied by public indifference. Since that time, the removal of the *Genius of Universal Emancipation* to the Seat of Government has rendered less imperious the establishment of a similar periodical in that quarter.

During my recent tour for the purpose of exciting the minds of the people by a series of discourses on the subject of slavery, every place that I visited gave fresh evidence of the fact, that a greater revolution in public sentiment was to be effected in the free states—*and particularly in New-England*—than at the south. I found contempt more bitter, opposition more active, detraction more relentless, prejudice more stubborn, and apathy more frozen, than among slave owners themselves. Of course, there were individual exceptions to the contrary. This state of things afflicted, but did not dishearten me. I determined, at every hazard, to lift up the standard of emancipation in the eyes of the nation, *within sight of Bunker Hill and in the birth place of liberty.* That standard is now unfurled; and long may it float, unhurt by the spoliations of time or the missiles of a desperate foe—yea, till every chain be broken, and every bondman set free! Let southern oppressors tremble—let their secret abettors tremble—let their northern apologists tremble—let all the enemies of the persecuted blacks tremble.

I deem the publication of my original Prospectus unnecessary, as it has obtained a wide circulation. The principles therein inculcated will be steadily pursued in this paper, excepting that I shall not array myself as the political partisan of any man. In defending the great cause of human rights, I wish to derive the assistance of all religions and of all parties.

Assenting to the "self-evident truth" maintained in the American Declaration of Independence, "that all men are created equal, and endowed by their Creator with certain inalienable rights—among which are life, liberty and the pursuit of happiness," I shall strenuously contend for the immediate enfranchisement of our slave population. In Park-street Church, on the Fourth of July, 1829, in an address on slavery, I unreflectingly assented to the popular but pernicious doctrine of gradual abolition. I seize this opportunity to make a full and unequivocal recantation, and thus publicly to ask pardon of my God, of my country, and of my brethren the poor slaves, for having uttered a sentiment so full of timidity, injustice and absurdity. A similar recantation, from my pen, was published in the Genius of Universal Emancipation at Baltimore, in September, 1829. My confidence in now satisfied.

I am aware, that many object to the severity of my language; but is there not cause for severity? I *will* be as harsh as truth, and as uncompromising as justice. On this subject, I do not wish to think, or speak, or write, with moderation. No! no! Tell a man whose house is on fire, to give a moderate alarm; tell him to moderately rescue his wife from the hand of the ravisher; tell the mother to gradually extricate her babe from the fire into which it has fallen;—but urge me not to use moderation in a cause like the present. I am in earnest—I will not equivocate—I will not excuse—I will not retreat a single inch—

AND I WILL BE HEARD. The apathy of the people is enough to make every statue leap from its pedestal, and to hasten the resurrection of the dead.

It is pretended, that I am retarding the cause of emancipation by the coarseness of my invective, and the precipitancy of my measures. The *charge is not true.* On this question my influence,—humble as it is,—is felt at this moment to a considerable extent, and shall be felt in coming years—not perniciously, but beneficially—not as a curse, but as a blessing; and posterity will bear testimony that I was right. I desire to thank God, that he enables me to disregard "the fear of man which bringeth a snare," and to speak his truth in its simplicity and power. And here I close with this fresh dedication:

> *Oppression! I have seen thee, face to face,*
> *And met thy cruel eye and cloudy brow;*
> *But thy soul-withering glance I fear not now—*
> *For dread to prouder feelings doth give place*
> *Of deep abhorrence! Scorning the disgrace*
> *Of slavish knees that at thy footstool bow,*
> *I also kneel—but with far other vow*
> *Do hail thee and thy herd of hirelings base:—*
> *I swear, while life-blood warms my throbbing veins,*
> *Still to oppose and thwart, with heart and hand,*
> *Thy brutalizing sway – till Afric's chains*
> *Are burst, and Freedom rules the rescued land,—*
> *Trampling Oppression and his iron rod:*
> *Such is the vow I take—SO HELP ME GOD!*

The Liberator, 1:1 (January 1, 1831).

WILLIAM LLOYD GARRISON COMMENTS ON WALKER'S APPEAL (1831)

Believing, as we do, that men should never do evil that good may come; that a good end does not justify wicked means in the accomplishment of it; and that we ought to suffer, as did our Lord and his apostles, unresistingly—knowing that vengeance belongs to God, and he will certainly repay it where it is due;—believing all this, and that the Almighty will deliver the oppressed in a way which they know not, we deprecate the spirit and tendency of this Appeal. Nevertheless, it is not for the American people, as a nation, to denounce it as bloody or monstrous. Mr. Walker but pays them in their own coin, but follows their own creed, but adopts their own language. *We* do not preach rebellion—no, but submission and peace. Our

enemies may accuse us of striving to stir up the slaves to revenge but their accusations are false, and made only to excite the prejudices of the whites, and to destroy our influence. We say, that the possibility of a bloody insurrection at the south fills us with dismay; and we avow, too, as plainly, that if any people were ever justified in throwing off the yoke of their tyrants, the slaves are that people. It is not we, but our guilty countrymen, who put arguments into the mouths, and swords into the hands of the slaves. Every sentence that they write—every word that they speak—every resistance that they make, against foreign oppression, is a call upon their slaves to destroy them. Every Fourth of July celebration must embitter and inflame the minds of the slaves. And the late dinners, and illuminations, and orations, and shoutings, at the south, over the downfall of the French tyrant, Charles the Tenth, furnish so many reasons to the slaves why they should obtain their own rights by violence.

Some editors have affected to doubt where the deceased Walker wrote this pamphlet.—On this point, skepticism need not stumble: the Appeal bears the strongest internal evidence of having emanated from his own mind. No white man could have written in language so natural and enthusiastic.

The Liberator, 1:2 (January 8, 1831).

A CONTEMPORARY ACCOUNT OF NAT TURNER'S REVOLT (1831)

The Banditti

. . . A fanatic preacher by the name of Nat Turner (Gen. Nat Turner) who had been taught to read and write, and permitted to go about preaching in the country, was at the bottom of this infernal brigandage. He was artful, impudent and vindictive, without any cause or provocation, that could be assigned. —He was the slave of Mr. Travis. He and another slave of Mr. T. a young fellow, by the name of Moore, were two of the leaders. Three or four others were first concerned and most active.—

They had 15 others to join them. And by importunity or threats they prevailed upon about 20 others to cooperate in the scheme of massacre. We cannot say how long they were organizing themselves—but they turned out on last Monday early (the 22d) upon their nefarious expedition. . . . They were mounted to the number of 40 or 50; and with knives and axes—knocking on the head, or cutting the throats of their victims. They had few firearms among them—and scarcely one, if one, was fit for use. . . . But as they went from house to house, they drank ardent spirits—and it is supposed, that in consequence of their being intoxicated,—or from mere fatigue, they paused in their murderous career about 12 o'clock on Monday.

A fact or two, before we continue our narrative. These wretches are now estimated to have committed sixty-one murders! Not a white person escaped at all the houses they visited except two. One was a little child at Mrs. Waller's, about 7 or 8 years of age, who had sagacity enough to Creep up a chimney; and the other was Mrs. Barrow, whose husband was murdered in his cotton patch, though he had received some notice in the course of the morning of the murderous deeds that were going on; but placed no confidence in the story and fell victim to his incredulty. His wife bid herself between weather-boarding, and the unplastered lathing, and escaped, the wretches not taking time to hunt her out. It was believed that one of the brigands had taken up a spit against Mr. Barrow, because he had refused him one of his female slaves for a wife.

Early on Tuesday morning, they attempted to renew their bloody work. They made an attack upon Mr. Blunt, a gentleman who was very unwell with the gout, and who instead of flying determined to brave them out. He had several pieces of firearms, perhaps seven or eight, and he put them into the hands of his own slaves, who nobly and gallantly stood by him. They repelled the brigands—killed one, wounded and took prisoner (Gen. Moore), and we believe took a third who was not wounded at all. . . .

The militia of Southampton had been most active in ferreting out the fugitives from their hiding places. . . . But it deserves to be said to the credit of many of the slaves whom gratitude had bound to their masters, that they had manifested the greatest alacrity in detecting and apprehending many of the brigands. They had brought in several and a fine spirit had been shown in many of the plantations of confidence on the part of the masters, and gratitude on that of the slaves. It is said that from 40 to 50 blacks were in jail—some of whom were known to be concerned with the murders, and others suspected. The courts will discriminate the innocent from the guilty.

It is believed that all the brigands were slaves—and most, if not all these, the property of kind and indulgent masters. It is not known that any of them had been the runaways of the swamps and only one of them was a free man of color. He had afterwards returned to his own house, and a party sent there to apprehend him. He was accidently seen concealed in his yard and shot. . . .

Nat, the ringleader, who calls himself General, pretends to be a Baptist preachers great enthusiast—declares to his comrades that he is commissioned by Jesus Christ, and proceeds under his inspired directions—that the late singular appearance of the sun was the sign for him, &c., &c., is among the number not yet taken. The story of his having been killed at the bridge, and of two engagements there, is ungrounded. It is believed he cannot escape.

The General is convinced, from various sources of information, that there existed no general concert among the slaves. —Circumstances impossible to have been feigned, demonstrate the entire ignorance on the subject of all the slaves in the counties around Southampton, among whom he has never known more perfect order and quiet to prevail.

Richmond *Enquirer*,
August 30, 1831.

FROM NAT TURNER'S CONFESSION (1831)

Agreeable to his own appointment, on the evening he was committed to prison, with permission of the jailer, I visited NAT on Tuesday the 1st November, when, without being questioned at all, commenced his narrative in the following words:—

SIR,—You have asked me to give a history of the motives which induced me to undertake the late insurrection, as you call it—To do so I must go back to the days of my infancy, and even before I was born. I was thirty-one years of age the 2d of October last, and born the property of Benj. Turner, of this county. In my childhood a circumstance occurred which made an indelible impression on my mind, and laid the ground work of that enthusiasm, which has terminated so fatally to many, both white and black, and for which I am about to atone at the gallows. It is here necessary to relate this circumstance—trifling as it may seem, it was the commencement of that belief which has grown with time, and even now, sir, in this dungeon, helpless and forsaken as I am, I cannot divest myself of. Being at play with other children, when three or four years old, I was telling them something, which my mother overhearing, said it had happened before I was born—I stuck to my story, however, and related somethings which went, in her opinion, to confirm it—others being called on were greatly astonished, knowing that these things had happened, and caused them to say in my hearing, I surely would be a prophet, as the Lord had shewn me things that had happened before my birth. And my father and mother strengthened me in this my first impression, saying in my presence, I was intended for some great purpose, which they had always thought from certain marks on my head and breast—[a parcel of excrescences which I believe are not at all uncommon, particularly among negroes, as I have seen several with the same. In this case he has either cut them off or they have nearly disappeared]—My grand mother, who was very religious, and to whom I was much attached—my master, who belonged to the church, and other religious persons who visited the house, and whom I often saw at prayers, noticing the singularity of my manners, I suppose, and my uncommon intelligence for a child, remarked I had too much sense to be raised, and if I was, I would never be of any service to any one as a slave—To a mind like mine, restless, inquisitive and observant of every thing that was passing, it is easy to suppose that religion was the subject to which it would be directed, and although this subject principally occupied my thoughts—there was nothing that I saw or heard of to which my attention was not directed—The manner in which I learned to read and write, not only had great influence on my own mind, as I acquired it with the most perfect ease, so much so, that I have no recollection whatever of learning the alphabet—but to the astonishment of the family, one day, when a book was shewn me to keep me from crying, I began spelling the names of different objects—this was a source of wonder to all in the neighborhood, particularly the blacks—and this learning was constantly improved at all opportunities—when I got large enough to go to work, while employed, I was reflecting on many things that would present themselves to my imagination, and whenever an opportunity occurred of looking at a book, when the school children were getting their lessons, I would find many things that the fertility of my own imagination had depicted to me before; all my time, not devoted to my master's service, was spent either in prayer, or in making experiments in casting different things in moulds made of earth, in attempting to make paper, gunpowder, and many other experiments, that although I could not perfect, yet convinced me of its practicability if I had the means. I was not addicted to stealing in my youth, nor have ever been—Yet such was the confidence of the negroes in the neighborhood, even at this early period of my life, in my superior judgment, that they would often carry me with them when they were going on any roguery, to plan for them. Growing up among them, with this confidence in my superior judgment, and when this, in their opinions, was perfected by Divine inspiration, from the circumstances already alluded to in my infancy, and which belief was ever afterwards zealously inculcated by the austerity of my life and manners, which became the subject of remark by white and black.—Having soon discovered to be great, I must appear so, and therefore studiously avoided mixing in society, and wrapped myself in mystery, devoting my time to fasting and prayer—By this time, having arrived to man's estate, and hearing the scriptures commented on at meetings, I was struck with that particular passage which says : "Seek ye the kingdom of Heaven and all things shall be added unto you." I reflected much on this passage, and prayed daily for light on this subject—As I was praying one day at my plough, the spirit spoke to me, saying "Seek ye the kingdom of Heaven and all things shall be added unto you." *Question*—what do you mean by the Spirit. *Ans.* The Spirit that spoke to the prophets in former days—and I was greatly astonished, and for two years prayed continually, whenever my duty would permit—and then again I had the same revelation, which fully confirmed me in the impression that I was ordained for some great purpose in the hands of the Almighty. Several years rolled round, in which many events occurred to strengthen me in this my belief. At this time I reverted in my mind to the remarks made of me in my childhood, and the things that had been shewn me—and as it had been said of me in my childhood by those by whom I had been taught to pray, both white and black, and in whom I had the greatest confidence, that I had too much sense to be raised, and if I was, I would never be of any use to any one as a slave. Now finding I had arrived to man's estate, and was a slave, and these revelations being made known to me, I began to direct my attention to this great object, to fulfil the purpose for which, by this time, I felt assured I was intended. Knowing the influence I had obtained over the minds of my fellow servants, (not by the means of conjuring and such like tricks—for to them I always spoke of such things with contempt) but by the communion of the Spirit whose revelations I often communicated to them, and they believed and said my wisdom came from God. I now began to prepare them for my purpose, by telling them something was about to happen that would terminate in fulfilling the great promise that had been made to me—About this time I was placed under an overseer, from whom I ran away—and after remaining in the woods thirty days, I returned, to the astonishment of the negroes on the plantation, who thought I had made my escape to some other part of the country, as my father had done before. But the reason of my return was, that the Spirit appeared to me and said I had my wishes directed to the things of this world, and not to the kingdom of Heaven, and that I should return to the service of my earthly master—"For he who knoweth his Master's will, and doeth it not, shall be beaten with many stripes, and thus, have I chastened you." And the negroes found fault, and murmured against me, saying that if they had my sense they would not serve any master in the world. And about this time I had a vision—and I saw white spirits and black spirits engaged in battle, and the sun was darkened—the thunder rolled in the Heavens, and blood flowed in streams—and I heard a voice saying, "Such is your luck, such you are called to see, and let it come rough or smooth, you must surely bare it." I now withdrew myself as much as my situation would permit, from the intercourse of my fellow servants, for the avowed purpose of serving the Spirit more fully—and it appeared to me, and reminded me of the things it had already shown me, and that it would then reveal to me the knowledge of the elements, the revolution of the planets, the operation of tides, and changes of the seasons. After this revelation in the year 1825, and the knowledge of the elements being made known to me, I sought more than ever to obtain true holiness before the great day of judgment should appear, and then I began to receive the true knowledge of faith. And from the first steps of righteousness until the last, was I made perfect; and the Holy Ghost was with me, and said, "Behold me as I stand in the Heavens"—and I looked and saw the forms of men in different attitudes—and there were lights in the sky to which the children of darkness gave other names than what they really were—for they were the lights of the Saviour's hands, stretched forth from east to west, even as they were extended on the cross on Calvary for the redemption of sinners. And I wondered greatly at these miracles, and prayed to be informed of a certainty of the meaning thereof—and shortly afterwards, while laboring in the field, I discovered drops of blood on the corn as though it were dew from heaven—and I communicated it to many, both white and black, in the neighborhood—and I then found on the leaves in the woods hieroglyphic characters, and numbers, with the forms of men in different attitudes, portrayed in blood, and representing the figures I had seen before in the heavens. And now the Holy Ghost had revealed itself to me, and made plain the miracles it had shown me—For as the blood of Christ had been shed on this earth, and had ascended to heaven for the salvation of sinners, and was now returning to earth again in the form of dew—and as the leaves on the trees bore the impression of the figures I had seen in the heavens, it was plain to me that the Saviour was about to lay down the yoke he had borne for the sins of men, and the great day of judgment was at hand. About this time I told these things to a white man, (Etheldred T. Brantley) on whom it had a wonderful effect—and he ceased from his wickedness, and was attacked immediately with a cutaneous eruption, and blood ozed from the pores of his skin, and after praying and fasting nine days, he was healed, and the Spirit appeared to me again, and said, as the Saviour had been baptised so should we be also—and when the white people would not let us be baptised by the church, we went down into the water together, in the sight of many who reviled us, and were baptised by the Spirit—After this I rejoiced greatly, and gave thanks to God. And on the 12th of May, 1828, I heard a loud noise in the heavens, and the Spirit instantly appeared to me and said the Serpent was loosened, and Christ had laid down the yoke he had borne for the sins of men, and that I should take it on and fight against the Serpent, for the time was fast approaching when the first should be last and the last should be first. *Ques.* Do you not find yourself mistaken now? *Ans.* Was not Christ crucified. And by signs in the heavens that it would make known to me when I should commence the great work—and until the first sign appeared, I should conceal it from the knowledge of men—And on the appearance of the sign, (the eclipse of the sun last February) I should arise and prepare myself, and slay my enemies with their own weapons. And immediately on the sign appearing in the heavens, the seal was removed from my lips, and I communicated the great work laid out for me to do, to four in whom I had the greatest confidence, (Henry, Hark, Nelson, and Sam)—It was intended by us to have begun the work of death on the 4th July last—Many were the plans formed and rejected by us, and it affected my mind to such a degree, that I fell sick, and the time passed without our coming to any determination how to commence—Still forming new schemes and rejecting them, when the sign appeared again, which determined me not to wait longer.

Since the commencement of 1830, I had been living with Mr. Joseph Travis, who was to me a kind master, and placed the greatest confidence in me; in fact, I had no cause to complain of his treatment to me. On Saturday evening, the 20th of August, it was agreed between Henry, Hark and myself, to prepare a dinner the next day for the men we expected, and then to concert a plan, as we had not yet determined on any. Hark, on the following morning, brought a pig, and Henry brandy, and being joined by Sam, Nelson, Will and Jack, they turpared in the woods a dinner, where, about three o'clock, I joined them.

Q. Why were you so backward in joining them?

A. The same reason that had caused me not to mix with them for years before.

I saluted them on coming up, and asked Will how came he there, he answered, his life was worth no more than others, and his liberty as dear to him. I asked him if he thought to obtain it? He said he would, or loose his life. This was enough to put him in full confidence. Jack, I knew, was only a tool in the hands of Hark, it was quickly agreed we should commence at home (Mr. J. Travis') on that night, and until we had armed and equipped ourselves, and gathered sufficient force, neither age nor sex was to be spared, (which was invariably adhered to.) We remained at the feast until about two hours in the night, when we went to the house and found Austin; they all went to the cider press and drank, except myself. On returning to the house, Hark went to the door with an axe, for the purpose of breaking it open, as we knew we were strong enough to murder the family, if they were awaked by the noise; but reflecting that it might create an alarm in the neighborhood, we determined to enter the house secretly, and murder them whilst sleeping. Hark got a ladder and set it against the chimney, on which I ascended, and hoisting a window, entered and came down stairs, unbarred the door, and removed the guns from their places. It was then observed that I must spill the first blood. On which, armed with a hatchet, and accompanied by Will, I entered my master's chamber, it being dark, I could not give a death blow, the hatchet glanced from his head, he sprang from the bed and called his wife, it was his last word, Will laid him dead, with a blow of his axe, and Mrs. Travis shared the same fate, as she lay in bed. The murder of this family, five in number, was the work of a moment, not one of them awoke; there was a little infant sleeping in a cradle, that was forgotten, until we had left the house and gone some distance, when Henry and Will returned and killed it; we got here, four guns that would shoot, and several old muskets, with a pound or two of powder. We remained some time at the barn, where we paraded; I formed them in a line as soldiers, and after carrying them through all the manoeuvres I was master of, marched them off to Mr. Salathul Francis', about six hundred yards distant. Sam and Will went to the door and knocked. Mr. Francis asked who was there, Sam replied, it was him, and he had a letter for him, on which he got up and came to the door, they immediately seized him, and dragging him out a little from the door, he was dispatched by repeated blows on the head; there was no

other white person in the family. We started from there for Mrs. Reese's, maintaining the most perfect silence on our march, where finding the door unlocked, we entered, and murdered Mrs. Reese in her bed, while sleeping; her son awoke, but it was only to sleep the sleep of death, he had only time to say who is that, and he was no more. From Mrs. Reese's we went to Mrs. Turner's, a mile distant, which we reached about sunrise, on Monday morning. Henry, Austin, and Sam, went to the still, where, finding Mr. Peebles, Austin shot him, and the rest of us went to the house; as we approached, the family discovered us, and shut the door. Vain hope! Will, with one stroke of his axe, opened it, and we entered and found Mrs. Turner and Mrs. Newsome in the middle of a room, almost frightened to death. Will immediately killed Mrs. Turner, with one blow of his axe. I took Mrs. Newsome by the hand, and with the sword I had when I was apprehended, I struck her several blows over the head, but not being able to kill her, as the sword was dull. Will turning around and discovering it, despatched her also. A general destruction of property and search for money and ammunition, always succeeded the murders. By this time my company amounted to fifteen, and nine men mounted, who started for Mrs. Whitehead's, (the other six were to go through a by way to Mr. Bryant's and rejoin us at Mrs. Whitehead's,) as we approached the house we discovered Mr. Richard Whitehead standing in the cotton patch, near the lane fence; we called him over into the lane, and Will, the executioner, was near at hand, with his fatal axe, to send him to an untimely grave. As we pushed on to the house, I discovered some one run round the garden, and thinking it was some of the white family, I pursued them, but finding it was a servant girl belonging to the house, I returned to commence the work of death, but they whom I left, had not been idle; all the family were already murdered, but Mrs. Whitehead and her daughter Margaret. As I came round to the door I saw Will pulling Mrs. Whitehead out of the house, and at the step he nearly severed her head from her body, with his broad axe. Miss Margaret, when I discovered her, had concealed herself in the corner, formed by the projection of the cellar cap from the house; on my approach she fled, but was soon overtaken, and after repeated blows with a sword, I killed her by a blow on the head, with a fence rail. By this time, the six who had gone by Mr. Bryant's, rejoined us, and informed me they had done the work of death assigned them. We again divided, part going to Mr. Richard Porter's, and from thence to Nathaniel Francis', the others to Mr. Howell Harris', and Mr. T. Doyles. On my reaching Mr. Porter's, he had escaped with his family. I understood there, that the alarm had already spread, and I immediately returned to bring up those sent to Mr. Doyles, and Mr. Howell Harris'; the party I left going on to Mr. Francis', having told them I would join them in that neighborhood. I met these sent to Mr. Doyles' and Mr. Harris' returning, having met Mr. Doyle on the road and killed him; and learning from some who joined them, that Mr. Harris was from home, I immediately pursued the course taken by the party gone on before; but knowing they would complete the work of death and pillage, at Mr. Francis' before I could there, I went to Mr. Peter Edwards', expecting to find them there, but they had been here also. I then went to Mr. John T. Barrow's, they had been here and murdered him. I pursued on their track to Capt. Newit Harris', where I found the greater part mounted, and ready to start; the men now amounting to about forty, shouted and hurraed as I rode up, some were in the yard, loading their guns, others drinking. They said Captain Harris and his family had escaped, the property in the house they destroyed, robbing him of money and other valuables. I ordered them to mount and march instantly, this was about nine or ten o'clock, Monday morning. I proceeded to Mr. Levi Waller's, two or three miles distant. I took my station in the rear, and as it 'twas my object to carry terror and devastation wherever we went, I placed fifteen or twenty of the best armed and most to be relied on, in front, who generally approached the houses as fast as their horses could run; this was for two purposes, to prevent their escape and strike terror to the inhabitants—on this account I never got to the houses, after leaving Mrs. Whitehead's, until the murders were committed, except in one case. I sometimes got in sight in time to see the work of death completed, viewed the mangled bodies as they lay, in silent satisfaction, and immediately started in quest of other victims—Having murdered Mrs. Waller and ten children, we started for Mr. William Williams'—having killed him and two little boys that were there; while engaged in this, Mrs. Williams fled and got some distance from the house, but she was pursued, overtaken, and compelled to get up behind one of the company, who brought her back, and after showing her the mangled body of her lifeless husband, she was told to get down and lay by his side, where she was shot dead. I then started for Mr. Jacob Williams, where the family were murdered—Here we found a young man named Drury, who had come on business with Mr. Williams—he was pursued, overtaken and shot. Mrs. Vaughan was the next place we visited—and after murdering the family here, I determined on starting for Jerusalem—Our number amounted now to fifty or

sixty, all mounted and armed with guns, axes, swords and clubs—On reaching Mr. James W. Parkers' gate, immediately on the road leading to Jerusalem, and about three miles distant, it was proposed to me to call there, but I objected, as I knew he was gone to Jerusalem, and my object was to reach there as soon as possible; but some of the men having relations at Mr. Parker's it was agreed that they might call and get his people. I remained at the gate on the road, with seven or eight; the others going across the field to the house, about half a mile off. After waiting some time for them, I became impatient, and started to the house for them, and on our return we were met by a party of white men, who had pursued our blood-stained track, and who had fired on those at the gate, and dispersed them, which I new nothing of, not having been at that time rejoined by any of them—Immediately on discovering the whites, I ordered my men to halt and form, as they appeared to be alarmed—The white men, eighteen in number, approached us in about one hundred yards, when one of them fired, (this was against the positive orders of Captain Alexander P. Peete, who commanded, and who had directed the men to reserve their fire until within thirty paces) And I discovered about half of them retreating, I then ordered my men to fire and rush on them; the few remaining stood their ground until we approached within fifty yards, when they fired and retreated. We pursued and overtook some of them who we thought we left dead; (they were not killed) after pursuing them about two hundred yards, and rising a little hill, I discovered they were met by another party, and had haulted, and were re-loading their guns, (this was a small party from Jerusalem who knew the negroes were in the field, and had just tied their horses to await their return to the road, knowing that Mr. Parker and family were in Jerusalem, but knew nothing of the party that had gone in with Captain Peete; on hearing the firing they immediately rushed to the spot and arrived just in time to arrest the progress of these barbarous villains, and save the lives of their friends and fellow citizens.) Thinking that those who retreated first, and the party who fired on us at fifty or sixty yards distant, had all only fallen back to meet others with amunition. As I saw them re-loading their guns, and more coming up than I saw at first, and several of my bravest men being wounded, the others became panick struck and squandered over the field; the white men pursued and fired on us several times. Hark had his horse shot under him, and I caught another for him as it was running by me; five or six of my men were wounded, but none left on the field; finding myself defeated here I instantly determined to go through a private way, and cross the Nottoway river at the Cypress Bridge, three miles below Jerusalem, and attack that place in the rear, as I expected they would look for me on the other road, and I had a great desire to get there to procure arms and amunition. After going a short distance in this private way, accompanied by about twenty men, I overtook two or three who told me the others were dispersed in every direction. After trying in vain to collect a sufficient force to proceed to Jerusalem, I determined to return, as I was sure they would make back to their old neighborhood, where they would rejoin me, make new recruits, and come down again. On my way back, I called at Mrs. Thomas's, Mrs. Spencer's, and several other places, the white families having fled, we found no more victims to gratify our thirst for blood, we stopped at Majr. Ridley's quarter for the night, and being joined by four of his men, with the recruits made since my defeat, we mustered now about forty strong. After placing out sentinels, I laid down to sleep, but was quickly roused by a great racket; starting up, I found some mounted, and others in great confusion; one of the sentinels having given the alarm that we were about to be attacked, I ordered some to ride round and reconnoitre, and on their return the others being more alarmed, not knowing who they were, fled in different ways, so that I was reduced to about twenty again; with this I determined to attempt to recruit, and proceed on to rally in the neighborhood, I had left. Dr. Blunt's was the nearest house, which we reached just before day; on riding up the yard, Hark fired a gun. We expected Dr. Blunt and his family were at Maj. Ridley's, as I knew there was a company of men there; the gun was fired to ascertain if any of the family were at home; we were immediately fired upon and retreated, leaving several of my men. I do not know what became of them, as I never saw them afterwards. Pursuing our course back and coming in sight of Captain Harris', where we had been the day before, we discovered a party of white men at the house, on which all deserted me but two, (Jacob and Nat,) we concealed ourselves in the woods until near night, when I sent them in search of Henry, Sam, Nelson, and Hark, and directed them to rally all they could, at the place we had had our dinner the Sunday before, where they would find me, and I accordingly returned there as soon as it was dark and remained until Wednesday evening, when discovering white men riding around the place as though they were looking for some one, and none of my men joining me, I concluded Jacob and Nat had been taken, and compelled to betray me. On this I gave up all hope for the present; and on

Thursday night after having supplied myself with provisions from Mr. Travis's, I scratched a hole under a pile of fence rails in a field, where I concealed myself for six weeks, never leaving my hiding place but for a few minutes in the dead of night to get water which was very near; thinking by this time I could venture out, I began to go about in the night and eaves drop the houses in the neighborhood; pursuing this course for about a fortnight and gathering little or no intelligence, afraid of speaking to any human being, and returning every morning to my cave before the dawn of day. I know not how long I might have led this life, if accident had not betrayed me, a dog in the neighborhood passing by my hiding place one night while I was out, was attracted by some meat I had in my cave, and crawled in and stole it, and was coming out just as I returned. A few nights after, two negroes having started to go hunting with the same dog, and passed that way, the dog came again to the place, and having just gone out to walk about, discovered me and barked, on which thinking myself discovered, I spoke to them to beg concealment. On making myself known they fled from me. Knowing then they would betray me, I immediately left my hiding place, and was pursued almost incessantly until I was taken a fortnight afterwards by Mr. Benjamin Phipps, in a little hole I had dug out with my sword, for the purpose of concealment, under the top of a fallen tree. On Mr. Phipps' discovering the place of my concealment, he cocked his gun and aimed at me. I requested him not to shoot and I would give up, upon which he demanded my sword. I delivered it to him, and he brought me to prison. During the time I was pursued, I had many hair breadth escapes, which your time will not permit you to relate. I am here loaded with chains, and willing to suffer the fate that awaits me.

I here proceeded to make some inquiries of him after assuring him of the certain death that awaited him, and that concealment would only bring destruction on the innocent as well as guilty, of his own color, if he knew of any extensive or concerted plan. His answer was, I do not. When I questioned him as to the insurrection in North Carolina happening about the same time, he denied any knowledge of it; and when I looked him in the face as though I would search his inmost thoughts, he replied, "I see sir, you doubt my word; but can you not think the same ideas, and strange appearances about this time in the heaven's might prompt others, as well as myself, to this undertaking." I now had much conversation with and asked him many questions, having forborne to do so previously, except in the cases noted in parenthesis;

but during his statement, I had, unnoticed by him, taken notes as to some particular circumstances, and having the advantage of his statement before me in writing, on the evening of the third day that I had been with him, I began a cross examination, and found his statement corroborated by every circumstance coming within my own knowledge or the confessions of others whom had been either killed or executed, and whom he had not seen nor had any knowledge since 22d of August last, he expressed himself fully satisfied as to the impracticability of his attempt. It has been said he was ignorant and cowardly, and that his object was to murder and rob for the purpose of obtaining money to make his escape. It is notorious, that he was never known to have a dollar in his life; to swear an oath, or drink a drop of spirits. As to his ignorance, he certainly never had the advantages of education, but he can read and write, (it was taught him by his parents,) and for natural intelligence and quickness of apprehension, is surpassed by few men I have ever seen. As to his being a coward, his reason as given for not resisting Mr. Phipps, shews the decision of his character. When he saw Mr. Phipps present his gun, he said he knew it was impossible for him to escape as the woods were full of men; he therefore thought it was better to surrender, and trust to fortune for his escape. He is a complete fanatic, or plays his part most admirably. On other subjects he possesses an uncommon share of intelligence, with a mind capable of attaining any thing; but warped and perverted by the influence of early impressions. He is below the ordinary stature, though strong and active, having the true negro face, every feature of which is strongly marked. I shall not attempt to describe the effect of his narrative, as told and commented on by himself, in the condemned hole of the prison. The calm, deliberate composure with which he spoke of his late deeds and intentions, the expression of his fiend-like face when excited by enthusiasm, still bearing the stains of the blood of helpless innocence about him; clothed with rags and covered with chains; yet daring to raise his manacled hands to heaven, with a spirit soaring above the attributes of man; I looked on him and my blood curdled in my veins.

I will not shock the feelings of humanity, nor wound afresh the bosoms of the disconsolate sufferers in this unparalleled and inhuman massacre, by detailing the deeds of their fiend-like barbarity. There were two or three who were in the power of these wretches, had they known it, and who escaped in the most providential manner. There were two whom they thought they left dead on the field at Mr. Parker's, but who

were only stunned by the blows of their guns, as they did not take time to re-load when they charged on them. The escape of a little girl who went to school at Mr. Waller's, and where the children were collecting for that purpose. excited general sympathy. As their teacher had not arrived, they were at play in the yard, and seeing the negroes approach, ran up on a dirt chimney (such as are common to log houses,) and remained there unnoticed during the massacre of the eleven that were killed at this place. She remained on her hiding place till just before the arrival of a party, who were in pursuit of the murderers, when she came down and fled to a swamp, where, a mere child as she was, with the horrors of the late scene before her, she lay concealed until the next day, when seeing a party go up to the house, she came up, and on being asked how she escaped, replied with the utmost simplicity, "The Lord helped her." She was taken up behind a gentleman of the party, and returned to the arms of her weeping mother. Miss Whitehead concealed herself between the bed and the mat that supported it, while they murdered her sister in the same room, without discovering her. She was afterwards carried off, and concealed for protection by a slave of the family, who gave evidence against several of them on their trial. Mrs. Nathaniel Francis, while concealed in a closet heard their blows, and the shrieks of the victims of these ruthless savages; they then entered the closet where she was concealed, and went out without discovering her. While in this hiding place, she heard two of her women in a quarrel about the division of her clothes. Mr. John T. Baron, discovering them approaching his house, told his wife to make her escape, and scorning to fly, fell fighting on his own threshold. After firing his rifle, he discharged his gun at them, and then broke it over the villain who first approached him, but he was overpowered, and slain. His bravery, however, saved from the hands of these monsters, his lovely and amiable wife, who will long lament a husband so deserving of her love. As directed by him, she attempted to escape through the garden, when she was caught and held by one of her servant girls, but another coming to her rescue, she fled to the woods, and concealed herself. Few indeed, were those who escaped their work of death. But fortunate for society, the hand of retributive justice has overtaken them; and not one that was known to be concerned has escaped.

Turner, Nat. 1881. *The Confession, Trial and Execution of Nat Turner, the Negro Insurrectionist; Also a List of Persons Murdered in the Insurrection in Southampton County, Virginia, on the 21st and 22nd of August, 1831, with Introductory Remarks.* Petersburg, VA: J. B. Edge.

CONDITIONS OF FREE BLACKS IN PENNSYLVANIA (1832)

Appendix to Memorial to Pennsylvania Legislature.

1. In connexion with the foregoing memorial, we beg leave to offer the following statement of facts for the information of all who desire to be correctly informed on the subjects to which they relate.

2. By a statement published by order of the guardians of the poor in 1832, it appears that out of 549 outdoor poor relieved during the year, only 22 were persons of color, being about 4 per cent of the whole number, while their ratio of the population of the city and suburbs exceeds 8 1/4 per cent. By a note appended to the printed report of the guardians of the poor, above referred to, it appears that the colored paupers admitted into the almshouse for the same period, did not exceed 4 per cent of the whole number.

3. In consequence of the neglect of the assessors, to distinguish, in their assessment, the property of people of color from that of others, it is not easy to ascertain the exact amount of taxes paid by us. But an attempt has been made to remedy this defect by a reference to receipts kept by tax-payers. The result thus obtained must necessarily be deficient, and fall short of the amount really paid by people of color; because it is fair to presume that we could not find receipts for all the money paid in taxes, and because no returns have been made except where receipts were found. From these imperfect returns, however, it is ascertained that we pay not less than 2500 dollars annually, while the sum expended for the relief of our poor, out of the public funds has rarely, if ever, exceeded $2000 a year. The amount of rents paid by our people, is found to exceed $100,000 annually.

4. Many of us, by our labor and industry have acquired a little property; and have become freeholders. Besides which, we have no less than six Methodist meeting houses, two Presbyterian, two Baptist, one Episcopalean, and one public hall, owned exclusively by our people, the value of which, in the aggregate, is estimated to exceed $100,000. To these may be added, two Sunday schools, two tract societies, two Bible societies, two temperance societies, and one female literary institution.

5. We have among ourselves, more than fifty beneficent societies, some of which are incorporated, for mutual aid in time of sickness and distress. The members of these societies are bound by rules and regulations, which tend to promote industry and morality among them. For any disregard or violation of these rules,—for intemperance or immorality of any kind, the members are liable to be suspended or expelled. These societies expend annually for the relief of their members when sick or disabled, or in distress, upwards of $7000, out of funds raised among themselves for mutual aid. It is also worthy of remark, that we cannot find a single instance of one of the members of either of these societies being convicted in any of our courts. One instance only has occurred of a member being brought up and accused before a court; but this individual was acquitted. Notwithstanding the difficulty of getting places for our sons as apprentices, to learn mechanical trades, owing to the prejudices with which we have to contend, there are between four and five hundred people of color in the city and suburbs who follow mechanical employments.

6. While we thankfully embrace the opportunity for schooling our children, which has been opened to us by public munificence and private benevolence, we are still desirous to do our part in the accomplishment of so desirable an object. Such of us as are of ability to do so, send our children to school at our own expense. Knowing by experience the disadvantages many of us labor under for want of early instruction; we are anxious to give our children a suitable education to fit them for the duties and enjoyments of life. In making the above statement of facts, our only object is, to prevent a misconception of our real condition; and to counteract those unjust prejudices against us, which the prevalence of erroneous opinions in regard to us, is calculated to produce.

We know that the most effectual method of refuting, and rendering harmless, false and exaggerated accounts of our degraded condition, is by our conduct; by living consistent, orderly and moral lives. Yet we are convinced that many good and humane citizens of this commonwealth, have been imposed upon, and induced to give credit to statements injurious to our general character and standing. At this important crisis, pregnant with great events, we deem it a duty we owe to ourselves and to our white friends, and to the public in general, to present to their candid and impartial consideration, the above statements. We ask only to be judged fairly and impartially. We claim no exemption from the frailties and imperfections of our common nature. We feel that we are men of like passions and feelings with others of a different color, liable to be drawn aside by temptation, from the paths of rectitude. But we think that in the aggregate we will not suffer by a comparison with our white neighbors whose opportunities of improvement have been no greater than ours. By such a comparison, fairly and impartially made, we are willing to be judged.

We have been careful in our exhibit of facts, to produce nothing but what may be sustained by legal evidence; by which we mean such facts as are susceptible of proof in a court of law. We have submitted our statements, with the sources whence they are drawn, to some of the intelligent citizens of Philadelphia who can testify to their substantial accuracy. All of which is respectfully submitted to a candid public.

Hazard's Register, June 1832.

FREDERICK DOUGLASS DESCRIBES SLAVE RESISTANCE (1834)

If at any one time of my life, more than another, I was made to drink the bitterest dregs of slavery, that time was during the first six months of my stay with this man Covey. We worked all weathers. It was never too hot, or too cold; it could never rain, blow, snow, or hail too hard for us to work in the field. Work, work, work, was scarcely more than the order of the day than of the night. The longest days were too short for him, and the shortest nights were too long for him. I was somewhat unmanageable at the first, but a few months of this discipline tamed me. Mr. Covey succeeded in breaking me—in body, soul, and spirit. My natural elasticity was crushed; my intellect languished; the disposition to read departed, the cheerful spark that lingered about my eye died out; the dark night of slavery closed in upon me, and behold a man transformed to a brute!

Sunday was my only leisure time. I spent this under some large tree, in a sort of beast-like stupor between sleeping and waking. At times I would rise up and a flash of energetic freedom would dart through my soul, accompanied with a faint beam of hope that flickered for a moment, and then vanished. I sank down again mourning over my wretched condition. I was sometimes tempted to take my life and that of Covey, but was prevented by a combination of hope and fear. My sufferings, as I remember them now, seem like a dream rather than like a stern reality.

Our house stood within a few rods of the Chesapeake bay, whose broad bosom was ever white with sails from every quarter of the habitable globe. Those beautiful vessels, robed in white, and so delightful to the eyes of free men, were to me so many shrouded ghosts, to terrify and torment me with thoughts of my wretched condition. I have often, in the deep stillness of a summer's Sabbath, stood all alone upon the banks of that noble bay, and traced, with saddened heart and tearful eye, the countless number of sails moving off to the mighty ocean. The sight of these always affected me powerfully. My thoughts would compel utterance; and there, with no audience but the Almighty, I would pour out my soul's complaint in my rude way with an apostrophe to the moving multitude of ships. . . .

I shall never be able to narrate half the mental experience through which it was my lot to pass, during my stay at Covey's. I was completely wrecked, changed, and bewildered; goaded almost to madness at one time, and at another reconciling myself to my wretched condition. All the kindness I had received at Baltimore, all my former hopes and aspirations for usefulness in the world, and even the happy moments spent in the exercises of religion, contrasted with my then present lot, served but to increase my anguish.

I suffered bodily as well as mentally. I had neither sufficient time in which to eat, or to sleep, except on Sundays. The overwork, and the brutal chastisements of which I was the victim, combined with that evergnawing and soul devouring thought—"I am a slave—and a slave for life—a slave with no rational ground to hope for freedom"—rendered me a living embodiment of mental and physical wretchedness.

Douglass, Frederick. 1951. "Frederick Douglass and the Slave-Breaker, 1834." In *A Documentary History of the Negro People in the United States.* Volume I. Herbert Aptheker, ed. New York: Carol Publishing Group.

ABOLITIONIST LITERATURE AND THE U.S. MAIL (1835)

Report on the Delivery of Abolition Materials in the Southern States by Postmaster General Amos Kendall.

A new question has arisen in the administration of this Department. A number of individuals have established an association in the Northern and Eastern States and raised a large sum of money, for the purpose of effecting the immediate abolition of Slavery in the Southern States. One of the means reported to has been the printing of a large mass of newspapers, pamphlets, tracts, and almanacs, containing exaggerated, and in some instances, false accounts of the treatment of slaves, illustrated with cuts calculated to operate on the passions of the colored men, and produce discontent, assassination, and servile war. These they attempted to disseminate throughout the slaveholding States, by the agency of the public mails.

As soon as it was ascertained that the mails contained these productions, great excitement arose, particularly in Charleston, S. C., and to ensure the safety of the mail in its progress Southward, the postmaster at that place agreed to retain them in his office until he could obtain instructions from the Postmaster General. In reply to his appeal, he was informed, that it was a subject upon which the Postmaster General had no legal authority to instruct him. The question again came up from the Postmaster at New York, who had refused to send the papers by the steamboat mail to Charleston, S. C. He was also answered that the Postmaster General possessed no legal authority to give instructions on the subject; but as the undersigned had no doubt that the circumstances of the case justified the detention of the papers, he did not hesitate to say so. Important principles are involved in this question, and it merits the grave consideration of all departments of the Government.

It is universally conceded, that our States are united only for certain purposes. There are interests, in relation to which they are believed to be as independent of each other as they were before the constitution was formed. The interest which the people of some of the States have in slaves, is one of them. No State obtained by the union any right whatsoever over slavery in any other State, nor did any State lose any of its power over it, within its own borders. On this subject, therefore, if this view be correct, the States are still independent, and may fence round and protect their interest in slaves, by such laws and regulations as in their sovereign will they may deem expedient.

Nor have the people of one State any more right to interfere with this subject in another State, than they have to interfere with the internal regulations, rights of property, or domestic police, of a foreign nation. If they were to combine and send papers among the laboring population of another nation, calculated to produce discontent and rebellion, their conduct would be good ground of complaint on the part of that nation; and, in case it were not repressed by the United States, might be, if perseveringly persisted in, just cause of war. The mutual obligations of our several States to suppress attacks by their citizens on each others' reserved rights and interests, would seem to be greater, because by entering into the Union, they have lost the right of redress which belongs to nations wholly independent. Whatever claim may be set up, or maintained, to a right of free discussion within their own borders of the institutions and laws of other communities, over which they have no rightful control,

few will maintain that they have a right, unless it be obtained by compact or treaty, to carry on such discussions within those communities, either orally, or by the distribution of printed papers, particularly if it be in violation of their peculiar laws, and at the hazard of their peace and existence. The constitution of the United States provides that "the citizens of each State shall be entitled to all privileges and immunities of citizens in the several States," but this clause cannot confer on the citizens of one State, higher privileges and immunities in another, than the citizens of the latter themselves posses. It is not easy, therefore, to perceive how the citizens of the Northern States can possess or claim the privilege of carrying on discussions within the Southern States, by the distribution of printed papers, which the citizens of the latter are forbidden to circulate by their own laws.

Neither does it appear that the United States acquired, by the constitution, any power whatsoever over this subject except a right to prohibit the importation of slaves after a certain date. On the contrary, that instrument contains evidences, that one object of the Southern States, in adopting it, was to secure to themselves a more perfect control over this interest, and cause it to be respected by the sister States. In the exercise of their reserved rights, and for the purpose of protecting this interest, and ensuring the safety of their people, some of the States have passed laws, prohibiting under heavy penalties, the printing or circulation of papers like those in question, within their respective territories. It has never been alleged that these laws are incompatible with the constitution and laws of the United States. Nor does it seem possible that they can be so, because they relate to a subject over which the United States cannot rightfully assume any control under that constitution, either by law or otherwise. If these principles be sound, it will follow that the State laws on this subject, are, within the scope of their jurisdiction, the supreme laws of the land, obligatory alike on all persons, whether private citizens, officers of the State, or functionaries of the General Government.

The constitution makes it the duty of the United States "to protect each of the States against invasion; and, on application of the Legislature, or of the Executive, (when the Legislature cannot be convened) against domestic violence." There is no quarter whence domestic violence is so much to be apprehended, in some of the States, as from the servile population, operated upon by mistaken or designing men. It is to obviate danger from this quarter, that many of the State laws, in relation to the circulation of incendiary papers, have been enacted. Without claiming for the General Government the power to pass laws prohibiting discussions of any sort, as a means of protecting States from domestic violence, it may safely be assumed, that the United States have no right, through their officers or departments, knowingly to be instrumental in producing within the several states, the very mischief which the constitution commands them to repress. It would be an extraordinary construction of the powers of the general Government, to maintain that they are bound to afford the agency of their mails and post offices, to counteract the laws of the States, in the circulation of papers calculated to produce domestic violence; when it would, at the same time, be one of their most important constitutional duties to protect the States against the natural, if not necessary consequences produced by that very agency.

The position assumed by this Department, is believed to have produced the effect of withholding its agency, generally, in giving circulation to the obnoxious papers in the Southern States. Whether it be necessary more effectually to prevent, by legislative enactments, the use of the mails, as a means of evading or violating the constitutional laws of the States in reference to this portion of their reserved rights, is a question which, it appears to the undersigned, may be submitted to Congress, upon a statement of the facts, and their own knowledge of the public necessities.

"Report of the Postmaster General," *House Documents,* 24th Cong., 1st sess., Appendix 9.

THE GAG RESOLUTIONS (1836)

The main question was then stated, viz: that the House do agree to the resolutions reported by the committee, which are as follows:

1. *Resolved,* That Congress possesses no constitutional authority to interfere, in any way, with the institution of slavery in any of the States of this confederacy.

2. *Resolved,* That Congress ought not to interfere, in any way, with slavery in the District of Columbia.

And whereas, it is extremely important and desirable that the agitation of this subject should be finally arrested, for the purpose of restoring tranquillity to the public mind, your committee respectfully recommend the adoption of the following additional resolution, viz:

3. *Resolved,* That all petitions, memorials, resolutions, propositions, or papers, relating in any way or to any extent whatever to the subject of slavery, or the aboli-

tion of slavery, shall, without being either printed or referred, be laid upon the table, and that no further action whatever shall be had thereon.

Journal of the House of Representatives, 24th Cong., 1st sess. May 25, 1836.

JOHN C. CALHOUN'S "SLAVERY A POSITIVE GOOD" (1837)

February 6, 1837

I do not belong, said Mr. C., to the school which holds that aggression is to be met by concession. Mine is the opposite creed, which teaches that encroachments must be met at the beginning, and that those who act on the opposite principle are prepared to become slaves. In this case, in particular. I hold concession or compromise to be fatal. If we concede an inch, concession would follow concession—compromise would follow compromise, until our ranks would be so broken that effectual resistance would be impossible. We must meet the enemy on the frontier, with a fixed determination of maintaining our position at every hazard. Consent to receive these insulting petitions, and the next demand will be that they be referred to a committee in order that they may be deliberated and acted upon. At the last session we were modestly asked to receive them, simply to lay them on the table, without any view to ulterior action. . . . I then said, that the next step would be to refer the petition to a committee, and I already see indications that such is now the intention. If we yield, that will be followed by another, and we will thus proceed, step by step, to the final consummation of the object of these petitions. We are now told that the most effectual mode of arresting the progress of abolition is, to reason it down; and with this view it is urged that the petitions ought to be referred to a committee. That is the very ground which was taken at the last session in the other House, but instead of arresting its progress it has since advanced more rapidly than ever. The most unquestionable right may be rendered doubtful, if once admitted to be a subject of controversy, and that would be the case in the present instance. The subject is beyond the jurisdiction of Congress—they have no right to touch it in any shape or form, or to make it the subject of deliberation or discussion. . . .

As widely as this incendiary spirit has spread, it has not yet infected this body, or the great mass of the intelligent and business portion of the North; but unless it be speedily stopped, it will spread and work upwards till it brings the two great sections of the Union into deadly conflict. This is not a new impression with me. Several years since, in a discussion with one of the Senators from Massachusetts (Mr. Webster), before this fell spirit had showed itself, I then predicted that the doctrine of the proclamation and the Force Bill— that this Government had a right, in the last resort, to determine the extent of its own powers, and enforce its decision at the point of the bayonet, which was so warmly maintained by that Senator, would at no distant day arouse the dormant spirit of abolitionism. I told him that the doctrine was tantamount to the assumption of unlimited power on the part of the Government, and that such would be the impression on the public mind in a large portion of the Union. The consequence would be inevitable. A large portion of the Northern States believed slavery to be a sin, and would consider it as an obligation of conscience to abolish it if they should feel themselves in any degree responsible for its continuance, and that this doctrine would necessarily lead to the belief of such responsibility. I then predicted that it would commence as it has with this fanatical portion of society, and that they would begin their operations on the ignorant, the weak, the young, and the thoughtless,—and gradually extend upwards till they would become strong enough to obtain political control, when he and others holding the highest stations in society, would, however reluctant, be compelled to yield to their doctrines, or be driven into obscurity. But four years have since elapsed, and all this is already in a course of regular fulfillment.

Standing at the point of time at which we have now arrived, it will not be more difficult to trace the course of future events now than it was then. They who imagine that the spirit now abroad in the North, will die away of itself without a shock or convulsion, have formed a very inadequate conception of its real character; it will continue to rise and spread, unless prompt and efficient measures to stay its progress be adopted. Already it has taken possession of the pulpit, of the schools, and, to a considerable extent, of the press; those great instruments by which the mind of the rising generation will be formed.

However sound the great body of the non-slaveholding States are at present, in the course of a few years they will be succeeded by those who will have been taught to hate the people and institutions of nearly one-half of this Union, with a hatred more deadly than one hostile nation ever entertained towards another. It is easy to see the end. By the necessary course of events, if left to themselves, we must become, finally, two people. It is impossible under the deadly hatred which must spring up between the two great nations, if the present causes are permitted to operate unchecked, that we should continue under the same political system. The conflicting elements would burst the Union asunder, powerful as are the links which hold it together. Abolition and the Union cannot coexist. As the friend of the Union I openly proclaim it,—and the sooner it is known the better. The former may now be controlled, but in a short time it will be beyond the power of man to arrest the course of events. We of the South will not, cannot, surrender our institutions. To maintain the existing relations between the two races, inhabiting that section of the Union, is indispensable to the peace and happiness of both. . . . But let me not be understood as admitting, even by implication, that the existing relations between the two races in the slaveholding States is an evil:—far otherwise; I hold it to be a good, as it has thus far proved itself to be to both, and will continue to prove so if not disturbed by the fell spirit of abolition. I appeal to facts. Never before has the black race of Central Africa, from the dawn of history to the present day, attained a condition so civilized and so improved, not only physically, but morally and intellectually.

In the meantime, the white or European race, has not degenerated. It has kept pace with its brethren in other sections of the Union where slavery does not exist. It is odious to make comparison; but I appeal to all sides whether the South is not equal in virtue, intelligence, patriotism, courage, disinterestedness, and all the high qualities which adorn our nature.

But I take higher ground. I hold that in the present state of civilization, where two races of different origin, and distinguished by color, and other physical differences, as well as intellectual, are brought together, the relation now existing in the slaveholding States between the two, is, instead of an evil, a good—a positive good. I feel myself called upon to speak freely upon the subject where the honor and interests of those I represent are involved. I hold then, that there never has yet existed a wealthy and civilized society in which one portion of the community did not, in point of fact, live on the labor of the other. Broad and general as is this assertion, it is fully borne out by history. This is not the proper occasion, but, if it were, it would not be difficult to trace the various devices by which the wealth of all civilized communities has been so unequally divided, and to show by what means so small a share has been allotted to those by whose labor it was produced, and so large a share given to the non-producing classes. The devices are almost innumerable, from the brute force and gross superstition of ancient times, to the subtle and artful fiscal contrivances of modern. I might well challenge a comparison between them and the more direct, simple, and patriarchal mode by which the labor of the African race is, among us, commanded by the European. I may say with truth, that in few countries so much is left to the share of the laborer, and so little exacted from him, or where there is more kind attention paid to him in sickness or infirmities of age. Compare his condition with the tenants of the poor houses in the more civilized portions of Europe—look at the sick, and the old and infirm slave, on one hand, in the midst of his family and friends, under the kind superintending care of his master and mistress, and compare it with the forlorn and wretched condition of the pauper in the poorhouse. But I will not dwell on this aspect of the question; I turn to the political; and here I fearlessly assert that the existing relation between the two races in the South, against which these blind fanatics are waging war, forms the most solid and durable foundation on which to rear free and stable political institutions. It is useless to disguise the fact. There is and always has been in an advanced stage of wealth and civilization, a conflict between labor and capital. The condition of society in the South exempts us from the disorders and dangers resulting from this conflict; and which explains why it is that the political condition of the slaveholding States has been so much more stable and quiet than that of the North. . . .

> McLaughlin, Andrew C. 1914. *Readings in the History of the American Nation.* New York: D. Appleton and Company.

A SLAVE MAROON IS KILLED (1837)

From the New Orleans Picayune of the 19th.

SQUIRE, THE OUTLAW. This notorious black scoundrel was yesterday killed by a Spaniard in the swamp near the Bayou road. It will be remembered by all our citizens that Squire was the negro who has so long prowled about the marshes in the rear of the city, a terror to the community, and for whose head a reward of two thousand dollars was offered some years ago. The life of this negro has been one of crime and total depravity. The annals of the city furnish records of his cruelty, crime, and murder. He had killed several white men in this place before he fled to the swamp, and has, up to the time of his death, eluded with a dexterity worthy of a more educated villain, all the searching efforts of justice to capture him. He has lived for the last three years an outlaw in the marshes in the rear of the city. Many years since he had his right arm shot off; he is said, notwithstanding this

deprivation, to have been an excellent marksman, but with the use of his left arm. Inured by hardships and exposure to the climate, he has subsisted in the woods, and carried on, until this time, his deeds of robbery and murder with the most perfect impunity—the marshes surrounding the city being almost impenetrable to our citizens. This demi-devil has for a long time ruled as the "Brigand of the Swamp." A supposition has always found believers that there was an encampment of outlaw negroes near the city, and that Squire was their leader. He has done much mischief in the way of decoying slaves to his camp, and in committing depredation upon the premises of those who live on the outskirts of the city. His destruction is hailed by old and young, as a benefit to society. A Spaniard was yesterday morning in the swamp, and proved the successful enemy of this foe to society. Squire raised his gun to shoot him, but failed, the gun have snapped. Immediately the Spaniard rushed upon him with a big stick—he gave him a blow which brought him to the ground, when his brains were literally beat out by the infuriated man. Proud of his victory, the conqueror came into the city, and reported what he had done. On hearing that Squire was dead, the authorities determined to have his body hauled to the city, and forthwith appointed a guard of men to repair to the swamp and bring it in. About two o'clock yesterday his body was exhibited on the public square of the First Municipality.

The Liberator, August 11, 1837.

ALTON *OBSERVER* EDITORIAL (1837)

September 11, 1837

To the Friends of the Redeemer in Alton

Dear Brethren, It is at all times important that the friends of truth should be united. It is especially so at the present time, when iniquity is coming in like a flood. I should be false to my covenant vows, and false to every feeling in my heart, were I to refuse making any personal sacrifice to effect so desirable an object. Having learned that there is a division of sentiments among the brethren, as it regards the propriety of my continuing longing to fill the office of Editor of the "Alton *Observer*," I do not hesitate a moment to submit the question to your decision. Most cheerfully I will resign my post, if in your collective wisdom you think the cause we all profess to love will thereby be promoted. And in coming to a decision on this question, I beseech you as a favour—may I not enjoin it as a duty?—that you act without any regard to my personal feelings. I should be false to the Master I serve, and of whose gospel I am a minister, should I allow my own interests, (real or supposed,) to be placed in competition with his. Indeed, I have no interest, no wish, at least I think I have none; I know I wrought to have none other than such as are subordinate to his will. Be it yours, brethren, to decide what is best for the cause of truth, most for the glory of God, and the salvation of souls, and rest assured—whatever my own private judgment may be—of my cordial acquiescence in your decision.

I had, at first, intended to make an unconditional surrender of the editorship into your hands. But as such a course might be liable to misconstructions, I have, by the advice of a beloved brother, determined to leave the whole matter with you. I am ready to go forward if you say so, and equally ready to yield to a successor, if such be your opinion. Yet let me say, promptly, that in looking back over my past labours as Editor of the "Observer," while I see many imperfections, and many errors and mistakes, I have, nevertheless, done the best I could. This I say in the fear of God; so that if I am to continue [as] the Editor, you must not, on the whole, expect a much better paper than you have had.

Should you decide that I ought to give place to a successor, I shall expect the two following conditions to be fulfilled.

1. That you will assume in its behalf, all my obligations contracted in consequence of my connection with the "Observer." Some of them were contracted immediately on behalf of the "Observer," and some in supporting my family while its Editor.

2. As I have now spent four among the best years of my life in struggling to establish the "Observer," and place it on its present footing, I shall expect you will furnish me with a sum sufficient to enable me to remove myself and family to another field of labour. More I do not ask, and I trust this will not be thought unreasonable. I would not ask even this had I the means myself, but I have not.

3. On these conditions I surrender into your hands the "Observer's" subscription list, now amounting to more than two thousand one hundred names, and constantly increasing, together with all the dues coming to the establishment. A list of both of the debts and cred its accompanies this communication.

May the spirit of wisdom, dear brethren, guide you to a wise and unanimous decision—to a decision which God will approve and ratify, and which shall redound to the glory of his name.

Yours affectionately,

Elijah P. Lovejoy

Alton [IL] *Observer,* September 11, 1837.

WENDELL PHILLIPS EULOGIZES ELIJAH P. LOVEJOY (1837)

"The Murder of Lovejoy"

MR. CHAIRMAN:—We have met for the freest discussion of these resolutions, and the events which gave rise to them [Cries of "Question," "Hear him," "Go on," "No gagging," etc.] I hope I shall be permitted to express my surprise at the sentiments of the last speaker, surprise not only at such sentiments from such a man, but at the applause they have received within these walls. A comparison has been drawn between the events of the Revolution and the tragedy at Alton. We have heard it asserted here, in Fanueil Hall, that Great Britain had a right to tax the Colonies, and we have heard the mob at Alton, the drunken murderers of Lovejoy, compared to those patriot fathers who threw the tea overboard! [Great applause.] Fellow-citizens, is this Fanueil Hall doctrine? ["no, no."] The mob at Alton were met to wrest from a citizen his just rights,—met to resist the laws. We have been told that our fathers did the same; and the glorious mantle of Revolutionary precedent has been thrown over the mobs of our day. To make out their title to such defense, the gentleman says that the British Parliament had a *right* to tax these Colonies. It is manifest that, without this, his parallel falls to the ground; for Lovejoy had stationed himself within constitutional bulwarks. He was not only defending the freedom of the press, but he was under his own roof, in arms with the sanction of the civil authority. The men who assailed him went against and over the laws. The mob, as the gentleman terms it,—mob forsooth! Certainly we sons of the tea-spillers are a marvelously patient generation!—the "orderly mob" which assembled in the Old South to destroy the teat were met to resist, not the laws, but illegal exactions. Shame on the American who calls the tea-tax and stamp-act *laws!* Our fathers resisted, not the King's prerogative, but the King's usurpation. To find any other account, you must read our Revolutionary history upside down. Our state archives are loaded with arguments of John Adams to prove the taxes laid by the British Parliament unconstitutional,—beyond its power. It was not till this was made out that the men of New England rushed to arms. The arguments of the Council Chamber and the House of Representatives preceded and sanctioned the contest. To draw the conduct of our ancestors into a precedent for mobs, for a right to resist laws we ourselves have enacted, is an insult to their memory. The difference between the excitements of those days and our own, which the gentleman in kindness to the latter has overlooked, is simply this: the men of that day went for the right, as secured by the laws. They were the people rising to sustain the laws and constitution of the Province. The rioters of our day go for their own wills, right or wrong. Sir, when I heard the gentleman lay down principles which place the murderers of Alton side by side with Otis and Hancock, with Quincy and Adams, I thought those pictured lips [pointing to the portraits in the Hall] would have broken into voice to rebuke the recreant American – the slanderer of the dead. [Great applause and counter applause.] The gentleman said that he should sink into insignificance if he dared to gainsay the principles of these resolutions. Sir, for the sentiments he has uttered, on soil consecrated by the prayers of Puritans and the blood of patriots, the earth should have yawned and swallowed him up.

Fellow-citizens, I cannot take back my words. Surely the Attorney-General, so long and well-known here, needs not the aid of your hisses against one so young as I am,—my voice never before heard within these walls!

Another ground has been taken to excuse the mob, and throw doubt and discredit on the conduct of Lovejoy and his associates. Allusion has been made to what lawyers understand very well,—the "conflict of laws." We are told that nothing but the Mississippi River rolls between St. Louis and Alton; and the conflict of laws somehow or other gives the citizens of the former a right to find fault with the defender of the press for publishing his opinions so near their limits. Will the gentleman venture that argument before lawyers? How the laws of the two States could be said to come into conflict in such circumstances I question whether any lawyer in this audience can explain or understand. No matter whether the line that divides one sovereign State from another be an imaginary one or ocean-wide, the moment you cross it the State you leave is blotted out of existence, so far as you are concerned. The Czar might as well claim to control the deliberations of Fanueil Hall, as the laws of Missouri demand reverence, or the shadow of obedience, from an inhabitant of Illinois.

I must find some fault with the statement which has been made of the events in Alton. It has been asked why Lovejoy and his friends did not appeal to the executive,—trust their defense to the police of the city. It has been hinted that, from hasty and ill-judged excitement, the men within the building provoked a quarrel, and that he fell in the course of it, one mob resisting another. Recollect, Sir, that they did act with the approbation and sanction of the Mayor. In strict truth, there was no executive to appeal to for protection. The Mayor acknowledged that he could not protect them. They asked him if it was lawful for them to defend themselves. He told them it was, and sanctioned their assembling in arms to do so. They were not, then, a mob; they were in some sense the *posse comitatus,* adopted for the occasion into the police of the city, acting under the order of a magistrate. It was civil authority resisting lawless violence. Where, then, was the imprudence? Is the doctrine to be sustained here, that it is imprudent for men to aid magistrates in executing the laws?

Men are continually asking each other, Had Lovejoy a right to resist? Sir, I protest against the question, instead of answering it. Lovejoy did not resist, in the sense they mean. He did not throw himself back on the natural right of self-defense. He did not cry anarchy, and let slip the dogs of civil war, careless of the horrors which would follow.

Sir, as I understand this affair, it was not an individual protecting his property; it was not one body of armed men resisting another, and making the streets of a peaceful city run blood with their contentions. It did not bring back the scenes in some old Italian cities, where family met family, and faction met faction, and mutually trampled the laws under foot. No; the men in that house were regularly *enrolled,* under the sanction of the Mayor. These relieved each other every other night. About thirty men were in arms on the night of the sixth, when the press was landed. The next evening, it was not thought necessary to summon more than half that number; among these was Lovejoy. It was, therefore, you perceived, Sir, the police of the city resisting rioters,—civil government breasting itself to the shock of lawless men.

Here is no question about the right of self-defense. It is in fact simply this: Has the civil magistrate a right to put down a riot?

Some persons seem to imagine that anarchy existed at Alton from the commencement of these disputes. Not at all. "No one of us," says an eyewitness and a comrade of Lovejoy, "has taken up arms during these disturbances but at the command of the Mayor." Anarchy did not settle down on that devoted city till Lovejoy breathed his last. Till then the law, represented in his person, sustained itself against its foes. When he fell, civil authority was trampled under foot. He had "planted himself on his constitutional rights,"—appealed to the laws,—claimed the protection of the civil authority,—taken refuge under "the broad shield of the Constitution. When through that he was pierced and fell, he fell but one sufferer in a common catastrophe." He took refuge under the banner of liberty,—amid its folds; and when he fell, its glorious stars and stripes, the emblem of free institutions, around which cluster so many heart-stirring memories, were blotted out in the martyr's blood.

It has been stated, perhaps inadvertently, that Lovejoy or his comrades fired first. This is denied by those who have the best means of knowing. Guns were first fired by the mob. After being twice fired on, those within the building consulted together and deliberately returned the fire. But suppose they did fire first. They had a right to do so; not only the right which every citizen has to defend himself, but the further right which every civil officer has to resist violence. Even if Lovejoy fired the first gun, it would not lessen his claim to our sympathy, or destroy his title to be considered a martyr in defense of a free press. The question now is, Did he act within the Constitution and the laws? The men who fell in State Street on the 5th of March, 1770, did more than Lovejoy is charged with. They were the *first* assailants. Upon some slight quarrel they pelted the troops with every missile within reach. Did this bate one jot of the eulogy with which Hancock and Warren hallowed their memory, hailing them as the first martyrs in the cause of American liberty?

If, Sir, I had adopted what are called Peace principles, I might lament the circumstances in this case. But all you who believe, as I do, in the right and duty of magistrates to execute the laws, join with me and brand as base hypocrisy the conduct of those who assemble year after year on the 4th of July, to fight over the battles of the Revolution, and yet "damn with faint praise," or load with obloquy, the memory of this man, who shed his blood in defense of life, liberty, property, and the freedom of the press!

Throughout that terrible night I find nothing to regret but this, that within the limits of our country, civil authority should have been so prostrated as to oblige a citizen to arm in his own defense, and to arm in vain. The gentleman says Lovejoy was presumptuous and imprudent,—he "died as the fool dieth." And a reverend clergyman of the city tells us that no citizen has a right to publish opinions disagreeable to the community! If any mob follows such publication, on *him* rests its guilt! He must wait, forsooth, till the people come up to it and agree with him! This libel on liberty goes on to say that the want of right to speak as we think is an evil inseparable from republican institu-

tions! If this be so, what are they worth? Welcome the despotism of the Sultan, where one knows what he may publish and what he may not, rather than the tyranny of this many-headed monster, the mob, where we know not what we may do or say, till some fellow-citizen has tried it, and paid for the lesson with his life. This clerical absurdity chooses as a check for the abuses of the press, not the *law,* but the dread of a mob. By so doing, it deprives not only the individual and the minority of their rights, but the majority also, since the expression of *their* opinion may sometimes provoke disturbance from the minority. A few men may make a mob as well as many. The majority, then, have no right, as Christian men, to utter their sentiments, if by any possibility it may lead to a mob! Shades of Hugh Peters and John Cotton, save us from such pulpits!

Imprudent to defend the liberty of the press! Why? Because the defense was unsuccessful? Does success gild crime into patriotism, and the want of it change heroic self-devotion to imprudence? Was Hampden imprudent when he drew the sword and threw away the scabbard? Yet he, judged by that single hour, was unsuccessful. After a short exile, the race he hated sat again upon the throne.

Imagine yourself present when the first news of Bunker Hill battle reached a New England town. The tale would have to run thus: "The patriots are routed,—the redcoats victorious,—Warren lies dead upon the field." With what scorn would that *Tory* have been received, who should have charged Warren with *imprudence!* Who should have said that, bred a physician, he was "out of place" in that battled, and "died as the *fool dieth*"! [Great applause.] How would the intimation have been received, that Warren and his associates should have waited a better time? But if success be indeed the only criterion of prudence, *Respice finem,*—wait till the end.

Presumptuous to assert the freedom of the press on American ground! It is the assertion of such freedom before the age? So much before the age as to leave one no right to make it because it displeases the community? Who invents this libel on his country? It is this very thing which entitles Lovejoy to greater praise. The disputed right which provoked the Revolution—taxation without representation—is far beneath that for which he died. [Here there was a strong and general expression of disapprobation.] One word, gentlemen. As much as *thought* is better than money, so much is the cause in which Lovejoy died nobler than a mere question of taxes. James Otis thundered in this Hall when the King did but touch his *pocket.* Imagine, if you can, his indignant eloquence, had England offered to put a gag upon his lips. [Great applause.]

The question that stirred the Revolution touched our civil interests. *This* concerns us not only as citizens, but as immortal beings. Wrapped up in its fate, saved or lost with it, are not only the voice of the statesman, but the instructions of the pulpit, and the progress of our faith.

The clergy "marvelously out of place" where free speech is battled for,—liberty of speech on national sins? Does the gentleman remember that freedom to preach was first gained, dragging in its train freedom to print? I thank the clergy here present, as I reverence their predecessors, who did not so far forget their country in their immediate profession as to deem it duty to separate themselves from the struggle of '76,—the Mayhews and Coopers, who remembered they were citizens before they were clergymen.

Mr. Chairman, from the bottom of my heart I thank that brave little band at Alton for resisting. We must remember that Lovejoy had fled from city to city,—suffered the destruction of three presses patiently. At length he took counsel with friends, men of character, of tried integrity, of wide views, of Christian principle. They thought the crisis had come: it was full time to assert the laws. They saw around them, not a community like our own, of fixed habits, of character moulded and settled, but one "in the gristle, not yet hardened into the bone of manhood." The people there, children of our older States, seem to have forgotten the blood-tried principles of their fathers the moment they lost sight of our New England hills. Something was to be done to show them the priceless value of the freedom of the press, to bring back and set right their wandering and confused ideas. He and his advisors looked out on a community, staggering like a drunken man, indifferent to their rights and confused in their feelings. Deaf to argument, haply they ought be stunned into sobriety. They saw that of which we cannot judge, the *necessity* of resistance. Insulted law called for it. Public opinion, fast hastening on the downward course, must be arrested.

Does not the event show they judged rightly? Absorbed in a thousand trifles, how has the nation all at once come to a stand? Men begin, as in 1776 and 1640, to discuss principles, to weigh characters, to find out where they are. Haply we may awake before we are borne over the precipice.

I am glad, Sir, to see this crowded house. It is good for us to be here. When Liberty is in danger, Fanueil Hall has the right, it is her duty, to strike the key-note for these United States. I am glad, for one reason, that remarks such as those to which I have alluded have been uttered here. The passage of these resolutions, in spite of this opposition, led by the Attorney-General of the Commonwealth, will show more clearly, more decisively, the deep indignation with which Boston regards this outrage.

Phillips, Wendell. 1863. *Speeches, Lectures, and Letters.* Boston: James Redpath.

ANTI-SLAVERY ADVOCATES ENDORSE ADDITIONAL REFORMS (1837)

The termination of the present year will complete the seventh volume of the *Liberator:* we have served, therefore, a regular apprenticeship in the cause of LIBERTY, and are now prepared to advocate it upon a more extended scale.

In commencing this publication, we had but a single object in view—the total abolition of American slavery, and as a just consequence, the complete enfranchisement of our colored countrymen. As the first step towards this sublime result, we found the overthrow of the American Colonization Society to be indispensable—containing, as it did, in its organization, all the elements of prejudice, caste, and slavery.

In entering upon our eighth volume, the abolition of slavery will still be the grand object of our labors, though not, perhaps, so exclusively as heretofore. There are other topics, which, in our opinion, are intimately connected with the great doctrine of inalienable human rights; and which, while they conflict with no religious sect, or political party, as such, are pregnant with momentous consequences to the freedom, equality, and happiness of mankind. These we shall discuss as time and opportunity may permit.

The motto upon our banner has been, from the commencement of our moral warfare, "OUR COUNTRY IS THE WORLD—OUR COUNTRYMEN ARE ALL MANKIND." We trust that it will be our only epitaph. Another motto we have chosen is, UNIVERSAL EMANCIPATION. Up to this time we have limited its application to those who are held in this country, by Southern taskmasters, as marketable commodities, goods and chattels, and implements of husbandry. Henceforth we shall use it in its widest latitude: the emancipation of our whole race from the dominion of man, from the thralldom of self, from the government of brute force, from the bondage of sin—and bringing them under the dominion of God, the control of an inward spirit, the government of the law of love, and into the obedience and liberty of Christ, who is *the same,* yesterday, TODAY, and forever."

It has never been our design, in conducting the

Liberator, to require of the friends of emancipation any political or sectarian shibboleth [specific creed]; though, in consequence of the general corruption of all political parties and religious sects, and of the obstacles which they have thrown into the path of emancipation, we have been necessitated to reprove them all. Nor have we any intention—at least, not while ours professes to be an anti-slavery publication, distinctively and eminently—to assail or give the preference to any sect or party. We are bound by no denominational trammels; we are not political partisans; we have taken upon our lips no human creed: we are guided by no human authority; we cannot consent to wear the livery of any fallible body. The abolition of American slavery we hold to be COMMON GROUND, upon which men of all creeds, complexions and parties, if they have true humanity in their hearts, may meet on amicable and equal terms to effect a common object. But whoever marches on to that ground, loving his creed, or sect, or party, or any worldly interest, or personal reputation or property, or friends, or wife, or children, or life itself, more than the cause of bleeding humanity,—or expecting to promote his political designs, or to enforce his sectarian dogmas, or to drive others from the ranks on account of their modes of faith,—will assuredly prove himself to be unworthy of his abolition profession, and his real character will be made manifest to all, for severe and unerring tests will be applied frequently: it will not be possible for him to make those sacrifices, or to endure those trials, which unbending integrity to the cause will require. For ourselves, we care not who is found upon this broad platform of our common nature: if he will join hands with us, in good faith, to undo the heavy burdens and break the yokes of our enslaved countrymen, we shall not stop to inquire whether he is a Trinitarian or Unitarian, Baptist or Methodist, Catholic or Covenanter, Presbyterian or Quaker, Swedenborgian or Perfectionist. However widely we may differ in our views on other subjects, we shall not refuse to labor with him against slavery, in the same phalanx, if he refuse not to labor with us. Certainly no man can truly affirm that we have sought to bring any other religious or political tests into this philanthropic enterprise than these:—"Thou shalt love thy neighbor as thyself" "Whatsoever ye would that men should do to you, do ye even so to them"— "Remember those in bonds as bound with them."

Next to the overthrow of slavery, the cause of PEACE will command our attention. The doctrine of non-resistance as commonly received and practiced by Friends, or Quakers, and certain members of other religious denominations, we conceive to be utterly indefensible in its application to national wars: not that it "goes too far," but that it does not go far enough. If a nation may not redress its wrongs by physical force, if it may not repel or punish a foreign enemy who comes to plunder, enslave or murder its inhabitants then it may not resort to arms to quell an insurrection, or send to prison or suspend upon a gibbet any transgressors upon its soil. If the slaves of the South have not an undoubted right to resist their masters in the last resort, then no man, or body of men, may appeal to the law of violence in self-defense—for none have ever suffered, or can suffer, more than they. If, when men are robbed of their earnings, their liberties, their personal ownership, their wives and children, they may not resist, in no case can physical resistance be allowable, either in an individual or collective capacity.

Now the doctrine we shall endeavor to inculcate is, that the kingdoms of this world are to become the kingdoms of our Lord and of his Christ; consequently, that they are all to be supplanted, whether they are called despotic, monarchical, or republican, and lie only who is King of kings, and Lord of lords, is to rule in righteousness. The kingdom of God is to be established IN ALL THE EARTH, and it shall never be destroyed, but it shall "BREAK IN PIECES AND CONSUME ALL OTHERS": its elements are righteousness and peace, and joy in the Holy Ghost; without are dogs, and sorcerers, and whoremongers, and murderers, and idolaters, and whatsoever loveth and maketh a lie. Its government is one of love, not of military coercion or physical restraint: its laws are not written upon parchment, but upon the hearts of its subjects—they are not conceived in the wisdom of man, but framed by the Spirit of God: its weapons are not carnal, but spiritual. Its soldiers are clad in the whole armor of God, having their loins girt, about with truth, and having on the breastplate of righteousness; their feet are shod with the preparation of the gospel of peace; with the shield of faith they are able to quench all the fiery darts of the wicked, and they wear the helmet of salvation, and wield the sword of the spirit, which is the word of God. Hence, when smitten on the one cheek, they turn the other also; being defamed, they entreat; being deviled, they bless; being persecuted, they suffer it; they take joyfully the spoiling of their goods; they rejoice, inasmuch as they are partakers of Christ's sufferings; they are sheep in the midst of wolves; in no Extremity whatever, even if their enemies are determined to nail them to the cross with Jesus, and if they, like him, could summon legions of angels to their rescue, will they resort to the law of violence.

As to the governments of this world, whatever their titles or forms, we shall endeavor to prove that, in their essential elements, and as at present administered, they are all Anti-Christ; that they can never, by human wisdom, be brought into conformity to the will of God; that they cannot be maintained except by naval and military power; that all their penal enactments, being a dead letter without an army to carry them into effect, are virtually written in human blood; and that the followers of Jesus should instinctively shun their stations of honor, power, and emolument—at the same time "submitting to every ordinance of man, for the Lord's sake," and offering no physical resistance to any of their mandates, however unjust or tyrannical. The language of Jesus is, "My kingdom is not of this world, else would my servants fight." Calling his disciples to him, he said to them, "Ye know that they which are accustomed to rule over the Gentiles, exercise lordship Over them; and their great ones exercise authority upon them. *But so it* SHALL NOT *be* among You; but whosoever will be great among you, shall be your minister; and whosoever of you will be the chiefest, shall be servant of all. For even the Son of man came not to be ministered unto, but to minister, and to give his life a ransom for many."

Human governments are to be viewed as judicial punishments. If a people turn the grace of God into lasciviousness, or make their liberty, an occasion for anarchy, or if they refuse to belong to the "one fold and one Shepherd,"—they shall be scourged by governments of their own choosing, and burdened with taxation, and subjected to physical control, and torn by factions, and made to eat the fruit of their evil doings, until they are prepared to receive the liberty and the rest which remain, on earth as well as in heaven, for THE PEOPLE OF GOD. This is in strict accordance with the arrangement of Divine Providence.

So long as men contemn the perfect government of the Most High, persons, just so long will they desire to usurp authority over each other—just so long will they pertinaciously cling to human governments, *fashioned in the likeness and* administered *in the spirit of their own disobedience.* Now, if the prayer of our Lord be not a mockery; if the Kingdom of God is to come universally, and his will to be alone ON EARTH AS IT IS IN HEAVEN; and if, in that kingdom, no carnal weapon can be wielded, and swords are beaten into ploughshares, and spears into pruning-hooks, and there is none to molest or make afraid, and no statute-book but the Bible, and no judge but Christ; then why are not Christians obligated to come out NOW, and be separate from "the kingdoms of this world," which are all based upon THE PRINCIPLE OF VIO-

LENCE, and which require their officers and servants to govern and be governed by that principle? . . .

These are among the views we shall offer in connection with the heaven-originated cause of PEACE—views which any person is at liberty to controvert in our columns, and for which no man or body of men is responsible but ourselves. If any man shall affirm that the anti-slavery cause, as such, or any anti-slavery society, is answerable for our sentiments on this subject, to him may be justly applied the apostolic declaration, "the truth is not in him." We regret, indeed, that the principles of abolitionists seem to be quite unsettled upon a question of such vast importance, and so vitally connected with the bloodless overthrow of slavery. It is time for all our friends to know where they stand. If those whose yokes they are endeavoring to break by the fire and hammer of God's word, would not, in their opinion, be justified in appealing to physical force, how can they justify others of a different complexion in doing the same thing? And if they conscientiously believe that the slaves would be guiltless in shedding the blood of their merciless oppressors, let them say so unequivocally—for there is no neutral ground in this matter, and the time is near when they will be compelled to take sides.

As our object is universal emancipation—to redeem woman as well as man from a servile to an equal condition—we shall go for the RIGHTS OF WOMAN to their utmost extent.

The Liberator, December 15, 1837.

PRO-SLAVERY MOB ATTACKS ABOLITIONIST MEETING AT PENNSYLVANIA HALL (1838)

Text of Angelina Grimké Weld's Speech at Pennsylvania Hall

Men, brethren and fathers—mothers, daughters and sisters, what came ye out for to see? A reed shaken with the wind? Is it curiosity merely, or a deep sympathy with the perishing slave, that has brought this large audience together? [A yell from the mob without the building.] Those voices without ought to awaken and call out our warmest sympathies. Deluded beings! "they know not what they do." They know not that they are undermining their own rights and their own happiness, temporal and eternal. Do you ask, "what has the North to do with slavery?" Hear it—hear it. Those voices without tell us that the spirit of slavery is *here,* and has been roused to wrath by our abolition speeches and conventions: for surely liberty would not foam and tear herself with rage, because her friends are multiplied daily, and meetings are held in quick succession to set forth her virtues and extend her peaceful kingdom. This opposition shows that slavery has done its deadliest work in the hearts of our citizens. Do you ask, then, "what has the North to do?" I answer, cast out first the spirit of slavery from your own hearts, and then lend your aid to convert the South. Each one present has a work to do, be his or her situation what it may, however limited their means, or insignificant their supposed influence. The great men of this country will not do this work; the church will never do it. A desire to please the world, to keep the favor of all parties and of all conditions, makes them dumb on this and every other unpopular subject. They have become worldly-wise, and therefore God, in his wisdom, employs them not to carry on his plans of reformation and salvation. He hath chosen the foolish things of the world to confound the wise, and the weak to overcome the mighty.

As a Southerner I feel that it is my duty to stand up here to-night and bear testimony against slavery. I have seen it—I have seen it. I know it has horrors that can never be described. I was brought up under its wing: I witnessed for many years its demoralizing influences, and its destructiveness to human happiness. It is admitted by some that the slave is not happy under the *worst* forms of slavery. But I have *never* seen a happy slave. I have seen him dance in his chains, it is true; but he was not happy. There is a wide difference between happiness and mirth. Man cannot enjoy the former while his manhood is destroyed, and that part of the being which is necessary to the making, and to the enjoyment of happiness, is completely blotted out. The slaves, however, may be, and sometimes are, mirthful. When hope is extinguished, they say, "let us eat and drink, for to-morrow we die." [Just then stones were thrown at the windows,—a great noise without, and commotion within.] What is a mob? What would the breaking of every window be? What would the levelling of this Hall be? Any evidence that we are wrong, or that slavery is a good and wholesome institution? What if the mob should now burst in upon us, break up our meeting and commit violence upon our persons—would this be any thing compared with what the slaves endure? No, no: and we do not remember them "as bound with them," if we shrink in the time of peril, or feel unwilling to sacrifice ourselves, if need be, for their sake. [Great noise.] I thank the Lord that there is yet life left enough to feel the truth, even though it rages at it—that conscience is not so completely seared as to be unmoved by the truth of the living God.

Many persons go to the South for a season, and are hospitably entertained in the parlor and at the table of the slave-holder. They never enter the huts of the slaves; they know nothing of the dark side of the picture, and they return home with praises on their lips of the generous character of those with whom they had tarried. Or if they have witnessed the cruelties of slavery, by remaining silent spectators they have naturally become callous—an insensibility has ensued which prepares them to apologize even for barbarity. Nothing but the corrupting influence of slavery on the hearts of the Northern people can induce them to apologize for it; and much will have been done for the destruction of Southern slavery when we have so reformed the North that no one here will be willing to risk his reputation by advocating or even excusing the holding of men as property. The South know it, and acknowledge that as fast as our principles prevail, the hold of the master must be relaxed. [Another outbreak of mobocratic spirit, and some confusion in the house.]

How wonderfully constituted is the human mind! How it resists, as long as it can, all efforts made to reclaim from error! I feel that all this disturbance is but an evidence that our efforts are the best that could have been adopted, or else the friends of slavery would not care for what we say and do. The South know what we do. I am thankful that they are reached by our efforts. Many times have I wept in the land of my birth, over the system of slavery. I knew of none who sympathized in my feelings—I was unaware that any efforts were made to deliver the oppressed—no voice in the wilderness was heard calling on the people to repent and do works meet for repentance—and my heart sickened within me. Oh, how should I have rejoiced to know that such efforts as these were being made. I only wonder that I had such feelings. I wonder when I reflect under what influence I was brought up that my heart is not harder than the nether millstone. But in the midst of temptation I was preserved, and my sympathy grew warmer, and my hatred of slavery more inveterate, until at last I have exiled myself from my native land because I could no longer endure to hear the wailing of the slave. I fled to the land of Penn; for here, thought I, sympathy for the slave will surely be found. But I found it not. The people were kind and hospitable, but the slave had no place in their thoughts. Whenever questions were put to me as to his condition, I felt that they were dictated by an idle curiosity, rather than by that deep feeling which would lead to effort for his rescue. I therefore shut up my grief in my own heart. I remembered that I was a Carolinian, from a state which framed this iniquity by law. I knew that throughout her territory was continual suffering, on the one part, and continual brutality and sin on the other. Every Southern breeze wafted to me the discordant tones of weeping and wailing, shrieks and groans, mingled with prayers and blasphemous curses. I thought there was no hope; that the wicked would go on in his wickedness, until he had destroyed both himself and his country. My heart sunk within me at the abominations in the midst of which I had been born and educated. What will it avail, cried I in bitterness of spirit, to expose to the gaze of strangers the horrors and pollutions of slavery, when there is no ear to hear nor heart to feel and pray for the slave. The language of my soul was, "Oh tell it not in Gath, publish it not in the streets of Askelon." But how different do I feel now! Animated with hope, nay, with an assurance of the triumph of liberty and good will to man, I will lift up my voice like a trumpet, and show this people their transgression, their sins of omission towards the slave, and what they can do towards affecting Southern mind, and overthrowing Southern oppression.

We may talk of occupying neutral ground, but on this subject, in its present attitude, there is no such thing as neutral ground. He that is not for us is against us, and he that gathereth not with us, scattereth abroad. If you are on what you suppose to be neutral ground, the South look upon you as on the side of the oppressor. And is there one who loves his country willing to give his influence, even indirectly, in favor of slavery—that curse of nations ? God swept Egypt with the besom of destruction, and punished Judea also with a sore punishment, because of slavery. And have we any reason to believe that he is less just now?—or that he will be more favorable to us than to his own "peculiar people?" [Shoutings, stones thrown against the windows, &c.]

There is nothing to be feared from those who would stop our mouths, but they themselves should fear and tremble. The current is even now setting fast against them. If the arm of the North had not caused the Bastille of slavery to totter to its foundation, you would not hear those cries. A few years ago, and the South felt secure, and with a contemptuous sneer asked, "Who are the abolitionists? The abolitionists are nothing?"—Ay, in one sense they were nothing, and they are nothing still. But in this we rejoice, that "God has chosen things that are not to bring to nought things that are." [Mob again disturbed the meeting.]

We often hear the question asked, "What shall we do?" Here is an opportunity for doing something now. Every man and every woman present may do something by showing that we fear not a mob, and, in the midst of threatenings and revilings, by opening our mouths for the dumb and pleading the cause of those who are ready to perish.

To work as we should in this cause, we must know what Slavery is. Let me urge you then to buy the books which have been written on this subject and read them, and then lend them to your neighbors. Give your money no longer for things which pander to pride and lust, but aid in scattering "the living coals of truth" upon the naked heart of this nation,—in circulating appeals to the sympathies of Christians in behalf of the outraged and suffering slave. But, it is said by some, our "books and papers do not speak the truth." Why, then, do they not contradict what we say? They cannot. Moreover the South has entreated, nay commanded us to be silent; and what greater evidence of the truth of our publications could be desired?

Women of Philadelphia! allow me as a Southern woman, with much attachment to the land of my birth, to entreat you to come up to this work. Especially let me urge you to petition. *Men* may settle this and other questions at the ballot-box, but you have no such right; it is only through petitions that you can reach the Legislature. It is therefore peculiarly *your* duty to petition. Do you say, "It does no good?" The South already turns pale at the number sent. They have read the reports of the proceedings of Congress, and there have seen that among other petitions were very many from the women of the North on the subject of slavery. This fact has called the attention of the South to the subject. How could we expect to have done more as yet? Men who hold the rod over slaves, rule in the councils of the nation: and they deny our right to petition and to remonstrate against abuses of our sex and of our kind. We have these rights, however, from our God. Only let us exercise them: and though often turned away unanswered, let us remember the influence of importunity upon the unjust judge, and act accordingly. The fact that the South look with jealousy upon our measures shows that they are effectual. There is, therefore, no cause for doubting or despair, but rather for rejoicing.

It was remarked in England that women did much to abolish Slavery in her colonies. Nor are they now idle. Numerous petitions from them have recently been presented to the Queen, to abolish the apprenticeship with its cruelties nearly equal to those of the system whose place it supplies. One petition two miles and a quarter long has been presented. And do you think these labors will be in vain? Let the history of the past answer. When the women of these States send up to Congress such a petition, our legislators will arise as did those of England, and say, "When all the maids and matrons of the land are knocking at our doors we must legislate." Let the zeal and love, the faith and works of our English sisters quicken ours—that while the slaves continue to suffer, and when they shout deliverance, we may feel the satisfaction of *having done what we could.*

Webb, Samuel. 1838. *History of Pennsylvania Hall Which was Destroyed by a Mob on the 17th of May, 1838.* Philadelphia: Merrihew and Gunn.

THE PLIGHT OF THE *AMISTAD* CAPTIVES (1839)

As much interest and curiosity exist in the community, respecting the Africans now confined at New Haven, we take pleasure in laying before our readers the following letter from a gentleman who was appointed to visit them, and make report of their situation.

To the committee on behalf of the African prisoners at New Haven. Gentlemen—Having been deputed to visit the company of African captives now in confinement at New Haven, I hasten to lay before you a few particulars respecting their situation. I found them occupying four or five apartments, under the care of the U.S. marshal, N. Wilcox, Esq. and his assistant, Mr. Pendleton. They seem to be made as comfortable as is consistent with their situation, excepting that they need opportunities for exercise in the open air.

This, I hope, will be secured as soon as the marshal returns from New London, where he has gone to take an inventory of the slaver and its contents. A faithful and accomplished physician, Charles Hooker, M. D., of New Haven, is devoting to all the professional attention they need. Five or six of them are in the hospital apartment, and some of the rest are slightly affected with bowel complaints. They have all been decently clothed in cotton shirts and trowsers by the care of the marshal, and will have flannel provided as soon as the physician shall direct. Care is also taken as to their food.

They were not as destitute of clothing when taken near our shore, as has been represented in the papers, but had clothing, probably found on board the slaver, which they did not wear in consequence of the intolerable heat when confined in the hold of the slaver. Great curiosity is felt to see these victims of the slave-trade, the first that have been known in Connecticut for a great many years.

Multitudes visit the prison, the keeper charging each one a New York shilling, the avails of which, after a just compensation for his trouble, he purposes to expend for the benefit of the prisoners, or for some other charitable object. Objections have been made to this course, but I found some of the most intelligent and humane of the citizens satisfied that the sympathy produced by it is rather favorable than otherwise to the prisoners, and also useful in raising their spirits, &c.

Joseph Cinquez, the leader, is in the cell with other prisoners; his countenance bears a resemblance to the prints that are hawked about our streets. He is less cheerful than many of the others. They all appear to be persons of quiet minds and a mild and cheerful temper; there are no contentions among them; even the poor children, three girls and one boy, who are in a room by themselves, seem to be uniformly kind and friendly.

I took along with me an old African man, who said he could speak the Congo language, in hopes thereby of attaining the means of communication with them, as the newspapers said they speak the Congo; but they all say the are not Congoes. Many of them say Manding, whence it is supposed they are Mandingoes, though it is not unlikely there are persons of several tribes among them.

Unremitted efforts will be made to obtain the means of communication with these unfortunate persons, who have been committed to prison and bound over to be tried for their lives, without an opportunity to say a word for themselves, and without a word communicated to them explanatory of their situation.

They are detained by the marshal on two processes; one the commitment for trial on a charge of murder; and the other the claim upon them as property by the Spaniards who pretend to be their owners, and by the American captors who have lobbied for salvage.

It is believed there are a number of Africans in this city, or various tribes, some of whom will be able to communicate with them.

Very respectfully,

JOSHUA LEAVITT 143 Nassau street, Friday evening, September 6th.

P. S. it is expected that some of those native Africans will go to New Haven this evening with a member of the committee.

New York Commercial Advertiser, August 28–September 25, 1839.

EXCESSIVE PUNISHMENT
OF SLAVES (1839)

Testimony of Mr. William Poe.

Mr. Poe is a native of Richmond, Virginia, and was formerly a slaveholder. He was for several years a merchant in Richmond, and subsequently in Lynchburg, Virginia. A few years since, he emancipated his slaves, and removed to Hamilton County, Ohio, near Cincinnati, where he is a highly respected ruling elder in the Presbyterian church. He says,—

"I am pained exceedingly, and nothing but my duty to God, to the oppressors, and to the poor down-trodden slaves, who go mourning all their days, could move me to say a word. I will state to you a *few* cases of the abuse of the slaves, but time would fail, if I had language to tell how many and great are the inflictions of slavery even in its mildest form."

Benjamin James Harris, a wealthy tobacconist of Richmond, Virginia, whipped a slave girl fifteen years old to death. While he was whipping her, his wife heated a smoothing iron, put it on her body in various places, and burned her severely. The verdict of the coroner's inquest was, "Died of excessive whipping." He was tried in Richmond, and acquitted. I attended the trial. Some years after, this same Harris whipped another slave to death. The man had not done so much work as was required of him. After a number of protracted and violent scourgings, with short intervals between, the slave died under the lash. Harris was tried, and again acquitted, because none but blacks saw it done. The same man afterwards whipped another slave severely, for not doing work to please him. After repeated and severe floggings in quick succession, for the same cause, the slave, in despair of pleasing him, cut off his own hand. Harris soon after became a bankrupt, went to New Orleans to recruit his finances, failed, removed to Kentucky, became a maniac, and died.

A captain in the United States' Navy, who married a daughter of the collector of the port of Richmond, and resided there, became offended with his negro boy, took him into the meat house, put him upon a stool, crossed his hands before him, tied a rope to them, threw it over a joist in the building, drew the boy up so that he could just stand on the stool with his toes, and kept him in that position, flogging him severely at intervals, until the boy became so exhausted that he reeled off the stool, and swung by his hands until he died. The master was tried and acquitted.

In Goochland County, Virginia, an overseer tied a slave to a tree, flogged him again and again with great severity, then piled brush around him, set it on fire, and burned him to death. The overseer was tried and imprisoned. The whole transaction may be found on the records of the court.

In traveling, one day, from Petersburg to Richmond, Virginia, I heard cries of distress at a distance, on the road. I rode up, and found two white men, beating a slave. One of them had hold of a rope, which was passed under the bottom of a fence; the other end was fastened around the neck of the slave, who was thrown flat on the ground, on his face, with his back bared. The other was beating him furiously with a large hickory.

A slaveholder in Henrico County, Virginia, had a slave who used frequently to work for my father. One morning he came into the field with his back completely *cut up,* and mangled from his head to his heels. The man was so stiff and sore he could scarcely walk. This same person got offended with another of his slaves, knocked him down, and struck out one of his eyes with a maul. The eyes of several of his slaves were injured by similar violence.

In Richmond, Virginia, a company occupied as a dwelling a large warehouse. They got angry with a negro lad, one of their slaves, took him into the cellar, tied his hands with a rope, bored a hole through the floor, and passed the rope up through it. Some of the family drew up the boy, while others whipped. This they continued until the boy died. The warehouse was owned by a Mr. Whitlock, on the site of one formerly owned by a Mr. Philpot.

Joseph Chilton, a resident of Campbell County, Virginia, purchased a quart of tanners' oil, for the purpose, as he said, of putting it on one of his negro's heads, that he had sometime previous pitched or tarred over, for running away.

In the town of Lynchburg, Virginia, there was a negro man put in prison, charged with having pillaged some packages of goods, which he, as head man of a boat, received at Richmond, to be delivered at Lynchburg. The goods belonged to A. B. Nichols, of Liberty, Bedford County, Virginia. He came to Lynchburg, and desired the jailor to permit him to whip the negro, to make him confess, as there was *no proof against him.* Mr. Williams, (I think that is his name,) a pious Methodist man, a great stickler for law and good order, professedly a great friend to the black man, delivered the negro into the hands of Nichols. Nichols told me that he took the slave, tied his wrists together, then drew his arms down so far below his knees as to permit a staff to pass above the arms under the knees, thereby placing the slave in a situation that he could not move hand or foot. He then commenced his bloody work, and continued, at intervals, until 500 blows were inflicted. I received this statement from Nichols himself, who was, by the way, a *son of the land of "steady habits,"* where there are many like him, if we may judge from their writings, sayings, and doings."

Weld, Theodore Dwight. 1839. *American Slavery as It Is: Testimony of a Thousand Witnesses.* New York: American Anti-Slavery Society.

SLAVES EXECUTED FOR KILLING OVERSEER (1841)

Fruits of Slavery.

From the Opelousas (La.) Gazette. EXECUTION. On Monday last, three slaves belonging to Mrs. Preston of this place, were executed for the murder of John Moore. The circumstances of the murder are these. Mr. Moore, being the overseer of Mrs. Preston, discovered some whiskey in the cabins of the slaves, and threatened to punish them for it the next day (Monday). It seems, however, that three or four of the negroes had previously resolved upon the death of Moore, and in order to avoid the threatened punishment, fixed upon that as a fit occasion to accomplish their hellish designs. Three of them, Zachariah, Jeffrey, and William, (Mrs. P's carriage driver and a confidential servant,) went to the house of Mr. Moore; Jeffrey went in and began to beg off from the promised punishment, while Zachariah pretended to be making a fire, (it being nearly day light,) and William stood at the door. Moore having refused to forgive them their offence, Jeffrey leaped upon him, and began choking him, calling to the others to assist, both of whom did so, holding him while Jeffrey held him by the throat. After they had, as they thought, strangled their victim, they took him out of the house, when he again struggled violently, and Zachariah struck him with a billet of wood, fracturing the skull, causing instant death. After the murder, they saddled Moore's horse, and throwing him across the saddle, carried him about a mile into the woods, and left him near the road, with his coat off and one foot in the stirrup, in order to induce the belief that his horse had thrown him, and had caused his death by dragging, the girth being broken, and the horse standing not far off from his master. All the above facts were elicited on the trial, and were confessed by the criminals after they were convicted. Another negro belonging to the same lady, was put upon his trial for the same offence, and was acquitted, but it has been ascertained since, that he participated in the crime—his name is Morris—and we regret that he cannot be tried again and hanged.

The Liberator, February 5, 1841.

JOHN QUINCY ADAMS DEFENDS THE *AMISTAD* CAPTIVES (1841)

. . . I appear here on the behalf of thirty-six individuals, the life and liberty of every one of whom depend on the decision of this Court. . . . Three or four of them are female children, incapable, in the judgment of our laws, of the crime of murder or piracy, or, perhaps, of any other crime. Yet, from the day when the vessel was taken possession of by one of our naval officers, they have all been held as close prisoners, now for the period of eighteen long months. . . .

The Constitution of the United States recognizes the slaves, held within some of the States of the Union, only in their capacity of persons—persons held to labor or service in a State under the laws thereof—persons constituting elements of representation in the popular branch of the National Legislature persons, the migration or importation of whom should not be prohibited by Congress prior to the year 1808. The Constitution no where recognizes them as property. The words slave and slavery are studiously excluded from the Constitution. Circumlocutions are the figleaves under which the parts of the body politic are decently concealed. Slaves, therefore, in the Constitution of the United States are persons, enjoying rights and held to the performance of duties. . . .

The persons aforesaid, described as slaves, are Negroes and persons of color, who have been transported from Africa in violation of the laws of the United States. . . . The Court should enable the United States to send the Negroes home to Africa . . . in pursuance of the law of Congress passed March 3, 1829, entitled "An act in addition to the acts prohibiting the slave-trade." . . .

The President . . . signed [an] order for the delivery of MEN to the control of an officer of the navy to be carried beyond sea. . . . The District Judge, contrary to all [the] anticipations of the Executive, decided that the thirty-six Negroes . . . brought before the Court . . . were FREEMEN; that they had been kidnapped in Africa; that they did not own . . . Spanish names; . . . that they were not correctly described in the passport, but were new Negroes . . . fully entitled to their liberty.

Well was it for the country—well was it for the President of the United States himself that he paused before stepping over this Rubicon! . . . The indignation of the freemen of Connecticut, might not tamely endure the sight, of thirty-six free persons, though Africans, fettered and manacled in their land of freedom, to be transported beyond the seas, to perpetual hereditary servitude or to death, by the servile submission of an American President to the insolent dictation of a foreign minister. . . .

[President Van Buren informed his subordinates that] if the decree of the Judge should be in our favor, and you can steal a march upon the Negroes by foreclosing their right of appeal, ship them off without mercy and without delay: and if the decree should be in their favor, fail not to enter an instantaneous appeal to the Supreme Court where the chances may be more hostile to self-emancipated slaves.

Was ever such a scene of Lilliputian trickery enacted by the rulers of a great, magnanimous, and Christian nation? Contrast it with that act of self-emancipation, by which the savage, heathen barbarians Cinque and Grabeau liberated themselves and their fellow suffering countrymen from Spanish slave traders, and which the Secretary of State . . . denominates lawless violence. . . . Cinque and Graveau are uncooth and barbarous names. Call them Harmodius and Aristogiton, and go back for moral principle three thousand years to the fierce and glorious democracy of Athens. They too resorted to lawless violence, and slew the tyrant to redeem the freedom of their country. . . .

I said, when I began this plea, that my final reliance for success in this case was on this Court as a court of JUSTICE; and in the confidence this fact inspired, that, in the administration of justice, in a case of no less importance than the liberty and the life of a large number of persons, this Court would not decide but on a due consideration of all the rights, both natural and social, of everyone of these individuals. . . . I have avoided, purposely avoided . . . a recurrence to those first principles of liberty which might well have been invoked in the argument of this cause. I have shown that [the *Amistad*'s crew members] . . . were acting at the time in a way that is forbidden by the laws of Great Britain, of Spain and of the United States, and . . . that these Negroes were free and had a right to assert their liberty. . . .

On the of February, 1804, now more than thirty-seven years past, my name was entered, and yet stands recorded, on both the rolls, as one of the Attorneys and Counsellors of this Court. . . . I stand before the same Court, but not before the same judges—nor aided by the same associates—nor resisted by the same opponents. As I cast my eyes along those seats of honor and public trust, now occupied by you, they

seek in vain for one of those honored and honorable persons whose indulgence listened then to my voice. Marshall—Cushing—Chase—Washington—Johnson—Livingston—Todd—Where are they? . . . Gone! Gone! All gone! . . . In taking, then, my final leave of this Bar, and of this Honorable Court, I can only ejaculate a fervent petition to Heaven, that every member of it may go to his final account with as little of earthly frailty to answer for as those illustrious dead. . . .

Adams, John Quincy. 1841. *Argument of John Quincy Adams, before the Supreme Court of the United States, in the Case of the United States, Appellants, vs. Cinque, and Others, Africans, Captured in the Schooner Amistad. Delivered on February 24, and March 1, 1841.* New York: S. W. Benedict.

RUMORS OF REVOLT (1841)

From the N. O. Bulletin.

INTENDED REVOLT OF SLAVES. —Intelligence was received yesterday by the packet steamer Clipper from Bayou Sara, of a systematized plan on the part of the negroes to rise up and murder the whites. The news, greatly exaggerated in its repetition, has created quite a sensation in town. The plain truth is certainly sufficient to occasion serious apprehensions. The particulars that we have received are these:

The overseer of the plantation of Robt. J. Barrow, of West Feliciana, having occasion to rise from his bed late, in one of the recent hot nights, heard what he believed to be negroes conversing on one of the quarters. On silently approaching the vicinity, and listening, he overheard two of the slaves discussing the subject of a rising against the whites. This led to the examination the next morning of the two fellows, when they confessed the fact, and gave information that led to the arrest of several others. The alarm was immediately spread abroad, arrests were made in various plantations, and it was found by the confessions that they all agreed in the main facts, that there was to be a general rise, and that the 1st of August was the day agreed upon.

A white man, a carpenter, who had lately done a lot of work for Mr. Barrow, was also arrested on suspicion, and examined. He said he had nothing to do with the plot—that he had never said any thing to the negroes on the subject, but acknowledged that they frequently spoke to him, and informed him all about it.

This white man, with about 40 negroes, all of whom had confessed their knowledge of the intended rising, were in jail at St. Francisville, guarded by a company of volunteers. Their examination by a competent tribunal, was to have commenced yesterday at 10 a.m.

At Woodville, we learn numerous slaves were confined in the jail, having confessed to the same facts as those arrested in Feliciana.

Capt. Laurent states that on stopping at Point Coupee, to communicate information of the situation of the affairs above, several gentlemen recollected occurrences of recent date which tended to confirm the suspicion that the slaves of their section were parties to the wicked plot. Doct.—— said he had been asked what day of the month it was, by more negroes, within the last ten days, than in seven years before—and there had been unusual assemblies of the slaves, in rather by-places, for several Sundays past.

Some of the negroes have confessed that the combination was from Bayou Sara to Natchez.

It may not be amiss to remark, that the plantations in Feliciana and Wilkinson county, from which the slaves were taken who are imprisoned, are owned by the most wealthy and respectable planters of the State, whose kind and humane treatment of their slaves is proverbial.

The Liberator, August 6, 1841.

ADVERTISEMENTS FOR FUGITIVE SLAVES (1841)

Life in New Orleans.

$100 Reward. Ran away from the subscriber, on the 10th inst., a negro man, who calls himself MOSES, but will no doubt give himself some other name. Said negro is about 28 years old, of a light black complexion, about 5 feet 5 inches in height, well made; has some of his fore teeth out, both upper and under; has had a small slit in each ear, made with a knife, about three-fourths of an inch from the lower tip; though healed up, it may be discovered on examination; speaks affably, is quite intelligent, and can read well. He is an old hand at running away.

$25 Reward. Ran away from the subscriber, on the 24th ult., the girl MARY, alias JANE. She is of a griffe color, about 19 years old, full face and large lips, and has the mark of a whip under one of her eyes, and on the back of her neck. The above reward will be paid to any person who will return her to the subscriber.

G. VANDREUL, 213, Poydras St.

$10 Reward. Ran away from the subscriber, on the

14th inst., a negro man, named ROBERT, but passes frequently under the assumed name of Sam; age 35 years or thereabouts; is five feet 6 or 8 inches in height; thin visage, having been lately sick; of dark complexion, having a dark expression of countenance, with a scar on his left cheek, inclining towards his mouth. He had on when he left, a pair of jans blue pants, a white linen dress coat, and linen shoes with broad plaits.

The above reward will be given for the apprehension of the same Bob or Sam, by application to H. F. Wade, 56 Tchoupitoulas. It is supposed he will endeavor to leave the city; and the captains of vessels are hereby forewarned not to carry him off, under the penalty of the law.

H. F. WADE.

$5 Reward. Lost, about two weeks ago, a large, black bull dog, with a wound in the right eye, had on a leather collar, with a rope attached to it. The above reward will be given to whoever will return him to

E. STONE, cor. New Levee and
Lafayette sts.

Ran away or stolen, the slave CAROLINE, from my residence in Carrolton, on the 7th inst. Said negress is about 14 years old, slim and delicate made, under lip quite thick, and mark of a burn on one of her arms. I warn all steamboats to be on the lookout, for I believe she will be trying to go up the river. I will pay a reward of $20 for her delivery in jail in this city, or delivered to me in Carrolton.

G. B. MASON.

Scars—burns—whip marks—teeth knocked out—slit ears!!—behold the march of humanity! The foregoing are copied from the New Orleans Picayune and the Bulletin. —Philanthropist. *The Liberator*, September 3, 1841.

SOLOMON NORTHUP DESCRIBES A SLAVE AUCTION (1841)

In the first place we were required to wash thoroughly, and those with beards to shave. We were then furnished with a new suit each, cheap, but clean. The men had hat, coat, shirt, pants and shoes; the women frocks of calico, and handkerchief to bind about their heads. We were now conducted into a large room in the front part of the building to which the yard was attached, in order to be properly trained, before the admission of customers. The men were arranged on one side of the room, the women at the other. The tallest was placed at the head of the row, then the next tallest, and so on in the order of their respective heights. Emily was at the foot of the line of women. Freeman [Theophilus Freeman, owner of the slave-pen.] charged us to remember our places; exhorted us to appear smart and lively—sometimes threatening, and again, holding out various inducements. During the day he exercised us in the art of "looking smart," and of moving to our places with exact precision.

After being fed, in the afternoon, we were again paraded and made to dance. Bob, a colored boy, who had some time belonged to Freeman, played on the violin. Standing near him, I made bold to inquire if he could play the "Virginia Reel." He answered he could not, and asked me if I could play. Replying in the affirmative, he handed me the violin. I struck up a tune, and finished it. Freeman ordered me to continue playing, and seemed well pleased, telling Bob that I far excelled him—a remark that seemed to grieve my musical companion very much.

Next day many customers called to examine Freeman's "new lot." The latter gentleman was very loquacious, dwelling at much length upon our several good points and qualities. He would make us hold up our heads, walk briskly back and forth, while customers would feel of our hands and arms and bodies, turn us about, ask us what we could do, make us open our mouths and show our teeth, precisely as a jockey examines a horse which he is about to barter for or purchase. Sometimes a man or woman was taken back to the small house in the yard, stripped, and inspected more minutely. Scars upon a slave's back were considered evidence of a rebellious or unruly spirit, and hurt his sale.

An old gentleman, who said he wanted a coachman, appeared to take a fancy to me. From his conversation with Burch [Freeman's business associate], I learned be was a resident in the city. I very much desired that he would buy me, because I conceived it would not be difficult to make my escape from New Orleans on some northern vessel. Freeman asked him fifteen hundred dollars for me. The old gentleman insisted it was too much as times were very hard. Freeman, however, declared that I was sound of health, of a good constitution, and intelligent. He made it a point to enlarge upon my musical attainments. The old gentleman argued quite adroitly that there was nothing extraordinary about the Negro, and finally, to my regret, went out, saying he would call again. During the day, however, a number of sales were made. David and Caroline were purchased together by a Natchez

planter. They left us, grinning broadly, and in a most happy state of mind, caused by the fact of their not being separated. Sethe was sold to a planter of Baton Rouge, her eyes flashing with anger as she was led away.

The same man also purchased Randall. The little fellow was made to jump, and run across the floor, and perform many other feats, exhibiting his activity and condition. All the time the trade was going on, Eliza was crying aloud, and wringing her hands. She besought the man not to buy him, unless he also bought herself and Emily. She promised, in that case, to be the most faithful slave that ever lived. The man answered that he could not afford it, and then Eliza burst into a paroxysm of grief, weeping plaintively. Freeman turned round to her, savagely, with his whip in his uplifted hand, ordering her to stop her noise, or he would flog her. He would not have such work—such snivelling; and unless she ceased that minute, he would take her to the yard and give her a hundred lashes. Yes, he would take the nonsense out of her pretty quick—if he didn't, might he be d—d. Eliza shrunk before him, and tried to wipe away her tears, but it was all in vain. She wanted to be with her children, she said, the little time she had to live. All the frowns and threats of Freeman, could not wholly silence the afflicted mother. She kept on begging and beseeching them, most piteously, not to separate the three. Over and over again she told them how she loved her boy. A great many times she repeated her former promises—how very faithful and obedient she would be; how hard she would labor day and night, to the last moment of her life, if he would only buy them all together. But it was of no avail; the man could not afford it. The bargain was agreed upon, and Randall must go alone. Then Eliza ran to him; embraced him passionately; kissed him again and again; told him to remember her—all the while her tears falling in the boy's face like rain.

Freeman damned her, calling her a blubbering, bawling wench, and ordered her to go to her place, and behave herself, and be somebody. He swore he wouldn't stand such stuff but a little longer. He would soon give her something to cry about, if she was not mighty careful, and that she might depend upon.

The planter from Baton Rouge, with his new purchase, was ready to depart.

"Don't cry, mama. I will be a good boy. Don't cry," said Randall, looking back, as they passed out of the door.

What has become of the lad, God knows. It was a mournful scene indeed. I would have cried myself if I had dared.

Northup, Solomon. 1975. *Twelve Years a Slave*. Sue Eakin and Joseph Logsdon, eds. Baton Rouge: Louisiana State University Press.

OBSERVATIONS ON THE EDUCATION OF SLAVES (1841)

So far from any provision being made for the education of the slaves, it is either entirely prohibited or universally discouraged. In some of the states the education of the slave is expressly forbidden by law, and any attempt made to educate them, whether by whites or black, is severely punished. In some of the less important slaveholding states, instruction in letters is not prohibited by law; but it is effectually prevented by public opinion. Such is the case in Kentucky.

The following are a few specimens of the laws which forbid the education of slaves. *Jay's Inquiry*—p. 136.

"A law of South Carolina passed in 1800, authorizes the infliction of twenty lashes on every slave found in an assembly convened for the purpose of 'mental instruction,' held in a confined or secret place, although in the presence of a white. Another law imposes a fine of £100 on any person who may teach a slave to write. An act of Virginia, of 1829, declares every meeting of slaves at any school by day or night, for instruction in reading or writing, an unlawful assembly; and any justice may inflict twenty lashes on each slave found in such school.

"In North Caroline, to teach a slave to read or write, or to sell or give him any book (bible not excepted) or pamphlet, is punished with thirty-nine lashes, or imprisonment if the offender be a free negro, but if a white, then with a fine of 200 dollars. The reason for this law assigned in its preamble is, that 'teaching slaves to read and write, tends to excite dissatisfaction in their minds, and to produce insurrection and rebellion.

"In Georgia, if a white teach a free negro or slave to read or write, he is fined 500 dollars, and imprisoned at the discretion of the court; if the offender be a colored man, bond or free, he is to be fined or whipped at the discretion of the court. Of course a father may be flogged for teaching his own child. This barbarous law was enacted in 1829.

"In Louisiana, the penalty for teaching slaves to read or write, is one year's imprisonment.

These are specimens of the efforts made by slave legislatures, to enslave the minds of their victims; and we have surely no reason to hope that their souls are regarded with more compassion."

The reason honestly assigned in the preamble to the North Carolina law, i.e., that "teaching slaves to read or write tends to excite dissatisfaction in their minds, and to produce insurrection and rebellion," is doubtless the ground of all these prohibitory enactments. The law of South Carolina in 1740 says, "The allowing of slaves to read would be attended with many inconveniences." In plain English, education is regarded as positively inconsistent with slavery, and its prohibition as indispensable to the continuance of the system.

But let us see what is the extent of instruction in those states which do not expressly interdict it by statute. We have specified Kentucky as an example of this nature, and she is perhaps the fairest specimen among all the slaveholding states. The following testimony is quoted from the address of the Kentucky Synod already referred to.

"Slavery dooms thousands of human beings to hopeless ignorance. Throughout our whole land, so far as we can learn, there is but one school in which, during the week, slaves can be taught. Here and there a family is found, where humanity and religion impel the master, mistress, or children, to the laborious task of private instruction. But after all, what is the utmost amount of instruction given to slaves? Those of the Word, that they may make corn and cotton, and buy and sell, and get gain, meet this cry at the bar of God? and what shall the hundreds of money-making and money-loving masters, who have grown rich by the toil and sweat of their slaves, and left their souls to perish, say when they go with them to the judgment of the great day?"

The following testimony with regard to the slaves in Alabama, is from a letter published in the Southern Religious Telegraph, and is dated June 20, 1836:

"'Yesterday afternoon, I attended divine service in this place. The afternoon sermon is always intended especially for the blacks. The number present yesterday was probably over 400. Rev. Mr. Houp informed me that preaching was not kept up regularly in any other Methodist church in Middle Alabama except Montgomery. I have myself visited all the Presbyterian churches belonging to Tuscaloosa and South Alabama Presbyteries, except Mobile and three others, and have found the blacks almost entirely neglected in all but two."

"The Rev. Mr. Converse, who was at one period an agent of the Colonization Society, and resided for some time in Virginia, states in a discourse before the Vermont Colonization Society, that 'almost nothing is done to instruct the slaves in the principles and duties of the Christian religion. The laws of the south strictly forbid their being taught to read; and they make no provision for their being orally instructed. Ministers sometimes preach to them under peculiar and severe restrictions of the law. But with all that has yet been done, the majority are emphatically heathens, and what is very strange, heathens in the midst of a land of sabbaths and of churches, of bibles and of Christians . . . Pious masters (with honorable exceptions) are criminally negligent of giving religious instruction to their slaves . . . They can and do instruct their own children, and perhaps their house servants; while those called 'field hands' live, and labor, and die, without being told by their pious masters (?) that Jesus Christ died to save sinners."

The following is the testimony of Dr. Nelson, late President of Marion College, Missouri, a Presbyterian Clergyman of high respectability, who was born and educated in Tennessee, and till forty years old, a slaveholder.

"'I have been asked concerning the religious instruction of slaves; and I feel safe in answering that in general it amounts to little or nothing. Hundreds and thousand never hear of a Saviour; and of those who are familiar with his name, few have any comprehension of its meaning. I remember one grey headed negro, with whom I tried to talk concerning his immortal soul. I pointed to the hills and told him God made them. He said he did not believe any body made the hills. I asked another slave about Jesus Christ. I found he had heard his name, but thought he was the son of the Governor of Kentucky."

To show how masters, even professedly religious ones, often discourage attention to the subject of religion among their slaves, we give the following extract from the "Report on the Condition of the People of Colour in the State of Ohio."

"Said a coloured woman to us the other day, 'When I was little I used to long to read. After prayers, master would often leave the bible and hymn book on the stand, and I would sometimes open them to see if the letters would not tell me something. When he came and catched me looking in them, he would always strike me and sometimes knock me down.'"

Executive Committee of the American Anti-Slavery Committee. 1841. *Slavery and the International Slave Trade in the United States of America,* London: Thomas Ward and Co.

PRIGG V. PENNSYLVANIA (1842)

We have not the slightest hesitation in holding that, under and in virtue of the Constitution, the owner of a slave is clothed with entire authority, in every State in the Union, to seize and recapture his slave, whenever he can do it without any breach of the peace or any illegal violence. . . .

It is scarcely conceivable that the slaveholding states would have been satisfied with leaving to the legislation of the non-slaveholding states, a power of regulation, in the absence of that of Congress, which would or might practically amount to a power to destroy the rights of the owner. If the argument, therefore, of a concurrent power in the states to act upon the subject-matter in the absence of legislation by Congress, be well founded; then, if Congress had never acted at all, or if the act of Congress should be repealed without providing a substitute, there would be a resulting authority in each of the states to regulate the whole subject at its pleasure; and to dole out its own remedial justice, or withhold it at its pleasure and according to its own views of policy and expediency. Surely such a state of things never could have been intended, under such a solemn guarantee of right and duty. On the other hand, construe the right of legislation as exclusive in Congress, and every evil, and every danger vanishes. The right and the duty are then co-extensive and uniform in remedy and operation throughout the whole Union. The owner has the same security, and the same remedial justice, and the same exemption from state regulation and control, through however many states he may pass with his fugitive slave in his possession, in transitu, to his own domicile. But, upon the other supposition, the moment he passes the state line, he becomes amenable to the laws of another sovereignty, whose regulations may greatly embarrass or delay the exercise of his rights, and even be repugnant to those of the state where he first arrested the fugitive. Consequences like these show that the nature and objects of the provision imperiously require, that, to make it effectual, it should be construed to be exclusive of state authority. We adopt the language of this Court in *Sturgis v. Crowninshield,* 4 Wheat. Rep. 193, and say, that "it has never been supposed that the concurrent power of legislation extended to every possible case in which its exercise by the states has not been expressly prohibited. The confusion of such a practice would be endless." And we know no case in which the confusion and public inconvenience and mischiefs thereof, could be more completely exemplified than the present.

These are some of the reasons, but by no means all, upon which we hold the power of legislation on this subject to be exclusive in Congress. To guard, however, against any possible misconstruction of our views, it is proper to state, that we are by no means to be understood in any manner whatsoever to doubt or to interfere with the police power belonging to the states in virtue of their general sovereignty. That police power extends over all subjects within the territorial limits of the states; and has never been conceded to the United States. It is wholly distinguishable from the right and duty secured by the provision now under consideration; which is exclusively derived from and secured by the Constitution of the United States, and owes its whole efficacy thereto. We entertain no doubt whatsoever, that the states, in virtue of their general police power, possess full jurisdiction to arrest and restrain runaway slaves, and remove them from their borders, and otherwise to secure themselves against their depredations and evil example, as they certainly may do in cases of idlers, vagabonds, and paupers. The rights of the owners of fugitive slaves are in no just sense interfered with, or regulated by such a course; and in many cases, the operations of this police power, although designed essentially for other purposes, for the protection, safety, and peace of the state, may essentially promote and aid the interests of the owners. But such regulations can never be permitted to interfere with or to obstruct the just rights of the owner to reclaim his slave, derived from the Constitution of the United States; or with the remedies prescribed by Congress to aid and enforce the same.

Upon these grounds, we are of opinion that the act of Pennsylvania upon which this indictment is founded, is unconstitutional and void. It purports to punish as a public offence against that state, the very act of seizing and removing a slave by his master, which the Constitution of the United States was designed to justify and uphold. The special verdict finds this fact, and the State Courts have rendered judgment against the plaintiff in error upon that verdict. That judgment must, therefore, be reversed, and the cause remanded to the Supreme Court of Pennsylvania; with directions to carry into effect the judgment of this Court rendered upon the special verdict in favour of the plaintiff in error.

26 Pet. 539 (1842).

AN ACCOUNT OF SLAVE SUICIDE (1843)

The following anecdote was related to us on last Monday by a gentleman recently from Georgia, now in this city: George, a slave, belonged to a family in the State of Georgia, near the Ochmulgee River whom he served faithfully. He was an excellent mechanic and during the life of his owners or claimants (for he never had an owner) they would take no money for him, and

in consequence of his faithfulness to them, at their death, George was willed a freeman!

Poor George then looked upon himself as one of the lords, even of the accursed soil of Georgia. But George was doomed to disappointment. The unjust heirs broke the will, seized his person, and thrust him into the dark caverns of slavery again! Bound for a new residence, they started down the Ochmulgee. George was on board the steamboat bound for his destination, but the vicious robbers of his liberty knew not where. George looked sad, and talked but little.

The steamer glided along, with a crowd of guests, unconscious of their weary fellow passenger. In the night a splash was heard which awakened the attention of boatmen, passengers; all looked with anxiety, but seeing all appeared to be safe, it was just a conclusion, that this must have been the noise occasioned by the falling in of the bank of the river. Morning came, the grindstone of the boat was missed, information was given, and search being made, George was gone, they knew not where.

The river was ordered to be scoured by the eager master, thirsting after the blood of the mechanic. It was scoured and George was found with the grindstone tied to his neck. Reposing in the depth of the Ochmulgee, preferring as a man, Death before slavery! George had tasted liberty!!!

The Liberator, October 20, 1843.

A FUGITIVE SLAVE CORRESPONDS WITH HIS FORMER MASTER (1844)

March 23, 1844, Detroit, Michigan.

Dear Sir:—I am happy to inform you that you are not mistaken in the man whom you sold as property, and received pay for as such. But I thank God that I am not property now, but am regarded as a man like yourself, and although I live far north, I am enjoying a comfortable living by my own industry. If you should ever chance to be traveling this way, and will call on me, I will use you better than you did me while you held me as a slave. Think not that I have any malice against you, for the cruel treatment which you inflicted on me while I was in your power. As it was the custom of your country, to treat your fellow men as you did me and my little family, I can freely forgive you.

I wish to be remembered in love to my aged mother, and friends; please tell her that if we should never meet again in this life, my prayer shall be to God that we may meet in Heaven, where parting shall be no more.

You wish to be remembered to King and Jack. I am pleased, sir, to inform you that they are both here, well, and doing well. They are both living in Canada West. They are now the owners of better farms than the men are who once owned them.

You may perhaps think hard of us for running away from slavery, but as to myself, I have but one apology to make for it, which is this: I have only to regret that I did not start at an earlier period. I might have been free long before I was. I think it is very probable that I should have been a toiling slave on your property to-day, if you had treated me differently.

To be compelled to stand by and see you whip and slash my wife without mercy, when I could afford her no protection, not even by offering myself to suffer the lash in her place, was more than I felt it to be the duty of a slave husband to endure, while the way was open to Canada. My infant child was also frequently flogged by Mrs. Gatewood, for crying, until its skin was bruised literally purple. This kind of treatment was what drove me from home and family, to seek a better home for them. But I am willing to forge the past. I should be pleased to hear from you again, on the reception of this and should also be very happy to correspond with you often, if it should be agreeable to yourself. I subscribe myself a friend to the oppressed, and Liberty forever.

HENRY BIBB.

Bibb, Henry. 1849. *Narrative of the Life and Adventures of Henry Bibb, an American Slave, Written by Himself.* New York: Author.

EDITORIAL SUPPORTING MANUMISSION (1844)

"Cassius M. Clay has announced his determination to emancipate all his slaves in the course of the present year. Mr. Clay is a very large slave-holder, and is said to be the richest man in Kentucky."

The right spirit in Kentucky. It seems by the above that C. M. Clay is about to liberate his slaves, we suppose he don't believe that negro slavery is sanctified by two hundred years legislation, neither does he believe that he ought to have black or white slaves, it is somewhat strange to us to see that these Clays differ so widely, there must be some difference in the Clay they are made of, we hope the mantle of C. M. C. will fall on H. Clay. We might also add, and that the mantle of Birney and Brisbane may fall on the Clay so to change the temper of this monster as to make it useful to those that wish to use it for emancipation. This Clay has been a slave-holder for forty years, certainly this

period is long enough to convince him of the great evil of holding human beings in slavery, we think that he has reaped the cost of these 60 slaves before this, if he has not in the length of time we have stated his being a slave-holder. In speaking of Slavery we don't intend to array ourselves against any particular party, Whig or Democrat, but intend as far as our abilities extend to dig at the root of the evil.

Palladium of Liberty, 1:9 (March 27, 1844).

MURDER IN OHIO (1844)

"Outrage and Death"

On Wednesday the 6th of March, a colored man was attacked on the east end of the lower bridge at Zanesville, by three unhung ruffians who beat him so that he died on the 16th. We ask, where is the hand of justice? Is this bareface murder to go unnoticed, and these prowling wolves to go unpunished? If so the very ground will cry out against it, and the voice will be justice, justice.

This man had one of his own color with him but what does this avail when we are deprived of justice in the courts of law and equity, therefore, the scape gallows and midnight assassin, can, and does attack us and take our lives, rob our houses, defile our wives and daughters, at the same time the law protects them by the color of the skin, and they under this very act, passed in 1807, shelter themselves, and say here is nothing but negroes, we can do just as we please. Lawmakers, look at this and give us our testimony that we may be able to protect ourselves when our lives are at stake.

Palladium of Liberty, 1:10 (April 3, 1844).

ANTI-ABOLITION RIOTING IN PHILADELPHIA (1844)

July 18, 1844.

"Pennsylvania Hall". This riotous and bloody city has just completed another terrible tragedy, which will probably beget another and another, till even ruffianism itself shall grow weary and sick of its dreadful deeds, and mobocracy be sated with human carnage.

The immediate cause of these frightful outbreaks is unquestionably to be attributed to the formation of the Native American Party—a party which should be discountenanced by every friend of human brotherhood, which is animated by a spirit hostile to our race, which is anti-republican and tyrannical in its purposes, which makes hatred of one particular class of our fellow countrymen an act of patriotism, and which occupies a position that, sooner or later, if it be not abandoned, will assuredly spread a civil war throughout the country, and lead to scenes of desolation and horror too awful even for the imagination to contemplate.

In the present instance, the blame is as usual, thrown upon the Irish population; and no doubt they are very much to blame. But, insulted, proscribed and denounced as they are by the party to which we have alluded, is it surprising that they have been goaded to deeds of madness, which, but for the provocation given to them, they never would have committed? However justly, therefore, they deserve to be censured, let the weight of censure rest the most heavily on the party which arrogantly styles itself the Native American party. There will be no safety, no repose, no end to mobocratic excesses, until that party every where be resolved into its original elements, and cease to wound the heart and vex the ear of the suffering humanity.

But the primary cause of these sanguinary conflicts finds its root in southern slavery, which fosters the spirit of caste, tramples all law and order under foot, and revels in human blood. It was in Louisiana, among slaveholders, that this native party originated. They were fearful that the warm appeals of Daniel O'Connell and Father Mathew to the Irish in this country, to join with the abolitionists for the overthrow of slavery, and vote for no candidate known to be a slaveholder or an apologist for slavery, would be heartily responded to by them; and therefore they contrived this scheme to exclude them from office and the ballot box. But the Irish have disregarded the noble entreaties of their countrymen at home, and instead of aiding the anti-slavery movement, have basely turned their backs upon it; and verily, they have their reward.

Philadelphia has endeavored (and most successfully) to surpass all other places in murderous opposition to the cause of negro emancipation. To propitiate southern slavemongers, and secure southern trade, she has treated abolitionists as outlaws, broken up their meetings by mobocratic assaults, burnt the dwellings and brutally maltreated the persons of many of her colored inhabitants, given Pennsylvania Hall to the consuming fire, &c. &c; and her reward has been, the loss of seventy million of dollars at the South, the blackning of her character with infamy throughout the civilized world, incendiary and bloody riots, and fiendish anarchy. Behold how awful, how just, and how swift has been the retribution of Heaven! Alleluia! For the Lord God omnipotent reigneth!! Truly, they who sow the wind, shall reap the whirlwind; and what shall be the end of these things!

Pennsylvania Freeman, 14:18 (July 1844)

A PLEA FOR TOLERANCE (1844)

"Prejudice"

This evil is as much with the people of color as almost any thing that exists. We see it every day, without turning to the right or the left. Every man and woman wants to be heard, or else nothing at all; for instance, if any project is got up, Mr. A. or B. wants to lead, in doing this they must of course get up an excitement for the purpose of carrying their point and instead of doing this manfully as they should, as good citizens, and as one that loves union and harmony with his fellow men, and to secure peace in the community. We go for perfect union among our people without which nothing can be done. We may labor, we may write, print, and do any thing pertaining to our welfare, and it will all be abortive. We at most give up the ship at times, when we see such a contrary spirit existing among our people. We take the liberty to name some of the several creeds, as they think they had better be out of the world, than out of the fashion.

Whig, democrat, abolitionist, pro-slavery conventionist, anti-conventionist, district school, anti-district school, lofer, anti-lofer, and so on we are afraid till time shall end. In making this enumeration we have some exceptions to this rule, we have as true hearts among us as any party, sect or denomination. All these misrule men cry out we don't want disunion and at the same time are the very ones that's guilty of sowing discord among men, and will say oh how I hate party strife, I would not have it for the world, even if we have an election for this that or the other, some one of these people loving men will commence this discord and continue it till they are met in public by a discided disapprobation. In this state society goes on among our colored people, to a greater or less extent, we say to such to cease this roubling or we cannot do any thing in the great cause of humanity, we say this because we know that there are other things of more importance, for us to engage in, we say to such with all good feeling that nothing can be done while this spirit exists amongst us as a people.

Palladium of Liberty, 1:28 (August 21, 1844).

A FORMER SLAVE DESCRIBES PUNISHMENT METHODS (1845)

There were four house-slaves in this family, including myself, and though we had not, in all respects, so hard work as the field hands, yet in many things our condition was much worse. We were constantly exposed to the whims and passions of every member of the family; from the least to the greatest their anger was wreaked upon us. Nor was our life an easy one, in the hours of our toil or in the amount of labor performed. We were always required to sit up until all the family had retired; then we must be up at early dawn in summer, and before day in winter. If we failed, through weariness or for any other reason, to appear at the first morning summons, we were sure to have our hearing quickened by a severe chastisement. Such horror has seized me, lest I might not hear the first shrill call, that I have often in dreams fancied I heard that unwelcome call, and have leaped from my couch and walked through the house and out of it before I awoke. I have gone and called the other slaves, in my sleep, and asked them if they did not hear master call. Never, while I live, will the remembrance of those long, bitter nights of fear pass from my mind.

But I want to give you a few specimens of the abuse which I received. During the ten years that I lived with Mrs. Banton, I do not think there were as many days, when she was at home, that I, or some other slave, did not receive some kind of beating or abuse at her hands. It seemed as though she could not live nor sleep unless some poor back was smarting, some head beating with pain, or some eye filled with tears, around her. Her tender mercies were indeed cruel. She brought up her children to imitate her example. Two of them manifested some dislike to the cruelties taught them by their mother, but they never stood high in favor with her; indeed, any thing like humanity or kindness to a slave, was looked upon by her as a great offence.

Her instruments of torture were ordinarily the raw hide, or a bunch of hickory-sprouts seasoned in the fire and tied together. But if these were not at hand, nothing came amiss. She could relish a beating with a chair, the broom, tongs, shovel, shears, knife-handle, the heavy heel of her slipper; her zeal was so active in these barbarous inflictions, that her invention was wonderfully quick, and some way of inflicting the requisite torture was soon found out.

One instrument of torture is worthy of particular description. *This was an oak club, a foot and a half in length and an inch and a half square.* With this delicate weapon she would beat us upon the hands and upon the feet until they were blistered. This instrument was carefully preserved for a period of four years. Every day, for that time, I was compelled to see that hated tool of cruelty lying in the chair by my side. The least degree of delinquency either in not doing all the appointed work, or in look or behavior, was visited with a beating from this oak club. That club will always be a prominent object in the picture of horrors of my life of more than twenty years of bitter bondage.

When about nine years old I was sent in the evening to catch and kill a turkey. They were securely sleeping in a tree—their accustomed resting place for the night. I approached as cautiously as possible, selected the victim I was directed to catch, but just as I grasped him in my hand, my foot slipped and he made his escape from the tree and fled beyond my reach. I returned with a heavy heart to my mistress with the story of my misfortune. She was enraged beyond measure. She determined at once that I should have a whipping of the worst kind, and she was bent upon adding all the aggravations possible. Master had gone to bed drunk, and was now as fast asleep as drunkards ever are. At any rate he was filling the house with the noise of his snoring and with the perfume of his breath. I was ordered to go and call him—wake him up—and ask him to be *kind* enough to give me fifty good smart lashes. To be *whipped* is bad enough—to *ask* for it is worse—to ask a drunken man to whip you is too bad. I would sooner have gone to a nest of rattlesnakes, than to the bed of this drunkard. But go I must. Softly I crept along, and gently shaking his arm, said with a trembling voice, "Master, Master, Mistress wants you to wake up." This did not go the extent of her command, and in a great fury she called out—"What, you wont ask him to whip you, will you?" I then added "Mistress wants you to give me fifty lashes." A bear at the smell of a lamb, was never roused quicker. "Yes, yes, that I will; I'll give you such a whipping as you will never want again." And sure enough so he did. He sprang from the bed, seized me by the hair, lashed me with a handful of switches, threw me my whole length upon the floor, beat, kicked and cuffed me worse than he would a dog, and then threw me, with all his strength out of the door more dead than alive. There I lay for a long time scarcely able and not daring to move, till I could hear no sound of the furies within, and then crept to my couch, longing for death to put an end to my misery. I had no friend in the world to whom I could utter one word of complaint, or to whom I could look for protection.

Clarke, Lewis Garrard and Joseph C. Lovejoy. 1845. *Narrative of the Sufferings of Lewis Clarke During a Captivity of More than Twenty-Five Years, Among the Algerines of Kentucky, One of the So Called Christian States of North America.* Boston: D. H. Ela.

FREDERICK DOUGLASS DESCRIBES HIS LIFE IN SLAVERY (1845)

I had left Master Thomas's house, and went to live with Mr. Covey, on the 1st of January, 1833. I was now, for the first time in my life, a field hand. In my new employment, I found myself even more awkward than a country boy appeared to be in a large city. I had been at my new home but one week before Mr. Covey gave me a very severe whipping, cutting my back, causing the blood to run, and raising ridges on my flesh as large as my little finger. The details of this affair are as follows: Mr. Covey sent me, very early in the morning of one of our coldest days in the month of January, to the woods, to get a load of wood. He gave me a team of unbroken oxen. He told me which was the in-hand ox, and which the off-hand one. He then tied the end of a large rope around the horns of the in-hand ox, and gave me the other end of it, and told me, if the oxen started to run, that I must hold on upon the rope. I had never driven oxen before, and of course I was very awkward. I, however, succeeded in getting to the edge of the woods with little difficulty; but I had got a very few rods into the woods, when the oxen took fright, and started full tilt, carrying the cart against trees, and over stumps, in the most frightful manner. I expected every moment that my brains would be dashed out against the trees. After running thus for a considerable distance, they finally upset the cart, dashing it with great force against a tree, and threw themselves into a dense thicket. How I escaped death, I do not know. There I was, entirely alone, in a thick wood, in a place new to me. My cart was upset and shattered, my oxen were entangled among the young trees, and there was none to help me. After a long spell of effort, I succeeded in getting my cart righted, my oxen disentangled, and again yoked to the cart. I now proceeded with my team to the place where I had, the day before, been chopping wood, and loaded my cart pretty heavily, thinking in this way to tame my oxen. I then proceeded on my way home. I had now consumed one half of the day. I got out of the woods safely, and now felt out of danger. I stopped my oxen to open the woods gate; and just as I did so, before I could get hold of my oxrope, the oxen again started, rushed through the gate, catching it between the wheel and the body of the cart, tearing it to pieces, and coming within a few inches of crushing me against the gate-post. Thus twice, in one short day, I escaped death by the merest chance. On my return, I told Mr. Covey what had happened, and how it happened. He ordered me to return to the woods again immediately. I did so, and he followed on after me. Just as I got into the woods, he came up and told me to stop my cart, and that he would teach me how to trifle away my time, and break gates. He then went to a large gum-tree, and with his axe cut three large switches, and, after trimming them up neatly with his pocket-knife, he ordered me to take off my clothes. I made him no answer, but stood with my clothes on. He repeated his order. I still made him no answer, nor did I move to strip myself. Upon this he rushed at me with the fierceness of a tiger, tore off my clothes, and lashed me till he had worn out his switches, cutting me so savagely as to leave the marks visible for a long time after. This whipping was the first of a number just like it, and for similar offences.

I lived with Mr. Covey one year. During the first six months, of that year, scarce a week passed without his whipping me. I was seldom free from a sore back. My awkwardness was almost always his excuse for whipping me. We were worked fully up to the point of endurance. Long before day we were up, our horses fed, and by the first approach of day we were off to the field with our hoes and ploughing teams. Mr. Covey gave us enough to eat, but scarce time to eat it. We were often less than five minutes taking our meals. We were often in the field from the first approach of day till its last lingering ray had left us; and at saving-fodder time, midnight often caught us in the field binding blades.

Covey would be out with us. The way he used to stand it, was this. He would spend the most of his afternoons in bed. He would then come out fresh in the evening, ready to urge us on with his words, example, and frequently with the whip. Mr. Covey was one of the few slaveholders who could and did work with his hands. He was a hardworking man. He knew by himself just what a man or a boy could do. There was no deceiving him. His work went on in his absence almost as well as in his presence; and he had the faculty of making us feel that he was ever present with us. This he did by surprising us. He seldom approached the spot where we were at work openly, if he could do it secretly. He always aimed at taking us by surprise. Such was his cunning, that we used to call him, among ourselves, "the snake." When we were at work in the cornfield, he would sometimes crawl on his hands and knees to avoid detection, and all at once he would rise nearly in our midst, and scream out, "Ha, ha! Come, come! Dash on, dash on!" This being his mode of attack, it was never safe to stop a single minute. His comings were like a thief in the night. He appeared to us as being ever at hand. He was under every tree, behind every stump, in every bush, and at every window, on the plantation. He would sometimes mount his horse, as if bound to St. Michael's, a distance of seven miles, and in half an hour afterwards you would see him coiled up in the corner of the wood-fence, watching every motion of the slaves. He would, for this purpose, leave his horse tied up in the woods. Again, he would sometimes walk up to us, and give us orders as though he was upon the point of starting on a long journey, turn his back upon us, and make as though he was going to the house to get ready; and, before he would get half way thither, he would turn short and crawl into a fence-corner, or behind some tree, and there watch us till the going down of the sun.

Mr. Covey's FORTE consisted in his power to deceive. His life was devoted to planning and perpetrating the grossest deceptions. Every thing he possessed in the shape of learning or religion, he made conform to his disposition to deceive. He seemed to think himself equal to deceiving the Almighty. He would make a short prayer in the morning, and a long prayer at night; and, strange as it may seem, few men would at times appear more devotional than he. The exercises of his family devotions were always commenced with singing; and, as he was a very poor singer himself, the duty of raising the hymn generally came upon me. He would read his hymn, and nod at me to commence. I would at times do so; at others, I would not. My non-compliance would almost always produce much confusion. To show himself independent of me, he would start and stagger through with his hymn in the most discordant manner. In this state of mind, he prayed with more than ordinary spirit. Poor man! such was his disposition, and success at deceiving, I do verily believe that he sometimes deceived himself into the solemn belief, that he was a sincere worshipper of the most high God; and this, too, at a time when he may be said to have been guilty of compelling his woman slave to commit the sin of adultery. The facts in the case are these: Mr. Covey was a poor man; he was just commencing in life; he was only able to buy one slave; and, shocking as is the fact, he bought her, as he said, for A BREEDER. This woman was named Caroline. Mr. Covey bought her from Mr. Thomas Lowe, about six miles from St. Michael's. She was a large, able-bodied woman, about twenty years old. She had already given birth to one child, which proved her to be just what he wanted. After buying her, he hired a married man of Mr. Samuel Harrison, to live with him one year; and him he used to fasten up with her every night! The result was, that, at the end of the year, the miserable woman gave birth to twins. At this result Mr. Covey seemed to be highly pleased, both with the man and the wretched woman. Such was his joy, and that of his wife, that nothing they could do for Caroline during her confinement was too good, or too hard, to be done. The children were regarded as being quite an addition to his wealth.

If at any one time of my life more than another, I was made to drink the bitterest dregs of slavery, that time was during the first six months of my stay with Mr. Covey. We were worked in all weathers. It was never too hot or too cold; it could never rain, blow, hail, or snow, too hard for us to work in the field. Work, work, work, was scarcely more the order of the day than of the night. The longest days were too short for him, and the shortest nights too long for him. I was somewhat unmanageable when I first went there, but a few months of this discipline tamed me. Mr. Covey succeeded in breaking me. I was broken in body, soul, and spirit. My natural elasticity was crushed, my intellect languished, the disposition to read departed, the cheerful spark that lingered about my eye died; the dark night of slavery closed in upon me; and behold a man transformed into a brute!

Sunday was my only leisure time. I spent this in a sort of beast-like stupor, between sleep and wake, under some large tree. At times I would rise up, a flash of energetic freedom would dart through my soul, accompanied with a faint beam of hope, that flickered for a moment, and then vanished. I sank down again, mourning over my wretched condition. I was sometimes prompted to take my life, and that of Covey, but was prevented by a combination of hope and fear. My sufferings on this plantation seem now like a dream rather than a stern reality.

Our house stood within a few rods of the Chesapeake Bay, whose broad bosom was ever white with sails from every quarter of the habitable globe. Those beautiful vessels, robed in purest white, so delightful to the eye of freemen, were to me so many shrouded ghosts, to terrify and torment me with thoughts of my wretched condition. I have often, in the deep stillness of a summer's Sabbath, stood all alone upon the lofty banks of that noble bay, and traced, with saddened heart and tearful eye, the countless number of sails moving off to the mighty ocean. The sight of these always affected me powerfully. My thoughts would compel utterance; and there, with no audience but the Almighty, I would pour out my soul's complaint, in my rude way, with an apostrophe to the moving multitude of ships:—

"You are loosed from your moorings, and are free; I am fast in my chains, and am a slave! You move merrily before the gentle gale, and I sadly before the bloody whip! You are freedom's swift-winged angels, that fly round the world; I am confined in bands of iron! O that I were free! O, that I were on one of your gallant decks, and under your protecting wing! Alas! betwixt me and you, the turbid waters roll. Go on, go on. O that I could also go! Could I but swim! If I could fly! O, why was I born a man, of whom to make a brute! The glad ship is gone; she hides in the dim distance. I am left in the hottest hell of unending slavery. O God, save me! God, deliver me! Let me be free! Is there any God? Why am I a slave? I will run away. I will not stand it. Get caught, or get clear, I'll try it. I had as well die with ague as the fever. I have only one life to lose. I had as well be killed running as die standing. Only think of it; one hundred miles straight north, and I am free! Try it? Yes! God helping me, I will. It cannot be that I shall live and die a slave. I will take to the water. This very bay shall yet bear me into freedom. The steamboats steered in a northeast course from North Point. I will do the same; and when I get to the head of the bay, I will turn my canoe adrift, and walk straight through Delaware into Pennsylvania. When I get there, I shall not be required to have a pass; I can travel without being disturbed. Let but the first opportunity offer, and, come what will, I am off. Meanwhile, I will try to bear up under the yoke. I am not the only slave in the world. Why should I fret? I can bear as much as any of them. Besides, I am but a boy, and all boys are bound to some one. It may be that my misery in slavery will only increase my happiness when I get free. There is a better day coming. "

Douglass, Frederick and William Lloyd Garrison. 1845. *Narrative of the Life of Frederick Douglass, an American Slave*. Boston: Anti-Slavery Office.

THE NORTH STAR EDITORIAL (1847)

We are now about to assume the management of the editorial department of a newspaper, devoted to the cause of Liberty, Humanity and Progress. The position is one which, with the purest motives, we have long desired to occupy. It has long been our anxious wish to see, in this slave-holding, slave-trading, and Negro-hating land, a printing-press and paper, permanently established, under the complete control and direction of the immediate victims of slavery and oppression.

Animated by this intense desire, we have pursued our object, till on the threshold of obtaining it. Our press and printing materials are bought, and paid for. Our office secured, and is well situated, in the centre of business, in this enterprising city. Our office Agent,

an industrious and amiable young man, thoroughly devoted to the interests of humanity, has already entered upon his duties. Printers well recommended have offered their services, and are ready to work as soon as we are prepared for the regular publication of our paper. Kind friends are rallying round us, with words and deeds of encouragement. Subscribers are steadily, if not rapidly coming in, and some of the best minds in the country are generously offering to lend us the powerful aid of their pens. The sincere wish of our heart, so long and so devoutly cherished seems now upon the eve of complete realization.

It is scarcely necessary for us to say that our desire to occupy our present position at the head of an Anti-slavery Journal, has resulted from no unworthy distrust or ungrateful want of appreciation of the zeal, integrity, or ability of the noble band of white laborers, in this department of our cause; but, from a sincere and settled conviction that such a Journal, if conducted with only moderate skill and ability, would do a most important and indispensable work, which it would be wholly impossible for our white friends to do for us.

It is neither a reflection on the fidelity, nor a disparagement of the ability of our friends and fellow-laborers, to assert what "common sense affirms and only folly denies," that the man who has *suffered the wrong* is the man to *demand redress,*—that the man STRUCK is the man to CRY OUT—and that he who has *endured the cruel pangs of Slavery* is the man to *advocate Liberty.* It is evident we must be our own representatives and advocates, not exclusively, but peculiarly—not distinct from, but in connection with our white friends. In the grand struggle for liberty and equality now waging, it is meet, right and essential that there should arise in our ranks authors and editors, as well as orators, for it is in these capacities that the most permanent good can be rendered to our cause.

Hitherto the immediate victims of slavery and prejudice, owing to various causes, have had little share in this department of effort: they have frequently undertaken, and almost as frequently failed. This latter fact has often been urged by our friends against our engaging in the present enterprise; but, so far from convincing us of the impolicy of our course, it serves to confirm us in the necessity, if not the wisdom of our undertaking. That others have failed, is a reason for OUR earnestly endeavoring to succeed. Our race must be vindicated from the embarrassing imputations resulting from former non-success. We believe that what *ought* to be done, *can* be done. We say this, in no self-confident or boastful spirit, but with a full sense of our weakness and unworthiness, relying upon the Most High for wisdom and strength to support us in our righteous undertaking. We are not wholly unaware of the duties, hardships and responsibilities of our position. We have easily imagined some, and friends have not hesitated to inform us of others. Many doubtless are yet to be revealed by that infallible teacher, experience. A view of them solemnize, but do not appal us. We have counted the cost. Our mind is made up, and we are resolved to go forward.

In aspiring to our present position, the aid of circumstances has been so strikingly apparent as to almost stamp our humble aspirations with the solemn sanctions of a Divine Providence. Nine years ago, as most of our readers are aware, we were held as a slave, shrouded in the midnight ignorance of that infernal system—sunken in the depths of senility and degradation—registered with four footed beasts and creeping things—regarded as property—compelled to toil without wages—with a heart swollen with bitter anguish—and a spirit crushed and broken. By a singular combination of circumstances we finally succeeded in escaping from the grasp of the man who claimed us as his property, and succeeded in safely reaching New Bedford, Mass. In this town we worked three years as a daily laborer on the wharves. Six years ago we became a Lecturer on Slavery. Under the apprehension of being re-taken into bondage, two years ago we embarked for England. During our stay in that country, kind friends, anxious for our safety, ransomed us from slavery, by the payment of a large sum. The same friends, as unexpectedly as generously, placed in our hands the necessary means of purchasing a printing press and printing materials. Finding ourself now in a favorable position for aiming an important blow at slavery and prejudice, we feel urged on in our enterprise by a sense of duty to God and man, firmly believing that our effort will be crowned with entire success.

The North Star, December 3, 1847.

ABRAHAM LINCOLN'S "SPOT RESOLUTIONS" (1847)

Presented to the United States House of Representatives, on December 22, 1847.

Whereas the President of the United States, in his message of May 11, 1846, has declared that "the Mexican Government not only refused to receive him, [the envoy of the United States,] or listen to his propositions, but, after a long-continued series of menaces, has at last invaded *our territory* and shed the blood of our fellow-citizens on our *own soil.*"

And again, in his message of December 8, 1846, that "we had ample cause of war against Mexico long before the breaking out of hostilities; but even then we forbore to take redress into our own hands until Mexico herself became the aggressor, by invading *our soil* in hostile array, and shedding the blood of our citizens:"

And yet again, in his message of December 7, 1847, that "the Mexican Government refused even to hear the terms of adjustment which he [our minister of peace] was authorized to propose, and finally, under wholly unjustifiable pretexts, involved the two countries in war, by invading the territory of the State of Texas, striking the first blow, and shedding the blood of our citizens on *our own soil.*"

And whereas this House is desirous to obtain a full knowledge of all the facts which go to establish whether the particular spot on which the blood of our citizens was so shed was or was not at that time *our own soil:* Therefore,

Resolved By the House of Representatives, That the President of the United States be respectfully requested to inform this House—

1st. Whether the spot on which the blood of our citizens was shed, as in his messages declared, was or was not within the territory of Spain, at least after the treaty of 1819, until the Mexican revolution.

2d. Whether that spot is or is not within the territory which was wrested from Spain by the revolutionary Government of Mexico.

3d. Whether that spot is or is not within a settlement of people, which settlement has existed ever since long before the Texas revolution, and until its inhabitants fled before the approach of the United States army.

4th. Whether that settlement is or is not isolated from any and all other settlements by the Gulf and the Rio Grande on the south and west, and by wide uninhabited regions on the north and east.

5th. Whether the people of that settlement, or a majority of them, or any of them, have ever submitted themselves to the government or laws of Texas or the United States, by consent or compulsion, either by accepting office, or voting at elections, or paying tax, or serving on juries, or having process served upon them, or in any other way.

6th. Whether the people of that settlement did or did not flee from the approach of the United States army, leaving unprotected their homes and their growing crops, *before* the blood was shed, as in the messages stated; and whether the first blood, so shed, was or was not shed within the enclosure of one of the people who had thus fled from it.

7th. Whether our *citizens,* whose blood was shed, as in his message declared, were or were not, at that time, armed officers and soldiers, sent into that settlement by the military order of the President, through the Secretary of War.

8th. Whether the military force of the United States was or was not sent into that settlement after General Taylor had more than once intimated to the War Department that, in his opinion, no such movement was necessary to the defence or protection of Texas.

Journal of the House of Representatives of the United States, 1847–1848. December 22, 1847.

JONES V. VAN ZANDT (1847)

MR. JUSTICE WOODBURY delivered the opinion of the court.

This case comes here on a division of opinion in the Circuit Court of Ohio.   The subject matter of the original suit was debt for a penalty of $500, under the act of Congress of February 12th, 1793, for concealing and harbouring a fugitive slave belonging to the plaintiff. . . .

It remains to consider the fifth and sixth divisions of opinion under this head. They are, whether the act of Congress, under which the action is brought, is repugnant either to the constitution, or the ordinance "for the government of the territory northwest of the river Ohio."

This court has already, after much deliberation, decided that the act of February 12th, 1793, was not repugnant to the constitution. The reasons for their opinion are fully explained by Justice Story in *Prigg v. Pennsylvania,* 16 Pet. 611.

In coming to that conclusion they were fortified by the idea, that the constitution itself, in the clause before cited, flung its shield, for security, over such property as is in controversy in the present case, and the right to pursue and reclaim it within the limits of another State.

This was only carrying out, in our confederate form of government, the clear right of every man at common law to make fresh suit and recapture of his own property within the realm. . . .

But the power by national law to pursue and regain most kinds of property, in the limits of a foreign government, is rather an act of comity than strict right; and hence, as the property in persons might not thus be recognized in some of the States in the Union, and

its reclamation not be allowed through either courtesy or right, this clause was undoubtedly introduced into the constitution, as one of its compromises, for the safety of that portion of the Union which did permit such poverty, and which otherwise might often be deprived of it entirely by its merely crossing the line of an adjoining State. 3 Madison Papers, 1569, 1589.

This was thought to be too harsh a doctrine in respect to any title to property—of a friendly neighbour, not brought nor placed in another State, under its laws, by the owner himself, but escaping there against his consent, and often forthwith pursued in order to be reclaimed.

The act of Congress, passed only four years after the constitution was adopted, was therefore designed merely to render effective the guaranty of the constitution itself; and a course of decisions since, in the courts of the States and general government, has for half a century exhibited great uniformity in favor of the validity as well as expediency of the act. . . .

That this act of Congress, then, is not repugnant to the constitution, must be considered as among the settled adjudications of this court.

The last question on which a division is certified relates to the ordinance of 1787, and the supposed repugnancy to it of the act of Congress of 1793.

The ordinance prohibited the existence of slavery in the territory northwest of the river Ohio among only its own people. Similar prohibitions have from time to time been introduced into many of the old States. But this circumstance does not affect the domestic institution of slavery, as other States may choose to allow it among their people, nor impair their rights of property under it, when their slaves happen to escape to other States. These other States, whether northwest of the river Ohio, or on the eastern side of the Alleghanies, if out of the Union, would not be bound to surrender fugitives, even for crimes, it being, as before remarked, an act of comity, or imperfect obligation. *Holmes v. Jennison et al.,* 14 Pet. 540 . . .

But in relation to inhabitants of other States, if they escape into the limits of States within the ordinance, and if the constitution allow them, when fugitives from labor, to be reclaimed, this does not interfere with their own laws as to their own people, nor do acts of Congress interfere with them, which are rightfully passed to carry these constitutional rights into effect there, as fully as in other portions of the Union.

Before concluding, it may be expected by the defendant that some notice should be taken of the argument, urging on us a disregard of the constitution and the act of Congress in respect to this subject, on account of the supposed inexpediency and invalidity of all laws recognizing slavery or any right of property in man. But that is a political question, settled by each State for itself; and the federal power over it is limited and regulated by the people of the States in the constitution itself, as one of its sacred compromises, and which we possess no authority as a judicial body to modify or overrule.

Whatever may be the theoretical opinions of any as to the expediency of some of those compromises, or of the right of property in persons which they recognize, this court has no alternative, while they exist, but to stand by the constitution and laws with fidelity to their duties and their oaths. Their path is a strait and narrow one, to go where that constitution and the laws lead, and not to break both by traveling without or beyond them. . . .

5 How. 215 (1847).

"THE RUNAWAY SLAVE AT PILGRIM'S POINT" (1848)

By Elizabeth Barrett Browning

I.

I STAND on the mark beside the shore
Of the first white pilgrim's bended knee,
Where exile turned to ancestor,
And God was thanked for liberty.
I have run through the night, my skin is as dark,
I bend my knee down on this mark . . .
I look on the sky and the sea.

II.

O pilgrim-souls, I speak to you!
I see you come out proud and slow
From the land of the spirits pale as dew . . .
And round me and round me ye go!
O pilgrims, I have gasped and run
All night long from the whips of one
Who in your names works sin and woe.

III.

And thus I thought that I would come
And kneel here where I knelt before,
And feel your souls around me hum
In undertone to the ocean's roar;
And lift my black face, my black hand,
Here, in your names, to curse this land
Ye blessed in freedom's evermore.

IV.

I am black, I am black;

And yet God made me, they say.
But if He did so, smiling back
He must have cast His work away
Under the feet of His white creatures,
With a look of scorn,—that the dusky features
Might be trodden again to clay.

V.

And yet He has made dark things
To be glad and merry as light.
There's a little dark bird sits and sings;
There's a dark stream ripples out of sight;
And the dark frogs chant in the safe morass,
And the sweetest stars are made to pass
O'er the face of the darkest night.

VI.

But we who are dark, we are dark!
Ah, God, we have no stars!
About our souls in care and cark
Our blackness shuts like prison bars:
The poor souls crouch so far behind,
That never a comfort can they find
By reaching through the prison-bars.

VII.

Indeed, we live beneath the sky, . . .
That great smooth Hand of God, stretched out
On all His children fatherly,
To bless them from the fear and doubt,
Which would be, if, from this low place,
All opened straight up to His face
Into the grand eternity.

VIII.

And still God's sunshine and His frost,
They make us hot, they make us cold,
As if we were not black and lost:
And the beasts and birds, in wood and fold,
Do fear and take us for very men!
Could the weep-poor-will or the cat of the glen
Look into my eyes and be bold?

IX.

I am black, I am black!—
But, once, I laughed in girlish glee;
For one of my colour stood in the track
Where the drivers drove, and looked at me—
And tender and full was the look he gave:
Could a slave look so at another slave?—
I look at the sky and the sea.

X.

And from that hour our spirits grew
As free as if unsold, unbought:
Oh, strong enough, since we were two
To conquer the world, we thought!
The drivers drove us day by day;
We did not mind, we went one way,
And no better a liberty sought.

XI.

In the sunny ground between the canes,
He said "I love you" as he passed:
When the shingle-roof rang sharp with the rains,
I heard how he vowed it fast:
While others shook, he smiled in the hut
As he carved me a bowl of the cocoa-nut,
Through the roar of the hurricanes.

XII.

I sang his name instead of a song;
Over and over I sang his name—
Upward and downward I drew it along
My various notes; the same, the same!
I sang it low, that the slave-girls near
Might never guess from aught they could hear,
It was only a name.

XIII.

I look on the sky and the sea—
We were two to love, and two to pray,—
Yes, two, O God, who cried to Thee,
Though nothing didst Thou say.
Coldly Thou sat'st behind the sun!
And now I cry who am but one,
How wilt Thou speak to-day?—

XIV.

We were black, we were black!
We had no claim to love and bliss:
What marvel, if each turned to lack?
They wrung my cold hands out of his,—
They dragged him . . . where ? . . . I crawled to
touch
His blood's mark in the dust! . . . not much,
Ye pilgrim-souls, . . . though plain as this!

XV.

Wrong, followed by a deeper wrong!
Mere grief's too good for such as I,
So the white men brought the shame ere long
To strangle the sob of my agony.
They would not leave me for my dull

Wet eyes!—it was too merciful
To let me weep pure tears and die.

XVI.

I am black, I am black!—
I wore a child upon my breast
An amulet that hung too slack,
And, in my unrest, could not rest:
Thus we went moaning, child and mother,
One to another, one to another,
Until all ended for the best:

XVII.

For hark ! I will tell you low . . . low . . .
I am black, you see,—
And the babe who lay on my bosom so,
Was far too white . . . too white for me;
As white as the ladies who scorned to pray
Beside me at church but yesterday;
Though my tears had washed a place for my knee.

XVIII.

My own, own child! I could not bear
To look in his face, it was so white.
I covered him up with a kerchief there;
I covered his face in close and tight:
And he moaned and struggled, as well might be,
For the white child wanted his liberty—
Ha, ha! he wanted his master right.

XIX.

He moaned and beat with his head and feet,
His little feet that never grew—
He struck them out, as it was meet,
Against my heart to break it through.
I might have sung and made him mild—
But I dared not sing to the white-faced child
The only song I knew.

XX.

I pulled the kerchief very close:
He could not see the sun, I swear,
More, then, alive, than now he does
From between the roots of the mango . . . where
. . . I know where. Close! a child and mother
Do wrong to look at one another,
When one is black and one is fair.

XXI.

Why, in that single glance I had
Of my child's face, . . . I tell you all,
I saw a look that made me mad . . .

The master's look, that used to fall
On my soul like his lash . . . or worse!
And so, to save it from my curse,
I twisted it round in my shawl.

XXII.

And he moaned and trembled from foot to head,
He shivered from head to foot;
Till, after a time, he lay instead
Too suddenly still and mute.
I felt, beside, a stiffening cold, . . .
I dared to lift up just a fold . . .
As in lifting a leaf of the mango-fruit.

XXIII.

But my fruit . . . ha, ha!—there, had been
(I laugh to think on't at this hour! . . .)
Your fine white angels, who have seen
Nearest the secret of God's power, . . .
And plucked my fruit to make them wine,
And sucked the soul of that child of mine,
As the humming-bird sucks the soul of the flower.

XXIV.

Ha, ha, for the trick of the angels white!
They freed the white child's spirit so.
I said not a word, but, day and night,
I carried the body to and fro;
And it lay on my heart like a stone . . . as chill.
—The sun may shine out as much as he will:
I am cold, though it happened a month ago.

XXV.

From the white man's house, and the black man's hut,
I carried the little body on,
The forest's arms did round us shut,
And silence through the trees did run:
They asked no question as I went,—
They stood too high for astonishment,—
They could see God sit on His throne.

XXVI.

My little body, kerchiefed fast,
I bore it on through the forest . . . on:
And when I felt it was tired at last,
I scooped a hole beneath the moon.
Through the forest-tops the angels far,
With a white sharp finger from every star,
Did point and mock at what was done.

XXVII.

Yet when it was all done aright, . . .

Earth, 'twixt me and my baby, strewed,
All, changed to black earth, . . . nothing white, . . .
A dark child in the dark,—ensued
Some comfort, and my heart grew young:
I sate down smiling there and sung
The song I learnt in my maidenhood.

XXVIII.

And thus we two were reconciled,
The white child and black mother, thus:
For, as I sang it, soft and wild
The same song, more melodious,
Rose from the grave whereon I sate!
It was the dead child singing that,
To join the souls of both of us.

XXIX.

I look on the sea and the sky!
Where the pilgrims' ships first anchored lay,
The free sun rideth gloriously;
But the pilgrim-ghosts have slid away
Through the earliest streaks of the morn.
My face is black, but it glares with a scorn
Which they dare not meet by day.

XXX.

Ah!—in their 'stead, their hunter sons!
Ah, ah! they are on me—they hunt in a ring—
Keep off! I brave you all at once—
I throw off your eyes like snakes that sting!
You have killed the black eagle at nest, I think:
Did you never stand still in your triumph, and shrink
From the stroke of her wounded wing?

XXXI.

(Man, drop that stone you dared to lift!—)
I wish you, who stand there five a-breast,
Each, for his own wife's joy and gift,
A little corpse as safely at rest
As mine in the mangos!—Yes, but she
May keep live babies on her knee,
And sing the song she liketh best.

XXXII.

I am not mad: I am black.
I see you staring in my face—
I know you, staring, shrinking back—
Ye are born of the Washington-race:
And this land is the free America:
And this mark on my wrist . . . (I prove what I say)
Ropes tied me up here to the flogging-place.

XXXIII.

You think I shrieked then? Not a sound!
I hung, as a gourd hangs in the sun.
I only cursed them all around,
As softly as I might have done
My very own child!—From these sands
Up to the mountains, lift your hands,
O slaves, and end what I begun!

XXXIV.

Whips, curses; these must answer those!
For in this UNION, you have set
Two kinds of men in adverse rows,
Each loathing each: and all forget
The seven wounds in Christ's body fair;
While HE sees gaping everywhere
Our countless wounds that pay no debt.

XXXV.

Our wounds are different. Your white men
Are, after all, not gods indeed,
Nor able to make Christs again
Do good with bleeding. We who bleed . . .
(Stand off!) we help not in our loss!
We are too heavy for our cross,
And fall and crush you and your seed.

XXXVI.

I fall, I swoon! I look at the sky:
The clouds are breaking on my brain;
I am floated along, as if I should die
Of liberty's exquisite pain—
In the name of the white child, waiting for me
In the death-dark where we may kiss and agree,
White men, I leave you all curse-free
In my broken heart's disdain!

The Liberty Bell, January 20, 1848.

CALHOUN'S EXPOSITION ON THE SOUTHERN ETHOS (1849)

*Excerpts from "The Southern Address"
by John C. Calhoun*

The conflict commenced not long after the acknowledgment of our independence, and has gradually increased until it has arrayed the great body of the North against the South on this most vital subject. In the progress of this conflict, aggression has followed aggression, and encroachment encroachment, until they have reached a point when a regard for your peace and safety will not permit us to remain longer silent. The object of this address is to give you a clear, correct, but brief account of the whole series of aggression and encroachments on your rights, with a statement of the dangers to which they expose you. Our object in making it is not to cause excitement, but to put you in full possession of all the facts and circumstances necessary to a full and just conception of a deep-seated disease, which threatens great danger to you and the whole body politic. We act on the impression, that in a popular government like ours, a true conception of the actual character and state of a disease is indispensable to effecting a cure.

Not to go further back, the difference of opinion and feeling in reference to the relation between the two races, disclosed itself in the Convention that framed the Constitution, and constituted one of the greatest difficulties in forming it. After many efforts, it was overcome by a compromise, which provided in the first place, that representative and direct taxes shall be apportioned among the States according to their respective numbers; and that, in ascertaining the number of each, five slaves shall be estimated as three. In the next, that slaves escaping into States where slavery does not exist, shall not be discharged from servitude, but shall be delivered up on claim of the party to whom their labor or service is due. In the third place, that Congress shall not prohibit the importation of slaves before the year 1808; but a tax not exceeding ten dollars may be imposed on each imported. And finally, that no capitation or direct tax shall be laid, but in proportion to federal numbers; and that no amendment of the Constitution, prior to 1808, shall affect this provision, nor that relating to the importation of slaves.

So satisfactory were these provisions, that the second, relating to the delivering up of fugitive slaves, was adopted unanimously, and all the rest, except the third, relative to the importation of slaves until 1808, with almost equal unanimity. They recognize the existence of slavery, and make a specific provision for its protection where it was supposed to be the most exposed. They go further, and incorporate it, as an important element, in determining the relative weight of the several States in the Government of the Union, and the respective burden they should bear in laying capitation and direct taxes. It was well understood at the time, that without them the Constitution would not have been adopted by the Southern States, and of course that they constituted elements so essential to the system that it never would have existed without them. The Northern States, knowing all this, ratified the Constitution, thereby pledging their faith, in the most solemn manner, sacredly to observe them. How that faith has been kept and that pledge redeemed we shall next proceed to show.

With few exceptions of no great importance, the South had no cause to complain prior to the year 1819—a year, it is to be feared, destined to mark a train of events, bringing with them many, and great, and fatal disasters, on the country and its institutions. With it commenced the agitating debate on the question of the admission of Missouri into the Union. We shall pass by for the present this question, and others of the same kind, directly growing out of it, and shall proceed to consider the effects of that spirit of discord, which it roused up between the two sections. It first disclosed itself in the North, by hostility to that portion of the Constitution which provides for the delivering up of fugitive slaves. In its progress it led to the adoption of hostile acts, intended to render it of non-effect, and with so much success that it may be regarded now as practically expunged from the Constitution. How this has been effected will be next explained.

After a careful examination, truth constrains us to say, that it has been by a clear and palpable evasion of the Constitution. It is impossible for any provision to be more free from ambiguity or doubt. It is in the following words: "No person held to service, or labor, in one State, under the laws thereof, escaping into another State, shall, in consequence of any law or regulation therein, be discharged from such service or labor, but shall be delivered up on claim of the party to whom such service or labor may be due." All is clear. There is not an uncertain or equivocal word to be found in the whole provision. What shall not be done, and what shall be done, are fully and explicitly set forth. The former provides that the fugitive slave shall not be discharged from his servitude by any law or regulation of the State wherein he is found; and the latter, that he shall be delivered up on claim of his owner.

We do not deem it necessary to undertake to refute the sophistry and subterfuges by which so plain a provision of the Constitution has been evaded, and, in effect, annulled. It constitutes an essential part of the constitutional compact, and of course the supreme law of the land. As such it is binding on all, the Federal and State Governments, the States and the individuals composing them. The sacred obligation of compact, and the solemn injunction of the supreme law, which legislators and judges, both Federal and State, are bound by oath to support, all unite to enforce its fulfilment, according to its plain meeting and true intent. What that meaning and intent are, there was no diversity of opinion in the better days of the Republic, prior to 1819. Congress, State Legislatures, State and Federal Judges and Magistrates, and people, all spontaneously placed the same interpretation on it. During that period none interposed impediments in the way of the owner seeking to recover his fugitive slave; nor did any deny his right to have every proper facility to enforce his claim to have him delivered up. It was then nearly as easy to recover one found in a Northern State, as one found in a neighboring Southern State. But this has passed away, and the provision is defunct, except perhaps in two States. [Indiana and Illinois.]

These are grave and solemn and admonitory words, from a high source. They confirm all for which the South has ever contended, as to the clearness, importance, and fundamental character of this provision, and the disastrous consequences which would inevitably follow from its violation. But in spite of these solemn warnings, the violation, then commenced, and which they were intended to rebuke, has been full and perfectly consummated. The citizens of the South, in their attempt to recover their slaves, now meet, instead of aid and co-operation, resistance in every form; resistance from hostile acts of legislation, intended to baffle and defeat their claims by all sorts of devices, and by interposing every description of impediment—resistance from judges and magistrates—and finally, when all these fail, from mobs, composed of whites and blacks, which, by threats or force, rescue the fugitive slave from the possession of his rightful owner. The attempt to recover a slave, in most of the Northern States, cannot now be made without the hazard of insult, heavy pecuniary loss, imprisonment, and even of life itself. Already has a worthy citizen of Maryland lost his life [Mr. Kennedy, of Hagerstown, Maryland.] in making an attempt to enforce his claim to a fugitive slave under this provision.

But a provision of the Constitution may be violated indirectly as well as directly; by doing an act in its nature inconsistent with that which is enjoined to be done. Of the form of violation, there is a striking instance connected with the provision under consideration. We allude to secret combinations which are believed to exist in many of the Northern States, whose object is to entice, decoy, entrap, inveigle, and seduce slaves to escape from their owners, and to pass them secretly and rapidly, by means organized for the purpose, into Canada, where they will be beyond the reach of the provision. That to entice a slave, by whatever artifice, to abscond from his owner, into a non-slaveholding State, with the intention to place him beyond the reach of the provision, or prevent his recovery, by concealment or otherwise, is as completely repugnant to it, as its open violation would be, is too clear to admit of doubt or to require illustration.

And yet, as repugnant as these combinations are to the true intent of the provision, it is believed, that, with the above exception, not one of the States, within whose limits they exist, has adopted any measure to suppress them, or to punish those by whose agency the object for which they were formed is carried into execution. On the contrary, they have looked on, and witnessed with indifference, if not with secret approbation, a great number of slaves enticed from their owners, and placed beyond the possibility of recovery, to the great annoyance and heavy pecuniary loss of the bordering Southern States.

There remains to be noticed another class of aggressive acts of a kindred character, but which instead of striking at an express and specific provision of the Constitution, aims directly at destroying the relation between the two races at the South, by means subversive in their tendency of one of the ends for which the Constitution was established. We refer to the systematic agitation of the question by the Abolitionists, which, commencing about 1835, is still continued in all possible forms. Their avowed intention is to bring about a state of things that will force emancipation on the South. To unite the North in fixed hostility to slavery in the South, and to excite discontent among the slaves with their condition, are among the means employed to effect it. With a view to bring about the former, every means are resorted to in order to render the South, and the relation between the two races there, odious and hateful to the North. For this purpose societies and newspapers are everywhere established, debating clubs opened, lecturers employed, pamphlets and other publications, pictures and petitions to Congress, resorted to, and directed to that single point, regardless of truth or decency; while the circulation of incendiary publications in the South, the agitation of the subject of abolition in Congress, and the employment of emissaries are relied on to excite discontent among the slaves. This agitation, and the use of these means, have been continued with more or less activity for a series of years, not without doing much towards effecting the object intended. We regard both object and means to be aggressive and dangerous to the rights of the South, and subversive, as stated, of one of the ends for which the Constitution was established. Slavery is a domestic institution. It belongs to the States, each for itself to decide, whether it shall be established or not; and if it be established, whether it should be abolished or not. Such being the clear and unquestionable right of the States, it follows necessarily that it would be a flagrant act of aggression on a State, destructive of its rights, and subversive of its independence, for the Federal Government, or one or more States, or their people, to undertake to force on it the emancipation of its slaves. But it is a sound maxim in politics, as well as law and morals, that no one has a right to do that indirectly what he cannot do directly, and it may be added with equal truth, to aid, abet, or countenance another in doing it. And yet the Abolitionists of the North, openly avowing their intention, and resorting to the most efficient means for the purpose, have been attempting to bring about a state of things to force the Southern States to emancipate their slaves, without any act on the part of any Northern State to arrest or suppress the means by which they propose to accomplish it. They have been permitted to pursue their object, and to use whatever means they please, if without aid or countenance, also without resistance or disapprobation. What gives a deeper shade to the whole affair, is the fact, that one of the means to effect their object, that of exciting discontent among our slaves, tends directly to subvert what its preamble declares to be one of the ends for which the Constitution was ordained and established: "to ensure domestic tranquillity," and that in the only way in which domestic tranquillity is likely ever to be disturbed in the South. Certain it is, that an agitation so systematic—having such an object in view, and sought to be carried into execution by such means—would, between independent nations, constitute just cause of remonstrance by the party against which the aggression was directed, and if not heeded, an appeal to arms for redress. Such being the case where an aggression of the kind takes place among independent nations, how much more aggravated must it be between confederated States, where the Union precludes an appeal to arms, while it affords a medium through which it can operate with vastly increased force and effect? That it would be perverted to such a use, never entered into the imagination of the generation which formed and adopted the Constitution, and, if it had been supposed it would, it is certain that the South never would have adopted it.

Calhoun, John C. 1851. *The Works of John C. Calhoun.* Richard K. Crallé, ed. Columbia, SC: A. S. Johnston.

HENRY BIBB DESCRIBES SLAVE SUPERSTITION AND CONJURING (1849)

There is much superstition among the slaves. Many of them believe in what they call "conjuration," tricking, and witchcraft; and some of them pretend to understand the art, and say that by it they can prevent their masters from exercising their will over their slaves. Such are often applied to by others, to give them power to prevent their masters from flogging them.

The remedy is most generally some kind of bitter root; they are directed to chew it and spit towards their masters when they are angry with their slaves. At other times they prepare certain kinds of powders, to sprinkle about their masters dwellings. This is all done for the purpose of defending themselves in some Peaceable manner, although I am satisfied that there is no virtue at all in it. I have tried it to perfection when I was a slave at the South. I was then a young man, full of life and vigor, and was very fond of visiting our neighbors slaves, but had no time to visit only Sundays, when I could get a permit to go, or after night, when I could slip off without being seen. If it was found out, the next morning I was called up to give an account of myself for going off without permission, and would very often get a flogging for it.

I got myself into a scrape at a certain times, by going off in this way, and I expected to be severely punished for it. I had a strong notion of running off, to escape being flogged, but was advised by a friend to go to one of those conjurers, who could prevent me from being flogged. I went and informed him of the difficulty. He said if I would pay him a small sum, he would prevent my being flogged. After I had paid him, he mixed up some alum, salt and other stuff into a powder, and said I must sprinkle it about my master, if he should offer to strike me; this would prevent him. He also gave me some kind of bitter root to chew, and spit towards him, which would certainly prevent my being flogged. According to order I used his remedy, and for some cause I was let pass without being flogged that time.

I had then great faith in conjuration and witchcraft, I was led to believe that I could do almost as, I pleased, without being flogged. So on the next Sabbath my conjuration was fully tested by my going off, and staying away until Monday morning, without permission. When I returned home, my master declared that he would punish me for going off; but I did not believe that he could do it, while I had this root and dust; and as he approached me, I commenced talking saucy to him. But he soon convinced me that there was no virtue in them. He soon became so enraged at me for saucing him, that he grasped a handful of switches and punished me severely, in spite of all my roots and powders.

But there was another old slave in that neighborhood, who professed to understand all about conjuration, and I thought I would try his skill. He told me that the first one was only a quack, and if I would only pay him a certain amount in cash, that he would tell me how to prevent any person from striking me. After I had paid him his charge, he told me to go to the cow-pen after night, and get some fresh cow manure, and mix it with red pepper and white people's hair, all to be put into a pot over the fire, and scorched until it could be ground into snuff. I was then to sprinkle it about my master's bedroom, in his hat and boots, and it would prevent him from ever abusing me in any way. After I got it all ready prepared, the smallest pinch of it scattered over a room, was enough to make a horse sneeze from the strength of it; but it did no good. I tried it to my satisfaction. It was my business to make fires in my master's chamber, night and morning. Whenever I could get a chance, I sprinkled a Little of this dust about the linen of the bed, where they would breathe it on retiring. This was to act upon them as what is called a kind of love powder, to change their sentiments of anger, to those of love, towards me, but this all proved to be vain imagination. The old man had my money, and I was treated no better for it.

One night when I went in to make a fire, I availed myself of the opportunity of sprinkling a very heavy charge of this powder about my master's bed. Soon after their going to bed, they began to cough and sneeze. Being close around the house, watching and listening, to know what the effect would be, I heard them ask each other what in the world it could be, that made them cough and sneeze so. All the while, I was trembling with fear, expecting every moment I should be called and asked if I knew any thing about it. After this, for fear they might find me out in my dangerous experiments upon them, I had to give them up, for the time being. I was then convinced that running away was the most effectual way by which a slave could escape cruel punishment.

As all the instrumentalities which I as a slave, could bring to bear upon the system, had utterly failed to palliate my sufferings, all hope and consolation fled. I must be a slave for life, and suffer under the lash or die. The influence which this had only tended to make me more unhappy. I resolved that I would be free if running away could make me so. I had heard that Canada was a land of liberty, somewhere in the North; and every wave of trouble that rolled across my breast, caused me to think more and more about Canada, and liberty. But more especially after having been flogged, I have fled to the highest hills of the forest, pressing my way to the North for refuge; but the river Ohio was my limit. To me it was an impassable gulf. I had no rod wherewith to smite the stream, and thereby divide the waters. I had no Moses to go before me and lead the way from bondage to a promised land. Yet I was in a far worse state than Egyptian bondage; for they had houses and land; I had none; they had oxen and sheep; I had none; they had a wise counsel, to tell them what to do, and where to go, and even to go with them; I had none. I was surrounded by opposition on every hand. My friends were few and far between. I have often felt when running away as if I had scarcely a friend on earth.

Bibb, Henry. 1849. *Narrative of the Life and Adventures of Henry Bibb, an American Slave, Written by Himself.* New York: Author.

SEWARD'S "HIGHER LAW" SPEECH (1850)

Excerpts from William H. Seward's "Higher Law" Speech

Mr. SEWARD: I mean to say that Congress can hereafter decide whether any states, slave or free, can be framed out of Texas. If they should never be framed out of Texas, they never could be admitted.

How is the original equality of the states proved? It rests on a syllogism of Vattel, as follows: All men are equal by the law of nature and of nations. But states are only lawful aggregations of individual men, who severally are equal. Therefore, states are equal in natural rights. All this is just and sound. But assuming the same premises, to wit, that all men are equal by the law of nature and of nations, the right of property in slaves falls to the ground; for one who is equal to another cannot be the owner or property of that other. But you answer, that the Constitution recognizes property in slaves. It would be sufficient, then, to reply, that this constitutional recognition must be void, because it is repugnant to the law of nature and of nations. But I deny that the Constitution recognizes property in man. I submit, on the other hand, most respectfully, that the Constitution not merely does not affirm that principle, but, on the contrary, altogether excludes it.

The Constitution does not *expressly* affirm anything on the subject; all that it contains is two incidental allusions to slaves. These are, first, in the provision establishing a ratio of representation and taxation; and secondly, in the provision relating to fugitives from labor. In both cases, the Constitution designedly mentions slaves, not as slaves, much less as chattels, but as *persons.* That this recognition of them as persons was designed is historically known, and I think was never denied. . . .

I deem it established, then, that the Constitution does not recognize property in man, but leaves that question, as between the states, to the law of nature and of nations. That law, as expounded by Vattel, is founded on the reason of things. When God had created the earth, with its wonderful adaptations, He gave dominion over it to man, absolute human dominion. The title of that dominion, thus bestowed, would have been incomplete, if the lord of all terrestrial things could himself have been the property of his fellow-man.

The right to *have* a slave implies the right in some one to *make* the slave; that right must be equal and mutual, and this would resolve society into a state of perpetual war. But if we grant the original equality of the states, and grant also the constitutional recognition as slaves as property, still the argument we are considering fails. Because the states are not parties to the Constitution as states; it is the Constitution of the people of the United States.

But even if the states continue under the constitution as states, they nevertheless surrendered their equality as states, and submitted themselves to the sway of the numerical majority, with qualifications or checks; first, of the representation of three-fifths of slaves in the ratio of representation and taxation; and, secondly, of the equal representation of states in the Senate.

The proposition of an established classification of states as *slave states* and *free states,* as insisted on by some, and into *northern* and *southern,* as maintained by others, seems to me purely imaginary, and of course the supposed equilibrium of those classes a mere conceit. This must be so, because, when the Constitution was adopted, twelve of the thirteen states were slave states, and so there was no equilibrium. And so as to the classification of states as northern states and southern states. It is the maintenance of slavery by law in a state, not parallels of latitude, that makes it a southern state; and the absence of this, that makes it a northern state. And so all the states, save one, were southern states, and there was no equilibrium. But the Constitution was made not only for southern and northern states, but for states neither northern nor southern, namely, the western states, their coming being foreseen and provided for.

It needs no argument to show that the idea of a joint stock association, or a copartnership, as applicable even by its analogies to the United States, is erroneous, with all the consequences fancifully deduced from it. The United States are a political state, or organized society, whose end is government, for the security, welfare, and happiness of all who live under its protection. The theory I am combating reduces the objects of government to the mere spoils of conquest. Contrary to a theory so debasing, the preamble of the Constitution not only asserts the sovereignty to be, not in the states, but in the people, but also promulgates the objects of the Constitution:

"We, the people of the United States, in order to

form a *more perfect union,* establish justice, insure domestic tranquillity, provide for the *common defence,* promote the GENERAL WELFARE, and secure the *blessings of liberty,* do ordain and establish this Constitution. "

Objects sublime and benevolent! They exclude the very idea of conquests, to be either divided among states or even enjoyed by them, for the purpose of securing, not the blessings of liberty, but the evils of slavery. There is a novelty in the principle of the proposed compromise which condemns it. Simultaneously with the establishment of the Constitution, Virginia ceded to the United States her domain, which then extended to the Mississippi, and was even claimed to extend to the Pacific Ocean. Congress accepted it, and unanimously devoted the domain to freedom, in the language from which the ordinance now so severely condemned was borrowed. Five states have already been organized on this domain, from all of which, in pursuance of that ordinance, slavery is excluded. How did it happen that this theory of the equality of states, of the classification of states, of the equilibrium of states, of the title of the states, to common enjoyment of the domain, or to an equitable and just partition between them, was never promulgated, nor even dreamed of, by the slave states, when they unanimously consented to that ordinance?

There is another aspect of the principle of compromise which deserves consideration. It assumes that slavery, if not the only institution in a slave state, is at least a ruling institution, and that this characteristic is recognized by the Constitution. But *slavery* is only *one* of many institutions there. Freedom is equally an institution there. Slavery is only a temporary, accidental, partial, and incongruous one. Freedom on the contrary, is a perpetual, organic, universal one, in harmony with the Constitution of the United States. The slaveholder himself stands under the protection of the latter, in common with all the free citizens of the state. But it is, moreover, an indispensable institution. You may separate slavery from South Carolina, and the state will still remain; but if you subvert freedom there, the state will cease to exist. But the principle of this compromise gives complete ascendancy in the slave states, and in the Constitution of the United States, to the subordinate, accidental, and incongruous institution, over its paramount antagonist. To reduce this claim of slavery to an absurdity, it is only necessary to add that there are only two states in which slaves are a majority, and not one in which the slaveholders are not a very disproportionate minority.

But there is yet another aspect in which this principle must be examined. It regards the domain only as a possession, to be enjoyed either in common or by partition by the citizens of the old states. It is true, indeed, that the national domain is ours. It is true it was acquired by the valor and with the wealth of the whole nation. But we hold, nevertheless, no arbitrary power over it. We hold no arbitrary authority over anything, whether acquired lawfully or seized by usurpation. The Congress regulates our stewardship; the Constitution devotes the domain to union, to justice, to defence, to welfare, and to liberty.

But there is a higher law than the Constitution, which regulates our authority over the domain, and devotes it to the same noble purposes. The territory is a part, no inconsiderable part, of the common heritage of mankind, bestowed upon them by the Creator of the universe. We are his stewards, and must so discharge our trust as to secure in the highest attainable degree their happiness. How momentous that trust is, we may learn from the instructions of the founder of modern philosophy:

Slavery has never obtained anywhere by express legislative authority, but always by trampling down laws higher than any mere municipal laws—the laws of nature and of nations. There can be no oppression in superadding the sanction of Congress to the authority which is so weak and so vehemently questioned. And there is some possibility, if not probability, that the institution may obtain a foothold surreptitiously, if it shall not be absolutely forbidden by our own authority.

Sir, those who would alarm us with the terrors of revolution have not well considered the structure of this government, and the organization of its forces. It is a democracy of property and persons, with a fair approximation towards universal education, and operating by means of universal suffrage. The constituent members of this democracy are the only persons who could subvert it; and they are not the citizens of a metropolis like Paris, or of a region subjected to the influences of a metropolis like France; but they are husbandmen, dispersed over this broad land, on the mountain and on the plain, and on the prairie, from the ocean to the Rocky Mountains, and from the great lakes to the gulf; and this people are now, while we are discussing their imaginary danger, at peace and in their happy homes, as unconcerned and uninformed of their peril as they are of events occurring in the moon. Nor have the alarmists made due allowance in their calculations for the influence of conservative reaction, strong in any government, and irresistible in a rural republic, operating by universal suffrage. That principle of reaction is due to the force of the habits of acquiescence and loyalty among the people. No man better understood this principle than MACHIAVELLI, who has told us, in regard to factions, that "no safe reliance can be placed in the force of nature and the bravery of words, except it be corroborated by custom." Do the alarmists remember that this government has stood sixty years already without exacting one drop of blood?—that this government has stood sixty years, and yet treason is an obsolete crime? That day, I trust, is far off when the fountains of popular contentment shall be broken up; but whenever it shall come, it will bring forth a higher illustration than has ever yet been given of the excellence of the democratic system; for then it will be seen how calmly, how firmly, how nobly, a great people can act in preserving their Constitution; whom "love of country moveth, example teacheth, company comforteth, emulation quickeneth, and glory exalteth."

Seward, William H. 1853. *The Works of William H. Seward*. George E. Baker, ed. New York: Redfield.

FUGITIVE SLAVE ACT (1850)

Section 1

Be it enacted by the Senate and House of Representatives of the United States of America in Congress assembled, That the persons who have been, or may hereafter be, appointed commissioners, in virtue of any act of Congress, by the Circuit Courts of the United States, and Who, in consequence of such appointment, are authorized to exercise the powers that any justice of the peace, or other magistrate of any of the United States, may exercise in respect to offenders for any crime or offense against the United States, by arresting, imprisoning, or bailing the same under and by the virtue of the thirty-third section of the act of the twenty-fourth of September seventeen hundred and eighty-nine, entitled "An Act to establish the judicial courts of the United States" shall be, and are hereby, authorized and required to exercise and discharge all the powers and duties conferred by this act.

Section 2

And be it further enacted, That the Superior Court of each organized Territory of the United States shall have the same power to appoint commissioners to take acknowledgments of bail and affidavits, and to take depositions of witnesses in civil causes, which is now possessed by the Circuit Court of the United States; and all commissioners who shall hereafter be appointed for such purposes by the Superior Court of any organized Territory of the United States, shall possess all the powers, and exercise all the duties, conferred by law upon the commissioners appointed by the Circuit Courts of the United States for similar purposes, and shall moreover exercise and discharge all the powers and duties conferred by this act.

Section 3

And be it further enacted, That the Circuit Courts of the United States shall from time to time enlarge the number of the commissioners, with a view to afford reasonable facilities to reclaim fugitives from labor, and to the prompt discharge of the duties imposed by this act.

Section 4

And be it further enacted, That the commissioners above named shall have concurrent jurisdiction with the judges of the Circuit and District Courts of the United States, in their respective circuits and districts within the several States, and the judges of the Superior Courts of the Territories, severally and collectively, in term-time and vacation; shall grant certificates to such claimants, upon satisfactory proof being made, with authority to take and remove such fugitives from service or labor, under the restrictions herein contained, to the State or Territory from which such persons may have escaped or fled.

Section 5

And be it further enacted, That it shall be the duty of all marshals and deputy marshals to obey and execute all warrants and precepts issued under the provisions of this act, when to them directed; and should any marshal or deputy marshal refuse to receive such warrant, or other process, when tendered, or to use all proper means diligently to execute the same, he shall, on conviction thereof, be fined in the sum of one thousand dollars, to the use of such claimant, on the motion of such claimant, by the Circuit or District Court for the district of such marshal; and after arrest of such fugitive, by such marshal or his deputy, or whilst at any time in his custody under the provisions of this act, should such fugitive escape, whether with or without the assent of such marshal or his deputy, such marshal shall be liable, on his official bond, to be prosecuted for the benefit of such claimant, for the full value of the service or labor of said fugitive in the State, Territory, or District whence he escaped: and the better to enable the said commissioners, when thus appointed, to execute their duties faithfully and efficiently, in conformity with the requirements of the Constitution of the United States and of this act, they are hereby authorized and empowered, within their counties respectively, to appoint, in writing under their hands, any one or more suitable persons, from time to time, to execute all such warrants and other process as may be issued by them in the lawful performance of their respective duties; with authority to such commissioners, or the persons to be appointed by them, to execute process as aforesaid, to summon and call to their aid the bystanders, or posse comitatus of the proper county, when necessary to ensure a faithful observance of the clause of the Constitution referred to, in conformity with the provisions of this act; and all good citizens are hereby commanded to aid and assist in the prompt and efficient execution of this law, whenever their services may be required, as aforesaid, for that purpose; and said warrants shall run, and be executed by said officers, any where in the State within which they are issued.

Section 6

And be it further enacted, That when a person held to service or labor in any State or Territory of the United States, has heretofore or shall hereafter escape into another State or Territory of the United States, the person or persons to whom such service or labor may be due, or his, her, or their agent or attorney, duly authorized, by power of attorney, in writing, acknowledged and certified under the seal of some legal officer or court of the State or Territory in which the same may be executed, may pursue and reclaim such fugitive person, either by procuring a warrant from some one of the courts, judges, or commissioners aforesaid, of the proper circuit, district, or county, for the apprehension of such fugitive from service or labor, or by seizing and arresting such fugitive, where the same can be done without process, and by taking, or causing such person to be taken, forthwith before such court, judge, or commissioner, whose duty it shall be to hear and determine the case of such claimant in a summary manner; and upon satisfactory proof being made, by deposition or affidavit, in writing, to be taken and certified by such court, judge, or commissioner, or by other satisfactory testimony, duly taken and certified by some court, magistrate, justice of the peace, or other legal officer authorized to administer an oath and take depositions under the laws of the State or Territory from which such person owing service or labor may have escaped, with a certificate of such magistracy or other authority, as aforesaid, with the seal of the proper court or officer thereto attached, which seal shall be sufficient to establish the competency of the proof, and with proof, also by affidavit, of the identity of the person whose service or labor is claimed to be due as aforesaid, that the person so arrested does in fact owe service or labor to the person or persons claiming him

or her, in the State or Territory from which such fugitive may have escaped as aforesaid, and that said person escaped, to make out and deliver to such claimant, his or her agent or attorney, a certificate setting forth the substantial facts as to the service or labor due from such fugitive to the claimant, and of his or her escape from the State or Territory in which he or she was arrested, with authority to such claimant, or his or her agent or attorney, to use such reasonable force and restraint as may be necessary, under the circumstances of the case, to take and remove such fugitive person back to the State or Territory whence he or she may have escaped as aforesaid. In no trial or hearing under this act shall the testimony of such alleged fugitive be admitted in evidence; and the certificates in this and the first [fourth] section mentioned, shall be conclusive of the right of the person or persons in whose favor granted, to remove such fugitive to the State or Territory from which he escaped, and shall prevent all molestation of such person or persons by any process issued by any court, judge, magistrate, or other person whomsoever.

Section 7

And be it further enacted, That any person who shall knowingly and willingly obstruct, hinder, or prevent such claimant, his agent or attorney, or any person or persons lawfully assisting him, her, or them, from arresting such a fugitive from service or labor, either with or without process as aforesaid, or shall rescue, or attempt to rescue, such fugitive from service or labor, from the custody of such claimant, his or her agent or attorney, or other person or persons lawfully assisting as aforesaid, when so arrested, pursuant to the authority herein given and declared; or shall aid, abet, or assist such person so owing service or labor as aforesaid, directly or indirectly, to escape from such claimant, his agent or attorney, or other person or persons legally authorized as aforesaid; or shall harbor or conceal such fugitive, so as to prevent the discovery and arrest of such person, after notice or knowledge of the fact that such person was a fugitive from service or labor as aforesaid, shall, for either of said offences, be subject to a fine not exceeding one thousand dollars, and imprisonment not exceeding six months, by indictment and conviction before the District Court of the United States for the district in which such offence may have been committed, or before the proper court of criminal jurisdiction, if committed within any one of the organized Territories of the United States; and shall moreover forfeit and pay, by way of civil damages to the party injured by such illegal conduct, the sum of one thousand dollars for each fugitive so lost as aforesaid, to be recovered by action of debt, in any of the District or Territorial Courts aforesaid, within whose jurisdiction the said offence may have been committed.

Section 8

And be it further enacted, That the marshals, their deputies, and the clerks of the said District and Territorial Courts, shall be paid, for their services, the like fees as may be allowed for similar services in other cases; and where such services are rendered exclusively in the arrest, custody, and delivery of the fugitive to the claimant, his or her agent or attorney, or where such supposed fugitive may be discharged out of custody for the want of sufficient proof as aforesaid, then such fees are to be paid in whole by such claimant, his or her agent or attorney; and in all cases where the proceedings arc before a commissioner, he shall be entitled to a fee of ten dollars in full for his services in each case, upon the delivery of the said certificate to the claimant, his agent or attorney; or a fee of five dollars in cases where the proof shall not, in the opinion of such commissioner, warrant such certificate and delivery, inclusive of all services incident to such arrest and examination, to be paid, in either case, by the claimant, his or her agent or attorney. The person or persons authorized to execute the process to be issued by such commissioner for the arrest and detention of fugitives from service or labor as aforesaid, shall also be entitled to a fee of five dollars each for each person he or they may arrest, and take before any commissioner as aforesaid, at the instance and request of such claimant, with such other fees as may be deemed reasonable by such commissioner for such other additional services as may be necessarily performed by him or them; such as attending at the examination, keeping the fugitive in custody, and providing him with food and lodging during his detention, and until the final determination of such commissioners; and, in general, for performing such other duties as may be required by such claimant, his or her attorney or agent, or commissioner in the premises, such fees to be made up in conformity with the fees usually charged by the officers of the courts of justice within the proper district or county, as near as may be practicable, and paid by such claimants, their agents or attorneys, whether such supposed fugitives from service or labor be ordered to be delivered to such claimant by the final determination of such commissioner or not.

Section 9

And be it further enacted, That, upon affidavit made by the claimant of such fugitive, his agent or attorney, after such certificate has been issued, that he has reason to apprehend that such fugitive will he rescued by force from his or their possession before he can be taken beyond the limits of the State in which the arrest is made, it shall be the duty of the officer making the arrest to retain such fugitive in his custody, and to remove him to the State whence he fled, and there to deliver him to said claimant, his agent, or attorney. And to this end, the officer aforesaid is hereby authorized and required to employ so many persons as he may deem necessary to overcome such force, and to retain them in his service so long as circumstances may require. The said officer and his assistants, while so employed, to receive the same compensation, and to be allowed the same expenses, as are now allowed by law for transportation of criminals, to be certified by the judge of the district within which the arrest is made, and paid out of the treasury of the United States.

Section 10

And be it further enacted, That when any person held to service or labor in any State or Territory, or in the District of Columbia, shall escape therefrom, the party to whom such service or labor shall be due, his, her, or their agent or attorney, may apply to any court of record therein, or judge thereof in vacation, and make satisfactory proof to such court, or judge in vacation, of the escape aforesaid, and that the person escaping owed service or labor to such party. Whereupon the court shall cause a record to be made of the matters so proved, and also a general description of the person so escaping, with such convenient certainty as may be; and a transcript of such record, authenticated by the attestation of the clerk and of the seal of the said court, being produced in any other State, Territory, or district in which the person so escaping may be found, and being exhibited to any judge, commissioner, or other office, authorized by the law of the United States to cause persons escaping from service or labor to be delivered up, shall be held and taken to be full and conclusive evidence of the fact of escape, and that the service or labor of the person escaping is due to the party in such record mentioned. And upon the production by the said party of other and further evidence if necessary, either oral or by affidavit, in addition to what is contained in the said record of the identity of the person escaping, he or she shall be delivered up to the claimant, And the said court, commissioner, judge, or other person authorized by this act to grant certificates to claimants or fugitives, shall, upon the production of the record and other evidences aforesaid, grant to such claimant a certificate of his right to take any such person identified and proved to be owing service or labor as aforesaid, which certificate shall authorize such claimant to seize or arrest and transport such person to the State or Territory from which he escaped: Provided, That nothing herein contained shall be construed as requiring the production of a transcript of such record as evidence as aforesaid. But in its absence the claim shall be heard and determined upon other satisfactory proofs, competent in law.

Approved, September 18, 1850.

TYPICAL WORK PRACTICES OF SLAVE LABORERS (1850)

It is expected that servants should rise early enough to be at work by the time it is light. In sections of country that are sickly, it will be found conducive to health in the fall to make the hands eat their breakfast before going into the dew. In winter, as the days are short and nights long, it will be no encroachment upon their necessary rest to make them eat breakfast before daylight. One properly taken care of, and supplied with good tools, is certainly able to do more work than under other circumstances. While at work, they should be brisk. If one is called to you or sent from you, and he does not move briskly, chastise him at once. If this does not answer, repeat the dose and double the quantity. When at work, I have no objection to their whistling or singing some lively tune, but no drawling tunes are allowed in the field, for their motions are almost certain to keep time with the music.

In winter, a hand may be pressed all day, but not so in summer. In the first of the spring, a hand need not be allowed any more time at noon than is sufficient to eat. As the days get longer and warmer, a longer rest is necessary. In May, from one and a half to two hours; in June, two and a half; in July and August, three hours at noon. If the day is unusually sultry, a longer time is better. When the weather is oppressive, it is best for all hands to take a nap at noon. It is refreshing, and they are better able to stand pressing the balance of the day. Hands by being kept out of the sun during the hottest of the day have better health and can do more work through the season than those who take what they call a good steady gait and work regularly from morning till night. They will certainly last much longer.

If the corn for feeding is in the shuck, the husking should be done at noon; and all corn for milling should, during summer, be shelled at noon, that as the nights are short the hands may be ready for bed at an early hour.

If water be not convenient in the field where the hands are at work, instead of having it brought from a distance in buckets, it will be found more convenient to have a barrel fixed on wheels and carried full of water to some convenient place, and let a small boy or girl with a bucket supply the hands from the barrel. Some persons make each negro carry a jug or large gourd full of water to the field every morning, and this has to serve for the day.

During the fall and winter, hands may be made to pack at night what cotton has been ginned in the day. The women may be required to spin what little roping will be necessary for plough lines and to make some heavy bed-quilts for themselves. Besides this, there is very little that can properly be done of nights.

Tattler. "Management of Negroes," *Southern Cultivator* 8 (November 1850).

EDITORIAL FROM *THE SOUTH CAROLINA HERALD* OF FAIRFIELD, SOUTH CAROLINA (1851)

We have been frequently charged with being hostile to the present Federal Government. We are so, and for the following very satisfactory reasons, among many others.

Because, for the last thirty years, it has proven a withering and unmitigated curse upon the South, having robbed us during this period of not less than one thousand millions, to build up Northern interests and institutions.

Because it has, by its late action, destroyed the sovereignty and equality of fifteen States of this Confederacy, and degraded them to the condition of colonial dependencies.

Because it has ceased to afford us protection in any particular, its whole aim being to break down and destroy the South.

Because it is an Abolition Government, striking directly at the institutions and domestic policy of the section in which we live, its whole legislation being shaped to this end, and having this only for its object.

Because in fine, it has most signally failed, as an experiment of the capacity of the people for self-government, inasmuch as the rights of one section has been trampled under foot, to gratify the fanaticism and lust for power of the other.

We are in favour of its dissolution or disunion—
Because it will bring wealth and greatness to the south, under a Southern Confederacy, which must inevitably arise from dissolution.

Because it will afford us protection in our persons, property, &c.

Because it will kill off the foul spirit of abolition, by taking away the food it feeds on.

Because it will put an end to kidnapping and border thieving, and restore peace and security to the frontier States.

Because it will promote the case of religion, morality, and civilisation, in the South.

Because it will build up a system of internal improvements, increase the number of schools, colleges, &c.

Because it will destroy entirely pauperism, by enabling every man, not physically diseased, to earn his daily bread, and accumulate, from the abundance of our prosperity, a fortune for himself in a short time.

Because it will renew and perpetuate the experiment of the capability of the people for self-government.

Because, even if the Slavery Question is settled, the seeds of discord have been too deeply sown by the North, ever to bring forth any other fruit than hostility, and constant wrangling between the two sections.

Because the Union is too large, and composed of too various interests, ever to harmonise together.

Because we honestly believe the Almighty never intended that the generous and noble Southerner should constitute one people, with the cold, calculating, plundering Yankee.

The Anti-Slavery Reporter (New Series), 6:61
(January 1, 1851)

SOUTHERN ENTHUSIASM FOR THE FUGITIVE SLAVE ACT (1851)

The following article is taken from the Charleston Mercury:—

If it is true that thirty thousand fugitive slaves are in the non-slaveholding States, there cannot be much difficulty in applying the provisions of the Fugitive Slave Act of Congress, in a sufficient number of cases, to test effectually the force of the Federal Government in every anti-slavery State in the Union. The following suggestions are respectfully submitted:—

1. In each Southern State the several District Southern Rights Associations may combine, by constituting a general committee for each State.

2. Every slave-owner, from whom any slaves have run away within the last ten years, should report their names and descriptions of their personal appearance, together with any information which might aid in the discovery of their present location.

3. These reports should be laid before the general committee of the State.

4. Each general State Committee should appoint an agent, with instructions to travel through the non-slaveholding States, and collect all the information to be there found concerning the fugitive slaves. Reports, showing their names, personal appearance, location, and history, should be made by these agents to the general committee appointing them.

5. By comparing the reports of the owners with those of the agents, many fugitive slaves would soon be identified, and their owners, advised and aided by the Associations, could proceed to reclaim them according to the forms of the Act of Congress.

6. The enforcement of this law, with the restoration of Southern property, or the rendering of society at the North, by the persevering resolution to test the strength of the United States Government in a conflict with fanaticism, is an alternative worthy of those who associate for the protection of Southern rights.

7. Whenever the issue is made, those who have an interest in the preservation of property, by the maintenance of law, will have to defend property in slavery, or abandon the law and peril their own security.

8. Faction and insurrection will probably conquer the Federal Government, whose officers, from President Fillmore and his Cabinet to the United States Marshal of New York, are shrinking from their sworn duty; and the impotence of the Union, except against the South, will be manifested.

9. The selfish politicians, and their parties, who have coaxed and patted Abolitionists for their votes, will find, like Actæon, the dogs at their own throats.

10. Seward and Hale must either lead the revolution, or be its victims. Anti-Slavery, being only the present war-cry of the party opposed to law and social order, will be forgotten, when once disorder and the reign of terror begin.

11. From the North will come disunion and civil war, and the people of Massachusetts and New York, who scoff at the state sovereignty, must have the insurrectionary Government of triumphant mobs.

12. Against those will "the Star Spangled Banner of the Union" in Southern hands be waved, sustained by the cannon and the sword; or far from their intestine anarchy and civil broils will the South pursue the prosper-

ous path of peace, under the flag which will float over their "glorious Union."–SCIPIO.

The Anti-Slavery Reporter (New Series), 6:61 (January 1, 1851).

EXTRACT OF A LETTER FROM JOHN G. WHITTIER TO JOSEPH STURGE, DATED AMESBURY, JAN. 7, 1851, ON THE FUGITIVE SLAVE LAW OF THE UNITED STATES.

Since I last wrote, we have been greatly distressed by the operation of the wicked Fugitive Slave Law upon our poor coloured fellow-citizens. I have never felt so keenly the shame, and sin, and cruelty of slavery, as for the last few months; and in labouring to awaken the popular feeling against this terrible enactment, I have found it exceedingly difficult to speak and act with the moderation and prudence which should charcterise the efforts of a Christian reformer. In my weak state of health the excitement has been very trying to me. I felt bound, in the interim, on the occasion of declining the nomination of Senator in the State by the democratic party, to declare that *I could not obey the law, that I should treat it as null and void, and open my door to the hunted fugitive in spite of its cruel provisions.* It cannot be obeyed by any man who professes to be a Christian or a friend of his kind; and it is a sad thing to have morality and justice on one side, and law on the other. But so it is; and while I deprecate with my whole heart any virulent resistance, I see no way left for us than to disobey the unrighteous act, and bear the penalty of fine and prison.

A case has just occurred in Philadelphia which shows, in a true light, the character of this law. A coloured man was seized by constables, under a false pretence, dragged before the slave commissioner, and although he produced two witnesses to prove him a free man, he was pronounced a slave, on the oath of a wretch who was then awaiting his trial for kidnapping, and hurried off to Maryland. Happily an officer of respectability accompanied the kidnappers and their victim to his pretended owner, who, on seeing him, had to honesty to declare *that the man was not his slave!*

Since writing the above, a poor young coloured man has been sent back into slavery from New York. Our noble friend, Lewis Tappan, made strenuous, but unavailing, efforts to save him; thou wilt doubtless get from him a full account of the case.

Our State legislature is now in session, and it is pretty certain that Charles Sumner—the true friend of peace and freedom, and every good word and work—will be chosen U.S. Senator, for six years from the 1st of 3d month next. He will, if elected, take the place which Daniel Webster has dishonoured.

Thou wilt be sorry to hear that the *Non-Slaveholder* has ceased to exist. Our dear friends, Samuel Richards and A. L. Pannock, sustained it a very long time, almost unaided. Nevertheless, the concern to avoid, as far as practicable, the use of slave products, is increasing, especially in our Society.

The Anti-Slavery Reporter (New Series), 6:62 (February 1, 1851)

PSEUDO-SCIENTIFIC THEORIES OF SLAVE BEHAVIOR (1851)

"Diseases and Peculiarities of the Negro Race," by Dr. Samuel Cartwright.

Drapetomania, or the Disease Causing Negroes to Run Away. Drapetomania is from δραπετηζ *[drapetes]*, a runaway slave, and μανια [mania], *mad or crazy.* It is unknown to our medical authorities, although its diagnostic symptom, the absconding from service, is well known to our planters and overseers, as it was to the ancient Greeks who expressed, by the single word δραπετηζ, the fact of the absconding, and the relation that the fugitive held to the person he fled from. I have added to the word meaning runaway slave, another Greek term, to express the disease of the mind causing him to abscond. In noticing a disease not heretofore classed among the long list of maladies that man is subject to, it was necessary to have a new term to express it. The cause in the most of cases, that induces the negro to run away from service, is as much a disease of the mind as any other species of mental alienation, and much more curable, as a general rule. With the advantages of proper medical advice, strictly followed, this troublesome practice that many negroes have of running away, can be almost entirely prevented, although the slaves be located on the borders of a free state, within a stone's throw of the abolitionists. I was born in Virginia, east of the Blue Ridge, where negroes were numerous, and studied medicine some years in Maryland, a slave state, separated from Pennsylvania, a free state, by Mason & Dixon's line–a mere air line, without wall or guard. I long ago observed that some persons considered as very good, and others as very bad masters, often lost their negroes by their absconding from service; while the slaves of another class of persons, remarkable for order and good discipline, but not praised or blamed as either good or bad masters, never ran away, although no guard or forcible means were used to prevent them. The same management which prevented them from walking over a mere nominal, unguarded line, will prevent them from running away anywhere.

To ascertain the true method of governing negroes, so as to cure and prevent the disease under consideration, we must go back to the Pentateuch, and learn the true meaning of the untranslated term that represents the negro race. In the name there given to that race, is locked up the true art of governing negroes in such a manner that the they cannot run away. The correct translation of that term declares the Creator's will in regard to the negro; it declares him to be the submissive knee-bender. In the anatomical conformation of his knees, we see "*genu flexit*" written in his physical structure, being more flexed or bent, than any other kind of man. If the white man attempts to oppose the Deity's will, by trying to make the negro anything else than "the submissive knee-bender," (which the Almighty declared he should be,) by trying to raise him to a level with himself, or by putting himself on an equality with the negro; or if he abuses the power which God has given him over his fellow-man, by being cruel to him, or punishing him in anger, or by neglecting to protect him from the wanton abuses of his fellow-servants and all others, or by denying him the usual comforts and necessaries of life, the negro will run away; but if he keeps him in the position that we learn from the Scriptures he was intended to occupy, that is, the position of submission; and if his master or overseer be kind and gracious in his hearing towards him, without condescension, and at the same time ministers to his physical wants, and protects him from abuses, the negro is spell-bound, and cannot run away. . . .

According to my experience, the "genu flexit"—the awe and reverence, must be exacted from them, or they will despise their masters, become rude and ungovernable, and run away. On Mason and Dixon's line, two classes of persons were apt to lose their negroes: those who made themselves too familiar with them, treating them as equals, and making little or no distinction in regard to color; and, on the other hand, those who treated them cruelly, denied them the common necessaries of life, neglected to protect them against the abuses of others, or frightened them by a blustering manner of approach, when about to punish them for misdemeanors. Before the negroes run away, unless they are frightened or panic-struck, they become sulky and dissatisfied. The cause of this sulkiness

and dissatisfaction should be inquired into and removed, or they are apt to run away or fall into the negro consumption. When sulky and dissatisfied without cause, the experience of those on the line and elsewhere, was decidedly in favor of whipping them out of it, as a preventive measure against absconding, or other bad conduct. It was called whipping the devil out of them.

If treated kindly, well fed and clothed, with fuel enough to keep a small fire burning all night—separated into families, each family having its own house—not permitted to run about at night to visit their neighbors, to receive visits or use intoxicating liquors, and not overworked or exposed too much to the weather, they are very easily governed—more so than any other people in the world. When all this is done, if any one of more of them, at any time, are inclined to raise their heads to a level with their master or overseer, humanity and their own good require that they should be punished until they fall into that submissive state which it was intended for them to occupy in all after-time, when their progenitor received the name of Canaan or "submissive knee-bender." They have only to be kept in that state and treated like children, with care, kindness, attention and humanity, to prevent and cure them from running away.

Dysaethesia Aethiopica, or Hebetude of Mind and Obtuse Sensibility of Body—a Disease Peculiar to Negroes—Called by Overseers, "Rascality." Dysaethesia Aethiopica is a disease peculiar to negroes, affecting both mind and body in a manner as well expressed by dysaesthesia, the name I have given it, as could be by a single term. There is both mind and sensibility, but both seem to be difficult to reach by impressions from without. There is a partial insensibility of the skin, and so great a hebetude of the intellectual faculties, as to be like a person half asleep, that is with difficulty aroused and kept awake. It differs from every other species of mental disease, as it is accompanied with physical signs or lesions of the body discoverable to the medical observer, which are always present and sufficient to account for the symptoms. It is much more prevalent among free negroes living in clusters by themselves, than among slaves on our plantations, and attacks only such slaves as live like free negroes in regard to diet, drinks, exercise, etc. It is not my purpose to treat of the complaint as it prevails among free negroes, nearly all of whom are more or less afflicted with it, that have not got some white person to direct and to take care of them. To narrate its symptoms and effects among them would be to write a history of the ruins and dilapidation of Hayti, and every spot of earth they have ever had uncontrolled possession over for any length of time. I propose only to describe its symptoms among slaves.

From the careless movements of the individuals affected with the complaint, they are apt to do much mischief, which appears as if intentional, but is mostly owing to the stupidness of mind and insensibility of the nerves induced by the disease. Thus, they break, waste and destroy everything they handle,—abuse horses and cattle,—tear, burn or rend their own clothing, and, paying no attention to the rights of property, steal others, to replace what they have destroyed. They wander about at night, and keep in a half nodding sleep during the day. They slight their work,—cut up corn, cane, cotton or tobacco when hoeing it, as if for pure mischief. They raise disturbances with their overseers and fellow-servants without cause or motive, and seem to be insensible to pain when subjected to punishment. The fact of the existence of such a complaint, making man like an automaton or senseless machine, having the above or similar symptoms, can be clearly established by the most direct and positive testimony. That it should have escaped the attention of the medical profession, can only be accounted for because its attention has not been sufficiently directed to the maladies of the negro race. Otherwise a complaint of so common an occurrence on badly-governed plantations, and so universal among free negroes, or those who are not governed at all,—a disease radicated in physical lesions and having its peculiar and well marked symptoms and its curative indications, would not have escaped the notice of the profession. The northern physicians and people have noticed the symptoms, but not the disease from which they spring. They ignorantly attribute the symptoms to the debasing influence of slavery on the mind without considering that those who have never been in slavery, or their fathers before them, are the most afflicted, and the latest from the slave-holding South the least. The disease is the natural offspring of negro liberty—the liberty to be idle, to wallow in filth, and to indulge in improper food and drinks.

Cartwright, Samuel A. "Diseases and Peculiarities of the Negro Race," *DeBow's Review.* Vol. XI (July, August, September, and November 1851).

"ELIZA'S DRAMATIC ESCAPE," FROM *UNCLE TOM'S CABIN* (1852)

Chapter VII—The Mother's Struggle

It is impossible to conceive of a human creature more wholly desolate and forlorn than Eliza, when she turned her footsteps from Uncle Tom's cabin.

Her husband's suffering and dangers, and the danger of her child, all blended in her mind, with a confused and stunning sense of the risk she was running, in leaving the only home she had ever known, and cutting loose from the protection of a friend whom she loved and revered. Then there was the parting from every familiar object,—the place where she had grown up, the trees under which she had played, the groves where she had walked many an evening in happier days, by the side of her young husband,—everything, as it lay in the clear, frosty starlight, seemed to speak reproachfully to her, and ask her whither could she go from a home like that?

But stronger than all was maternal love, wrought into a paroxysm of frenzy by the near approach of a fearful danger. Her boy was old enough to have walked by her side, and, in an indifferent case, she would only have led him by the hand; but now the bare thought of putting him out of her arms made her shudder, and she strained him to her bosom with a convulsive grasp, as she went rapidly forward.

The frosty ground creaked beneath her feet, and she trembled at the sound; every quaking leaf and fluttering shadow sent the blood backward to her heart, and quickened her footsteps. She wondered within herself at the strength that seemed to be come upon her; for she felt the weight of her boy as if it had been a feather, and every flutter of fear seemed to increase the supernatural power that bore her on, while from her pale lips burst forth, in frequent ejaculations, the prayer to a Friend above—"Lord, help! Lord, save me!"

If it were *your* Harry, mother, or your Willie, that were going to be torn from you by a brutal trader, tomorrow morning,—if you had seen the man, and heard that the papers were signed and delivered, and you had only from twelve o'clock till morning to make good your escape,—how fast could *you* walk? How many miles could you make in those few brief hours, with the darling at your bosom,—the little sleepy head on your shoulder,—the small, soft arms trustingly holding on to your neck?

For the child slept. At first, the novelty and alarm kept him waking; but his mother so hurriedly repressed every breath or sound, and so assured him that if he were only still she would certainly save him, that he clung quietly round her neck, only asking, as he found himself sinking to sleep,

"Mother, I don't need to keep awake, do I?"

"No, my darling; sleep, if you want to."

"But, mother, if I do get asleep, you won't let him get me?"

"No! so may God help me!" said his mother, with a paler cheek, and a brighter light in her large dark eyes.

"You're *sure*, an't you, mother?"

"Yes, *sure!*" said the mother, in a voice that startled herself; for it seemed to her to come from a spirit within, that was no part of her; and the boy dropped his litle weary head on her shoulder, and was soon asleep. How the touch of those warm arms, the gentle breathings that came in her neck, seemed to add fire and spirit to her movements! It seemed to her as if strength poured into her in electric streams, from every gentle touch and movement of the sleeping, confiding child. Sublime is the dominion of the mind over the body, that, for a time, can make flesh and nerve impregnable, and string the sinews like steel, so that the weak become so mighty.

The boundaries of the farm, the grove, the wood lot, passed by her dizzily, as she walked on; and still she went, leaving one familiar object after another, slacking not, pausing not, till reddening daylight found her many a long mile from all traces of any familiar objects upon the open highway.

She had often been, with her mistress, to visit some connections, in the little village of T—, not far from the Ohio river, and knew the road well. To go thither, to escape across the Ohio river, were the first hurried outlines of her plan of escape; beyond that, she could only hope in God.

When horses and vehicles began to move along the highway, with that alert perception peculiar to a state of excitement, and which seems to be a sort of inspiration, she became aware that her headlong pace and distracted air might bring on her remark and suspicion. She therefore put the boy on the ground, and, adjusting her dress and bonnet, she walked on at as rapid a pace as she thought consistent with the preservation of appearances. In her little bundle she had provided a store of cakes and apples, which she used as expedients for quickening the speed of the child, rolling the apple some yards before them, when the boy would run with all his might after it; and this ruse, often repeated, carried them over many a half-mile.

After a while, they came to a thick patch of woodland, through which murmured a clear brook. As the child complained of hunger and thirst, she climbed over the fence with him; and, sitting down behind a large rock which concealed them from the road, she gave him a breakfast out of her little package. The boy wondered and grieved that she could not eat; and when, putting his arms round her neck, he tried to wedge some of his cake into her mouth, it seemed to her that the rising in her throat would choke her.

"No, no, Harry darling! mother can't eat till you are safe! We must go on—on—till we come to the river!" And she hurried again into the road, and again constrained herself to walk regularly and composedly forward.

She was many miles past any neighborhood where she was personally known. If she should chance to meet any who knew her, she reflected that the well-known kindness of the family would be of itself a blind to suspicion, as making it an unlikely supposition that she could be a fugitive. As she was also so white as not to be known as of colored lineage, without a critical survey, and her child was white also, it was much easier for her to pass on unsuspected.

On this presumption, she stopped at noon at a neat farmhouse, to rest herself, and buy some dinner for her child and self; for, as the danger decreased with the distance, the supernatural tension of the nervous system lessened, and she found herself both weary and hungry.

The good woman, kindly and gossiping, seemed rather pleased than otherwise with having somebody come in to talk with; and accepted, without examination, Eliza's statement, that she "was going on a little piece, to spend a week with her friends,"—all which she hoped in her heart might prove strictly true.

An hour before sunset, she entered the village of T—, by the Ohio river, weary and foot-sore, but still strong in heart. Her first glance was at the river, which lay, like Jordan, between her and the Canaan of liberty on the other side.

It was now early spring, and the river was swollen and turbulent; great cakes of floating ice were swinging heavily to and fro in the turbid waters. Owing to the peculiar form of the shore on the Kentucky side, the land bending far out into the water, the ice had been lodged and detained in great quantities, and the narrow channel which swept round the bend was full of ice, piled one cake over another, thus forming a temporary barrier to the descending ice, which lodged, and formed a great, undulating raft, filling up the whole river, and extending almost to the Kentucky shore.

Eliza stood, for a moment, contemplating this unfavorable aspect of things, which she saw at once must prevent the usual ferry-boat from running, and then turned into a small public house on the bank, to make a few inquiries.

The hostess, who was busy in various fizzing and stewing operations over the fire, preparatory to the evening meal, stopped, with a fork in her hand, as Eliza's sweet and plaintive voice arrested her.

"What is it?" she said.

"Isn't there any ferry or boat, that takes people over to B—, now?" she said.

"No, indeed!" said the woman; "the boats has stopped running. "

Eliza's look of dismay and disappointment struck the woman, and she said, inquiringly,

"May be you're wanting to get over?—anybody sick? Ye seem mighty anxious?"

"I've got a child that's very dangerous," said Eliza. "I never heard of it till last night, and I've walked quite a piece today, in hopes to get to the ferry. "

"Well, now, that's onlucky," said the woman, whose motherly sympathies were much aroused; I'm re'lly consarned for ye. Solomon!" she called, from the window, towards a small back building. A man, in leather apron and very dirty hands, appeared at the door.

"I say, Sol," said the woman, "is that ar man going to tote them bar'ls over tonight?"

"He said he should try, if 't was any way prudent," said the man.

"There's a man a piece down here, that's going over with some truck this evening, if he durs' to; he'll be in here to supper tonight, so you'd better set down and wait. That's a sweet little fellow," added the woman, offering him a cake.

But the child, wholly exhausted, cried with weariness. "Poor fellow! he isn't used to walking, and I've hurried him on so," said Eliza.

"Well, take him into this room," said the woman, opening into a small bed-room, where stood a comfortable bed. Eliza laid the weary boy upon it, and held his hands in hers till he was fast asleep. For her there was no rest. As a fire in her bones, the thought of the pursuer urged her on; and she gazed with longing eyes on the sullen, surging waters that lay between her and liberty.

Here we must take our leave of her for the present, to follow the course of her pursuers.

Though Mrs. Shelby had promised that the dinner should be hurried on table, yet it was soon seen, as the thing has often been seen before, that it required more than one to make a bargain. So, although the order was fairly given out in Haley's hearing, and carried to Aunt Chloe by at least half a dozen juvenile messengers, that dignitary only gave certain very gruff snorts, and tosses of her head, and went on with every operation in an unusually leisurely and circumstantial manner.

For some singular reason, an impression seemed to reign among the servants generally that Missis would not be particularly disobliged by delay; and it was wonderful what a number of counter accidents oc-curred constantly, to retard the course of things. One luckless wight contrived to upset the gravy; and then gravy had to be got up *de novo,* with due care and formality, Aunt Chloe watching and stirring with dogged precision, answering shortly, to all suggestions of haste, that she "warn't a going to have raw gravy on the table, to help nobody's catchings." One tumbled down with the water, and had to go to the spring for more; and another precipitated the butter into the path of events; and there was from time to time giggling news brought into the kitchen that "Mas'r Haley was mighty oneasy, and that he couldn't sit in his cheer no ways, but was a walkin' and stalkin' to the winders and through the porch."

"Sarves him right!" said Aunt Chloe, indignantly. "He'll get wus nor oneasy, one of these days, if he don't mend his ways. *His* master'll be sending for him, and then see how he'll look!"

"He'll go to torment, and no mistake," said little Jake.

"He desarves it!" said Aunt Chloe, grimly, "he's broke a many, many, many hearts,—I tell ye all!" she said, stopping, with a fork uplifted in her hands, "it's like what Mas'r George reads in Ravelations,—souls a callin' under the altar! and a callin' on the Lord for vengeance on sich!—and by and by the Lord he'll hear 'em—so he will!"

Aunt Chloe, who was much revered in the kitchen, was listened to with open mouth; and, the dinner being now fairly sent in, the whole kitchen was at leisure to gossip with her, and to listen to her remarks.

"Sich'll be burnt up forever, and no mistake, won't ther?" said Andy.

"I'd be glad to see it, I'll be boun'," said little Jake.

"Chil'en!" said a voice, that made them all start. It was Uncle Tom, who had come in, and stood listening to the conversation at the door.

"Chil'en!" he said, "I'm afeard you don't know what ye're sayin'. Forever is a *dre'ful* word, chil'en; it's awful to think on 't. You oughtenter wish that ar to any human crittur."

"We wouldn't to anybody but the soul-drivers," said Andy; "nobody can help wishing it to them, they's so awful wicked."

"Don't natur herself kinder cry out on 'em?" said Aunt Chloe. "Don't dey tear der suckin' baby right off his mother's breast, and sell him, and der little children as is crying and holding on by her clothes,—don't dey pull 'em off and sells 'em? Don't dey tear wife and husband apart?" said Aunt Chloe, beginning to cry, "when it's jest takin' the very life on 'em?—and all the while does they feel one bit, don't dey drink and smoke, and take it oncommon easy? Lor, if the devil don't get them, what's he good for?" And Aunt Chloe covered her face with her checked apron, and began to sob in good earnest.

"Pray for them that spitefully use you, the good book says," says Tom.

"Pray for 'em!" said Aunt Chloe; "Lor, it's too tough! I can't pray for 'em."

"It's natur, Chloe, and natur 's strong," said Tom, "but the Lord's grace is stronger; besides, you oughter think what an awful state a poor crittur's soul 's in that'll do them ar things,—you oughter thank God that you an't *like* him, Chloe. I'm sure I'd rather be sold, ten thousand times over, than to have all that ar poor crittur's got to answer for."

"So 'd I, a heap," said Jake. "Lor, *shouldn't* we cotch it, Andy?"

Andy shrugged his shoulders, and gave an acquiescent whistle.

"I'm glad Mas'r didn't go off this morning, as he looked to," said Tom; "that ar hurt me more than sellin', it did. Mebbe it might have been natural for him, but 't would have come desp't hard on me, as has known him from a baby; but I've seen Mas'r, and I begin ter feel sort o' reconciled to the Lord's will now. Mas'r couldn't help hisself; he did right, but I'm feared things will be kinder goin' to rack, when I'm gone Mas'r can't be spected to be a pryin' round everywhar, as I've done, a keepin' up all the ends. The boys all means well, but they 's powerful car'less. That ar troubles me."

The bell here rang, and Tom was summoned to the parlor.

"Tom," said his master, kindly, "I want you to notice that I give this gentleman bonds to forfeit a thousand dollars if you are not on the spot when he wants you; he's going today to look after his other business, and you can have the day to yourself. Go anywhere you like, boy."

"Thank you, Mas'r," said Tom.

"And mind yourself," said the trader, "and don't come it over your master with any o' yer nigger tricks; for I'll take every cent out of him, if you an't thar. If he'd hear to me, he wouldn't trust any on ye—slippery as eels!"

"Mas'r," said Tom,—and he stood very straight,—"I was jist eight years old when ole Missis put you into my arms, and you wasn't a year old. 'Thar,' says she, 'Tom, that's to be *your* young Mas'r; take good care on him,' says she. And now I jist ask you, Mas'r, have I ever broke word to you, or gone contrary to you, 'specially since I was a Christian?"

Mr. Shelby was fairly overcome, and the tears rose to his eyes.

"My good boy," said he, "the Lord knows you say but the truth; and if I was able to help it, all the world shouldn't buy you."

"And sure as I am a Christian woman," said Mrs. Shelby, "you shall be redeemed as soon as I can any bring together means. Sir," she said to Haley, "take good account of who you sell him to, and let me know."

"Lor, yes, for that matter," said the trader, "I may bring him up in a year, not much the wuss for wear, and trade him back."

"I'll trade with you then, and make it for your advantage," said Mrs. Shelby.

"Of course," said the trader, "all 's equal with me; li'ves trade 'em up as down, so I does a good business. All I want is a livin', you know, ma'am; that's all any of us wants, I, s'pose."

Mr. and Mrs. Shelby both felt annoyed and degraded by the familiar impudence of the trader, and yet both saw the absolute necessity of putting a constraint on their feelings. The more hopelessly sordid and insensible he appeared, the greater became Mrs. Shelby's dread of his succeeding in recapturing Eliza and her child, and of course the greater her motive for detaining him by every female artifice. She therefore graciously smiled, assented, chatted familiarly, and did all she could to make time pass imperceptibly.

At two o'clock Sam and Andy brought the horses up to the posts, apparently greatly refreshed and invigorated by the scamper of the morning.

Sam was there new oiled from dinner, with an abundance of zealous and ready officiousness. As Haley approached, he was boasting, in flourishing style, to Andy, of the evident and eminent success of the operation, now that he had "farly come to it."

"Your master, I s'pose, don't keep no dogs," said Haley, thoughtfully, as he prepared to mount.

"Heaps on 'em," said Sam, triumphantly; "thar's Bruno—he's a roarer! and, besides that, 'bout every nigger of us keeps a pup of some natur or uther."

"Poh!" said Haley,—and he said something else, too, with regard to the said dogs, at which Sam muttered,

"I don't see no use cussin' on 'em, no way."

"But your master don't keep no dogs (I pretty much know he don't) for trackin' out niggers."

Sam knew exactly what he meant, but he kept on a look of earnest and desperate simplicity.

"Our dogs all smells round considable sharp. I spect they's the kind, though they han't never had no practice. They's *far* dogs, though, at most anything, if you'd get 'em started. Here, Bruno," he called, whistling to the lumbering Newfoundland, who came pitching tumultuously toward them.

"You go hang!" said Haley, getting up. "Come, tumble up now."

Sam tumbled up accordingly, dexterously contriving to tickle Andy as he did so, which occasioned Andy to split out into a laugh, greatly to Haley's indignation, who made a cut at him with his riding-whip.

"I 's 'stonished at yer, Andy," said Sam, with awful gravity. "This yer's a seris bisness, Andy. Yer mustn't be a makin' game. This yer an't no way to help Mas'r."

"I shall take the straight road to the river," said Haley, decidedly, after they had come to the boundaries of the estate. "I know the way of all of 'em,—they makes tracks for the underground."

"Sartin," said Sam, "dat's de idee. Mas'r Haley hits de thing right in de middle. Now, der's two roads to de river,—de dirt road and der pike,—which Mas'r mean to take?"

Andy looked up innocently at Sam, surprised at hearing this new geographical fact, but instantly confirmed what he said, by a vehement reiteration.

"Course," said Sam, "I'd rather be 'clined to 'magine that Lizy 'd take de dirt road, bein' it's the least travelled."

Haley, notwithstanding that he was a very old bird, and naturally inclined to be suspicious of chaff, was rather brought up by this view of the case.

"If yer warn't both on yer such cussed liars, now!" he said, contemplatively as he pondered a moment.

The pensive, reflective tone in which this was spoken appeared to amuse Andy prodigiously, and he drew a little behind, and shook so as apparently to run a great risk of failing off his horse, while Sam's face was immovably composed into the most doleful gravity.

"Course," said Sam, "Mas'r can do as he'd ruther, go de straight road, if Mas'r thinks best,—it's all one to us. Now, when I study 'pon it, I think de straight road de best, *deridedly*."

"She would naturally go a lonesome way," said Haley, thinking aloud, and not minding Sam's remark.

"Dar an't no sayin'," said Sam; "gals is pecular; they never does nothin' ye thinks they will; mose gen'lly the contrary. Gals is nat'lly made contrary; and so, if you thinks they've gone one road, it is sartin you'd better go t' other, and then you'll be sure to find 'em. Now, my private 'pinion is, Lizy took der road; so I think we'd better take de straight one."

This profound generic view of the female sex did not seem to dispose Haley particularly to the straight road, and he announced decidedly that he should go the other, and asked Sam when they should come to it.

"A little piece ahead," said Sam, giving a wink to Andy with the eye which was on Andy's side of the head; and he added, gravely, "but I've studded on de matter, and I'm quite clar we ought not to go dat ar way. I nebber been over it no way. It's despit lonesome, and we might lose our way,—whar we'd come to, de Lord only knows."

"Nevertheless," said Haley, "I shall go that way."

"Now I think on 't, I think I hearn 'em tell that dat ar road was all fenced up and down by der creek, and thar, an't it, Andy?"

Andy wasn't certain; he'd only "hearn tell" about that road, but never been over it. In short, he was strictly noncommittal.

Haley, accustomed to strike the balance of probabilities between lies of greater or lesser magnitude, thought that it lay in favor of the dirt road aforesaid. The mention of the thing he thought he perceived was involuntary on Sam's part at first, and his confused attempts to dissuade him he set down to a desperate lying on second thoughts, as being unwilling to implicate Liza.

When, therefore, Sam indicated the road, Haley plunged briskly into it, followed by Sam and Andy.

Now, the road, in fact, was an old one, that had formerly been a thoroughfare to the river, but abandoned for many years after the laying of the new pike. It was open for about an hour's ride, and after that it was cut across by various farms and fences. Sam knew this fact perfectly well,—indeed, the road had been so long closed up, that Andy had never heard of it. He therefore rode along with an air of dutiful submission, only groaning and vociferating occasionally that 't was "despt rough, and bad for Jerry's foot."

"Now, I jest give yer warning," said Haley, "I know yer; yer won't get me to turn off this road, with all yer fussin'—so you shet up!"

"Mas'r will go his own way!" said Sam, with rueful submission, at the same time winking most portentously to Andy, whose delight was now very near the explosive point.

Sam was in wonderful spirits,—professed to keep a very brisk lookout,—at one time exclaiming that he saw "a gal's bonnet" on the top of some distant eminence, or calling to Andy "if that thar wasn't 'Lizy' down in the hollow;" always making these exclamations in some rough or craggy part of the road, where the sudden quickening of speed was a special inconvenience to all parties concerned, and thus keeping Haley in a state of constant commotion.

After riding about an hour in this way, the whole party made a precipitate and tumultuous descent into a barn-yard belonging to a large farming establishment. Not a soul was in sight, all the hands being employed in the fields; but, as the barn stood conspicuously and plainly square across the road, it was evident that their journey in that direction had reached a decided finale.

"Wan't dat ar what I telled Mas'r?" said Sam, with an air of injured innocence. "How does strange gentleman spect to know more about a country dan de natives born and raised?"

"You rascal!" said Haley, "you knew all about this."

"Didn't I tell yer I *knowd,* and yer wouldn't believe me? I telled Mas'r 't was all shet up, and fenced up, and I didn't spect we could get through,—Andy heard me."

It was all too true to be disputed, and the unlucky man had to pocket his wrath with the best grace he was able, and all three faced to the right about, and took up their line of march for the highway.

In consequence of all the various delays, it was about three-quarters of an hour after Eliza had laid her child to sleep in the village tavern that the party came riding into the same place. Eliza was standing by the window, looking out in another direction, when Sam's quick eye caught a glimpse of her. Haley and Andy were two yards behind. At this crisis, Sam contrived to have his hat blown off, and uttered a loud and characteristic ejaculation, which startled her at once; she drew suddenly back; the whole train swept by the window, round to the front door.

A thousand lives seemed to be concentrated in that one moment to Eliza. Her room opened by a side door to the river. She caught her child, and sprang down the steps towards it. The trader caught a full glimpse of her just as she was disappearing down the bank; and throwing himself from his horse, and calling loudly on Sam and Andy, he was after her like a hound after a deer. In that dizzy moment her feet to her scarce seemed to touch the ground, and a moment brought her to the water's edge. Right on behind they came; and, nerved with strength such as God gives only to the desperate, with one wild cry and flying leap, she vaulted sheer over the turbid current by the shore, on to the raft of ice beyond. It was a desperate leap—impossible to anything but madness and despair; and Haley, Sam, and Andy, instinctively cried out, and lifted up their hands, as she did it.

The huge green fragment of ice on which she alighted pitched and creaked as her weight came on it, but she staid there not a moment. With wild cries and desperate energy she leaped to another and still another cake; stumbling—leaping—slipping—springing upwards again! Her shoes are gone—her stockings cut from her feet—while blood marked every step; but she saw nothing, felt nothing, till dimly, as in a dream, she saw the Ohio side, and a man helping her up the bank.

"Yer a brave gal, now, whoever ye ar!" said the man, with an oath.

Eliza recognized the voice and face for a man who owned a farm not far from her old home.

"O, Mr. Symmes!—save me—do save me—do hide me!" said Elia.

"Why, what's this?" said the man. "Why, if 'tan't Shelby's gal!"

"My child!—this boy!—he'd sold him! There is his Mas'r," said she, pointing to the Kentucky shore. "O, Mr. Symmes, you've got a little boy!"

"So I have," said the man, as he roughly, but kindly, drew her up the steep bank. "Besides, you're a right brave gal. I like grit, wherever I see it."

When they had gained the top of the bank, the man paused.

"I'd be glad to do something for ye," said he; "but then there's nowhar I could take ye. The best I can do is to tell ye to go *thar,*" said he, pointing to a large white house which stood by itself, off the main street of the village. "Go thar; they're kind folks. Thar's no kind o' danger but they'll help you,—they're up to all that sort o' thing."

"The Lord bless you!" said Eliza, earnestly.

"No 'casion, no 'casion in the world," said the man. "What I've done's of no 'count."

"And, oh, surely, sir, you won't tell any one!"

"Go to thunder, gal! What do you take a feller for? In course not," said the man. "Come, now, go along like a likely, sensible gal, as you are. You've arnt your liberty, and you shall have it, for all me."

The woman folded her child to her bosom, and walked firmly and swiftly away. The man stood and looked after her.

"Shelby, now, mebbe won't think this yer the most neighborly thing in the world; but what's a feller to do? If he catches one of my gals in the same fix, he's welcome to pay back. Somehow I never could see no kind o' critter a strivin' and pantin', and trying to clar theirselves, with the dogs arter 'em and go agin 'em. Besides, I don't see no kind of 'casion for me to be hunter and catcher for other folks, neither."

So spoke this poor, heathenish Kentuckian, who had not been instructed in his constitutional relations, and consequently was betrayed into acting in a sort of Christianized manner, which, if he had been better situated and more enlightened, he would not have been left to do.

Haley had stood a perfectly amazed spectator of the scene, till Eliza had disappeared up the bank, when he turned a blank, inquiring look on Sam and Andy.

"That ar was a tolable fair stroke of business," said Sam.

"The gal 's got seven devils in her, I believe!" said Haley. "How like a wildcat she jumped!"

"Wal, now," said Sam, scratching his head, "I hope Mas'r'll 'scuse us trying dat ar road. Don't think I feel spry enough for dat ar, no way!" and Sam gave a hoarse chuckle.

"*You* laugh!" said the trader, with a growl.

"Lord bless you, Mas'r, I couldn't help it now," said Sam, giving way to the long pent-up delight of his soul. "She looked so curi's, a leapin' and springin'—ice a crackin'—and only to hear her,—plump! ker chunk! ker splash! Spring! Lord! how she goes it!" and Sam and Andy laughed till the tears rolled down their cheeks.

"I'll make ye laugh t' other side yer mouths!" said the trader, laying about their heads with his riding-whip.

Both ducked, and ran shouting up the bank, and were on their horses before he was up.

"Good-evening, Mas'r!" said Sam, with much gravity. "I berry much spect Missis be anxious 'bout Jerry. Mas'r Haley won't want us no longer. Missis wouldn't hear of our ridin' the critters over Lizy's bridge tonight;" and, with a facetious poke into Andy's ribs, he started off, followed by the latter, at full speed,—their shouts of laughter coming faintly on the wind.

Stowe, Harriet Beecher. 1852. *Uncle Tom's Cabin; or, Life Among the Lowly.* Cleveland, OH: Jewett, Proctor and Worthington.

ABOLITIONIST CRITICISM OF *UNCLE TOM'S CABIN* (1852)

The appalling liabilities which constantly impend over such slaves as have "kind and indulgent masters" are thrillingly illustrated in various personal narratives; especially in that of "Uncle Tom," over whose fate every reader will drop the scalding tear, and for whose character the highest reverence will be felt. No insult, no outrage, no suffering could ruffle the Christ-like meekness of his spirit, and shake the steadfastness of his faith. Towards his merciless oppressors, he cherished no animosity, and breathed nothing of retaliation. Like his Lord and Master, he was willing to be "led as a lamb to the slaughter," returning blessing for cursing, and anxious only for the salvation of his enemies. His character is sketched with great power and rare religious perception. It triumphantly exemplifies the nature, tendency and results of CHRISTIAN NON-RESISTANCE. We are curious to know whether Mrs. Stowe is a believer in the duty of non-resistance for the white man, under all possible outrage and peril, as well as for the black man; whether she is for self-defense on her own part, or that of her husband or friends or country, in case of malignant assault, or whether she impartially disarms all mankind in the name of Christ, be the danger or suffering what it may. We are curious to know this, because our opinion of her, as a religious teacher, would be greatly strengthened or lessened, as the inquiry might terminate. That all the slaves at the South ought, "if smitten on the one cheek, to turn the other also"—to repudiate all carnal weapons, shed no blood, "be obedient to their masters," wait for a peaceful deliverance, and abstain for all insurrectionary movements—is every where taken for granted, because the VICTIMS ARE BLACK. They cannot be animated by a Christian spirit, and yet return blow for blow, or conspire for the destruction of their oppressors. They are required by the Bible to put away all wrath, to submit to every conceivable outrage without resistance, to suffer with Christ if they would reign with him. None of their advocates may seek to inspire them to imitate the example of the Greeks, the Poles, the Hungarians, our Revolutionary sires; for such teaching would evince a most unchristian and blood-thirsty disposition. For them there is no hope of heaven, unless they give the most liberal interpretations to the non-resisting injunctions contained in the Sermon on the Mount, touching the treatment of enemies. It is for them, though despoiled of all their rights and deprived of all protection, to "threaten not, but to commit the keeping of their souls to God in well-doing, as unto a faithful Creator." Nothing can be plainer than that such conduct is obligatory upon them; and when, through the operations of divine grace, they are enabled to manifest a spirit like this, it is acknowledged to be worthy of great commendation, as in the case of "Uncle Tom." But, for those whose skin is of a different complexion, the case is materially altered. When they are spit upon and buffeted, outraged and oppressed, talk not then of a non-resisting Saviour—it is fanaticism! Talk not of overcoming evil with good—it is madness! Talk not of peacefully submitting to chains and stripes—it is base servility! Talk not of servants being obedient to their masters—let the blood of tyrants flow! How is this to be explained or reconciled? Is there one law of submission and non-resistance for the black man, and another law of rebellion and conflict for the white man? When it is the whites who are trodden in the dust, does Christ justify them in taking up arms to vindicate their rights? And when it is the blacks who are thus treated, does Christ require them to be patient, harmless, long-suffering, and forgiving? And are there two Christs?

The Liberator, March 26, 1852.

FREE SOIL PARTY PLATFORM OF PRINCIPLES (1852)

Having assembled in National Convention as the delegates of the Free Democracy of the United States, united by a common resolve to maintain rights against wrongs, and freedom against slavery—confiding in the intelligence, the patriotism, and the discriminating justice of the American people—putting our trust in God for the triumph of our cause, and invoking His guidance in our endeavours to advance it—we now submit, for the candid judgment of all men, the following declaration of principles and measures:—

First.—That Governments, deriving their just powers from the consent of the governed, are instituted among men to secure to all those inalienable rights of life, liberty, and the pursuit of happiness, with which they are endowed by their Creator, and of which none can be deprived by valid legislation, except for crime.

Second.—That the true mission of Democracy is to maintain the liberties of the people, the sovereignty of the States, and the perpetuity of the Union, by the impartial application to public affairs, without sectional discrimination, of the fundamental principles of equal rights, strict justice, and economical administration.

Third.—That the Federal Government is one of limited powers, derived solely from the Constitution, and the grants of power therein ought to be strictly construed by all the departments and agents of the Government; and it is inexpedient and dangerous to exercise doubtful constitutional powers.

Fourth.—That the early history of the Government clearly shows the settled policy to have been, not to extend, nationalise, and encourage, but to limit, localise, and discourage slavery; and to this policy, which should never have been departed from, the Government ought forthwith to return.

Fifth.—That the Constitution of the United States, ordained to form a more perfect union, to establish justice, and secure the blessings of liberty, expressly denies to the General Government any power to deprive any person of life, liberty, or property, without due process of law; and therefore the Government, having no more power to make a slave than to make a king, and no more power to establish slavery than to establish monarchy, should at once proceed to relieve itself from all responsibilities for the extenstion of slavery, wherever it possesses constitutional power to legislate for its extenstion.

Sixth.—That to the preserving and importunate demands of the slave power for more slave States, new slave territories, and the nationalisation of slavery, our distinct and final answer is—No more slave states, no slave territories, no nationalised slavery, and no national legislation for the extradition of slaves.

Seventh.—That the Act of Congress, known as the Compromise measures of 1850—by making the admission of a sovereign State contingent upon the adoption of other measures, demanded by the special interest of slavery—by their omission to guarantee freedom in free territories—by their attempt to impose unconstitutional limitations of the power of Congress and the people to admit new States—by their provisions for the assumption of five millions of the State debt of Texas, and for the payment of five millions more and the cession of a large territory to the same State under menace, as an inducement to the relinquishment of a groundless claim—and by their invasion of the sovereignty of the States and the liberties of the people, through the enactments of an unjust, oppressive, and unconstitutional Fugitive Slave Law, are proved to be incompatible with all the principles and maxims of Democracy, and wholly inadequate to the settlement of the questions of which they are claimed to be an adjustment.

Eighth.—That no permanent settlement of the slavery question can be looked for, except in the practical recognition of the truth that slavery is sectional and freedom national—by the total separation of the General Government from slavery, and the exercise of its legitimate and constitutional influence on the side of freedom—and by leaving to the States the whole subject of slavery and the extradition of fugitives from service.

[The next five resolutions have reference to the general politics of the country; we, therefore, pass them over, and proceed to others having reference to the anti-slavery cause.]

Fourteenth.—That slavery is a sin against God and a crime against man, the enormity of which no law nor usage can sanction or mitigate, and that Christianity and humanity alike demand its abolition.

Fifteenth.—That the Fugitive Slave Act of 1850 is repugnant to the Constitution, to the principles of the common law, to the spirit of Christianity, and to the sentiments of the civilised world—we therefore deny its binding force upon the American people, and demand its immediate and total repeal.

Sixteenth.—That the doctrine that any human law is a finality, and not subject to modification or repeal, is not in accordance with the creed of the founders of our Government, and is dangerous to the liberties of our people.

Seventeenth.—That the independence of Hayti ought to be recognised by our Government, and our commercial relations with it placed on the footing of the most favoured nations.

Eighteenth.—That it is the imperative duty of the General Government to protect all persons, of whatever colour, visiting any of the United States, from unjust and illegal imprisonment, or any other infringement of their rights.

Nineteenth.—That we recommend the introduction into all treaties hereafter to be negotiated between the United States and foreign nations of some provision for the amicable settlement of difficulties by a resort to decisive arbitration.

Twentieth.—That the Free Democratic party is not organised to aid either the Whig or the Democratic section of the great slave Compromise party of the nation, but to defeat them both; and that, repudiating and renouncing both as hopelessly corrupt, and utterly unworthy of confidence, the purpose of the Free Democracy is to take possession of the Federal Government, and administer it for the better protection of the rights and interests of the whole people.

Twenty-first.—That we inscribe on our banner, Free Soil, Free Speech, Free Labour, and Free Men, and under it will fight on, and fight ever, until a triumphant victory shall reward our exertions.

The Anti-Slavery Reporter (New Series), 7:81 (September 1, 1852).

SLAVE KINSHIP NETWORKS (1852)

"Genealogy"

"Breathes there a man with soul so dead".   I was born in Charleston, South Carolina in the year 1852. The place of my birth and the conditions under which I was born are matters over which, of course, I had no control. If I had, I should have altered the conditions, but I should not have changed the place; for it is a grand old city, and I have always felt proud of my citizenship. My father and my grandfather were born there, and there they died—my grandfather at the age of seventy-two, my father at seventy-six. My great grandfather came, or rather was brought, from Africa. It is said he bore the distinguishing marks of royalty on his person and was a fine looking man—fine looking for a Negro I believe is the usual qualification—at least that is what an old lady once told my own father who had inherited the good looks of his grandsire.

I do not know the name my great grandfather bore in Africa, but when he arrived in this country he was given the name, Clement, and when he found he needed a surname—something he was not accustomed to in his native land—he borrowed that of the man who bought him. It is a very good name, and as we have held the same for more than a hundred and fifty years, without change or alteration, I think, therefore, we are legally entitled to it. His descendants up to the close of the Civil War, seemed with rare good fortune under the Providence of God, to have escaped many of the more cruel hardships incident to American slavery.

I may be permitted to add that on the arrival of my progenitor in this country he was not allowed to enter into negotiation with the Indians, and thereby acquire a large tract of land. Instead, an axe was placed in his hands and he therefore became in some sort, a pioneer of American civilization.

My father and my mother were both under the "yoke," but were held by different families. They made their home with my father's people who were, of all slave holders, the very best; and it was here that I spent the first years of my life.

My mother went to her work early each morning, and came home after the day's work was done. My brother, older than I, accompanied her, but I being too young to be of practical service, was left to the care of my grandmother—and what a dear old christian she was! At this time her advanced age and past faithful service, rendered her required duties light, so that she had ample time to care for me. Her patient endeavor to impress upon my youthful mind the simple principles of a christian life shall never be forgotten, and I trust her efforts have not been altogether in vain. She was born in the hands of the family where she passed her entire life; and it would be a revelation to many of the present day to know to what extent her counsel and advice was sought and heeded by the household—white and black.

Our household was large; beside the owners, three maiden ladies (sisters) there were a dozen servants, some like my father, worked out and paid wages, but all:

> *Claimed kindred here*
> *And had their claims allowed.*

For there never was a better ordered establishment, nor were there ever better examples of christian womanhood than that of the three ladies who presided over it; and it is especially worthy of note that all the servants who were old enough, could read, and some of them had mastered the three "R's," having been taught by these ladies or their predecessors. Before the beginning of the Civil War these kind ladies liberated all their slaves, and it is no reflection on the Negro that many of the liberated ones refused to leave them. There were many considerations that prompted them to decline their proffered freedom; in some cases husband and wife were not fellow-servants, and one was unwilling to leave the other. All those who accepted their liberty were sent to Liberia. I know of one who returned after the, war to visit relatives and friends. He had been quite successful in his new home, and he gave good account of those who had left Charleston with him. Some had died, others were doing well. He found one of the good ladies still living and had the great pleasure of relating his story to her. When, after a brief stay in the city, he took his departure, he carried with him many tokens of remembrance from their kind benefactress for himself and those at home.

Aleckson, Sam. 1929. *Before the War, and After the Union. An Autobiography.* Boston: Gold Mind Publishing Co.

HARRIET BEECHER STOWE WRITES TO WILLIAM LLOYD GARRISON (1853)

Cabin, Dec. 19

Mr. Garrison. Dear Sir:. After seeing you, I enjoyed the pleasure of a personal interview with Mr.

Douglass and I feel bound in justice to say that the impression was far more satisfactory than I had anticipated.

There does not appear to be any deep underlying stratum of bitterness—he did not seem to me malignant or revengeful. I think that it was only a temporary excitement and one which he will outgrow.

I was much gratified with the growth and development both of his mind and heart. I am satisfied that his change of sentiments was not a mere political one but a genuine growth of his own conviction. A vigorous reflective mind like his cast among those holding new sentiments is naturally led to modified views.

At all events, he holds no opinion which he cannot defend, with a variety and richness of thought and expression and an aptness of illustration which show it to be a growth from the soil of this own mind with a living root and not a twig broken off other men's thoughts and stuck down to subserve a temporary purpose.

His plans for the elevation of his own race, are manly, sensible, comprehensive, he has evidently observed carefully and thought deeply and will I trust act efficiently.

You speak of him as an apostate—I cannot but regard this language as unjustly severe—Why is he any more to be called an apostate for having spoken ill tempered things of former friends than they for having spoken severely and cruelly as they have of him?—Where is this work of excommunication to end—Is there but one true anti-slavery church and all others infidels?—Who shall declare which it is.

I feel bound to remonstrate with this—for the same reason that I do with slavery—because I think it, an injustice. I must say still further, that if the first allusion to his family concerns was unfortunate this last one is more unjustifiable still—I am utterly surprised at it—as a friend to you, and to him I view it with the deepest concern and regret.

What Douglass is really, time will show—I trust that he will make no further additions to the already unfortunate controversial literature of the cause. Silence in this case will be eminently—golden.

I must indulge the hope you will reason at some future time to alter your opinion and that what you now cast aside as worthless shall yet appear to be a treasure.

There is abundant room in the antislavery field for him to perform a work without crossing the track or impeding the movement of his old friends and perhaps in some future time meeting each other from opposite quarters of a victorious field you may yet shake hands together.

I write this letter because in the conversation I had

with you, and also with Miss Weston I admitted so much that was unfavorable to Mr. Douglass that I felt bound in justice to state the more favorable views which had arisen to my mind.

Very sincerely your friend,
H. B. Stowe

Garrison, Wendell Phillips, and Francis Jackson Garrison. 1885–1889. *William Lloyd Garrison, 1805–1879; The Story of His Life Told by His Children,* vol. 3. New York: The Century Co.

THE ROLE OF THE OVERSEER (1853)

Chapter XV: Of the Delegated Power of Overseers.

All the Power of the owner over his Slave is held and exercised also by Overseers and Agents. We have, thus far, considered chiefly the power of the slave *owner.* It has been seen, likewise, that essentially the same power is lodged in the *hirer of* a slave. Incidentally, the power of *overseers and agents* has been alluded to. But we must now take a more distinct view of this feature of slavery. It has been expressed thus:

"*All the power of the master over the slave may be exercised, not by himself only, in person, but by any one whom he may depute as his agent.*" (Stroud's Sketch, p. 44.)

Considering the judicial authority vested in the slave owner, whoever he may be, (drunk or sober,) and the duty of the "sheriffs" and public negro whippers to execute his decisions, (as already noticed,) this *additional* power of delegating his magisterial dignity and authority to whomsoever (drunk or sober) he may think proper, becomes a very remarkable one. Irresponsible himself, and absolute, he commits the same authority over the slave to a subordinate despot, responsible solely to himself.

LOUISIANA, by express statute, enacts as follows "The *condition of a slave* BEING MERELY A PASSIVE ONE, his subordination to his master, AND ALL WHO REPRESENT HIM, *is not susceptible of any modification or restriction,* (except in what can excite the slave to the commission of crime,) in such manner that he owes to his master and to *all his family* a respect WITHOUT BOUNDS and an ABSOLUTE OBEDIENCE, and he is consequently to execute all the orders which he receives from him or from them." (1 Martin's Digest, 616.)

Thus does "the innocent legal relation" of slave ownership confer on every slave owner a power which no magistrate or government holds over *him,* or over any subject or citizen; and, not content with this, it clothes him with the prerogative of transferring this authority, not only *by the sale* of the slave, but by verbal commission while he yet owns him. His wife, his housekeeper, his overseer, and even his young children share his unlimited power and authority over the slave, though at the age of threescore! Instead of controlling his own children, the slave is controlled by the children of his master, and by hired overseers.

The *exception,* in the statute just cited, informs us that when the slave is "incited to crime" by the commands of his tyrant, whom he may not resist, he may nevertheless be held responsible for the crime! In its practical bearings, the law can effect nothing else, unless it be the martyrdom of the slave. Whatever crime he may be commanded to commit, he can lodge no information against his master, he can bear no testimony against him. If he persists in refusing to assist in the commission of the crime, his master may lawfully "chastise" him with the "moderate correction" that may cause his death, and then, if he "offers" resistance, he may be lawfully killed!

Louisiana is said to be the only State with an express statute on the topic of the master's delegated authority, but the usage, recognized by the Courts as law, universally exists. "In the other slave States," says Stroud, (p. 44,) the subjoined extract from Mr. Stephen's delineation of Slavery in the West Indies will, it is believed, accurately express the law and the practice:

"The slave is liable to be coerced or punished by the whip, *and to be tormented by every species of personal ill-treatment,* subject only to the exceptions already mentioned, (i.e., the deprivation of life and limb,) *by the attorney, manager, overseer, driver, and every other person to whose government and control* the owner may choose to subject him, as fully as by the owner himself. Nor is any special mandate or express general power necessary for this purpose; *it is enough that the inflictor of the violence is set over the slave for the moment, or by the owner or by any of his delegates or sub-delegates, of whatever rank or character.*" (Stephen's Slavery, p. 46.) This power of deputation by the master is one of the degrading and distinguishing features of *negro* slavery. It was not permitted by the laws of villeinage." (Stroud, p. 45. See 9 Coke's Reports, 76 A, &c. See Stephen, supra.)

The following description of "*overseers*" is from William Wirt's *Life of Patrick Henry:* "Last and lowest, (i.e., of the different classes of society in Virginia,) a *feculum* of beings called *overseers;* the most abject, degraded, unprincipled race, always cap in hand to the Dons who employed them, and furnishing materials for the exercise of their pride, insolence, and spirit of domination."

The great majority of slaves, male and female, labor

on plantations, under the charge of these "overseers." The "house servants," as already seen by the statute of Louisiana, are under absolute subjection to every member of the family. Slaves hired out, waiters at hotels, &c., are, in this particular, in no better condition. Almost every where, they are controlled by others, in addition to the direct control of their owners.

Goodell, William. 1853. *The American Slave Code in Theory and Practice: Its Distinctive Features Shown by Its Statutes, Judicial Decisions, and Illustrative Facts.* New York: American & Foreign Anti-Slavery Society.

THE FUGITIVE SLAVE AS A HEROIC FIGURE (1855)

Liberty; Or Jim Bow-Legs.

In 1855 a trader arrived with the above name, who, on examination, was found to possess very extraordinary characteristics. As a hero and adventurer, some passages of his history were most remarkable. His schooling had been such as could only be gathered on plantations under brutal overseers, or while fleeing, or in swamps, in prisons, or on the auction-block, in which conditions he was often found. Nevertheless, in these circumstances, his mind got well-stored with vigorous thoughts, neither books nor friendly advisers being at his command, yet his native intelligence, as it regarded human nature, was extraordinary. His resolution and perseverance never faltered. In all respects he was a remarkable man. He was a young man, weighing about 180 pounds, of uncommon muscular strength. He was born in the State of Georgia, Oglethorpe county, and was owned by Dr. Thomas Stephens, of Lexington. On reaching the vigilance committee in Philadelphia, his story was told, many times over, to one and another. Taking all of the facts into consideration respecting the courageous career of this successful adventurer for freedom, his case is by far more interesting than any that I have yet referred to. Indeed, for the good of the cause, and the honor of one who gained his liberty by periling his life so frequently, being shot several times, making six unsuccessful attempts to escape from the South, numberless times chased by bloodhounds, captured, sold and imprisoned repeatedly, living for months in the woods, swamps and caves, subsisting mainly on parched corn and berries. His narrative ought, by all means, to be published, though I doubt very much whether many could be found who could persuade themselves to believe one-tenth part of this story.

His master, finding him not available on account of his absconding propensities, would gladly have offered him for sale. He was once taken to Florida for that purpose, but, generally, traders being wide awake, on inspecting him, would almost invariably pronounce him a damn rascal, because he would never fail to eye them sternly as they inspected him. The obedient and submissive slave is always recognized by hanging his head, and looking on the ground when looked at by a slaveholder. This lesson Jim Hall never learned. Hence he was not trusted. His head and chest, and, indeed, his entire structure, as solid as a rock, indicated that physically he was no ordinary man, and not being under the influence of non-resistance, he had occasionally been found to be rather a formidable customer. His father was a full-blooded Indian, brother to the noted Chief Billy Bow-Legs. His mother was quite black, and of unmixed blood. For five or six years, the greater part of Jim's time was occupied in trying to escape, and being in prison for sale, to punish him for running away.

His mechanical genius was excellent, so was his geographical abilities. He could make shoes, or do carpenter work handily, though he had never had the chance to learn. As to traveling by night or day, he was always road-ready, and having an uncommon memory, could give exceedingly good accounts of what he saw. When he entered a swamp, and had occasion to take a nap, he took care, first, to decide upon the posture he must take, so that if come upon unexpectedly by the hounds and slave-hunters, he might know, in an instant, which way to steer to defeat them. He always carried a liquid, which he had prepared, to prevent hounds from scenting him, which he said had never failed him. As soon as the hounds came to the spot where he had rubbed his legs and feet with said liquid, they could follow him no further, but howled and turned immediately. A large number of friends of the slave saw this man, and would sit long, and listen with the most undivided attention to his narrative, none doubting for a moment its entire truthfulness. Strange as his story was, there was so much natural simplicity in his manners and countenance, one could not refrain from believing him.

Williams, James. 1893. *Life and Adventures of James Williams, a Fugitive Slave, with a Full Description of the Underground Railroad.* Philadelphia: Sickler.

A DESCRIPTION OF THE DOMESTIC SLAVE TRADE (C. 1855)

When the day came for them to leave, some, who seemed to have been willing to go at first, refused, and were handcuffed together and guarded on their way to the cars by white men. The women and children were driven to the depot in crowds, like so many cattle, and the sight of them caused great excitement among master's negroes. Imagine a mass of uneducated people shedding tears and yelling at the tops of their voices in anguish and grief.

The victims were to take the cars from a station called Clarkson turnout, which was about four miles from master's place. The excitement was so great that the overseer and driver could not control the relatives and friends of those that were going away, as a large crowd of both old and young went down to the depot to see them off. Louisiana was considered by the slaves as a place of slaughter, so those who were going did not expect to see their friends again. While passing along, many of the negroes left their masters' fields and joined us as we marched to the cars; some were yelling and wringing their hands, while others were singing little hymns that they were accustomed to for the consolation of those that were going away, such as

"When we all meet in heaven,
There is no parting there;
When we all meet in heaven,
There is parting no more."

We arrived at the depot and had to wait for the cars to bring the others from the Sumterville Jail, but they soon came in sight, and when the noise of the cars died away we heard wailing and shrieks from those in the cars. While some were weeping, others were fiddling, picking banjo, and dancing as they used to do in their cabins on the plantations. Those who were so merry had very bad masters, and even though they stood a chance of being sold to one as bad or even worse, yet they were glad to be rid of the one they knew.

While the cars were at the depot, a large crowd of white people gathered, and were laughing and talking about the prospect of negro traffic; but when the cars began to start and the conductor cried out, "all who are going on this train must get on board without delay," the colored people cried out with one voice as though the heavens and earth were coming together, and it was so pitiful, that those hard hearted white men who had been accustomed to driving slaves all their lives, shed tears like children. As the cars moved away we heard the weeping and wailing from the slaves as far as human voice could be heard; and from that time to the present I have neither seen nor heard from my two sisters, nor any of those who left Clarkson depot on that memorable day.

Stroyer, Jacob. 1890. *My Life in the South.* Salem: Salem Observer Book and Job Print.

SLAVE RESISTANCE: THE CASE OF MARGARET GARNER (1856)

The Cincinnati Slaves—Another Thrilling Scene in the Tragedy.

Gov. Chase, of Ohio, made a requisition upon Gov. Morehead, of Kentucky, for the slave woman Peggy, charged with the murder of her child at Cincinnati. It was understood that Peggy was held subject to this demand; but on Friday, the 7th, she was sent to Louisville, and shipped on board the *Henry Lewis,* which left that port on the evening of that day for the South. The Cincinnati *Commercial* gives an account of the whole affair, which we abridge somewhat.

On Thursday, Joe Cooper, of Springfield, left for Frankfort, with the requisition. It is supposed that his errand leaked out, for when he reached Frankfort, Gaines with the negroes was on his way to Louisville. Gov. Morehead granted the necessary documents, and when Cooper returned from his fruitless search, he expressed himself warmly indignant at the conduct of Gaines, saying that that individual had trifled with him and deceived him, and had insulted the dignity of the Commonwealth of Kentucky.

"On the train of cars for Frankfort, which conveyed Cooper, were four slaves of Gaines, being sent South. They had attempted to escape after the flight of Margaret and the others, but had been overtaken on the Kentucky side. One of them was a very likely and rather pretty mulatto girl, which our informant said Cooper had a great notion to buy, to save her from the Southern excursion to which she was destined. These negroes were in charge of Marshal Butts, of Covington, who did not permit them to tarry at Frankfort, but put them on the first train for Louisville, and with them Margaret. So that, it appears, Cooper arrived in Frankfort before Margaret was taken away. After Cooper's interview with the Governor, he took the first train for Louisville, and reached that town two hours after the *Henry Lewis* had started. He then returned to Cincinnati."

Now comes the most interesting part of the story. The *Henry Lewis,* on her passage down the river, came in collision with another steamer and was much damaged, and several lives were lost. The *Commercial* gives the narrative of events as follows:—

"When the accident occurred to the *Henry Lewis,* the negroes were in the nursery, (as a place between the cabin and steerage in the stern of the boat is called,) ironed by couples. After the disaster, they were heard calling for help and to be relieved of their handcuffs. Some one happened to be on hand to save them. Margaret had her child–the infant that she hit on the head with the shovel when arrested here—in her arms; but by the shock of the boat that came to the assistance of the *Lewis,* (as one story goes,) she was thrown into the river with her child and a white woman, who was one of the steerage passengers, and who was standing by her at the moment. This woman and the child were drowned, but a black man, the cook on the *Lewis,* sprang into the river, and saved Margaret, who, it is said, displayed frantic joy when told that her child was drowned, and said she would never reach alive Gaines' Landing, in Arkansas, the point to which she was shipped—thus indicating her intention to drown herself.

"Another report is, that, as soon as she had an opportunity, she threw her child into the river, and jumped after it. Still another story has it, that she tried to jump upon the boat alongside, but fell short. It is only certain that she was in the river with her child, and that it was drowned, while she was saved by the prompt energy of the cook. We are told by one of the officers of the boat, that Peggy was the only female among the slaves. It is probable, therefore, that the story about the good-looking mulatto girl, who was being sent South, and attracted attention and sympathy, is a romance. The last that was seen of Peggy, she was on the *Hungarian,* crouching like a wild animal near the stove, with a blanket wrapped around her. Our readers will, we presume, be struck with the dramatic features of the Fugitive Slave Case, and that it progresses like a plot wrought by some master of tragedy.

"First, there were the flight and the crossing of the frozen river in the twilight of morning, the place of fancied security, the surprise by the officers, the fight with them, the murder of the child, the arrest, the scenes about the court-room and in the jail, the long suspense, the return to Kentucky, the removal to Frankfort, the separation there, the approach of the messenger with the requisition for Peggy, her removal to Louisville, the pursuit of the messenger, the boat on which she was to have been taken South leaving two hours ahead of Cooper, with the writ from Gov. Morehead—then the speedy catastrophe to the steamer, the drowning of the babe of the heroine, and her own rescue, as if yet saved for some more fearful and startling act of the tragedy; and, lastly, the curtain falls leaving her wet and dismal, on a boat bound South, perfectly careless as to her own fate only determined never to set foot on the soil of Arkansas. There is something fearfully tragic about this, which must occur to every mind, and we shall look with much interest for information on the catastrophe which will complete the dramatic unity of the affair.

"And here an incident, related to us as occurring during the awful moments when the *Henry Lewis* was sinking and breaking, suggests itself to us. It is not wholly authentic, but its worth telling, anyhow. Marshal Butts, of Covington, who had charge of the negroes, is said to have been inflated somewhat with the importance of his position, and talked of his charge as his niggers, and displayed an immense amount of cutlery and fire-arms, with which he expressed himself resolved to slaughter whole armies of Abolitionists; and it happened that he exchanged some sharp words with a gentleman on the steamer about the Fugitive Slave case, &c. When the accident occurred, he was in his room, and one of the tables rolling against his door, he could not get out, and yelled tremendously for assistance. Some persons heard him, and went to work cutting a hole through the roof to let him out. The most active of those so engaged was the man with whom he had had the quarrel.

"When a hole was made large enough to let the rescuer and the prisoner communicate with each other, but not sufficient to crawl through, the man with the axe learned for the first time whom he was laboring to save, and called out "Hallo, Butts, is that you? D—n you, if I'd known that, you might have drowned. And [after a moment's reflection] you shall any how, if you won't give your word to let those niggers go." There was no time to be lost, and Butts, fearing that he might be left to perish said—"To tell the truth now, I don't own the niggers; if I did, I'd let 'em go. I'm only the agent." "Well," said the man holding the axe of deliverance or death, "take the irons off them, any how." That Butts agreed to do, and the opening being enlarged, he crawled out and began to inquire with some anxiety, "Where's them d—n niggers?" and was much gratified when he found that only the baby was lost.

The Liberator, March 21, 1856.

"BEECHER'S BIBLES" ARE SENT TO KANSAS (1856)

Sharp's Rifles and the Bible.

The Rev. H.W. Beecher to the New Haven Colony for Kansas.   C.B. Lines, New Haven, Ct:

DEAR SIR—Allow me to address you, and through you the gentlemen of your Company, on the eve of your departure for Kansas. I hope and believe that you will find a settlement there to be a means of great personal prosperity. You are not, like the early settlers of New Haven, going upon a doubtful enterprise, to a poor soil, in a severe climate, the ocean on one side, and the wilderness of a continent on every side. You will not go far from us. In our day, we measure by time, rather than distance: by hours, not miles. You will not be as far from your old homes as one Sabbath is from another. And yet you go upon an errand not one *whit* less Christian and less heroic than that of our common ancestors, who founded New Haven. You are pioneers of towns and cities; you are the seeds of Christianity—the germs of civilization. You will put down your feet in a wilderness: in a year it will be a populous place. And where the morning sun now rises on herds of wild buffalo, couched deep in wild grass, in your own life time it will bring forth the cry of multitudes and the noise of a city. Nevertheless, such perils have been coiled about the young State of Kansas that it is an act of courage to settle there, if a man goes with the true spirit of American institutions. To go there determined to transplant to its soil that tree of liberty which, under God, has in older States borne and shook down from its boughs all the fruits of an unparalleled prosperity, requires heroic courage. It is a pleasure and an honor to us to be in any way connected with such an enterprise, by furnishing to the emigrant material or moral aid. I have personally felt a double interest in your company, because it springs from New Haven, my father's birth-place and home of my ancestors. A friend and parishioner [A. Studwell] desires me to present to you twenty-five copies of the Bible. This is the charter of all charters, the constitution of all constitutions, the source and spring of Christian manliness. This book will be at the foundation of your State. It will teach you to value your rights, and inspire you to defend them. The donor has caused to be inscribed upon them: "Be ye steadfast and unmovable."

It is a shame that, in America, amidst our free institutions, anything else should be needed but *moral* instrumentalities. But you do need more. You will be surrounded by men who have already committed the wickedest wrongs, and the most atrocious crimes. They will scruple at nothing by which slavery can be fastened upon the young State. To send forth companies of men with their families amid those who have been bred to regard helplessness as a lawful prey to strength, would be a piece of unjustifiable cruelty. I send to you, therefore, as I promised, the arms required for twenty-five men. I have not the least fear that a hundred men, bred under New England influences, will be too eager or too warlike. You have been taught to create wealth, and not to rob it: to rely upon intelligence and rectitude for defence; and you will not be in danger of erring on the side of violence. But you are sent for the defence of great rights. You have no liberty to betray them by cowardice. There are times when self-defence is a religious duty. If that duty was ever imperative, it is now, and in Kansas. I do not say that you have barely the right to defend yourselves and your liberties; I say that it is a duty from which you cannot shrink, without leaving your honor, your manhood, your Christian fidelity behind you. But this invincible courage will be a shield to you. You will not need to use arms when it is known that you have them, and are determined to employ them in extremities. It is the very essence of that spirit which slavery breeds to be arrogant toward the weak, and cowardly before the strong. If you are willing to lose your lives, you will save them. If, on the other hand, you are found helpless, the miscreants of slavery would sweep you from Kansas like grass from the prairies before autumnal fires. If you are known to be fearless men, prepared for emergencies, Slavery, like the lion, will come up, and gazing into the eyes of courageous men, will stop, cower, and creep away into ambush. I trust that the perils which, a few months ago, hung like a cloud over that fair State, are lifting and passing away. May you find an unobstructed peace. *Then,* let these muskets hang over your doors, as the old revolutionary muskets do in many a New England dwelling. May your children in another generation look upon them with pride and say, "Our fathers' courage saved this fair region from blood and slavery." We will not forget you. Every morning's breeze shall catch the blessings of our prayers, and roll them westward to your prairie homes. May your sons be large-hearted as the heavens above their heads; may your daughters fill the land as the flowers do the prairies, only sweeter and fairer than they.

I am, in the bonds of the gospel, and in
the firm faith of Liberty, truly yours,

H.W. BEECHER.

Brooklyn, Friday, March 28, 1856.

The Liberator, April 11, 1856.

EDITORIAL RESPONSES TO THE BROOKS-SUMNER AFFAIR (1856)

New York Tribune *(May 23, 1856)*

By the news from Washington it will be seen that Senator Sumner has been savagely and brutally assaulted, while sitting in his seat in the Senate chamber, by the

Hon. Mr. Brooks of South Carolina, the reason assigned therefore being that the Senator's remarks on Mr. Butler of South Carolina, who is uncle to the man who made the attack. The particulars show that Mr. Sumner was struck unawares over the head by a loaded cane and stunned, and then the ruffianly attack was continued with many blows, the Hon. Mr. Keitt of South Carolina keeping any of those around, who might be so disposed, from attempting a rescue. No meaner exhibition of Southern cowardice—generally miscalled Southern chivalry—was ever witnessed. It is not in the least a cause for wonder that a member of the national House of Representatives, assisted by another as a fender-off, should attack a member of the national Senate, because, in the course of a constitutional argument, the last had uttered words which the first chose to consider distasteful. The reasons for the absence of collision between North and South—collision of sentiment and person—which existed a few years back, have ceased; and as the South has taken the oligarchic ground that Slavery ought to exist, irrespective of color—that there must be a governing class and a class governed—that Democracy is a delusion and a lie—we must expect that Northern men in Washington, whether members or not, will be assaulted, wounded or killed, as the case may be, so long as the North will bear it. The acts of violence during this session—including one murder—are simply overtures to the drama of which the persecutions, murders, robberies and war upon the Free-State men in Kansas, constitute the first act. We are either to have Liberty or Slavery. Failing to silence the North by threats, notwithstanding the doughfaced creatures who so long misrepresented the spirit of the Republic and of the age, the South now resorts to actual violence. It is reduced to a question whether there is to be any more liberty of speech south of Mason and Dixon's line, even in the ten miles square of the District of Columbia. South of that, liberty has long since departed; but whether the common ground where the national representatives meet is to be turned into a slave plantation where Northern members act under the lash, the bowie-knife and the pistol, is a question to be settled. That Congress will take any action in view of this new event, we shall not be rash enough to surmise; but if the Northern people are not generally the poltroons they are taken for by the hostile slavebreeders and slavedrivers of the South, they will be heard from. As a beginning, they should express their sentiments upon this brutal and dastardly outrage in their popular assemblies. The Pulpit should not be silent.

If, indeed, we go on quietly to submit to such outrages, we deserve to have our names flattened, our skins blacked, and to be placed at work under taskmasters; for we have lost the noblest attributes of freemen, and are virtually slaves.

Boston, Massachusetts, Atlas *(May 24, 1856)*

The outrage in the Senate, on Thursday last is without a parallel in the legislative history of the country. Nothing has heretofore seemed so bold, so bad, so alarming. There have been affrays, more or less serious, in the House, for the House is a popular, and therefore, a tumultuous body; there have been rencounters in the streets, for the streets are arenas in which any assassin may display his prowess; but never before has the sanctity of the Senate Chamber been violated; never before has an intruder ventured to carry into those privileged precincts his private hostilities; never before has a Senator been struck down in his seat, and stretched, by the hand of a lawless bully, prostrate, bleeding, and insensible upon the floor. The wrong is full of public importance; and we almost forget the private injury of Mr. Sumner in the broad temerity of the insult which has been offered to the country, to Massachusetts, to the Senate. This first act of violence may pass into a precedent; what a single creature has done today, a hundred, equally barbarous, may attempt tomorrow; until a band of alien censors may crowd the galleries, and the lobbies, and even the floor of the Senate, and by the persuasive arguments of the bludgeon, the bowie knife, and the revolver, effectually refute and silence any member who may dare to utter, with some thing of force and freedom, his personal convictions. The privileges which we have fondly supposed were conferred with the Senatorial dignity; the right to characterize public measures and public men, with no responsibility, save to God and to conscience; the freedom of debate, without which its forms are a mere mockery—these will all disappear; and in their place we shall have the government of a self-constituted and revolutionary tribunal, overawing the Senate, as the Jacobins of Paris overawed the National Assembly of France, as the soldiers of Cromwell intimidated the Parliament of Great Britain. Shall we have, did we say? We have it already. There is freedom of speech in Washington, but it is only for the champions of slavery. There is freedom of the press, but only of the press which extenuates or defends political wrongs. Twice already the South, failed in the arguments of reason, has resorted to the argument of folly. Driven from every position, constantly refuted in its reasoning, met and repulsed when it has resorted to invective, by an invective more vigorous than its own, at first astonished and then crazed by the changing and bolder tone of Northern man, the South has taken to expedients with which long use has made it familiar, and in which years of daily practice have given it a nefarious skill. Thank God, we know little of these resources in New England! We have our differences, but they are differences controlled by decency. We have our controversies, but we do not permit their warmth to betray us into brutality; we do not think it necessary to shoot, to slash, or to stun the man with whom we may differ upon political points. The controversial ethics of the South are of another character, and they find their most repulsive illustration in the event of Thursday.

The barbarian who assaulted Mr. Sumner, and who sought in the head of his bludgeon for an argument which he could not find in his own, complained that South Carolina have been insulted by the Senator from Massachusetts, and that his venerable uncle had been spoken of in disrespectful terms! If every State, the public policy of which is assailed in the Senate, had been entitled to send to Washington a physical champion, we should long ago have despatched thither our brauniest athlete. If every nephew, whose uncle provokes criticism by public acts, is to rush into the Senate, the champion of his kinsman, we shall have a nepotism established quite unauthorized by the Constitution! The South complains of hard words, of plain speech, of licentious language! Have its members then been accustomed to bridle their tongues, to control their tempers, to moderate their ire, to abstain from personalities? What indeed have we had from that quarter, save one long stream of vituperation, one endless rain of fish-wife rhetoric, one continuous blast of feverish denunciation and passionate threat? Let the world judge between us. We have borne and forborne. We have been patient until patience has become ignominious. There are wrongs which no man of spirit will suffer tamely; there are topics which it is impossible to discuss with coldness; there are injuries which must lend fire to language, and arouse the temper of the most stolid. Mr. Sumner's speech is before the country and it is for the country to decide whether it does or does not justify the violence with which it has been met. Our Senator comments freely upon the character of the Kansas bill, upon the apologies which have been made for it, in Congress, upon the readiness of the Administration to promote the schemes of its supporters, upon the unparalleled injuries which have been inflicted upon the unfortunate people of Kansas. Others have spoken upon the same topics with equal plainness, although not perhaps with equal ability. Mr. Sumner is singularly well sustained in all his positions,

in his opinions of the bill, and in his estimate of Douglas and Butler, by the mind and heart, not only of his constituents, but of the whole North. The time had come for plain and unmistakable language, and it has been uttered. There are those who profess to believe that Northern rhetoric should always be emasculated, and that Northern members should always take care to speak humbly and with "bated breath." They complain with nervous fastidiousness that Mr. Sumner was provoking. So were Mr. Burke and Mr. Sheridan, when in immoderate language they exposed the wrongs of India and the crimes of Hastings; so was Patrick Henry, when he plead against the parsons; so was Tristram Burges, when he silenced Randolph of Roanoke; so was Mr. Webster, when, in the most remarkable oration of modern times, he launched the lightning of his overwhelming invective, while every fibre of his great frame was full of indignation and reproach. Smooth speeches will answer for smooth times; but there is a species of oratory, classic since the days of Demosthenes, employed without a scruple upon fit occasions, in all deliberative assemblies, perfectly well recognized, and sometimes absolutely necessary. Who will say that Kansas, and Atchison, and Douglas together, were not enough to inspire and justify a new Philippic?

But we care not what Mr. Sumner said, nor in what behalf he was pleading. We know him only as the Senator of Massachusetts; we remember only that the commonwealth has been outraged. Had the Senator of any other State been subjected to a like indignity, we might have found words in which to express our abhorrence of the crime; but now we can only say, that every constituent of Mr. Sumner ought to feel that the injury is his own, and that it is for him to expect redress. A high-minded Senate, would vindicate its trampled dignity; a respectable House of Representatives would drive the wrong-doer from its benches; in a society unpolluted by barbarism, the assaulter of an unarmed man, would find himself the object of general contempt. We can hardly hope that such a retribution will visit the offender; but Massachusetts, in other and better times, would have had a right confidently to anticipate the expulsion of Preston Brooks from the house of Representatives. We leave it to others to decide how far it may be fit and proper for her officially to express her sense of this indignity. For our own part, we think she can rely upon the generosity and the justice of her sister states, that an outrage so indefensible will meet with a fitting rebuke from the people, if not from the representatives of the people. And if in this age of civilization, brute force is to control the government of the country, striking down our senators, silencing debate, and leaving us only the name of Freedom, there are remedies with which Massachusetts has found it necessary to meet similar exigencies in the past, which she will not hesitate to employ in the future.

Pittsburgh, Pennsylvania, Gazette
(May 24, 1856)

The news of the cowardly attack on Mr. Sumner by a villainous South Carolinian, stirred up a deeper indignation among our citizens, yesterday, than we have ever before witnessed. It was an indignation that pervaded all classes and conditions of men. The assault was deliberately planned, being made in the presence and under the encouragement of a crowd of bullies, when Mr. Sumner was alone, unarmed and defenceless, and it was conducted so brutally—fifty blows being inflicted upon an unresisting victim, until the weapon of attack was used up, and not one hand raised among the bystanders to stay the fury of the perfidious wretch, that every feeling of human nature revolts at the exhibition. Barbarians and savages would not be guilty of such unmanliness; and even the vulgar blackguards who follow the business of bruisers and shoulder-hitters would have a far higher sense of fair play than was shown by these patterns of chivalry. A universal cry of "Shame!" would go up from the lips of the people, if, unfortunately, the people did not, in view of this and similar outrages, feel a bitter shamefacedness at their own degradation in having to submit to them.

It is time, now, to inaugurate a change. It can no longer be permitted that all the blows shall come from one side. If Southern men will resort to the fist to overawe and intimidate Northern men, blow must be given back for blow. Forbearance and kindly deportment are lost upon these Southern ruffians. It were as well to throw pearls before swine as turn one cheek to them when the other is smitten. Under the circumstances now prevailing, neither religion nor manhood requires submission to such outrages. Northern men must defend themselves; and if our present representatives will not fight, when attacked, let us find those who will. It is not enough, now, to have backbone; there must be strong right arms, and a determination to use them. The voters of the Free States, in vindication of their own manliness will, hereafter, in addition to inquiring of candidates. Will you vote so-and-so, have to enlarge the basis of interrogation, and demand an affirmative answer to the question, Will you fight? It has come to that, now, that Senators and Representatives cannot enjoy the right of free speech or free discussion, without being liable to brutal assaults; and they must, of necessity, arm themselves with swordcanes or revolvers. To think of enduring quietly such attacks as that upon Mr. SUMNER, is craven and pusillanimous.—These cut-throat Southrons will never learn to respect Northern men until some one of their number has a rapier thrust through his ribs, or feels a bullet in his thorax. It is lamentable that such should be the case; but it is not in human nature to be trampled on.

THE FREE-LABOUR PRODUCE MOVEMENT (1857)

The following excerpt is taken from E. Burritt's Citizen of the World

It is certainly the fact, that movements involving political excitement and fervid speech-making present an attraction to the great majority of anti-slavery men of this country, which the quiet free-labour enterprise does not offer them. In seeking to introduce into the Southern States the enriching industry of free sinews, and to shew here and there, by repeated demonstrations, that cotton, sugar, rice, &c., may be grown by those unbought sinews more profitably than by slave-labour, although we undermine powerfully the system of Slavery, we do not array against the slaveholders that sharp and wordy antagonism which is the chief characteristic of political action. We would not institute any comparison between these two forms of effort. There is plenty of room and occasion for both. The noiseless free-labor movement has this particular merit at least: it is designed to operate in the very heart of the old Slave States, and directly upon those interests interwoven with their "peculiar institution." It is an agency calculated to make the most salutary impression upon the planter, and the poor unfortunate white man whom slavery has degraded and oppressed. We are persuaded that it is the necessary complement to all other efforts for the extinction of the cruel system of human bondage. As such, we would earnestly solicit for it the co-operation of all the friends of freedom and humanity. Let them glance at all the other operations, political, religious, and philanthropic, directed against that system at this moment, and they will find that they are almost entirely confined to the Free States, or to the Territories, and designed to affect public sentiment an action north of Mason and Dixon's line. What other effort has been set on foot for the express purpose of enlightening the people south of that line, in regard to the wrong, and waste, and wretchedness of the iniquitous system they uphold? Are there any agents, missionaries, tracts, or other instrumentalities employed to this end in those States? No. All the influences put forth upon them on this subject by the North are merely indirect and incidental. The free-labour enterprise, on the other hand, makes the South its especial field of exertion. It penetrates to the very citadel of the slave-power. It makes every acre tilled by free sinews over against the planter's estate a mute but most intelligible anti-slavery lecture, illustrated with cuts, contrasting his wasteful economy with the productive and fertilizing industry of well-paid toil. It presents a simple picture-book to the slave, with the alphabet of freedom reduced to his understanding. It comes in as a valuable auxiliary to the poor white man, to inspire him with self-respect, and to make him feel that he belongs to the great democracy of free-labour, which shall triumph gloriously in the end. For each of these three parties composing the population of the South, it works in the spirit of good-will, aiming to promote their best interests. And good-will is the most energetic sentiment wherewith to work for humanity. It works without flagging, through good and evil report. All its implements are shaped and pointed for constructions. It displaces, supplants, supersedes. It does not aim at mere demolition or uprooting. It does not seek to create a blank; but is ever erecting something. This sentiment is the motive force of the free-labour enterprise; and we hope this fact will commend it to the hearty and generous support of all the friends of freedom and righteousness who may become acquainted with its operations.

The Anti Slavery Reporter (New Series), 5:3 (March 2, 1857).

DRED SCOTT DECISION (1857)

Dred Scott, Plaintiff in Error, v. John F. A. Sandford. December Term, 1856

Justice Catron, Justice Wayne, Justice Nelson, Justice Grier, Justice Daniel, and Justice Campbell concurring in separate opinions. Justice McLean and Justice Curtis dissenting in separate opinions. Now, as we have already said in an earlier part of this opinion, upon a different point, the right of property in a slave is distinctly and expressly affirmed in the Constitution. The right to traffic in it, like an ordinary article of merchandise and property, was guaranteed to the citizens of the United States, in every State that might desire it, for twenty years. And the Government in express terms is pledged to protect it in all future time, if the slave escapes from his owner. This is done in plain

words too plain to be misunderstood. And no word can be found in the Constitution which gives Congress a greater power over slave property, or which entitles property of that kind to less protection than property of any other description. The only power conferred is the power coupled with the duty of guarding and protecting the owner in his rights.

Upon these considerations, it is the opinion of the court that the act of Congress which prohibited a citizen from holding and owning property of this kind in the territory of the United States north of the line therein mentioned, is not warranted by the Constitution, and is therefore void; and that neither Dred Scott himself, nor any of his family, were made free by being carried into this territory; even if they had been carried there by the owner, with the intention of becoming a permanent resident.

We have so far examined the case, as it stands under the Constitution of the United States, and the powers thereby delegated to the Federal Government.

But there is another point in the case which depends on State power and State law. And it is contended, on the part of the plaintiff, that he is made free by being taken to Rock Island, in the State of Illinois, independently of his residence in the territory of the United States; and being so made free, he was not again reduced to a state of slavery by being brought back to Missouri.

Our notice of this part of the case will be very brief; for the principle on which it depends was decided in this court, upon much consideration, in the case of *Strader et al. v. Graham,* reported in 10th Howard, 82. In that case, the slaves had been taken from Kentucky to Ohio, with the consent of the owner, and afterwards brought back to Kentucky. And this court held that their status or condition, as free or slave, depended upon the laws of Kentucky, when they were brought back into that State, and not of Ohio; and that this court had no jurisdiction to revise the judgment of a State court upon its own laws. This was the point directly before the court, and the decision that this court had not jurisdiction turned upon it, as will be seen by the report of the case.

So in this case. As Scott was a slave when taken into the State of Illinois by his owner, and was there held as such, and brought back in that character, his status, as free or slave, depended on the laws of Missouri, and not of Illinois.

It has, however, been urged in the argument, that by the laws of Missouri he was free on his return, and that this case, therefore, cannot be governed by the case of *Strader et al. v. Graham,* where it appeared, by the laws of Kentucky, that the plaintiffs continued to be slaves on their return from Ohio. But whatever doubts or opinions may, at one time, have been entertained upon this subject, we are satisfied, upon a careful examination of all the cases decided in the State courts of Missouri referred to, that it is now firmly settled by the decisions of the highest court in the State, that Scott and his family upon their return were not free, but were, by the laws of Missouri, the property of the defendant; and that the Circuit Court of the United States had no jurisdiction, when, by the laws of the State, the plaintiff was a slave, and not a citizen.

Moreover, the plaintiff, it appears, brought a similar action against the defendant in the State court of Missouri, claiming the freedom of himself and his family upon the same grounds and the same evidence upon which he relies in the case before the court. The case was carried before the Supreme Court of the State; was fully argued there; and that court decided that neither the plaintiff nor his family were entitled to freedom, and were still the slaves of the defendant; and reversed the judgment of the inferior State court, which had given a different decision. If the plaintiff supposed that this judgment of the Supreme Court of the State was erroneous, and that this court had jurisdiction to revise and reverse it, the only mode by which he could legally bring it before this court was by writ of error directed to the Supreme Court of the State, requiring it to transmit the record to this court. If this had been done, it is too plain for argument that the writ must have been dismissed for want of jurisdiction in this court. The case of *Strader and others v. Graham* is directly in point; and, indeed, independent of any decision, the language of the 25th section of the act of 1789 is too clear and precise to admit of controversy.

But the plaintiff did not pursue the mode prescribed by law for bringing the judgment of a State court before this court for revision, but suffered the case to be remanded to the inferior State court, where it is still continued, and is, by agreement of parties, to await the judgment of this court on the point. All of this appears on the record before us, and by the printed report of the case.

And while the case is yet open and pending in the inferior State court, the plaintiff goes into the Circuit Court of the United States, upon the same case and the same evidence, and against the same party, and proceeds to judgment, and then brings here the same case from the Circuit Court, which the law would not have permitted him to bring directly from the State court. And if this court takes jurisdiction in this form, the result, so far as the rights of the respective parties are concerned, is in every respect substantially the same as if it had in open violation of law entertained jurisdiction over the judgment of the State court upon a writ of error, and revised and reversed its judgment upon the ground that its opinion upon the question of law was erroneous. It would ill become this court to sanction such an attempt to evade the law, or to exercise an appellate power in this circuitous way, which it is forbidden to exercise in the direct and regular and invariable forms of judicial proceedings.

Upon the whole, therefore, it is the judgment of this court, that it appears by the record before us that the plaintiff in error is not a citizen of Missouri, in the sense in which that word is used in the Constitution; and that the Circuit Court of the United States, for that reason, had no jurisdiction in the case, and could give no judgment in it. Its judgment for the defendant must, consequently, be reversed, and a mandate issued, directing the suit to be dismissed for want of jurisdiction.

19 How. 393 (1857).

EDITORIAL RESPONSE TO THE DRED SCOTT DECISION (1857)

Pittsburgh, Pennsylvania, Gazette (March 7, 1857)

We do not know how other persons may feel in view of the recent *dicta* of the Supreme Court in the case of Dred Scott, an abstract of which was published in our telegraphic column on Saturday morning, but it appears to us that the almost diabolical spirit it evinces in going out of the way to Freedom at the expense of Slavery, ought to be sufficient to arouse to indignation the coolest and most torpid of northern men. The decision is a fitting crown to the aborted tyranny which has just submerged with Pierce; an iron clasp, well forged to link the dead with the living administration. It comes pat upon the recent inaugural, "rounds and caps it to the tyrant's eye" and just fills up the cup of inequity.

What matter is it that this decision upsets those we have on record? New lights have arisen with the progress of revolving years, and Story and Marshall, Jefferson, Madison, and Monroe hide their twinkling lights before the full-orbed glory of Douglas, Pierce and Davis. The Supreme Court has aimed a blow at State Sovereignty which is baser and more iniquitous than any thing we had before conceived of. The State of Illinois for example, under this decision in her legislative capacity, has no power to enact such a law as can make a slave coming there with the consent of his master a freeman! The decision that the Court has no jurisdiction in this case make all the other remarks from the bench touching the ordinance of 1787, and the compromise of 1820, mere *obiter dicta,* it is true, but the fact that the Court has gone out of its way to say what it has, shows its animus, and trumpets to the four corners of the earth the eager alacrity with which it echoes the mouthings of demagogues like Pierce and Douglas. We may henceforth throw to the winds the reasoning of Story and the decisions of Marshall, so far as this court is concerned, and submit to seeing the government surrendered, bound hand and foot to the same power which has given Kansas over to blood and desolation, elevated a weak old man to the executive chair, given the Treasury, the Post Office, the Army, the Navy and the Department of the Interior to be its willing servants and exhilarated and energized by its success, pressed on to the Supreme Court, made that the echo of its will and left no place for hope to rest upon, but the virtue of the masses of the people, to which we must henceforth appeal. Let them come in their might and at the ballot box root up the rotten fabric to its foundations which four years of misrule has served so much to weaken, and which the four years to come will doubtless not improve or strengthen.

New York Tribune (March 11, 1857)

It is impossible to exaggerate the importance of the recent decision of the Supreme Court. The grounds and methods of that decision we have exposed elsewhere; and we now turn from them to contemplate the great fact which it establishes—the fact that *Slavery is National;* and that, until that remote period when different Judges, sitting in this same Court, shall reverse this wicked and false judgment, the Constitution of the United States is nothing better than the bulwark of inhumanity and oppression.

It is most true that this decision is bad law; that it is based on false historical premises and wrong interpretations of the Constitution; that it does not at all represent the legal or judicial opinion of the Nation; that it is merely a Southern sophism clothed with the dignity of our highest Court. Nevertheless there it is; the final action of the National Judiciary, established by the founders of the Republic to interpret the Constitution, and to embody the ultimate legal conclusions of the whole people—an action proclaiming that in the view of the Constitution *slaves are property.* The inference is plain. If slaves are recognized as property by the Constitution, of course no local or State law can either prevent property being carried through an individual

State or Territory, or forbid its being sold as such wherever its owner may choose to hold it. This is all involved in the present decision; but let a single case draw from the Court an official judgment that slaves can be held and protected under National law, and we shall see men buying slaves for the New York market. There will be no legal power to prevent it. At this moment, indeed, any wealthy New York jobber connected with the Southern trade can put in his next orders: "Send me a negro cook, at the lowest market value! Buy me a waiter! Balance my account with two chambermaids and a truckman!" Excepting the interference of the Underground Railroad and the chance of loss, there will be nothing to stop this. But then these underhanded efforts for stealing property must, of course, be checked by our Police. Mr. Matsell will have no more right to allow gentlemen's servants to be spirited away by burgarious Abolitionists than gentlemen's spoons. They are property under even stronger pledges of security than mere lifeless chattels. The whole power of the State—the military, the Courts and Governor of the State of New York—will necessarily be sworn to protect each New York slave-owner from the robbery or burglary of his negro. If they are not sufficient, why then the United States Army and Navy can be called upon to guard that singular species of property which alone of all property the Constitution of the United States has especially recognized. Slaves can be kept in Boston; Mr. Toombs can call the roll of his chattels on the slope of Bunker Hill; auctions of black men may be held in front of Faneuil Hall, and the slave-ship, protected by the guns of United States frigates, may land its dusky cargo at Plymouth Rock. The free hills of Vermont, the lakes of Maine, the valleys of Connecticut, the city where the ancient Oak of Liberty has wisely fallen, may be traversed by the gangs of the negro-driver, and enriched by the legitimate commerce of the slave-pen. Are we told that public opinion will prevent this? What can public opinion do against the Supreme Court and all the power of the United States? Shall not a citizen of this Union have the right to take and hold his property, his horses, his oxen, his dogs, his slaves, wherever it seems to him good? According to the law now established, the Free-State men of Kansas are robbers, for they attack the Constitutional and inalienable rights of property. The bogus laws of which they presume to complain, but which the mild and paternal punishment of death is not to protect from infractions, are just and necessary laws for the safety of those sacred rights. The number of Free Soil men in that Territory can make no difference hereafter, as it has made none hitherto. Slavery is there, as the ownership of horses or land is there, by supreme national law. Of what use, then, to contend for such a shadow as the difference between a Free and a Slave Constitution? Or what sense in that old fiction of State Rights? The States have no rights as respects Freedom; their rights consist only in establishing and strengthening Slavery—nothing more.

Another most pregnant change is wrought by this decision, in respect of the Northern people. We have been accustomed to regard Slavery as a local matter for which we were in no wise responsible. As we have been used, to say, it belonged to the Southern States alone, and they must answer for it before the world. We can say this no more. Now, wherever the stars and stripes wave, they protect Slavery and represent Slavery. The black and cursed stain is thick on our hands also. From Maine to the Pacific, over all future conquests and annexations, wherever in the islands of western seas, or in the South American Continent, or in the Mexican Gulf, the flag of the Union, by just means or unjust, shall be planted, there it plants the curse, and tears, and blood, and unpaid toil of this "institution." The Star of Freedom and the stripes of bondage are henceforth one. American Republicanism and American Slavery are for the future synonymous. This, then, is the final fruit. In this all the labors of our statesmen, the blood of our heroes, the life-long cares and toils of our forefathers, the aspirations of our scholars, the prayers of good men, have finally ended! America the slavebreeder and slaveholder!

Albany, New York, Evening Journal
(March 19, 1857)

Five of its nine silk gowns are worn by Slaveholders. More than half its long Bench is filled with Slaveholders. Its Chief Justice is a Slaveholder. The Free States with double the population of the Slave State, do not have half the Judges. The majority represent a minority of 350,000. The minority represent a majority of twenty Millions!

It has long been so. Originally there were three Northern and three Southern Judges. But the South soon got the bigger share of the black robes, and kept them. Of the thirty-eight who have sat there in judgment, twenty-two were nurtured "on plantation." The Slave States have been masters of the Court fifty-seven years, the Free States but eleven! The Free States have had the majority only seven years, this century. Even the Free State Judges are chosen from Slavery extending parties. Presidents nominate, and Senates confirm none other. Three times a new Judgeship has been created, and every time it has been filled with a Slave-holder. The advocate who pleads there against Slavery, wastes his voice in its vaulted roof, and upon ears stuffed sixty years with cotton. His case is judged before it is argued, and his client condemned before he is heard.

DESCRIPTION OF GANG LABOR ON A KENTUCKY PLANTATION (1857)

The year 1857 was at hand. Fifteen slaves had been left on the farm to do the winter work. These were kept busy husking and shelling corn, taking same to the mill, then to the distillery and made into liquor. That year of 1857 there were from five to six hundred barrels of liquor made and stored in the cellar. Master at this time was about sixty years of age and he married a girl about seventeen. He returned to the farm with his young wife, twelve slaves besides the stewardess, named Rosa, and trouble soon began. Rosa was well fitted for her position and she had a general oversight of all the slaves. She was an octoroon and had the confidence of Master who trusted her to the utmost.

New slaves were brought in every few days and these were set to work during the summer, clearing land when there was no other work, their hours of labor being from 16 to 18 each day.

The slaves were divided into gangs, and over each gang was a Boss, who was also one of the slaves. At four o'clock each morning, the bell was rung and each Boss had to see that his gang was up and ready to commence the day's work. They marched by gangs to the tables set up under some trees in the yard, where breakfast was served for which one half hour was allowed, after which each Boss marched his gang to the fields or to the kind of work laid out for them. The overseer rode on horse back from one gang to another seeing that all were kept busy. If he saw two or three idle, or talking to each other, if no satisfactory reason could be given, a whipping was sure to follow. At no time were three allowed to talk together unless the overseer was present. At twelve o'clock the gangs were marched to the tables for dinner, and one hour was allowed for dinner and rest, and then they were marched again to their work, where they remained as long as there was daylight to work by, and then they were marched once more to the tables for supper, after which they went to their cabins, each cabin being occupied by from ten to twelve persons, men and women were in separate cabins, except where they were married, and such had cabins by themselves. At ten o'clock the bell was rung when all must go to bed, or at half past ten, when the overseer made his rounds, if any were found up they were taken to the punishment room, and in the morning Master administered such punishment as he thought best. The punishment was a certain number of lashes from the whip for the first offence and more if the offence was repeated, with the addition of an iron weight tied to their backs for a number of days or weeks according to the Master's pleasure, these weights to be carried during the day while they were at work.

The year of which we are writing, about two hundred slaves were gathered on the stock farm, and in the fall most of them were marched off to the several slave markets in the same manner as before described, fastened to a long chain with the women who could walk following, and the women and children not able to walk in wagons. Of the two hundred, 170 were taken, leaving thirty to run the farm and do the winter work. This lot was taken to Bardstown, thence to Louisville, where they were put aboard of boats rigged with stalls similar to horse stalls into which the slaves were placed and chained until they reached Vicksburg or other places where markets were held.

Johnson, Isaac. 1901. *Slavery Days in Old Kentucky.* Ogdensburg, NY: Republican & Journal Co. Printing.

GEORGE FITZHUGH VIEWS SLAVERY A CONDITION OF NATURE (1857)

"The Universal Law of Slavery"

He the Negro is but a grown up child, and must be governed as a child, not as a lunatic or criminal. The master occupies toward him the place of parent or guardian. We shall not dwell on this view, for no one will differ with us who thinks as we do of the negro's capacity, and we might argue till dooms-day in vain, with those who have a high opinion of the negro's moral and intellectual capacity.

Secondly. The negro is improvident; will not lay up in summer for the wants of winter; will not accumulate in youth for the exigencies of age. He would become an insufferable burden to society. Society has the right to prevent this, and can only do so by subjecting him to domestic slavery. In the last place, the negro race is inferior to the white race, and living in their midst, they would be far outstripped or outwitted in the chaos of free competition. Gradual but certain extermination would be their fate. We presume the maddest abolitionist does not think the negro's providence of habits and money-making capacity at all to compare to those of the whites. This defect of character would alone justify enslaving him, if he is to remain here. In

Africa or the West Indies, he would become idolatrous, savage and cannibal, or be devoured by savages and cannibals. At the North he would freeze or starve.

We would remind those who deprecate and sympathize with negro slavery, that his slavery here relieves him from a far more cruel slavery in Africa, or from idolatry and cannibalism, and every brutal vice and crime that can disgrace humanity; and that it christianizes, protects, supports and civilizes him; that it governs him far better than free laborers at the North are governed. There, wife-murder has become a mere holiday pastime; and where so many wives are murdered, almost all must be brutally treated. Nay, more; men who kill their wives or treat them brutally, must be ready for all kinds of crime, and the calendar of crime at the North proves the inference to be correct. Negroes never kill their wives. If it be objected that legally they have no wives, then we reply, that in an experience of more than forty years, we never yet heard of a negro man killing a negro woman. Our negroes are not only better off as to physical comfort than free laborers, but their moral condition is better.

The negro slaves of the South are the happiest, and, in some sense, the freest people in the world. The children and the aged and the infirm work not at all, and yet have all the comforts and necessaries of life provided for them. They enjoy liberty, because they are oppressed neither by care nor labor. The women do little hard work, and are protected from the despotism of their husbands by their masters. The negro men and stout boys work, on the average, in good weather, not more than nine hours a day. The balance of their time is spent in perfect abandon. Besides they have their Sabbaths and holidays. White men, with so much of license and liberty, would die of ennui; but negroes luxuriate in corporeal and mental repose. With their faces upturned to the sun, they can sleep at any hour; and quiet sleep is the greatest of human enjoyments. "Blessed be the man who invented sleep." 'Tis happiness in itself—and results from contentment with the present, and confident assurance of the future.

A common charge preferred against slavery is, that it induces idleness with the masters. The trouble, care and labor, of providing for wife, children and slaves, and of properly governing and administering the whole affairs of the farm, is usually borne on small estates by the master. On larger ones, he is aided by an overseer or manager. If they do their duty, their time is fully occupied. If they do not, the estate goes to ruin. The mistress, on Southern farms, is usually more busily, usefully and benevolently occupied than any one on the farm. She unites in her person, the offices of wife, mother, mistress, housekeeper, and sister of charity. And she fulfills all these offices admirably well. The rich men, in free society, may, if they please, lounge about town, visit clubs, attend the theatre, and have no other trouble than that of collecting rents, interest and dividends of stock. In a well constituted slave society, there should be no idlers. But we cannot divine how the capitalists in free society are to put to work. The master labors for the slave, they exchange industrial value. But the capitalist, living on his income, gives nothing to his subjects. He lives by mere exploitations.

Fitzhugh, George. 1857. *Cannibals All!, or, Slaves Without Masters*. Richmond, VA: A. Morris.

JAMES HENRY HAMMOND'S "MUD-SILL THEORY" (1858)

Speech to the U.S. Senate, March 4, 1858.

But sir, the greatest strength of the South arises from the harmony of her political and social institutions. This harmony gives her a frame of society, the best in the world, and an extent of political freedom, combined with entire security, such as no other people ever enjoyed upon the face of the earth. Society precedes government; creates it, and ought to control it; but as far as we can look back in historic times we find the case different; for government is no sooner created than it becomes too strong for society, and shapes and molds, as well as controls it. In later centuries the progress of civilization and of intelligence has made the divergence so great as to produce civil wars and revolutions; and it is nothing now but the want of harmony between governments and societies which occasions all the uneasiness and trouble and terror that we see abroad. It was this that brought on the American Revolution. We threw off a government not adapted to our social system, and made one for ourselves. The question is, how far have we succeeded? The South, so far as that is concerned, is satisfied, content, happy, harmonious, and prosperous.

In all social systems there must be a class to do the menial duties, to perform the drudgery of life. That is, a class requiring but a low order of intellect and but little skill. Its requisites are vigor, docility, fidelity. Such a class you must have, or you would not have that other class which leads progress, civilization, and refinement. It constitutes the very mud-sill of society and of political government; and you might as well attempt to build a house in the air, as to build either the one or the other, except on the mud-sills. Fortunately for the South, she found a race adapted to that purpose to her hand. A race inferior to her own, but eminently qualified in temper, in vigor, in docility, in capacity to stand the climate, to answer all her purposes. We use them for our purpose, and call them slaves. We are old-fashioned at the South yet; it is a word discarded now by ears polite; I will not characterize that class at the North by that term; but you have it; it is there; it is everywhere; it is eternal.

The Senator from New York said yesterday that the whole world had abolished slavery. Ay, the name, but not the thing; and all the powers of the earth cannot abolish it. God only can do it when he repeals the fiat, "the poor ye always have with you;" for the man who lives by daily labor, and scarcely lives at that, and who has to put out his labor in the market, and take the best he can get for it; in short, your whole hireling class of manual laborers and operatives, as you call them, are essentially slaves. The difference between us is, that our slaves are hired for life and well compensated; there is no starvation, no begging, no want of employment among our people, and not too much employment either. Yours are hired by the day, not cared for, and scantily compensated, which may be proved in the most deplorable manner, at any hour, in any street in any of your large towns. Why, sir, you meet more beggars in one day, in any single street of the city of New York, than you would meet in a lifetime in the whole South. We do not think that whites should be slaves either by law or necessity. Our slaves are black, of another, inferior race. The *status* in which we have placed them is an elevation. They are elevated from the condition in which God first created them, by being made our slaves. None of that race on the whole face of the globe can be compared with the slaves of the South, and they know it. They are happy, content, unaspiring, and utterly incapable, from intellectual degradation, ever to give us any trouble by their aspirations.

Your slaves are white, of your own race; you are brothers of one blood. They are your equals in natural endowment of intellect, and they feel galled by their degradation. Our slaves do not vote. We give them no political power. Yours do vote, and, being the majority, they are the depositories of all your political power. If they knew the tremendous secret, that the ballot-box is stronger than an army with bayonets, and could combine, where would you be? Your society would be reconstructed, your government reconstructed, your property divided, not as they have mistakenly attempted to initiate such proceedings by meeting in parks, with arms in their hands, but by the quiet process of the ballot-box. You have been making war upon us to our very hearthstones. How would you like for us to send lecturers and agitators North, to teach these people this, to aid and assist in combining, and to lead them?

United States Congress. 1858. *The Congressional Globe, Thirty-fifth Congress, First Session.* Washington, DC: John C. Rives.

ABRAHAM LINCOLN'S "HOUSE DIVIDED" SPEECH (1858)

Mr. President and Gentlemen of the Convention.

If we could first know where we are, and whither we are tending, we could then better judge what to do, and how to do it.

We are now far into the fifth year, since a policy was initiated, with the avowed object, and confident promise, of putting an end to slavery agitation.

Under the operation of that policy, that agitation has not only, not ceased, but has constantly augmented.

In my opinion, it will not cease, until a crisis shall have been reached, and passed.

"A house divided against itself cannot stand."

I believe this government cannot endure, permanently half slave and half free.

I do not expect the Union to be dissolved—I do not expect the house to fall—but I do expect it will cease to be divided.

It will become all one thing, or all the other.

Either the opponents of slavery, will arrest the further spread of it, and place it where the public mind shall rest in the belief that it is in course of ultimate extinction; or its advocates will push it forward, till it shall become alike lawful in all the States, old as well as new—North as well as South.

Have we no tendency to the latter condition?

Let any one who doubts, carefully contemplate that now almost complete legal combination-piece of machinery so to speak-compounded of the Nebraska doctrine, and the Dred Scott decision. Let him consider not only what work the machinery is adapted to do, and how well adapted; but also, let him study the history of its construction, and trace, if he can, or rather fail, if he can, to trace the evidences of design, and concert of action, among its chief bosses, from the beginning.

But, so far, Congress only, had acted; and an endorsement by the people, real or apparent, was indispensable, to save the point already gained, and give chance for more.

The new year of 1854 found slavery excluded from more than half the States by State Constitutions, and from most of the national territory by Congressional prohibition.

Four days later, commenced the struggle, which ended in repealing that Congressional prohibition.

This opened all the national territory to slavery; and was the first point gained.

This necessity had not been overlooked; but had been provided for, as well as might be, in the notable argument of "squatter sovereignty," otherwise called "sacred right of self government," which latter phrase, though expressive of the only rightful basis of, any government, was so perverted in this attempted use of it as to amount to just this: That if any one man choose to enslave another, no third man shall be allowed to object.

That argument was incorporated into the Nebraska bill itself, in the language which follows: "It being the true intent and meaning of this act not to legislate slavery into any Territory or state, not exclude it therefrom; but to leave the people thereof perfectly free to form and regulate their domestic institutions in their own way, subject only to the Constitution of the United States."

Then opened the roar of loose declamation in favor of "Squatter Sovereignty," and "Sacred right of self government."

"But," said opposition members, "let us be more specific—let us amend the bill so as to expressly declare that the people of the territory may exclude slavery." Not we, said the friends of the measure; and down they voted the amendment.

While the Nebraska bill was passing through congress, a law case, involving the question of a negroe's freedom, by reason of his owner having voluntarily taken him first into a free state and then a territory covered by the congressional prohibition, and held him as a slave, for a long time in each, was passing through the U.S. Circuit Court for the District of Missouri; and both Nebraska bill and law suit were brought to a decision in the same month of May, 1854. The negroe's name was "Dred Scott," which name now designates the decision finally made in the case.

Before the then next Presidential election, the law case came to, and was argued in the Supreme Court of the United States; but the decision of it was deferred until after the election. Still, before the election, Senator Trumbull, on the floor of the Senate, requests the leading advocate of the Nebraska bill to state his opinion whether the people of a territory can constitutionally exclude slavery from their limits; and the latter answers, "That is a question for the Supreme Court."

The election came. Mr. Buchanan was elected, and

the endorsement, such as it was, secured. That was the second point gained. The endorsement, however, fell short of a clear popular majority by nearly four hundred thousand votes, and so, perhaps, was not overwhelmingly reliable and satisfactory.

The outgoing President, in his last annual message, as impressively as possible echoed back upon the people the weight and authority of the endorsement.

The Supreme Court met again; did not announce their decision, but ordered a re-argument.

The Presidential inauguration came, and still no decision of the court; but the incoming President, in his inaugural address, fervently exhorted the people to abide by the forthcoming decision, whatever it might be.

Then, in a few days, came the decision.

The reputed author of the Nebraska bill finds an early occasion to make a speech at this capitol endorsing the Dred Scott Decision, and vehemently denouncing all opposition to it.

The new President, too, seizes the early occasion of the Silliman letter to endorse and strongly construe that decision, and to express his astonishment that any different view had ever been entertained.

At length a squabble springs up between the President and the author of the Nebraska bill, on the mere question of fact, whether the Lecompton Constitution was or was not, in any just sense, made by the people of Kansas; and in that squabble the latter declares that all he wants is a fair vote for the people, and that he cares not whether slavery be voted down or voted up. I do not understand his declaration that he cares not whether slavery be voted down or voted up, to be intended by him other than as an apt definition of the policy he would impress upon the public mind—the principle for which he declares he has suffered much, and is ready to suffer to the end.

And well may he cling to that principle. If he has any parental feeling, well may he cling to it. That principle, is the only shred left of his original Nebraska doctrine. Under the Dred Scott decision, "squatter sovereignty" squatted out of existence, tumbled down like temporary scaffolding—like the mould at the foundry served through one blast and fell back into loose sand—helped to carry an election, and then was kicked to the winds. His late joint struggle with the Republicans, against the Lecompton Constitution, involves nothing of the original Nebraska doctrine. That struggle was made on a point, the right of a people to make their own constitution, upon which he and the Republicans have never differed.

The several points of the Dred Scott decision, in connection with Senator Douglas' "care not" policy, constitute the piece of machinery, in its present state of advancement. This was the third point gained.

The working points of that machinery are:

First, that no negro slave, imported as such from Africa, and no descendant of such slave can ever be a citizen of any State, in the sense of that term as used in the Constitution of the United States.

This point is made in order to deprive the negro, in every possible event, of the benefit of this provision of the United States Constitution, which declares, that—

"The citizens of each State shall be entitled to all privileges and immunities of citizens in the several States."

Secondly, that "subject to the Constitution of the United States," neither Congress nor a Territorial Legislature can exclude slavery from any United States territory.

This point is made in order that individual men may fill up the territories with slaves, without danger of losing them as property, and thus to enhance the chances of permanency to the institution through all the future.

Thirdly, that whether the holding a negro in actual slavery in a free State, makes him free, as against the holder, the United States courts will not decide, but will leave to be decided by the courts of any slave State the negro may be forced into by the master.

This point is made, not to be pressed immediately; but, if acquiesced in for a while, and apparently indorsed by the people at an election, then to sustain the logical conclusion that what Dred Scott's master might lawfully do with Dred Scott, in the free State of Illinois, every other master may lawfully do with any other one, or one thousand slaves, in Illinois, or in any other free State.

Auxiliary to all this, and working hand in hand with it, the Nebraska doctrine, or what is left of it, is to educate and mould public opinion, at least Northern public opinion, to not care whether slavery is voted down or voted up.

This shows exactly where we now are, and partially also, whither we are tending.

It will throw additional light on the latter, to go back, and run the mind over the string of historical facts already stated. Several things will now appear less dark and mysterious than they did when they were transpiring. The people were to be left "perfectly free" "subject only to the Constitution." What the Constitution had to do with it, outsiders could not then see. Plainly enough now, it was an exactly fitted niche, for the Dred Scott decision to afterwards come in, and declare the perfect freedom of the people, to be just no freedom at all.

Why was the amendment, expressly declaring the right of the people to exclude slavery, voted down? Plainly enough now, the adoption of it would have spoiled the niche for the Dred Scott decision.

Why was the court decision held up? Why, even a Senator's individual opinion withheld, till after the Presidential election? Plainly enough now, the speaking out then would have damaged the "perfectly free" argument upon which the election was to be carried.

Why the outgoing President's felicitation on the endorsement? Why the delay of a reargument? Why the incoming President's advance exhortation in favor of the decision?

These things look like the cautious patting and petting a spirited horse, preparatory to mounting him, when it is dreaded that he may give the rider a fall.

And why the hasty after endorsements of the decision by the President and others?

We can not absolutely know that all these exact adaptations are the result of preconcert. But when we see a lot of framed timbers, different portions of which we know have been gotten out at different times and places and by different workmen—Stephen, Franklin, Roger and James, for instance—and when we see these timbers joined together, and see they exactly make the frame of a house or a mill, all the tenons and mortices exactly fitting, and all the lengths and proportions of the different pieces exactly adapted to their respective places, and not a piece too many or too few—not omitting even scaffolding—or, if a single piece be lacking, we can see the place in the frame exactly fitted and prepared to yet bring such piece in—in such a case, we find it impossible to not believe that Stephen and Franklin and Roger and James all understood one another from the beginning, and all worked upon a common plan or draft drawn up before the first lick was struck.

It should not be overlooked that, by the Nebraska bill, the people of a State as well as Territory, were to be left "perfectly free" "subject only to the Constitution."

Why mention a State? They were legislating for territories, and not for or about States. Certainly the people of a State are and ought to be subject to the Constitution of the United States; but why is mention of this lugged into this merely territorial law? Why are the people of a territory and the people of a state therein lumped together, and their relation to the Constitution therein treated as being precisely the same?

While the opinion of the Court, by Chief Justice Taney, in the Dred Scott case, and the separate opinions of all the concurring Judges, expressly declare that the Constitution of the United States neither permits Congress nor a Territorial legislature to exclude slavery from any United States territory, they all omit to declare whether or not the same Constitution permits a state, or the people of a State, to exclude it.

Possibly, this was a mere omission; but who can be quite sure, if McLean or Curtis had sought to get into the opinion a declaration of unlimited power in the people of a state to exclude slavery from their limits, just as Chase and Macy sought to get such declaration, in behalf of the people of a territory, into the Nebraska bill—I ask, who can be quite sure that it would not have been voted down, in the one case, as it had been in the other.

The nearest approach to the point of declaring the power of a State over slavery, is made by Judge Nelson. He approaches it more than once, using the precise idea, and almost the language too, of the Nebraska act. On one occasion his exact language is, "except in cases where the power is restrained by the Constitution of the United States, the law of the State is supreme over the subject of slavery within its jurisdiction."

In what cases the power of the states is so restrained by the U.S. Constitution, is left an open question, precisely as the same question, as to the restraint on the power of the territories was left open in the Nebraska act. Put that and that together, and we have another nice little niche, which we may, ere long, see filled with another Supreme Court decision, declaring that the Constitution of the United States does not permit a state to exclude slavery from its limits.

And this may especially be expected if the doctrine of "care not whether slavery be voted down or voted up," shall gain upon the public mind sufficiently to give promise that such a decision can be maintained when made.

Such a decision is all that slavery now lacks of being alike lawful in all the States.

Welcome or unwelcome, such decision is probably coming, and will soon be upon us, unless the power of the present political dynasty shall be met and overthrown.

We shall lie down pleasantly dreaming that the people of Missouri are on the verge of making their State free; and we shall awake to the reality, instead, that the Supreme Court has made Illinois a slave State.

To meet and overthrow the power of that dynasty, is the work now before all those who would prevent that consummation.

That is what we have to do.

But how can we best do it?

There are those who denounce us openly to their own friends, and yet whisper us softly, that Senator Douglas is the aptest instrument there is, with which to effect that object. They do not tell us, nor has he told us, that he wishes any such object to be effected.

They wish us to infer all, from the facts, that he now has a little quarrel with the present head of the dynasty; and that he has regularly voted with us, on a single point, upon which, he and we, have never differed.

They remind us that he is a very great man, and that the largest of us are very small ones. Let this be granted. But "a living dog is better than a dead lion." Judge Douglas, if not a dead lion for this work, is at least a caged and toothless one. How can he oppose the advances of slavery? He don't care anything about it. His avowed mission is impressing the "public heart" to care nothing about it.

A leading Douglas Democratic newspaper thinks Douglas' superior talent will be needed to resist the revival of the African slave trade.

Does Douglas believe an effort to revive that trade is approaching? He has not said so. Does he really think so? But if it is, how can he resist it? For years he has labored to prove it is a sacred right of white men to take negro slaves into the new territories. Can he possibly show that it is less a sacred right to buy them where they can be bought cheapest? And, unquestionably they can be bought cheaper in Africa than in Virginia.

He has done all in his power to reduce the whole question of slavery to one of a mere right of property; and as such, how can he oppose the foreign slave trade—how can he refuse that trade in that "property" shall be "perfectly free"—unless he does it as a protection to the home production? And as the home producers will probably not ask the protection, he will be wholly without a ground of opposition.

Senator Douglas holds, we know, that a man may rightfully be wiser to-day than he was yesterday—that he may rightfully change when he finds himself wrong.

But, can we for that reason, run ahead, and infer that he will make any particular change, of which he, himself, has given no intimation? Can we safely base our action upon any such vague inference?

Now, as ever, I wish to not misrepresent Judge Douglas' position, question his motives, or do ought that can be personally offensive to him.

Whenever, if ever, he and we can come together on principle so that our great cause may have assistance from his great ability, I hope to have interposed no adventitious obstacle.

But clearly, he is not now with us—he does not pretend to be—he does not promise to ever be.

Our cause, then, must be entrusted to, and conducted by its own undoubted friends—those whose hands are free, whose hearts are in the work—who do care for the result.

Two years ago the Republicans of the nation mustered over thirteen hundred thousand strong.

We did this under the single impulse of resistance to a common danger, with every external circumstance against us.

Of strange, discordant, and even, hostile elements, we gathered from the four winds, and formed and fought the battle through, under the constant hot fire of a disciplined, proud, and pampered enemy.

Did we brave all then, to falter now?—now—when that same enemy is wavering, dissevered and belligerent?

The result is not doubtful. We shall not fail—if we stand firm, we shall not fail.

Wise councils may accelerate or mistakes delay it, but, sooner or later the victory is sure to come.

Lincoln, Abraham. "The House Divided Speech, June 16, 1858." In *Abraham Lincoln, a Documentary Portrait through His Speeches and Writings*. Don E. Fehrenbacher, ed. Stanford, CA: Stanford University Press, 1964.

OBSERVATIONS ON HEALTH CARE OF SLAVES (1858)

I propose to offer a few practical observations on the above subject [health of Negroes], and it is one to which I fear, many planters and managers are wont to bestow too little attention. I am persuaded that they can do much to promote the health of their Negroes by timely care and attention, and thus avoid, in some measure, what I have often heard them say gives them the greatest trouble in the management of their plantations, namely *the sickness amongst negroes.*

Their food should be sound, of sufficient quantity, well cooked, and served at regular intervals. It is better, as a general rule to have it cooked for them than to give them their allowances to be cooked by themselves, as is frequently done. I am aware that they prefer to cook for themselves, but there are always some negroes on every place who are too careless and indolent to cook their food in a proper manner; consequently they eat it but imperfectly cooked, if not entirely raw. With their meat and bread they should have vegetables of some kind and at least *three times* a week, and where it is practicable, it were better that they have them daily.

The next thing in importance is the water which they drink. The purest and best is *cistern water.* I will here state, as the result of my experience and observation as a physician in the low lands of Louisiana during the Cholera epidemics of 1849 and '50, that those places on which cistern water alone was used were nearly exempt from that dreadful disease. The few cases that did occur on those places were attributable to some imprudence in eating, or to the drinking of unwholesome water. On one plantation, where the disease made fearful havoc 'till the negroes were removed to the woods and given *cistern water,* it was ascertained that it was their custom to make use of stagnant water from a lagoon near the quarter. Spring and well water, so much used in many parts of the Southern and Western States, contains salts which are unwholesome, and in some instances positively deleterious. The water of the Mississippi River, when filtered or settled, is better than this, but not so good as *cistern water.* The cost of cisterns prevents many planters from having them, in that the greatest of blessings, health. Negroes generally drink *too much* water when they are in the field at work; this they should not do, and more especially when much heated.

Every one who has seen much of the Negro knows how susceptible he is to the effects of cold and atmospheric vicissitudes. The sickness and mortality from the winter diseases, Pleurisy and Pneumonia, are distressing, besides being the cause of a serious loss to the planters. Being impossible to carry on the work of a plantation without some degree of exposure of the hands to the rains and colds in the winter, it becomes a matter of much importance that their *clothing* be particularly attended to at this season. Besides the heavy linsey clothing, the hats and shoes given them, I would recommend that each should wear a *flannel under shirt.* The beneficial effects from wearing this garment are very great and have been verified in many instances within my knowledge, but in none more strongly than on a certain plantation in this county where the hands are very much exposed, being obliged too travel between two and three miles from their quarters to get to a part of their work. The past has been a very wet winter. They were often out in the cold rains and mud, yet they seemed to suffer no inconvenience from the exposure, as there was no case of sickness amongst them; nor has there been a case of Pneumonia on the place in many years. I ascribe their exemption from disease, in a great measure, to the wearing of flannel shirts. They should be put on as soon as the cold weather beings in the fall, and worn til the warm weather in Spring. When one is inclined to be sickly, besides the shirt, give him *drawers* of the same material. The importance of giving their negroes *flannel* cannot be too strongly urged upon the attention of planters.

In the summer, negroes should be made to wear hats to protect their heads from the rays of the sun; this is very important with unacclimated negroes, who are more apt to be sunstruck.

Their houses should be good, their beds comfortable, with plenty of comforts and blankets for the cold nights of Winter. A negro is unfit for a good day's work without sleep. Their houses, as well as the quarter lot, should be kept free from all filth. This matter will demand the frequent attention of the owner, or manager, as the negro is proverbially filthy in his mode of living.

The free unrestrained use of whisky and tobacco by negroes is highly injurious to them, though they have an innate desire for both. It is better not to allow them to have the former at all, except as a medicine, and the latter only in small quantities and at regular intervals. When sick they require constant care and attention, and it is very important to prevent them from indulging their appetites for food, as they will frequently do if not held in restraint. They should not be allowed to remain in their houses, but placed in the hospital as soon as taken sick. Here they can be attended to with much less inconvenience, and their chances for recovery are greater than when left at their own houses. Calomel (an excellent remedy in the hands of one who knows its proper use) is in very many cases injurious to sick negroes, given as it is so indiscriminately. I am persuaded that many cases of fever can be cured.

Butterfield, Ralph. 1858. "Health of Negroes." In *American Cotton Planter and Soil of the South,* 2 (September).

VERMONT PERSONAL LIBERTY LAW (1858)

An Act to Secure Freedom to All Persons Within This State

It is hereby enacted, &c.

Section 1. No person within this State shall be considered as property, or subject, as such, to sale, purchase, or delivery; nor shall any person, within the limits of this State, at this time, be deprived of liberty or property without due process of law.

Section 2. Due process of law, mentioned in the preceding section of this Act shall, in all cases, be defined to mean the usual process and forms in force by the laws of this State, and issued by the courts thereof; and under such process, such person shall be entitled to a trial by jury.

Section 3. Whenever any person in this State shall be deprived of liberty, arrested, or detained, on the ground that such person owes service or labor to another person, not an inhabitant of this State, either party may claim a trial by jury; and, in such case, challenges shall be allowed to the defendant agreeably to sections four and five of chapter one hundred and eleven of the compiled statutes.

Section 4. Every person who shall deprive or attempt to deprive any other person of his or her liberty, contrary to the preceding sections of this Act, shall, on conviction thereof, forfeit and pay a fine not exceeding two thousand dollars nor less than five hundred dollars, or be punished by imprisonment in the State Prison for a term not exceeding ten years: Provided, that nothing in said preceding sections shall apply to, or affect the right to arrest or imprison under existing laws for contempt of court.

Section 5. Neither descent near or remote from an African, whether such African is or may have been a slave or not, nor color of skin or complexion, shall disqualify any person from being, or prevent any person from becoming, a citizen of this State, nor deprive such person of the rights and privileges thereof.

Section 6. Every person who may have been held as a slave, who shall come, or be brought, or be in this State, with or without the consent of his or her master or mistress, or who shall come, or be brought, or be, involuntarily or in any way in this State, shall be free.

Section 7. Every person who shall hold, or attempt to hold, in this State, in slavery, or as a slave, any person mentioned as a slave in the sixth section of this act, or any free person, in any form, or for any time, however short, under pretence that such person is or has been a slave, shall, on conviction thereof, be imprisoned in the State Prison for a term not less than one year, nor more than fifteen years, and be fined not exceeding two thousand dollars.

Section 8. All Acts and parts of Acts inconsistent with the provisions of this Act are hereby repealed.

Section 9. This Act shall take effect from its passage.

Approved November 25, 1858.

Child, Lydia Maria. 1860. *The Duty of Civil Disobedience to the Fugitive Slave Act: An Appeal to the Legislators of Massachusetts.* Boston: American Anti-Slavery Society.

SOUTHERN EDITORIAL RESPONSE TO THE HARPERS FERRY RAID (1859)

Charleston, South Carolina, Mercury *(October 18, 1859)*

Our despatches this morning give us some particulars of a serious outbreak among the employees on the government works at Harpers Ferry, Virginia, in which the negros, led on by some infuriated abolitionists, have been forced to co-operate. The trains were stopped and telegraphic wires cut, and, as the despatch informs us, the whole town was in possession of the insurgents. It will be seen, however, that the most active means have been put into execution to quell the disturbance; that several companies of artillery and infantry have proceeded to the scene, and, no doubt, before this reaches the eye of our readers, perfect quiet has been again established. We regret, however, that our telegraphic agent closed his reports so early, as it would have been exceedingly gratifying to learn that the miserable leaders of this unfortunate and disgraceful affair had received their just deserts.

Richmond, Virginia, Whig *(October 18, 1859)*

The telegraphic despatches in another column, concerning the outbreak at Harpers Ferry, are stirring enough for ordinary purposes. We believe the affair, however, to be greatly exaggerated, as such occurrences usually are. There is at least no cause for uneasiness elsewhere in the State, notwithstanding the reports concerning the complicity of the negroes in the business.—Indeed, we rather incline to the belief that the entire report of the affair is pretty much of a humbug. That there is something of a riot there, on the part of a few of the operatives, we have no doubt; but the object of the rebels is to take possession of the public funds which were deposited there on Saturday.

Our goodly city was in a state of the liveliest excitement all yesterday evening. The military, particularly, were in great commotion. The Governor, we learn, has ordered the whole volunteer Regiment to the scene of disturbance. Company "F," under command of Col. Cary left at 8 o'clock last night—the Fredricksburg mail train having been detained for their accommodation. The remainder of the Regiment, consising of six or seven companies, will leave at 6 o'clock this morning. The Governor accompanied Col. Cary's company last night—and we slightly incline to the opinion that Harpers Ferry will be captured, and the rebels put down, especially as the military from the surrounding country and Old Point, Baltimore, Washington, and Alexandria, have been ordered to the scene of action. We think these are almost enough to put an end to the "war" during the course of the week—provided all hands stand firm, as they no doubt will, with some exceptions.

The "soldiers" took leave of their wives and little ones last night amid such weeping and wailing, not expecting ever to see them more! It was a heart-rending scene, to be sure. We endeavored to procure a lock of the hair of several of the "soldiers," as a memento of them, in case they should fight, bleed and die in the service of their country; but they were too much afflicted by the parting scene to pay any attention to our request. We expect to see half of the "soldiers" back at least.—But good fortune to them all.

Nashville, Tennessee, Union and American *(October 21, 1859)*

We publish to-day full telegraphic particulars of the riot at Harpers Ferry, a briefer outline of which had heretofore appeared in our columns. The first report attributed the riot to the fact that a contractor on the Government works had absconded, leaving his employees unpaid, who had seized the arsenal with the purpose of securing Government funds and paying themselves. Later accounts seem conclusive that it was a concerted attempt at insurrection, aided by leading Northern Abolitionists. The papers of Brown, the leader, are said to have fallen into the hands of Gov. Wise, and to include among them letters from Gerrit Smith, Fred Douglass and others. We shall hear more in a few days, when, no doubt, the whole plot will be disclosed.

In the mean time, the facts already before us show that Abolitionism is working out its legitimate results, in encouraging fanatics to riot and revolution. The "harmless republicanism" out of which there is serious talk even here of making a national party, to defeat the Democracy, fosters and sustains, and is formidable only from the zeal of, the class within its ranks who incited this insurrection. Of the capacity of the South to defend and protect herself, we have no doubt. But when called on to do this, as at Harpers Ferry, she must know who are her friends and who are her enemies. She can have no political association with men who are only watching a safe opportunity to cut the throats of her citizens. It will not do for Northern Republicans to attribute this outbreak to the fanaticism of a few zealots. The Republican party of the North is responsible for it. It is the legitimate result of Sewardism. It is the commencement of what Seward spoke of as the "irrepressible conflict." The South will hold the whole party of Republicans responsible for the blood-shed at Harpers Ferry. For the fanatics engaged there would never have dared the attempt at insurrection but for the inflammatory speeches and writings of Seward, Greeley, and the other Republican leaders. Waiting for the details before saying more, we refer the reader to the accounts of the insurrection published in another place in this paper.

JOHN BROWN'S LAST SPEECH (1859)

November 2, 1859

I have, may it please the Court, a few words to say. In the first place, I deny everything but what I have all along admitted,—the design on my part to free the slaves. I intended certainly to have made a clean thing of that matter, as I did last winter, when I went into Missouri and there took slaves without the snapping of a gun on either side, moved them through the country, and finally left them in Canada. I designed to have done the same thing again, on a larger scale. That was all I intended. I never did intend murder, or treason, or the destruction of property, or to excite or incite slaves to rebellion, or to make insurrection.

I have another objection; and that is, it is unjust that I should suffer such a penalty. Had I interfered in the manner which I admit, and which I admit has been fairly proved (for I admire the truthfulness and candor of the greater portion of the witnesses who have testified in this case),—had I so interfered in behalf of the rich, the powerful, the intelligent, the so-called great, or in behalf of any of their friends,—either father, mother, brother, sister, wife, or children, or any of that class,—and suffered and sacrificed what I have in this interference, it would have been all right; and every man in this court would have deemed it an act worthy of reward rather than punishment.

This court acknowledges, as I suppose, the validity of the law of God. I see a book kissed here which I suppose to be the Bible, or at least the new Testament. That teaches me that all things whatsoever I would that men should do to me, I should do even so to them. It teaches me, further, to remember them that are in bonds, as bound with them. I endeavored to act up to that instruction. I say, I am yet too young to understand that God is any respecter of persons. I believe that to have interfered as I have done—as I have always freely admitted I have done—in behalf of His despised poor, was not wrong, but right. Now, if it is deemed necessary that I should forfeit my life for the furtherance of the ends of justice, and mingle my blood further with the blood of my children and with the blood of millions in this slave country whose rights are disregarded by wicked, cruel, and unjust enactments,—I submit; so let it be done!

Let me say one word further. I feel entirely satisfied with the treatment I have received in my trial. Considering all the circumstances, it has been more generous than I expected. But I feel no consciousness of guilt. I have stated from the first what was my intention, and what was not. I never had any design against the life of any person, nor any disposition to commit treason, or excite slaves to rebel, or make any general insurrection. I never encouraged any man to do so, but always discouraged any idea of that kind.

Let me say, also, a word in regard to the statements made by some of those connected with me. I hear it has been stated by some of them that I have induced them to join me. But the contrary is true. I do not say this to injure them, but as regretting their weakness. There is not one of them but joined me of his own expense. A number of them I never saw, and never had a word of conversation with, till the day they came to me; and that was for the purpose I have stated.

Now I have done.

American State Trials. J. D. Lawson, ed. Vol. VI, p. 800

A VIRGINIAN CHASTISES NORTHERN ABOLITIONISTS (1859)

"No Interference with Slavery in the States"

Muscoe R. H. Garnett of Virginia. United States House of Representatives, December 7, 1859.

The gentleman from New York [Mr. CLARK] told us yesterday that he never knew an Abolitionist in New York; he in whose district the church of Doctor Cheever reverberates, Sunday after Sunday, with sentiments of treason and bloodshed; he in whose State a Senator was chosen, to represent the people in this Congress, marked above all others by his bold, imperturbable calculations, by his deep-laid plans, by his acting upon a calculated system, where you can mark out his course, step by step, from year to year—all connected parts of one whole—who, as my friend from South Carolina [Mr. KEITT] showed yesterday, before he ever entered the Senate, uttered sentiments the same in substance though not in form as Helper's—a Senator who preaches up to the country that there is an irrepressible conflict between the two sections of the country, which must result in the overthrow of one or the other—a Senator who is a representative man of his party, whom they intend to nominate for the presidency, and if they do not do it, it will be only because they are scared out of it! No Abolitionists in New York or in the North! when at Albany one hundred minute guns were fired there in mourning for the death of John Brown! No Abolitionists in

Natick! when a large public meeting of sympathy was held for Brown, of which a Senator from the State of Massachusetts was present! No Abolitionists in Massachusetts! when, in the Senate of Massachusetts, they found nearly a majority in favor of adjourning on the day of the execution of Brown! No Abolitionists at Cleveland! when, as a friend from Indiana tells me, that city was draped in mourning, and five thousand men were attending a public meeting, to express their sentiments upon that event, upon the day of the execution of Brown!

You do not mean to interfere with slavery in the States! So the gentleman from Ohio [Mr. SHERMAN] told us yesterday, though his remarks are somewhat diluted in the report of them which appears in the Globe to-day. He and his party do not mean to interfere with slavery in the States; but they mean to hold southern people to the yoke, and to organize Territory after Territory, into which no southern man shall be permitted to go with his property. They mean to hem us in, as with a wall of fire, as I think Mr. SEWARD said, until the institution is so cribbed and confined that it will perish for want of sustenance. They do not mean to interfere with slavery in the States, and yet when a band of assassins violate the sacred soil of my native State, we hear not one word of denunciation from you. You do not mean to interfere with slavery in the States, and yet you find societies at the North planning deliberately to render the institution valueless upon the borders, by running off the slaves, until the owners are compelled to sell them to the South, or to emancipate and give them up to you. You do not mean to interfere with slavery in the States, and yet, though the Constitution guarantees the right of reclaiming fugitives from labor, laws are passed refusing to allow us the use of northern jails; you turn your judges out of office if they assist in enforcing the law for the reclamation of fugitives from labor, and you attack and use violence against our citizens when they appear there to reclaim their property. Call you this no interference with slavery in the States? Call you the incessant war against it waged from your press, your pulpit, and your hustings, no interference with slavery in the States? Why do you not carry on this crusade against monarchy in Europe, or against aristocracy in England, if it is a mere desire to correct public evils all over the world? Why not organize a society against slavery in Cuba and Brazil? Why not inaugurate political crusades against every system of government that we disapprove in every part of the world? No, sir; these benefits, those kind offices are reserved for us—for your brethren, your fellows of the southern States.

Years ago, as far back as 1836, Governor Marcy then Governor of the State of New York, advised the Legislature of that State to pass laws preventing and suppressing incendiary appeals of abolition societies—few in number at that time—inciting the slaves to insurrection. These few societies have become numerous. Their principles are the shibboleth of the great political party of the North. Yet what Governor of any of the northern States dare now make such a recommendation as Mr. Marcy made twenty-three years ago! When Walker organizes a company of filibusters and descends on Nicaragua, a country with which we are at peace, you appeal to the neutrality laws that are properly on your statute books—you say we have no right to allow our territory to be used for organizing piratical expeditions against a friendly foreign Power; and you call on the President of the United States to use the Army and Navy to suppress such expeditions, and to protect this foreign Power from them. And you do so properly. Nay, when Commodore Paulding exceeds his legal power in order to execute this law; when he does what he has no right to do in making a descent on this foreign country, you pass resolutions of approval. But here we are—no foreign State—we are confederated States; here we are, no half-barbarian Nicaragua, but your brethren of the Anglo-Saxon race; your fellow-citizens under a common flag, under the pretended protection of a common Constitution—and which one of your States will pass laws suppressing these expeditions against the South? Which one of your States will pass neutrality laws to punish the men who advise and the men who take part in these piratical expeditions against the peace and safety of the southern States? So far from it, when you discover men actually concerned in them, you allow them, with impunity, to publish statements declaring that they take themselves to Canada to evade United States process. With impunity your Senators rise in the other end of the Capitol and denounce the Federal judiciary, because of its process to summon them as witnesses. With impunity, men high in your society, men at the head of your literary circles, men like Dr. Howe, acknowledge their complicity by supplying money and arms to expeditions aimed against the South, and then they flee from the jurisdiction of the Federal court.

United States Congress. *The Congressional Globe: The Official Proceedings of Congress,* 36th Cong., 1st sess. Washington, DC: John C. Rives.

EDITORIAL UPON JOHN BROWN'S HANGING (1859)

North and South.

Half the troubles of mankind have arisen from misunderstandings. There is just now some small danger that a misunderstanding may engender trouble between the North and the South. Each section of the country misunderstands the other. Each is excited and disposed to be angry; and if an opportunity offers, there may be a quarrel between them before a chance is afforded for mutual explanation and candid interchange of opinion.

The South imagines that the Northern people sympathize with John Brown, and regard him as a martyr. Among others, Governor Wise, of Virginia, and Governor Gist, of South Carolina, entertain, and endeavor to disseminate this opinion. Yet it is a notorious fallacy. The bulk of the Northern people have no sympathy whatever with John Brown. They regard him as a man who broke his country's laws willfully, who caused the death of innocent men, and who has been justly punished for his crimes. This is the view taken by the great conservative body of the Northern people, including most of the merchants, farmers, mechanics, and citizens generally. Members of the Republican party—while owning to some tenderness for Brown on account of his sincerity and manliness—still admit that he was rightly punished. Of those who deem him a martyr, and censure Virginia for having executed the law, there is a mere handful—Cheever, Emerson, Phillips, and a select party of radical abolitionists, who have never had any following worth mention.

On the other hand, the North is apt to be misled by the vaporing of Southern newspapers and Southern politicians, clamoring for disunion. These newspapers and these politicians misapprehend and misrepresent the true sentiments of the South. The disunion party—so far as we are enabled to learn—is no stronger in the South than the radical abolition party in the North. Both are mere noisy minorities. A great number of the Southern newspapers are party political organs, whose sole aim is the elevation of this or that politician to a Governorship or to the Presidency. They assume and promulgate extreme views in the hope of currying favor with the masses of the Southern people. Their nonsense does not deserve a moment's serious attention. In the event of disunion, gravely as the North would suffer at first, the South would be at least as great a sufferer in the end. Seven-eighths of the fiscal revenue of the Confederacy is collected in the North; in the event of disunion the South would need to impose new and very onerous taxes on its people to support a central Government. In the border States it would be morally impossible to maintain the slave institution; for, in the absence of the present Constitutional compact and the Fugitive Slave Law, no restraint, legal or moral, would interpose to prevent organized slave stampedes. The foreign trade of the country would continue, as now, to be carried on at the North; for trade dépôts can not be created by laws; they are the offspring of natural causes, over which Legislatures have no control; and all that the South would gain would be some additional charges on its imports to defray the cost of bonding them in New York in transit for the Southern country. These considerations are quite familiar to the intelligent statesmen of the South. They weigh with the planters. We of the North may rest assured that, whatever politicians and political newspapers may say, the Southern people, as a body, are decidedly opposed to disunion.

We hope that the patriotic men who have seats in Congress will interchange these mutual explanations—that the Northern members, as a body, will express their conviction that, whatever admiration some may feel for the fortitude of Old Brown, he was justly punished; and, on the other hand, that the leading Southern men will denounce the disunionists of the South in the terms which are suitable.

It is really too bad that a parcel of politicians of both sections, none of whom have any real claim to authority, should be allowed to endanger the edifice which, in eighty years, has reached so grand an elevation. One can not help thinking that John Brown's gibbet would be a fitting tail-piece to the career of some of the knaves who—seeking nothing beyond personal gain or the gratification of private ambition—are pandering to the worst passions of the mob in both sections of the country, and doing all that in them lies to plunge a peaceful and contented people into the horrors of civil war.

Harper's Weekly, December 17, 1859.

A SOUTHERNER DEFENDS THE EXPANSION OF SLAVERY (1860)

"Why Slavery Must Be Protected in the Territories"

Albert Gallatin Brown of Mississippi.   January 3, 1860

I have been asked elsewhere—and probably there is a whispering in the mind of some one who hears me to

the same effect now—why are you so tenacious of this principle of protection to slavery in the Territories? What do you expect to accomplish by it? With that frankness which I trust is a part of my character, I will tell you why I am so tenacious. I know that you can never plant slavery in the Territories unless you afford it protection—protection based on statutory law. Without such protection, there never will be another slave Territory; and without slave Territories you can never have slave States. You have, I believe, five Territories now. You are already called on, during the present session, to organize three more. These Territories will rapidly populate, and as rapidly come knocking at the door for admission into the Union. You commenced with thirteen States only a little more than three quarters of a century ago—dating from the birth of the Constitution, not so long as that—and now you have thirty-three, five Territories already organized, and three asking for organization. Of these thirty-three States, fifteen are slaveholding States, and eighteen are non-slaveholding. Under your present policy, all the Territories outstanding, organized and unorganized, and all the territory to be acquired hereafter, will but add to the number of free States; and then, sir, the boast made on the other side of the Chamber, that when they get the power they will so mold the Constitution, according to the forms of the Constitution itself, as to give them uncontrolled sway—will be carried out with all its force and all its power. It cannot be long, under the present order of things, before the anti-slavery sentiment of this country will have brought into the Union, and added to the non-slaveholding States now in the Union, a sufficient number of States to give them the two thirds required to change the Constitution. That being done, the enunciation so vauntingly made by the distinguished Senator from New York, and followed up by others, that you mean to crush out slavery under the forms of the Constitution, will have been accomplished. I see that things are rapidly drifting in that direction. I see that we can have no more slave States unless we can plant slavery in the Territories; and I see that that cannot be done unless you protect the slaveholder in his rights. If we can have no more slave States, then twenty years will not pass before a change of the Constitution will enable the anti-slavery sentiments of the North, under the forms and guarantees of the Constitution, as amended, to overthrow slavery.

I hope I am understood. I am tenacious upon this point, because I want to multiply the number of slave States. I want to multiply the number of slave States because I am, and always have been, a genuine constitutional Union man. I love the Union of our fathers, and yield to no man in deep, earnest, heartfelt devotion to it. They made a slaveholding Union. Washington and Jefferson and Madison, and other illustrious patriots, who took a prominent part in the formation of the Union, were themselves slaveholders, and they gave to slave property the guarantees which the Constitution contains, as expounded by the Supreme Court. By the Union which they made I am ready to stand; for it I am ready to fall; and I will never stand idly by, and see, by your timid time-serving policy, that Union undermined and forced to tumble into ruins.

Nor am I willing to take the position which the President assigns me, of entrenchment behind the courts. No, sir. No man has higher veneration for courts of justice than I have. No man entertains a deeper, more heartfelt reverence for the judges of that illustrious court, which to-day sits in this Capitol, than I do. Sir, I venerate, I revere, I almost reverence these old judges; but when I see them on their trembling limbs treading your streets, I cannot disguise from my own mind that all these old men, in the lapse of a few years, not more than fifteen or twenty at most; must pass from the stage of active existence. The venerable Chief Justice is already over eighty years of age; I am told that the majority of his associates are over seventy. How long can these old men hold out? When they are gone, and the gentlemen on the other side of the Chamber shall have taken possession of the executive and legislative Government, what will happen? That bench now adorned by a Taney, by a Catron, by a Nelson, and by other illustrious judges, will be occupied by such gentlemen as those on the other side of the Chamber. When that day comes, what will become of the Dred Scott decision behind which I am asked to entrench myself? Sir, it will pass away as "the baseless fabric of a vision." These Senators and other persons outside the Chamber who sympathize with them, will carry their opinions upon the bench, and will as remorselessly overturn the decision rendered by the present judges as they would overturn a decision sounding in mere dollars and cents. Yet, sir, with these facts before us, seeing them as we do, we are asked to give up all struggle to maintain our constitutional rights through the law-making power of the Government, and to rely entirely on the courts. Sir, others may pursue that course which to them seems best; I will pursue my own, and leave to time, the great tester of all truths, to determine whether I am not right.

United States Congress. *The Congressional Globe: The Official Proceedings of Congress*, 36th Cong., 1st sess. Washington, DC: John C. Rives.

ON THE IMMORALITY OF SLAVERY (1860)

Interesting Correspondence.

The following letter to the Rev. J. W. LOGUEN from his old Mistress, and his reply to her, will be read with interest by our readers. Mr. L. is a clergyman and gentleman of high standing in this community; and any attempt to capture him will involve consequences that we hardly dare picture to our imagination. "Letter from Mrs. Logue."

Maury Co., State of Tennessee,
February 20th, 1860.

To JARM:—I now take my pen to write you a few lines, to let you know how we all are. I am a cripple, but I am still able to get about. The rest of the family are all well. Cherry is as well as common. I write you these lines to let you know the situation we are in—partly in consequence of your running away and stealing Old Rock, our fine mare. Though we got the mare back, she was never worth much after you took her; and as I now stand in need of some funds, I have determined to sell you; and I have had an offer for you, but did not see fit to take it. If you will send me one thousand dollars and pay for the old mare, I will give up all claim I have to you. Write to me as soon as you get these lines, and let me know if you will accept my proposition. In consequence of your running away, we had to sell Abe and Ann and twelve acres of land; and I want you to send me the money that I may be able to redeem the land that you was the cause of our selling, and on receipt of the above named sum of money, I will send you your bill of sale. If you do not comply with my request, I will sell you to some one else, and you may rest assured that the time is not far distant when things will be changed with you. Write to me as soon as you get these lines. Direct your letter to Bigbyville, Maury County, Tennessee. You had better comply with my request.

I understand that you are a preacher. As the Southern people are so bad, you had better come and preach to your old acquaintances. I would like to know if you read your Bible? If so can you tell what will become of the thief if he does not repent? and, if the blind lead the blind, what will the consequence be? I deem it unnecessary to say much more at present. A word to the wise is sufficient. You know where the liar has his part. You know that we reared you as we reared our own children; that you was never abused, and that shortly before you ran away, when your master asked you if you would like to be sold, you said you would not leave him to go with any body.

                                            Sarah Logue.

"Mr. Loguen's Reply"

Syracuse, N. Y., March 28, 1860.

MRS. SARAH LOGUE:—Yours of the 20th of February is duly received, and I thank you for it. It is a long-time since I heard from my poor old mother, and I am glad to know she is yet alive, and as you say, "as well as common." What that means I don't know. I wish you had said more about her.

You are a woman; but had you a woman's heart you could never have insulted a brother by telling him you sold his only remaining brother and sister, because he put himself beyond your power to convert him into money.

You sold my brother and sister, ABE and ANN, and 12 acres of land, you say, because I run away. Now you have the unutterable meanness to ask me to return and be your miserable chattel, or in lieu thereof send you $1,000 to enable you to redeem the *land,* but not to redeem my poor brother and sister! If I were to send you money it would be to get my brother and sister, and not that you should get land. You say you are a *cripple,* and doubtless you say it to stir my pity, for you know I was susceptible in that direction. I do pity you from the bottom of my heart. Nevertheless I am indignant beyond the power of words to express, that you should be so sunken and cruel as to tear the hearts I love so much all in pieces; that you should be willing to impale and crucify us out of all compassion for your poor *foot* or *leg.* Wretched woman! Be it known to you that I value my freedom, to say nothing of my mother, brothers and sisters, more than your whole body; more, indeed, than my own life; more than all the lives of all the slaveholders and tyrants under Heaven.

You say you have offers to buy me, and that you shall sell me if I do not send you $1,000, and in the same breath and almost in the same sentence, you say, "you know we raised you as we did our own children." Woman, did you raise your *own children* for the market? Did you raise them for the whipping-post? Did you raise them to be drove off in a coffle in chains? Where are my poor bleeding brothers and sisters? Can you tell? Who was it that sent them off into sugar and cotton fields, to be kicked, and cuffed, and whipped, and to groan and die; and where no kin can hear their groans, or attend and sympathize at their dying bed, or follow in their funeral? Wretched woman! Do you say *you* did not do it? Then I reply, your husband did, and *you* approved the deed—and the very letter you sent me shows that your heart approves it all. Shame on you.

But, by the way, where is your husband? You don't speak of him. I infer, therefore, that he is dead; that he has gone to his great account, with all his sins against my poor family upon his head. Poor man! gone to meet the spirits of my poor, outraged and murdered people, in a world where Liberty and Justice are MASTERS.

But you say I am a thief, because I took the old mare along with me. Have you got to learn that I had a better right to the old mare, as you called her, than MANASSETH LOGUE had to me? Is it a greater sin for me to steal his horse, than it was for him to rob my mother's cradle and steal me? If he and you infer that I forfeit all my rights to you, shall not I infer that you forfeit all your rights to me? Have you got to learn that human rights are mutual and reciprocal, and if you take my liberty and life, you forfeit me your own liberty and life? Before God and High Heaven, is there a law for one man which is not law for every other man?

If you or any other speculator on my body and rights, wish to know how I regard my rights, they need but come here and lay their hands on me to enslave me. Did you think to terrify me by presenting the alternative to give my money to you, or give my body to Slavery? Then let me say to you, that I meet the proposition with unutterable scorn and contempt. The proposition is an outrage and an insult. I will not budge one hair's breadth. I will not breath a shorter breath, even to save me from your persecutions. I stand among a free people, who, I thank God, sympathize with my rights, and the rights of mankind; and if your emissaries and venders come here to re-inslave me, and escape the unshrinking vigor of my own right arm, I trust my strong and brave friends, in this City and State, will be my rescuers and avengers.

                                        Yours, &c.,
                                        J. W. Loguen.

Loguen, Jermain W. 1859. *The Rev. J. W. Loguen, as a Slave and as a Freeman. A Narrative of Real Life.* Syracuse, NY: J. G. K. Truair & Co.

ILLEGAL IMPORTATION OF AFRICANS AS SLAVES (1860)

The Africans of the Slave Bark, Wildfire

Key West, Florida, May 20, 1860.

On the morning of the 30th of April last, the United States steamer *Mohawk,* Lieutenant Craven commanding, came to anchor in the harbor of this place, having in tow a bark of the burden of about three hundred and thirty tons, supposed to be the bark *Wildfire*, lately owned in the city of New York. The bark had on board five hundred and ten native Africans, taken on board in the River Congo, on the west side of the continent of Africa. She had been captured a few days previously by Lieutenant Craven within sight of the northern coast of Cuba, as an American vessel employed in violating our laws against the slave-trade. She had left the Congo River thirty-six days before her capture.

Soon after the bark was anchored we repaired on board, and on passing over the side saw, on the deck of the vessel, about four hundred and fifty native Africans, in a state of entire nudity, in a sitting or squatting posture, the most of them having their knees elevated so as to form a resting place for their heads and arms. They sat very close together, mostly on either side of the vessel, forward and aft, leaving a narrow open space along the line of the centre for the crew of the vessel to pass to and fro. About fifty of them were full-grown young men, and about four hundred were boys aged from ten to sixteen years. It is said by persons acquainted with the slave-trade and who saw them, that they were generally in a very good condition of health and flesh, as compared with other similar cargoes, owing to the fact that they had not been so much crowded together on board as is common in slave voyages, and had been better fed than usual. It is said that the bark is capable of carrying, and was prepared to carry, one thousand, but not being able without inconvenient delay to procure so many, she sailed with six hundred. Ninety and upward had died on the voyage. But this is considered as comparatively a small loss, showing that they had been better cared for than usual. Ten more have died since their arrival, and there are about forty more sick in the hospital. We saw on board about six or seven boys and men greatly emaciated, and diseased past recovery, and about a hundred that showed decided evidences of suffering from inanition, exhaustion, and disease. Dysentery was the principal disease. But notwithstanding their sufferings, we could not be otherwise than interested and amused at their strange looks, motions, and actions. The well ones looked happy and contented, and were ready at any moment to join in a song or a dance whenever they were directed to do so by "Jack"—a little fellow as black as ebony, about twelve years old, having a handsome and expressive face, an intelligent look, and a sparkling eye. The sailors on the voyage had dressed "Jack" in sailor costume, and had made him a great pet. When we were on board "Jack"

carried about in his hand a short cord, not only as the emblem but also as the instrument of his brief delegated authority. He would make the men and boys stand up, sit down, sing, or dance just as he directed. When they sang "Jack" moved around among them as light as a cat, and beat the time by slapping his hands together, and if any refused to sing, or sang out of time, Jack's cord descended on their backs. Their singing was monotonous. The words we did not understand. We have rarely seen a more happy and merry-looking fellow than "Jack."

From the deck we descended into the cabin, where we saw sixty or seventy women and young girls, in Nature's dress, some sitting on the floor and others on the lockers, and some sick ones lying in the berths. Four or five of them were a good deal tattooed on the back and arms, and we noticed that three had an arm branded with the figure "7," which, we suppose, is the merchant's mark.

On the day of their arrival the sickest, about forty in all, were landed and carried to a building on the public grounds belonging to Fort Taylor, and Doctors Whitehurst and Skrine employed as medical attendants. We visited them in the afternoon. The United States Marshal had procured for all of them shirts, and pants for the men, and some benevolent ladies of the city had sent the girls and women gowns. Six or eight were very sick; the others did not appear to be in any immediate danger of dying. We were very much amused by a young lad about fifteen years old, not much sick, who had got on, probably for the first time in his life, a whole shirt, and who seemed to be delighted with every body and every thing he saw. He evidently thought the speech of the white man was very funny. When a few words were spoken to him he immediately repeated them with great glee. Pointing to Dr. Skrine, we said "Doctor." He said "Doctor." And then pointing to Dr. Whitehurst, we said "Doctor too." He said "Doctor too." The doctors had selected from the bark a woman about twenty-four years of age to assist the nurse in taking care of the sick. She had been dressed in a clean calico frock, and looked very respectable.

About sundown they all lay down for the night upon a camp bed, and were covered over with blankets. And now a scene took place which interested us very much, but which we did not understand and can not explain. The woman standing up slapped her hands together once or twice, and as soon as all were silent she commenced a sort of recitation, song, or prayer, in tone and manner much like a chanting of the Litany in Catholic churches, and every few moments the voices of ten or fifteen others were heard in the same tone, as if responding. This exercise continued about a minute. Now what could this be? It looked and sounded to us very much like Christians chanting together an evening prayer on retiring to rest. And yet we feel quite assured that none of these persons had ever heard of Christ, or had learned Christian practices, or possessed much, if any, knowledge of God as a Creator or Preserver of the world. We suspect that it was not understood by them as a religious exercise at all, but as something which they had been trained to go through at the barracoons in Africa or on board the ship.

In two days after the arrival of the bark the Marshal had completed a large, airy building at Whitehead's Point, a little out of the town, for the reception and accommodation of these people; and after getting them clad as well as he could in so short a time, they were all landed on the fort wharf, and carried in carts to their quarters. On arriving there they all arranged themselves along the sides of the building, as they had been accustomed to do on the decks of the vessel, and squatted down in the same manner. It took the Marshal and his assistants some little time, and no small efforts, to give the Africans to understand that they were free to move about, to go out and come in at will.

They learned this in the course of a few hours, however, and general merriment and hilarity prevailed. We visited them in the afternoon, and have done so several times since; and we confess that we have been struck, as many others have been, with the expression of intelligence displayed in their faces, the beauty of their physical conformation, and the beauty of their teeth. We have been accustomed to think that the civilized negroes of our own country were superior, in point of intelligence and physical development, to the native Africans; but judging only by the eye, we think it would be difficult to find, any where in our own country, four hundred finer and handsomer-looking boys and girls than these are. To be sure you often saw the elongated occiput, the protruded jaws, and the receding forehead; but you also often saw a head as round, with features as regular as any European's, except the universal flat noses. Little "Jack" has a head as round as an apple.

A number of these negroes—perhaps twelve or fifteen in all—have been more or less at and about Loando, a Portuguese town on the coast, and have learned to speak a little Portuguese. Through an interpreter we learned from them that some four or five—perhaps more, but probably not many—had been baptized at the Roman Catholic missionary station at Loando. Francisco, a young man, says he was baptized by a Franciscan friar in Loando; that he was a slave in Africa, and does not wish to return there. He says he had rather be a slave to the white man in this country. Salvador, a bright-looking, smart lad, has been baptized. Constantia says she was baptized in Loando. She does not remember her father; she was stolen away when she was young, and was sold by her brother. Antonia and Amelia are both fine-looking young women, aged about twenty, and were both baptized at Loando. Madia, a pagan, unbaptized, aged about twenty, has obtained among the white people here who have visited the quarters the name of "The Princess," on account of her fine personal appearance and the deference that seemed to be paid to her by some of her companions. The persons we have here mentioned, including some eight or ten others, evidently do not belong to the same tribe that the rest do. Indeed the whole number is evidently taken from different tribes living in the interior of Africa, but the greater number are "Congos." The women we have named have cut or shaved the hair off the back part of their head, from a point on the crown to the back part of either ear. It is the fashion of their tribe. None of the other women are thus shorn. Many of the men, women, boys, and girls have filed their front teeth—some by sharpening them to a point, and others by cutting down the two upper front teeth. The persons above named have their teeth in a natural state. Perhaps fifty in all are tattooed more or less.

Travelers describe the natives of Congo as being small of stature, cheerful, good-humored, unreflecting, and possessed of little energy either of mind or body. Negro indolence is carried with them to the utmost excess. The little cultivation that exists, entirely carried on by the females, is nearly limited to the manioc root, which they are not very skillful in preparing. Their houses are put together of mats made from the fibre of the palm-tree, and their clothes and bedding consist merely of matted grass.

The President, on receiving news of the capture of the *Wildfire,* sent a special message to Congress on the subject, from which we give an extract below. The subsequent capture of another slave ship with more Africans will probably lead to some enactment on the subject. The President says: "The expenditure for the Africans captured on board the *Wildfire* will not be less than one hundred thousand dollars, and may considerably exceed that sum. But it will not be sufficient for Congress to limit the amount appropriated to the case of the *Wildfire.* It is probable, judging from the increased activity of the slave-trade and the vigilance of our cruisers, that several similar captures may be made before the end of the year. An appropriation ought, therefore, to be granted large enough to cover such contingencies. The period has arrived when it is indispensable to provide some specific legislation for the guidance of the Executive on this subject. With this view, I would suggest that Congress might authorize the President to enter into a general agreement with the Colonization Society, binding them to receive, on the coast of Africa from our agent there, all the captured Africans which may be delivered to him, and to maintain them for a limited period, upon such terms and conditions as may combine humanity toward these unfortunates with a just economy. This would obviate the necessity of making a new bargain with every new capture, and would prevent delay and avoid expense in the disposition of the captured. The law might then provide that, in all cases where this may be practicable, the captor should carry the negroes directly to Africa, and deliver them to the American agent there, afterward bringing the captured vessel to the United States for adjudication.

Harper's Weekly, June 2, 1860.

PRO-SECESSION EDITORIAL (1860)

"What Shall the South Carolina Legislature Do?"

The issue before the country is the extinction of slavery. No man of common sense, who has observed the progress of events, and who is not prepared to surrender the institution, with the safety and independence of the South, can doubt that the time for action has come—now or never. The Southern States are now in the crisis of their fate; and, if we read aright the signs of the times, nothing is needed for our deliverance, but that the ball of revolution be set in motion. There is sufficient readiness among the people to make it entirely successful. Co-operation will follow the action of any State. The example of a forward movement only is requisite to unite Southern States in a common cause. Under these circumstances the Legislature of South Carolina is about to meet. It happens to assemble in advance of the Legislature of any other State. Being in session at this momentous juncture—the Legislature of that State which is most united in the policy of freeing the South from Black Republican domination— the eyes of the whole country, and most especially of the resistance party of the Southern States, is intently turned upon the conduct of this body. We have innumerable assurances that the men of action in each and all of the Southern States, earnestly desire South Carolina to exhibit promptitude and decision in this conjuncture. Other states are torn and divided, to a greater or less extent, by old party issues. South Carolina alone is not. Any practical move would enable the people of other States to rise above their past divisions, and lock shields on the broad ground of Southern security. The course of our Legislature will either greatly stimulate and strengthen, or unnerve the resistance elements of the whole South. A Convention is the point to which their attention will be chiefly directed.

The question of calling a Convention by our Legislature does not necessarily involve the question of separate or co-operative action. That is a question for the Convention when it assembles, under the circumstances which shall exist when it assembles. All desire the action of as many Southern States as possible, for the formation of a Southern Confederacy. But each should not delay and wait on the other. As these States are separate sovereignties, each must act separately; and whether one or the other acts first or last, we suppose is of no sort of consequence. What is really essential is this—that by the action of one or more States, there shall be the *reasonable probability* that a Southern Confederacy will be formed. We say probability,—because there is no certainty in the future of human affairs; and in the position in which the South will be placed by the election of an Abolitionist white man as President of the United States, and an Abolitionist colored man as Vice President of the United States, we should not hesitate, somewhat to venture. The existence of slavery is at stake. The evils of submission are too terrible for us to risk them, from vague fears of failure, or a jealous distrust of our sister Cotton States. We think, therefore, that the approaching Legislature should provide for the assembling of a Convention of the people of South Carolina, as soon as it is ascertained that Messrs. LINCOLN and HAMLIN will have a majority in the Electoral Colleges for President and Vice President of the United States. The only point of difficulty is as to *the* time *when the Convention* shall *assemble.* In our judgment, it should assemble *at the earliest possible time* consistent with the opportunity for co-operative action of other Southern States, which may, like ourselves, be determined not to submit to Black Republican domination at Washington. Delay is fatal, while our move will retard no willing State from co-operation. South Carolina, as a sovereign State, is bound to protect her people, but she should so act as to give the other Southern States the opportunity of joining in this policy. The Governors of Alabama, Mississippi and Georgia can act simultaneously. With this qualification, the *earliest time is the best,* for the following reasons:

1. Our great agricultural staples are going to market. The sooner we act, the more of these staples we will have on hand, to control the conduct of the people of the North and of foreign nations, to secure a peaceful result for our deliverance. Thousands at the North, and millions in Europe, need our Cotton to keep their looms in operation. Let us act, before we have parted with our agricultural productions for the season.

2. The commercial and financial interests of the South require that we should act speedily in settling our relations towards the North. Suspense is embarrassment and loss. Decision, with separation, will speedily open new sources of wealth and prosperity, and relieve the finances of the South through the establishment of new channels. In all changes of Government, respect should be had to all classes of the people, and the least possible loss be inflicted on any.

3. The moral effect of promptitude will be immense. Delay will dispirit our friends, and inspire confidence in our enemies. The evils against which we are to provide are not the growth of yesterday. They have been gathering head for thirty years. We have tried, again and again, to avert them by compromise and submission. Submission has failed to avert them; and wise, prompt and resolute action is our last and only course for safety.

4. Black Republican rule at Washington will not commence until the 4th of March next—four short months. Before that time all that South Carolina or the other Southern States intend to do, should be done. The settlement of our relations towards the General Government, in consequence of our measures of protection, should be completed during the existing Administration.

5. It is exceedingly important, also, that our measures should be laid as soon as possible before *the present Congress.* The secession of one or more States from the Union must be communicated to the President of the United States. He has done all he could to arrest the sectional madness of the North. He knows that we are wronged and endangered by Black Republican ascendancy, and he will not, we have a right to suppose, lend himself to carry out their bloody policy.

6. By communication from the President of the United States, as well as by the withdrawal from Congress of the members of the seceding States, the question of the right of a State to secede from the Union, with the question of a Force Bill, must arise in Congress for action. The Representatives from the other Southern States will most probably be forced either to continue members of a body which orders the sword to be drawn against the seceding States, or they must leave it. They will most probably leave it; and thus the South will be brought together by action in Congress, even though they fail to co-operate at once by their State authorities. It will not be wise to pretermit either of these intrumentalities for the union and co-action of the Southern States; but, it is our opinion, that Congress is the best place to unite them. By prompt action, and through the question of secession in Congress, the agitations which must ensue, will not only tend to unite the Southern members of Congress, but to unite and stimulate State action in the States they represent. We conclude, therefore, by urging the Legislature about to assemble, to provide for the calling a Convention, as soon as it is ascertained that Messrs. LINCOLN and HAMLIN have the majority in the Electoral Colleges for President and Vice President of the United States; and that this Convention shall assemble at the earliest day practicable, consistent with the knowledge of our course by our sister Southern States. To this end we would respectfully suggest Nov. 22d and 23d as the day of election, and December 15th as the time of assembling the Convention of the people of South Carolina.

The Charleston Mercury, November 3, 1860.

HINTON ROWAN HELPER APPEALS TO WHITE SOUTHERNERS (1860)

In 1856, there were assessed for taxation in the State of New York

Acres of land: 30,080,000.   Valued at $1,112,133,136

Average value per acre: $36.97.   North Carolina

Acres of land: 32,450,560.   Valued at $98,800,636

Average value per acre: $3.06.   It is difficult for us to make any remarks on the official facts above. Our indignation is struck almost dumb at this astounding and revolting display of the awful wreck that slavery is leaving behind it in the South. We will however, go into a calculation for the purpose of ascertaining as nearly as possible, in this one particular, how much North Carolina has lost by the retention of slavery. As we have already seen, the average value per acre of land in the State of New York is $36.97; in North Carolina it is only $3.06; why is it so much less, or even any less, in the latter than in the former? The answer is, *slavery.* In soil, in climate, in minerals, in water-power for manufactural purposes, and in area of territory, North Carolina has the advantage of New York, and, with the exception of slavery, no plausible reason can possibly be assigned why land should not be *at least* as valuable in the valley of the Yadkin as it is along the banks of the Genesee.

The difference between $36.97 and $3.06 is $33.91, which, multiplied by the whole number of acres of land in North Carolina, will show, in this one particular, the enormous loss that Freedom has sustained on account of Slavery in the Old North State. Thus: 32,450,560 acres at $33.91. . . . $1,100,398,489.

Let it be indelibly impressed on the mind, however, that this amount, large as it is, is only a moity of the sum it has cost to maintain slavery in North Carolina. From time to time, hundreds upon hundreds of millions of dollars have left the State, either in search of profitable, permanent investment abroad, or in the shape of profits to Northern merchants and manufacturers, who have become the moneyed aristocracy of the country by supplying to the South such articles of necessity, utility, and adornment, as would have been produced at home but for the pernicious presence of the peculiar institution.

A reward of Eleven Hundred Millions of Dollars is offered for the conversion of the lands of North Carolina into free soil. The lands themselves, desolate and impoverished under the fatal foot of slavery, offer the reward. How, then, can it be made to appear that the abolition of slavery in North Carolina, and indeed, throughout all the Southern States—for slavery is exceedingly inimical to them all—is not demanded by every consideration of justice, prudence, and good sense? In 1850, the total value of all the slaves of the State, at the rate of four hundred dollars per head, amounted to less than one hundred and sixteen millions of dollars. Is the sum of one hundred and sixteen millions of dollars more desirable than the sum of eleven hundred millions of dollars? When a man has land for sale, does he reject thirty-six dollars per acre and take three? Non-slaveholding whites! look well to your interests! Many of you have lands; comparatively speaking, you have nothing else. Abolish slavery, and you will enhance the value of every league, your own and your neighbors', from three to thirty-six dollars per acre. Your little tract containing two hundred acres, now valued at the pitiful sum of only six hundred dollars, will then be worth seven thousand. Your children, now deprived of even the meager advantages of common schools, will then reap the benefits of a collegiate education. Your rivers and smaller streams, now wasting their waters in idleness, will then turn the wheels of multitudinous mills. Your bays and harbors,

now unknown to commerce, will then swarm with ships from every enlightened quarter of the globe. Non-slaveholding whites! look well to your interests!

Would the slaveholders of North Carolina lose anything by the abolition of slavery? Let us see. According to their own estimate, their slaves are worth, in round numbers, say, one hundred and twenty millions of dollars. There are in the State twenty-eight thousand slaveholders, owning, it may be safely assumed, an average of at least five hundred acres of land each—fourteen millions of acres in all. This number of acres, multiplied by thirty-three dollars and ninety-one cents, the difference in value between free soil and slave soil, makes the enormous sum of four hundred and seventy-four millions of dollars—showing that, by the abolition of slavery, the slaveholders themselves would realize a net profit of not less than three hundred and fifty-four millions of dollars!

Compensation to the slaveholders for the negroes now in their possession! The idea is preposterous. The suggestion is criminal. The demand is unjust, wicked, monstrous, damnable. Shall we pat the bloodhounds of slavery for the sake of doing them a favor? Shall we free the curs of slavery in order to make them rich at our expense? Shall we pay the whelps of slavery for the privilege of converting them into decent, honest, upright men? No, never! The non-slaveholders expect to gain, and will gain, something by the abolition of slavery; but slaveholders themselves will, by far, be the greater gainers; for, in proportion to population, they own much larger and more fertile tracts of land, and will, as a matter of course, receive the lion's share of the increase in the value of not only real estate, but also of other genuine property, of which they are likewise the principal owners. How ridiculously absurd, therefore, is the objection, that, if we liberate the slaves, we ruin the masters! Not long since, a gentleman in Baltimore, a native of Maryland, remarked in our presence that he was an abolitionist because he felt that it was right and proper to be one; "but," inquired he, "are there not, in some of the States, many widows and orphans who would be left in destitute circumstances, if their negroes were taken from them?" In answer to the question, we replied that slavery had already reduced thousands and tens of thousands of non-slaveholding widows and orphans to the lowest depths of poverty and ignorance, and that we did not believe one slaveholding widow and three orphans were of more, or even of as much consequence as five non-slaveholding widows and fifteen orphans. "You are right," exclaimed the gentleman, "I had not viewed the subject in that light before; I perceive you go in for the greatest good to the greatest number." Emancipate the negroes, and the ex-slave-holding widow would still retain her lands and tenements, which, in consequence of being surrounded by the magic influences of liberty, would soon render her far more wealthy and infinitely more respectable, than she could possibly ever become while trafficking in human flesh.

The fact is, every slave in the South costs the State in which he resides at least three times as much as he, in the whole course of his life, is worth to his master. Slavery benefits no one but its immediate, individual owners, and them only in a pecuniary point of view, and at the sacrifice of the dearest rights and interests of the whole mass of non-slaveholders, white and black. Even the masters themselves, as we have already shown, would be far better off without it than with it. To all classes of society the institution is a curse; an especial curse is it to those who own it not. Non-slaveholding whites! look well to your interests!

Helper, Hinton Rowan. 1860. *The Impending Crisis of the South: How to Meet It.* New York: A. B. Burdick.

SEXUAL EXPLOITATION OF FEMALE SLAVES (1860)

I had entered my sixteenth year, and every day it became more apparent that my presence was intolerable to Mrs. Flint. Angry words frequently passed between her and her husband. He had never punished me himself, and he would not allow any body else to punish me. In that respect, she was never satisfied; but, in her angry moods, no terms were too vile for her to bestow upon me. Yet I, whom she detested so bitterly, had far more pity for her than he had, whose duty it was to make her life happy. I never wronged her, or wished to wrong her; and one word of kindness from her would have brought me to her feet.

After repeated quarrels between the doctor and his wife, he announced his intention to take his youngest daughter, then four years old, to sleep in his apartment. It was necessary that a servant should sleep in the same room, to be on hand if the child stirred. I was selected for that office, and informed for what purpose that arrangement had been made. By managing to keep within sight of people, as much as possible during the day time, I had hitherto succeeded in eluding my master, though a razor was often held to my throat to force me to change this line of policy. At night I slept by the side of my great aunt, where I felt safe. He was too prudent to come into her room. She was an old woman, and had been in the family many years. Moreover, as a married man, and a professional man,

he deemed it necessary to save appearances in some degree. But he resolved to remove the obstacle in the way of his scheme; and he thought he had planned it so that he should evade suspicion. He was well aware how much I prized my refuge by the side of my old aunt, and he determined to dispossess me of it. The first night the doctor had the little child in his room alone. The next morning, I was ordered to take my station as nurse the following night. A kind Providence interposed in my favor. During the day Mrs. Flint heard of this new arrangement, and a storm followed. I rejoiced to hear it rage.

After a while my mistress sent for me to come to her room. Her first question was, "Did you know you were to sleep in the doctor's room?"

"Yes, ma'am."

"Who told you?"

"My master."

"Will you answer truly all the questions I ask?"

"Yes, ma'am."

"Tell me, then, as you hope to be forgiven, are you innocent of what I have accused you?"

"I am."

She handed me a Bible, and said, "Lay your hand on your heart, kiss this holy book, and swear before God that you tell me the truth."

I took the oath she required, and I did it with a clear conscience.

"You have taken God's holy word to testify your innocence," said she. "If you have deceived me, beware! Now take this stool, sit down, look me directly in the face, and tell me all that has passed between your master and you."

I did as she ordered. As I went on with my account her color changed frequently, she wept, and sometimes groaned. She spoke in tones so sad, that I was touched by her grief. The tears came to my eyes; but I was soon convinced that her emotions arose from anger and wounded pride. She felt that her marriage vows were desecrated, her dignity insulted, but she had no compassion for the poor victim of her husband's perfidy. She pitied herself as a martyr; but she was incapable of feeling for the condition of shame and misery in which her unfortunate, helpless slave was placed.

Yet perhaps she had some touch of feeling for me; for when the conference was ended, she spoke kindly, and promised to protect me. I should have been much comforted by this assurance if I could have had confidence in it; but my experiences in slavery had filled me with distrust. She was not a very refined woman, and had not much control over her passions. I was an object of her jealousy, and, consequently, of her hatred; and I knew I could not expect kindness or confidence from her under the circumstances in which I was placed. I could not blame her. Slave-holders' wives feel as other women would under similar circumstances. The fire of her temper kindled from small sparks, and now the flame became so intense that the doctor was obliged to give up his intended arrangement.

I knew I had ignited the torch, and I expected to suffer for it afterwards; but I felt too thankful to my mistress for the timely aid she rendered me to care much about that. She now took me to sleep in a room adjoining her own. There I was an object of her especial care, though not of her especial comfort, for she spent many a sleepless night to watch over me. Sometimes I woke up, and found her bending over me. At other times she whispered in my ear, as though it was her husband who was speaking to me, and listened to hear what I would answer. If she startled me, on such occasions, she would glide stealthily away; and the next morning she would tell me I had been talking in my sleep, and ask who I was talking to. At last, I began to be fearful for my life. It had been often threatened; and you can imagine, better than I can describe, what an unpleasant sensation it must produce to wake up in the dead of night and find a jealous woman bending over you. Terrible as this experience was, I had fears that it would give place to one more terrible.

My mistress grew weary of her vigils; they did not prove satisfactory. She changed her tactics. She now tried the trick of accusing my master of crime, in my presence, and gave my name as the author of the accusation. To my utter astonishment, he replied, "I don't believe it; but if she did acknowledge it, you tortured her into exposing me." Tortured into exposing him! Truly, Satan had no difficulty in distinguishing the color of his soul! I understood his object in making this false representation. It was to show me that I gained nothing by seeking the protection of my mistress; that the power was still all in his own hands. I pitied Mrs. Flint. She was a second wife, many years the junior of her husband; and the hoary-headed miscreant was enough to try the patience of a wiser and better woman. She was completely foiled, and knew not how to proceed. She would gladly have had me flogged for my supposed false oath; but, as I have already stated, the doctor never allowed any one to whip me. The old sinner was politic. The application of the lash might have led to remarks that would have exposed him in the eyes of his children and grandchildren. How often did I rejoice that I lived in a town where all the inhabitants knew each other! If I had been on a remote plantation, or lost among the multitude of a crowded city, I should not be a living woman at this day.

The secrets of slavery are concealed like those of the Inquisition. My master was, to my knowledge, the father of eleven slaves. But did the mothers dare to tell who was the father of their children? Did the other slaves dare to allude to it, except in whispers among themselves? No, indeed! They knew too well the terrible consequences.

Jacobs, Harriet A. 1860. *Incidents in the Life of a Slave Girl, Written by Herself.* Lydia Maria Frances Child, ed. Boston: Author.

BOOKER T. WASHINGTON DESCRIBES THE SLAVE'S LIVING CONDITIONS (C. 1860)

The cabin was not only our living-place, but was also used as the kitchen for the plantation. My mother was the plantation cook. The cabin was without glass windows; it had only openings in the side which let in the light, and also the cold, chilly air of winter. There was a door to the cabin—that is, something that was called a door—but the uncertain hinges by which it was hung, and the large cracks in it, to say nothing of the fact that it was too small, made the room a very uncomfortable one. In addition to these openings there was, in the lower right-hand corner of the room, the "cat-hole,"—a contrivance which almost every mansion or cabin in Virginia possessed during the antebellum period. The "cat-hole" was a square opening, about seven by eight inches, provided for the purpose of letting the cat pass in and out of the house at will during the night. In the case of our particular cabin I could never understand the necessity for this convenience, since there were at least a half-dozen other places in the cabin that would have accommodated the cats. There was no wooden floor in our cabin, the naked earth being used as a floor.

In the centre of the earthen floor there was a large, deep opening covered with boards, which was used as a place in which to store sweet potatoes during the winter. An impression of this potato-hole is very distinctly engraved upon my memory, because I recall that during the process of putting the potatoes in or taking them out I would often come into possession of one or two, which I roasted and thoroughly enjoyed. There was no cooking-stove on our plantation, and all the cooking for the whites and slaves my mother had to do over an open fireplace, mostly in pots and "skillets." While the poorly built cabin caused us to suffer with cold in the winter, the heat from the open fireplace in summer was equally trying.

The early years of my life, which were spent in the

little cabin, were not very different from those of thousands of other slaves. My mother, of course, had little time in which to give attention to the training of her children during the day. She snatched a few moments for our care in the early morning before her work began, and at night after the day's work was done. One of my earliest recollections is that of my mother cooking a chicken late at night, and awakening her children for the purpose of feeding them. How or where she got it I do not know. I presume, however, it was procured from our owner's farm. Some people may call this theft. If such a thing were to happen now, I should condemn it as theft myself. But taking place at the time it did, and for the reason that it did, no one could ever make me believe that my mother was guilty of thieving. She was simply a victim of the system of slavery. I cannot remember having slept in a bed until after our family was declared free by the Emancipation Proclamation. Three children—John, my older brother, Amanda, my sister, and myself—had a pallet on the dirt floor, or, to be more correct, we slept in and on a bundle of filthy rags laid upon the dirt floor.

I was asked not long ago to tell something about the sports and pastimes that I engaged in during my youth. Until that question was asked it had never occurred to me that there was no period of my life that was devoted to play. From the time that I can remember anything, almost every day of my life has been occupied in some kind of labour; though I think I would now be a more useful man if I had had time for sports. During the period that I spent in slavery I was not large enough to be of much service, still I was occupied most of the time in cleaning the yards, carrying water to the men in the fields, or going to the mill, to which I used to take the corn, once a week, to be ground. The mill was about three miles from the plantation. This work I always dreaded. The heavy bag of corn would be thrown across the back of the horse, and the corn divided about evenly on each side; but in some way, almost without exception, on these trips, the corn would so shift as to become unbalanced and would fall off the horse, and often I would fall with it. As I was not strong enough to reload the corn upon the horse, I would have to wait, sometimes for many hours, till a chance passer-by came along who would help me out of my trouble. The hours while waiting for some one were usually spent in crying. The time consumed in this way made me late in reaching the mill, and by the time I got my corn ground and reached home it would be far into the night. The road was a lonely one, and often led through dense forests. I was always frightened. The woods were said to be full of soldiers who had deserted from the army, and I had

been told that the first thing a deserter did to a Negro boy when he found him alone was to cut off his ears. Besides, when I was late in getting home I knew I would always get a severe scolding or a flogging.

I had no schooling whatever while I was a slave, though I remember on several occasions I went as far as the schoolhouse door with one of my young mistresses to carry her books. The picture of several dozen boys and girls in a schoolroom engaged in study made a deep impression upon me, and I had the feeling that to get into a schoolhouse and study in this way would be about the same as getting into paradise.

So far as I can now recall, the first knowledge that I got of the fact that we were slaves, and that freedom of the slaves was being discussed, was early one morning before day, when I was awakened by my mother kneeling over her children and fervently praying that Lincoln and his armies might be successful, and that one day she and her children might be free. In this connection I have never been able to understand how the slaves throughout the South, completely ignorant as were the masses so far as books or newspapers were concerned, were able to keep themselves so accurately and completely informed about the great National questions that were agitating the country. From the time that Garrison, Lovejoy, and others began to agitate for freedom, the slaves throughout the South kept in close touch with the progress of the movement. Though I was a mere child during the preparation for the Civil War and during the war itself, I now recall the many late-at-night whispered discussions that I heard my mother and the other slaves on the plantation indulge in. These discussions showed that they understood the situation, and that they kept themselves informed of events by what was termed the "grape-vine" telegraph.

During the campaign when Lincoln was first a candidate for the Presidency, the slaves on our far-off plantation, miles from any railroad or large city or daily newspaper, knew what the issues involved were. When war was begun between the North and the South, every slave on our plantation felt and knew that, though other issues were discussed, the primal one was that of slavery. Even the most ignorant members of my race on the remote plantations felt in their hearts, with a certainty that admitted of no doubt, that the freedom of the slaves would be the one great result of the war, if the Northern armies conquered. Every success of the Federal armies and every defeat of the Confederate forces was watched with the keenest and most intense interest. Often the slaves got knowledge of the results of great battles before the white people received it. This news was usually gotten from the coloured man who was sent to the post-office for the mail. In our case the post-office was about three miles from the plantation and the mail came once or twice a week. The man who was sent to the office would linger about the place long enough to get the drift of the conversation from the group of white people who naturally congregated there, after receiving their mail, to discuss the latest news. The mail-carrier on his way back to our master's house would as naturally retail the news that he had secured among the slaves, and in this way they often heard of important events before the white people at the "big house," as the master's house was called.

I cannot remember a single instance during my childhood or early boyhood when our entire family sat down to the table together, and God's blessing was asked, and the family ate a meal in a civilized manner. On the plantation in Virginia, and even later, meals were gotten by the children very much as dumb animals get theirs. It was a piece of bread here and a scrap of meat there. It was a cup of milk at one time and some potatoes at another. Sometimes a portion of our family would eat out of the skillet or pot, while some one else would eat from a tin plate held on the knees, and often using nothing but the hands with which to hold the food. When I had grown to sufficient size, I was required to go to the "big house" at meal-times to fan the flies from the table by means of a large set of paper fans operated by a pulley. Naturally much of the conversation of the white people turned upon the subject of freedom and the war, and I absorbed a good deal of it. I remember that at one time I saw two of my young mistresses and some lady visitors eating ginger-cakes, in the yard. At that time those cakes seemed to me to be absolutely the most tempting and desirable things that I had ever seen; and I then and there resolved that, if I ever got free, the height of my ambition would be reached if I could get to the point where I could secure and eat ginger-cakes in the way that I saw those ladies doing.

Washington, Booker T. 1901. *Up from Slavery; an Autobiography.* New York: Doubleday, Page & Co.

FRÉMONT'S PROCLAMATION OF EMANCIPATION (1861)

Proclamation.

Headquarters Western Department, *Saint Louis, August 30, 1861.*

Circumstances, in my judgment, of sufficient urgency render it necessary that the commanding general of this department should assume the administrative powers of the State. Its disorganized condition, the helplessness of the civil authority, the total insecurity of life, and the devastation of property by bands of murderers and marauders, who infest nearly every county of the State, and avail themselves of the public misfortunes and the vicinity of a hostile force to gratify private and neighborhood vengeance, and who find an enemy wherever they find plunder, finally demand the severest measures to repress the daily-increasing crimes and outrages which are driving off the inhabitants and ruining the State.

In this condition the public safety and the success of our arms require unity of purpose, without let or hinderance to the prompt administration of affairs. In order, therefore, to suppress disorder, to maintain as far as now practicable the public peace, and to give security and protection to the persons and property of loyal citizens, I do hereby extend and declare established martial law throughout the State of Missouri.

The lines of the army of occupation in this State are for the present declared to extend from Leavenworth, by way of the posts of Jefferson City, Rolla, and Ironton, to Cape Girardeau, on the Mississippi River.

All persons who shall be taken with arms in their hands within these lines shall be tried by court-martial, and if found guilty will be shot.

The property, real and personal, of all persons in the State of Missouri who shall take up arms against the United States, or who shall be directly proven to have taken an active part with their enemies in the field, is declared to be confiscated to the public use, and their slaves, if any they have, are hereby declared freemen.

All persons who shall be proven to have destroyed, after the publication of this order, railroad tracks, bridges, or telegraphs shall suffer the extreme penalty of the law.

All persons engaged in treasonable correspondence, in giving or procuring aid to the enemies of the United States, in fomenting tumults, in disturbing the public tranquillity by creating and circulating false reports or incendiary documents, are in their own interests warned that they are exposing themselves to sudden and severe punishment.

All persons who have been led away from their allegiance are required to return to their homes forthwith. Any such absence, without sufficient cause, will be held to be presumptive evidence against them.

The object of this declaration is to place in the hands of the military authorities the power to give instantaneous effect to existing laws, and to supply such deficiencies as the conditions of war demand. But this is not intended to suspend the ordinary tribunals of the country, where the law will be administered by the civil officers in the usual manner, and with their customary authority, while the same can be peaceably exercised.

The commanding general will labor vigilantly for the public welfare, and in his efforts for their safety hopes to obtain not only the acquiescence but the active support of the loyal people of the country.

J. C. FRÉMONT,

Major-General, Commanding.

Official Records of the War of the Rebellion—Series I: Volume 3– Correspondence, Orders, and Returns, Relating Specially to Operations in Arkansas, the Indian Territory, Kansas, and Missouri, from May 10 to November 19, 1861.

LINCOLN'S PLAN FOR COMPENSATED EMANCIPATION (1862)

March 6, 1862

Fellow-Citizens of the Senate and House of Representatives:

I recommend the adoption of a joint resolution by your honorable bodies, which shall be substantially as follows: *Resolved,* that the United States ought to cooperate with any state which may adopt gradual abolishment of slavery, giving to such state pecuniary aid, to be used by such state, in its discretion, to compensate for the inconveniences, public and private, produced by such change of system.

If the proposition contained in the resolution does not meet the approval of Congress and the country, there is the end; but if it does command such approval, I deem it of importance that the states and people immediately interested should be at once distinctly notified of the fact, so that they may begin to consider whether to accept or reject it. The Federal government would find its highest interest in such a measure as one of the most efficient means of self-preservation. The leaders of the existing insurrection entertain the hope that this government will ultimately be forced to acknowledge the independence of some part of the disaffected region, and that all the slave states north of such part will then say, "The Union for which we have struggled being already gone, we now choose to go with the Southern section." To deprive them of this hope substantially ends the rebellion, and the initiation of emancipation completely deprives them of it as to all the states initiating it.

The point is not that *all* the states tolerating slavery would very soon, if at all, initiate emancipation but that, while the offer is equally made to all, the more northern shall by such initiation make it certain to the more southern that in no event will the former ever join the latter in their proposed confederacy. I say "initiation" because, in my judgment, gradual and not sudden emancipation is better for all. In the mere financial or pecuniary view, any member of Congress with the census tables and Treasury reports before him can readily see for himself how very soon the current expenditures of this war would purchase, at fair valuation, all the slaves in any named state. Such a proposition on the part of the general government sets up no claim of a right by Federal authority to interfere with slavery within state limits, referring, as it does, the absolute control of the subject in each case to the state and its people immediately interested. It is proposed as a matter of perfectly free choice with them.

In the annual message last December, I thought fit to say "the Union must be preserved, and hence all indispensable means must be employed." I said this not hastily but deliberately. War has been made and continues to be an indispensable means to this end. A practical reacknowledgment of the national authority would render the war unnecessary, and it would at once cease. If, however, resistance continues, the war must also continue; and it is impossible to foresee all the incidents which may attend and all the ruin which may follow it. Such as may seem indispensable or may obviously promise great efficiency toward ending the struggle must and will come.

The proposition now made (though an offer only), I hope it may be esteemed no offense to ask whether the pecuniary consideration tendered would not be of more value to the states and private persons concerned than are the institution and property in it in the present aspect of affairs.

While it is true that the adoption of the proposed resolution would be merely initiatory, and not within itself a practical measure, it is recommended in the hope that it would soon lead to important practical results. In full view of my great responsibility to my God and to my country, I earnestly beg the attention of Congress and the people to the subject.

ABRAHAM LINCOLN.

Richardson, James D., ed. 1897. *A Compilation of the Messages and Papers of the Presidents.* Vol. 7. New York: Bureau of National Literature.

EMANCIPATION OF SLAVES IN WASHINGTON, D. C. (1862)

An Act for the Release of certain Persons held to Service or Labor in the District of Columbia

Section 1. *Be it enacted by the Senate and House of Representatives of the United States of America in Congress assembled,* That all persons held to service or labor within the District of Columbia by reason of African descent are hereby discharged and freed of and from all claim to such service or labor; and from and after the passage of this act neither slavery nor involuntary servitude, except for crime, whereof the party shall be duly convicted, shall hereafter exist in said District.

Section 2. *And be it further enacted,* That all persons loyal to the United States, holding claims to service or labor against persons discharged therefrom by this act, may, within ninety days from the passage thereof, but not thereafter, present to the commissioners hereinafter mentioned their respective statements or petitions in writing, verified by oath or affirmation, setting forth the names, ages, and personal description of such persons, the manner in which said petitioners acquired such claim, and any facts touching the value thereof, and declaring his allegiance to the Government of the United States, and that he has not borne arms against the United States during the present rebellion, nor in any way given aid or comfort thereto: *Provided,* That the oath of the party to the petition shall not be evidence of the facts therein stated.

Section 3. *And be it further enacted,* That the President of the United States, with the advice and consent of the Senate, shall appoint three commissioners, residents of the District of Columbia, any two of whom shall have power to act, who shall receive the petitions above mentioned, and who shall investigate and determine the validity and value of the claims therein presented, as aforesaid, and appraise and apportion, under the proviso hereto annexed, the value in money of the several claims by them found to be valid: *Provided, however,* That the entire sum so appraised and apportioned shall not exceed in the aggregate an amount equal to three hundred dollars for each person shown to have been so held by lawful claim: *And provided, further,* That no claim shall be allowed for any slave or slaves brought into said District after the passage of this act, nor for any slave claimed by any person who has borne arms against the Government of the United States in the present rebellion, or in any way given aid or comfort thereto, or which originates in or by virtue of any transfer heretofore made, or which shall hereafter be made by any person who has in any manner aided or sustained the rebellion against the Government of the United States.

Section 4. *And be it further enacted,* That said commissioners shall, within nine months from the passage of this act, make a full and final report of their proceedings, findings, and appraisement, and shall deliver the same to the Secretary of the Treasury, which report shall be deemed and taken to be conclusive in all respects, except as hereinafter provided; and the Secretary of the Treasury shall, with like exception, cause the amounts so apportioned to said claims to be paid from the Treasury of the United States to the parties found by said report to be entitled thereto as aforesaid, and the same shall be received in full and complete compensation: *Provided,* That in cases where petitions may be filed presenting conflicting claims, or setting up liens, said commissioners shall so specify in said report, and payment shall not be made according to the award of said commissioners until a period of sixty days shall have elapsed, during which time any petitioner claiming an interest in the particular amount may file a bill in equity in the Circuit Court of the District of Columbia, making all other claimants defendants thereto, setting forth the proceedings in such case before said commissioners and their actions therein, and praying that the party to whom payment has been awarded may be enjoined from receiving the same; and if said court shall grant such provisional order, a copy thereof may, on motion of said complainant, be served upon the Secretary of the Treasury, who shall thereupon cause the said amount of money to be paid into said court, subject to its orders and final decree, which payment shall be in full and complete compensation, as in other cases.

Section 5. *And be it further enacted,* That said commissioners shall hold their sessions in the city of Washington, at such place and times as the President of the United States may direct, of which they shall give due and public notice. They shall have power to subpoena and compel the attendance of witnesses, and to receive testimony and enforce its production, as in civil cases before courts of justice, without the exclusion of any witness on account of color; and they may summon before them the persons making claim to service or labor, and examine them under oath; and they may also, for purposes of identification and appraisement, call before them the persons so claimed. Said commissioners shall appoint a clerk, who shall keep files and [a] complete record of all proceedings before them, who shall have power to administer oaths and affirmations in said proceedings, and who shall issue all lawful process by them ordered. The Marshal of the District of Columbia shall personally, or by deputy, attend upon the sessions of said commissioners, and shall execute the process issued by said clerk.

Section 6. *And be it further enacted,* That said commissioners shall receive in compensation for their services the sum of two thousand dollars each, to be paid upon the filing of their report; that said clerk shall receive for his services the sum of two hundred dollars per month; that said marshal shall receive such fees as are allowed by law for similar services performed by him in the Circuit Court of the District of Columbia; that the Secretary of the Treasury shall cause all other reasonable expenses of said commission to be audited and allowed, and that said compensation, fees, and expenses shall be paid from the Treasury of the United States.

Section 7. *And be it further enacted,* That for the purpose of carrying this act into effect there is hereby appropriated, out of any money in the Treasury not otherwise appropriated, a sum not exceeding one million of dollars.

Section 8. *And be it further enacted,* That any person or persons who shall kidnap, or in any manner transport or procure to be taken out of said District, any person or persons discharged and freed by the provisions of this act, or any free person or persons with intent to re-enslave or sell such person or person into slavery, or shall re-enslave any of said freed persons, the person of persons so offending shall be deemed guilty of a felony, and on conviction thereof in any court of competent jurisdiction in said District, shall be imprisoned in the penitentiary not less than five nor more than twenty years.

Section 9. *And be it further enacted,* That within twenty days, or within such further time as the commissioners herein provided for shall limit, after the passage of this act, a statement in writing or schedule shall be filed with the clerk of the Circuit court for the District of Columbia, by the several owners or claimants to the services of the persons made free or manumitted by this act, setting forth the names, ages, sex, and particular description of such persons, severally; and the said clerk shall receive and record, in a book by him to be provided and kept for that purpose, the said statements or schedules on receiving fifty cents each therefor, and no claim shall be allowed to any claimant or owner who shall neglect this requirement.

Section 10. *And be it further enacted,* That the said clerk and his successors in office shall, from time to time, on demand, and on receiving twenty-five cents therefor, prepare, sign, and deliver to each person made free or manumitted by this act, a certificate under the seal of said court, setting out the name, age, and description of such person, and stating that such person was duly manumitted and set free by this act.

Section 11. *And be it further enacted,* That the sum of one hundred thousand dollars, out of any money in the Treasury not otherwise appropriated, is hereby appropriated, to be expended under the direction of the President of the United States, to aid in the colonization and settlement of such free persons of African descent now residing in said District, including those to be liberated by this act, as may desire to emigrate to the Republics of Hayti or Liberia, or such other country beyond the limits of the United States as the President may determine: *Provided,* The expenditure for this purpose shall not exceed one hundred dollars for each emigrant.

Section 12. *And be it further enacted,* That all acts of Congress and all laws of the State of Maryland in force in said District, and all ordinances of the cities of Washington and Georgetown, inconsistent with the provisions of this act, are hereby repealed.

Approved, April 16, 1862.

U.S. Congress. *U.S. Statutes at Large.* 37th Cong., 2nd sess, ch. 54.

LINCOLN RESPONDS TO DAVID HUNTER'S PROCLAMATION (1862)

Proclamation.

Whereas, there appears in the public prints what purports to be a proclamation of Major-General Hunter in the words and figures following, to wit:

General Orders No. 11. Headquarters Department of the South, *Hilton Head, S. C., May 9, 1862.*

The three States of Georgia, Florida and South Carolina, comprising the Military Department of the South, having deliberately declared themselves no longer under the protection of the United States of America and having taken up arms against the said United States it becomes a military necessity to declare them under martial law. This was accordingly done on the 25th day of April, 1862. Slavery and martial law in a free country are altogether incompatible; the persons in these three States—Georgia, Florida and South Carolina—heretofore held as slaves are therefore declared forever free.

David Hunter,

Major-General, Commanding.

And whereas, the same is producing some excitement and misunderstanding:

Therefore, I, Abraham Lincoln, President of the United States, proclaim and declare that the Government of the United States had no knowledge, information or belief of an intention on the part of General Hunter to issue such a proclamation nor has it yet any authentic information that the document is genuine. And further that neither General Hunter nor any other commander or person has been authorized by the Government of the United States to make proclamations declaring the slaves of any State free; and that the supposed proclamation now in question whether genuine or false is altogether void so far as respects such declaration.

I further make known that whether it be competent for me as Commander-in-Chief of the Army and Navy to declare the slaves of any State or States free, and whether at any time in any case it shall have become a necessity indispensable to the maintenance of the Government to exercise such supposed power are questions which under my responsibility I reserve to myself and which I cannot feel justified in leaving to the decision of commanders in the field. These are totally different questions from those of police regulations in armies and camps.

On the 6th day of March last by a special message I recommended to Congress the adoption of a joint resolution to be substantially as follows:

Resolved, That the United States ought to co-operate with any State which may adopt a gradual abolishment of slavery, giving to such State pecuniary aid to be used by such State in its discretion to compensate for the inconveniences public and private produced by such change of system.

The resolution in the language above quoted was adopted by large majorities in both branches of Congress and now stands an authentic, definite and solemn proposal of the nation to the States and people most immediately interested in the subject-matter. To the people of those States I now earnestly appeal; I do not argue, I beseech you to make the argument for yourselves; you cannot if you would be blind to the signs of the times; I beg of you a calm and an enlarged consideration of them, ranging if it may be far above personal and partisan politics. This proposal makes common cause for a common object casting no reproaches upon any; it acts not the Pharisee. The changes it contemplates would come gently as the dews of Heaven, not rending or wrecking anything. Will you not embrace it! So much good has not been done by one effort in all past time as in the Providence of God it is now your high privilege to do. May the vast future not have to lament that you have neglected it.

In witness whereof I have hereunto set my hand and caused the seal of the United States to be affixed.

Done at the city of Washington this nineteenth day of May, in the year of our Lord one thousand eight hundred and sixty-two, and of the Independence of the United States the eighty-sixth.

Abraham Lincoln.

By the President:

William H. Seward,

Secretary of State.

Official Records of the War of the Rebellion—Series II, Volume I: Miscellaneous Records Relating to the Negro in the Early Stage of the Rebellion.

PUNISHMENT OF A SLAVE TRADER (1862)

The Execution of Gordon, the Slave-Trader.

Not the least important among the changes which are taking place in the current of national policy and public opinion is evidenced by the fact that on Friday, 21st February, in this city, Nathaniel Gordon was hung for being engaged in the slave-trade. For forty years the slave-trade has been pronounced piracy by law, and to engage in it has been a capital offense. But the sympathy of the Government and its officials has been so often on the side of the criminal, and it seemed so absurd to hang a man for doing at sea that which, in half the Union, is done daily without censure on land, that no one has ever been punished under the Act. The Administration of Mr. Lincoln has turned over a new leaf in this respect. Henceforth the slave-trade will be abandoned to the British and their friends. The hanging of Gordon is an event in the history of our country.

He was probably the most successful and one of the worst of the individuals engaged in the trade. A native of Maine, he had engaged in the business many years since, and had always eluded justice. The particular voyage which proved fatal to him was undertaken in 1860. The following summary of the case we take from the *Times:*

It was in evidence (given by Lieutenant Henry D. Todd, U.S.N.) that the ship *Erie* was first discovered by the United States steamer *Mohican,* on the morning of the 8th day of August, 1860; that she was then about fifty miles outside of the River Congo, on the West Coast of Africa, standing to the northward, with all sail set; that she was flying the American flag, and that a gun from the *Mohican* brought her to.

It was shown by Lieutenant Todd that he went on board himself about noon, and took command of the prize. He found on board of the *Erie,* which our readers will remember was but 500 tons burden, eight hundred and ninety-seven (897) negroes, men, women, and children, ranging from the age of six months to forty years. They were half children, one-fourth men, and one-fourth women, and so crowded when on the main deck that one could scarcely put his foot down without stepping on them. The stench from the hold was fearful, and the filth and dirt upon their persons indescribably offensive.

At first he of course knew nothing about them, and until Gordon showed him, he was unable to stow them or feed them—finally he learned how, but they were stowed so closely that during the entire voyage they appeared to be in great agony. The details are sickening, but as fair exponents of the result of this close stowing, we will but mention that running sores and cutaneous diseases of the most painful as well as contagious character infected the entire load. Decency was unthought of; privacy was simply impossible—nastiness and wretchedness reigned supreme. From such a state of affairs we are not surprised to learn that, during the passage of fifteen days, twenty-nine of the sufferers died, and were thrown overboard.

It was proved by one of the seamen that he, with others, shipped on the *Erie,* believing her to be bound upon a legitimate voyage, and that, when at sea they suspected, from the nature of the cargo, that all was not right, which suspicion they mentioned to the Captain (Gordon), who satisfied them by saying that he was on a lawful voyage, that they had shipped as sailors, and would do better to return to their duties than to talk to him.

Subsequently they were told that they had shipped on a slaver, and that for every negro safely landed they should receive a dollar.

The negroes were taken on board the ship on the 7th day of August, 1860, and the entire operation of launching and unloading nearly nine hundred negroes, occupied but three quarters of an hour, or less time than a sensible man would require for his dinner. As the poor creatures came over the side Gordon would take them by the arm, and shove them here or there, as the case might be, and if by chance their persons were covered from entire exposure by a strip of rag, he would, with his knife, cut it off, fling it overboard, and send the wretch naked with his fellows.

Several of the crew testified, all agreeing that Gordon acted as Captain; that he engaged them; that he ordered them; that he promised them the $1 per capita; that he superintended the bringing on board the negroes; and that he was, in fact, the master-spirit of the entire enterprise.

For this crime Gordon was arrested, tried, and, mainly through the energy of District-Attorney Smith, convicted, and sentenced to death. Immense exertions were made by his friends and the slave-trading interest to procure a pardon, or at least a commutation of his sentence, from President Lincoln, but without avail. He was sentenced to die on 21st.

Harper's Weekly, March 8, 1862.

THE PRAYER OF TWENTY MILLIONS (1862)

To Abraham Lincoln,
President of the United States:

DEAR SIR: I do not intrude to tell you—for you must know already—that a great proportion of those who triumphed in your election, and of all who desire the unqualified suppression of the rebellion now desolating our country, are sorely disappointed and deeply pained by the policy you seem to be pursuing with regard to the slaves of rebels. I write only to set succinctly and unmistakably before you what we require, what we think we have a right to expect, and of what we complain.

I. We require of you, as the first servant of the Republic, charged especially and preeminently with this duty, that you EXECUTE THE LAWS. Most emphatically do we demand that such laws as have been recently enacted, which therefore may fairly be presumed to embody the public will and to be dictated by the *present* needs of the republic, and which, after due consideration, have received your personal sanction, shall by you be carried into full effect and that you publicly and decisively instruct your subordinates that such laws exist, that they are binding on all functionaries and citizens, and that they are to be obeyed to the letter.

II. We think you are strangely and disastrously remiss in the discharge of your official and imperative duty with regard to the emancipating provisions of the new Confiscation Act. Those provisions were designed to fight Slavery with Liberty. They prescribe that men loyal to the Union, and willing to shed their blood in her behalf, shall no longer be held, with the nation's consent, in bondage to persistent, malignant traitors, who for twenty years have been plotting and for sixteen months have been fighting to divide and destroy our country. Why these traitors should be treated with tenderness by you, to the prejudice of the dearest rights of loyal men, we cannot conceive.

III. We think you are unduly influenced by the

councils, the representations, the menaces, of certain fossil politicians hailing from the Border Slave States. Knowing well that the heartily, unconditionally loyal portion of the white citizens of those States do not expect nor desire that Slavery shall be upheld to the prejudice of the Union—(for the truth of which we appeal not only to every Republican residing in those States, but to such eminent loyalists as H. Winter Davis, Parson Brownlow, the Union Central Committee of Baltimore, and to the *Nashville Union*)—we ask you to consider that Slavery is everywhere the inciting cause and sustaining base of treason: the most slaveholding sections of Maryland and Delaware being this day, though under the Union flag, in full sympathy with the rebellion, while the free labor portions of Tennessee and of Texas, though writhing under the bloody heel of treason, are unconquerably loyal to the Union.

So emphatically is this the case that a most intelligent Union banker of Baltimore recently avowed his confident belief that a majority of the present legislature of Maryland, though elected as and all professing to be Unionists, are at heart desirous of the triumph of the Jeff Davis conspiracy, and when asked how they could be won back to loyalty, replied—"Only by the complete abolition of slavery."

It seems to us the most obvious truth, that whatever strengthens or fortifies Slavery in the Border States strengthens also treason, and drives home the wedge intended to divide the Union. Had you, from the first, refused to recognize in those States, as here, any other than unconditional loyalty—that which stands for the Union, whatever may become of Slavery—those States would have been, and would be, far more helpful and less troublesome to the defenders of the Union than they have been, or now are.

IV. We think timid counsels in such a crisis calculated to prove perilous, and probably disastrous. It is the duty of a Government so wantonly, wickedly assailed by rebellion as ours has been, to oppose force to force in a defiant, dauntless spirit. It cannot afford to temporize with traitors, nor with semi-traitors. It must not bribe them to behave themselves, nor make them fair promises in the hope of disarming their causeless hostility. Representing a brave and high-spirited people, it can afford to forfeit any thing else better than its own self-respect, or their admiring confidence, For our Government even to seek, after war has been made on it, to dispel the affected apprehensions of armed traitors that their cherished privileges may be assailed by it, is to invite insult and encourage hopes of its own downfall. The rush to arms of Ohio, Indiana, Illinois, is the true answer at once to the rebel raids of John Morgan and the traitorous sophistries of Beriah Magoffin.

V. We complain that the Union cause has suffered, and is now suffering immensely, from mistaken deference to rebel Slavery. Had you sir, in your Inaugural Address, unmistakably given notice that, in case the rebellion already commenced, were persisted in, and your efforts to preserve the Union and enforce the laws should be resisted by armed force, *you would recognize no loyal person as rightfully held in Slavery by a traitor,* we believe the rebellion would therein have received a staggering if not fatal blow. At that moment, according to the returns of the most recent elections, the Unionists were a large majority of the voters of the slave States. But they were composed in good part of the aged, the feeble, the wealthy, the timid—the young, the reckless, the aspiring, the adventurous, had already been largely lured by the gamblers and negro-traders, the politicians by trade and the conspirators by instinct, into the toils of treason. Had you then proclaimed that rebellion would strike the shackles from the slaves of every traitor, the wealthy and the cautious would have been supplied with a powerful inducement to remain loyal.

As it was, every coward in the South soon became a traitor from fear; for loyalty was perilous, while treason seemed comparatively safe. Hence the boasted unanimity of the South—a unanimity based on Rebel terrorism and the fact that immunity and safety were found on that side, danger and probable death on ours. The Rebels, from the first, have been eager to confiscate, imprison, scourge, and kill; we have fought wolves with the devices of sheep. The result is just what might have been expected. Tens of thousands are fighting in the Rebel ranks today whose original bias and natural leanings would have led them into ours.

VI. We complain that the Confiscation Act which you approved is habitually disregarded by your Generals, and that no word of rebuke for them from you has yet reached the public ear. Fremont's Proclamation and Hunter's Order favoring Emancipation were promptly annulled by you; while Halleck's Number Three, forbidding fugitives from slavery to rebels to come within his lines—an order as unmilitary as inhuman, and which received the hearty approbation of every traitor in America—with scores of like tendency, have never provoked even your remonstrance.

VII. We complain that the officers of your armies have habitually repelled rather than invited the approach of slaves who would have gladly taken the risks of escaping from their Rebel masters to our camps, bringing intelligence often of inestimable value to the Union cause. We complain that those who *have* thus escaped to us, avowing a willingness to do for us whatever might be required, have been brutally and madly repulsed, and often surrendered to be scourged, maimed, and tortured by the ruffian traitors who pretend to own them. We complain that a large proportion of our regular Army officers, with many of the volunteers, evince far more solicitude to uphold slavery than to put down the rebellion.

And finally, we complain that you, Mr. President, elected as a Republican, knowing well what an abomination Slavery is, and how emphatically it is the core and essence of this atrocious rebellion, seem never to interfere with these atrocities, and never give a direction to your military subordinates, which does not appear to have been conceived in the interest of Slavery rather than of freedom.

VIII. On the face of this wide earth, Mr. President, there is not one disinterested, determined, intelligent champion of the Union cause who does not feel that all attempts to put down the rebellion and at the same time uphold its inciting cause are preposterous and futile—that the rebellion, if crushed out to-morrow, would be renewed within a year if Slavery were left in full vigor—that army officers who remain to this day devoted to Slavery can at best be but half-way loyal to the Union—and that every hour of deference to Slavery is an hour of added and deepened peril to the Union. I appeal to the testimony of your ambassadors in Europe. It is freely at your service, not at mine. Ask them to tell you candidly whether the seeming subserviency of your policy to the slaveholding, slavery-upholding interest, is not the perplexity, the despair of statesmen of all parties, and be admonished by the general answer!

IX. I close as I began with the statement that what an immense majority of the loyal millions of your countrymen require of you is a frank, declared, unqualified, ungrudging execution of the laws of the land, more especially of the Confiscation Act. That act gives freedom to the slaves of rebels coming within our lines, or whom those lines may at any time enclose— we ask you to render it due obedience by publicly requiring all your subordinates to recognize and obey it. The rebels are everywhere using the late anti-negro riots in the North, as they have long used your officers' treatment of negroes in the South, to convince the slaves that they have nothing to hope from a Union success—that we mean in that case to sell them into a bitter bondage to defray the cost of the war.

Let them impress this as a truth on the great mass of their ignorant and credulous bondmen, and the Union will never be restored—never. We cannot conquer ten millions of people united in solid phalanx against us, powerfully aided by Northern sympathizers and European allies. We must have scouts, guides, spies, cooks, teamsters, diggers, and choppers from the blacks of the South, whether we allow them to fight for us or not, or we shall be babbled and repelled.

As one of the millions who would gladly have avoided this struggle at any sacrifice but that of principle and honor, but who now feel that the triumph of the Union is indispensable not only to the existence of our country but to the well-being of mankind, I entreat you to render a hearty and unequivocal obedience to the law of the land.

Yours,
Horace Greeley

New York *Tribune*, August 19, 1862.

LINCOLN'S RESPONSE TO HORACE GREELEY (1862)

New York Tribune, *August 19, 1862.*

Executive Mansion, Washington, August 22, 1862.
Hon. Horace Greeley:
DEAR SIR: I have just read yours of the nineteenth, addressed to myself through the New-York *Tribune*. If there be in it any statements or assumptions of fact which I may know to be erroneous, I do not now and here controvert them. If there be in it any inferences which I may believe to be falsely drawn, I do not now and here argue against them. If there be perceptible in it an impatient and dictatorial tone, I waive it in deference to an old friend, whose heart I have always supposed to be right.

As to the policy I "seem to be pursuing," as you say, I have not meant to leave any one in doubt.

I would save the Union. I would save it the shortest way under the Constitution. The sooner the National authority can be restored, the nearer the Union will be "the Union as it was." If there be those who would not save the Union unless they could at the same time *save* Slavery, I do not agree with them. If there be those who would not save the Union unless they could at the same time *destroy* Slavery, I do not agree with them. My paramount object in this struggle *is* to save the Union, and is *not* either to save or destroy Slavery. If I could save the Union without freeing *any* slave, I would do it; and if I could save it by freeing *all* the slaves, I would do it; and if I could do it by freeing some and leaving others alone, I would also do that. What I do about Slavery and the colored race, I do because I believe it helps to save this Union; and what I forbear, I forbear because I do not believe it would help to save the Union. I shall do *less* whenever I shall believe what I am doing hurts the cause, and I shall do *more* whenever I shall believe doing more will help the cause. I shall try to correct errors when shown to be errors and I shall adopt new views so fast as they shall appear to be true views. I have here stated my purpose according to my view of *official* duty, and I intend no modification of my oft-expressed *personal* wish that all men, everywhere, could be free.

Yours,
A. Lincoln.

The Christian Times and Illinois Baptist, September 3, 1862.

JEFFERSON DAVIS' PROCLAMATION REGARDING BLACK TROOPS (1862)

Adjt. and Insp. General's Office, *Richmond [Va.], December 24, 1862.*

General Orders, No. 111.

I. The following proclamation of the President is published for the information and guidance of all concerned therein:

By the President of the Confederate States. a Proclamation. Now therefore, I Jefferson Davis, President of the Confederate States of America, and in their name do pronounce and declare the said Benjamin F. Butler to be a felon deserving of capital punishment. I do order that he be no longer considered or treated simply as a public enemy of the Confederate States of America but as an outlaw and common enemy of mankind, and that in the event of his capture the officer in command of the capturing force do cause him to be immediately executed by hanging; and I do further order that no commissioned officer of the United States taken captive shall be released on parole before exchange until the said Butler shall have met with due punishment for his crimes.

And whereas the hostilities waged against this Confederacy by the forces of the United States under the command of said Benjamin F. Butler have borne no resemblance to such warfare as is alone permissible by the rules of international law or the usages of civilization but have been characterized by repeated atrocities and outrages, among the large number of which the following may be cited as examples:

Peaceful and aged citizens, unresisting captives and non-combatants, have been confined at hard labor with balls and chains attached to their limbs, and are still so held in dungeons and fortresses. Others have been subjected to a like degrading punishment for selling medicines to the sick soldiers of the Confederacy.

The soldiers of the United States have been invited and encouraged by general orders to insult and outrage the wives, the mothers and the sisters of our citizens.

Helpless women have been torn from their homes and subjected to solitary confinement, some in fortresses and prisons and one especially on an island of barren sand under a tropical sun; have been fed with loathsome rations that had been condemned as unfit for soldiers, and have been exposed to the vilest insults.

Prisoners of war who surrendered to the naval forces of the United States on agreement that they should be released on parole have been seized and kept in close confinement.

Repeated pretexts have been sought or invented for plundering the inhabitants of the captured city by fines levied and exacted under threat of imprisoning recusants at hard labor with ball and chain.

The entire population of the city of New Orleans have been forced to elect between starvation, by the confiscation of all their property, and taking an oath against conscience to bear allegiance to the invaders of their country.

Egress from the city has been refused to those whose fortitude withstood the test, even to lone and aged women and to helpless children; and after being ejected from their homes and robbed of their property they have been left to starve in the streets or subsist on charity.

The slaves have been driven from the plantations in the neighborhood of New Orleans till their owners would consent to share the crops with the commanding general, his brother Andrew J. Butler, and other officers; and when such consent had been extorted the slaves have been restored to the plantations and there compelled to work under the bayonets of guards of U.S. soldiers.

Where this partnership was refused armed expeditions have been sent to the plantations to rob them of everything that was susceptible of removal, and even slaves too aged or infirm for work have in spite of their entreaties been forced from the homes provided by the owners and driven to wander helpless on the highway.

By a recent general order (No. 91) the entire property in that part of Louisiana lying west of the Mississippi River has been sequestrated for confiscation and officers have been assigned to duty with orders to "gather up and collect the personal property and turn over to the proper officers upon their receipts such of said property as may be required for the use of the U.S. Army; to collect together all the other personal property and bring the same to New Orleans and cause it to be sold at public auction to the highest bidders"—an order which if executed condemns to punishment by starvation at least a quarter of a million of human beings of all ages, sexes and conditions; and of which the execution although forbidden to military officers by the orders of President Lincoln is in accordance with the confiscation law of our enemies which he has directed to be enforced through the agency of civil officials. And finally the African slaves have not only been excited to insurrection by every license and encouragement but numbers of them have actually been armed for a servile war—a war in its nature far exceeding in horrors the most merciless atrocities of the savages.

And whereas the officers under the command of the said Butler have been in many instances active and zealous agents in the commission of these crimes, and no instance is known of the refusal of any one of them to participate in the outrages above narrated.

And whereas the President of the United States has by public and official declaration signified not only his approval of the effort to excite servile war within the Confederacy but his intention to give aid and encouragement thereto if these independent States shall continue to refuse submission to a foreign power after the 1st day of January next, and has thus made known that all appeals to the laws of nations, the dictates of reason and the instincts of humanity would be addressed in vain to our enemies, and that they can be deterred from the commission of these crimes only by the terms of just retribution:

Now therefore I, Jefferson Davis, President of the Confederate States of America and acting by their authority, appealing to the Divine Judge in attestation that their conduct is not guided by the passion of revenge but that they reluctantly yield to the solemn duty of repressing by necessary severity crimes of which their citizens are the victims, do issue this my proclamation, and by virtue of my authority as Commander-in-Chief of the Armies of the Confederate States do order——

1. That all commissioned officers in the command of said Benjamin F. Butler be declared not entitled to be considered as soldiers engaged in honorable warfare but as robbers and criminals deserving death, and that they and each of them be whenever captured reserved for execution.

2. That the private soldiers and non-commissioned officers in the army of said Butler be considered as only the instruments used for the commission of the crimes perpetrated by his orders and not as free agents; that they therefore be treated when capture as prisoners of war with kindness and humanity and be sent home on the usual parole that they will in no manner aid or serve the United States in any capacity during the continuance of this war unless duly exchanged.

3. That all negro slaves captured in arms be at once delivered over to the executive authorities of the respective States to which they belong to be dealt with according to the laws of said States.

4. That the like orders be executed in all cases with respect to all commissioned officers of the United States when found serving in company with armed slaves in insurrection against the authorities of the different States of this Confederacy.

In testimony whereof I have signed these presents and caused the seal of the Confederate States of America to be affixed thereto at the city of Richmond on this 23d day of December, in the year of our Lord one thousand eight hundred and sixty-two.

Jeff'n Davis.

By the President: J. P. Benjamin,
Secretary of State.

II. Officers of the Army are charged with the observance and enforcement of the foregoing orders of the President. Where the evidence is not full or the case is for any reason of a doubtful character it will be referred through this office for the decision of the War Department.

By order:

S. Cooper, *Adjutant and Inspector General.*

U.S. War Department. 1880–1901. *The War of the Rebellion: A Compendium of the Official Records of the Union and Confederate Armies—Series II, Vol. 5.* Washington, DC: Government Printing Office.

EMANCIPATION PROCLAMATION (1863)

By the President of the United States of America:

A Proclamation. Whereas on the 22nd day of September, A. D. 1862, a proclamation was issued by the President of the United States, containing, among other things, the following, to wit:

That on the 1st day of January, A. D. 1863, all persons held as slaves within any State or designated part of a State the people whereof shall then be in rebellion against the United States shall be then, thenceforward, and forever free; and the executive government of the United States, including the military and naval authority thereof, will recognize and maintain the freedom of such persons and will do no act or acts to repress such persons, or any of them, in any efforts they may make for their actual freedom.

That the executive will on the 1st day of January aforesaid, by proclamation, designate the States and parts of States, if any, in which the people thereof, respectively, shall then be in rebellion against the United States; and the fact that any State or the people thereof shall on that day be in good faith represented in the Congress of the United States by members chosen thereto at elections wherein a majority of the qualified voters of such States shall have participated shall, in the absence of strong countervailing testimony, be deemed conclusive evidence that such State and the people thereof are not then in rebellion against the United States.

Now, therefore, I, Abraham Lincoln, President of the United States, by virtue of the power in me vested as Commander-In-Chief of the Army and Navy of the United States in time of actual armed rebellion against the authority and government of the United States, and as a fit and necessary war measure for suppressing said rebellion, do, on this 1st day of January, A. D. 1863, and in accordance with my purpose so to do, publicly proclaimed for the full period of one hundred days from the first day above mentioned, order and designate as the States and parts of States wherein the people thereof, respectively, are this day in rebellion against the United States the following, to wit:

Arkansas, Texas, Louisiana (except the parishes of St. Bernard, Plaque mines, Jefferson, St. John, St. Charles, St. James, Ascension, Assumption, Terrebonne, Lafourche, St. Mary, St. Martin, and Orleans, including the city of New Orleans), Mississippi, Alabama, Florida, Georgia, South Carolina, North Carolina, and Virginia (except the forty-eight counties designated as West Virginia, and also the counties of Berkeley, Accomac, Northhampton, Elizabeth City, York, Princess Anne, and Norfolk, including the cities of Norfolk and Portsmouth), and which excepted parts are for the present left precisely as if this proclamation were not issued.

And by virtue of the power and for the purpose aforesaid, I do order and declare that all persons held as slaves within said designated States and parts of States are, and henceforward shall be, free; and that the Executive Government of the United States, including the military and naval authorities thereof, will recognize and maintain the freedom of said persons.

And I hereby enjoin upon the people so declared to be free to abstain from all violence, unless in necessary self-defense; and I recommend to them that, in all case when allowed, they labor faithfully for reasonable wages.

And I further declare and make known that such persons of suitable condition will be received into the armed service of the United States to garrison forts, positions, stations, and other places, and to man vessels of all sorts in said service.

And upon this act, sincerely believed to be an act of justice, warranted by the Constitution upon military necessity, I invoke the considerate judgment of mankind and the gracious favor of Almighty God.

Lincoln, Abraham. "The Emancipation Proclamation," in *Documents of American History*, ed. Henry Steele Commager (New York: Appleton-Century-Crofts, 1963).

THE CONFEDERATE CONGRESS REACTS TO BLACK TROOPS (1863)

May 1, 1863.

The resolutions having been read as follows, viz:

1. Resolved by the Congress of the Confederate States of America, In response to the message of the President, transmitted to Congress at the commencement of the present session, that, in the opinion of Congress, the commissioned officers of the enemy ought not to be delivered to the authorities of the respective States, as suggested in the said message, but all captives taken by the Confederate forces ought to be dealt with and disposed of by the Confederate Government.

2. That, in the judgment of Congress, the proclamations of the President of the United States, dated, respectively, September twenty-second, eighteen hundred and sixty-two, and January first, eighteen hundred and sixty-three, and the other measures of the Government of the United States and its authorities, commanders, and forces, designed or tending to emancipate slaves in the Confederate States, or to abduct such slaves, or to incite them to insurrection, or to employ negroes in war against the Confederate States, or to overthrow the institution of African slavery and bring on a servile war in these States, would, if successful, produce atrocious consequences, and they are inconsistent with the spirit of those usages which in modern warfare prevail among civilized nations, they may therefore be properly and lawfully repressed by retaliation.

3. That in every case wherein, during the present war, any violation of the laws or usages of war among civi-

lized nations shall be or has been done and perpetrated by those acting under the authority of the Government of the United States on the persons or property of citizens of the Confederate States or of those under the protection or in the land or naval service of the Confederate States or of any State of the Confederacy, the President of the Confederate States is hereby authorized to cause full and ample retaliation to be made for every such violation in such manner and to such extent as he may think proper.

4. That every white person being a commissioned officer, or acting as such, who, during the present war, shall command negroes or mulattoes in arms against the Confederate States, or who shall arm, train, organize, or prepare negroes or mulattoes for military service against the Confederate States, or who shall voluntarily aid negroes or mulattoes in any military enterprise, attack, or conflict in such service, shall be deemed as inciting servile insurrection, and shall, if captured, be put to death or be otherwise punished, at the discretion of the court.

5. Every person being a commissioned officer, or acting as such, in the service of the enemy, who shall, during the present war, excite, attempt to excite, or cause to be excited a servile insurrection, or who shall incite or cause to be incited a slave to rebel, shall, if captured, be put to death or be otherwise punished, at the discretion of the court.

6. Every person charged with an offense punishable under the preceding resolutions shall, during the present war, be tried before the military court attached to the army or corps by the troops of which he shall have been captured or by such other military court as the President may direct and in such manner and under such regulations as the President shall prescribe, and, after conviction, the President may commute the punishment in such manner and on such terms as he may deem proper.

7. All negroes and mulattoes who shall be engaged in war, or be taken in arms against the Confederate States, or shall give aid and comfort to the enemies of the Confederate States, shall, when captured in the Confederate States, be delivered to the authorities of the State or States in which they shall be captured to be dealt with according to the present or future laws of such State or States.

Mr. Gray called the question.
Mr. Lyons demanded the yeas and nays;

which were ordered,
and are recorded as follows, viz:
Yeas . . . 29
Nays . . . 27

Journal of the Congress of the Confederate States of America, 1861–1865, Volume 6.

THE HUMAN TOLL OF SLAVERY (1863)

Selection from Journal of a Residence on a Georgian Plantation.

Before closing this letter, I have a mind to transcribe to you the entries for today recorded in a sort of day-book, where I put down very succinctly the number of people who visit me, their petitions and ailments, and also such special particulars concerning them as seem to me worth recording. You will see how miserable the physical condition of many of these poor creatures is; and their physical condition, it is insisted by those who uphold this evil system, is the only part of it which is prosperous, happy, and compares well with that of Northern laborers. Judge from the details I now send you; and never forget, while reading them, that the people on this plantation are well off, and consider themselves well off, in comparison with the slaves on some of the neighboring [communities].

Fanny has had six children; all dead but one. She came to beg to have her work in the field lightened.

Nanny has had three children; two of them are dead. She came to implore that the rule of sending them into the field three weeks after their confinement might be altered.

Leah, Caesar's wife, has had six children; three are dead.

Sophy, Lewis's wife, came to beg for some old linen. She is suffering fearfully; has had ten children; five of them are dead. The principal favor she asked was a piece of meat, which I gave her.

Sally, Scipio's wife, has had two miscarriages and three children born, one of whom is dead. She came complaining of incessant pain and weakness in her back. This woman was a mulatto daughter of a slave called Sophy, by a white man of the name of Walker, who visited the plantation.

Charlotte, Renty's wife, had had two miscarriages, and was with child again. She was almost crippled with rheumatism, and showed me a pair of poor swollen knees that made my heart ache. I have promised her a pair of flannel trousers, which I must forthwith set about making.

Sarah, Stephen's wife: this woman's case and history were alike deplorable. She had had four miscarriages, had brought seven children into the world, five of whom were dead, and was again with child. She complained of dreadful pains in the back, and an internal tumor which swells with the exertion of working in the fields; probably, I think, she is ruptured. She told me she had once been mad and had run into the woods, where she contrived to elude discovery for some time, but was at last tracked and brought back, when she was tied up by the arms, and heavy logs fastened to her feet, and was severely flogged. After this she contrived to escape again, and lived for some time skulking in the woods, and she supposes mad, for when she was taken again she was entirely naked. She subsequently recovered from this derangement, and seems now just like all the other poor creatures who come to me for help and pity. I suppose her constant childbearing and hard labor in the fields at the same time have produced the temporary insanity.

Kemble, Frances Anne. 1863. *Journal of a Residence on a Georgian Plantation in 1838–1839.* London: Longman, Greene, Longman, Roberts & Green.

NATIONAL FREEDMEN'S RELIEF ASSOCIATION GUIDELINES (1864)

Rules and Regulations.

Adopted February 26, 1864, by the National Freedmen's Relief Association, with regard to the schools and teachers under its auspices, in General Saxton's Department.   1. All present contracts with teachers shall terminate with the close of their respective schools, in the summer of this year, and the publication of these regulations in the *Freedmen's Advocate* shall be a sufficient notice thereof.

2. All appointments of teachers shall henceforth be annual, or for the current school season; but teachers who are, or have been, in the employ of the Association, shall, when recommended by the Superintendent, be entitled to preference, the qualifications being equal; and, if reappointed, to salary, during thirty days' vacation or absence from their field of labor; but, in order to secure such preference, application for reappointment must be made to the President of the Association, by or before the first day of September.

3. The school season shall be held to commence of the 15th of October, subject, however, to local variations, according to the judgment of the Superintendent; and all teachers who may be absent from the Department, must be ready to embark from New York, when called upon after the 1st of October.

4. Teachers shall be entitled to salary from the date of their departure from New York, up to the date of their departure from their field of labor, if actively engaged in teaching in the meanwhile, and shall not be liable to deduction on account of illness of less than thirty days duration.

5. The subsistence of teachers on the passage from New York, shall be paid by the Association, as will that on the return passage, when they shall have been six months in its employ; but not otherwise, except in case of disabling illness.

6. Teachers who resign in less than three months, except in case of disabling illness, or who shall be discharged for cause, shall be entitled to receive but half salary for the time of actual service, the Association reserving the right to terminate all contracts with teachers, on thirty days' notice, without prejudice to the claims of those in good standing.

7. Unacclimated teachers, and those whose locations are unwholesome, may be absent from their posts between the 15th of July and the 15th of October, with the consent of the Superintendent, for a longer time than the thirty days' vacation specified, without prejudice to their standing with the Association; but the schools shall be kept open as long as practicable, without danger to health; and no school need be closed, the teacher of which is willing and desirous to keep it open during said vacation.

8. All teachers, in addition to their regular work, are expected to interest themselves in the moral, religious, and social improvement of the families of their pupils, to visit them in their homes, to instruct the women and girls in sewing and domestic economy, to encourage and take part in religious meetings and Sunday Schools, but to avoid all peculiarly denominational or sectarian controversy.

9. Each teacher shall, before the 10th of every month, render to the Superintendent a full report of the condition of the school under her charge during the previous month, which reports, shall, as received, be forwarded to the Chairman of the House Committee, by the Superintendent, with remarks upon such schools as shall have been personally visited by him during the month. And the Superintendent shall, during the months of January, April, and July, transmit to said

Chairman a full report of the condition of all the schools under his charge during the preceding quarter, which reports shall include an inventory of all books, school furniture, and other property belonging to the Association, and a list of such articles as may be needed for the schools, the dwellings of the Superintendent and teachers, and for the orphan asylum at Fernandina.

10. In case the Superintendent shall have serious cause of complaint against any teacher, and such teacher shall refuse to be guided by his advice, he shall transmit a formal statement of charges to the Chairman of the House Committee, having first submitted the same to such teacher, and allowed eight days for the preparation of a counter statement, or defense, in order that the cause may be adjudged by the Association. And the Superintendent shall have authority to suspend such teacher until final decision, when, in his judgment, such action shall be required; and the thirty days' notice before reserved, shall be held to date from such suspension. But the teacher shall have the option, by resignation, to prevent the transmissions of the charges in question.

GEO. C. WARD,

Secretary.

Rules and Regulations. Adopted February 26, 1864, by the National Freedmen's Relief Association, with Regard to the Schools and Teachers under Its Auspices, in General Saxton's Department. [n. p.] 1864. Printed Ephemera Collection; Portfolio 235, Folder 1. Library of Congress. Washington, DC.

THE WADE-DAVIS MANIFESTO (1864)

August 5, 1864

We have read without surprise, but not without indignation, the Proclamation of the President of the 8th of July.

The President, by preventing this bill from becoming a law, holds the electoral votes of the Rebel States at the dictation of his personal ambition.

If those votes turn the balance in his favor, is it to be supposed that his competitor, defeated by such means will acquiesce?

If the Rebel majority assert their supremacy in those States, and send votes which elect an enemy of the Government, will we not repel his claims?

And is not that civil war for the Presidency, inaugurated by the votes of Rebel States?

Seriously impressed with these dangers, Congress,

"the proper constitutional authority," formally declared that there are no State Governments in the Rebel States, and provided for their erection at a proper time; and both the Senate and the House of Representatives rejected the Senators and Representatives chosen under the authority of what the President calls the Free Constitution and Government of Arkansas.

The President's proclamation *"holds for naught"* this judgment, and discards the authority of the Supreme Court, and strides headlong toward the anarchy his Proclamation of the 8th of December inaugurated.

If electors for President be allowed to be chosen in either of those States, a sinister light will be cast on the motives which induced the President to "hold for naught" the will of Congress rather than his Government in Louisiana and Arkansas.

That judgment of Congress which the President defies was the exercise of an authority exclusively vested in Congress by the Constitution to determine what is the established Government in a State, and in its own nature and by the highest judicial authority binding on all other departments of the Government. . . .

A more studied outrage on the legislative authority of the people has never been perpetrated.

Congress passed a bill; the President refused to approve it, and then by proclamation puts as much of it in force as he sees fit, and proposes to execute those parts by officers unknown to the laws of the United States and not subject to the confirmation of the Senate!

The bill directed the appointment of Provisional Governors by and with the advice and consent of the Senate.

The President, after defeating the law, proposes to appoint without law, and without the advice and consent of the Senate, *Military* Governors for the Rebel States!

He has already exercised this dictatorial usurpation in Louisiana, and he defeated the bill to prevent its limitation. . . .

The President has greatly presumed on the forbearance which the supporters of his Administration have so long practiced, in view of the arduous conflict in which we are engaged, and the reckless ferocity of our political opponents.

But he must understand that our support is of a cause and not of a man; that the authority of Congress is paramount and must be respected; that the whole body of the Union men of Congress will not submit to be impeached by him of rash and unconstitutional legislation; and if he wishes our support, he must confine himself to his executive duties—to obey and execute, not make the laws—to suppress by arms armed Rebellion, and leave political reorganization to Congress.

If the supporters of the Government fail to insist on this, they become responsible for the usurpations which they fail to rebuke, and are justly liable to the indignation of the people whose rights and security, committed to their keeping, they sacrifice.

Let them consider the remedy for these usurpations, and, having found it, fearlessly execute it.

McPherson, Edward, ed. 1865. *Political History of the Rebellion.* Washington, DC: Philp & Solomons.

FORTY ACRES AND A MULE (1865)

Special Field Order No. 15.

Hdqrs. Mil. Div. of the Mississippi. In the Field, Savannah, Ga.

January 16th, 1865.

I. The islands from Charleston, south, the abandoned rice fields along the rivers for thirty miles back from the sea, and the country bordering the St. Johns river, Florida, are reserved and set apart for the settlement of the negroes now made free by the acts of war and the proclamation of the President of the United States.

II. At Beaufort, Hilton Head, Savannah, Fernandina, St. Augustine and Jacksonville, the blacks may remain in their chosen or accustomed vocations—but on the islands, and in the settlements hereafter to be established, no white person whatever, unless military officers and soldiers detailed for duty, will be permitted to reside; and the sole and exclusive management of affairs will be left to the freed people themselves, subject only to the United States military authority and the acts of Congress. By the laws of war, and orders of the President of the United States, the negro is free and must be dealt with as such. He cannot be subjected to conscription or forced military service, save by the written orders of the highest military authority of the Department, under such regulations as the President or Congress may prescribe. Domestic servants, blacksmiths, carpenters and other mechanics, will be free to select their own work and residence, but the young and able-bodied negroes must be encouraged to enlist as soldiers in the service of the United States, to contribute their share towards maintaining their own freedom, and securing their rights as citizens of the United States.

Negroes so enlisted will be organized into companies, battalions and regiments, under the orders of the United States military authorities, and will be paid, fed and clothed according to law. The bounties paid on enlistment may, with the consent of the recruit, go to assist his family and settlement in procuring agricultural implements, seed, tools, boots, clothing, and other articles necessary for their livelihood.

III. Whenever three respectable negroes, heads of families, shall desire to settle on land, and shall have selected for that purpose an island or a locality clearly defined, within the limits above designated, the Inspector of Settlements and Plantations will himself, or by such subordinate officer as he may appoint, give them a license to settle such island or district, and afford them such assistance as he can to enable them to establish a peaceable agricultural settlement. The three parties named will subdivide the land, under the supervision of the Inspector, among themselves and such others as may choose to settle near them, so that each family shall have a plot of not more than (40) forty acres of tillable ground, and when it borders on some water channel, with not more than 800 feet water front, in the possession of which land the military authorities will afford them protection, until such time as they can protect themselves, or until Congress shall regulate their title. The Quartermaster may, on the requisition of the Inspector of Settlements and Plantations, place at the disposal of the Inspector, one or more of the captured steamers, to ply between the settlements and one or more of the commercial points heretofore named in orders, to afford the settlers the opportunity to supply their necessary wants, and to sell the products of their land and labor.

IV. Whenever a negro has enlisted in the military service of the United States, he may locate his family in any one of the settlements at pleasure, and acquire a homestead, and all other rights and privileges of a settler, as though present in person. In like manner, negroes may settle their families and engage on board the gunboats, or in fishing, or in the navigation of the inland waters, without losing any claim to land or other advantages derived from this system. But no one, unless an actual settler as above defined, or unless absent on Government service, will be entitled to claim any right to land or property in any settlement by virtue of these orders.

V. In order to carry out this system of settlement, a general officer will be detailed as Inspector of Settlements and Plantations, whose duty it shall be to visit the settlements, to regulate their police and general management, and who will furnish personally to each head of a family, subject to the approval of the President of the United States, a possessory title in writing, giving as near as possible the description of boundaries; and who shall adjust all claims or conflicts that may arise under the same, subject to the like approval, treating such titles altogether as possessory. The same general officer will also be charged with the enlistment and organization of the negro recruits, and protecting their interests while absent from their settlements; and will be governed by the rules and regulations prescribed by the War Department for such purposes.

VI. Brigadier General R. Saxton is hereby appointed Inspector of Settlements and Plantations, and will at once enter on the performance of his duties. No change is intended or desired in the settlement now on Beaufort [Port Royal] Island, nor will any rights to property heretofore acquired be affected thereby.

By Order of Major General W. T. Sherman

L. M. DAYTON

Assistant Adjutant-General

The War of the Rebellion: A Compilation of the Official Records of the Union and Confederate Armies. Published under the direction of The Hon. Elihu Root, Secretary of War, by Brig. Gen. Fred C. Ainsworth, Chief of Records and Pension Office, War Department and Mr. Joseph W. Kirkley, vol. XLVII/2. Washington, DC: Government Printing Office, 1891.

EDITORIAL OPPOSING "BLACK LAWS" (1865)

The Black Laws.

Illinois has repealed her black laws, and indeed she could hardly help wiping the stain from her face when her neighbor Missouri was lifting her whole body out of the slough. The black laws of Illinois, although Illinois is a free State, were as much a part of the code of slavery as any slave law of Arkansas or Mississippi; for they were the work of what was called the Democratic party, and that party was the minister of slavery. In Illinois, for instance, all colored persons were presumed to be slaves unless they could prove themselves to be free; in other words, were held to be guilty until they proved their innocence: thus directly reversing the first humane maxim of the common law. By another act, if any negro or mulatto came into the State and staid ten days, he was to be fined fifty dollars, and sold indefinitely to pay the fine.

We read such things incredulously, in the light of to-day. The wicked folly of selecting for outrage a special class of the population, and that class the most innocent and defenseless, is so like a caprice of Ashantee society, or a measure of Patagonian statesmanship, that it is quite impossible to believe that it was tolerated in the great, prosperous, and enlightened State of Illinois. It explains the curiously inhuman and heartless tone of Mr. Douglas in speaking of the colored race. He lived in the midst of this senseless and fierce prejudice, and he rose by pandering to it.

The black laws of Illinois were another proof of the fearful demoralization which slavery had wrought in this country, and upon which it counted for easy success in its rebellion. When slavery saw that Pierce and Buchanan, two successive Presidents, were its most abject tools; when it saw every Northern city ready to take by the throat any man who fiercely denounced it; when it saw even in Boston a rich merchant and noted citizen named Fay, with the Mayor of the city, turning a meeting for condemnation of slavery into the street; when it read such laws as these of Illinois; when it saw the city of New York cringing beneath its frown and fawning upon its contemptuous smile, how could it help believing that Franklin Pierce wrote the truth to Jefferson Davis when he said that the blood would flow this side of Mason and Dixon's line rather than the other, and suppose, with Robert Toombs, that any man could drink all the blood that would be shed in the war.

Now that Illinois has repealed her black laws, is it too much to hope that New York will do the same thing? The Constitution of the State allows colored citizens to vote, provided that they have lived twice as long in the State and county, and paid twice as much tax as any other voter. The other voters may be ignorant and brutal sots, who are nuisances and pests in any country, and these may be intelligent, industrious, thrifty, valuable citizens; but the Constitution of New York, enslaved by the same mean and inhuman prejudice which dictated the black laws of Illinois, declares that ignorance and brutality are politically preferable to intelligence and thrift.

If intelligence is to be the condition of active citizenship, it is a test which every body can understand, and which most people will approve. But to make it dependent upon complexion is as wise as to rest it upon the color of the hair or the breadth of the shoulders. The monstrous subjection of this country to the prejudice against color is not, as many who are under its influence suppose, "a natural instinct;" it is only the natural result of a system which arbitrarily and forcibly makes color the sign of hopeless servitude. If red-haired men or men over six feet in height were enslaved and imbruted for centuries, there would be exactly the same "natural aversion" to them which is gravely alleged by many otherwise sensible people against the colored race.

Missouri has emancipated herself; Illinois has

thrown off her black laws. Suppose that sensible men and women now emancipate themselves from the black law of a most cruel and senseless prejudice.

Harper's Weekly, February 11, 1865.

FREEDMEN'S BUREAU ACT (1865)

Chap. XC. An Act to Establish a Bureau for the Relief of Freedmen and Refugees.

Be it enacted by the Senate and House of Representatives of the United States of America an Congress assembled, That there is hereby established in the War Department, to continue during the present war of rebellion, and for one year thereafter, a bureau of refugees, freedmen, and abandoned lands, to which shall be committed, as hereinafter provided, the supervision and management of all abandoned lands, and the control of all subjects relating to refugees and freedmen from rebel states, or from any district of country within the territory embraced in the operations of the army, under such rules and regulations as may be prescribed by the head of the bureau and approved by the President. The said bureau shall be under the management and control of a commissioner to be appointed by the President, by and with the advice and consent of the Senate, whose compensation shall be three thousand dollars per annum, and such number of clerks as may be assigned to him by the Secretary of War, not exceeding one chief clerk, two of the fourth class, two of the third class, and five of the first class. And the commissioner and all persons appointed under this act, shall, before entering upon their duties, take the oath of office prescribed in an act entitled "An act to prescribe an oath of office, and for other purposes," approved July second, eighteen hundred and sixty-two, and the commissioner and the chief clerk shall, before entering upon their duties, give bonds to the treasurer of the United States, the former in the sum of fifty thousand dollars, and the latter in the sum of ten thousand dollars, conditioned for the faithful discharge of their duties respectively, with securities to be approved as sufficient by the Attorney-General, which bonds shall be filed in the office of the first comptroller of the treasury, to be by him put in suit for the benefit of any injured party upon any breach of the conditions thereof.

Section 2. *And be it further enacted,* That the Secretary of War may direct such issues of provisions, clothing, and fuel, as he may deem needful for the immediate and temporary shelter and supply of destitute and suffering refugees and freedmen and their wives and children, under such rules and regulations as he may direct.

Section 3. *And be it further enacted,* That the President may, by and with the advice and consent of the Senate, appoint an assistant commissioner for each of the states declared to be in insurrection, not exceeding ten in number, who shall, under the direction of the commissioner, aid in the execution of the provisions of this act; and he shall give a bond to the Treasurer of the United States, in the sum of twenty thousand dollars, in the form and manner prescribed in the first section of this act. Each of said commissioners shall receive an annual salary of two thousand five hundred dollars in full compensation for all his services. And any military officer may be detailed and assigned to duty under this act without increase of pay or allowances. The commissioner shall, before the commencement of each regular session of congress, make full report of his proceedings with exhibits of the state of his accounts to the President, who shall communicate the same to congress, and shall also make special reports whenever required to do so by the President or either house of congress; and the assistant commissioners shall make quarterly reports of their proceedings to the commissioner, and also such other special reports as from time to time may be required.

Section 4. *And be it further enacted,* That the commissioner, under the direction of the President, shall have authority to set apart, for the use of loyal refugees and freedmen, such tracts of land within the insurrectionary states as shall have been abandoned, or to which the United States shall have acquired title by confiscation or sale, or otherwise, and to every male citizen, whether refugee or freedman, as aforesaid, there shall be assigned not more than forty acres of such land, and the person to whom it was so assigned shall be protected in the use and enjoyment of the land for the term of three years at an annual rent not exceeding six per centum upon the value of such land, as it was appraised by the state authorities in the year eighteen hundred and sixty, for the purpose of taxation, and in case no such appraisal can be found, then the rental shall be based upon the estimated value of the land in said year, to be ascertained in such manner as the commissioner may by regulation prescribe. At the end of said term, or at any time during said term, the occupants of any parcels so assigned may purchase the land and receive such title thereto as the United States can convey, upon paying therefor the value of the land, as ascertained and fixed for the purpose of determining the annual rent aforesaid.

Section 5. And be it further enacted, That all acts

and parts of acts inconsistent with the provisions of this act, are hereby repealed.

Approved, March 3, 1865.

United States Congress. *United States Statutes at Large,* 38th Cong., 2nd Sess., ch. 90.

MARTIN R. DELANY OFFERS ADVICE TO FREEDMEN (1865)

July 23, 1865
St. Helena Island, South Carolina

It was only a War policy of the Government, to declare the slaves of the South free, knowing that the whole power of the South, laid in the possession of the Slaves. But I want you to understand, that we would not have become free, had we not armed ourselves and fought out our independence.

. . . People say that you are too lazy to work, that you have no intelligence to get on for yourselves, without being guided and driven to the work by overseers. They have often told you, Sam, you lazy nigger, you don't earn your salt. . . . *He* never earned a single dollar in his life. You men and women, every one of you around me, made thousands and thousands of dollars. Only you were the means for your master to lead the idle and inglorious life, and to give his children the education which he denied to you for fear you may awake to conscience. I say it is a lie, and a blasphemous lie, and I will prove it to be so. . . . If I look around me, I tell you, all the houses on this Island and in Beaufort, they are all familiar to my eye, they are the same structures which I have met with in Africa. They have all been made by the negroes, you can see it by their rude exterior. I tell you they (White men) cannot teach you anything, and they could not make them because they have not the brain to do it. . . .

I am going to tell you now, *what* you are worth. As you know Christopher Columbus landed here in 1492. They came here only for the purpose to dig gold, gather precious pearls, diamonds and all sorts of jewels, only for the proud Aristocracy of the White Spaniards and Portuguese, to adorn their persons, to have brooches for their breasts, earrings for their ears, Bracelets for their ankles and rings for their limbs and fingers. They found here (red men) Indians whom they obliged to dig and work and slave for them—but they found out that they had taken some blacks (Africans) along with them and put *them* to work—they could stand it—and yet the Whites say they are superior to our race, though they could not stand it. (At the present day in some of the Eastern parts of Spain, the Spaniard there [having been once conquered by the black race] have black eyes, black hair, black complexion. They have Negroe blood in them!!) The work was so profitable which those poor blacks did, that in the year 1502 Charles the V. gave permission to import into America yearly 4,000 blacks. The profit of these sales was so immense, that afterwards even the Virgin Queen of England and James the II took part in the Slave trade and were accumulating great wealth for the Treasury of the Government. And so you *always* have been the means of riches.

I tell you I have been all over Africa . . . and I tell you (as I told to the Geographical Faculty in London) that those people there, are a well-driving class of cultivators, and I never saw or heard of one of our brethern there to travel without taking seeds with him as much as he can carry and to sow it wherever he goes to, or to exchange it with his brethern.

So you ought further to know, that all the spices, cotton, rice and coffee has only been brought over by *you,* from the land of our brethern.

Your masters who lived in opulence, kept you to hard work by some contemptible being called overseer—who chastised and beat you whenever he pleased—while your master lived in some Northern town or in Europe to squander away the wealth only you acquired for him.

. . . Now tell me from all you have heard from me, are you not worth anything? Are you those men whom they think, God only created as a curse and for a slave? Whom they do not consider their equals? As I said before the Yankees are smart; there are good ones and bad ones. The good ones, if they are good they are very good, if they are bad, they are very bad. But the worst and most contemptible, and even worse than even your masters were, are those Yankees, who hired themselves as *overseers.*

Believe not in these School teachers, Emissaries, Ministers, and agents, because they never tell you the truth, and I particularly warn you against those Cotton Agents, who come honey mouthed unto you, their only intent being to make profit by your inexperience.

If there is a man who comes to you, who will meddle with your affairs, send him to one of your more enlightened brothers, who shall ask him who he is, what business he seeks with you, etc.

Believe none but those Agents who are sent out by Government, to enlighten and guide you. I am an officer in the service of the U.S. Government, and ordered to aid Gen'l Saxton, who has been only lately appointed Asst. Comr for South Carolina. So is Gen'l Wild Asst Comr for Georgia.

When Chief Justice Chase was down here to speak to

you, some of those malicious and abominable New York papers derived from it that he only seeks to be elected by you as President. I have no such ambition, I let them have for a President a white or a black one. I don't care who it be—it may be who has a mind to. I shall not be intimidated whether by threats or imprisonment, and no power will keep me from telling you the truth. So I expressed myself even at Charleston, the hotbed of those scoundrels, your old masters, without fear or reluctance.

So I will come to the main purpose for which I have come to see you. As before the whole South depended upon you, now the *whole country* will depend upon you. I give you an advice how to get along. Get up a community and get all the lands you can—if you cannot get any singly.

Grow as much vegetables, etc, as you want for your families; on the other part of the land you cultivate Rice and Cotton. Now for instance 1 Acre will grow a crop of Cotton of $90—now a land with 10 Acres will bring $900 every year: if you cannot get the land all yourself—the community can, and so you can divide the profit. There is Tobacco for instance (Virginia is the great place for Tobacco). There are whole squares at Dublin and Liverpool named after some place of Tobacco notoriety, so you see of what enormous value your labor was to the benefits of your masters. Now you understand that I want you to be the producers of this country. It is the wish of the Government for you to be so. We will send friends to you, who will further instruct you how to come to the end of our wishes. You see that by so adhering to your views, you will become a wealthy and powerful population.

Now I look around me and notice a man, barefooted, covered with rags and dirt. Now I ask, what is that man doing, for whom he is working. I hear that he works for that and that farmer for 30 cents a day. I tell you that must not be. That would be cursed slavery over again. I will not have it, the Government will not have it, and the Government shall hear about it. I will tell the Government. I will tell you slavery is over, and shall never return again. We have now 200,000 of our men well drilled in arms and used to War fare and I tell you it is with you and them that slavery shall not come back again, if you are determined it will not return again.

Stoeber, Lt. Edward M. and Bvt. Maj. Taylor. July 24, 1865. "Memorandum of Extracts from Speech by Major Delany, African, at the Brick Church, St. Helena Island, South Carolina, Sunday, July 23, 1865." Submitted by Lt. Alexander Whyte, Jr., to Col. Charles H. Howard, Records of the Assistant Commissioners, South Carolina (Letters Received), Freedmen's Bureau. National Archives. Washington, DC.

MAINTAINING ORDER AMONG FREEDMEN (1865)

Town of Opelousas, [Louisiana]

ORDINANCE Relative to the Police of Recently Emancipated Negroes or Freedmen, Within the Corporate Limits of the Town of Opelousas. Whereas the relations formerly subsisting between master and slave have become changed by the action of the controlling authorities; and whereas it is necessary to provide for the proper policing and government of the recently emancipated negroes or freedmen, in their new relations to the municipal authorities;

Section 1. Be it therefore ordained by the Board of Police of the Town of Opelousas: that no negro or freedman shall be allowed to come within the limits of the Town of Opelousas without special permission from his employer specifying the object of his visit and the time necessary for the accomplishment of the same. Whoever shall violate this provision shall suffer imprisonment and two days' work on the public streets, or shall pay a fine of two dollars and fifty cents.

Section 2. Be it further ordained that every negro or freedman who shall be found on the streets of Opelousas after 10 o'clock at night without a written pass or permit from his employer, shall be imprisoned and compelled to work five days on the public streets, or pay a fine of five dollars.

Section 3. No negro or freedman shall be permitted to rent or keep a house within the limits of the town under any circumstances, and any one thus offending shall be ejected, and compelled to find an employer or leave the town within twenty-four hours. The lessor or furnisher of the house leased or kept as above shall pay a fine of ten dollars for each offence.

Section 4. No negro or freedman shall reside within the limits of the Town of Opelousas who is not in the regular service of some white person or former owner, who shall be held responsible for the conduct of said freedman. But said employer or former owner may permit said freedman to hire his time, by special permission in writing, which permission shall not extend over twenty-four hours at any one time. Any one violating the provisions of this section shall be imprisoned and compelled to work for two days in the public streets, or pay a fine of five dollars.

Section 5. No public meetings or congregations of negroes or freedmen shall be allowed within the limits of the Town of Opelousas, under any circumstances or for any purpose, without the permission of the Mayor or President of the Board. This prohibition is not intended, however, to prevent freedmen from attending the usual church services conducted by established ministers of religion. Every freedman violating this law shall be imprisoned and made to work five days on the public streets.

Section 6. No negro or freedman shall be permitted to preach, exhort, or otherwise declaim to congregations of colored people without a special permission from the Mayor or President of the Board of Police, under the penalty of a fine of ten dollars or twenty days' work on the public streets.

Section 7. No freedman who is not in the military service shall be allowed to carry fire-arms or any kind of weapons within the limits of the Town of Opelousas, without the special permission of his employer, in writing, and approved by the Mayor or President of the Board of Police. Any one thus offending shall forfeit his weapons and shall be imprisoned and made to work five days on the public streets or pay a fine of five dollars in lieu of said work.

Section 8. No freedman shall sell, barter or exchange any articles or merchandise of traffic within the limits of Opelousas, without permission from his employer or the Mayor or President of the Board, under the penalty of the forfeiture of said articles, and imprisonment and one day's labor, or a fine of one dollar in lieu of said work.

Section 9. Any freedman found drunk within the limits of the Town shall be imprisoned and made to labor five days on the public streets, or pay five dollars in lieu of said labor.

Section 10. Any freedman not residing in Opelousas, who shall be found within its corporate limits after the hour of 3 o'clock P. M., on Sunday, without a special written permission from his employer or the Mayor, shall be arrested and imprisoned and made to work two days on the public streets, or pay two dollars in lieu of said work.

Section 11. All the foregoing provisions apply to freedmen and freedwomen, or both sexes.

Section 12. It shall be the special duty of the Mayor or President of the Board to see that all the provisions of this ordinance are faithfully executed.

Section 13. Be it further ordained, that this ordinance is to take effect from and after its first publication.

Ordained the 3rd day of July, 1865.

(*Signed*) E. D. ESTILLETTE,
President of the Board of Police

(*Signed*) JOS. D. RICHARD,
Clerk

Warmoth, Henry Clay. 1930. *War, Politics and Reconstruction.* New York: Macmillan Company.

CIVIL WAR AMENDMENTS (1865, 1868, 1870)

Amendment XIII (1865)

Section 1. Neither slavery nor involuntary servitude, except as a punishment for crime whereof the party shall have been duly convicted, shall exist within the United States, or any place subject to their jurisdiction.

Section 2. Congress shall have power to enforce this article by appropriate legislation.

Amendment XIV (1868)

Section 1. All persons born or naturalized in the United States, and subject to the jurisdiction thereof, are citizens of the United States and of the State wherein they reside. No State shall make or enforce any law which shall abridge the privileges or immunities of citizens of the United States; nor shall any State deprive any person of life, liberty, or property, without due process of law; nor deny to any person within its jurisdiction the equal protection of the laws.

Section 2. Representatives shall be apportioned among the several States according to their respective numbers, counting the whole number of persons in each State, excluding Indians not taxed. But when the right to vote at any election for the choice of electors for President and Vice-President of the United States, Representatives in Congress, the Executive and Judicial officers of a State, or the members of the Legislature thereof, is denied to any of the male inhabitants of such State, being twenty-one years of age, and citizens of the United States, or in any way abridged, except for participation in rebellion, or other crime, the basis of representation therein shall be reduced in the proportion which the number of such male citizens shall bear to the whole number of male citizens twenty-one years of age in such State.

Section 3. No person shall be a Senator or Representative in Congress, or elector of President and Vice President, or hold any office, civil or military, under the United States, or under any State, who, having previously taken an oath, as a member of Congress, or as an officer of the United States, or as a member of any State legislature, or as an executive or judicial officer of any State, to support the Constitution of the United States, shall have engaged in insurrection or rebellion against the same, or given aid or comfort to the enemies thereof. But Congress may by a vote of two-thirds of each House, remove such disability.

Section 4. The validity of the public debt of the United States, authorized by law, including debts incurred for payment of pensions and bounties for services in suppressing insurrection or rebellion, shall not be questioned. But neither the United States nor any State shall assume or pay any debt or obligation incurred in aid of insurrection or rebellion against the United States, or any claim for the loss or emancipation of any slave; but all such debts, obligations, and claims shall be held illegal and void.

Section 5. The Congress shall have the power to enforce, by appropriate legislation, the provisions of this article.

Amendment XV (1870)

Section 1. The right of citizens of the United States to vote shall not be denied or abridged by the United States or by any State on account of race, color, or previous condition of servitude.

Section 2. The Congress shall have power to enforce this article by appropriate legislation.

U.S. Const. amend. XIII–XV.

EDUCATIONAL OPPORTUNITIES FOR FREEDMEN (1866)

Education of the Freedmen

"The Freedmen," said our martyr President, "are the Wards of the Nation." "Yes," replied Mr. Stanton, "Ward in Chancery." What is our duty to them as their guardians? Clearly, to clothe them if they are naked; to teach them if they are ignorant; to nurse them if they are sick, and to adopt them if they are homeless and motherless. They have been slaves, war made them freedmen, and peace must make them freemen. They must be shielded from unjust laws and unkindly prejudices; they must be instructed in the true principles of social order and democratic government; they must be prepared to take their place by-and-by in the great army of voters as lately they filled up the ranks in the great army of fighters. The superstitions, the vices, the unthriftiness, the loitering and indolent habits which slavery foisted on the whites and blacks alike, who were cursed by its presence in their midst, must be dispelled and supplanted by all the traits and virtues of a truly Christian civilization.

The North, that liberated the slave, has not been remiss in its duty to the freedman. The common school has kept step to the music of the advancing army. *Wilson's Readers* have followed Grant's soldiers everywhere. Many of the colored troops on the march had primers in their boxes and primers in their pockets. They were namesakes, but not of the same family. Charleston had not been captured more than a week before the schools for freedmen and poor whites were opened there. It is proposed now to educate all the negroes and poor whites in the South—as a political necessity; in order that henceforth there may be no other insurrections, the result of ignorance, either on the part of the late slave or that late slaveholder. Ignorance has cost us too much to be suffered to disturb us again. In free countries it is not the intelligent but the ignorant who rebel. Ambitious men could never induce an enlightened people to overthrow a free Government. It was because there were over 600,000 white adults in the slave States, and 4,000,000 of slaves who could neither read nor write, that Davis and Toombs and Slidell had power to raise armies against the nation. Let us prevent all social upheavals in the future by educating all men now.

The National Freedmen's Relief Association of New York—of which Francis George Shaw is President and Joseph B. Collins Treasurer—has been the most active of the agencies in relieving the wants and dispelling the ignorance of the freedman. It has expended during the last four years three quarters of a million of dollars in clothing the naked; in establishing the freedmen on farms; in supplying them with tools; in founding orphan homes; in distributing school-books and establishing schools. They have over two hundred teachers in the South at this time. They support orphan homes in Florida and South Carolina. They teach ten thousand children, and large numbers of adults. They have instituted industrial schools to educate the negro women to be thrifty housewives. They are continually laboring, in brief, to make the negroes self-reliant and self-supporting. They appeal for additional aid. There are but a thousand teachers for freedmen in all the Southern States; whereas twenty thousand could find immediate employment. The National Relief Association could find pupils for 5000. It has but 200. As the work is a good and great one, and as the officers of this Society are eminent citizens of New York, we heartily commend their appeal to the generosity of our readers.

Harper's Weekly, February 10, 1866.

FIRST CIVIL RIGHTS ACT (1866)

Chapter. XXXI.—An Act to protect all Persons in the United States in their Civil Rights, and furnish the Means of their Vindication.

Be it enacted by the Senate and House of Representatives of the United States of America in Congress assembled, That all persons born in the United States and not subject to any foreign power, excluding Indians not taxed, are hereby declared to be citizens of the United States; and such citizens, of every race and color, without regard to any previous condition of slavery or involuntary servitude, except as a punishment for crime whereof the party shall have been duly convicted, shall have the same right, in every State and Territory in the United States, to make and enforce contracts, to sue, be parties, and give evidence, to inherit, purchase, lease, sell, hold, and convey real and personal property, and to full and equal benefit of all laws and proceedings for the security of person and property, as is enjoyed by white citizens, and shall be subject to like punishment, pains, and penalties, and to none other, any law, statute, ordinance, regulation, or custom, to the contrary notwithstanding.

Section 2. *And be it further enacted,* That any person who, under color of any law, statute, ordinance, regulation, or custom, shall subject, or cause to be subjected, any inhabitant of any State or Territory to the deprivation of any right secured or protected by this act, or to different punishment, pains, or penalties on account of such person having at any time been held in a condition of slavery or involuntary servitude, except as a punishment for crime whereof the party shall have been duly convicted, or by reason of his color or race, than is prescribed for the punishment of white persons, shall be deemed guilty of a misdemeanor, and, on conviction, shall be punished by fine not exceeding one thousand dollars, or imprisonment not exceeding one year, or both, in the discretion of the court.

Section 3. *And be it further enacted,* That the district courts of the United States, within their respective districts, shall have, exclusively of the courts of the several States, cognizance of all crimes and offenses committed against the provisions of this act, and also, concurrently with the circuit courts of the United States, of all causes, civil and criminal, affecting persons who are denied or cannot enforce in the courts or judicial tribunals of the State or locality where they may be any of the rights secured to them by the first section of this act. . . . The jurisdiction in civil and criminal matters hereby conferred on the district and circuit courts of the United States shall be exercised and enforced in conformity with the laws of the United States, so far as such laws are suitable to carry the same into effect; but in all cases where such laws are not adapted to the object, or are deficient in the provisions necessary to furnish suitable remedies and punish offences against law, the common law, as modified and changed by the constitution and statutes of the State wherein the court having jurisdiction of the cause, civil or criminal, is held, so far as the same is not inconsistent with the Constitution and laws of the United States, shall be extended to and govern said courts in the trial and disposition of such cause, and, if of a criminal nature, in the infliction of punishment on the party found guilty.

Section 4. *And be it further enacted,* That the district attorneys, marshals, and deputy marshals of the United States, the commissioners appointed by the circuit and territorial courts of the United States, with powers of arresting, imprisoning, or bailing offenders against the laws of the United States, the officers and agents of the Freedmen's Bureau, and every other officer who may be specially empowered by the President of the United States, shall be, and they are hereby, specially authorized and required, at the expense of the United States, to institute proceedings against all and every person who shall violate the provisions of this act, and cause him or them to be arrested and imprisoned, or bailed, as the case may be, for trial before such court of the United States or territorial court as by this act has cognizance of the offense. And with a view to affording reasonable protection to all persons in their constitutional rights of equality before the law, without distinction of race or color, or previous condition of slavery or involuntary servitude, except as a punishment for crime, whereof the party shall have been duly convicted, and to the prompt discharge of the duties of this act, it shall be the duty of the circuit courts of the United States and the superior courts of the Territories of the United States, from time to time, to increase the number of commissioners, so as to afford a speedy and convenient means for the arrest and examination of persons charged with a violation of this act; and such commissioners are hereby authorized and required to exercise and discharge all the powers and duties conferred on them by this act, and the same duties with regard to offences created by this act, as they are authorized by law to exercise with regard to other offences against the laws of the United States.

Section 5. *And be it further enacted,* That it shall be the duty of all marshals and deputy marshals to obey and execute all warrants and precepts issued under the provisions of this act, when to them directed; and should any marshal or deputy marshal refuse to receive such warrant or other process when tendered, or to use all proper means diligently to execute the same, he shall, on conviction thereof, be fined in the sum of one thousand dollars, to the use of the person upon whom the accused is alleged to have committed the offence. And the better to enable the said commissioners to execute their duties faithfully and efficiently, in conformity with the Constitution of the United States and the requirements of this act, they are hereby authorized and empowered, within their counties respectively, to appoint, in writing, under their hands, any one or more suitable persons, from time to time, to execute all such warrants and other process as may be issued by them in the lawful performance of their respective duties; and the persons so appointed to execute any warrant or process as afore said shall have authority to summon and call to their aid the bystanders or posse comitatus of the proper county, or such portion of the land or naval forces of the United States, or of the militia, as may be necessary to the performance of the duty with which they are charged, and to insure a faithful observance of the clause of the Constitution which prohibits slavery, in conformity with the provisions of this act; and said warrants shall run and be executed by said officers anywhere in the State or Territory within which they are issued.

Section 6. *And be it further enacted,* That any person who shall knowingly and wilfully obstruct, hinder, or prevent any officer, or other person charged with the execution of any warrant or process issued under the provisions of this act, or any person or persons lawfully assisting him or them, from arresting any person for whose apprehension such warrant or process may have been issued, or shall rescue or attempt to rescue such person from the custody of the officer, other person or persons, or those lawfully assisting as aforesaid, when so arrested pursuant to the authority herein given and declared, or shall aid, abet, or assist any person so arrested as aforesaid, directly or indirectly, to escape from the custody of the officer or other person legally authorized as aforesaid, or shall harbor or conceal any person for whose arrest a warrant or process shall have been issued as aforesaid, so as to prevent his discovery and arrest after notice or knowledge of the fact that a warrant has been issued for the apprehension of such person, shall, for either of said offences, be subject to a fine not exceeding one thousand dollars, and imprisonment not exceeding six months, by indictment and conviction before the district court of the United States for the district in which said offence may have been committed, or before the proper court of criminal jurisdiction, if committed within any one of the organized Territories of the United States.

Section 7. *And be it further enacted,* That the district attorneys, the marshals, their deputies, and the clerks of the said district and territorial courts shall be paid for their services the like fees as may be allowed to them for similar services in other cases; and in all cases where the proceedings are before a commissioner, he shall be entitled to a fee of ten dollars in full for his services in each case, inclusive of all services incident to such arrest and examination. The person or persons authorized to execute the process to be issued by such commissioners for the arrest of offenders against the provisions of this act shall be entitled to a fee of five dollars for each person he or they may arrest and take before any such commissioner as aforesaid, with such other fees as may be deemed reasonable by such commissioner for such other additional services as may be necessarily performed by him or them, such as attending at the examination, keeping the prisoner in custody, and providing him with food and lodging during his detention, and until the final determination of such commissioner, and in general for performing such other duties as may be required in the premises; such fees to be made up in conformity with the fees usually charged by the officers of the courts of justice within the proper district or county, as near as may be practicable, and paid out of the Treasury of the United States on the certificate of the judge of the district within which the arrest is made, and to be recoverable from the defendant as part of the judgment in case of conviction.

Section 8. *And be it further enacted,* That whenever the President of the United States shall have reason to believe that offenses have been or are likely to be committed against the provisions of this act within any judicial district, it shall be lawful for him, in his discretion, to direct the judge, marshal, and district attorney of such district to attend at such place within the district, and for such time as he may designate, for the purpose of the more speedy arrest and trial of persons charged with a violation of this act; and it shall be the duty of every judge or other officer, when any such requisition shall be received by him, to attend at the place and for the time therein designated.

Section 9. *And be it further enacted,* That it shall be lawful for the President of the United States, or such person as he may empower for that purpose, to employ such part of the land or naval forces of the United States, or of the militia, as shall be necessary to prevent the violation and enforce the due execution of this act.

Section 10. *And be it further enacted,* That upon all questions of law arising in any cause under the provisions of this act a final appeal may be taken to the Supreme Court of the United States.

Schuyler Colfax,

Speaker of the House of Representatives.

La Fayette S. Foster,

President of the Senate, *pro tempore.*

U.S. Congress. *United States Statutes at Large,* 39th Cong., 1st sess., Ch. 31.

EDITORIAL SUPPORTING THE CIVIL RIGHTS BILL (1866)

The Civil Rights Bill

The Civil Rights Bill was drawn with simplicity and care for a very necessary purpose. It declares who are citizens of the United States, defines their rights, prescribes penalties for violating them, and provides the means of redress. The power to do this springs from the very nature and function of a supreme government. But the power being conceded, it is fair to demand that any measure of legislation shall be shown to be necessary, politic, and constitutional.

It is certainly essential to an intelligent use of language in the laws and common speech that the true meaning of citizenship should be defined. Nearly a fifth of the population of the country are colored. They are subject to the Government; they support the obligations and do the duty of citizens. Are they citizens or aliens? Can any thing be more unreasonable than to fear or hesitate to define their status? If they are not citizens, are they aliens, are they unnaturalized natives? Domiciled aliens and foreigners have the protection of law, indeed, but these are neither. They are native to the soil. They owe and perform the obligations of other citizens. Why not call them citizens?

That color was not originally a disability for citizenship is undeniable; for the citizens of the several States became, upon the adoption of the Constitution, citizens of the United States, and in some of the States at that time colored persons were not only citizens but voters. Naturalization and other laws in 1802 and 1803, by implication and directly, admit that color is not a disability. In 1843 Mr. Hugh S. Legare, Attorney-General of the United States, gave his opinion that a free colored man can be a citizen. But as the Government became thoroughly tainted with the spirit of slavery, the reluctance to acknowledge the fact increased and obscured the whole question. Mr. Marcy, as Secretary of State, held both opinions, that colored men were and were not citizens. Passports have been both issued and refused to them as citizens; and finally the spirit of slavery culminating in the Dred Scott decision, declared that a free negro was not a citizen. In 1862, under the Government purged of the influence of slavery, the question again arose, and Attorney-General Bates in a masterly opinion held that color was not a disqualification. But the baffled party of disunion still asserts the contrary. President Johnson in his veto of the Civil Rights Bill; admits a difference of opinion; and the Constitution, while it speaks of citizens, nowhere defines the term. It is therefore both timely and wise, at the close of a civil war which has abolished slavery, that the highest authority should declare distinctly who are citizens of the United States, and what are the rights to which citizens are entitled.

The policy of such a measure is plain from the fact that the civil rights of millions of the native population of the United States are destroyed in certain parts of the country on the ground of color; that this invasion springs from the spirit and habit of slavery, and that, if not corrected by the supreme authority, the inevitable result will be a confirmation of that spirit, and a consequent perpetual menace of the public peace by deepening the conviction of the outraged class of the population that the chance of legal redress is hopeless. The good policy is evident from the further fact that the country earnestly desires repose, but that repose is and ought to be impossible while millions of loyal and tried friends of the Government are exposed, to the vengeance of those who are still, and naturally, alienated from the Government. Nothing can tend so surely to confirm the peace of the Union as the kindly but firmly expressed intention of the Government to protect and enforce the equal civil rights of every citizen; understanding by civil rights, according to Chancellor Kent, "the right of personal security, the right of personal liberty, and the right to acquire and enjoy property." This is substantially the explanation given by President Johnson of the right conferred by the Emancipation Amendment. "Liberty," he said to the colored soldiers and to Judge Wairdlaw, "means freedom to work and enjoy the products of your own labor." The Civil Rights Bill merely secures that freedom; for no man enjoys the fruit of his labor if he can not own property, and sue and testify and convey.

But if the United States had the constitutional right to confer this freedom, can it be unconstitutional to defend it? If it were constitutional for the Government to insist that the late rebel States should recognize this liberty, can it not insist that they shall assent to its definition and protection? What else was the significance of the second clause of the amendment authorizing the Government to enforce it? Having freed a man from chattel slavery, is the Government bound to look on passively and see him reduced again to virtual slavery, by a State vagrant law, for a trivial offense? The President, indeed, asks in his veto whether the present laws are not sufficient to protect the rights of the freedmen. What rights? If they are neither citizens, nor domiciled aliens, nor foreigners, what rights have they? Clearly their status must be determined before their rights can be defined; and then, if existing remedies are adequate, they are not impaired by the bill. If they are not adequate, the bill is plainly necessary.

The President's objection to the bill as special legislation is a manifest misapprehension. The bill is universal in its application. If the rights of any citizen of whatever birth or color are invaded anywhere in the country the bill provides the remedy, without any exclusion or exception whatever. But the veto lays great weight upon the fact that "worthy, intelligent, and patriotic foreigners" must reside here five years before they can become citizens, and expresses the opinion that the bill discriminates against them in favor of those to whom the avenues of freedom and intelligence are just opened. But the President hardly puts the case fairly. Let us ask it in another way. If "worthy, intelligent, and patriotic foreigners" are to be made both citizens and voters at the end of a residence of five years, is it unreasonable that worthy, intelligent, and patriotic natives, all whose interests and affections are and always have been bound up with the country, should be made citizens, merely, at the end of twenty-one years? If it be objected that the mass of the natives in question are not intelligent, will it be asserted that the mass of the foreigners are so? If it be right to take a foreigner totally ignorant of our language and government and the whole spirit of our system and give him a vote at the end of five years, can it be wrong to take a man like Robert Small, who instinctively know and loves and struggles for the government, and at the end of three years of emancipation give him, not so much as a vote, but the name and rights of a citizen? That is a question which we do not find answered in the Message.

The objection that the bill interferes with rightful State legislation is not sustained by a careful consideration of the bill. If the United States may lawfully define the civil rights of their citizen's no State can lawfully impair those rights. The bill leaves the legislative discretion of the States unlimited by any thing but the fundamental civil rights of all citizens which the nation itself protects; and it gives the United States courts exclusive jurisdiction under an express clause of the Constitution.

But the most extraordinary objection urged by the President is that the Civil Rights Bill undertakes to settle questions of political economy. It is not easy to see precisely what is meant by this statement. The bill provides that all citizens shall have the same right to make contracts, to sue and be sued, to give evidence, to inherit and convey property. Is this settling questions of political economy? We should as soon have suspected that it was an attempt to solve astronomical problems.

But the serious objection to the veto lies in the fact, which is evident throughout, that the President thinks enough has been done to redeem the sacred honor of the United States, not of the separate States, pledged to the emancipated class. He says indeed that he will co-operate with Congress to protect them; but Congress has maturely considered and presented two methods of protection, and he rejects both. What is the President's plan? Is it to leave them to the Black Codes? Is it to call them free, thereby exasperating the late masters, and then suffer those masters unchecked to forbid them to own property, to bear arms, to testify, and to enjoy any of the rights of freedom? Is it to trust to time, and to hope that when the present generation, to whom we gave our word, is exterminated, some kind of justice may be done their posterity by those who come after us? The present danger to the Union is not in the direction feared by the President. It is not from the United States doing a simple Constitutional act of justice; it is from the States perpetuating the old injustice from which our troubles sprang. State rights interpreted by slavery brought us bitter alienation and bloody war. State rights interpreted by liberty can alone give us Constitutional unity and enduring peace.

Harper's Weekly, April 14, 1866.

CAUTIOUS ADVICE TO FREEDMEN (1866)

"Wholesome Advice to the Freedmen"

The *South Carolina Ledger,* a weekly paper published in the interests of the colored people, was established in Charleston sometime last autumn by T. Hurley & Co. In his last issue Mr. Hurley gives the following wholesome advice to the freedmen:

Cultivate by every means in your power the good opinion of your former master. Remember that they have suffered much and been severely tried the past five years. Bear in mind, too, that they have their prejudices and the prejudices of their fathers to contend against; and that, besides, they cannot, from their very circumstances, be expected to regard innovations in their midst in the same light that Northern Eutopians do.

But be patient. Recollect that when the time does come—that whatever claims or privileges are granted you by them—will, in their practical bearings, be worth to you far more than all the recognitions of the North. But anything suddenly forced upon the whites by any party hostile to the South—that you can never enjoy! In the North itself the negro's steps have been but of gradual measurement. We have heard some of your so-called friends say that nothing short of another revolution could save the cause; and you may be told by interested parties—vampires who feed on the "cause"—that, in the event of collision between yourselves and the whites—the North would stand by you. They would insinuate that, now you know the use of the cartridge-box, you should insist immediately on the ballot-box.

Yes the red man dared assert his claim to the fair country the Great Spirit had given him, and these men's fathers speedily "improved him off the face of the earth"; and their descendants to this day ignore the claims of the colored man, as in Connecticut and other States! Out on the canting hypocrites! Be not deceived by these men. If a collision occurs the government would of course be compelled to see order observed; but should a war of races ever ensue, the whites would join the whites, and the blacks join the blacks. Your most implacable enemies are to be found among the white soldiers. Their hatred towards your race seems to grow in intensity from the very moment they enter the service.

Staunton [Virginia] Vindicator, June 22, 1866.

INSECURITY OF FREEDMEN (1866)

Attempt to Revive the Slave-Trade.

Information has been received at the Navy Department of the capture of a slaver in Pensacola Bay, Fla., by the United States' sloop *Augustine,* having on board 150 freedmen, secured at Mobile, Alabama, and bound for Cuba. The system has been, to enlist coloured labourers about Mobile, run them up the railroad to Greenville, Ala., switch them on to the Pensacola road, and run down to a plantation in Florida, near the Escalabia river, place the negroes upon blat boats, float down to tide-water, ship them on board sloops, and, passing by Pensacola, gain the sea, and land their human freight in Slavery. Parties in New Orleans, Mobile, and New York, are implicated in the affair.

A Mobile paper of July 28th is responsible for the following:

"A sloop was overhauled in Mobile lower bay early on Tuesday morning, July 17, by the United-States' cutter, having on board fifty negroes, whom the parties were about to carry to Cuba and sell into Slavery. These negroes had been collected at different employment offices in Louisville, Nashville, and Memphis, under a promise of thirty dollars per month, to work on a plantation. The captain and crew of the ship were ironed and placed on board the sloop of war *Augustine* for safe keeping, and will be forwarded to Washington."

There are reasons for suspecting that steamers *Virgininga* and *George Williams,* and schooner *Sunnyside,* were interested in this slave-trade, and that the schooner *Charles Henry,* that cleared at Mobile on the 7th July, for Fowl river, with a cargo of lumber and labourers, was to take about 150 negroes to sea.

The Navy Department professes not to know of the truth of the above reports, but they are signally confirmed by the following from the Atlanta (Ga.) *Intelligencer,* a rebel paper:

"An enterprising genius has been in this city for some time past, engaged in collecting up negro boys between the ages of fifteen and twenty years. To a number of these unsuspecting youths he has represented himself as a son of the late President Lincoln, and pictured to them, in glowing terms, the splendours of a home he will take them to in Cuba, which place he gives them to understand is somewhere in the north. He agrees to pay 20 dollars per month, and defray all travelling expenses. On reaching Cuba they will receive all sorts of good clothes and plenty to eat, and light labour only required of them. How successful this swindling scamp has been we have no knowledge, and of his real purposes we are equally ignorant. That he has found dupes we can readily believe, and have not a doubt that many have been induced to leave comfortable homes. It has been observed that every western train bears hence large and small squads of negroes, many of whom have no knowledge of their destination. They have been employed, their present expenses are being paid, they receive kind treatment and flattering promises, and that is about all they know. If the truth would be known, there is sad work going on, and poor Cuffee is learning that his imaginary troubles did not end when his freedom was attained."

The Anti-Slavery Reporter (New Series), 14:11 (November 1, 1866).

THE CONDITIONS
OF THE FREEDMEN (1866)

Testimony of Major General Rufus Saxton before the U.S. Congress's Joint Committee on Reconstruction.

[Question] What is [the freedmen's] disposition in regard to purchasing land, and what is the disposition of the landowners in reference to selling land to Negroes?

[Answer] The object which the freedman has most at heart is the purchase of land. They all desire to get small homesteads and to locate themselves upon them, and there is scarcely any sacrifice too great for them to make to accomplish this object. I believe it is the policy of the majority of the farm owners to prevent Negroes from becoming landholders. They desire to keep the Negroes landless, and as nearly in a condition of slavery as it is possible for them to do. I think that the former slaveholders know really less about the freedmen than any other class of people. The system of slavery has been one of concealment on the part of the Negro of all his feelings and impulses; and that feeling of concealment is so ingrained with the very constitution of the Negro that he deceives his former master on almost every point. The freedman has no faith in his former master, nor has his former owner any faith in the capacity of the freedman. A mutual distrust exists between them. But the freedman is ready and willing to contract to work for any northern man. One man from the North, a man of capital, who employed large numbers of freedmen, and paid them regularly, told me, as others have, that he desired no better laborers; that he considered them fully as easy to manage as Irish laborers. That was my own experience in employing several thousands of them in cultivating the soil. I have also had considerable experience in employing white labor, having, as quartermaster, frequently had large numbers of laborers under my control.

[Question] If the Negro is put in possession of all his rights as a man, do you apprehend any danger of insurrection among them?

[Answer] I do not; and I think that is the only thing which will prevent difficulty. I think if the Negro is put in possession of all his rights as a citizen and as a man, he will be peaceful, orderly, and self-sustaining as any other man or class of men, and that he will rapidly advance. . . .

[Question] It has been suggested that, if the Negro is allowed to vote, he will be likely to vote on the side of his former master, and be inveigled in the support of a policy hostile to the government of the United States; do you share in that apprehension?

[Answer] I have positive information from Negroes, from the most intelligent freedmen in those States, those who are leaders among them, that they are thoroughly loyal, and know their friends, and they will never be found voting on the side of oppression. . . . I think it vital to the safety and prosperity of the two races in the south that the Negro should immediately be put in possession of all his rights as a man; and that the word "color" should be left out of all laws, constitutions, and regulations for the people; I think it vital to the safety of the Union that this should be done.

U.S. Congress, Joint Committee. 1866. *Report of the Joint Committee on Reconstruction, at the First Session, Thirty-ninth Congress.* Washington, DC: Government Printing Office.

EXTENSION OF VOTING RIGHTS
TO FREEDMEN IN THE DISTRICT
OF COLUMBIA (1867)

Chapter VI—An Act to regulate the elective Franchise in the District of Columbia.

Be it enacted by the Senate and House of Representatives of the United States of America in Congress assembled, That, from and after the passage of this act, each and every male person, excepting paupers and persons under guardianship, of the age of twenty-one years and upwards, who has not been convicted of any infamous crime or offence, and excepting persons who may have voluntarily given aid and comfort to the rebels in the late rebellion, and who shall have been born or naturalized in the United States, and who shall have resided in the said District for the period of one year, and three months in the ward or election precinct in which he shall offer to vote, next preceding any election therein, shall be entitled to the elective franchise, and shall be deemed an elector and entitled to vote at any election in said District, without any distinction on account of color or race.

Section 2. *And be it further enacted,* That any person whose duty it shall be to receive votes at any election within the District of Columbia, who shall wilfully refuse to receive, or who shall wilfully reject, the vote of any person entitled to such right under this act, shall be liable to an action of tort by the person injured, and shall be liable, on indictment and conviction, if such act was done knowingly, to a fine not exceeding five thousand dollars, or to imprisonment for a term not exceeding one year in the jail of said District, or to both.

Section 3. *And be it further enacted,* That if any person or persons shall wilfully interrupt or disturb any such elector in the exercise of such franchise, he or they shall be deemed guilty of a misdemeanor, and, on conviction thereof, shall be fined in any sum not to exceed one thousand dollars, or be imprisoned in the jail in said District for a period not to exceed thirty days, or both, at the discretion of the court.

Section 4. *And be it further enacted,* That it shall be the duty of the several courts having criminal jurisdiction in said District to give this act in special charge to the grand jury at the commencement of each term of the court next preceding the holding of any general or city election in said District.

Section 5. *And be it further enacted,* That the mayors and aldermen of the cities of Washington and Georgetown, respectively, on or before the first day of March, in each year, shall prepare a list of the persons they judge to be qualified to vote in the several wards of said cities in any election; to be qualified to vote in the several wards of said cities in any election; and said mayors and aldermen shall be in open session to receive evidence of the qualification of persons claiming the right to vote in any election therein, and for correcting said list, on two days in each year, not exceeding five days prior to the annual election for the choice of city officers, giving previous notice of the time and place of each session in some newspaper printed in said District.

Section 6. *And be it further enacted,* That on or before the first day of March the mayors and aldermen of said cities shall post up a list of voters thus prepared in one or more public places in said cities, respectively, at least ten days prior to said annual election.

Section 7. *And be it further enacted,* That the officers presiding at any election, shall keep and use the check-list herein required at the polls during the election of all officers, and no vote shall be received unless delivered by the voter in person, and not until the presiding officer has had opportunity to be satisfied of his identity, and shall find his name on the list, and mark it, and ascertain that his vote is single.

Section 8. *And be it further enacted,* That it is hereby declared unlawful for any person, directly or indirectly, to promise, offer, or give, or procure or cause to be promised, offered, or given, any money, goods, right in action, bribe, present, or reward, or any promise, understanding, obligation, or security for the payment or delivery of any money, goods, right in action, bribe, present, or reward, or any other valuable thing whatever, to any person with intent to influence his vote to be given at any election hereafter to be held within the District of Columbia; and every person so offending shall, on conviction thereof, be fined in any sum not exceeding two thousand dollars, or imprisoned not exceeding two years, or both, at the discretion of the court.

Section 9. *And be it further enacted,* That any person who shall accept, directly or indirectly, any money, goods, right in action, bribe, present, or reward, or any promise, understanding, obligation, or security for the payment or delivery of any money, goods, right in action, bribe, present, or reward, or any other valuable thing whatever, to influence his vote at any election hereafter to be held in the District of Columbia, shall, on conviction, be imprisoned not less than one year and be forever disfranchised.

Section 10. *And be it further enacted,* That all acts and parts of acts inconsistent with this act be, and the same are hereby repealed.

Schuyler Colfax,
Speaker of the House of Representatives.

La Fayette S. Foster,
President of the Senate, Pro Tempore.

U.S. Congress. *United States Statutes at Large,* 39th Cong., 2nd sess., ch. 6.

FIRST RECONSTRUCTION ACT (1867)

Chapter CLIII—An Act to provide for the more efficient Government of the Rebel States.

WHEREAS no legal State governments or adequate protection for life or property now exists in the rebel States of Virginia, North Carolina, South Carolina, Georgia, Mississippi, Alabama, Louisiana, Florida, Texas, and Arkansas; and whereas it is necessary that peace and good order should be enforced in said States until loyal and republican State governments can be legally established: Therefore,

Be it enacted by the Senate and House of Representative of the United States of America in Congress assembled, That said rebel States shall be divided into military districts and made subject to the military authority of the United States as hereinafter prescribed, and for that purpose Virginia shall constitute the first district; North Carolina and South Carolina the second district; Georgia, Alabama, and Florida the third district; Mississippi and Arkansas the fourth district; and Louisiana and Texas the fifth district.

Section 2. *And be it further enacted,* That it shall be the duty of the President to assign to the command of each of said districts an officer of the army, not below the rank of brigadier-general, and to detail a sufficient military force to enable such officer to perform his duties and enforce his authority within the district to which he is assigned.

Section 3. *And be it further enacted,* That it shall be the duty of each officer assigned as aforesaid, to protect all persons in their rights of person and property, to suppress insurrection, disorder, and violence, and to punish, or cause to be punished, all disturbers of the public peace and criminals; and to this end he may allow local civil tribunals to take jurisdiction of and to try offenders, or, when in his judgment it may be necessary for the trail of offenders, he shall have power to organize military commissions or tribunals for that purpose, and all interference under color of State authority with the exercise of military authority under this act, shall be null and void.

Section 4. *And be it further enacted,* That all persons put under military arrest by virtue of this act shall be tried without unnecessary delay, and no cruel or unusual punishment shall be inflicted, and no sentence of any military commission or tribunal hereby authorized, affecting the life or liberty of any person, shall be executed until it is approved by the officer in command of the district, and the laws and regulations for the government of the army shall not be affected by this act, except in so far as they conflict with its provisions: *Provided,* That no sentence of death under the provisions of this act shall be carried into effect without the approval of the President.

Section 5. *And be it further enacted,* That when the people of any one of said rebel States shall have formed a constitution of government in conformity with the Constitution of the United States in all respects, framed by a convention of delegates elected by the male citizens of said State, twenty-one years old and upward, of whatever race, color, or previous condition, who have been resident in said State for one year previous to the day of such election, except such as may be disfranchised for participation in the rebellion or for felony at common law, and when such constitution shall provide that the elective franchise shall be enjoyed by all such persons as have the qualifications herein stated for electors of delegates, and when such constitution shall be ratified by a majority of the persons voting on the question of ratification who are qualified as electors for delegates, and when such constitution shall have been submitted to Congress for examination and approval, and Congress shall have approved the same, and when said State, by a vote of its legislature elected under said constitution, shall have adopted the amendment to the Constitu-

tion of the United States, proposed by the Thirty-ninth Congress, and known as article fourteen, and when said article shall have become a part of the Constitution of the United States, said State shall be declared entitled to representation in Congress, and senators and representatives shall be admitted therefrom on their taking the oath prescribed by law, and then and thereafter the preceding sections of this act shall be inoperative in said State: *Provided,* That no person excluded from the privilege of holding office by said proposed amendment to the Constitution of the United States, shall be eligible to election as a member of the convention to frame a constitution for any of said rebel States, nor shall any such person vote for members of such convention.

Section 6. *And be it further enacted,* That until the people of said rebel States shall be by law admitted to representation in the Congress of the United States, any civil governments which may exist therein shall be deemed provisional only, and in all respects subject to the paramount authority of the United States at any time to abolish, modify, control, or supersede the same; and in all elections to any office under such provisional governments all persons shall be entitled to vote, and none others, who are entitled to vote, under the provisions of the fifth section of this act; and no person shall be eligible to any office under any such provisional governments who would be disqualified from holding office under the provisions of the third *article* of said constitutional amendment.

Schuyler Colfax.
Speaker of the House of Representatives.
La Fayette S. Foster,
President of the Senate, Pro Tempore.

U.S. Congress. *United States Statutes at Large,* 39th Cong., 2nd sess., ch. 153.

SECOND RECONSTRUCTION ACT (1867)

Chapter VI—An Act supplementary to an Act entitled "An Act to provide for the more efficient Government of the Rebel States," passed March second, eighteen hundred and sixty-seven, and to facilitate Restoration.

Be it enacted by the Senate and House of Representatives of the United States of America in Congress assembled, That before the first day of September, eighteen hundred and sixty-seven, the commanding general in each district defined by an act entitled "An act to provide for the more efficient government of the rebel States," passed March second, eighteen hundred sixty-seven, shall cause a registration to be made of the male citizens of the United States, twenty-one years of age and upwards, resident in each county or parish in the State or States included in his district, which registration shall include only those persons who are qualified to vote for delegates by the act aforesaid, and who shall have taken and subscribed the following oath or affirmation: "I,———, do solemnly swear (or affirm), in the presence of Almighty God, that I am a citizen of the State of———; that I have resided in said State for———months next preceding this day, and now reside in the county of———, or the parish of———, in said State (as the case may be); that I am twenty-one years old; that I have not been disfranchised for the participation in any rebellion or civil war against the United States, nor for felony committed against the laws of any State or of the United States; that I have never been a member of any State legislature, nor held any executive or judicial office in any State and afterwards engaged in insurrection or rebellion against the United States, or given aid or comfort to the enemies thereof; that I have never taken an oath as a member of Congress of the United States, or as a member of any State legislature, or as an executive or judicial officer of any State, to support the Constitution of the United States, or given aid or comfort to the enemies thereof; that I will faithfully support the Constitution and obey the laws of the United States, and will, to the best of my ability, encourage others so to do, so help me God"; which oath or affirmation may be administered by any registering officer.

Section 2. *And be it further enacted,* That after the completion of the registration hereby provided for in any State, at such time and places therein as the commanding general shall appoint and direct, of which at least thirty days' public notice shall be given, and election shall be held of delegates to a convention for the purpose of establishing a constitution and civil government for such State loyal to the Union, said convention in each State, except Virginia, to consist of the same number of members as the most numerous branch of the State legislature of such State in the year eighteen hundred and sixty, to be apportioned among the several districts, counties, or parishes of such State by the commanding general, giving to each representation in the ratio of voters registered as aforesaid as nearly as may be. The convention in Virginia shall consist of the same number of members as represented the territory now constituting Virginia in the most numerous branch of the legislature of said State in the year eighteen hundred and sixty, to be apportioned as aforesaid.

Section 3. *And be it further enacted,* That at said election the registered voters of each State shall vote for or against a convention to form a constitution therefore under this act. Those voting in favor of such a convention shall have written or printed on the ballots by which they vote for delegates, as aforesaid, the words "For a convention," and those voting against such a convention shall have written or printed on such ballots the words, "Against a convention." The persons appointed to superintend said election, and to make return of the votes given thereat, as herein provided, shall count and make return of the votes given for and against a convention; and the commanding general to whom the same shall have been returned shall ascertain and declare the total vote in each State for an d against a convention. If a majority of the votes given on that question shall be for a convention, then such convention shall be held as hereinafter provided; but if a majority of said votes shall be against a convention, then no such convention shall be held under this act: *Provided,* That such convention shall not be held unless a majority of all such registered voters shall have voted on the question of holding such convention.

Section 4. *And be it further enacted,* That the commanding general of each district shall appoint as many boards of registration as may be necessary, consisting of three loyal officers or persons, to make and complete the registration, superintend the election, and make return to him of the votes, list of voters, and of the person elected as delegates by a plurality of the votes cast at said election; and upon receiving said returns he shall open the same, ascertain the persons elected as delegates, according to the returns of the officers who conducted the said election, and make proclamation thereof; and if a majority of the votes given on that question shall be for a convention, the commanding general, within sixty days from the date of election, shall notify the delegates to assemble in convention, at a time and place to be mentioned in the notification, and said convention, when organized, shall proceed to frame a constitution and civil government according to the provisions of this act, and the act to which it is supplementary; and when the same shall have been so framed, said constitution shall be submitted by the convention for ratification to the persons registered under the provisions of this act at an election to be conducted by the officers or persons appointed or to be appointed by the commanding general, as hereinbefore provided, and to be held after the expiration of thirty days from the date of notice thereof, to be given by said convention; and the returns thereof shall be made to the commanding general of the district.

Section 5. *And be it further enacted,* That if, according to said returns, the constitution shall be ratified by a majority of the votes of the registered electors qualified as herein specified, cast at said election, at least one half of all the registered voters voting upon the question of such ratification, the president of the convention shall transmit a copy of the same, duly certified, to the President of the United States, who shall forthwith transmit the same to Congress, if then in session, and if not in session, then immediately upon its next assembling; and if it shall moreover appear to Congress that the election was one at which all the registered and qualified electors in the State had an opportunity to vote freely and without restraint, fear, or the influence of fraud, and if the Congress shall be satisfied that such constitution meets the approval of a majority of all the qualified electors in the State, and if the said constitution shall be declared by Congress to be in conformity with the provisions of the act to which this is supplementary, and the other provisions of said act shall have been complied with, and the said constitution shall be approved by Congress, the State shall be declared entitled to representation, and senators and representatives shall be admitted therefrom as therein provided.

Section 6. *And be it further enacted,* That all elections in the States mentioned in the said "Act to provide for the more efficient government of the rebel States," shall, during the operation of said act, be by ballot; and all officers making the said registration of voters and conducting said elections shall, before entering upon the discharge of their duties, take and subscribe the oath prescribed by the act approved July second, eighteen hundred and sixty-two, entitled "An act to prescribe an oath of office": *Provided,* That if any person shall knowingly and falsely take and subscribe any oath in this act prescribed, such person so offending and being thereof duly convicted shall be subject to the pains, penalties, and disabilities which by law are provided for the punishment of the crime of wilful and corrupt perjury.

Section 7. *And be it further enacted,* That all expenses incurred by the several commanding generals, or by virtue of any orders issued, or appointments made, by them, under or by virtue of this act, shall be paid out of any moneys in the treasury not otherwise appropriated.

Section 8. *And be it further enacted,* That the convention for each State shall prescribe the fees, salary, and compensation to be paid to all delegates and other officers and agents herein authorized or necessary to carry into effect the purposes of this act not herein otherwise provided for, and shall provide for the levy and collection of such taxes on the property in such State as may be necessary to pay the same.

Section 9. *And be it further enacted,* That the word "article," in the sixth section of the act to which this is supplementary, shall be construed to mean "section."

Schuyler Colfax,
Speaker of the House of Representatives.

B. F. Wade
President of the Senate Pro Tempore.

U.S. Congress. *United States Statutes at Large,* 40th Cong., 1st sess., ch. 6.

THIRD RECONSTRUCTION ACT (1867)

Chapter XXX.—An Act supplementary to an Act entitled "An Act to provide for the more efficient Government of the Rebel States," passed on the second day of March, eighteen hundred and sixty-seven, and the Act supplementary thereto, passed on the twenty-third day of March, eighteen hundred and sixty-seven.

Be it enacted by the Senate and House of Representatives of the United States of America in Congress assembled, That it is hereby declared to have been the true intent and meaning of the act of the second day of March, one thousand eight hundred and sixty-seven, entitled "An act to provide for the more efficient government of the rebel States," and of the act supplementary thereto, passed on the twenty-third day of March, in the year one thousand eight hundred and sixty-seven, that the governments then existing in the rebel States of Virginia, North Carolina, South Carolina, Georgia, Mississippi, Alabama, Louisiana, Florida, Texas, and Arkansas were not legal State governments; and that thereafter said governments, if continued, were to be continued subject in all respects to the military commanders of the respective districts, and to the paramount authority of Congress.

Section 2. *And be it further enacted,* That the commander of any district named in said act shall have power, subject to the disapproval of the General of the army of the United States, and to have effect till disapproved, whenever in the opinion of such commander the proper administration of said act shall require it, to suspend or remove from office, or from the performance of official duties and the exercise of official powers, any officer or person holding or exercising, or professing to hold or exercise, any civil or military office or duty in such district under any power, election, appointment or authority derived from, or granted by, or claimed other division thereof, and upon such suspension or removal such commander, subject to the disapproval of the General as aforesaid, shall have power to provide from time to time for the performance of the said duties of such officer or person so suspended or removed, by the detail of some competent officer or soldier or the army, or by the appointment of some other person, to perform the same, and to fill vacancies occasioned by death, resignation, or otherwise

Section 3. *And be it further enacted,* That the General of the army of the United States shall be invested with all the powers of suspension, removal, appointment, and detail granted in the preceding section to district commanders.

Section 4. *And be it further enacted,* That the acts of the officers of the army already done in removing in said districts persons exercising the functions of civil officers, and appointing others in their stead, are hereby confirmed: *Provided,* That any person heretofore or hereafter appointed by any district commander to exercise the functions of any civil office, may be removed either by the military officer in command of the district, or by the General of the army. And it shall be the duty of such commander to remove from office as aforesaid all persons who are disloyal to the government of the United States, or who use their official influence in any manner to hinder, delay, prevent, or obstruct the due and proper administration of this act and the acts to which it is supplementary.

Section 5. *And be it further enacted,* That the boards of registration provided for in the act entitled "An act supplementary to an act entitled 'An act to provide for the more efficient government of the rebel States,' passed March two, eighteen hundred and sixty-seven, and to facilitate restoration," passed March twenty-three, eighteen hundred and sixty-seven, shall have power, and it shall be their duty before allowing the registration of any person, to ascertain, upon such facts or information as they can obtain, whether such person is entitled to be registered under said act, and the oath required by said act shall not be conclusive on such question, and no person shall be registered unless such board shall decide that he is entitled thereto; and such board shall also have power to examine, under oath, (to be administered by any member of such board,) any one touching the qualification of any person claiming registration; but in every case of refusal by the board to register an applicant, and in every case of striking his name from the list as hereinafter provided, the board shall make a note or memorandum, which shall be returned with the registration list to the commanding general of the district, setting forth the grounds of such refusal or such striking from the list: *Provided,* That no person shall be disqualified as member of any board of registration by reason of race or color.

Section 6. *And be it further enacted,* That the true intent and meaning of the oath prescribed in said supplementary act is, (among other things,) that no person who has been a member of the legislature of any State, or who has held any executive or judicial office in any State, whether he has taken an oath to support the Constitution of the United States or not, and whether he was holding such office at the commencement of the rebellion, or had held it before, and who has afterwards engaged in insurrection or rebellion against the United States, or given aid or comfort to the enemies thereof, is entitled to be registered or to vote; and the words "executive or judicial office in any State" in said oath mentioned shall be construed to include all civil offices created by law for the administration of any general law of a State, or for the administration of justice.

Section 7. *And be it further enacted,* That the time for completing the original registration provided for in said act may, in the discretion of the commander of any district be extended to the first day of October, eighteen hundred sixty-seven; and the boards of registration shall have power, and it shall be their duty, commencing fourteen days prior to any election under said act, and upon reasonable public notice of the time and place thereof, to revise, for a period of five days, the registration lists, and upon being satisfied that any person not entitled thereto has been registered, to strike the name of such person from the list, and such person shall not be allowed to vote. And such board shall also, during the same period, add to such registry the names of all persons who at that time possess the qualifications required by said act who have not been already registered; and no person shall, at any time, be entitled to be registered or to vote by reason of any executive pardon or amnesty for any act or thing which, without such pardon or amnesty, would disqualify him from registration or voting.

Section 8. *And be it further enacted,* That section four of said last-named act shall be construed to authorize the commanding general named therein, whenever he shall deem it needful, to remove any member of a board of registration and to appoint another in his stead, and to fill any vacancy in such board.

Section 9. *And be it further enacted,* That all members of said boards of registration and all persons hereafter elected or appointed to office in said military districts, under any so-called State or municipal authority, or by detail or appointment of the district commanders, shall be required to take and to subscribe the oath of office prescribed by law for officers of the United States.

Section 10. *And be it further enacted,* That no district commander or member of the board of registration, or any of the officers or appointees acting under them, shall be bound in his action by any opinion of any civil officer of the United States.

Section 11. *And be it further enacted,* That all the provisions of this act and of the acts to which this is supplementary shall be construed liberally, to the end that all the intents thereof may be fully and perfectly carried out.

U.S. Congress. *United States Statutes at Large,* 40th Cong., 1st sess., ch. 30.

SUCCESSFUL EXPERIMENTS WITH LAND OWNERSHIP (1867)

How these experiments of the working of 1862 affected both those who superintended and those by whose labour it was carried out, may be seen by the following Extract:—"The success of one of our Superintendents in conducting two of the largest plantations for the Government was so great, that he has, in connection with some friends at the North, purchased eleven plantations, comprising about 8000 acres, and is carrying them on this season by means of the old men, the women, and children,—most of the young and able-bodied men being now enlisted in the army of the United States."—(*First Annual Report of the Educational Commission for Freedmen.*)

This Agent, there is little doubt, was Mr. Philbrick, whose operations are reported in the next Annual Report as having raised, at "perhaps a little lower than the average former cost," and with this inferior labour—mainly of women, children, and old men—two-thirds of an ordinary crop. In the same year these blacks were making sales of minor market commodities to at least 150,000 dollars.

Then, as to the Freedmen themselves. At the end of the first year, at the sale which took place in March, 1863, four plantations, containing 3,500 acres, were bought by the Freedmen living upon them. At the sales of 1864, further tracts of land were purchased by them for about 40,000 dollars. *All these purchases were made from the savings of two years.*

In relation to these facts, the *North American Review* declared it could be claimed that the coloured population of the Sea Islands had been brought in two years from a state of utter destitution and ignorance to absolute prosperity and partial education, under all the disadvantages of military occupation and actual war, *by two comparatively feeble Societies in Boston and New York, aided by one in Philadelphia.*

It ought to be added that the Negroes of these Islands were regarded as the most "animalized" in all the United States, and their whole previous condition to have made up as desperate a case, for this kind of effort, as could well be conceived.

National Freedmen's Aid Union. 1867. *The Industry of the Freedmen of America.* Birmingham, AL: National Freedmen's Aid Union.

FOURTH RECONSTRUCTION ACT (1868)

Chapter XXV

An Act to amend the Act passed March twenty-third, eighteen hundred and sixty-seven, entitled "An Act supplementary to 'An Act to provide for the more efficient Government of the rebel States' passed March second, eighteen hundred and sixty-seven, and to facilitate their Restoration.". *Be it enacted by the Senate and House of Representatives of the United States of America an Congress assembled,* That hereafter any election authorized by the act passed March twenty-three, eighteen hundred and sixty-seven, entitled "An act supplementary to 'An act to provide for the more efficient government of the rebel States,' passed March *two,* [second,] eighteen hundred and sixty-seven, and to facilitate their restoration,"shall be decided by a majority of the votes actually cast; and at the election in which the question of the adoption or rejection of any constitution is submitted, any person duly registered in the State may vote in the election district where he offers to vote when he has resided therein for ten days next preceding such election, upon presentation of his certificate of registration, his affidavit, or other satisfactory evidence, under such regulations as the district commanders may prescribe.

Section 2. *And be it further enacted,* That the constitutional convention of any of the States mentioned in the acts to which this is amendatory may provide that at the time of voting upon the ratification of the constitution the registered voters may vote also for members of the House of Representatives of the United States and for all elective officers provided for by the said constitution; and the same election officers who shall make the return of the votes cast on the ratification or rejection of the constitution, shall enumerate and certify the votes cast for members of Congress.

U.S. Congress. *United States Statutes at Large*, 40th Cong., 2nd sess., ch. 25.

THE FREEDMAN'S BUREAU REPORT (1870)

Operations in 1870—Report of General Howard

Gen. Howard's Annual Report on the Bureau of Refugees, Freedmen, and Abandoned Lands, shows that, in accordance with the Acts of Congress the force of officers and clerks has been reduced from 158 to 87. In Washington, 1,500 freedmen are cared for. The various asylums and sub-bureaus in the Southern towns are nearly all discontinued, and the work of the bureau is confined to the District of Columbia, where many of the destitute coloured people have been sent from all parts of the South. One man—sent from Louisiana—says Gen. Howard, is 113 years old. His early life was spent within sight of the hills on which this city is built, and he remembers well the first President, though he never was one of the famous "body-guard." This venerable man has given more than a century of productive labour to his country. Were his just wages paid him he would not now be an object of charity. And equally urgent is the case of nearly ever inmate of the asylum. No State nor city recognises them as citizens; no municipal government allows their claim for aid; unless, therefore, the United States Government continues to feed and clothe and shelter them, they must perish. I believe that Congress and the people will sanction whatever expenditures are necessary to support these national paupers, and to alleviate as far as possible their sufferings. The work of collecting and paying bounties to coloured soldiers has been continued through the year, and 1,087 of these claims have been collected and settled; 3,108 remain to be disposed of. The whole amount of back pay, bounties and pensions collected by the Bureau is 130,900. 65 dols.; all cases intrusted to the Commissioner—Gen. Howard—were settled without fees. The number of certificates and checks issued by the Treasury, and payable by Gen. Howard, was 9,107, representing 1,659,728. 86 dols. The whole amount paid since the passage of the Act (March, 1867) is 7,683,618. 61 dols. The evidence in 1,568 cases, filed by attorneys and claim agents, and suspended by the Second Auditor because the attorneys had failed to furnish the necessary evidence—by reason of death, retirement from business, willful negligence, or other causes—has been perfected through the agency of this Bureau. In addition to the above, 405 contested cases, referred to me by the Second Auditor have been taken up for investigation; and legal proceedings have been instituted against parties charged with frauds against the Government.

The educational branch of the Bureau has been continued to as great an extent as the limited fund would permit, and a good work has been achieved. The number of schools reported is 2,639; the number of teachers, 3,300, and the pupils, 149,581. The number of schools has increased—standing now at 94, with an attendance of 8,147. Appeals are coming in from all parts of the South for further help. Many school buildings, it is reported, must remain closed on account of the withdrawal of Government assistance; but I am obliged to reply to all these appeals: My funds are expanded; there is nothing more to give. All I can do is to counsel the freedmen to make every effort and sacrifice necessary to keep their schools open, and to agitate the subject of free schools until they secure their establishment. A very great work remains to be done before that result can be attained. The people of the Southern States have been too much occupied with material interests, the restoration of industrial order and political reconstruction, to give to the subject of education the attention which its importance demands.

The expenditures for educational purposes during the last year have been 976,853. 89 dols. This includes 25,000 dols. transferred to Wilberforce University, Ohio, and 12,000 dols. to Lincoln University, Pennsylvania, by Act of Congress. The expenditures of the Bureau for all purposes during the last year has been 1,579,129. 55 dols., and the balance on hand August 31, 1870, was 200,146. 52. This sum will not be sufficient to settle outstanding claims, and will be no more than is needed to support the hospital and asylum in this city, and meet other current expenses until the next session of Congress.

The Anti-Slavery Reporter, 17:7 (October 2, 1871).

CORRESPONDENCE BETWEEN SPANISH AND AMERICAN OFFICIALS ON THE MERITS OF ABOLITION (1871)

Letter from Spanish Consul to Gov. Reed.

New Orleans, March 14, 1871

Governor,—The undersigned, Consul of Spain in New Orleans, has the honour to submit to your consideration the following request:—

It ranks prominent among the official duties of the undersigned to have his Government faithfully and reliably informed of the general condition of the country to which he has had the honour to be accredited as consular representative.

The abolition of Slavery decreed by the Spanish Government for Cuba and Porto Rico will, undoubtedly, give rise to questions of great moment, which should be met and decided with the utmost care and impartial spirit; it is, therefore, very desirable that the opinion of his government be enlightened with such reliable data upon the subject as can be compiled in the country; and with such suggestions as experience may point out as just and proper.

To attain this end in the part allotted to him by virtue of his office, the undersigned begs leave to ask you to kindly consent in furnishing him at your earliest convenience, with such official and private information, recent statistics, &c., as will impartially show the results of abolition in your State, from an economical as well as a social point of view.

Your valuable opinion in the matter shall be gratefully received; and the undersigned shall take great pleasure in informing his Government of your kind compliance with his request.

The undersigned, finally, begs leave to tender the assurance of his highest personal regard, and to remain, very respectfully,

Your most obedient servant,
Carlos Vie

Governor Reed's Reply

Tallahassee, March 29, 1871

Sir,—Your favour of the 14th instant, referring to the decree of the Spanish Government abolishing Slavery in Cuba and Porto Rico, and inviting information in relation to the results and practical effects of the abolition of Slavery in this country, is received, and I have the honour to reply. It affords me great satisfaction to be able to say that the results in this State are decidedly beneficial to the people and the State.

The fact that freedom was accomplished by violence, and in opposition to the will of the slaveholder, instead of being inaugurated through concession and by his consent, has occasioned much embarrassment and prevented many advantages which would otherwise have been realised; but enough has been developed to show that it is highly conducive to the progress, wealth and prosperity of the State, as well as to the advancement of civilisation.

Before and for some time after the abolition of Slavery the theory of the South was, that the negroes would not work except under compulsion, and that cotton, the great staple of the South, could not be produced by free labour. The fallacy of this has been demonstrated by the cotton crop of 1870, which is equal to the average of the last four years before the war of undisturbed Slave labour.

It was also contended that, in freedom and deprived of the protection and care of their owners, the slaves would become vagrant and dissolute, and subject to disease and death, and soon the race would be exterminated.

It was confidently asserted that the reduction through this demoralisation would, in 1870, equal one-half the population of 1860. But what is the fact?

Though thousands perished during the war, and thousands more from being suddenly thrust out without subsistence or resource, destitute of medical attendance, and frequently subjected to vindictive opposition from their disappointed and enraged late owners, who still possessed the soil, still, from the census just completed, it is found that the negro population of the cotton States has increased since 1860 eight and three-fourths per cent.

In the State of Florida the increase in wealth and population, during the three years of Republican government just past, has been unparalleled in her previous history.

Her increase in population has been at least fifty per cent, and in industrial resources more than two hundred per cent.

The inevitable effect of Slavery is to concentrate the wealth in the hands of a few, while the effect of freedom is directly the opposite—to diffuse that wealth among the masses. Slavery degrades labour to a mere brute standard, while freedom ennobles it and makes it a fit associate with intellectual and moral cultivation.

In an educational and moral point of view the results of the abolition of Slavery are equally satisfactory, notwithstanding prejudice and intolerance have cheated the emancipated race of half its possible attainments. This branch of the subject opens a wide and interesting field of discussion and enquiry, which time will not permit me here to enter. The barbarism of Slavery and the beneficence of Freedom have been fully attested in the conduct and progress of the coloured race, even under all the adverse circumstances which have attended the country since emancipation, and I cannot but congratulate you and the nation which you represent on the recent decree of emancipation in Cuba and Porto Rico.

I have the honor to be, Sir,

With high respect,

Your obedient servant,

HARRISON REED,

Governor of Florida.

The Anti-Slavery Reporter, 17:7
(October 2, 1871).

SECOND CIVIL RIGHTS ACT (1875)

CXIV:—An act to protect all citizens in their civil and legal rights.

Whereas, it is essential to just government we recognize the equality of all men before the law, and hold that it is the duty of government in its dealings with the people to mete out equal and exact justice to all, of whatever nativity, race, color, or persuasion, religious or political; and it being the appropriate object of legislation to enact great fundamental principles into law: Therefore,

Be it enacted by the Senate and House of Representatives of the United States of America and Congress assembled, That all persons within the jurisdiction of the United States shall be entitled to the full and equal enjoyment of the accommodations, advantages, facilities, and privileges of inns, public conveyances on land or water, theaters, and other places of public amusement; subject only to the conditions and limitations established by law, and applicable alike to citizens of every race and color, regardless of any previous condition of servitude.

Section 2. That any person who shall violate the foregoing section by denying to any citizen, except for reasons by law applicable to citizens of every race and color, and regardless of any previous condition of servitude, the full enjoyment of any of the accommodations, advantages, facilities, or privileges in said section enumerated, or by aiding or inciting such denial, shall, for every such offense, forfeit and pay the sum of five hundred dollars to the person aggrieved thereby, to be recovered in an action of debt, with full costs; and shall also, for every such offense, be deemed guilty of a misdemeanor, and, upon conviction thereof shall be fined not less than five hundred nor more than one thousand dollars, or shall be imprisoned not less than thirty days nor more than one year: *Provided,* That all persons may elect to sue for the penalty aforesaid or to proceed under their rights at common law and by State statutes; and having so elected to proceed in the one mode or the other, their right to proceed in the other jurisdiction shall be barred. But this proviso shall not apply to criminal proceedings, either under this act or the criminal law of any State: *And provided further,* That a judgment for the penalty in favor of the party aggrieved, or a judgment upon an indictment, shall be a bar to either prosecution respectively.

Section 3. That the district and circuit courts of the United States shall have, exclusively of the courts of the several States, cognizance of all crimes and offenses against, and violations of, the provisions of this act; and actions for the penalty given by the preceding section may be prosecuted in the territorial district, or circuit courts of the United States wherever the defendant may be found, without regard to the other party; and the district attorneys, marshals, and deputy marshals of the United States, and commissioners appointed by the circuit and territorial courts of the United States, with powers of arresting and imprisoning or bailing offenders against the laws of the United States, are hereby specially authorized and required to institute proceedings against every person who shall violate the provisions of this act, and cause him to be arrested and imprisoned or bailed, as the case may be, for trial before such court of the United States, or territorial court, as by law has cognizance of the offense, except in respect of the right of action accruing to the person aggrieved; and such district attorneys shall cause such proceedings to be prosecuted to their termination as in other cases: *Provided,* That nothing contained in this section shall be construed to deny or defeat any right of civil action accruing to any person, whether by reason of this act or otherwise; and any district attorney who shall willfully fail to institute and prosecute the proceedings herein required, shall, for every such offense, forfeit and pay the sum of five hundred dollars to the person aggrieved thereby, to be recovered by an action of debt, with full costs, and shall, on conviction thereof, be deemed guilty of a misdemeanor, and be fined not less than one thousand nor more than five thousand dollars: *And provided further,* That a judgment for the penalty in favor of the party aggrieved against any such district attorney, or a judgment upon an indictment against any such district attorney, shall be a bar to either prosecution respectively.

Section 4. That no citizen possessing all other qualifications which are or may be prescribed by law shall be disqualified for service as grand or petit juror in any court of the United States, or of any State, on account of race, color, or previous condition of servitude; and any officer or other person charged with any duty in the selection or summoning of jurors who shall exclude or fail to summon any citizen for the cause aforesaid shall, on conviction thereof, be deemed guilty of a misdemeanor, and be fined not more than five thousand dollars.

Section 5. That all cases arising under the provisions of this act in the courts of the United States shall be reviewable by the Supreme Court of the United States, without regard to the sum in controversy, under the same provisions and regulations as are now provided by law for the review of other causes in said court.

Approved, March 1, 1875.

U.S. Congress. *United States Statutes at Large,* 43rd Cong., 2nd sess., ch. 114.

OBITUARY FOR WILLIAM LLOYD GARRISON (1879)

William Lloyd Garrison

The Committee of the British and Foreign Anti-Slavery Society place this day upon their records a notice of the death of their lamented friend and fellow-labourer WILLIAM LLOYD GARRISON, which has already been briefly chronicled in the last issue of the Society's Journal.

It was in the year 1833 that the Anti-Slavery Society first extended its welcome to William Lloyd Garrison, when he for the first time paid a visit to this country. He had then left the shores of the United States as the recognised leader of the forlorn hope of a cause then passing through the fiery ordeal of persecution and reproach.

He arrived here at the moment when the full tide of anti-slavery feeling in England was bearing down alike the opposition of the West Indian slave-owners and the reluctance of the government of this country.

When he visited England for the last time, two years ago, this Society once more gladly welcomed him at a meeting at which many of their friends were able to be present. It was then their privilege to hear him recount the history of that great anti-slavery triumph in the United States of America which had crowned the long and laborious work of himself and his coadjutors.

In recording the great loss to the cause of freedom which this Society and the emancipated people of America have alike to deplore, this Committee feel no little satisfaction in recurring to this last occasion of meeting with their friend, as affording a landmark in the history of the great cause which they all had at heart, and as an occasion for them to thank God and take courage, in view of the formidable work still before them, in the constant and determined assault upon the vast empire of slavery and the slave-trade which still exists in Cuba and in the Eastern world.

London, July 31st, 1879.

We have great pleasure in reprinting the following beautiful lines from the American poet Whittier, written expressly to commemorate the death of this eminent Abolitionist, in which he so eloquently describes the high and holy path of active service on behalf of right, and in redress of wrong, still open to those who have gone from a life of activity and love on earth to one of still greater activity and love in heaven: "Are they not all ministering spirits sent forth to minister for them who shall be heirs of salvation?"

> *The storm and peril overpast,*
> *The hounding hatred shamed and still;*
> *Go, soul of freedom! take at last*
> *The place which thou alone canst fill.*
> *Confirm the lesson taught of old,*
> *Life saved for self is lost, while they*
> *Who lose it in His service hold*
> *The lease of God's eternal day.*
> *Not for thyself, but for the slave*
> *Thy words of thunder shook the world;*
> *No selfish griefs or hatred gave*
> *The strength wherewith thy bolts were hurled.*
> *From lips that Sinai's trumpet blew*
> *We heard a tender undersong;*
> *Thy very wrath from pity grew,*
> *From love of man thy hate of wrong.*
> *Now past and present are as one;*
> *Thy life below is life above;*
> *Thy mortal years have but begun*
> *The immortality of love.*
> *Not for a soul like thine the calm*
> *Of selfish ease and joys of sense;*
> *But duty, more than crown or palm,*
> *Its own exceeding recompense.*
> *Go up and on! Thy day well done,*
> *Its morning promise well fulfilled,*
> *Arise to triumphs yet unwon,*
> *To holier tasks that God has willed.*
> *Go leave behind thee all that mars*
> *The work below of man for man;*
> *With the white legions of the stars*
> *Do service such as angels can.*
> *Wherever wrong shall right deny,*
> *Or suffering spirits urge their plea,*
> *Be thine a voice to smite the lie,*
> *A hand to set the captive free!*

The Anti-Slavery Reporter, 21:9 (August 1879).

FREDERICK DOUGLASS OFFERS REFLECTIONS UPON EMANCIPATION (1883)

Friends and Fellow Citizens: I could have wished that some one from among the younger men of Washington, some one with a mind more fruitful, with a voice more eloquent, with an oratorical ambition more lofty; more active, and more stimulating to high endeavor than mine, had been selected by your Committee of Arrangements, to give suitable utterance to the thoughts, feelings, and purposes, which this 21st anniversary of Emancipation in the District of Columbia is fitted to inspire. That such an one could have been easily found among the aspiring and promising young colored men of Washington, I am happy to know and am proud to affirm. They have been reared in the light of its new born freedom, qualified by its education, and by the elevating spirit of liberty, to speak the wise and grateful words befitting the occasion. The presence of one such, as your orator to-night, would be a more brilliant illustration of the wisdom and beneficence of the act of Emancipation, than any words of mine, however well chosen and appropriate. I represent the past, they the present. I represent the downfall of slavery, they the glorious triumphs of liberty. I speak of deliverance from bondage, they speak of concessions to liberty and equality. Their mission begins where my mission ends.

You will readily perceive that I have raised more questions than I shall be able for the present to answer. My general response to these inquiries is a mixed one. The sky of the American Negro is dark, but not rayless; it is stormy, but not cheerless. The grand old party of liberty, union, and progress, which has been his reliance and refuge so long, though less cohesive and strong than it once was, is still a power and has a future. I give you notice, that while there is a Democratic party there will be a Republican party. As the war for the Union recedes into the misty shadows of the past, and the Negro is no longer needed to assault forts and stop rebel bullets, he is in some sense, of less importance. Peace with the old master class has been war to the Negro. As the one has risen, the other has fallen. The reaction has been sudden, marked, and violent. It has swept the Negro from all the legislative halls of the Southern States, and from those of the Congress of the United States. It has, in many cases, driven him from the ballot box and the jury box. The situation has much in it for serious thought, but nothing to cause despair. Above all the frowning clouds that lower about our horizon, there is the steady light of stars, and the thick clouds that now obscure them, will in due season pass away.

Great, however, as is his advantage at this point, he is not altogether fortunate after all, as to the manner in which his claims are canvassed. His misfortune is that few men are qualified to discuss him candidly and impartially. They either exalt him too high or rate him too low. Americans can consider almost any other question more calmly and fairly than this one. I know of nothing outside of religion which kindles more wrath, causes wider differences, or gives

force and effect to fiercer and more irreconcilable antagonisms.

It was so in the time of slavery, and it is so now. Then, the cause was interest, now, the cause is pride and prejudice. Then, the cause was property. He was then worth twenty hundred millions to his owner. He is now worth uncounted millions to himself. While a slave there was a mountain of gold on his breast to keep him down—now that he is free there is a mountain of prejudice to hold him down.

Let any man now claim for the Negro, or worse still, let the Negro now claim for himself, any right, privilege or immunity which has hitherto been denied him by law or custom, and he will at once open a fountain of bitterness, and call forth overwhelming wrath.

It is his sad lot to live in a land where all presumptions are arrayed against him, unless we except the presumption of inferiority and worthlessness. If his course is downward he meets very little resistance, but if upward, his way is disputed at every turn of the road. If he comes in rags and in wretchedness, he answers the public demand for a negro, and provokes no anger, though he may provoke derision, but if he presumes to be a gentleman and a scholar, he is then entirely out of his place. He excites resentment and calls forth stern and bitter opposition. If he offers himself to a builder as a mechanic, to a client as a lawyer, to a patient as a physician, to a university as a professor, or to a department as a clerk, no matter what may be his ability or his attainments, there is a presumption based upon his color or his previous condition, of incompetency, and if he succeeds at all, he has to do so against this most discouraging presumption.

One ground of hope is found in the fact referred to in the beginning, and that is, the discussion concerning the Negro still goes on.

The country in which we live is happily governed by ideas as well as by laws, and no black man need despair while there is an audible and earnest assertion of justice and right on his behalf. He may be riddled with bullets, or roasted over a slow fire by the mob, but his cause cannot be shot or burned or otherwise destroyed. Like the impalpable ghost of the murdered Hamlet, it is immortal. All talk of its being a dead issue is a mistake. It may for a time be buried, but it is not dead. Tariffs, free trade, civil service, and river and harbor bills, may for a time cover it, but it will rise again, and again, and again, with increased life and vigor. Every year adds to the black man's numbers. Every year adds to his wealth and to his intelligence. These will speak for him.

There is a power in numbers, wealth and intelligence, which can never be despised nor defied. All efforts thus far to diminish the Negro's importance as a man and as a member of the American body politic, have failed. We are approaching a momentous canvass. If I do not misread the signs of the times, he will play an important part in the politics of the nation during the next Presidential campaign, and will play it well.

If you wish to suppress it, I counsel you, my fellow citizens, to remove its cause. The voice of popular complaint, whether it is heard in this country or in other countries, does not and can not rest upon dreams, visions, or illusions of any kind. There must be solid ground for it.

The demand for Negro rights would have ceased long since but for the existence of a sufficient and substantial cause for its continuance.

Fellow citizens, the present hour is full of admonition and warning. I despise threats, and remembering as I do the depths from which I have come, and the forlorn condition of those for whom I speak, I dare not assume before the American people an air of haughtiness, but on the other hand I can not forget that the Negro is now, and of right ought to be, an American citizen in the fullest sense of the word. This high position, I take it, was not accorded him in sport, mockery or deception. I credit the American people with sincerity.

The amendments to the Constitution of the United States mean this, or they are a cruel, scandalous and colossal sham, and deserve to be so branded before the civilized world. What Abraham Lincoln said in respect of the United States is as true of the colored people as of the relations of those States. They cannot remain half slave and half free. You must give them all or take from them all. Until this half-and-half condition is ended, there will be just ground of complaint. You will have an aggrieved class, and this discussion will go on. Until the public schools shall cease to be caste schools in every part of our country, this discussion will go on. Until the colored man's pathway to the American ballot box, North and South, shall be as smooth and as safe as the same is for the white citizen, this discussion will go on. Until the colored man's right to practice at the bar of our courts, and sit upon juries, shall be the universal law and practice of the land, this discussion will go on. Until the courts of the country shall grant the colored man a fair trial and a just verdict, this discussion will go on. Until color shall cease to be a bar to equal participation in the offices and honors of the country, this discussion will go on. Until the trades-unions and the workshops of the country shall cease to proscribe the colored man and prevent his children from learning useful trades, this discussion will go on. Until the American people shall make character, and

not color, the criterion of respectability, this discussion will go on. Until men like Bishops Payne and Campbell shall cease to be driven from respectable railroad cars at the South, this discussion will go on. In a word, until truth and humanity shall cease to be living ideas, and mankind shall sink back into moral darkness, and the world shall put evil for good, bitter for sweet, and darkness for light, this discussion will go on. Until all humane ideas and civilization shall be banished from the world, this discussion will go on.

When the nation was in peril; when the country was rent asunder at the center; when rebel armies were in the field, bold, defiant and victorious; when our recruiting sergeants were marching up and down our streets from early morn till late at night, with drum and fife, with banner and badge, footsore and weary; when the fate of the Republic trembled in the balance, and the hearts of loyal men were failing them for fear; when nearly all hope of subduing the rebellion had vanished, Abraham Lincoln called upon the colored men of this country to reach out their iron arms and clutch with their steel fingers the faltering banner of the Republic; and they rallied, and they rallied, full two hundred thousand strong. Ah! then, my friends, the claims of the Negro found the heart of the nation a little more tender and responsive than now. But I ask Americans to remember that the arms that were needed then may be needed again; and it is best that they do not convert the cheerful and loyal brows of six millions into a black Ireland.

A nation composed of all classes should be governed by no one class exclusively. All should be included, and none excluded. Thus aggrieved classes would be rendered impossible.

The question is sometimes asked, when, where and by whom the Negro was first suspected of having any rights at all? In answer to this inquiry it has been asserted that William Lloyd Garrison originated the Anti-slavery movement, that until his voice was raised against the American slave system, the whole world was silent. With all respect to those who make this claim I am compelled to dissent from it. I love and venerate the memory of William Lloyd Garrison. I knew him long and well. He was a grand man, a moral hero, a man whose acquaintance and friendship it was a great privilege to enjoy. While liberty has a friend on earth, and slavery an earnest enemy, his name and his works will be held in profound and grateful memory. To him it was given to formulate and thunder against oppression and slavery the testimonies of all ages. He revived, but did not originate.

Fellow-citizens—In view of the history now referred to, the low point at which he started in the race of life on this continent, and the many obstacles which had to be surmounted the Negro has reasons to be proud of his progress, if not of his beginning. He is a brilliant illustration of social and anthropological revolution and evolution.

We are now free, and though we have many of the consequences of our past condition to contend against, by union, effort, co-operation, and by a wise policy in the direction and the employment of our mental, moral, industrial and political powers, it is the faith of my soul, that we can blot out the handwriting of popular prejudice, remove the stumbling-blocks left in our way by slavery, rise to an honorable place in the estimation of our fellow-citizens of all classes, and make a comfortable way for ourselves in the world.

I have referred to the vast and wonderful changes which have taken place in the condition of the colored people of this country. We rejoice in those changes to-day, and we do well. We are neither wood nor stone, but men. We possess the sentiments common to right-minded men.

But do we know the history of those vast and marvellous changes and the means by which they were brought about? Do we comprehend the philosophy of our progress? Do we ever think of the time, the thought, the labor, the pain, the self-sacrifice, by which they were accomplished? Have we a just and proper conception of the noble zeal, the inflexible firmness, the heroic courage, and other grand qualities of soul, displayed by the reformers and statesmen through whose exertions these changes in our condition have been wrought out and the victory won?

The abolition of slavery in the District of Columbia was one of the most important events connected with the prosecution of the war for the preservation of the Union, and, as such, is worthy of the marked commemoration we have given it to-day. It was not only a staggering blow to slavery throughout the country, but a killing blow to the rebellion, and was the beginning of the end to both. It placed the National dignity and the National power on the side of emancipation. It was the first step toward a redeemed and regenerated nation. It imparted a moral and human significance to what at first seemed to the outside world, only a sanguinary war for empire.

It is, however, consoling to think that this limitation upon human foresight has helped us in the past and may help us in the future. Could William the Silent have foreseen the misery and ruin he would bring upon his country by taking up the sword against the Spanish Inquisition, he might have thought the sacrifice too great. Had William Lloyd Garrison foreseen that he would be hated, persecuted, mobbed, im-prisoned, and drawn through the streets of his beloved Boston with a halter about his neck, even his courage might have quailed, and the native hue of his resolution been sicklied o'er with the pale cast of thought. Could Abraham Lincoln have foreseen the immense cost, the terrible hardship, the awful waste of blood and treasure involved in the effort to retake and repossess the forts and arsenals and other property captured by the Confederate States; could he have forseen the tears of the widows and orphans, and his own warm blood trickling at the bidding of an assassin's bullet, he might have thought the sacrifice too great.

In every great movement men are prepared by preceding events for those which are to come. We neither know the evil nor the good which may be in store for us. Twenty-five years ago the system of slavery seemed impregnable. Cotton was king, and the civilized world acknowledged his sway. Twenty-five years ago no man could have foreseen that in less than ten years from that time no master would wield a lash and no slave would clank a chain in the United States.

Who at that time dreamed that Negroes would ever be seen as we have seen them to-day marching through the streets of this superb city, the Capital of this great Nation, with eagles on their buttons, muskets on their shoulders and swords by their sides, timing their high footsteps to the Star Spangled Banner and the Red, White and Blue? Who at that time dreamed that colored men would ever sit in the House of Representatives and in the Senate of the United States?

With a knowledge of the events of the last score of years, with a knowledge of the sudden and startling changes which have already come to pass, I am not prepared to say what the future will be.

There is but one destiny, it seems to me, left for us, and that is to make ourselves and be made by others a part of the American people in every sense of the word. Assimilation and not isolation is our true policy and our natural destiny. Unification for us is life: separation is death. We cannot afford to set up for ourselves a separate political party, or adopt for ourselves a political creed apart from the rest of our fellow citizens. Our own interests will be subserved by a generous care for the interests of the Nation at large. All the political, social and literary forces around us tend to unification.

Douglass, Frederick. 1883. *Address by Hon. Frederick Douglass, Delivered in the Congregational Church, Washington, D.C., April 16, 1883: on the Twenty-first Anniversary of Emancipation in the District of Columbia.* Washington, DC: Author.

Bibliography

—m—

Abel, Annie Heloise. 1992. *The American Indian as Slave-holder and Secessionist.* Lincoln: University of Nebraska Press.

Adams, John R. 1977. *Edward Everett Hale.* Boston: Twayne.

Adams, John R. 1989. *Harriet Beecher Stowe.* Boston: Twayne.

Allen, Richard. 1983. *The Experience and Gospel Labors of the Right Reverend Richard Allen Written by Himself.* Ed. George Singleton. Nashville, TN: Abingdon.

Allen, Will W. 1971. *Banneker: The Afro-American Astronomer.* Freeport, NY: Libraries Press.

Alonso, Harriet Hyman. 2002. *Growing Up Abolitionist: The Story of the Garrison Children.* Amherst: University of Massachusetts Press.

Alpers, Edward. 1975. *Ivory and Slaves.* Berkeley: University of California Press.

Altoff, Gerard T. 1996. *Amongst My Best Men: African-Americans and the War of 1812.* Put-in-Bay, OH: The Perry Group.

Anderson, Osborne Perry. 1974. *A Voice from Harpers Ferry: A Narrative of Events at Harpers Ferry.* New York: World View Forum.

Andrews, E. A. 1836. *Slavery and the Domestic Slave-Trade in the United States.* Baltimore, MD: Light and Stearns.

Aphornsuvan, Thanet. 1990. "James D. B. DeBow and the Political Economy of the Old South." Ph.D. dissertation, History Department, Binghamton University. Binghamton, NY.

Aptheker, Herbert. 1940. "The Quakers and Negro Slavery." *Journal of Negro History* 25 (July): 331–362.

Aptheker, Herbert. 1993. *American Negro Slave Revolts.* New York: International Publishers.

Herbert Aptheker. 1995. Private interview conducted in the subject's home by Malik Simba. San Jose, CA: May–June.

Ashworth, John. 1995. *Slavery, Capitalism, and Politics in the Antebellum Republic. Volume 1, Commerce and Compromise, 1820–1860.* New York: Cambridge University Press.

Atkin, Andrea M. 1995. "Converting America: The Rhetoric of Abolitionist Literature." Ph.D. dissertation, Department of English, University of Chicago, Chicago, Illinois.

Bailey, L. R. 1966. *The Indian Slave Trade in the Southwest.* Los Angeles, CA: Westernlore Press.

Bancroft, Frederick. 1928. *Calhoun and the South Carolina Nullification Movement.* Baltimore, MD: Johns Hopkins University Press.

Bancroft, Frederick. 1931. *Slave-Trading in the Old South.* Baltimore, MD: J. H. Furst.

Barber, John W. 1840. *A History of the Amistad Captives.* New Haven, CT: E. L. and J. W. Barber.

Barbour, Hugh, and J. William Frost. 1988. *The Quakers.* Westport, CT: Greenwood.

Barnes, Gilbert Hobbs. 1933. *The Anti-Slavery Impulse, 1830–1844.* Gloucester, MA: Peter Smith.

Barringer James G. 1987. "The African Methodist Church: 200 Years of Service to the Community." *Crisis* 94 (June/July): 40–43.

Barucky, Jerry M. 1969. "David Ross Locke: A Muckrake Man." M.A. Thesis, Bowling Green State University, Bowling Green, Ohio.

Bedini, Silvio A. 1972. *The Life of Benjamin Banneker.* New York: Charles Scribner's Sons.

Beecher, Edward. 1965. *Narrative of the Riots at Alton.* New York: E. P. Dutton.

Bell, Howard H. 1959. "The Negro Emigration Movement, 1849–1854: A Phase of Negro Nationalism." *Phylon* 20 (Summer): 132–142.

Bell, Howard H. 1962. "Negro Nationalism: A Factor in Emigration Projects, 1858–1861." *Journal of Negro History* 47: 42–53.

Bell, Howard H. 1969. *A Survey of the Negro Convention Movement, 1830–1861.* New York: Arno Press.

Belz, Herman. 1969. *Reconstructing the Union: Theory and Policy during the Civil War.* Ithaca, NY: Cornell University Press.

Bennett, Robert A. 1974. "Black Episcopalians: A History from the Colonial Period to the Present." *Historical Magazine of the Protestant Episcopal Church* 43 (September 3): 231–245.

Berland, Kevin, Jan Kirsten Gilliam, and Kenneth A. Lockridge, eds. 2001. *The Commonplace Book of William*

Byrd II of Westover. Chapel Hill: University of North Carolina Press.

Berlin, Ira. 1998. *Many Thousand Gone: The First Two Centuries of Slavery in North America.* Cambridge, MA: Harvard University Press.

Berlin, Ira. 2003. *Generations of Captivity: A History of African American Slaves.* Cambridge, MA: Harvard University Press.

Berlin, Ira, Marc Favreau, and Steven F. Miller, eds. 1998. *Remembering Slavery: Americans Talk about Their Personal Experiences of Slavery.* New York: Norton.

Billington, Ray Allen. 1953. *The Journal of Charlotte L. Forten.* New York: Collier.

Birmingham, Stephen. 1971. *The Grandees, America's Sephardic Elite.* New York: Harper and Row.

Birnbaum, Jonathan, and Clarence Taylor, eds. 2000. *Civil Rights Since 1787: A Reader on the Black Struggle.* New York: New York University Press.

Birney, Catherine H. 1885. *The Grimké Sisters.* Boston: Lee and Shepard.

Blackett, R. J. M. 1978. "Fugitive Slaves in Britain: The Odyssey of William and Ellen Craft." *Journal of American Studies* 12: 41–62.

Blakey, Michael. 1998. "The New York African Burial Ground Project: An Examination of Enslaved Lives, a Construction of Ancestral Ties." *Transforming Anthropology* 7 (1): 53–58.

Blassingame, John. 1972. *The Slave Community: Plantation Life in the Antebellum South.* New York: Oxford University Press.

Blassingame, John W., and Mae G. Henderson, eds. 1980–84. *Antislavery Newspapers and Periodicals, Volume I (1817–1845): Annotated Index of Letters in the Philanthropist, Emancipator, Genius of Universal Emancipation, Abolition Intelligencer, African Observer, and the Liberator.* Boston: G. K. Hall.

Blassingame, John W., Mae G. Henderson, and Jessica M. Dunn, eds. 1980–1984. *Antislavery Newspapers and Periodicals, Volume IV (1840–1860) and Volume V (1861–1871) Annotated Index of Letters in the National Anti-Slavery Standard.* Boston: G. K. Hall.

Bleser, Carol, ed. 1988. *Secret and Sacred: The Diaries of James Henry Hammond, a Southern Slaveholder.* New York: Oxford University Press.

Blight, David W. 1972. "The Martyrdom of Elijah P. Lovejoy." *Pennsylvania History* 39: 239–249.

Blockson, Charles L. 1987. *The Underground Railroad: First-Person Narratives of Escapes to Freedom in the North.* New York: Prentice-Hall.

Blue, Frederick J. 1973. *The Free Soilers: Third Party Politics, 1848–54.* Urbana: University of Illinois Press.

Blue, Frederick J. 1987. *Salmon P. Chase: A Life in Politics.* Kent, OH: Kent State University Press.

Bolton, Charles C. 1994. *Poor Whites of the Antebellum South: Tenants and Laborers in Central North Carolina and Northeast Mississippi.* Durham, NC: Duke University Press.

Boston Slave Riot, and Trial of Anthony Burns. 1854. Boston: Fetridge and Company.

Botkin, B. A., ed. 1941. *Slave Narratives: A Folk History of Slavery in the United States from Interviews with Former Slaves.* Washington, DC: U. S. Government Printing Office.

Boyd, James R. 1883. "William Still: His Life and Work to This Time." In William Still. *The Underground Railroad.* Philadelphia: William Still.

Brace, Joan. 1983. "From Chattel to Person: Martinique, 1635–1848." *Plantation Society.* 2 (1): 63–80.

Bracey, John. 1993. "Foreword." in *American Negro Slave Revolts.* New York: International Publishers.

Braithwaite, William. 1961. *The Second Period of Quakerism.* Cambridge: Cambridge University Press.

Brasch, Walter M. 2000. *Brer Rabbit, Uncle Remus, and the "Cornfield Journalist": The Tale of Joel Chandler Harris.* Macon, GA: Mercer University Press.

Brauer, Kinley. 1967. *Cotton versus Conscience: Massachusetts Whig Party Politics and Southwestern Expansion, 1843–1848.* Lexington: University of Kentucky Press.

Brawley, Benjamin. 1937. *Negro Builders and Heroes.* Chapel Hill: University of North Carolina Press.

Breathett, George. 1988. "Catholicism and the Code Noir in Haiti." *Journal of Negro History* 73 (1–4): 1–11.

Breen, Timothy, and Stephen Innes. 1982. "Seventeenth-Century Virginia's Forgotten Yeomen: The First Blacks." *Virginia Cavalcade* 32 (1): 10–19.

Brock, Peter. 1990. *The Quaker Peace Testimony, 1660–1914.* York, England: Ebor Press.

Brown, Henry Box. 2002. *Narrative of the Life of Henry Box Brown, Written by Himself.* New York: Oxford University Press.

Brown, John. 1969. *Provisional Constitution and Ordinances for the People of the United States.* Ed. Boyd Sutler. Weston, MA: M&S Press.

Brown, Josephine. 1856. *Biography of an American Bondman, By His Daughter.* Boston: R. F. Walcutt.

Brown, Richard H. 1966. "The Missouri Crisis, Slavery, and the Politics of Jacksonianism." *South Atlantic Quarterly* 65 (Winter): 55–72.

Brown, William Wells. 1847. *Narrative of William W. Brown, A Fugitive Slave, Written by Himself.* Boston: Anti-Slavery Office.

Bruce, Dickson D. 2001. *The Origins of African American Literature.* Charlottesville: University Press of Virginia.

Buhle, Paul. 2000. "The Sharecropper's Tale." In *Civil Rights: A Reader on the Black Struggle Since 1787.* Ed. Jonathan Birnbaum and Clarence Taylor. New York: New York University Press.

Burrison, John A. 1978. "Afro-American Folk Pottery in the South." *Southern Folklore Quarterly* 42 (2–3): 175–199.

Bush, Barbara 1996. "Hard Labor: Women, Childbirth, and Resistance in British Caribbean Slave Societies." In *More than Chattel: Black Women and Slavery in the Americas.* Ed. David Barry Gaspar and Darlene Clark Hine. Bloomington: Indiana University Press.

Byerman, Keith E. 1994. *Seizing the Word: History, Art, and Self in the Work of W. E. B. DuBois.* Athens: University of Georgia Press.

Cable, Mary. 1971. *Black Odyssey: The Case of the Slave Ship Amistad.* New York: Viking Press.

Cady, Edwin H. 1965. *John Woolman.* New York: Twayne.

Caldehead, William. 1972. "How Extensive Was the Border State Slave Trade? A New Look." *Civil War History* 18 (1): 42–55.

Campbell, Penelope. 1971. *Maryland in Africa: The Maryland State Colonization Society 1831–1857.* Urbana: University of Illinois Press.

Carretta, Vincent, and Phillip Gould, eds. 2001. *Genius in Bondage: Literature of the Black Atlantic.* Lexington: University Press of Kentucky.

Castel, Albert. 1958. *A Frontier State at War: Kansas, 1861–1865.* Ithaca, NY: Cornell University Press.

Ceplair, Larry. 1989. *The Public Years of Sarah and Angelina Grimké: Selected Writings, 1835–1839.* New York: Columbia University Press.

Chase, Henry. 1997. "Juneteenth in Texas." *American Visions* 12 (June–July): 44–49.

Chyet, Stanley F. 1962/3. "Aaron Lopez: A Study in Buenafama." *American Jewish Historical Quarterly* 52: 295–309.

Clemens, Cyril. 1936. *Petroleum Vesuvius Nasby.* Webster Groves, MO: International Mark Twain Society.

Clifford, Deborah Pickman. 1979. *Mine Eyes Have Seen the Glory.* Boston: Little, Brown.

The Code of the State of Georgia. 1861. Prepared by R. H. Clark, T. R. R. Cobb, and D. Irwin.

The Code of the State of Georgia. 1867. Revised and Corrected by David Irwin.

Coffin, Levi. 1876. *Reminiscences of Levi Coffin, Reputed President of the Underground Railroad.* Cincinnati, OH: Western Tract Society.

Collison, Gary. 1997. *Shadrach Minkins: From Fugitive Slave to Citizen.* Cambridge, MA: Harvard University Press.

Conyers, James L. Jr. 2000. *Richard Allen: An Apostle of Freedom.* Lawrenceville, NJ: Africa World Press.

Cooper, Richard. 1985. *John Chavis: To Teach a Generation.* Raleigh, NC: Creative Productions.

Cooper, William. 1978. *The South and the Politics of Slavery, 1828–1856.* Baton Rouge: Louisiana State University Press.

Cornelius, Janet. 1991. *"When I Can Read My Title Clear": Literacy, Slavery, and Religion in the Antebellum South.* Columbia: University of South Carolina Press.

Costanzo, Angelo. 1987. *Surprizing Narrative.* Westport, CT: Greenwood Press.

Covington, James W. 1995. *The Seminoles of Florida.* Gainesville: University Press of Florida.

Cox, LaWanda. 1981. *Lincoln and Black Freedom: A Study in Presidential Leadership.* Columbia: University of South Carolina Press.

Craft, William, and Ellen Craft. 1860. *Running a Thousand Miles for Freedom, or the Escape of William and Ellen Craft from Slavery.* London: William Tweedie.

Crane, Gregg. 2002. *Race, Citizenship, and Law in American Literature.* Cambridge: Cambridge University Press.

Crozier, Alice C. 1969. *The Novels of Harriet Beecher Stowe.* New York: Oxford University Press.

Curry, Leonard P. 1981. *The Free Black in Urban America, 1800–1850: The Shadow of the Dream.* Chicago: University of Chicago Press.

Curtin, Philip D. 1969. *The Atlantic Slave Trade: A Census.* Madison: University of Wisconsin Press.

Curtis, Michael Kent. 1997. "The 1837 Killing of Elijah Lovejoy by an Anti-abolition Mob: Free Speech, Republican Government, and the Privileges of American Citizens." *UCLA Law Review* 44 (April): 1109–1184.

Cushing, John D. 1961. "The Cushing Court and the Abolition of Slavery in Massachusetts: More Notes on the Quock Walker Case." *American Journal of Legal History* 5: 118–119.

Cusick, James G. 2003. *The Other War of 1812: The Patriot War and the American Invasion of Spanish East Florida.* Gainesville: University Press of Florida.

Daget, Serge. 1979. "British Repression of the Illegal French Slave Trade: Some Considerations." In *The Uncommon Market: Essays in the Economic History of the Atlantic Slave Trade.* Ed. Henry A. Gemery and Jan S. Hogendorn. New York: Academic Press.

Dal Lago, Enrico. 2005. *Agrarian Elites: American Slaveholders and Southern Italian Landowners, 1815-1861.* Baton Rouge: Louisiana State University Press.

Dallimore, Arnold. 1970. *George Whitefield.* London: Banner of Truth Trust.

Dangerfield, George. 1952. *The Era of Good Feelings.* New York: Harcourt, Brace and Company.

Davis, Charles T., and Henry Louis Gates, Jr., eds. 1985. *The Slave's Narrative.* New York: Oxford University Press.

Davis, David Brion. 1966. *The Problem of Slavery in Western Culture.* Oxford: Oxford University Press.

Davis, Hugh. 1990. *Joshua Leavitt, Evangelical Abolitionist.* Baton Rouge: Louisiana State University Press.

DeBoer, Clara Merritt. 1994. *Be Jubilant My Feet: African American Abolitionist in the American Missionary Association, 1839–1861.* New York: Garland.

DeBoer, Clara Merritt. 1995. *His Truth Is Marching On: African Americans Who Taught the Freedmen for the American Missionary Association, 1861–1890.* New York: Garland.

DeCamp, David. 1967. "African Day-Names in Jamaica." *Language* 43: 139–149.

DeCaro, Louis A. Jr. 2002. *Fire from the Midst of You: A Religious Life of John Brown.* New York: New York University Press.

Degler, Carl N. 1974. *The Other South: Southern Dissenters in the Nineteenth Century.* New York: Harper and Row.

Degler, Carl N. 1976. "Why Historians Change Their Minds." *Pacific Historical Review* 45: 167–184.

Degler, Carl N. 1978. "Experiencing Slavery." *Reviews in American History* 6: 277–282.

Delany, Martin R. 1852. *The Condition, Elevation, Emigration and Destiny of the Colored People of the United States, Politically Considered.* Philadelphia: Martin R. Delany.

Dillon, Merton L. 1966. *Benjamin Lundy and the Struggle for Negro Freedom.* Urbana: University of Illinois Press.

Dillon, Merton L. 1985. *Ulrich Bonnell Phillips: Historian of the Old South.* Baton Rouge: Louisiana State University Press.

Dillon, Merton L. 1986. "Benjamin Lundy: Quaker Radical." *Timeline* 3 (3): 28–41.

Dodson, Howard. 2002. *Jubilee: The Emergence of African-American Culture.* Washington, DC: National Geographic.

Donald, David, ed. 1956. *Lincoln Reconsidered: Essays on the Civil War Era.* New York: Knopf.

Donald, David. 1995. *Lincoln.* New York: Simon and Schuster.

Douglass, Frederick. 1855. *My Bondage and My Freedom.* New York: Miller, Orton.

Douglass, Frederick. 1845. *Narrative of the Life of Frederick Douglass, an American Slave: Written by Himself.* Boston: American Anti-Slavery Office.

Drake, Frederick C. 1970. "Secret History of the Slave Trade to Cuba Written by an American Naval Officer, 1861." *Journal of Negro History* 55: 218–235.

Drake, Thomas. 1954. *Quakers and Slavery in America.* New Haven, CT: Yale University Press.

Drake, Thomas E. n.d. "Thomas Garrett Quaker Abolitionist," In *Friends in Wilmington, 1738–1938.* Ed. Edward P Bartlett. Wilmington, OH.

DuBois, W. E. B., ed. 1902. *The Negro Artisan.* Atlanta, GA: Atlanta University Press.

DuBois, W. E. B. 1909. *John Brown.* Philadelphia: G. W. Jacobs.

DuBose, John Witherspoon. 1942. *The Life and Times of William Lowndes Yancey.* New York: Peter Smith.

Dumond, Dwight Lowell. 1959. *Antislavery Origins of the Civil War in the United States.* Ann Arbor: University of Michigan Press.

Dunaway, Wilma A. 2003. *The African-American Family in Slavery and Emancipation* and *Slavery in the American Mountain South.* Cambridge: Cambridge University Press.

Dunkelman, Mark H. 1999. "A Bold Break for Freedom." *American History* 34 (5): 22–28.

Dusinberre, William. 1996. *Them Dark Days: Slavery in the American Rice Swamps.* New York: Oxford University Press.

Eaton, Clement. 1964. *The Freedom-of-Thought Struggle in the Old South.* Baton Rouge: Louisiana State University Press.

Ebeogu, Afam. 1993. "Onomastics and the Igbo Tradition of Politics." *African Languages and Cultures* 6: 133–146.

Edwards, Lillie Johnson. 1996. "Episcopalians." In *Encyclopedia of African-American Culture and History.* Ed. Jack Salzman, David Lionel Smith, and Cornel West. New York: Macmillan.

Ellis, Richard. 1987. *The Union at Risk: Jacksonian, States' Rights and the Nullification Crisis.* New York: Oxford University Press.

Embree, Elihu, and Robert H. White. 1932. *The Emancipator.* Nashville, TN: B. H. Murphy.

Emmer, Pieter. 1981. "Abolition of the Abolished: The Illegal Dutch Slave Trade and the Mixed Courts." In *Abolition of the Atlantic Slave Trade.* Ed. James Walvin and David Eltis. Madison: University of Wisconsin Press.

Escott, Paul D. 1979. *Slavery Remembered: A Record of Twentieth-Century Slave Narratives.* Chapel Hill: University of North Carolina Press.

Estell, Kenneth, ed. 1994. *The African-American Almanac.* Detroit: Gale Research.

Etcheson, Nicole. 2004. *Bleeding Kansas: Contested Liberty in the Civil War Era.* Lawrence: University Press of Kansas.

Farrison, William Edward. 1969. *William Wells Brown: Author and Reformer.* Chicago: University of Chicago Press.

Faust, Drew Gilpin. 1977. "Evangelicalism and the Meaning of the Proslavery Argument: The Reverend Thornton Stringfellow of Virginia." *Virginia Magazine of History and Biography* 8 (January): 3–17

Faust, Drew Gilpin. 1979. "A Southern Stewardship: The Intellectual and the Proslavery Argument." *American Quarterly* 31 (Spring): 63–80.

Faust, Drew Gilpin. 1981. *The Ideology of Slavery: Proslavery Thought in the Antebellum South, 1830–1860.* Baton Rouge: Louisiana State University Press

Faust, Drew Gilpin. 1982. *James Henry Hammond and the Old South: A Design for Mastery.* Baton Rouge: Louisiana State University Press.

Fehrenbacher, Don E. 1980. *The South and Three Sectional Crises.* Baton Rouge: Louisiana State University Press.

Ferguson, Leland. 1992. *Uncommon Ground: Archaeology and Early African America, 1650–1800.* Washington, DC: Smithsonian Institution Press.

Fields, Barbara J. 1985. *Slavery and Freedom on the Middle Ground.* New Haven, CT: Yale University Press.

Filler, Louis. 1960. *The Crusade against Slavery.* New York: Harper.

Finkelman, Paul, ed., 1995. *His Soul Goes Marching On: Responses to John Brown and the Harpers Ferry Raid.* Charlottesville: University of Virginia Press.

Finkelman, Paul. 1996. "Legal Ethics and Fugitive Slaves: The Anthony Burns Case, Judge Loring, and Abolitionist Attorneys." *Cardozo Law Review* 17 (May): 1793–1858.

Fisher, Philip. 1985. *Hard Facts: Setting and Form in the American Novel.* New York: Oxford University Press.

Fishkin, Shelly Fisher, and Carla L. Peterson. 1990. "'We Hold These Truths to Be Self-Evident': The Rhetoric of Frederick Douglass' Journalism." In *Frederick Douglass: New Literary and Historical Essays.* Ed. Eric J. Sundquist. Cambridge: Cambridge University Press.

Fluche, Michael. 1979. "Joel Chandler and the Folklore of

Slavery." *Journal of American Studies* 9 (December): 347–363.

Foner, Eric. 1970. *Free Soil, Free Labor, Free Men: The Ideology of the Republican Party before the Civil War.* New York: Oxford University Press.

Foner, Eric. 1988. *Reconstruction: America's Unfinished Business, 1863–1877.* New York: Harper and Row.

Foner, Philip S. 1950. *Life and Writings of Frederick Douglass.* 5 vols. New York: International Publishers.

Foner, Philip S. 1964. *Frederick Douglass: A Biography.* New York: Citadel.

Foner, Philip S., and Josephine F. Pacheco. 1984. *Three Who Dared: Prudence Crandall, Margaret Douglass, Myrtilla Miner—Champions of Antebellum Black Education.* Westport, CT: Greenwood.

Forbes, Ella. 1998. *But We Have No Country: The 1851 Christiana, Pennsylvania, Resistance.* Cherry Hill, NJ: Africana Homestead Legacy.

Forbes, Robert Pierce. 1994. "Slavery and the Meaning of America, 1819–1837." Ph.D. diss., Yale University. New Haven, CT.

Fort, Bruce. 1999. "The Politics and Culture of Literacy in Georgia, 1800–1920." Ph.D. dissertation, University of Virginia, Charlottesville, VA.

Foster, Charles H. 1954. *The Rungless Ladder: Harriet Beecher Stowe and New England Puritanism.* Durham, NC: Duke University Press.

Fox-Genovese, Elizabeth. 1988. *Within the Plantation Household: Black and White Women of the South.* Chapel Hill: University of North Carolina Press.

Franklin, John H. 1995. *The Emancipation Proclamation.* Wheeling, IL: Harlan Davidson.

Franklin, John H., and Mass A. Alfred. 1994. *From Slavery to Freedom: A History of African Americans.* New York: McGraw-Hill.

Fredrickson, George M. 1988. *The Arrogance of Race: Historical Perspectives on Slavery, Racism, and Social Inequality.* Middletown, CT: Wesleyan University Press.

Freedom Southern Society Project. 1982–. *Freedom: A Documentary History of Emancipation, 1861–1867.* Cambridge: Cambridge University Press.

Freehling, Alison Goodyear. 1982. *Drift toward Dissolution: The Virginia Slavery Debate of 1831–1832.* Baton Rouge: Louisiana State University Press.

Freehling, William W. 1966. *Prelude to Civil War: The Nullification Controversy in South Carolina, 1818–1836.* New York: Harper and Row.

Freehling, William W. 1994. *The Reintegration of American History: Slavery and the Civil War.* New York: Oxford University Press.

Freehling, William W. 1990. *The Road to Disunion: Volume 1: Secessionists at Bay, 1776–1854.* New York: Oxford University Press.

French, David. 1976. "Elizur Wright, Jr., and the Emergence of Anti-Colonization Sentiments on the Connecticut Western Reserve." *Ohio History* 85 (Winter): 49–66.

Frey, Sylvia R. 1991. *Water from the Rock: Black Resistance in a Revolutionary Age.* Princeton, NJ: Princeton University Press.

Frost, J. William. 1978. "The Origins of the Quaker Crusade against Slavery: A Review of Recent Literature." *Quaker History* 67: 42–58.

Fry, Gladys-Marie. 1990. *Stitched from the Soul: Slave Quilts from the Ante-bellum South.* New York: Dutton Studio Books.

Fuentes, Carlos. 1992. *The Buried Mirror: Reflections on Spain and the New World.* Boston: Houghton Mifflin.

Fuller, Edmond. 1971. *Prudence Crandall: An Incident of Racism in Nineteenth-Century Connecticut.* Middletown, CT: Wesleyan University Press.

Galenson, David W. 1981. *White Servitude in Colonial America: An Economic Analysis.* Cambridge: Cambridge University Press.

Galloway, Lula Briggs, and Audrey Beatty. 1999. *Juneteenth, Ring the Bell of Freedom.* Saginaw, MI: National Association of Juneteenth Lineage.

Gamble, Douglas A. 1979. "Joshua Giddings and the Ohio Abolitionists: A Study in Radical Politics." *Ohio History* 88 (1): 37–56.

Gara, Larry. 1961. "William Still and the Underground Railroad." *Pennsylvania History* (1): 33–44.

Gara, Larry. 1996. *The Liberty Line: The Legend of the Underground Railroad.* Lexington: University Press of Kentucky.

Gatell, Frank Otto. 1958. "Conscience and Judgment: The Bolt of Massachusetts Conscience Whigs." *The Historian* 27 (November): 18–45.

Gates, Henry Louis, Jr. 1987. *Figures in Black: Words, Signs, and the "Racial" Self.* New York: Oxford University Press.

Gates, Henry Louis, Jr., ed. 1988. *Six Women's Slave Narratives.* New York: Oxford University Press.

Gaull, Marilyn. 1988. *English Romanticism: The Human Context.* New York: Norton.

Genovese, Eugene. 1974. *Roll, Jordan, Roll: The World the Slaves Made.* New York: Pantheon Books.

George, Carol V. R. 1973. *Segregated Sabbaths: Richard Allen and the Emergence of Independent Black Churches 1760–1840.* New York: Oxford University Press.

George, Christopher T. 2000. *Terror on the Chesapeake: The War of 1812 on the Bay.* Shippensburg, PA: White Mane Books.

Gerson, Noel B. 1965. *Harriet Beecher Stowe: A Biography,* New York: Praeger Publishers.

Gienapp, William E. 1987. *The Origins of the Republican Party, 1852–1856.* New York: Oxford University Press.

Gilje, Paul. 1996. *Rioting in America.* Bloomington: Indiana University Press.

Gilmore, Al-Tony, ed. 1978. *Revisiting Blassingame's* The Slave Community: *The Scholars Respond.* Westport, CT: Greenwood.

Goodheart, Lawrence B. 1982. "Tennessee's Antislavery

Movement Reconsidered: The Example of Elihu Embree." *Tennessee Historical Quarterly* 41 (3): 224–238.

Goodheart, Lawrence B. 1984. "Childrearing, Conscience and Conversion to Abolitionism: the Example of Elizur Wright, Jr. " *Psychohistory Review* 12: 24–33.

Goodheart, Lawrence B. 1990. *Abolitionist, Actuary, Atheist: Elizur Wright and the Reform Impulse.* Kent, OH: Kent State University Press.

Goodson, Susan H., et al. 1993. *The College of William and Mary: A History.* 2 vols. Williamsburg, VA: King and Queen Press.

Gossett, Thomas. 1965. *Race: The History of an Idea in America.* New York: Schocken.

Grant, Mary H. 1994. *Private Woman, Public Person: An Account of the Life of Julia Ward Howe from 1819 to 1868.* Brooklyn, NY: Carlson.

Gray, Lewis C. 1933. *History of Agriculture in the Southern United States to 1860,* 2 vols. Washington, DC: Carnegie Institution.

Green, Constance McLaughlin. 1956. *Eli Whitney and the Birth of American Technology.* Boston: Little, Brown.

Green, Fletcher M. 1930. *Constitutional Development in the South Atlantic States, 1776–1860: A Study in the Evolution of Democracy.* Chapel Hill: University of North Carolina Press.

Green, Richard L., ed. 1985. *A Salute to Black Scientists and Inventors.* New York: Empak.

Greenberg, Kenneth S. 1996. *The Confessions of Nat Turner and Related Documents.* Boston: St. Martin's Press.

Griffith, Cyril F. 1975. *The African Dream: Martin R. Delany and the Emergence of Pan-African Thought.* University Park: Penn State University Press.

Grimsted, David. 1998. *American Mobbing, 1828–1861: Toward Civil War.* New York: Oxford University Press.

Haas, Edward F., ed. 1983. *Louisiana's Legal Heritage.* New Orleans: Louisiana State Museum.

Hall, Gwendolyn Midlo. 1992. *Africans in Colonial Louisiana: The Development of Afro-Creole Culture in the Eighteenth Century.* Baton Rouge: Louisiana State University Press.

Hall, Mark. 1982. "The Proslavery Thought of J. D. B. De-Bow: A Practical Man's Guide to Economics." *Southern Studies* 21 (Spring): 97–104.

Hamer, Philip M. 1935. "British Consuls and the Negro Seamen's Act, 1850–1860." *Journal of Southern History* 1 (2): 138–168.

Hamer, Philip M. 1935. "Great Britain, the United States, and the Negro Seamen's Acts, 1822–1848." *Journal of Southern History* 1 (1): 3–28.

Hanaford, Phebe A. 1883. *Daughters of America, or Women of the Century.* Augusta, ME: True and Company.

Handler, Jerome S., and JoAnn Jacoby, 1996. "Slave Names and Naming in Barbados 1650–1830." *The William and Mary Quarterly,* 3d Series 53: 685–728.

Hanke, Lewis. 1949. *The Spanish Struggle for Justice in the Conquest of America.* Philadelphia: University of Pennsylvania Press.

Hansen, Joyce, and Gary McGowan. 1998. *Breaking Ground, Breaking Silence.* New York: Henry Holt and Company.

Harlan, Louis R. 1972. *Booker T. Washington: The Making of a Black Leader.* New York: Oxford University Press.

Harlan, Louis R. 1983. *Booker T. Washington: The Wizard of Tuskegee, 1901–1915.* New York: Oxford University Press.

Harrington, Spencer. 1993. "Bones and Bureaucrats: New York City's Great Cemetery Imbroglio." *Archaeology* (March/April): 28–38.

Harris, Robert L., Jr. 1981. "Charleston's Free Afro-American Elite: The Brown Fellowship Society and the Humane Brotherhood." *South Carolina Historical Magazine* 81: 289–310.

Harrison, John M. 1969. *The Man who Made Nasby: David Ross Locke.* Chapel Hill: University of North Carolina Press.

Harrison, Lowell. 1949. "Thomas Roderick Dew: Philosopher of the Old South." *Virginia Magazine of History and Biography* 57 (October): 390–404.

Harrold, Stanley C., Jr. 1976. "Forging an Antislavery Instrument: Gamaliel Bailey and the Formation of the Ohio Liberty Party." *Old Northwest* 2 (December): 371–87.

Harrold, Stanley C., Jr. 1986. *Gamaliel Bailey and Antislavery Union.* Kent, OH: Kent State University Press.

Harrold, Stanley C., Jr. 1977. "The Perspective of a Cincinnati Abolitionist: Gamaliel Bailey on Social Reform in America." *Bulletin of the Cincinnati Historical Society* 35 (Fall): 173–190.

Hatch, Alden. 1969. *The Byrds of Virginia,* New York: Holt, Rinehart and Winston.

Hatcher, William E. 1908. *John Jasper: The Unmatched Negro Philosopher and Preacher.* New York: F. H. Revell.

Haviland, Laura S. 1881. *A Woman's Life-Work: Labors and Experiences of Laura S. Haviland.* Chicago: Publishing Association of Friends.

Hayden, J. Carleton. 1971. "Conversion and Control: Dilemma of Episcopalians in Providing for the Religious Instruction of Slaves, Charleston, South Carolina, 1845–1860." *Historical Magazine of the Protestant Episcopal Church* 40 (June 2): 143–171.

Heidler, David. 1994. *Pulling the Temple Down: The Fire-Eaters and the Destruction of the Union.* Mechanicsburg, PA: Stackpole Books.

Heimert, Alan. 1966. *Religion and the American Mind: From Great Awakening to the Revolution.* Cambridge, MA: Harvard University Press.

Helper, Hinton Rowan. 1857. *The Impending Crisis of the South; How to Meet It.* New York: A. B. Burdock.

Henig, Gerald S. 1973. *Henry Winter Davis: Antebellum and Civil War Congressman from Maryland.* New York: Twayne Publishers.

Hersh, Blanche Glassman. 1978. *Slavery of Sex: Feminist-Abolitionists in America.* Urbana: University of Illinois Press.

Hewitt, Nancy A. 1986. "Feminist Friends: Agrarian Quakers and the Emergence of Women's Rights in America." *Feminist Studies* 12 (Spring): 27–49.

Hickey, Donald R. 1989. *The War of 1812: A Forgotten Conflict.* Urbana: University of Illinois Press.

Higginbotham, A. Leon, Jr., 1978. *In the Matter of Color.* New York: Oxford University Press.

Hine, Darlene Clark, Elsa Barkley Brown, and Rosalyn Terborg-Penn, eds. 1993. *Black Women in America, An Historical Encyclopedia.* Brooklyn, NY: Carlson.

Hinton, Richard J., ed. 1898. *Poems by Richard Realf: Poet, Soldier, Workman.* New York: Funk & Wagnalls Company.

Holt, Michael. 1978. *The Political Crisis of the 1850s.* New York: John Wiley and Sons.

Howe, Samuel G. [1864] 1969. *Report to the Freedmen's Inquiry Commission.* New York: Arno Press.

Hoyt, Edwin. 1970. *The Amistad Affair.* New York: Abelard-Schuman.

Hudson, Gossie. 1976. "John Chavis." In *Dictionary of Negro Biography.* Ed. Rayford W. Logan and Michael R. Winston. New York: Norton.

Huggins, Nathan Irvin. 1977. *Black Odyssey: The Afro-American Ordeal in Slavery.* New York: Pantheon Books.

Hume, David. 1987. "Of National Characters." In *Essays: Moral, Political, and Literary.* Indianapolis, IN: Liberty Classics.

Inscoe, John C. 1983. "Carolina Slave Names: An Index to Acculturation." *The Journal of Southern History* 49: 527–554.

Jaffa, Harry. 1959. *Crisis of the House Divided: An Interpretation of the Lincoln-Douglas Debates.* Garden City, NJ: Doubleday.

James, Isaac. 1954. *"The Sun Do Move": The Story of the Life of John Jasper.* Richmond, VA: Whittet and Shepperson.

Jay, William. 1853. "Introductory Remarks to the Reproof of the American Church Contained in the Recent History of the Protestant Episcopal Church in America, by the Bishop of Oxford. " In *Miscellaneous Writings on Slavery.* Boston: John P. Jewett.

Jefferson, Thomas. 1955. *Notes on Virginia.* Ed. William Peden. Chapel Hill: University of North Carolina Press.

Jeffery, Julie. 1961. *The Great Silent Army of Abolitionism: Women in the Antislavery Movement.* Chapel Hill: University of North Carolina Press.

Jeffreys, M. D. W. 1948. "Names of American Negro Slaves." *American Anthropologist* 50: 571–573.

Johannsen, Robert. 1989. *The Frontier, the Union, and Stephen A. Douglas.* Urbana: University of Illinois Press.

Johannsen, Robert. 1973. *Stephen A. Douglas.* New York: Oxford University Press.

Johnson, Charles, and Patricia Smith. 1998. *Africans in America: America's Journey Through Slavery.* New York: Harcourt, Brace, and Company.

Johnson, Michael P., and James L. Roark. 1982. "'A Middle Ground': Free Mulattoes and the Friendly Moralist Society of Ante-bellum Charleston." *Southern Studies* 21 (3): 246–265.

Johnson, Michael P., and James L. Roark, eds. 1984. *No Chariot Let Down: Charleston's Free People of Color on the Eve of the Civil War.* Chapel Hill: University of North Carolina Press.

Johnson, Rossiter. 1879. "Richard Realf." *Lippincott's Magazine* (March): 293–300.

Johnson, Walter. 1999. *Soul by Soul: Life Inside the Antebellum Slave Market.* Cambridge, MA: Harvard University Press.

Jones, Alfred Haworth. 1983. "Joel Chandler Harris: Tales of Uncle Remus." *American History Illustrated* 18 (3): 34–39.

Jones, Howard. 1987. *Mutiny on the* Amistad: *The Saga of a Slave Revolt and Its Impact on American Abolition, Law and Diplomacy.* New York: Oxford University Press.

Jones, Jacqueline. 1986. *Labor of Love, Labor of Sorrow: Black Women, Work and the Family, from Slavery to the Present.* New York: Vintage Books.

Jordan, Winthrop D. 1993. *Tumult and Silence at Second Creek: An Inquiry Into A Civil War Slave Conspiracy.* Baton Rouge: Louisiana State University Press.

Jordan, Winthrop D. 1968. *White over Black: American Attitudes Toward the Negro, 1550–1812.* Baltimore, MD: Penguin Books.

Joyner, Charles. 1984. *Down by the Riverside: A South Carolina Slave Community.* Urbana: University of Illinois Press.

Karcher, Carolyn L. 1980. *Shadow over the Promised Land: Slavery, Race, and Violence in Melville's America.* Baton Rouge: Louisiana State University Press.

Karcher, Carolyn L. 1994. *The First Woman in the Republic: A Cultural Biography of Lydia Maria Child.* Durham, NC: Duke University Press.

Keckley, Elizabeth. 1868. *Behind the Scenes; or, Thirty Years a Slave and Four Years in the White House.* New York: G. W. Carleton.

Kerber, Linda. 1967. "Abolitionists and Amalgamators: The New York City Race Riots of 1834." *New York History* 48 (January): 28–39.

Kerr-Ritchie, Jeffrey R. 1999. *Freedpeople in the Tobacco South, Virginia, 1860–1900.* Chapel Hill: University of North Carolina Press.

Kessell, John L. 2002. *Spain in the Southwest: A Narrative History of Colonial New Mexico, Arizona, Texas, and California.* Norman: University of Oklahoma Press.

King, Wilma 1996. "Suffer with Them till Death." In *More than Chattel: Black Women and Slavery in the Americas.* Ed. David Barry Gaspar and Darlene Clark Hine. Bloomington: Indiana University Press.

Kirkham, Bruce E. 1977. *The Building of Uncle Tom's Cabin,* Knoxville: University of Tennessee Press.

Klein, Herbert S. 1986. *African Slavery in Latin America and the Caribbean.* Oxford: Oxford University Press.

Klein, Philip S. 1962. *President James Buchanan: A Biography.* University Park: Pennsylvania State University Press.

Knee, Stuart E. 1985. "The Quaker Petition of 1791: A Challenge to Democracy in Early America." *Slavery & Abolition* 6 (September): 151–159.

Knight, Edgar W. 1930. "Notes on John Chavis." *North Carolina Historical Review* 7: 326–345.

Kolchin, Peter. 1993. *American Slavery, 1619–1877.* New York: Hill and Wang.

Kotlikoff, Laurence J., and Sebastian Pinera. 1977. "The Old South's Stake in the Inter-Regional Movement of Slaves, 1850–1860." *Journal of Economic History* 37 (2): 434–450.

Kraditor, Aileen S. 1969. *Means and Ends in American Abolitionism: Garrison and His Critics on Strategy and Tactics, 1834–1850.* New York: Pantheon Books.

Lambert, Frank. 1994. *Peddler in Divinity: George Whitefield and the Transatlantic Revivals.* Princeton, NJ: Princeton University Press.

Lane, Ann J., ed. 1971. *The Debate over Slavery: Stanley Elkins and His Critics.* Urbana: University of Illinois Press.

Lapsansky, Emma Jones. 1989. "Feminism, Freedom and Community: Charlotte Forten and Women Activists in Nineteenth-Century Philadelphia." *Pennsylvania Magazine of History and Biography* 113: 3–19.

Larison, Cornelius Wilson. 1988. *Sylvia Dubois: A Biografy of the Slav Who Whipt Her Mistres and Gand Her Fredom.*, Ed. Jared C. Lobdell. New York: Oxford University Press.

LaRoche, Cheryl, and Michael Blakey. 1997. "Seizing Intellectual Power: The Dialogue at the New York African Burial Ground." *Journal of Historical Archaeology* 31 (1): 85–96.

Latour, Arsène Lacarrière. 1816. *Historical Memoir of the War in West Florida and Louisiana in 1814–15: With an Atlas.* Ed. Gene A. Smith. Gainesville: The Historic New Orleans Collection and the University Press of Florida, 1999.

Lerner, Gerda. 1967. *The Grimké Sisters from South Carolina: Rebels Against Slavery.* Boston: Houghton Mifflin.

Levine, Robert. 1997. *Martin R. Delany, Frederick Douglass, and the Politics of Representative Identity.* Chapel Hill: University of North Carolina Press.

Lewis, David Levering. 1993. *W. E. B. DuBois: Biography of a Race.* New York: Henry Holt.

Little, Lawrence S. 2000. *Disciples of Liberty: The African Methodist Episcopal Church in the Age of Imperialism, 1884–1916.* Knoxville: University of Tennessee Press.

Lloyd, Arthur Young. 1939. *The Slavery Controversy, 1831–1860.* Chapel Hill: University of North Carolina Press.

Lockridge, Kenneth A. 1987. *The Diary, and Life, of William Byrd II of Virginia, 1674–1744.* Chapel Hill: University of North Carolina Press.

Logan, Shirley Wilson. 1995. *With Pen and Voice: A Critical Anthology of Nineteenth-Century African-American Women.* Carbondale: Southern Illinois University Press.

Louis XIV. 1998. *Le Code Noir.* Introduction and notes Robert Chesnais. Paris: L'Esprit frappeur.

Lovejoy, Paul. 2000. *Transformations in Slavery: A History of Slavery in Africa.* New York: Cambridge University Press.

Lowance, Mason I., Jr., Ellen E. Westbrook, and R. C. DeProspo, eds. 1994. *The Stowe Debate: Rhetorical Strategies in Uncle Tom's Cabin.* Amherst: University of Massachusetts Press.

Mabee, Carlton. 1970. *Black Freedom: The Nonviolent Abolitionists from 1830 Through the Civil War.* New York: Macmillan.

Mabee, Carlton. 1993. *Sojourner Truth: Slave, Prophet, Legend.* New York: New York University Press.

Macdonald, Robert R., John R. Kemp, and Edward F. Haas, eds. 1979. *Louisiana's Black Heritage.* New Orleans: Louisiana State Museum.

Mack, Mark E., and Cassandra Hill. 1995. "Pathologies Affecting Children in the African Burial Ground Population." *Newsletter of the African Burial Ground and Five Points Archaeological Projects* 1 (7): 4.

Maddex, Jack P., Jr. 1979. "'The Southern Apostasy' Revisited: The Significance of Proslavery Christianity." *Marxist Perspectives* 2 (Fall): 132–141.

Mails, Thomas E. 1992. *The Cherokee People: The Story of the Cherokees from Earliest Origins to Contemporary Times.* Tulsa, OK: Council Oaks Books.

Malin, James C. 1942. *John Brown and the Legend of Fifty-six.* Philadelphia: American Philosophical Society.

Malone, Dumas and Allen Johnson, eds. 1930. *Dictionary of American Biography.* New York: Charles Scribner's Sons.

Mannix, Daniel and Malcolm Cowley. 1962. *Black Cargoes: A History of the Atlantic Slave Trade.* New York: Viking.

Marcus, Jacob R. 1970. *The Colonial American Jew 1492–1776.* Detroit, MI: Wayne State University Press.

Mariambaud, Pierre. 1971 *William Byrd of Westover.* Charlottesville: University of Virginia Press.

Martin, Jonathan D. 2004. *Divided Mastery: Slave Hiring in the American South.* Cambridge, MA: Harvard University Press.

Mayer, Henry. 1998. *All on Fire: William Lloyd Garrison and the Abolition of Slavery.* New York: St. Martin's Press.

McAdoo Bill. 1983. *Pre–Civil War Black Nationalism.* New York: David Walker Press.

McClendon, R. Earl. 1933. "The *Amistad* Claims: Inconsistencies of Policy." *Political Science Quarterly* 48: 386–412.

McFeely, William S. 1991. *Frederick Douglass.* New York: . . Norton.

McGowan, James A. 1977. *Station Master on the Underground Railroad: The Life and Letters of Thomas Garrett.* Moylan, PA: Whimsie Press.

McLaurin, Melton A. 1991. *Celia, A Slave.* New York: Avon.

McNitt, Frank. 1972. *Navajo Wars: Military Campaigns,*

Slave Raids, and Reprisals. Albuquerque: University of New Mexico Press.

McPherson, James M. 1963. "The Fight against the Gag Rule: Joshua Leavitt and Antislavery Insurgency in the Whig Party, 1839–1842." *Journal of Negro History* 48 (July): 177–95.

McPherson, James. 1982. *Ordeal by Fire: The Civil War and Reconstruction.* New York: Knopf.

McReynolds, Edwin C. 1988. *The Seminoles.* Norman: University of Oklahoma Press.

Meier, August. 1963. *Negro Thought in America, 1880–1915.* Ann Arbor: University of Michigan Press.

Meltzer, Milton, and Patricia G. Holland, eds. 1982. *Lydia Maria Child: Selected Letters, 1817–1880.* Amherst: University of Massachusetts Press.

Menard, Russell R. 2001. *Migrants, Servants and Slaves: Unfree Labour in Colonial British America.* London: Variorum.

Merideth, Robert. 1964. "A Conservative Abolitionist at Alton: Edward Beecher's *Narrative.*" *Journal of Presbyterian History* 42 (March and June): 39–53, 92–103.

Merrill, Walter M. 1963. *Against Wind and Tide: A Biography of William Lloyd Garrison.* Cambridge, MA: Harvard University Press.

Miers, Suzanne. 1975. *Britain and the Ending of the Slave Trade.* New York: Longman.

Miles, Tiya. 2005. *The Story of an Afro-Cherokee Family in Slavery and Freedoom.* Berkeley: University of California Press.

Miller, Edward A. 1995. *Gullah Statesman: Robert Smalls from Slavery to Congress 1839–1915.* Columbia: University of South Carolina Press.

Miller, Floyd J. 1971. "The Father of Black Nationalism." *Civil War History* 17 (December): 310–319.

Miller, Floyd J. 1975. *The Search for a Black Nationality: Black Colonization and Emigration, 1787–1863.* Urbana: University of Illinois Press.

Miller, Kelly. 1916. "The Historic Background of the Negro Physician." *Journal of Negro History* 1 (2): 99–109.

Miller, William Lee. 1996. *Arguing About Slavery: The Great Battle in the United States Congress.* New York: Knopf.

Mills, Bruce. 1994. *Cultural Reformations: Lydia Maria Child and the Literature of Reform.* Athens: University of Georgia Press.

Mills, Gary B., 1977. *The Forgotten People: Cane River's Creoles of Color.* Baton Rouge: Louisiana State University Press.

Mirsky, Jeannette, and Allan Nevins. 1952. *The World of Eli Whitney.* New York: Macmillan.

Missall, John, and Mary Missall. 2004. *The Seminole Wars: America's Longest Indian Conflict.* Gainesville: University Press of Florida.

Mixon, Wayne. 1990. "The Ultimate Irrelevance of Race: Joel Chandler Harris and Uncle Remus in Their Time." *Journal of Southern History* 56 (3) : 457–480.

Moers, Ellen. 1996. *Literary Women.* London: Women's Press.

Mohler, Mark. 1926. "The Episcopal Church and National Reconciliation, 1865." *Political Science Quarterly* 41 (December): 567–95.

Monaghan, Jay. 1955. *Civil War on the Western Border, 1854–65.* Boston: Little, Brown.

Moore, Glover. 1953. *The Missouri Controversy, 1819–1821.* Lexington: University Press of Kentucky.

Moore, John Hebron. 1958. *Agriculture in Ante-Bellum Mississippi.* New York: Bookman Associates.

Moore, John Hebron. 1988. *The Emergence of the Cotton Kingdom in the Old Southwest: Mississippi, 1770–1860.* Baton Rouge, LA: Louisiana State University Press.

Morais, Herbert M. 1969. *The History of the Negro in Medicine.* New York: Publishers Company.

Morris, Thomas. 1974. *Free Men All: The Personal Liberty Laws of the North, 1780–1861.* Baltimore, MD: Johns Hopkins University Press.

Morris, Thomas. 1996. *Southern Slavery and the Law, 1619–1860.* Chapel Hill: University of North Carolina Press.

Morriss, Andrew P. 1995. "'This State Will Soon Have Plenty of Laws'—Lessons from One Hundred Years of Codification in Montana." *Montana Law Review* 56: 359–450.

Morrow, Ralph E. 1961. "The Proslavery Argument Revisited." *Mississippi Valley Historical Review* 47 (June): 79–93.

Murphy, Larry, J. Gordon Melton, and Gary L. Ward, eds. 1993. *Encyclopedia of African-American Religions.* New York: Garland.

Nash, Gary B. 1989. "New Light on Richard Allen: The Early Years of Freedom." *William and Mary Quarterly* 46 (2): 332–340.

Nash, Roderick W. 1961. "The Christiana Riot: An Evaluation of its National Significance." *Journal of the Lancaster County Historical Society* 64: 66–91.

Nash, Roderick W. 1961. "William Parker and the Christiana Riot." *Journal of Negro History* 46 (January): 24–31.

Newton, James, and Ronald Lewis, eds. 1978. *The Other Slaves: Mechanics, Artisans, and Craftsmen.* Boston: G. K. Hall.

Nichols, Alice. 1954. *Bleeding Kansas.* New York: Oxford University Press.

Nichols, Charles H. 1963. *Many Thousand Gone: The Ex-Slaves' Account of Their Bondage and Freedom.* Bloomington: Indiana University Press.

Nichols, Roy Franklin. 1948. *The Disruption of American Democracy.* New York: Macmillan.

Nogee, Joseph L. 1954. "The *Prigg* Case and Fugitive Slavery 1842–1850." *Journal of Negro History* 39 (April): 185–205.

Northrup, David, ed. 2002. *The Atlantic Slave Trade.* Boston: Houghton Mifflin.

Northup, Solomon. 1968. *Twelve Years a Slave.* Ed. Sue Eakin and Joseph Logsdon. Baton Rouge: Louisiana State University Press.

Nott, Josiah Clark. 1849. *Connection Between the Biblical and Physical History of Man.* New York: Bartlett and Welford.

Nott, Josiah Clark, and George R. Gliddon. 1854. *Types of Mankind.* Philadelphia, PA: Lippincott, Grambo, and Company.

Nott, Josiah Clark, and George R. Gliddon. 1857. *Indigenous Races of the Earth.* Philadelphia, PA: Lippincott.

Nye, Russel. 1949. *Fettered Freedom: Civil Liberties and the Slavery Controversy, 1830–1860.* East Lansing: Michigan State College Press.

O'Brien, William. 1961. "Did the Jennison Case Outlaw Slavery in Massachusetts?" *William and Mary Quarterly* 3d ser 17 (April): 219–241.

Oakes, James. 1982. *The Ruling Race.* New York: Knopf.

Oates, Stephen B. 1977. *With Malice Toward None: The Life of Abraham Lincoln.* New York: Harper and Row.

Oates, Stephen B. 1984. *To Purge This Land With Blood: A Biography of John Brown.* Amherst, MA: University of Massachusetts Press.

Oates, Stephen B. 1990. *The Fires of Jubilee: Nat Turner's Fierce Rebellion.* New York: Harper and Row.

Ogilvie, Marilyn Bailey. 1986. *Women in Science: Antiquity through the Nineteenth Century.* Cambridge, MA: MIT Press.

Othow, Helen Chavis. 2001. *John Chavis: African American Patriot.* Jefferson, NC: McFarland.

Owsley, Frank L. 1949. *Plain Folk of the Old South.* Baton Rouge: Louisiana State University Press.

Painter, Nell Irvin. 1988. "Martin R. Delany: Elitism and Black Nationalism." In *Black Leaders of the Nineteenth Century.* Ed. Leon Litwack and August Meier. Urbana: University of Illinois Press.

Painter, Nell Irvin. 1996. *Sojourner Truth: A Life, A Symbol.* New York: Norton.

Paludan, Philip Shaw. 1994. *The Presidency of Abraham Lincoln.* Lawrence: University Press of Kansas.

Parish, Peter J. 1989. *Slavery: History and Historians.* New York: Harper and Row.

Patton, Sharon. 1995. "Antebellum Louisiana Artisans: The Black Furniture Makers." *The International Review of African American Art* 12 (3): 15–23, 58–64.

Payne, Daniel Alexander. 1891. *History of the African Methodist Episcopal Church.* Nashville, TN: Publishing House of the A. M. E. Sunday School Union.

Pease, Jane H. 1969. "The Freshness of Fanaticism: Abby Kelley Foster." Ph.D. dissertation, Department of History, University of Rochester, Rochester, New York.

Pease, Jane H., and William H. Pease. 1975. *The Fugitive Slave Law and Anthony Burns: A Problem in Law Enforcement.* Philadelphia: Lippincott.

Pease, Jane H., and William H. Pease. 1990. *They Who Would Be Free: Blacks' Search for Freedom, 1830–1861.* Chicago: University of Chicago Press.

Pease, William H., and Jane H. Pease. 1971. "The Negro Convention Movement." In *Key Issues in the Afro-American Experience.* Ed. Nathan I. Huggins et al. New York: Harcourt, Brace, Jovanovich.

Pease, William, and Jane Pease. 1995. *James Louis Petigru: Southern Conservative, Southern Dissenter.* Athens: University of Georgia Press.

Peek, Phil. 1978. "Afro-American Material Culture and the Afro-American Craftsman." *Southern Folklore Quarterly* 42 (2–3): 109–134.

Pemberton, Doris Hollis. 1983. *Juneteenth at Comanche Crossing.* Austin, TX: Eakin Publications.

Perdue, Charles L., et al. 1976. *Weevils in the Wheat: Interviews with Virginia Ex-Slaves.* Charlottesville: University of Virginia Press.

Perdue, Theda. 1979. "The Development of Plantation Slavery before Removal." In *The Cherokee Indian Nation: A Troubled History.* Ed. Duane H. King. Knoxville: University of Tennessee Press.

Perry, Lewis, and Michael Fellman, eds. 1979. *Antislavery Reconsidered: New Perspectives on the Abolitionists.* Baton Rouge: Louisiana State University Press.

Peterson, Carla, L. 1995. *"Doers of the Word": African-American Women Speakers and Writers in the North (1830–1880).* New York: Oxford University Press.

Peterson, Merrill D. 1962. *The Jefferson Image in the American Mind.* New York: Oxford University Press.

Pieterse, Jan Nederveen. 1992. *White on Black: Images of African and Blacks in Western Popular Culture.* New Haven, CT: Yale University Press.

Pinkney, Alphonso 1976. *Red, Black, and Green; Black Nationalism in the United States.* Cambridge: Cambridge University Press.

Pittman, Chandra. 1998. "If Bones Could Speak." *Transforming Anthropology* 7 (1): 59–63.

Post, C. Gordon, ed. 1953. *A Disquisition on Government and Selections from the Discourse.* New York: Liberal Arts Press.

Potter, David M. 1976. *The Impending Crisis, 1848–1861.* New York: Harper and Row.

Powles, James M. 2000. "South Carolina Slave Robert Smalls Put His Ship-Piloting Skills to Good Use in an Audacious Break for Freedom." *America's Civil War* 13 (4): 8, 24, 62, 64.

Price, Michael. 1997. "Back to the Briar Patch: Joel Chandler Harris and the Literary Defense of Paternalism." *Georgia Historical Quarterly* 81 (3): 686–712.

Quarles, Benjamin. 1962. *Lincoln and the Negro.* New York: Oxford University Press.

Quarles, Benjamin. 1968. *Frederick Douglass.* New York: Oxford University Press.

Quarles, Benjamin. 1970. *Black Abolitionists.* New York: Oxford University Press.

Quarles, Benjamin. 1974. *Allies for Freedom: Blacks and John Brown.* New York: Oxford University Press.

Raboteau, Albert J. 1978. *Slave Religion: The "Invisible Institution" in the Antebellum South.* New York: Oxford University Press.

Raimond, Jean, and J. R. Watson, eds. 1992. *A Handbook to British Romanticism*. New York: St. Martin's.

Randell, Willard Sterne. 1993. *Thomas Jefferson: A Life*. New York: Henry Holt.

Rawick, George P. 1972, 1977, 1979. *The American Slave: A Composite Autobiography*. Westport, CT: Greenwood.

Rawley, James A. 1969. *Race and Politics: "Bleeding Kansas" and the Coming of the Civil War*. Philadelphia: J. B. Lippincott.

Realf, Richard. Testimony in "Mason Report" 1860. *U. S. Senate Committee Reports, 1859–60, II* (January 21): 91–113.

Ream, Debbie Williams. 1993. "Mine Eyes Have Seen the Glory." *American History Illustrated* 27 (1): 60–64.

Reed, Harry, 1994. *Platform for Change: The Foundation of the Northern Free Black Community, 1775–1865*. East Lansing: Michigan State University Press.

Reidy, Joseph P. 1992. *From Slavery to Agrarian Capitalism in the Cotton South: Central Georgia, 1800–1880*. Chapel Hill: University of North Carolina Press.

Remini, Robert. 1951. *Martin Van Buren and the Making of the Democratic Party*. New York: Columbia University Press.

Richards, Leonard L. *Gentlemen of Property and Standing: Anti-Abolition Mobs in Jacksonian America*. New York: Oxford University Press, 1975.

Richardson, Joe M. 1986. *Christian Reconstruction: The American Missionary Association and Southern Blacks, 1861–1890*. Athens: University of Georgia Press.

Richardson, Marilyn, ed. 1987. *Maria W Stewart, America's First Black Woman Political Writer*. Bloomington: Indiana University Press.

Riddleberger, Patrick W. 1966. *George Washington Julian, Radical Republican*. Indianapolis: Indiana Historical Bureau.

Ripley, C. Peter, ed. 1985. *The Black Abolitionist Papers: The British Isles, 1830–1865*. Chapel Hill: University of North Carolina Press.

Roach, Joseph. 1998. "Body of Law: The Sun King and the Code Noir." In *From the Royal to the Republican Body: Incorporating the Political in Seventeenth- and Eighteenth-Century France*. Ed. Sara E. Melzer and Kathryn Norberg. Berkeley: University of California Press.

Roane, Spencer. 1906. "Letters of Spencer Roane, 1788–1822." *New York Public Library Bulletin* 10: 167–180.

Robert, Joseph Clarke. 1941. *The Road from Monticello: A Study of the Virginia Slavery Debate of 1832*. Durham, NC: Duke University Press.

Robinson, Dean R. 2001. *Black Nationalism in American Politics and Thought*. Cambridge: Cambridge University Press.

Robinson, Donald. 1979. *Slavery in the Structure of American Politics*. New York: Norton.

Roper, John Herbert. 1984. *U. B. Phillips: A Southern Mind*. Macon, GA: Mercer University Press.

Rosenberg, Norman L. 1971. "Personal Liberty Laws and the Sectional Crisis, 1850–1861." *Civil War History* 17 (March): 25–45.

Ruggles, Jeffrey. 2003. *The Unboxing of Henry Brown*. Richmond: Library of Virginia.

Rycenga, Jennifer. 2001. "Maria Stewart, Black Abolitionist, and the Idea of Freedom." In *Frontline Feminisms: Women, War, and Resistance*. Ed. Marguerite R. Waller and Jennifer Rycenga. New York: Routledge.

Sala-Molins, Louis. 2003. *Le Code Noir ou le calvaire de Canaan*. Paris: Presses universitaires de France.

Salitan, Lucille, and Eve Lewis Perera, eds. 1994. *Virtuous Lives: Four Quaker Sisters Remember Family Life, Abolitionism, and Women's Suffrage*. New York: Continuum.

Sallinger, Sharon. 1987. *"To Serve Well and Faithfully" Labor and Indentured Servants in Pennsylvania*. Cambridge: Cambridge University Press.

Salzman, Jack, David Lionel Smith, and Corner West, eds. 1996. *Encyclopedia of African-American Culture and History*. New York: Macmillan Library Reference.

Savage, Sherman W. 1938. "The Origins of the Giddings Resolutions." *Ohio Archaeological and Historical Quarterly* 48 (October): 28–39.

Schafer, Joseph. 1936. "Stormy Days in Court—The *Booth* Case." *Wisconsin Magazine of History* 20 (September): 89–110.

Schwarz, Philip J. 2001. *Migrants against Slavery: Virginians and the Nation*. Charlottesville: University Press of Virginia.

Schwarz, Philip J. 1996. *Slave Laws in Virginia*. Athens: University of Georgia Press.

Sekora, John, and Darwin T. Turner, eds. 1982. *The Art of Slave Narrative: Original Essays in Criticism and Theory*. Macomb, IL: Western Illinois University.

Sewell, Richard H. 1976. *Ballots for Freedom: Antislavery Politics in the United States, 1837–1860*. New York: Oxford University Press.

Shade, William G. 1996. *Democratizing the Old Dominion: Virginia and the Second Party System, 1824–1861*. Charlottesville: University Press of Virginia.

Shapiro, Herbert. 1984. "The Impact of the Aptheker Thesis: A Retrospective View of American Negro Slave Revolts." *Science and Society* 48: 52–73.

Shick, Tom W. 1971. "A Quantitative Analysis of Liberian Colonization from 1820 to 1843 with Special Reference to Mortality." *Journal of African History* 12: 45–59.

Shore, Lawrence. 1986. *Southern Capitalists: The Ideological Leadership of an Elite, 1832–1885*. Chapel Hill: University of North Carolina Press.

Siebert, Wilbur H. 1898. *The Underground Railroad from Slavery to Freedom*. New York: Macmillan.

Skipper, Ottis Clark. 1958. *J. D. B. DeBow: Magazinist of the Old South*. Athens: University of Georgia Press.

Slaughter, Thomas. 1991. *Bloody Dawn: The Christiana Riot and Racial Violence in the Antebellum North*. New York: Oxford University Press.

Smedley, R. C. 1969. *History of the Underground Railroad*. New York: Arno Press.

Smith, Abbot Emerson. 1947. *Colonists in Bondage: White Servitude and Convict Labor in America 1607–1776.* Gloucester, MA: Peter Smith.

Smith, Elbert B. 1975. *The Presidency of James Buchanan.* Lawrence: University Press of Kansas.

Smith, John David. 1991. *An Old Creed for the New South: Proslavery Ideology and Historiography, 1865–1918.* Athens: University of Georgia Press. .

Smith, John David, and John C. Inscoe, eds. 1993. *Ulrich Bonnell Phillips: A Southern Historian and His Critics.* Athens: University of Georgia Press.

Smith, Marion. 1930. "The First Codification of the Substantive Common Law." *Tulane Law Review* 4: 178–189.

Smith, Venture. 1971. *A Narrative of the Life and Adventures of Venture Smith.* Boston: Beacon Press.

Smith Foster, Frances. 1979. *Witnessing Slavery: The Development of Ante-bellum Slave Narratives.* Madison: University of Wisconsin Press.

Snay, Mitchell. 1993. *Gospel of Disunion: Religion and Separatism in the Antebellum South.* Cambridge: Cambridge University Press.

Sobel, Mechal. 1987. *The World They Made Together: Black and White Values in Eighteenth-Century Virginia.* Princeton, NJ: Princeton University Press.

Soderlund, Jean R. 1985. *Quakers and Slavery: A Divided Spirit.* Princeton, NJ: Princeton University Press.

Sorin, Gerald. 1972. *Abolitionism: A New Perspective.* New York: Praeger Publishers.

Sox, David. 1999. *John Woolman, Quintessential Quaker, 1720–1772.* Richmond, IN: Friends United Press.

Spain, August O. 1951. *The Political Theory of John C. Calhoun.* New York: Bookman Associates.

Spector, Robert M. 1968. "The Quock Walker Cases (1781–83)—Slavery, Its Abolition, and Negro Citizenship in Early Massachusetts." *Journal of Negro History* 53 (January): 12–32.

Stampp, Kenneth M. 1942. "An Analysis of T. R. Dew's *Review of the Debate in the Virginia Legislature.*" *Journal of Negro History* 27 (October): 380–387.

Stanley, A. Knighton. 1979. *The Childrening: Congregationalism among Black People.* New York: Pilgrim Press.

Starling, Marion Wilson. 1981. *The Slave Narrative.* Boston: G. K. Hall.

Staudenraus, Philip J. 1961. *The African Colonization Movement, 1816–1865.* New York: Columbia University Press.

Stauffer, John. 2001. *The Black Hearts of Men: Radical Abolitionists and the Transformation of Race.* Cambridge: Harvard University Press.

Stearns, Charles. 1849. *Narrative of Henry Box Brown.* Boston: Brown and Stearns.

Stein, Robert Louis. 1988. *The French Sugar Business in the Eighteenth Century.* Baton Rouge: Louisiana State University Press.

Stephenson, Wendell. 1938. *Isaac Franklin: Slave Trader and Planter of the Old South.* Baton Rouge: Louisiana State University Press.

Sterling, Dorothy, ed. 1984. *We Are Your Sisters: Black Women in the Nineteenth Century.* New York: Norton.

Sterling, Dorothy. 1991. *Ahead of Her Time: Abby Kelley and the Politics of Anti-Slavery.* New York: Norton.

Stevens, Charles Emery. 1856. *Anthony Burns: A History.* Boston: John P. Jewett and Company.

Stevens, Elizabeth C. 2003. *Elizabeth Buffum Chace and Lillie Chace Wyman: A Century of Abolition, Suffragist and Workers' Rights Activism.* Jefferson, NC: McFarland.

Stevenson, Brenda, ed. 1988. *The Journals of Charlotte Forten Grimké.* New York: Oxford University Press.

Stewart, James Brewer. 1970. *Joshua Giddings and the Tactics of Radical Politics.* Cleveland: Case Western University Press.

Stewart, James Brewer. 1992. *William Lloyd Garrison and the Challenge of Emancipation.* Arlington Heights, IL: Harlan Davidson.

Stewart, James Brewer. 1996. *Holy Warriors: The Abolitionists and American Slavery.* New York: Hill and Wang.

Still, William. 1872. *The Underground Railroad.* Philadelphia: Porter and Coates.

Stimson, John Ward. 1903. "An Overlooked American Shelley." *The Arena* (July): 15–26.

Stout, Harry S. 1991 *The Divine Dramatist: George Whitefield and the Rise of Modern Evangelicalism.* Grand Rapids, MI: William B. Eerdmans.

Sutch, Richard. 1975. "The Breeding of Slaves for Sale and the Westward Expansion of Slavery." In *Race and Slavery in the Western Hemisphere.* Stanley L. Engerman and Eugene D. Genovese, eds. Princeton, NJ: Princeton University Press.

Tadman, Michael. 1996. *Speculators and Slaves: Masters, Traders, and Slaves in the Old South.* Madison: University of Wisconsin Press.

Takagi, Midori. 1999. "*Rearing Wolves to Our Own Destruction*": *Slavery in Richmond, Virginia, 1782–1865.* Charlottesville: University Press of Virginia.

Tallant, Harold D. 2003. *Evil Necessity: Slavery and Political Culture in Antebellum Kentucky.* Lexington: University Press of Kentucky.

Taylor, Yuval, ed. 1999. *I Was Born a Slave: An Anthology of Classic Slave Narratives.* Chicago: Lawrence Hill Books.

Taylor, Joe Gray. 1963. *Negro Slavery in Louisiana.* Baton Rouge: Louisiana Historical Association.

Thomas, Benjamin P. 1950. *Theodore Dwight Weld, Crusader for Freedom.* New Brunswick, NJ: Rutgers University Press.

Thomas, John L. 1963. *The Liberator: William Lloyd Garrison.* Boston: Little, Brown.

Thomas, Karen M. 1992. "Juneteenth Remembers Slavery, Celebrates Freedom." *Chicago Tribune* June 18, final edition: 1.

Thompson, Priscilla. 1986. "Harriet Tubman, Thomas Garrett, and the Underground Railroad." *Delaware History* 22 (September): 1–21.

Thornton, John K. 1991. "African Dimensions of the Stono Rebellion." *American Historical Review* 96 (October): 1101–1113.

Thornton, John. 1993. "Central African Names and African-American Naming-Patterns." *The William and Mary Quarterly*, 3d Series 50: 727–742.

Thorpe, Earl. 1971. *Black Historians: A Critique.* New York: William Morrow.

Tiainen-Anttila, Kaija. 1994. *The Problem of Humanity: Blacks in the European Enlightenment.* Helsinki: Finnish Historical Society.

Tiffany, Nina Moore. 1890. "Stories of the Fugitive Slaves, I: The Escape of William and Ellen Craft." *New England Magazine* 1: 528.

Tise, Edward. 1979. "The Interregional Appeal of Proslavery Thought: An Ideological Profile of the Antebellum American Clergy." *Plantation Society in the Americas* 1 (February): 63–72.

Trefousse, Hans L. 1963. *Benjamin Franklin Wade: Radical Republican from Ohio.* New York: Twayne.

Trefousse, Hans L. 1969. *The Radical Republicans: Lincoln's Vanguard for Racial Justice.* New York: Knopf.

Trotsky, Susan M., and Donna Olendorf, eds. 1992. *Contemporary Authors.* Vol. 137. Detroit: Gale Research.

Trueblood, David Elton. 1966. *The People Called Quakers.* Richmond, IN: Friends United Press.

Truth, Sojourner. 1991. *Narrative of Sojourner Truth; A Bondswoman of Olden Time.* Ed. Olive Gilbert. New York: Oxford University Press.

Tureaud, A. P. and C. C. Haydel. 1935. *The Negro in Medicine in Louisiana. National Medical Association Souvenir Program.* New Orleans, LA: Amistad Research Center.

Turnage, Sheila. 2002. "Stealing A Ship To Freedom." *American Legacy: Magazine of African-American History and Culture* 8 (1): 70–73, 75–76.

Udom, Essien. 1969. *Black Nationalism: A Search for Identity in America.* New York: Dell.

Venable, Austin L. 1942. "The Conflict between the Douglas and Yancey Forces in the Charleston Convention." *Journal of Southern History* 8 (May): 226–241.

Venable, Austin L. 1945. "The Role of William L. Yancey in the Secession Movement." M.A. Thesis, Department of History, Vanderbilt University, Nashville, Tennessee.

Vlach, John M. 1978. *The Afro-American Tradition in Decorative Arts.* Cleveland, OH: Cleveland Museum of Art.

Vlach, John M. 1991. *By the Work of Their Hands: Studies in Afro-American Folklife.* Ann Arbor, MI: UMI Research Press.

Von Frank, Albert J. 1998. *The Trials of Anthony Burns: Freedom and Slavery in Emerson's Boston.* Cambridge, MA: Harvard University Press.

Wade, Richard C. 1964. *Slavery in the Cities: The South, 1820–1860.* Oxford: Oxford University Press.

Walther, Eric H. 1992. *The Fire-Eaters.* Baton Rouge: Louisiana State University Press.

Ward, William. 1969. *The Royal Navy and the Slavers.* New York: Pantheon.

Washington, John E. 1942. *They Knew Lincoln.* New York: E. P. Dutton.

Webber, Thomas L. 1978. *Deep Like the Rivers: Education in the Slave Quarter Community, 1831–1865.* New York: Norton.

Weber, David J. 1992. *The Spanish Frontier in North America.* New Haven, CT: Yale University Press.

Weinstein, Allen, Frank Otto Gatell, and David Sarasohn, eds. 1968. *American Negro Slavery: A Modern Reader.* New York: Oxford University Press.

Wells, Tom Henderson. 1968. *The Slave Ship Wanderer.* Athens: University of Georgia Press.

Wesley, Charles H. 1942. "Manifests of Slave Shipments along the Waterways, 1808–1864." *Journal of Negro History* 27 (2): 155–174.

Whipple, Rev. George. 1876. *History of the American Missionary Association.* New York: 56 Reade Street AMA.

White, David O. 1984. "The Fugitive Blacksmith of Hartford: James W. C. Pennington." *The Connecticut Historical Society Bulletin* 49 (Winter): 4–29.

White, Deborah. 1985. *Ar'n't I a Woman: Female Slaves in the Plantation South.* New York: Norton.

Wiggins, William H. 1987. *O Freedom! Afro-American Emancipation Celebrations.* Knoxville: University of Tennessee Press.

Wiggins, William H. 1993. "Juneteenth: Tracking the Progress of an Emancipation Celebration." *American Visions* 8 (3, (June–July): 28–31.

Wikramanayake, Marina. 1973. *A World in Shadow: The Free Black in Ante-bellum South Carolina.* Columbia: University of South Carolina Press.

Wilkins, Thurman. 1988. *Cherokee Tragedy.* Norman: University of Oklahoma Press.

Williams, Heather Andrea. 2005. *Self-Taught: African American Education in Slavery and Freedom.* Chapel Hill: University of North Carolina Press.

Williamson, Laila. 1978. "Infanticide: An Anthropological Analysis." In *Infanticide and the Value of Life.* Ed. Marvin Kohl. New York: Prometheus Books.

Wish, Harvey. 1941. "The Revival of the African Slave Trade in the United States, 1856–1860." *Mississippi Valley Historical Review* 27: 569–588.

Wood, Peter H. 1974. *Black Majority: Negroes in Colonial South Carolina from 1670 through the Stono Rebellion.* New York: Norton.

Woodson, Carter G., ed. 1926. *The Mind of the Negro as Reflected in Letters Written During the Crisis, 1800–1860.* Washington, DC: Association for the Study of Negro Life and History.

Woodson, Carter G. 1968. *The Education of the Negro Prior to 1861.* New York: Arno Press.

Woolman, John. 1922. *The Journal and Essays of John Woolman.* Ed. A. M. Gunmere. New York: Macmillan.

Wright, Louis B., and Marion Tinling, eds. 1941. *The Secret Diary of William Byrd of Westover, 1709–1712.* Richmond, VA: Dietz Press.

Wyatt-Brown, Bertram. 1965. "The Abolitionists' Postal Campaign of 1835." *Journal of Negro History* 50 (October): 227–238.

Wyatt-Brown, Bertram. 1982. *Southern Honor: Ethics and Behavior in the Old South.* New York: Oxford University Press.

Wyly-Jones, Susan. 2001. "The 1835 Anti-Abolition Meetings in the South: a New Look at the Controversy over the Abolition Postal Campaign." *Civil War History* 47 (4): 289–309.

Wyman, Lillie Buffum Chace. 1903. "Reminiscences of Two Abolitionists." *New England Magazine* (January): 536–550.

Yang, Liwen. 1992. "John Brown's Role in the History of the Emancipation Movement of Black Americans." *Southern Studies* 3: 135–142.

Yellin, Jean Fagan. 1972. *The Intricate Knot: Black Figures in American Literature, 1776–1863.* New York: New York University Press.

Yellin, Jean Fagan, ed. 1987. *Incidents in the Life of a Slave Girl.* Cambridge, MA: Harvard University Press.

Yetman, Norman R. 1967. "The Background of the Slave Narrative Collection." *American Quarterly* 3: 535–553.

Zaborney, John J. 1999. "'They Are Out for Their Victuals and Clothes': Slave Hiring and Slave Family and Friendship Ties in Rural, Nineteenth-Century Virginia." In *Afro-Virginian History and Culture.* Ed. John Saillant. New York: Garland.

Zamir, Shamoon. 1995. *Dark Voices: W. E. B. DuBois and American Thought, 1888–1903.* Chicago: University of Chicago Press.

Zilversmit, Arthur. 1967. *The First Emancipation: The Abolition of Slavery in the North.* Chicago: University of Chicago Press.

Index

—m—